English for the Computer

English for the Computer

The SUSANNE Corpus and Analytic Scheme

□

GEOFFREY SAMPSON

CLARENDON PRESS · OXFORD
1995

Oxford University Press, Walton Street, Oxford OX2 6DP
Oxford New York
Athens Auckland Bangkok Bombay
Calcutta Cape Town Dar es Salaam Delhi
Florence Hong Kong Istanbul Karachi
Kuala Lumpur Madras Madrid Melbourne
Mexico City Nairobi Paris Singapore
Taipei Tokyo Toronto
and associated companies in
Berlin Ibadan

Oxford is a trade mark of Oxford University Press

Published in the United States
by Oxford University Press, Inc., New York

British Library Cataloguing in Publication Data
Data available

Library of Congress Cataloging in Publication Data
English for the computer : the SUSANNE corpus and analytic scheme
Geoffrey Sampson.
1. English language—Discourse analysis—Data processing.
2. English language—Research—Data processing. 3. Computational
linguistics. I. Title.
PE1074.5.S36 1995   425'.012—dc20   94–18387
ISBN 0–19–824023–6

1 3 5 7 9 10 8 6 4 2

Typeset by Graphicraft Typesetters Ltd., Hong Kong
Printed in Great Britain on acid-free paper by
Bookcraft (Bath) Ltd., Midsomer Norton

ᚠᚪᛏᛖᚱ·ᚠᛚᚢᚠᚱᛁᚦᛗ

If one asks what is the earliest monument of the English language, a standard answer is the Bewcastle Cross, which has stood in a remote Cumberland churchyard for perhaps thirteen centuries, and whose inscriptions have been read as commemorating Alhfrith, Under-King of the Deirans. (The interpretation is uncertain, depending on whether certain faint marks are seventh-century bind-runes or nineteenth-century vandalism.) Alhfrith is an interesting figure, whose actions arguably had greater consequences for the nature of our modern society than those of many whose names are better remembered. He embodied a conflict between British and European allegiances which has obvious echoes today. This book, by a latter-day Deiran, is inscribed to the memory of Alhfrith.

□

ACKNOWLEDGEMENTS

I SHOULD like to express my warmest thanks and appreciation to those who worked on or in association with the SUSANNE project: Hélène Knight, Tim Willis, Nancy Glaister, Robin Haigh, and David Tugwell. Since, formally, he was involved with the project only briefly, it is particularly important to record the fact that Robin Haigh in reality made massive contributions throughout the life of the project which were crucial to its success. If the contents of this book prove valuable to the research community, the credit is due in very large part to Robin Haigh.

I am grateful to the Economic and Social Research Council (UK) for sponsoring the SUSANNE project, and to the Speech Research Unit of the Royal Signals and Radar Establishment (now the Defence Research Agency), Malvern, for sponsoring related research which interacted with the SUSANNE project to their mutual benefit.

I thank Professor Alvar Ellegård of Gothenburg University for giving his blessing to the idea of developing and circulating a research resource based on the work of his team; Professor W. Nelson Francis and Andrew Mackie, of Brown University, Rhode Island, for help in checking details of the original Brown Corpus texts; and my former colleague Professor Geoffrey Leech, FBA, of the University of Lancaster, for introducing me to the practice of studying language through real-life examples.

I am grateful to Lou Burnard and Alan Morrison of the Oxford Text Archive for their work in making the SUSANNE Corpus readily accessible to computer users world-wide.

I acknowledge with thanks the permission of Mouton de Gruyter, Berlin, to reprint a passage from the published version of my contribution to the Nobel Symposium on Corpus Linguistics, Stockholm, August 1991.

G. R. S.

Guisborough, Yorks.
June 1993

☐
CONTENTS

□
ABBREVIATIONS

Dictionaries:

OALD3   *Oxford Advanced Learner's Dictionary of Current English*, 3rd edn., Oxford University Press. *OALD3* appeared in many successive printings with small differences of detail in the contents of individual articles; where such differences affect the definition of the scheme, *OALD3* refers to the original 1974 printing, which is the version from which CUVOALD86 and CUVOALD92 (see below) were derived.

LDOCE   *Longman Dictionary of Contemporary English*, Longman, 1978.

English grammars:

GCE   R. Quirk *et al.*, *A Grammar of Contemporary English*, Longman (Harlow), 1972.

CGEL   R. Quirk *et al.*, *A Comprehensive Grammar of the English Language*, Longman, 1985.

Corpus manuals (printed documents distributed with copies of the respective electronic corpora):

BCUM   "Brown Corpus Users' Manual": W. N. Francis and H. Kučera, *Manual of Information to Accompany a Standard Corpus of Present-Day Edited American English, for Use with Digital Computers*, Department of Linguistics, Brown University, Providence, Rhode Island. The first edition of this document was dated 1964; there have been several subsequent editions, in due course incorporating information relating to the "Tagged Brown Corpus", and references in the present work are to the edition dated 1989.

LCUM   "LOB Corpus Users' Manual": S. Johansson, *Manual of Information to Accompany the Lancaster-*

| | *Oslo/Bergen Corpus of British English, for Use with Digital Computers*, Department of English, University of Oslo, 1978. |
| *TLCUM* | The separate manual written to accompany the Tagged version of the LOB Corpus: S. Johansson, *The Tagged LOB Corpus Users' Manual*, Norwegian Computing Centre for the Humanities, Bergen, 1986. |

Other corpus-related reference works:

CEC	J. Svartvik and R. Quirk (eds.), *A Corpus of English Conversation*, C. W. K. Gleerup (Lund), 1980: gives technical information about the London-Lund Corpus and reproduces the contents of part of it.
CAE	R. G. Garside *et al.* (eds.), *The Computational Analysis of English: A Corpus-Based Approach*, Longman, 1987: gives various categories of information on the research background from which the present work emerges.

Initials are also used for successive versions of an electronic research resource:

| CUVOALD86 | refers to the computer-usable English dictionary developed by Roger Mitton of Birkbeck College, London (Mitton 1986) from the typesetting tape of *OALD3*. |
| CUVOALD92 | is the revised 1992 edition of this data file. |

Dates are quoted in this book in ISO *yyyy.mm.dd* format.

□ 1 □
AIMS AND BACKGROUND

This book has two purposes. First, it offers a draft of a comprehensive annotation scheme for representing the structure of the modern English language. This scheme attempts to specify a single predictable analysis for any form that is found in the language as it is used in practice, and to indicate all aspects of the grammar of English that are definite enough to be susceptible of formal annotation. And secondly, it introduces the reader to an electronic research resource, a body of English annotated in conformity with this scheme, which is available freely and without formality to anyone who would like to use it, and which is already in widespread use internationally. At the end of the book there is an explanation of how a copy of this SUSANNE Corpus can be obtained by anyone working at a computer with access to the Internet international network.[1]

Both the analytic scheme, and the annotated Corpus, may be of value to researchers in diverse domains. Specialists in English-language teaching, for instance, may find uses for a rigorous and comprehensive classification of the constructions occurring in authentic English[2] accompanied by a database allowing examples of any particular construction to be extracted at will. But the scheme and the Corpus have been developed in research environments oriented towards computer processing of human language — what is called Natural Language Processing, or "NLP" — and it is compu-

---

[1] The creation of the SUSANNE Corpus was sponsored by the Economic and Social Research Council (UK) under grant R000 23 1142 from 1988 to 1992. The name SUSANNE was chosen to stand for "Surface and underlying structural analyses of natural English".

[2] The term "authentic" is used in this book to describe examples of language that are drawn from real-life usage, such as the contents of the various electronic language corpora discussed later in this chapter, in contrast to language examples which are constructed by analysts in order to illustrate a discussion of language, and which may or may not be representative of naturally occurring forms. This use of the word "authentic" has been queried by several readers who find it inappropriate; the author is not altogether clear on the reason for this, but it may have to do with a special sense associated with the word within Marxist political philosophy. However, we need a word for the sense just spelled out, and in ordinary non-technical English no word seems to fit that sense more closely than "authentic". The topic of this book is remote from Marxist thought, so confusion is not likely to arise.

tational considerations which have been uppermost in the minds of those who participated in the SUSANNE enterprise.

The Need for Annotation Standards

Humans devote much of their energies to processing and exchanging information. Recently they have begun to devolve parts of this function on to the computer. Among humans, overwhelmingly the preferred medium of information exchange for most purposes is language in its spoken and written forms. But human languages are difficult things for computers to deal with: their often ambiguous and anarchic qualities create serious problems with respect to the computer's mechanical need for predictability, consistency, and order. Here and there, limited local successes have been achieved in the task of finding ways to enable computers to deal with human language. But in the 1990s it remains true as a broad generalization that computers, the machines Man has created for the task of processing information, cannot process it through the medium used by Man for that purpose. Human beings have to adapt to the computer when the two communicate, rather than the computer adapting to us.

If this state of affairs is to change, the path to change must involve intensive research on languages as they are actually used by human beings, conducted in a fashion calculated to yield findings of the well-defined, reproducible type which might be incorporated into improved NLP software systems. We need to be able to register the phenomena occurring in language samples and count how often different phenomena occur, in terms that will be understood in the same way by researchers at different sites (perhaps in different countries); and we have to be able to do this not just with artificially neat invented language samples, but with the messy realities of authentic language. Again, it is broadly true in the 1990s that we are not yet in a position to do this — for English, or to the author's knowledge for any other human language.

The present book attempts to meet this need for the English language in its two main (British and American) national standard varieties, and for one aspect of language structure: grammar (in a wide sense, including considerations that some would regard as semantic rather than strictly grammatical).

There is a great deal to a language other than grammar, but for computational NLP purposes grammar plays a central role. Almost any potential NLP application requires automatic *parsing* — that is,

the ability to extract the hierarchical grammatical structure underlying a linear sequence of words.

For some significant applications the role of parsing is fairly self-
evident: in the case of machine translation from one human language to another, for instance, it is understandable that the computer
needs to analyse the logic of a source-language input if it is to have
any chance of synthesizing a target-language output that succeeds in
expressing the same ideas, and similarly an intelligent front-end to
a database, allowing members of the public to extract information
from a computer by asking it questions in their own words, will
need to establish the logical structure of a user's query as a precon-
dition for identifying which stored item of information constitutes
an answer to that query. (And either of these applications will
require detailed knowledge of surface grammatical structures in order
to shape their outputs into user-friendly form — readable translations, or sensible-sounding, comprehensible answers to questions.)

But grammar and parsing are central also to NLP applications for
which they might prima facie seem irrelevant — according to
Obermeier (1989: 69), parsing is "[t]he central problem" in virtually all NLP applications. Text-to-speech systems, for instance, which
allow messages to be input to a machine in written form and output
by a mechanical "voice", perhaps for messages over a public address system, depend on grammatical analysis of the input texts to
determine an appropriate pattern of pitch and loudness variations
— "intonation" — on the syllables of the spoken words. Without
human-like intonation, synthesized speech quickly becomes intoler-
able to human hearers. Taking another area, one might imagine
that grammatical analysis had no place in automatic speech recognition — that is, the process of taking in speech sound as a pattern
of air pressure waves and identifying the sequence of words which
the waves represent. In fact, though, the physical airwaves alone
simply do not contain enough information uniquely to identify the
particular words the speaker intended to produce. Human hearers
can understand speech only because they unconsciously draw on
knowledge of the structural patterns of their language in order to
fill in the gaps of information missing from the physical signal.
Some of the research funding that has allowed this book to be
written was allotted specifically in the belief that the research programme from which it has emerged is likely to lead to improvements
in the performance of automatic speech recognition systems. Grammar is central to automatic natural language processing.

If it is accepted that NLP technology is largely about discovering
and using the grammatical structures underlying linear sequences of

words, the next step — explaining the need for a rigorously defined analytic scheme such as the one in this book — is easy.

In 1991, at the annual conference of the Association for Computational Linguistics at Berkeley, California, a workshop was held in which NLP researchers from nine institutions were given a range of authentic English sentences and were asked to specify, by annotating them with labelled bracketings, what their respective research groups would regard as the ideal analyses for these sentences — the target analyses which they would wish their automatic parsing systems[3] to assign to the examples. The nine sets of annotations were then compared. One cannot expect separate research groups' grammatical category labels to coincide, because choice of linguistic terminology is open-ended and the same technical term can be abbreviated in different ways, but the brackets themselves are a different matter: a particular sequence of words either is or is not bracketed together as a grammatical constituent. When one considers how long and fully the English language has been worked on, it might seem reasonable to expect different researchers' bracketings of sentences usually to coincide.

For three of the workshop examples, here are the total sets of bracketings that were identified by every workshop participant:

The famed Yankee Clipper, now retired, has been assisting [*as* [*a batting coach*]].
One of those capital-gains ventures, in fact, has saddled him [*with* [*Gore Court*]].
He said this constituted a [*very serious*] *misuse* [*of the* [*Criminal court*] *processes*].

Only a small fraction of the full range of grammatical structuring found in the examples was agreed on by all participants. (The phenomena causing divergent bracketings were listed in the workshop proceedings as including "punctuation, the employment of null nodes by the grammar, and the attachment of auxiliaries, negation, pre-infinitival *to*, adverbs, and other types of constituents". The proceedings also note that, if brackets agreed on by a majority though not necessarily all of the participants are included, then the resulting analyses come much closer to a complete identification of the examples' constituent structure.)

---

[3] This book draws a sharp distinction between the terms *system* and *scheme*. A parsing *scheme*, such as the SUSANNE scheme, is a set of categories and notational conventions allowing the grammatical properties of a text to be made explicit. A parsing *system* is a suite of computer software which, given a text as input, automatically discovers and outputs the grammatical structure of that text, represented in the notation of some parsing scheme.

The examples quoted do not seem to involve unusual or specially problematic English constructions; grammatically they are fairly simple. Authentic language is often much quirkier than this. Of course, sometimes different analysts will assign incompatible structures to the same example because they consciously hold conflicting theories about some grammatical construction included in the example: disagreements of this sort are necessary in a healthy science and will always occur. But it seems likely that most or all of the disparities between the analyses quoted above came about not because analysts positively disagreed with one another's views of English grammar, but simply because there exist no generally available public standards for grammatical analysis, which researchers could use wherever they had no positive theoretical reasons for choosing alternative analyses. Each research group is forced to define its own analytic norms from the ground up, for want of a public set of norms to fall back on.

The discipline has an acute requirement for explicit standards to be defined in this area. Such standards will not need to contain anything very original or surprising. There is no virtue in making public analytic norms idiosyncratic in any way, and they should conform to grammarians' consensus wherever consensus is discernible. But the results of the California workshop demonstrate that consensus alone will not take us far towards a comprehensive, explicit set of analytic norms for English grammar.

The SUSANNE scheme is a first public attempt to propose such a set of norms.

SUSANNE and Traditional Grammars

The SUSANNE scheme may be a first, very imperfect attempt to achieve the goals it has set itself, but it is obviously not the first attempt at a comprehensive description of English grammar. Such works have existed for centuries; very good ones have been produced in recent years, some of which have been heavily exploited by the SUSANNE research team, and many of them go far beyond anything in the present book in terms of richness of descriptive detail. What the SUSANNE scheme tries to do is different from what traditional grammars set out to do, rather in the way that the Domesday Book commissioned by William I after his conquest of England in the eleventh century differs from a conventional guidebook for visitors to England.

The guidebook sets out in more or less detail information on all sorts of features of the localities it describes — it takes up whatever topics the compilers think may interest a visitor, and the topics covered for one county will not necessarily always coincide with those for another. In the Lake District, geology challenges any visitor's attention, and the guidebook may take up geological matters at length; there is geology in the Midlands too, but a general-interest guidebook may not find it worth discussing.

Domesday Book, by contrast, consists of a series of terse statements about different places, always in the same format. It gives only set kinds of information, always the same kind of information for each place — just the information needed in order to levy taxes.

The SUSANNE scheme is similarly single-minded. Discussing any particular grammatical construction, it makes no attempt to set out all or even many of the humanly interesting properties that construction may possess; it aims merely to enable the analyst to decide unambiguously whether a particular form encountered in a text does or does not count in SUSANNE terms as an example of the construction, and, if it does, how to represent that fact in his annotation. A conventional grammatical description will often describe one construction as shading into a different construction, with clear cases at either end of the gradient but many intermediate cases sharing features of one construction and features of the other. The gradient may genuinely be continuous, but the SUSANNE scheme will try to impose some sharp boundary on it, grouping all the examples on one side of the boundary with one clear case and all the examples on the other side with the other clear case: computation needs sharpness and predictability. Domesday aimed to allow taxes to be levied on a nation comprehensively but fairly. SUSANNE aims to allow grammatical tree structures to be drawn for texts comprehensively but predictably.

In terms of richness of description, the SUSANNE scheme is intentionally very limited by comparison with a conventional grammar. In terms of comprehensiveness, SUSANNE in some ways goes rather further than conventional grammatical descriptions usually do. SUSANNE aims to prescribe a predictable analysis for everything that occurs in English; and there are many things that occur in written English, and which are often highly significant for practical NLP applications, which are felt to be only marginally part of the "English language" and tend to be overlooked by traditional grammatical description. Such things would include addresses, money sums, or even personal names, for instance.

These things have their own characteristic grammar: it is a fact about personal names occurring in English writing, for instance, that Christian names (forenames) precede surnames, that forenames are often replaced by initials but surnames usually not, and that certain terms (*Mr, Lady*) often precede a personal name while others (*BSc, OBE*) often follow one. These grammatical features can be as language-specific as are tense systems or the structure of relative clauses: in many East Asian languages, and in Hungarian, surnames precede individual names; postal addresses in many Continental European languages place town before street; Portuguese writes *2$50* where English writes £2.50 or $2.50. If one aims to build an automatic language-processing system to achieve some economically useful task, it is likely to be as important to deal successfully with these areas of language as with "core" areas of grammar, and they are included squarely within the purview of SUSANNE. Even punctuation tends to be neglected in conventional grammatical description, which is oriented primarily towards the spoken language;[4] but computer processing of written language obviously needs to be able to handle punctuation marks, and the SUSANNE scheme treats them as being as much a part of the English language as are verbs or nouns.

The Uses of the Scheme

NLP needs a rigorously defined analytic scheme for one thing because systems of automatic parsing require a clear target. It may be that in reality one English construction blends into another in a woolly way, but if we set out to create software systems for analysing the language we must make decisions about what specific performance on the part of such systems will count as success: such decisions are needed both to establish goals for the developers of systems, and to develop objective evaluation standards for those assessing systems developed by others. The SUSANNE scheme is one possible way of rendering such decisions explicit. It is certainly not the only possible way, and there is no suggestion that the

---

[4] At least, theoretical linguists conventionally explain their lack of interest in matters such as punctuation or the representation of money sums by arguing that linguistics ought to be concerned with spoken rather than with written language. However, linguists frequently discuss example sentences having highly ramified grammatical structures which are quite untypical of speech, and they tend to exclude from consideration linguistic phenomena characteristic of speech, such as the structure of "speech repairs". Arguably, the traditional agenda of linguistics has been determined less by considerations of spoken v. written language than by the question of what aspects of natural language are relevant to *logical* analysis: areas of language structure that lack a relationship with logic tend to be played down. For NLP purposes, though, logic is only one aspect of natural language.

SUSANNE scheme is the "correct" scheme or the "best" scheme — it is merely one explicit analytic scheme, offered to the research community for consideration.

Very probably, research groups working on automatic parsing systems in connection with particular applications will commonly have good reasons to reject various aspects of the SUSANNE scheme in favour of alternative conventions. But it is possible that even in such cases there will be areas of analysis where the choice of conventions is not critical, and the SUSANNE scheme might offer a saving of effort by allowing groups to avoid defining all aspects of their target parsing scheme from scratch.

Secondly, an explicit parsing scheme is needed for statistical approaches to NLP technology in order to allow linguistic items to be counted in a consistent way. Very often in English grammar there is a clear consensus that a particular word of a text heads a construction of a certain category, but there is some vagueness about whether a peripheral word or phrase is part of the construction or is a sister to it — is a tag question such as *does he?* subordinate to the preceding declarative clause, for instance, or are the two clauses concatenated? If such issues (and there are many of them) are left inexplicit then statistical data gathering will treat individual instances now one way, now another, leading to meaningless figures not just for one construction-type in each case but, typically, for three (the two which may be either sisters or mother and daughter, and the one which is mother to one or both). It is far better to gather statistics on *any* consistent basis than in this whimsical fashion. A principle guiding the development of the SUSANNE scheme was that it is more important that the recommended analysis of any particular linguistic form should be predictable than that it should be theoretically justifiable.

In the early years of computational linguistics data collections were small and individual research groups typically developed their own collections, with limited exchange of data between sites; but as the subject has matured and research resources have become larger, it has been appreciated that scientific efficiency calls for the investment in creating resources to be recouped by making them reusable by different groups. This requires publicly known annotation standards, allowing research groups routinely to exchange quantities of precise and unambiguous information about the contents of a language. At present not only, as we have seen, do the details of NLP researchers' labelled tree structures differ widely between research groups, but even the traditional terminology of linguistics is often heavily ambiguous. Terms such as "predicate" or "complement", for instance, are used in several quite incompatible senses. Again SUSANNE offers a set of standards which groups can, if they wish, declare as applicable to their exchanges of data, freeing them from the burden of developing explicit, detailed analytic conventions of their own in the area of grammar.

And the scheme has a further potential use which might give it value even if every individual detail of its notational conventions were rejected. It offers a conspectus or check-list allowing NLP researchers to monitor the scope of the total task and the extent to which particular systems have covered the entire language or left gaps. We have seen that traditional grammatical description tends to concentrate on "core" areas of language structure, overlooking matters such as the grammar of addresses, for instance, and it is easy to get into the habit of thinking that the concerns of traditional grammatical description define the scope of the discipline as a whole. SUSANNE has taken a different approach, evolving a scheme of formal annotation in response to the actual contents of a "fair sample" of the language rather than in response to the received agenda of grammatical discourse. Thus there is some reason to feel that the proportion of SUSANNE categories whose analysis is addressed by an NLP system offers a broadly meaningful estimate of the extent of coverage of that system, and that the relative size of different gaps in terms of ranges of SUSANNE categories un-addressed might offer a clue as to where extra research effort would most usefully be deployed. Furthermore, even if the research community rejects the particular analytic decisions incorporated in the SUSANNE scheme, the scheme at least identifies questions which an alternative scheme of annotation norms would have to decide in other ways. Future research groups will not need to waste time stumbling over these issues unexpectedly, as the SUSANNE team did in many cases.

The need that SUSANNE attempts to meet in the domain of English grammar is rather akin to the need which was met in the botanical domain in the eighteenth century by the Linnaean taxo-nomy. Before Linné, there were plenty of herbals that described the various plants of the world, accurately and often in great detail; but these works did not focus on the task of enabling a researcher to move easily and predictably from a specimen to a systematic, un-ambiguous identifying name. Linné saw plant kinds as shading con-tinuously into one another. As he put it: "Natura non facit saltus. Plantae omnes utrinque affinitatem monstrant, uti territorium in mappa geographica." But that did not stop him imposing bound-aries in this apparent continuum, as nineteenth-century European statesmen created colonial boundaries in the map of Africa. The arrangement of species and genera in the Linnaean system was artificial and in some respects conflicted with the natural (i.e. theoretically correct) arrangement, and Linné knew this very well — he spent part of his career producing fragments of a natural taxonomy, as an alternative to his artificial taxonomy; but the artificial system was based on concrete, objective features which made it practical to apply, and because it did not have to wait on the resolution of theoretical puzzles Linné could make it complete. Artificial though the Linnaean system was, it enabled the researcher to locate a definite name for any specimen (and to know that any other botanist in the world would use the same name for that specimen), and it gave him something approaching an exhaustive conspectus of the "data elements" which a more theoretical approach would need to be able to cope with.

If no one had ever done what Linné did, then Swedish biologists would continually be wondering what British biologists meant (indeed, biologists in Sussex would be wondering what biologists in Lancaster or Cambridge meant) by, say, cuckoo-pint, and whether cuckoo-pint, cuckoo flower, and ragged robin were one plant, two, or three. Since Linné, we all say *Arum maculatum* and we know what we are talking about. Computational linguistics up to now has been operating more or less on the cuckoo-pint standard. The SUSANNE scheme, using a system of code symbols as Linné used Latin to escape the ambiguities of traditional terminology, is a first attempt to improve on this situation. It is certainly not the last word on the subject. If this scheme is worth publishing, its value will ultimately lie in inaugurating a public process of evolving taxonomic standards which will surely lead in due course to schemes much fuller, more consistent, and more precise than the one specified in the chapters that follow.

SUSANNE *and Generative Grammar*

Computational approaches to natural language are commonly seen as having a particular affinity with the generative school of linguistic theory, which was inaugurated by Noam Chomsky's *Syntactic Structures* (Chomsky 1957) and dominated linguistic research during the late 1960s and 1970s — indeed the advent of the computer in the 1980s breathed new life into generative linguistics at a time when it was beginning to give ground to more humanistic modes of language study. Both computational linguistics and generative linguistics involve formal, quasi-mathematical styles of natural-language analysis. However, the taxonomic enterprise presented in this book has little in common with the assumptions underlying generative linguistics (which, for its part, has often dissociated itself rather sharply from taxonomic goals — see for instance Chomsky's pejorative use of the term "taxonomic model" (Chomsky 1964: 11), or various remarks by Katz (1971) on linguistics as "library science"). It will be as well to state these differences in order to avoid misunderstandings.

In the first place, a generative linguist might see any attempt to specify a comprehensive set of grammatical annotation conventions for the English language as unreasonably ambitious, considering that numerous books and articles have been and continue to be published which attempt to come closer to the ideal of defining a complete grammar of English, and generative authors repeatedly make the point that this ideal is not yet close to being achieved. However, a "grammar" in generative terms is a calculus which defines a boundary between valid and invalid word sequences (this is what the term "generate" means in this context); as Chomsky put it (1957: 13), "The fundamental aim in the linguistic analysis of a language L is to separate the *grammatical* sequences which are the sentences of L from the *ungrammatical* sequences which are not sentences of L and to study the structure of the grammatical sequences." But the present scheme makes no claim to draw a boundary between grammatical and ungrammatical sequences, which is the source of much of the difficulty of generative linguistics. The SUSANNE scheme aims only to provide predictable annotations for any forms that *do* occur in English; if, in achieving this, the scheme also implies annotations for hypothetical word-sequences that never occur, that is not a flaw in the scheme — it is a matter of no importance.

The present author is in fact sceptical about whether the concept of a boundary between valid and invalid word-sequences is applicable to natural languages. His own work on automatic parsing systems (see e.g. Sampson *et al.* 1989) makes no use of such a concept; it treats the parsing task as one of finding a labelled tree over a word-sequence which maximizes a continuous measure of similarity to the trees found in a database of correctly analysed examples, ruling no labelled tree out as illegal. Many writers have urged that it is actually quite difficult to construct English word-sequences which could not be meaningfully used in any circumstances, and that (Hockett 1968: 61) "*all* constraints in a language are of [a] more or less rubbery sort, yielding no definite boundary to the 'set of all possible sentences' ".

Sampson (1987*b*) examined this issue through a statistical analysis of the constructions occurring in a 40,000-word forerunner to the SUSANNE Corpus. This database contained labelled tree structures representing the surface grammar of the individual sentences included, and a "construction" was defined as a pairing of a mother label with a sequence of daughter labels, all drawn from a coarse alphabet of formal category labels, omitting many finer subcategories, in order to achieve a reasonable chance of encountering repetitions of the same construction. (The investigation reported used only constructions in which the mother label was "noun phrase".)

Even if there are rules in English which separate grammatical from ungrammatical sequences, a generative linguist would not predict that constructions violating the rules will never be found in practice; he would expect sporadic ungrammatical constructions to occur as a consequence of "performance errors" (Chomsky 1965: 3). But the generative view of natural language appears to predict a bimodal distribution, with a limited number of grammatical constructions repeating fairly often, and ungrammatical constructions occurring as one-offs or with low frequency because of essentially random performance factors. What emerged from the data was a quite different pattern. Plotting frequency of construction-type against proportion of the observed data accounted for by constructions belonging to types of not more than that frequency, on a log–log scale the data points were distributed evenly along a nearly straight line, with no discontinuity that might plausibly be identified with a grammatical/ungrammatical boundary. That is: as one considers lower frequencies, the number of different constructions having those frequencies increases smoothly and rapidly, so that (if the database used for this investigation is representative of the language as a whole) even when one thinks of a frequency so low that one would need to examine a vast amount of material to find one instance of a specified construction having that frequency, the likelihood that an example picked from a text at random will represent *some* construction of at least equal rarity will still be quite high. If an NLP system were based on a generative grammar, that grammar could not ignore very-low-frequency constructions as peripheral and probably ungrammatical, because a lot of authentic language is made up of constructions which individually have very low frequencies; but, equally, the grammar could not be based on an empirical investigation distinguishing constructions which occur, if only at very low frequencies, from hypothetical constructions that never occur at all, because the amount of material that would need to be checked is far too large for such an investigation to be feasible.[5]

Within the generative paradigm, furthermore, stating *an* analysis for a given grammatical construction is not the goal; generative linguistics as a theoretical science aims to discover the *correct* analysis (in terms of speakers' mental organization of their linguistic knowledge), and mere "observational adequacy" in a grammar (Chomsky 1964: ch. 2) is not highly regarded. If generative linguists took the SUSANNE enterprise to share this perspective, they would be right to see it as a grossly presumptuous exercise. But, for SUSANNE, "observational adequacy" is all that is attempted. As mentioned above, authentic English contains many phenomena that do not figure at all in theoretical linguists' grammars. First let us do a stocktaking of our material, and then we shall have among other things a better basis for theoretical work. From the point of view adopted in this book, to suggest that theoretically correct analyses of linguistic phenomena must be established before annotation conventions for those phenomena are promulgated would be like deferring the adoption of a systematic biological nomenclature until all questions about species relationships have been resolved through studies of nucleotide sequences in their chromosomes.

Another important difference of assumptions is that generative linguistics draws much of its motivation from a belief that the human ability to acquire and use languages depends on specialized cognitive machinery which is innate in all humans as part of the genetic endowment of our species, so that linguistics is in essence a "branch of cognitive psychology", as Chomsky put it (1968: 1). The idea that mankind possesses innate knowledge of language structure is linked to the idea that all human languages share common structural features ("linguistic universals") — features which a language must have in order to fit our innate language-processing machinery; and it implies that the study of universal features of language is more worthwhile than the study of features which differ from language to language, which cannot shed any light on our inherited cognitive machinery.

One practical consequence of this philosophical stance has been to reinforce the long-standing tendency of linguists, already mentioned above, to focus attention on "core" areas of language to the exclusion of more culture-specific areas. The structure of logically significant constructions such as the relative clause or the verbal

---

[5] The implications of these findings have been called into question by Taylor *et al.* (1989) and Briscoe (1990); but these papers involve serious misunderstandings, as discussed in Sampson (1992*b*: 440–5).

auxiliary system may conceivably be determined by innate psycho-logical machinery, and thus merits the generative linguist's atten-tion, but it is obvious that the structure of English postal addresses or references to sums of money are recent and local cultural devel-opments, not the reflection of cognitive principles biologically built into our minds, so to a generative linguist it may seem a waste of time to consider these areas of language.

It seems surprising how widely the doctrine of innate knowledge of language has won acceptance, since all the arguments classically put forward in its support turn out when scrutinized to rest on a series of logical fallacies (Sampson 1989*a*). But, even if that doctrine were well founded, it would scarcely be relevant in the context of NLP, which is an engineering discipline rather than a branch of pure science. The reason why society is willing to find resources to support NLP research lies in the hope that this work will yield software systems able to execute economically useful tasks. From that point of view it does not matter whether some aspect of lan-guage is psychologically innate or an acquired cultural feature: practical NLP systems need to be able to deal with addresses as well as with relative clauses.

And likewise the generative doctrine of "competence" and "per-formance" (Chomsky 1964: 10) — the idea that the proper subject of linguistic research is an ideal, relatively regular system of linguis-tic competence underlying the messy observable realities of speak-ers' performance — while it may possibly be appropriate to linguistics as a branch of psychology, loses its relevance in the NLP context. A computer software system executes a practical task, or it is noth-ing. The only kinds of language that actually occur in real life are the products of imperfect linguistic performance, so that is what NLP researchers must address themselves to. For the NLP researcher there is little point in speculating about the possibility that observed language results from extraneous interfering factors impinging on a neater system of linguistic competence within speakers' minds, because even if that were true a software system that dealt with an exclusively mental reality would be unusable.

Annotation Rules as Law

We have seen that the generative linguist might find the SUSANNE scheme too cursory a document to be capable of adequately cover-ing its declared domain. Readers approaching the scheme from other intellectual directions, though, on reading the hundreds of detailed annotation rules laid down in the following chapters, may well feel that the SUSANNE scheme is far more elaborate than it need be. The SUSANNE annotation conventions began life, ten years ago, as a terse document listing and briefly explaining a number of grammatical categories in a few pages; and the author confesses that he has often himself reacted with puzzlement and misgivings to the way in which the attempt to reconcile the experience of difficult cases with the need to maintain consistency and predictability in the application of the categories has led the definition of the scheme to balloon from a leaflet into a long book.

But consider the analogy with law. A legal system such as English Common Law is an attempt to give force to a few principles, such as equity, and a limited number of mechanisms such as contract and testamentary disposition. No one *wants* the law to be complicated; naïvely it might seem that a judge with a sound understanding of those few principles and mechanisms should be able to resolve the cases that come before him with no further ado — what need for piles of dusty law-books? Yet in real life, every day novel cases arise where fundamental principles alone fail to yield an unambiguous decision; there are arguments on both sides. We want the law to be consistent and predictable, so the mechanism of binding precedent has been invoked to require judges to harmonize their decisions with others made previously; and since there is no end to the variety of human circumstances, the precedents continue to heap themselves up. Of course we could sweep all this complexity away: we could instruct judges to follow the basic principles and, where these leave an issue open, to decide in favour of the older litigant, say. But we want our law to be less arbitrary than this: the complexity of precedent is a cost worth paying to make our system of law more just.

Likewise, one could sweep away most of the complexities of the SUSANNE scheme. One could choose a few simple rules for applying each annotation category, and follow them blindly even when they yield analyses which plainly misrepresent the true structure of English. But there would surely be little value in such a taxonomy. We cannot require our analytic scheme to represent the ultimate "correct grammar" of English, but at the same time the scheme should not be merely arbitrary. Linné's botanical taxonomy did not pretend to coincide with the natural classification of plants, but it did not group species together at random either. What is needed is a compromise between respect for the theoretically justifiable analysis where that is clear, and the need for analyses that can be applied consistently and predictably. Human language has much of the richness and continuing novelty of human life; so it may be inevitable that an adequate body of linguistic annotation rules will have something of the texture of a body of law.

Analytic Scheme and Analysed Corpus

"SUSANNE" is a scheme of analytic conventions, and a corpus of English annotated in accordance with those conventions. In terms of relative significance, the two things should be taken in that order. The primary purpose of the ten-year research effort which has led to the present book was to create a comprehensive and precise parsing scheme for English. The SUSANNE Corpus, together with other bodies of analysed English not in the public domain, served as test-beds for the development and debugging of the analytic scheme, and now that it has been electronically published the SUSANNE Corpus helps to specify the scheme, rather in the manner of a collection of type-specimens attached to a botanical taxonomy. But there are categories in the scheme (for instance, some low-frequency word-types) which happen not to be exemplified in the Corpus; in principle the SUSANNE team did not regard the fact that some known phenomenon failed to crop up in their data as a reason for omitting it from the analytic scheme, though obviously in practice the scheme is more likely to be adequate in areas where the data included relevant examples than in areas where they did not. There are undoubtedly still many individual cases where details of SUSANNE Corpus analyses conflict with the rules stated in the SUSANNE scheme, as laid down in this book; in such cases (provided the published scheme is consistent in itself) the scheme is authoritative and future versions of the Corpus need to be brought into conformity with it.

The role of the electronic corpus as adjunct to the scheme explains the limited size of the former: the SUSANNE Corpus comprises analyses of about 130,000 words of English. At the beginning of SUSANNE's ten-year gestation period, machine-readable samples of English equipped with structural annotations did not yet exist, so any statistical research on English grammar required such a resource to be created; one of the undertakings which led to the development of the SUSANNE scheme was the creation of a 40,000-word analysed corpus of British English (the "Lancaster-Leeds Treebank", discussed below) for use in a research project which was developing an automatic parsing system based on statistical techniques. More recently, though, as statistical approaches to NLP have become generally accepted by the research community, much larger analysed corpora have been created, outstripping either Lancaster-Leeds Treebank or SUSANNE Corpus in size; Mitchell Marcus of the University of Pennsylvania claimed in an unpublished paper dated January 1992 that his "Penn Treebank Project" had already annotated over 400,000 words of English with "skeletal syntactic structure", a figure that was predicted to double within months.[6]

There are alternative priorities here. Statistical research needs large populations of examples to yield reliable figures; in the case of language structure it is possible to produce large quantities of analysed material, at the cost of limiting the features indicated to those aspects of English grammatical structure which can be defined fairly easily without getting embroiled in questions of how to resolve awkward cases. Conversely, an analytic scheme which sets out to cover "all the grammar there is" and, ideally, to define a unique solution for every awkward case that may be encountered in the future must make a relatively minute examination of every instance in the data consulted, in order to have a reasonable chance of uncovering all the messy special situations: the cost of this is that the quantity of data that can be worked over is limited. It is questionable whether a research effort of the latter kind could in practice work with a corpus significantly larger than SUSANNE (cf. Black *et al.* 1993: 21), and likewise it is questionable whether an effort of the former kind could produce and undertake to conform to an analytic scheme comparable in degree of detail to the present scheme. To date no comparable body of conventions has been published by a research group working on larger-scale analysed corpora, nor have such corpora been equipped with annotations as detailed as those of SUSANNE.

The choice of whether to go for quantity of analysed material, or for comprehensiveness and precision of analytic scheme, is a choice between research strategies, either of which may be valid in different circumstances. Ultimately, the research community will need very large bodies of material, analysed in conformity with very comprehensive and precise schemes. In defence of the SUSANNE strategy, the author notes that the analogy with software engineering suggests that the best prospect of achieving this ultimate goal might come through first planning the analytic scheme in detail, and then applying it only when it is fully "stable".

Despite its limited size, the SUSANNE Corpus has proved to be

---

[6] A published version of the paper, received as this book was going to press (Marcus *et al.* 1993), gives a current figure of almost three million words.

a popular research resource in its own right even before publication of this book. Release 1 of the SUSANNE Corpus, including a documentation file giving a brief outline of the analytic categories, was first made publicly available via anonymous ftp (file transfer protocol) from the Oxford Text Archive in October 1992. By the nature of anonymous ftp the author has no way of knowing that any particular individual has taken a copy, unless that individual happens to contact him; but numerous people did get in touch with queries and comments. Within six months of initial release it appeared from messages received at the University of Sussex that the SUSANNE Corpus was already in use in academic and commercial research environments in many countries on at least four continents. Several users had commented favourably on the degree of analytic detail included in the SUSANNE annotations, by comparison with those of other analysed corpora.

The Scope of SUSANNE

SUSANNE as an analytic scheme is intended to cover the two principal national standard varieties of modern English, those of Britain and the USA, in a single scheme: it is based on both British and American written texts. (The SUSANNE Corpus itself consists purely of American English, but the scheme draws also on the Lancaster-Leeds Treebank, referred to above, which represented British English.) A limited amount of work has been done on extending the scheme to cover spoken English, and this is presented in Chapter 6.

The SUSANNE Corpus, as one would expect of a sizeable fair sample of modern English prose, contains occasional passages using archaic language or non-standard language varieties; there are even a few short poetry quotations. The analytic scheme takes account of the fact that such varieties of language occur sporadically in modern standard English prose, by specifying how linguistic phenomena characteristic of these varieties should be analysed within the framework of categories developed for the modern standard language. It does not attempt to extend that framework of categories, as would be necessary if one wished to provide an analytic scheme adequate for texts which as a whole exemplified varieties of English other than the modern standard language. For instance, the scheme notes explicitly that one may occasionally encounter a *thou* form of a verb, such as *goest*, and prescribes that it should be analysed as if it were a base form, *go*. In a scheme for annotating modern texts, it would be unjustifiable to introduce special complications for forms like *goest*, but in a scheme to be applied to the English of a few centuries ago it would certainly be necessary to create special analytic categories for such forms. Likewise, the scheme includes some resources for dealing with occasional technical items such as algebraic formulae when they occur sporadically in general prose, but it does not attempt to provide for the annotation of heavily technical material, such as mathematical or computational documents in which a significant fraction of the information is coded typographically by means other than linear sequences of sentences.

All the written material on which the SUSANNE scheme is based is published writing — the SUSANNE team did not use data from correspondence, for instance. The SUSANNE Corpus itself consists of prose extracts representing four narrowly defined genres of published English, as described in detail below. Readers interested in comparative genre studies may feel that the SUSANNE scheme is insufficiently broadly based in this respect (though the four genres used are quite different from one another). The author is inclined not to see this as a significant problem, because with respect to the structural features with which SUSANNE is concerned he does not believe that there exist large differences between genres of written English. Sampson and Haigh (1988) statistically analysed grammatical genre differences in the Lancaster-Leeds Treebank in order to locate the causes of what at a macroscopic level appear to be large structural contrasts between genres: mean sentence length in technical prose is almost twice the corresponding figure for fiction. Once attention shifted from these macroscopic effects towards their microscopic causes, however, the genre differences tended to melt away. There are a few individual grammatical phenomena which are characteristic of particular genres, most of which are obvious: fiction contains more direct speech than technical prose, for instance. But the large differences in sentence length turned out to be caused not by these phenomena, but by quite small inter-genre statistical differences in the propensity to realize particular constructions which are common to all genres in one way rather than another as sequences of daughter constituents. The recursive nature of grammatical structure means that even small statistical differences at the level of individual constructions multiply up and yield large overall differences at the level of sentences. If one is considering English grammar in terms of detailed grammatical analysis of individual examples, the microscopic point of view is the relevant one, and most of the differences found at this level fall well below the granularity of a scheme such as that of the present book. It may be that genres differ more sharply in terms of vocabulary; but grammatically speaking there is one written English language, with minor statistical differences between genres.

The largest grammatical unit recognized by the SUSANNE scheme is the paragraph. Documents commonly include structuring above the paragraph level, but it is not possible to study this through the medium of a Corpus of text extracts each of which is only 2,000 words long; the SUSANNE scheme does not purport to offer annotation standards for structure beyond the paragraph (and such structure in any case reflects relationships rather different from those of "grammar" in the ordinary sense).

It probably goes without saying that the SUSANNE scheme is intended to be applied to the English language and not to any other. There may be some structural features common to all human languages, and there are certainly many features common to the Indo-European languages which share a single ancestry with English; but the SUSANNE analytic scheme extends to a level of detail which goes far beyond the matters that can reasonably be seen as common even to the relatively closely related languages of Western Europe. No attention at all was paid, in developing the SUSANNE scheme, to the question whether a particular analytic category was applicable to English alone or had equivalents in other languages; the only issue regarded as relevant was whether, within English, the category is grammatically significant.

If researchers dealing with other languages set out to develop parsing schemes comparable to the present scheme for English, it is possible that they might find some of the general principles of the SUSANNE scheme useful in their own work, and the author would be delighted if that should be the case. But he would deprecate any suggestion that SUSANNE categories should be imposed on other languages (or that the SUSANNE approach to the analysis of English should be modified merely in order to make its annotations more similar to those appropriate for other languages).

For much of the twentieth century it was a truism of linguistics that each human language should be analysed in its own terms, and that importing analytic categories from the study of one language to that of another is likely to be harmful rather than helpful. In the last few decades this idea has been somewhat lost sight of. During the period of dominance of generative theory, the emphasis on psychologically grounded linguistic universals provided a theoretical reason for shifting attention away from the distinctive characteristics of individual languages. More recently, in Europe in the 1990s, the same trend has been reinforced by political developments; the growing role of the European Commission in setting research agendas has been associated with novel pressures on NLP researchers to adhere to analytic categories devised for the European languages as a class rather than for single languages individually. In the author's view this is a profound error, which will not advance EC goals but will only tend to produce poor science. The further one moves away from detailed examination of an individual language in its own terms, the less chance one has of replacing the centuries-old aprioristic categories of the schoolroom with categories that are empirically adequate to the realities of any particular language or languages.

The Research Background

In order to give the reader a clearer understanding of what the SUSANNE Corpus is like and why it is like that, it will be appropriate to recount something of the history of corpus linguistics in general and the particular programme of corpus-linguistics research from which the SUSANNE project emerged.

Corpus linguistics as it is usually understood today, that is the study of languages through the medium of large computer-readable authentic language samples, was inaugurated by the publication of the Brown Corpus of American English in 1964. Logically speaking there is of course no necessary relationship between the study of language through authentic samples and the use of computers: the computer is merely a tool that makes it practical to examine larger samples and extract information from them more rapidly. Corpus linguistics had been practised, without computers, long before the Brown Corpus: one notable example was Charles Fries's grammatical description of spoken English (Fries 1952), which avoided any use of traditional grammatical terminology in favour of newly coined categories derived empirically from the contents of a corpus of surreptitiously recorded telephone conversations. However, it happened that the dominance of generative theory during much of the 1960s and 1970s created a historical discontinuity between pre-computer and post-computer corpus linguistics. Generative linguists tended to be uninterested in or even hostile towards empirical, corpus-based research, for reasons that are not always easy to understand (Sampson 1975: ch. 4; Aarts and van den Heuvel 1985: 303–5), and as a result around the time that the Brown Corpus was published, and for many years afterwards, not much corpus-based linguistics was done — it was quite a long time after the Brown Corpus first became available that it began to be widely used.

When interest in corpus linguistics revived, the computer was becoming routinely available as a research tool to linguists, and once it is available no one would want to revert to manual methods in this domain, where data files tend to be massively large — computational linguists have acquired a reputation in university computing environments as regularly making larger demands on computer memory resources than representatives of any other academic discipline.[7] Thus "corpus linguistics" now means computer-based corpus linguistics, and it has only loose links with work carried out before the advent of the computer.

The Brown Corpus (see e.g. Francis and Kučera 1982, Leech 1987) was developed, by W. Nelson Francis and Henry Kučera of Brown University in Providence, Rhode Island, to be a one-million-word fair sample of edited American English prose which appeared in print in a particular year, namely 1961. The term "edited" refers to the fact that the coverage of the Brown Corpus is limited not merely to written rather than spoken language but, among written genres, to material which has been published and accordingly has been subjected to the editorial disciplines associated with publication.

Within that limited but large domain considerable effort was put into making the sample representative. It consists of 500 text extracts, each about 2,000 words long. The overall domain of edited English was divided into fifteen genres, such as press reportage, skills and hobbies, technical and scholarly prose, detective stories, etc., and the proportion of each genre within the total 500 texts was chosen by asking a number of suitable experts to offer numerical estimates of the relative significance of each genre within the total stream of edited English, and averaging their opinions: thus e.g. technical and scholarly writing accounts for eighty of the 500 extracts, science fiction for just six. Large catalogues of books, newspapers, and the like were consulted in order to make random selections of documents in the various genres; within any chosen document, a page number and line number were chosen at random, and a text extract harvested for the Corpus beginning at the first sentence-break following the chosen point and ending at the first sentence-break falling at least 2,000 words later. (Because each text extract consists of complete sentences, most of the 500 texts include a little over 2,000 words.) The extracts thus obtained were then converted into machine-readable form, using various coding conventions

---

[7] If this seems surprising, consider the fact that a subject such as chemistry, complex as it obviously is, ultimately concerns the interactions between atoms representing a hundred-odd distinct elements. The linguist's "atoms" are words, and even quite a small dictionary will list tens of thousands of different words, each with its own special and idiosyncratic properties.

to deal with typographical phenomena (such as italics v. roman) having no direct equivalence in computer character-sets.

Although, as mentioned above, the intellectual climate of the time caused the Brown Corpus to be somewhat neglected in the early years after publication, in due course a stream of related developments occurred.

In the first place, new corpora were produced. The Lancaster-Oslo/Bergen ("LOB") Corpus (Leech 1987) was developed, by Geoffrey Leech of Lancaster University and Stig Johansson and Knut Hofland in Norway, as a British English "twin" to the Brown Corpus, and was published in 1978. (Like Brown, LOB was based on documents published in 1961, in order to achieve a pair of resources differing only in terms of the national-variety variable.) The London-Lund Corpus of spoken British English (half a million words) was published in 1980 (Svartvik 1990). And, as computer power has grown, other and often much larger corpora have joined them, some in the public domain and others created for proprietary purposes, e.g. by dictionary publishers. The year 1991 saw the inauguration of the British National Corpus project, led by Oxford University Press, which is scheduled to produce a 100,000,000-word standard sample of written and spoken British English.

While new and larger corpora were developed, existing corpora were enriched by the addition of more sophisticated analytic apparatus, increasing their value as research resources. The original versions of Brown and LOB contained little more than direct electronic transcription of the typography of the source texts, though there was a small amount of analysis (for instance, full stops were distinguished as sentence-final or abbreviatory marks). But in 1979 and 1986 respectively "tagged" versions of Brown and LOB were published, in which each of their one-million-odd word-tokens was equipped with a code identifying its grammatical role: for instance *might* appears in the Tagged LOB Corpus as "might_MD" when acting as a modal verb, but as "might_NN" when functioning as a noun. Given the frequent grammatical ambiguity of English words taken in isolation, a data file in which words have grammatical tags is obviously far more useful as an information source than a corpus of "raw" texts.

The next stage beyond tagged corpora is that of analysed corpora, which display not just the grammatical roles of individual words but the larger grammatical structures of phrase, clause, and sentence into which the words fit. SUSANNE is one of the latest examples of an analysed corpus, and one whose analysis is relatively complete.

The Development of the SUSANNE Corpus

The present author first became involved in corpus linguistics when, in 1983, he began to collaborate with Geoffrey Leech and Roger Garside of Lancaster University on a research project directed by them whose goal was to produce a statistically based parsing system for English. The nature of the Lancaster parser is described e.g. in Garside and Leech (1987), Black *et al.* (1993); it uses the statistical optimizing concept described earlier in connection with the author's own work (he derived the idea from Leech and Garside).

The project accordingly needed an analysed corpus to serve as a source of grammatical statistics. Less obviously, it also needed a corpus to be analysed manually in order to develop explicit conventions defining what the desired output of the parsing system ought to be in numerous unclear cases. Because of the emphasis laid by the linguistics of the recent past on theoretical debate about a limited number of core, logically important constructions, it came as something of a surprise to many of us involved with the Lancaster parsing project to realize how frequently the received grammatical consensus left it entirely open what analysis is appropriate for the very diverse phenomena found in authentic material — and indeed how many open questions there are about the analysis even of core constructions, as more recently shown by the results of the California workshop discussed above.

Primary responsibility for developing an analysed corpus for the use of the Lancaster project was assigned to the present author. Initially, as already mentioned, a range of grammatical categories and symbols was listed in a document of a few pages drafted by Geoffrey Leech. The author used these categories to produce analyses of successive samples from the LOB Corpus, logging and making provisional decisions on the many precedents that arose in applying the categories to Corpus material; periodically the accumulated precedents were circulated and discussed in meetings of the whole research team, and the provisional decisions either confirmed or altered. This process resulted after two years in the manually analysed Lancaster-Leeds Treebank, together with a body of "case-law" governing the application of the analytic categories to difficult cases, the case-law document being rather longer than the corpus on whose analysis it was based.

A corpus of 40,000 words is not large for statistical purposes; and the Lancaster-Leeds analytic scheme, although rather well defined in its own terms, had limitations: in particular it described only the "surface" or "formal" grammatical structure of texts, ignoring their "logical" or "functional" grammar. Beginning in 1986, the present author directed a new programme of research on English-language parsing by stochastic optimization (that is, by computationally simulating Darwinian evolutionary techniques in order to maximize the plausibility of analyses for authentic input texts) which needed fuller statistical information on English grammar.[8] In 1988 the Economic and Social Research Council undertook to sponsor the SUSANNE project, whose aim was to go beyond these limitations by developing a larger analysed corpus, annotated in terms of a richer parsing scheme which should specify logical as well as surface grammar.

Producing a manually analysed corpus is a very labour-intensive and therefore expensive activity. It was clear that the SUSANNE project would have the best chance of success if, rather than attempting to carry out the entire work of annotating a new sample of raw texts, it began with a database as close as possible to the desired end-product and concentrated available resources on improving and adding to the information already present in that database. This is what we did. In 1988 several analysed corpora (apart from the Lancaster-Leeds Treebank) were already available; the SUSANNE project selected the "Gothenburg Corpus" as the most suitable starting-point for its own work. (Sampson 1991 gives details of the various analysed corpora available at the time and the reasons for choosing the Gothenburg Corpus.)

The Gothenburg Corpus (Ellegård 1978) is a manually analysed subset of the Brown Corpus, produced by Alvar Ellegård and his students at Gothenburg University in the 1970s. It contains sixty-four of the 500 Brown texts (hence the total of about 130,000 words); the sixty-four texts include sixteen from each of four Brown genre categories:

A press reportage;
G belles lettres, biography, memoirs, etc.;
J "learned" (technical and scholarly prose);
N adventure and Western fiction.

Details of the individual texts are included in the electronic documentation file accompanying Release 2 and upwards of the SUSANNE Corpus.

Research based on word-frequency data has suggested that the

[8] The author's programme of research on parsing by stochastic optimization has been sponsored by the Speech Research Unit of the Royal Signals and Radar Establishment, Malvern (contracts D/ER1/9/4/2062/151(RSRE), 1986–9, and D/ER1/9/4/2062/128(RSRE), 1989–91), and by the Science and Engineering Research Council and Ministry of Defence (joint grant GR/J06108, 1992–5).

fifteen Brown/LOB genre categories can be grouped into four broad types of prose (Hofland and Johansson 1982: 27), and it happens that categories A, G, J, and N exemplify each of these four types; so, although the Gothenburg Corpus contains only a fraction of the Brown material, there is some objective justification for seeing it as comparably representative.

In the Gothenburg Corpus, the prose of these texts is equipped with annotations representing its surface grammatical structure and also giving some limited indications of underlying logical structure, in cases where elements have been deleted or shifted from their logical position — it was largely this feature of the Gothenburg Corpus which made it specially attractive as the starting-point for the SUSANNE project. The grammatical annotations represent a hybrid type of grammatical analysis in which clauses and their immediate constituents are shown in phrase-structure terms, while the internal structure of phrases is coded in terms of Continental dependency grammar.

An extract from the Gothenburg Corpus is shown as Fig. 1.1. The grammatical structure annotations are in the columns towards the right, which in the first line run "ZDF1 S R".

Exploiting the information contained in the Gothenburg Corpus is not altogether straightforward. The method by which Gothenburg represents labelled tree structures in terms of linear character-strings is somewhat opaque, and it is also systematically ambiguous — that is, there are cases where labelled trees of distinct structures, correctly coded in accordance with the Gothenburg conventions, come out identical. Furthermore (a point that became apparent as the SUSANNE team began to work on the material) the contents of the Gothenburg Corpus are linear codings of tree structures in only a notional sense. The Gothenburg analysts did not actually draw labelled trees for the sentences of the chosen texts, and then transpose their trees into linear codes; instead they moved straight from the sentences to the linear codes, and at points where the grammar was complicated they sometimes allowed themselves to use the linear coding in ways that correspond to no particular tree structure. And finally, as Ellegård points out (1978: 8, 95) — and as is quite unavoidable when one has to rely on student labour rather than on that of salaried researchers — there is a significant incidence of errors and omissions in the Gothenburg material. These points are not made in a carping spirit, indeed the present author has great admiration for what Alvar Ellegård achieved in the circumstances in which he worked. The Gothenburg Corpus was much superior to the Lancaster-Leeds Treebank as a jumping-off point for what

```
000392000564HE          *N030460ZDF1        S        R
000392000565HANDED      N030460ZDF1         V        VD
000392000566THE         N030460ZDF1         O1       T
000392000567BAYONET     N030460ZDF1         O        N
000392000568TO          N030460ZDF1         KP       P
000392000569DEAN        N030460ZDF1         K        C
000392000570AND         *N030460ZDF2        Y        Y
000392000571KEPT        N030460ZDF2         V        VD
000392000572THE         N030460ZDF2         O1       T
000392000573PISTOL      *N030460ZDF2        4O       N
000393000574/ZJF11      *N030460ZDF1      1 O/
000393000575STAY        N030460ZJF11        V        VM
000393000576WELL        N030460ZJF11        A1       A
000393000577BACK        N030460ZJF11        A        A
000393000578OF          N030460ZJF11        A2P      P
000393000579ME          N030460ZJF11        A2       R
000393000580HE          *N030460ZDF1      2 S        R
000393000581SAID        N030460ZDF1        24V       VD
000394000582I-          *N030460ZDF1        S        R
000394000583-M          N030460ZDF1         V        B
000394000584GOING       N030460ZDF1         V1       VG
000394000585TO          N030460ZDF1         V11P     U
000394000586WALK        N030460ZDF1         V11      V
000394000587UP          N030460ZDF1         V11Q     A
000394000588TO          N030460ZDF1         BP       P
000394000589THE         N030460ZDF1         B1       T
000394000590HORSES      N030460ZDF1         B        NS
000394000591BOLD        N030460ZDF1         P        J
000394000592AS          N030460ZDF1         P1Q      Z
000394000593BRASS       N030460ZDF1         P1       N
000394000594/PDG11      N030460ZDF1         E/
000394000595PRETENDING  *N030460PDG11       V        VG
000394000596/PDF111     N030460PDG11        O/
000394000597I-          *N030460PDF111      S        R
000394000598-M          N030460PDF111       V        B
000394000599ONE         N030460PDF111       P        Q
000394000600OF          N030460PDF111       P1P      P
000394000601THE         N030460PDF111       P11      T
000394000602GUERRILLAS  N030460PDF111       4P1      NS
```

Figure 1.1

the SUSANNE project aimed to produce. Nevertheless, the factors mentioned may explain why the Gothenburg Corpus, although publicly available for a decade, had been very little used before our project.[9]

[9] Apart from the research by Ellegård himself which is reported in his 1978 book, the only other researcher known to have used the Gothenburg Corpus is Johan Elsness (e.g. Elsness 1984).

Since the Gothenburg Corpus is derived from the Brown Corpus, the texts in it are now over thirty years old. Some readers might wonder why we would have chosen such a source, considering that by the beginning of the SUSANNE project electronic corpora had become available which represent English of much more recent dates. Other things being equal, it might have been preferable to base SUSANNE on newer texts, but that possibility did not really arise: new corpora are raw corpora. The effort of adding analytic apparatus to sizeable language samples makes such large demands on highly qualified staff time that in practice the decisive question when one aims to develop more-fully annotated corpora is always likely to be "What existing resource comes closest to where we want to get to?", and that resource is likely to be a corpus which began life in its raw state many years earlier. The fact that the language is old is scarcely worth considering, if one is concerned with grammar. English grammar does not change very fast. There are a few points in the present book where considerations arise that would probably have arisen in a different form if the texts of the SUSANNE Corpus had belonged to the 1990s, but these points are trivial by comparison to the limitations that would have applied to the annotation if the SUSANNE project had had to base itself on a raw corpus. Brown, LOB, and London-Lund continue to be standard research resources in corpus linguistics, and are likely to remain such for many years to come.

(With studies of vocabulary it is a different matter — the use of words does change fast enough to make a thirty-year-old corpus inadequate for research on contemporary language. But the Brown and LOB Corpora are unsuitable for lexical research in any case, because they are too small; more than one million word-tokens are needed if one aims to gather evidence on the usage of any but the commonest individual words.)

The SUSANNE project set out to convert the annotations of the Gothenburg Corpus into an unambiguous and more transparent format, replacing idiosyncratic aspects of the Gothenburg analytic scheme with "consensus" alternatives. (For instance, the Gothenburg Corpus equates prepositional phrases with noun phrases, treating prepositions as premodifying elements akin to determiners — in the SUSANNE Corpus a prepositional phrase is a two-element construction having a preposition as one constituent and a noun phrase as the other.) The annotation scheme of the Lancaster-Leeds Treebank was to be used for those categories of information which it covered; and extensions were to be devised to the Lancaster-Leeds scheme in order to permit any further categories of grammatical information, such as logical structure, to be represented by notations which should integrate with the Lancaster-Leeds scheme into a coherent and comprehensive system of grammatical annotation.

The extended annotation scheme was required as a minimum to represent all those types of information about English texts for which the Gothenburg Corpus provided notations, and also to cover any other grammatical properties of English that are clear-cut enough to be the subject of formal annotation. The texts of the Gothenburg Corpus were to be completely annotated in terms of the revised and extended scheme, with the annotations derived automatically from the original Gothenburg annotations wherever possible, and created by manual methods wherever the Gothenburg annotations were erroneous or inadequate, or the relevant category of information was not covered by the Gothenburg scheme. (The SUSANNE Corpus was also required to restore typographic details of the original texts, such as punctuation and case differences, which were omitted from the Gothenburg Corpus.) The work of developing SUSANNE from the Gothenburg Corpus is described in Sampson (1992*a*).

Since the surface-structure Lancaster-Leeds annotation scheme had already been developed and "debugged" through detailed consideration of the awkward cases arising in tens of thousands of words of text, and was well documented, a policy was adopted that the extended scheme should only add to, but not modify, the Lancaster-Leeds annotations. The extended scheme was developed in a way similar to the process described earlier through which the Lancaster-Leeds scheme emerged. Initially the author proposed a set of notational extensions to handle additional categories of information, and then as the months went by the SUSANNE research team periodically brought forward problematic cases that arose in applying these extensions in practice, so that the eventual scheme presented in the following chapters incorporates many decisions that emerged from discussion in project meetings. It did not always prove possible to adhere rigidly to the principle that the Lancaster-Leeds surface scheme should be left unchanged — sometimes that scheme turned out to involve choices which were harmless so long as no attempt was made to indicate logical grammar, but which became indefensible once the domain of annotation was extended. In such cases we made well-defined modifications to the Lancaster-Leeds scheme. But cases of this sort were few, and in general the method of developing different aspects of the ultimate annotation system sequentially over a period of years seemed to work well: it restricted the proportion of the full complexity of ordinary English that had to be borne in mind at any one stage, and made it easier to reach well-considered decisions on those issues that were currently "up for grabs".

Ideally, a proposed standard annotation scheme would involve detailed consultation with other research groups working on English-language analysis internationally. The author was offered sponsorship by the Information Engineering Directorate of the UK Department of Trade and Industry for an intensive programme of international consultation, but unfortunately this project had to be abandoned as a consequence of unplanned developments in the author's career in 1990. It is worth stressing though that, even as it stands, the scheme presented in this book is much more than one individual's idea of how to represent English grammatical structure. It is the end-product of a team effort which lasted for a decade and at different times involved more than a dozen professional linguists and computer scientists. Many of the individual points in the scheme have emerged from repeated debates in which, week by week, various team members brought forward new empirical considerations in the attempt to thrash out the most practical solution for some awkward linguistic phenomenon; and the solution finally adopted was by no means always the one advocated by the present author. No claim is made that the SUSANNE analysis of a construction is always the best available analysis, if indeed the concept of a single best analysis applies; but it can at least be claimed that the SUSANNE analysis has often been selected after eliminating alternatives that seemed prima facie equally attractive but turned out to be problematical when applied in practice.

The later part of the period over which the SUSANNE Corpus was developed saw the emergence of the Text Encoding Initiative. The TEI is a multinational research effort, sponsored by various US agencies and by the European Commission, which aims to promulgate standards for electronic manipulation of natural language — it is concerned chiefly with matters such as encoding of typographic detail, but also includes linguistic structure in its purview. The first draft TEI Guidelines were published in 1990 (Sperberg-McQueen and Burnard 1990), and the definitive version appeared as the present work was going through proof in 1994. The present author has served on the TEI Analysis and Interpretation working group; at one point the chairman of that group, D. Terence Langendoen of the University of Arizona, proposed that the SUSANNE parsing scheme should be adopted as a recognized TEI standard. More recently the TEI has retreated from the concept of giving an official blessing to any schemes of substantive linguistic description, in favour of limiting itself to the definition of abstract formats for encoding whatever linguistic categories are preferred by individual analysts or groups; and this policy harmonizes better with the philosophy of the SUSANNE scheme itself, which (to repeat) does not claim to be the "best" scheme for annotating English grammatical structure, and which is published in the expectation that, if found useful, it will soon be modified.

Because of the timing of the two enterprises, it has not proved practical to make the early releases of the SUSANNE Corpus "TEI-conformant"; relevant aspects of the TEI Guidelines were not fixed early enough. But the format of the Corpus has been chosen with a view to moving to TEI conformance in later releases; when the TEI Guidelines are stable, and if they succeed in winning widespread acceptance as international standards, it is planned to turn SUSANNE into a fully TEI-conformant resource.

For comparison with Fig. 1.1, Fig. 1.2 displays the same section of text as it appears in the SUSANNE Corpus.

Limitations

Inevitably, not all the aims set for the SUSANNE Corpus have been fully achieved.

The most regrettable shortcoming in the finished Corpus, to the author's mind, is that it includes no indication of head–modifier relationships. In the phrase-structure grammatical formalism traditional in the English-speaking world, a sentence is diagrammed as a tree structure in which all the daughters of a non-terminal node are formally on a par with one another; informally, though, it is well understood that in many grammatical constructions one particular constituent is the head and the others are its modifiers, for instance in an adjective phrase such as *very wise* the adjective *wise* is the head and the qualifier *very* is its modifier. Continental dependency grammar formalizes this idea: it commonly draws trees in which the words of a sentence are associated with non-terminal as well as terminal nodes, so that the mother–daughter relationship between tree nodes is used to represent the head–modifier relationship. (It is not necessary to indicate the relationship this way: the same information can be encoded in ordinary phrase-structure trees, by adding some marker to one daughter of each non-terminal identifying it as the head daughter.) It is particularly unfortunate that headship indicators are missing in the SUSANNE Corpus, since this

```
N03:0460f  -   YB     <minbrk>          -      [Oh.Oh]
N03:0460g  -   PPHS1m He           He   he     [O[S[Nas:s.Nas:s]
N03:0460h  -   VVDt   handed            hand   [Vd.Vd]
N03:0460i  -   AT     the          the         [Ns:o.
N03:0460j  -   NN1c   bayonet           bayonet    .Ns:o]
N03:0460k  -   IIt    to           to          [P:u.
N03:0460m  -   NP1m   Dean         Dean        [Nns.Nns]P:u]
N03:0460n  -   CC     and          and         [S+.
N03:0460p  -   VVDv   kept         keep        [Vd.Vd]
N03:0460q  -   AT     the          the         [Ns:o.
N03:0470a  -   NN1c   pistol            pistol     .Ns:o]S+]S]
N03:0470b  -   YF     +.           -           .
N03:0470c  -   YIL    <ldquo>           -      [S.
N03:0470d  -   VV0v   +Stay stay   [Q:o[S*[V.V]
N03:0470e  -   RR     well         well   [R:p.
N03:0470f  -   RL     back         back        .
N03:0470g  -   IO     of           of          [Po.
N03:0470h  -   PPIO1  me           I          .Po]R:p]S*]Q:o]
N03:0470i  -   YIR    +<rdquo>          -           .
N03:0470j  -   YC     +,           -           .
N03:0470k  -   PPHS1m              he   he     [Nas:s.Nas:s]
N03:0470m  -   VVDv   said         say         [Vd.Vd]S]
N03:0470n  -   YF     +.           -           .
N03:0470p  -   YIL    <ldquo>           -           .
N03:0470q  -   PPIS1  +I           I      [Q[S[Nea:s.Nea:s]
N03:0470r  -   VBM    +<apos>m          be     [Vmut.
N03:0470s  -   VVGK   going        go          .Vmut]
N03:0470t  -   TO     to .         to          [Ti:z[Vi.
N03:0470u  -   VV0v   walk         walk        .Vi]
N03:0480a  -   RP     up           up          [R:q.R:q]
N03:0480b  -   IIt    to           to          [P:q.
N03:0480c  -   AT     the          the         [Np.
N03:0480d  -   NN2    horses            horse .Np]P:q]Ti:z]
N03:0480e  -   YC     +,           -           .
N03:0480f  -   JJ     bold         bold        [Jh:b.
N03:0480g  -   CSA    as           as          [P.
N03:0480h  -   NN1n   brass brass  .P]Jh:b]
N03:0480i  -   YC     +,           -           .
N03:0480j  -   VVGv   pretending        pretend    [Tg:b[Vg.Vg]
N03:0480k  -   PPIS1  I            I      [Fn:o[Nea:s.Nea:s]
N03:0480m  -   VBM    +<apos>m          be     [Vmb.Vmb]
N03:0480n  -   MC1    one          one         [Ms:e.
N03:0480p  -   IO     of           of          [Po.
N03:0480q  -   AT     the          the         [Np.
N03:0480r  -   NN2    guerrillas        guerrilla
                .Np]Po]Ms:e]Fn:o]Tg:b]S]
N03:0480s  -   YF     +.           -           .
```

Figure 1.2

information was partially encoded in the original Gothenburg Corpus; that aspect of the Gothenburg information was lost in the reformatted SUSANNE Corpus through a series of misunderstandings in the early stages of our project.

It is possible to defend the lack of headship marking in the SUSANNE scheme by pointing out that this concept is rather less clear than the various grammatical properties which are incorporated in the scheme: if SUSANNE did mark heads, it could not avoid theoretical controversy. There is not general agreement even on whether all constructions, or only some constructions, have heads; and, for constructions that have heads, there are sometimes large disagreements about which constituent is their head. (For instance, Vennemann (1984: 603–4) points out that some theorists regard the head of a noun phrase such as *the rose* as the noun, *rose*, while others regard the article *the* as the head. Anderson (1976: 6, 126) argues that the head of a phrase such as *a white rose* is *white*, and that the head of a construction such as *walk slowly* is *slowly*, but these concepts are contrary to many others' views.) However, it would be preferable if SUSANNE indicated headship, using any consistent theory of the concept, rather than merely ignoring it. It is hoped that this may be achieved in later releases of the Corpus; Chapter 2 defines notation allowing it to be done.

A second area ignored by the SUSANNE analytic scheme is anaphora: there is no attempt to mark identity of reference between referring items, for instance cases where an entity is introduced by a full noun phrase and subsequently identified by a pronoun. In straightforward cases, co-reference might have been indicated through an extended use of the index system defined in Chapter 5 for annotating logical/surface grammar disparities; but many examples of anaphora in English are less straightforward and could only be adequately indicated by a much subtler scheme. The fullest annotation scheme for anaphora known to the author is that developed by the Lancaster group (Fligelstone 1992). It would not be an easy matter to integrate this scheme, or any equivalent notation, with the SUSANNE annotation scheme, and there are no plans to develop the SUSANNE Corpus in this direction.

A third shortcoming of the SUSANNE scheme concerns logical scope relations — the aspect of logical structure which explains the ambiguity of, for instance, *Everyone in this room speaks two languages,* either as meaning that two particular languages are shared by all present or that each person has some two languages, not necessarily the same two in each case. Systems of formal logic which make scope relations explicit tend to do so using artificial structures which are far removed from the grammatical structure inherent in the English language, so that it is not easy to see how this aspect of the logic of natural language might be indicated by adding markings to a scheme of annotation that is centrally concerned with surface grammatical structure. At any event, no attempt has been made to do this.

The SUSANNE project did aim to identify word-meanings, by annotating ambiguous words with codes specifying which of the alternative senses listed in a published dictionary applies to the word in its context. A detailed scheme was worked out for achieving this, and during the latter stages of the project this scheme (which is explained in Chapter 2) was applied to a substantial portion of the Corpus. Unfortunately, it emerged by the time of initial public release of the Corpus that the quality of this particular aspect of the annotations was seriously flawed, so to date it has been omitted from public releases; it is possible that this failing will be remedied in due course.

Many readers will be able to think of small-scale grammatical distinctions which are overlooked by the analytic scheme. The task of developing an annotation scheme which represents "all the grammar there is" must ultimately be an unattainable ideal: Richard Sharman of the IBM UK Scientific Centre likens a natural language to a fractal object such as a coastline, which always continues to reveal further detail as it is examined more and more closely. One of the requirements for an NLP-oriented taxonomic scheme for a natural language is informed judgement about what levels of detail it is appropriate to specify for various areas of the language in the present state of the technology. The SUSANNE scheme incorporates many such judgements.

Apart from the above systematic limitations in the SUSANNE analytic scheme, there are inevitably many points where the scheme has been incorrectly applied to individual examples. For instance, Release 1 proved to contain many cases where the parsetree for a sentence was a normal labelled tree in SUSANNE terms, but misrepresented the meaning of the linguistic sequence to which it was attached, for instance by linking a postmodifying phrase or clause to the wrong level of the tree. These errors are being progressively eliminated in later releases; users finding errors are invited to notify the author with details (preferably by post rather than electronic mail).

It was the author's intention at one stage to provide an estimate in this book of the incidence of errors in the current release of the

Corpus. This might have been done by taking random extracts from Corpus texts, reanalysing them using the documented scheme but without consulting the analyses actually found in the Corpus, and counting discrepancies. However, by the point at which it would have been appropriate to undertake this, the author had grown too close to the analysed Corpus to do it adequately. It seemed probable that new analyses would be influenced by partial awareness of existing analyses, so that the discrepancy count would be unduly low; and an over-optimistic quality assessment would be worse than no assessment at all. Therefore no error count is provided here. After this book is circulated, it may be that someone coming fresh to the scheme will be willing to undertake the task, and if so the author would be glad to include such information in the documentation files accompanying future SUSANNE releases.

The Organization of this Book

The remainder of this book is organized as follows.

Chapter 2, "Fundamentals", defines the overall structure of the SUSANNE Corpus, explaining how its files are organized into records (one per word), each of which contains information in a fixed set of fields. It specifies how written texts are segmented into words (not always a straightforward matter in the case of hyphenation or punctuation marks, for instance) and how the relatively rich typography of printed texts is encoded into a computer character-set. Some aspects of Chapter 2, for instance the discussion of record structure, describe an individual research resource rather than a general scheme of linguistic annotation; but aspects such as the word-division principles define standards which are applicable outside the SUSANNE Corpus.

The contents of all following chapters define general annotation standards potentially applicable to any English-language texts.

Chapters 3, "Word Classes", 4, "Surface Grammar", and 5, "Logical Grammar", represent the heart of the book, specifying and exemplifying the grammatical annotation conventions constituting the SUSANNE parsing scheme; the chapter titles are self-explanatory.

Finally, Chapter 6, "Speech", defines and exemplifies the additional conventions that have been worked out to date for annotating the special phenomena found in spoken English.

Chapters 2 to 6 consist mainly of numerous rules or conventions, with frequent cross-references. To facilitate these, the text is divided into sections of one or a few paragraphs, which are numbered consecutively within each chapter, prefixed by the chapter number before a stop. Thus "§ 4.40" refers to the fortieth section of Chapter 4, on "Surface Grammar".

□ 2 □
FUNDAMENTALS

The Structure of the Corpus

§ **2.1**   The SUSANNE Corpus consists of sixty-four data files corresponding to the sixty-four Brown texts on which it is based (and having three-character names corresponding to the names of the respective Brown text files, from "A01" to "N18"), together with a documentation file (giving a skeleton outline of the analytic scheme described in this book) named "SUSANNE.doc". Each data file is about 83 kilobytes in size: 5.3 megabytes for the Corpus in total, excluding the documentation file.

§ **2.2**   Each SUSANNE file is divided into lines (records), and within each line fields are separated by the tab character (code 09). Apart from control codes, the character-set of the SUSANNE Corpus is restricted to a subset of the ninety-four graphic character allocations of the International Reference Version (IRV) of ISO 646:1983 *Information Processing — ISO 7-bit coded character set for information interchange*, which are as follows (codes shown in hexadecimal):

!	"	#	¤	%	&	'	(	)	*	+	,	−	.	/
21	22	23	24	25	26	27	28	29	2A	2B	2C	2D	2E	2F
0	1	2	3	4	5	6	7	8	9	:	;	<	=	>	?
30	31	32	33	34	35	36	37	38	39	3A	3B	3C	3D	3E	3F
@	A	B	C	D	E	F	G	H	I	J	K	L	M	N	O
40	41	42	43	44	45	46	47	48	49	4A	4B	4C	4D	4E	4F
P	Q	R	S	T	U	V	W	X	Y	Z	[	\	]	^	_
50	51	52	53	54	55	56	57	58	59	5A	5B	5C	5D	5E	5F
`	a	b	c	d	e	f	g	h	i	j	k	l	m	n	o
60	61	62	63	64	65	66	67	68	69	6A	6B	6C	6D	6E	6F
p	q	r	s	t	u	v	w	x	y	z	{	|	}	~
70	71	72	73	74	75	76	77	78	79	7A	7B	7C	7D	7E

The following twelve members of this character-set are never used in current releases of the SUSANNE Corpus[1] (and the space character, hexadecimal 20, classified by ISO 646 as a control character is also not used):

#	¤	'	/	\	^	_	`	{			}	~
23	24	27	2F	5C	5E	5F	60	7B	7C	7D	7E

§ 2.3 Where graphic entities outside the IRV set need to be encoded, this is done wherever possible by means of the "public entity definitions" of annex D to ISO 8879:1986, *Information Processing — Text & Office Systems — Standard Generalized Markup Language (SGML)*, enclosed in angle brackets: for instance the character $ is represented as *<dollar>*. ISO 8879 public entity names are also used in some cases where the IRV characters are insufficiently precise. Thus hexadecimal 27 conflates apostrophe and closing inverted comma with the prime symbol which abbreviates *feet*, and in SUSANNE representations of source texts these marks are distinguished. Detailed information about the coding of non-IRV characters is given below.

§ 2.4 Within each file the material is organized in a "vertical" format with one text word on each line: see the extract shown in Fig. 1.2. ("Words" for this purpose include many items such as punctuation marks, paragraph-boundary markers, enclitics such as -*n't*, "ghosts" showing the logical position of moved constituents, all of which occur on separate leaf nodes of the tree structures prescribed by the SUSANNE parsing scheme.) Each line contains six fields separated by tabs, as follows:

1. reference number;
2. status field;
3. wordtag;
4. word field;
5. lemma field;
6. parse field.

§ 2.5 Consider, for instance, the line of Fig. 1.2 which (in its full form, including the sense-coding omitted from the lemma field in early releases of SUSANNE, as discussed in Chapter 1) runs:

```
N03:0480j - VVGv pretending pretend_1.1 [Tg:b[Vg.Vg]
```

---

[1] The present work defines uses for some of these characters in potential future enriched Corpus releases; in any release which does use one or more of them, this fact will be recorded in the accompanying documentation file.

§ **2.6** The *reference number*, N03:0480j in the example, is a nine-byte code which gives each text word a reference that is unique across the SUSANNE Corpus. The first three bytes are the text name (in the example, N03) and thus remain constant through all records in a single SUSANNE file, and the fourth byte is always colon. Bytes five to eight are a four-digit number identifying the line on which the relevant word occurs in the "Bergen I" version of the Brown Corpus (*BCUM*, p. 7), which in turn is identical to the original Brown line-numbering except that where a word was broken over a line-end in the original corpus the whole of the word appears on the former line in Bergen I. (Brown line-numbers increase within a text; they normally increment in tens, but an occasional line-number ends in a digit other than zero as a consequence of accidents of the original Brown coding process in 1963–4.) The ninth byte is a lower-case letter used in the SUSANNE Corpus to differentiate the successive words contained in a single Brown line; successive SUSANNE records corresponding to a Brown line are lettered continuously beginning from "a", omitting "l" and "o" to avoid confusion with digits.[2]

§ **2.7** The *status field* contains a single byte showing whether the item in the word field is, or is part of, a form to which one of the following special categories applies; in a line to which none of the categories applies (the great majority of lines), the status field contains a hyphen:

E a misprint or linguistic solecism in the original text (for details on the treatment of misprints, see §§ 2.85 ff. below);
A an abbreviation, marked as such by ending in an abbreviatory stop;
S a "symbol" — a combination of one or more alphanumeric characters not forming a genuine word and not marked as an abbreviation by a stop (e.g. an acronym, or an algebraic variable).

Where a misprint cannot be located within a single line, for instance because an entire word is omitted, a continuous sequence of lines within which the error occurs each have E in their status field.

§ **2.8** The categories "abbreviation" and "symbol" are borrowed from the Brown Corpus (see *BCUM*, pp. 13, 16); they are not part of the SUSANNE annotation scheme, but are information which is

---

[2] Four-digit line numbers are thus constant across successive releases of the SUSANNE Corpus. The lettering of individual SUSANNE records however is subject to change between releases, where details of the grammatical analysis are revised.

included in Brown (in a different format) and which it seemed undesirable to discard in creating the SUSANNE Corpus. In connection with the distinction drawn in the Brown Corpus between "abbreviations" and "symbols", it is worth bearing in mind that orthographic practice in the early 1960s marked abbreviations with stops much more commonly than is now the case (*OALD3* observes, in the preface to its appendix listing "Common Abbreviations", that "Full points . . . are usually omitted in modern style"). Perhaps for this reason, the Brown Corpus treated absence of an abbreviatory stop as criterial for classifying an item as a "symbol" rather than an "abbreviation": many items are marked as "symbols" which would be called abbreviations in ordinary parlance. For instance, *min* for *minutes* is labelled as a symbol; when *centimetres* appears as *cm* it is treated as a symbol but when it appears as *cm.* it is an abbreviation; the acronym *U.S.A.* is an abbreviation but *NATO* is a symbol. The SUSANNE Corpus simply reflects Brown practice unmodified in this respect. (SUSANNE has changed the Brown system by moving the indication of abbreviation or symbol status out of the word field into a separate field, since it is desirable for the contents of the word field to be as close as possible to the typography of the original texts.)

There is a special problem about abbreviations which occur in sentence-final position. The Brown Corpus encoded these sometimes as "symbols", and sometimes as "abbreviations" having an abbreviatory stop followed by a separate, sentence-final stop; but only one stop will have occurred in the source texts in either case. Where the Brown Corpus uses the latter coding, the SUSANNE Corpus treats the single stop of the source text as the sentence-final punctuation mark (which in accordance with general SUSANNE practice is placed on a line of its own), and does not also include an abbreviatory stop with the abbreviation. That is, an abbreviation at the end of a sentence may be marked by either A or S in the status field but will not have a closing full stop in the word field (it may have internal stops — *U.S.A* at sentence end would appear as shown).

Whenever an abbreviation in the SUSANNE Corpus contains internal full stops, each of these is an abbreviatory stop. The Brown notation would be capable of distinguishing a case where an abbreviation contains an internal full stop serving some function other than abbreviation: no such case occurs in the SUSANNE Corpus, and no SUSANNE notation is defined for this theoretical possibility.

In principle it would be possible for a misprint to appear in an abbreviation or symbol, but again no example is found in the

SUSANNE Corpus and hence it was not necessary to provide separate fields for the different flags.

§ 2.9   The *wordtag* is drawn from a set of wordtags based on the "Lancaster" tagset (*CAE*, appendix B), but incorporating considerable further information. For instance, VVGv identifies *pretending* as the present participle of a verb that can be either transitive or intransitive. The SUSANNE wordtag-set is listed in § 3.73, and problematic boundaries between adjacent wordtags are defined in §§ 3.74 ff.

§ 2.10   The *word field* contains the text word itself. §§ 2.16–32 discuss how typographical details of the original texts are coded. §§ 2.33–45 discuss the principles by which words are divided. Whenever a continuous sequence of non-blank characters in the original text is divided into separate words in the SUSANNE Corpus (for instance, when a punctuation mark is placed on a separate line of the Corpus from the word to which it is appended), the symbol + is prefixed to each word-field form which is not preceded by whitespace in the text.

§ 2.11   The *lemma field* relates the text word to the entries and subentries of two standard published dictionaries widely used by computational linguists. In the case of non-dictionary words, e.g. proper names, numerals, punctuation marks, a hyphen appears in the lemma field. The class of words to which lemma coding is applied, and the full details of the coding scheme, are defined in §§ 2.46–74. In a standard case, such as "pretend_1.1" in the example, the earlier, alphabetical part shows the base form of the word, and the later, numerical part identifies the sense in which the word is used in the context.

The spelling and orthographic details (e.g. hyphenation) of base forms conform to that of the relevant headword in *OALD3*. The numerical part of the dictionary field refers to the numbering of senses in *LDOCE*. For instance, *pretending* in the example above is lemma-coded "pretend_1.1" because in its context the word *pretending* is an example of the *LDOCE* headword **pretend**[1] used in subsense 1, "to give an appearance of (something that is not true), with the intention of deceiving". References in this book to dictionary headwords will appear in bold type.

§ 2.12   The *parse fields* for the successive words of a paragraph display the grammatical structure assigned to the paragraph, in a manner which is fairly straightforward in practice but somewhat complicated to explain. A parsetree, with leaf nodes labelled by wordtags, is represented as a labelled bracketing, in which labels appear inside their brackets (to the right of an opening bracket and to the left of a closing bracket).[3] The string of labelled brackets corresponding to a parsetree is divided into segments at each point where a closing bracket is immediately followed by an opening bracket. Each resulting segment will contain exactly one leaf-node label, immediately surrounded by brackets, and possibly having labels and brackets for higher nodes to left and/or to right. Each segment is placed in the parse field of the line for the word corresponding to the leaf node contained in that segment; but, since the wordtag itself appears in a field of its own on each line, the wordtag and its surrounding brackets are represented by a full-stop character, hexadecimal 2E, in the parse field. (The justification for moving wordtags out of the parse field into a separate field is that some Corpus users may find it convenient to be able to access wordtags without examining the coding of higher-level grammatical structure.)

For instance, the labelled tree for the one-sentence paragraph *Where in Europe was he going now?* G06:0950 is as shown in Fig. 2.1, which corresponds to the labelled bracketing:

[O [S? [Rq:q [RRQq] [P [II] [Nns [NP1g] Nns] P] Rq:q] [Vosb [VBDZ] Vosb] [Nas:s [PPHS1m] Nas:s] [Vrg [VVGi] Vrg] [Rw:t [RTo] Rw:t] S?] [YQ] O]

and this is divided among SUSANNE lines as follows (showing only relevant fields):

wordtag	word field	parse field
RRQq	Where	[O[S?[Rq:q.
II	in	[P.
NP1g	Europe	[Nns.Nns]P]Rq:q]
VBDZ	was	[Vosb.Vosb]
PPHS1m	he	[Nas:s.Nas:s]
VVGi	going	[Vrg.Vrg]
RTo	now	[Rw:t.Rw:t]S?]
YQ	+?	.O]

§ 2.13   Since it is hoped in due course to produce a version of the SUSANNE Corpus which marks the head/dependent distinction among constituents of a construction, it will be appropriate at this point to define a notation which can be used for this purpose. An appropriate notation would replace full stop in the parse field by

---

[3] In Release 1 of the Corpus, brackets surrounding "full constituents" (§ 4.22) were square but "ghosts" (ibid.) were surrounded by angle brackets. This notational distinction was redundant, and from Release 2 onwards all parse-field brackets are square.

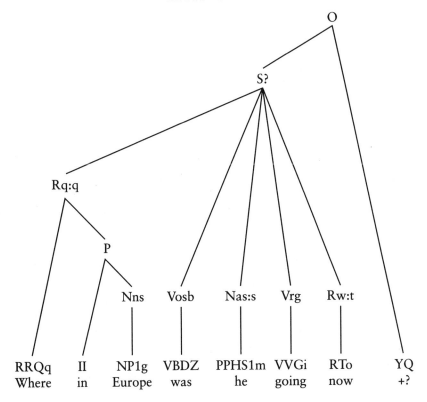

Figure 2.1

the apex mark "^" for any word that heads its construction, and would replace square brackets by angle brackets for a construction that heads the higher construction of which it is a daughter.

Thus, assuming that the head of a prepositional phrase is the preposition, that an interrogative clause is headed by its finite verb, and that paragraphs have no heads, then the above annotations, with the contents of the parse fields modified to mark headship, would read:

wordtag	word field	parse field
RRQq	Where	[O[S?[Rq:q^
II	in	[P^
NP1g	Europe	[Nns^Nns]P]Rq:q]
VBDZ	was	<Vosb^Vosb>
PPHS1m	he	[Nas:s^Nas:s]
VVGi	going	[Vrg^Vrg]

```
RTo        now        [Rw:t^Rw:t]S?]
YQ         +?         .O]
```

§ 2.14   The SUSANNE parsing scheme is based on constituent structure trees, which divide up text into stretches of greater or lesser inclusiveness (from words at the lowest level to paragraphs at the highest), and label each stretch in ways that identify aspects of its nature and relationship to the next-larger stretch within which it is included. Some general terminology for talking about constituent structure tree analyses is defined here.

The unique node which dominates all other nodes in a constituent structure tree is the *root* node of the tree; those nodes which dominate no other nodes (and which correspond to the individual words) are the *leaf* or *terminal* nodes of the tree. We shall say that a node dominates a word or a sequence of words if it dominates the leaf nodes representing the word(s). Each node of a tree bears a label. A non-terminal node-label may consist of more than one part; the internal structure of non-terminal node-labels is defined in Chapter 4.

The term *constituent* is often used for any of the stretches of text recognized by a constituent structure analysis, that is, any continuous sequence of words which corresponds to the full set of leaf nodes dominated by some one node at some level in the tree. Thus, in the example *the quality of mercy is not strained,* one would say that the word-sequence *of mercy* "is a constituent", because in any plausible analysis there will be a single node dominating just these two words and bearing a label that shows them to form a prepositional phrase, whereas the sequences *quality of,* or *mercy is not,* are "not constituents" — for either of these word-sequences, any node in a plausible analysis that dominates all words in the sequence will also dominate other words outside the sequence.

There is a difficulty in using the term "constituent" alone for this concept: that word identifies a stretch of text in relation to the larger stretch which contains it, so that the stretch of text dominated by a root node cannot itself be called a "constituent" (there is nothing for it to be a constituent of). Often it is more appropriate to discuss a stretch of text dominated by a node in relation to the smaller stretches that make it up; that is, alongside the term *constituent* which "looks upward" in a tree we need a symmetrical term which "looks downward", and we use the term *tagma* for this. Thus, a paragraph is a tagma, although it is not a constituent; a word is a constituent, but not a tagma; a text stretch dominated by a node intermediate between root and leaves is simultaneously a tagma and a constituent of a higher tagma.

Within the SUSANNE scheme most tagmas are categorized as either *phrases* or *clauses*; these terms are taken from ordinary grammatical terminology, but the distinction between them is made sharp and is very important for the correct application of the SUSANNE scheme.

Relationships between adjacent nodes in a tree are described using obvious family-relationship metaphors, with the convention that all nodes are female. Thus if node A and node B are immediately below node C, then A and B are *daughters* of C, C is the *mother* of A and B, and A and B are *sisters*. In conformity with widespread usage in linguistics, the term *immediate constituent* (abbreviated *IC*) is often used as a synonym of "daughter" in this sense.

The term *IC* is often suffixed to the name of a tagma category to refer to a constituent whose mother is of the given category. Thus the terms *clause IC, phrase IC* stand for an IC *of* a clause or phrase respectively — they do not mean "IC *which is* a clause/phrase".

§ 2.15 The reference number and status fields are sufficiently defined by the remarks in §§ 2.6–7 above. The contents of the wordtag and parse fields are defined in detail in Chapters 3–5. Within the rest of the present chapter there follow sections giving detailed specifications of the contents of the word field and lemma field.

The Word Field

§ 2.16 The word field contains the text of the Corpus itself, divided among successive lines into segments corresponding to the successive leaf nodes of the parsing structures prescribed by the SUSANNE parsing scheme. On the principles used for segmenting text into words, see §§ 2.33–45.

SUSANNE parsetrees treat the material they analyse as a strictly linear string of segments. Accordingly, grammatically relevant typographic phenomena (such as italicization) which occur together with, rather than before or after, individual words are coded as pairs of typographic-shift "words" placed at either end of the domains to which they apply, as discussed in §§ 2.22–3.

§ 2.17 Among the ninety-four characters of the ISO 646 IRV character-set, the four characters – + < > have special meanings when they occur in the word field, and never represent themselves. All other characters represent themselves except when enclosed between < >.

The hyphen indicates absence of text, in cases where a leaf node of a SUSANNE parsetree represents the logical position or "ghost" of a grammatical constituent which has been deleted or moved to a different position in surface structure — for details see Chapter 5. (The class of SUSANNE lines having a hyphen in the word field is identical to the class having YG in the wordtag field.)

The plus sign is prefixed to a character-string which in the original text was printed continuously with the content of the preceding non-empty word field, rather than separated by whitespace. In general the leaf nodes of SUSANNE parsetrees correspond to words in the ordinary typographic sense, but there are many cases where typographic words are split between successive leaf nodes and in these cases the plus sign appears in the word field: for instance, punctuation marks are separated from the preceding word, so that a comma will normally appear in the word field as:

```
+,
```

and many hyphenated words are divided (cf. §§ 2.36 ff.), so that the typographic word *term-end* appears in successive word fields as:

```
term
+<hyphen>
+end
```

The characters < > enclose codes for graphic phenomena which are not directly represented in the ISO 646 IRV character-set. A number of these codes are specific to the SUSANNE Corpus, and these are defined below. All other codes used are drawn from the sets of public entity names listed in ISO 8879:1986, annex D. For instance, the text word *Schönberg* is represented in the SUSANNE word field as *Sch<ouml>nberg*.[4]

§ 2.18   The level of typographic detail represented in SUSANNE word fields is limited by the nature of the original Brown Corpus. This filtered out certain elements of and distinctions in the source texts, in some cases because inclusion was regarded as inappropriate and in other cases because the technology of the time made inclusion cumbersome. (In the original Brown Corpus even the upper/lower case distinction had to be indicated by special coding, since the computing equipment available in the 1960s used all-upper-case character-sets. The "Bergen I" version of the Brown Corpus (*BCUM*, p. 7), on which the SUSANNE Corpus is based, recoded the original

---

[4] ISO public entity names are used with ISO permission as stated in the following notice, which is copied here in accordance with ISO requirements:

© International Organization for Standardization 1986
Permission to copy in any form is granted for use with conforming SGML systems and applications as defined in ISO 8879, provided this notice is included in all copies.

Brown files using a larger, modern character-set, but Bergen I contains no information that was not in the original version of Brown.) Very rarely there are instances where the source text appears to have been coded in the Brown Corpus in a fashion that is not perfectly in accord with the declared Brown coding principles. In a few cases distinctions lost in the Brown Corpus have been reconstructed in the SUSANNE Corpus (the distinction between opening and closing single inverted commas has been reinstated, and characters recorded in the Brown Corpus simply as "uncoded characters" have been replaced by entity names representing the characters of the original texts);[5] but in general the creation of the SUSANNE Corpus has not gone behind Brown to the texts from which Brown was derived.

Accordingly, the following sections §§ 2.19–32, like § 2.8 above, have a rather different status from the bulk of this book; they do not deal with rules for the annotation of English in general, but discuss how SUSANNE deals with certain analytic apparatus that was already incorporated into the particular texts on which it is based.

§ **2.19**   The Corpus text includes only the body of the source text, omitting titles, running heads, tables, picture captions, footnotes, and superscript references to footnotes in the text body. The Brown Corpus preserved typographical errors found in the source texts, and listed them under the bibliographical details for the respective texts given in *BCUM*; the SUSANNE Corpus retains those errors which *BCUM* list, and aims to eliminate any other errors encountered — all such cases are logged in SUSANNE.doc.

§ **2.20**   Formulae, defined as "[c]ombinations of letters, numbers, and other symbols which also include operator symbols (such as +, =, exponents, subscripts)" (*BCUM*, p. 12), are replaced by the symbol *<formul>*, which is treated in the SUSANNE Corpus as a single "word".

§ **2.21**   Two levels of text structure above the sentence level are recognized: "major" and "minor" divisions. According to *BCUM*, p. 10, a major division is:

---

[5] Several Brown "uncoded characters" represented the section symbol § or pilcrow ¶, represented in SUSANNE by the ISO names *<sect>*, *<para>*. Various uncoded characters in the press texts were short ornamental rules of various designs placed centrally in a newspaper column to separate two sequences of paragraphs. SUSANNE represents these using codes beginning "crule" (for "centred rule"), as follows:

<crule1>	plain rule
<crule2>	rule having a filled bulge at its centre
<crule3>	rule having open bulges at both ends
<crule4>	row of three asterisks

the largest subdivision of the text that falls within the sample. If a whole sample falls within a single chapter of a book, for example, [major division] codings are used for the largest subheads, if any, within the chapter. But if a sample straddles a chapter break, these codings are used for the chapter heading

— while:

Even in the case of elaborately subdivided material, [minor division codings] are used for all subdivisions below the largest, down to and including the paragraph. (ibid.)

The Brown classification of headings as "major" and "minor" appears to depend on typography rather than logical structure, where these considerations conflict: thus the dateline of a newspaper story (which would commonly be printed continuously with the opening of the story proper) is classified as a minor heading, although it applies to the whole of a story which may contain subheadings displayed on separate lines and classified as major headings. (We have seen that the SUSANNE scheme does not purport to represent the logical structure of texts above the paragraph level.) A simple boundary between paragraphs is always treated as a minor division even in texts that contain no higher-level division.

Where a major or minor text division is introduced by a heading, the text of the heading is surrounded by the markers:

    <bmajhd>   *<emajhd>*

or

    <bminhd>   *<eminhd>*

respectively. Headings are printed in all-capitals, with no indications of italics or "other graphic features" (*BCUM*, p. 10). Where a text division lacks a heading, it is separated from adjacent divisions by one of the symbols:

    <majbrk>   *<minbrk>*

as appropriate. (Thus, in practice, the commonest text-division marking is *<minbrk>* representing paragraph boundary.) These symbols are consistently included where a headingless division in the original text coincides with the *beginning* of a Corpus extract; they are consistently omitted where such a division coincides with the *end* of a Corpus extract. The SUSANNE Corpus has modified the Brown system in one respect: separate newspaper stories within a single text are always bounded by "major" text division symbols (in the Brown Corpus such boundaries are sometimes unmarked).

§ 2.22 Outside headings, italics and bold-face are distinguished from plain type (though underlining is not distinguished from italics); stretches of text having these typographical features are surrounded by the markers:

<bital> *<eital>*
<bbold> *<ebold>*

The Brown principles for placing these markers relative to punctuation marks which neutralize e.g. the italic/roman distinction are discussed in *BCUM*, p. 14. Occasionally, permuting the Brown ordering of typographical-shift markers relative to adjacent text elements allows a more natural grammatical structure (with paired beginning and end markers appearing as daughters of the same higher node) without implying any change in the physical appearance of the text; in such cases the SUSANNE Corpus adopts the permutation.

§ 2.23 All the text-division and typographic-shift markers just listed are treated in the SUSANNE Corpus as "words" of the text, having their own separate terminal nodes. They are logically akin to items such as brackets, inverted commas, and other punctuation marks which are likewise allocated terminal nodes in SUSANNE parsetrees.[6]

§ 2.24 In general, character-sequences including closing inverted commas and other punctuation marks are regularized within the Brown Corpus in such a way that the inverted commas precede the other marks. This means that a sentence which in the original source reads *You said, "He's coming?"* is encoded as if it read *You said, "He's coming"?* (*BCUM*, p. 14, expresses regret that the Brown Corpus eliminated this distinction; it notes an exception relating to typographic shifts.) Also, no consistent distinction is made between presence and absence of a space immediately following a punctuation mark. The SUSANNE use of plus sign to mark absence of preceding whitespace is determined purely by occurrence of whitespace in the Brown Corpus, and does not attempt to reconstruct this aspect of the source texts. A text-division marker counts as whitespace, but a plus sign may follow an italics or bold-face marker if typography changes within a typographic word.

§ 2.25 Line-breaks, and those line-end hyphens which the Brown

---

[6] An exception is cases where the two end-points of a typographical shift contain a proper part of what is in other respects a single word, as in (G13:1140, roman/italics as in original):

it's the *monogamous* relationship that is *dis*honest

In such a case it is preferable to treat *<bital>dis<eital>honest* as a single grammatical unit than to postulate an artificial "word" *dis*.

team judged to be "soft", are ignored. Quoted material which in the source text was printed "blocked", whether by indentation, use of smaller type, or irregular line-breaks in the case of verse, is represented as if enclosed in double inverted commas.

§ 2.26 Among the various typographical marks which appear as horizontal lines of different lengths, the Brown Corpus makes a two-way distinction between (hard) hyphens and dashes. Where a symbol encoded in the Brown Corpus as a hyphen is preceded by a space and followed by a number, it can be inferred to be functioning as a minus sign. (A sequence including a minus sign functioning as a binary operator is replaced by *<formul>*, but unary minus signs occur in negative numbers.) Accordingly, the SUSANNE Corpus makes a three-way distinction in its word fields, using the ISO public entity names *<mdash>*, *<hyphen>*, *<minus>*. These symbols carry no implication about the distinctiveness or otherwise of the respective marks in the original sources. The hyphen character itself appears in SUSANNE word fields only as an indicator of absence of text in the case of an empty "ghost" constituent.

§ 2.27 Numerals including fractions regularly occur in the Brown Corpus in forms such as "1-1/2" (meaning "one and a half"). *BCUM* do not discuss these forms, but it seems likely that they reflect forms such as $1\frac{1}{2}$ in the source texts; accordingly the SUSANNE Corpus represents them with ISO public entity names, e.g. *1<frac12>*. Two fraction symbols occur for which no ISO public entity names have been defined, namely $\frac{7}{2}$ and $\frac{1}{16}$; these are coded as *<frac72>* and (since the ISO convention limits entity names to six characters) *<fra116>*.

§ 2.28 The Brown Corpus neutralized the distinction between ampersand & and plus sign + in source texts, representing either by a common code. However, the few instances of this code which occur in the SUSANNE texts all appear from context likely to represent ampersand rather than plus sign, and are shown as ampersand in SUSANNE word fields.

§ 2.29 The solidus character "/" is represented by the ISO entity name *<sol>*; the motive for making this substitution is that the solidus occurs less than ten times in SUSANNE texts, and for practical computing purposes it is convenient to have a reasonable range of ASCII characters that are known not to occur in one's data files. Each character which does occur in the SUSANNE Corpus is represented by not fewer than 200 tokens.

§ 2.30 Greek letters are represented in the SUSANNE Corpus by ISO public entity names from the "Greek Alphabetic Characters" rather than the "Greek Symbols" set (e.g. α is *<agr>* rather than *<alpha>*); although Greek letters occur in the Corpus in a technical rather than linguistic context, the Brown Corpus does not preserve distinctions between letter-shapes such as ε v. ε which are relevant for correct use of the "Greek Symbols" set.

§ 2.31 The only diacritic recognized is the diaeresis/umlaut, which is encoded using ISO public entity names *<auml>*, *<euml>*, etc. All other diacritics were eliminated in the construction of the Brown Corpus. Thus a word such as *régime* in a source text will appear in the SUSANNE word field as *regime*, though in the lemma field its base form is shown as *r<eacute>gime* (since *OALD3* prints the acute).

§ 2.32 A complete list of entity names used in the SUSANNE Corpus is as follows. Note that the closing single inverted comma is distinguished in a SUSANNE word field, as *<rsquo>*, from the apostrophe, coded as *<apos>*, although the marks are physically identical in source texts and are not distinguished in the Brown Corpus. For the reason given in the preceding paragraph, some of these entity names occur only in the lemma field rather than the word field.

<agr>	α
<agrave>	à
<apos>	apostrophe
<auml>	ä
<bbold>	begin bold type
<bgr>	β
<bital>	begin italics
<blank>	space (used in lemma field where the dictionary form of a word includes internal word-space, see § 2.61)
<bmajhd>	begin major heading
<bminhd>	begin minor heading
<ccedil>	ç
<crule1> *<crule2>* *<crule3>* *<crule4>*	centred rule (see note to § 2.18)
<deg>	°
<dollar>	$
<eacute>	é
<ebold>	end bold type
<egr>	ε
<egrave>	è
<eital>	end italics
<emajhd>	end major heading
<eminhd>	end minor heading

<formul>	unspecified formula
<fra116>	$\frac{1}{16}$
<frac12>	$\frac{1}{2}$
<frac14>	$\frac{1}{4}$
<frac72>	$\frac{7}{2}$
<ggr>	γ
<hellip>	used in this book to represent the ellipsis mark, "...", occurring in a Corpus text
<hyphen>	hyphen
<iuml>	ï
<khgr>	χ
<ldquo>	opening double inverted commas
<lgr>	λ
<lsquo>	opening single inverted comma
<majbrk>	major text division
<mdash>	dash
<mgr>	μ
<minbrk>	paragraph boundary or other minor text division
<minus>	minus sign
<ntilde>	ñ
<oelig>	œ
<ouml>	ö
<para>	¶
<pgr>	π
<phgr>	ϕ
<prime>	′ (occurs in SUSANNE abbreviating *feet*, and in algebraic variables, e.g. *a*′)
<Prime>	″ (occurs in SUSANNE abbreviating *inches*)
<rdquo>	closing double inverted commas
<rgr>	ρ
<rsquo>	closing single inverted comma
<sect>	§
<sol>	/
<thgr>	θ

Word Segmentation

§ 2.33 Broadly, text is distributed across records in SUSANNE files on a one-word-per-line basis. But it is necessary to be precise about what counts as a "word" in this context. In some cases, how much of an English text counts as one word is not well defined in ordinary parlance: for instance, hyphenation is often used in order to represent an intermediate case between a loose compound formed from two or more independent words and a fixed compound ranking as a single word. In other cases, it is clear where word boundaries would normally be placed but the task of representing the grammatical structure of texts makes it necessary to deviate from standard concepts of "word": thus, punctuation marks are not usually regarded as separate words, and are written continuously with adjacent words, but, in the grammar of written English, punctuation marks commonly function as grammatical units at a high level (they are often immediate constituents of clauses), so in the SUSANNE Corpus punctuation marks are normally split off from the words to which they are adjacent and placed on lines of their own. The following sections survey the rules by which text is segmented across consecutive records in SUSANNE files. For simplicity of exposition, the segments into which Corpus text is divided by these rules are referred to simply as "words", irrespective of whether they coincide with words in the ordinary sense; thus, in the present work, a written comma is described as a word.

Where a word as segmented by the rules given here is printed immediately adjacent to the preceding word in the original text, not separated from it by whitespace, this fact is recorded in the word field of the corresponding record by a plus sign prefixed to the word.

§ 2.34   Whitespace in the original text is a sufficient (though not a necessary) condition for a SUSANNE word boundary. (One might not want to treat a word divided across lines by a "soft hyphen" as a pair of units for grammatical analysis, but this issue does not arise in the SUSANNE Corpus because soft hyphens were eliminated from the Brown Corpus on which SUSANNE is based — cf. § 2.25.) There are cases where a sequence of two or more orthographic words separated by space(s), e.g. *up to date*, are regarded as functioning grammatically as a single word ("grammatical idioms", see §§ 3.55 ff.), but they are nevertheless assigned separate records — their grammatical idiom status is shown by wordtagging and higher-level tagging.

Word boundaries are placed within material printed continuously in a number of circumstances.

§ 2.35   The Germanic genitive suffix is treated as a separate word; *John's, boys'* appear as:

John
+*<apos>s*

boys
+*<apos>*

Likewise enclitics — reduced forms of the word *not* and of various auxiliary verbs — are treated as separate words; thus *won't, cannot, he'll* are split across SUSANNE lines as:

wo
+n<apos>t

can .
+not

he
+<apos>ll

The same treatment is applied to less standardized informal contractions of multi-word sequences; thus the form *shouldda* which occurs in the sequence *"But they shouldda brought in Tokyo, too", added Old Scrapiron.* A11:1360 is represented in the Corpus as:

should
+da

— with *+da* identified in the lemma field as a version of the word *have*.

§ 2.36 Hyphenated sequences are normally segmented on either side of the hyphen; for instance, *bus-fare* would be represented as:

bus
+<hyphen>
+fare

This approach is taken even when the units linked by hyphens include affixes that could not normally occur as independent orthographic words:

re
+<hyphen>
+entrant

multi
+<hyphen>
+media

sea
+<hyphen>
+scape

The British *co-operate* will be split into separate words, though the different orthographic convention of American *coöperate* means that the same lexical item will be one word in this spelling.

Earlier corpora, such as the LOB Corpus, used a different rule, by which items linked by hyphens were invariably treated as single words. But this rule is incompatible with correct parsing in cases like *pre- and post-editing*, where part of the "hyphenated word" is co-ordinated with an element outside that word, or *Japan's extra-marital sex-seeking salarymen* (*The Times* 1991.12.27, p. 6), where a hyphen links *seeking* to a phrase *extra-marital sex* which includes an internal space; and it sometimes yields bizarre "words" (the phrase *the New York-Los Angeles route* is deemed to contain a word *York-Los*). The SUSANNE scheme does not use it.

§ 2.37   Hyphenations are treated as single SUSANNE words only in limited circumstances. Where the sequence linked by hyphens would need to be treated as a "grammatical idiom" if split into separate words, or in other cases where at least one of the forms linked by a hyphen has no recognized independent function (whether as word or affix), the hyphenation is not split up. (The concept "grammatical idiom" is defined in §§ 3.55 ff., and lists of idioms are included in § 3.73.) Examples of hyphenations treated as single SUSANNE words would therefore include the adjectives *up-to-date* (where the corresponding form with spaces, *up to date*, is a recognized grammatical idiom) and *over-all* (which is not on the list of recognized grammatical idioms, because it never normally occurs with space in place of hyphen, but for which a decision to split would lead to analysis as an idiom); the noun *cubby-hole*, where the form *cubby* in modern standard English has no use except as part of this word; the hyphenated form in *a B-52 bomber*, where the aircraft model name is an arbitrary alphanumeric formula, the elements of which have no significance to the average English speaker; and cases such as *"Je-sus", he breathed,* or *A-a-a-tishoo!*, where hyphens are used to indicate some peculiarity of pronunciation rather than to separate logically distinct parts of a compound. (Contrast *B-52* with *H-bomb*, where many readers will know that the *H* stands for *hydrogen* and accordingly the sequence is represented as:

H
+*<hyphen>*
+*bomb*

with the first word tagged as a chemical symbol; or *they won the match 3-0*, where the hyphen is understood as linking the two side's individual scores, so *3-0* is divided into three words.[7]) Hyphenated names of individual persons, e.g. *Jean-Marie*, or "double-barrelled"

---

[7] In *an out-of-bounds slice* A14:1220 the hyphenation as a whole is not recognized as an idiom, but *out of* is one; therefore the second hyphen but not the first is given a separate SUSANNE line.

surnames such as *Armstrong-Jones*, are treated as single words even if their separate components are well-known names. (But the hyphenation in *the Mason-Dixon line* is split, because Mason and Dixon were two individuals.)

A hyphenation will be split up even if the use of hyphens rather than spaces is crucial to its grammar. For instance, the "hyphenated words" of *The September-October term jury* A01:0070, *at oil-water interfaces* J05:1470, *in term-end presentments* A01:0030 are orthographically near-mandatory in order to turn the compounds into noun premodifiers, and some of them could not occur as compounds in any grammatical environment without a linking hyphen. Nevertheless, these compounds are not "grammatical idioms" — they are formed by productive rules; and they are divided into three SUSANNE words each, e.g.:

> *the*
> *September*
> *+<hyphen>*
> *+October*
> *term*
> *jury*

§ 2.38   Punctuation marks other than apostrophes (and other than the exceptional cases of hyphens just discussed) are treated as independent words; the sentence

> *"Come here"*.

would be segmented as:

> *<ldquo>*
> *+Come*
> *here*
> *+<rdquo>*
> *+.*

Double inverted commas are treated as single words, represented using ISO public entity names; three dots as an ellipsis mark is one word (but four dots, for sentence-final ellipsis, is treated as two words — ellipsis followed by full stop); colon immediately followed by dash is treated as a single word.

The individual form *and/or* is treated as a single word, and character-sequences are not split at a solidus in the case of arbitrary alphanumeric formulae (such as *3/60* in *a Sun 3/60 workstation*), or in a numerical date such as *3/4/93* for "3rd of April 1993" (or, in

American usage, "4th of March 1993"). Furthermore certain occurrences of the solidus character in the Brown Corpus appear to be used in order to represent fraction characters such as $\frac{1}{2}$ in the original texts (cf. § 2.27), and in the SUSANNE Corpus these are represented by ISO entity names. Where solidus occurs in the original texts in other ways, with an independent meaning such as "or" or "per", it is placed on a line of its own. Full stop (American "period") is treated as an independent word only when representing sentence boundary, not as decimal point or abbreviation marker.[8]

Brackets (American "parentheses") are normally treated as separate words, but for cases where brackets are analysed as part of a "label" see the footnote to wordtag MCb in § 3.73.

§ 2.39   Sequences written solidly which comprise a numeral and a unit are segmented into separate SUSANNE words; *$25.00, 32°F, 6″* (for "six inches") are represented respectively as:

<dollar>
+25.00

32
+<deg>F

6
+<Prime>

and likewise *25%* is represented as:

25
+%

§ 2.40   When a numeral is prefixed by an abbreviation such as *p.* or *pp.* (for "page(s)"), *#* (for "number"), etc. — a word tagged NNm or NNmm by the SUSANNE wordtagging scheme — the abbreviation and the numeral are treated as separate words even if written solid.

§ 2.41   A numeral containing integer and fractional part, e.g. $3\frac{1}{2}$, is not split but treated as a single word, *3<frac12>*.

§ 2.42   In principle, the treatment of formal equations or inequalities as single words or as sequences depends on whether they are integrated into the surrounding English text. Thus, in a case such as

---

[8] When a numeral is followed by a full stop as (part of) a heading, the full stop is grouped with the numeral as a single MCb word (see MCb in § 3.73). However, punctuation marks other than full stop in this environment are separated from the numeral. Thus:

[Oh *<bmajhd>* *1._*MCb *INTRODUCTION_*NN1n *<emajhd>* Oh] J01:0010
[Oh *<bmajhd>* *II_*MCr *+:_*YN [Dp *SOME OF . . .* Dp] *<emajhd>* Oh] J23:0010

but when <bital> h <eital> = 2<bital>c<eital>, the downwash is . . .
J74.183, the formula is treated as five separate words (wordtagged
YTL FOx YTR IIx FOx, see § 3.73) and the sequence *when <bital>*
h <eital> = 2<bital>c<eital> is analysed as an Fa clause (§ 4.288);
if on the other hand the same formula were displayed on a line of
its own, it would be treated as a single word, tagged FOqx. In the
SUSANNE Corpus, however, this policy is overridden by the fact
that the Brown Corpus often represented formulae by a single "formula" code (§ 2.20), so that we cannot recover the original structure
of the formulae concerned.

§ 2.43   An acronym written solid is treated as a single SUSANNE
word even if it can alternatively appear with spacing (in which case
it is split into separate words which are analysed as forming a
"grammatical idiom", see § 3.61); thus *USA* or *U.S.A.* are one word
each, wordtagged NP1c, and *U. S. A.* is three words forming an
NP1c= idiom.

§ 2.44   There are occasional cases where alphanumeric code
material which is written solid but is logically compound is split
across SUSANNE lines — thus, in the passage *The x-ray diffraction*
pattern of the material, taken with CuKα radiation, indicated . . .
J04:1320, the form *CuKα* is represented as:

CuK
+<agr>

— however such cases are too isolated within the SUSANNE Corpus to permit a general rule to be stated.

§ 2.45   The policy set out in the preceding sections, by segmenting text relatively finely, aims to achieve a situation in which the
task of representing the correct grammatical analysis of a text is
hardly ever made difficult by the need to accommodate a logically
complex form under a single terminal node. Unfortunately, however, some such difficulties do arise. This happens when an affix
written solidly with an adjacent stem is logically in construction
with a constituent including more than that stem; this is most frequent when the latter constituent is a hyphenation (e.g. *a couple of*
Indian take-aways, where the plural suffix applies to the compound
noun *take-away*, or *absent-mindedly*, where the suffixes *-ed* and *-ly*
apply to the sequence *absent-mind*), but it can also happen when an
affix is in construction with a sequence of words separated by spaces,
as in *a New Yorker* where the *-er* suffix applies to the whole name
New York.

One suffix which would create this problem very frequently is the
genitive *-'s* ending; constructions like *the King of England's hat*, where

the genitive suffix is in construction with a multi-word tagma, are notorious. The SUSANNE analytic scheme has avoided this particular problem by treating the Germanic genitive suffix as a separate word. Ultimately the way to avoid all such problems would be to do the same with other affixes, dividing up the examples just discussed into *take – away s, absent – mind ed ly, a New York er,* so that the separate morphemes could be linked up into whatever structures are logically appropriate irrespective of typography. This was felt to be too radical a solution for a relatively marginal problem to be appropriate for the SUSANNE scheme. Instead, examples such as those quoted are divided across lines by applying the general word-segmentation rules to the multi-word sequence which is in construction with an affix, and leaving the affix attached as part of whichever among the resulting words it is typographically linked to, thus yielding sequences such as:

> *take*
> *+<hyphen>*
> *+aways*

> *absent*
> *+<hyphen>*
> *+mindedly*

> *a*
> *New*
> *Yorker*

These word-sequences are then analysed as best they can be within the available range of categories: in the cases illustrated, *aways* is word-tagged as a plural noun (along with plurals of quoted words, as in too *many ifs and buts*), *mindedly* as an (otherwise non-existent) adverb, *Yorker* as a common noun like *Londoner*, and the entire phrases are analysed as respectively plural noun phrase, adverbial phrase, and singular noun phrase without any attempt to show that they contain intermediate-level constituents *take-away, absent-mind, New York*.

The Lemma Field

§ 2.46 The lemma field shows the base form of the word which occurs in the word field, together with the sense in which the word is used in the relevant context.

BASE FORM

§ 2.47   For SUSANNE purposes the authoritative orthography for
the base form of a word is taken as being that of the relevant
headword in *OALD3* as represented in the computer-usable version
CUVOALD86 developed by Roger Mitton. The chief respects in
which a text form can differ from its base form are these:

- The text form may have a grammatical inflexion: the forms *had
  children walked* are lemmatized as *have child walk* respectively.
- The text form may contain non-inherent capitalization: the forms
  Had WALKING ROBERTSON are lemmatized as *have walk
  Robertson* respectively.
- The orthography of the text form may be non-standard, whether
  as the result of a misprint (the form *assesment* J08:0270 is
  lemmatized as *assessment*), as a deliberate representation of
  general, regional, or idiosyncratic non-standard spoken usage
  (the forms *+n't git we-ell* are lemmatized as *not get well* respectively), or because of contrasts between alternative orthographic conventions (the form *flavor* is lemmatized as *flavour*).

Not all "words", in the sense of items appearing in the word field
of lines in SUSANNE files, are appropriately assigned a base form.
This concept would make little sense in the case of numerals or
punctuation marks, for instance; in the case of abbreviations one
might feel that the base form ought to be the unabbreviated equivalent, but the SUSANNE Corpus has not taken that path. The class
of words assigned base forms in SUSANNE dictionary fields is the
class of wordforms (word-field contents) on lines which meet all the
following criteria:

- the wordform includes only alphabetic characters, apostrophe,
  and hyphen, and includes at least one alphabetic character
  (symbols for alphabetic characters bearing diacritics, e.g. *<iuml>*,
  count as alphabetic characters);
- the status field does not contain A or S;
- the wordtag is not GG (i.e. genitive suffix — SUSANNE places
  "apostrophe-s" on a line of its own separate from the word to
  which it is suffixed, but no base form is defined for this enclitic),
  and does not begin FO... (formula), FW... (foreign word), or
  ZZ... (letter of the alphabet);
- the wordform is not a roman numeral.

In lines not meeting one or more of the above criteria, the dictionary field contains a hyphen character.

INFLEXIONS

§ **2.48** SUSANNE base forms reduce:

- plural nouns to their singulars;
- accusative pronouns to their nominatives;
- comparative and superlative adjectives and adverbs to the corresponding absolute forms;
- third-person singular, past-tense, and present- and past-participle forms of verbs to the corresponding uninflected forms (and likewise *am*, *are* are lemmatized as *be*).

Past-tense forms of modal verbs (*might*, *would*, etc.) are reduced to *may*, *will*, etc.[9] Pseudo-adjectives made by adding past-participle endings to noun stems (e.g. *mustachioed*, wordtagged JJ, or *bellied* in *pot-bellied*, wordtagged JJh) are given the corresponding singular noun (e.g. *mustachio*, *belly*) as base form.[10] Plural pronouns are not reduced to singulars, and possessive pronouns are not reduced to nominatives; thus *these his* stand as their own base forms rather than being reduced to *this he*. Other productive suffixes are treated as derivational rather than inflexional and are left to stand in the lemma field: for instance ordinal numbers are not reduced to cardinals, adverbs in *-ly* are not reduced to adjectives, nouns in *-er* are not reduced to verb stems.

§ **2.49** When a wordform bearing one of the inflexions identified above does duty as another part of speech, the inflexion is regarded as an integral part of the word in this use and is not removed in the lemma field.[11] Thus *following* as a verbal present participle is lemmatized as *follow*, but as a preposition (or noun) it is its own base form. The word *united* is etymologically a past participle (and past tense), with the base form *unite*, but when used as an adjective it is its own base form: in *United States* the form *United* is lemmatized as *united*. Decisions about whether to include a suffix in the lemma field are made in terms of the wordtag assigned to the text word in context, which in turn is determined by principles set out in §§ 3.74 ff.

§ **2.50** Where a word is inflected as a plural noun and hence wordtagged NN2, the corresponding singular form is given as the

---

[9] The verb *ought* is treated as its own base form, and is not classified as a past tense by any aspect of the SUSANNE analytic scheme.

[10] In the case of *gimbaled* G04:0870 the stem is a noun which is listed by *OALD3* as defective (cf. § 2.52 below), hence the form is lemmatized as *gimbals*.

[11] Where an inflected word is part of a "grammatical idiom" (§ 3.55), the inflexion is removed in the lemma field: in *so called* the form *called* is lemmatized as *call*.

base form even in cases where, if this form had occurred in the text, the SUSANNE wordtagging rules would treat it as a verbal participle (§ 3.76); for instance *testings* G08:0660 is lemmatized as *testing*, though a nominal use of *testing* would be wordtagged VVGt and lemmatized as *test*.

§ 2.51   Non-English inflexions in borrowed words are ignored except where the inflexion is incorporated into English as the functional equivalent of one of the above native inflexions. Thus *phenomena* acts in English as well as in Greek as the plural of *phenomenon*, which is therefore its base form; but in the phrases *per diem*, *de facto*, the words *diem*, *facto* are shown unchanged in the lemma field — they are not replaced by *dies*, *factum* (or *facere*). Likewise in proper names including foreign words, such as the radio-station name *Bayerische Rundfunk* G06:1570 or the street names *Buena Vista Terrace* G08:0420, *Rue de L'Arcade* G12:0400, the words *Bayerische buena l<apos>* are lemmatized as shown although, in the original languages, they are inflected or modified forms of *Bayerisch bueno la*.

§ 2.52   In the case of defective words which exist in inflected forms but whose uninflected equivalents are missing from the language, the SUSANNE scheme does not postulate artificial base forms: if (according to *OALD3*) no uninflected version of a word exists, the inflected text form stands in the lemma field as its own base form.

This arises most commonly with noun plurals. For instance, *OALD3* (perhaps surprisingly in some cases) lists no singular counterparts for *archives clothes cuff-links remains surroundings*, so the plural forms are used in the lemma field.[12] On the other hand, the plural noun *thanks* is listed in *OALD3* as an inflected form of a singular noun **thank**, so (although *OALD3* notes that the singular form occurs only in compounds) *thank* appears as the base form.[13] Uncountable nouns in *-ics* are lemmatized as they stand, whether or not a corresponding noun in *-ic* exists in the language: *dynamics* as a singular noun is lemmatized as *dynamics*.

---

[12] If *cuff-links* occurred hyphenated in a text, the SUSANNE word-segmentation rules (cf. § 2.36) would cause it to be treated as a series of separate words each assigned a base form independently, and *links* has the base form *link*. But the Corpus contains *cufflinks* written solid (at A14:0350); this is therefore a single SUSANNE word and is given the base form *cuff<hyphen>links* by reference to the *OALD3* subentry **cuff-links**.

[13] If Corpus usage contradicts *OALD3* claims about word defectiveness, the lemma field follows the logic of Corpus usage: thus *OALD3* lists *aborigines* as plural-only, but text G04 consistently uses *aborigine* as a singular and *aborigines* as its plural, therefore both forms are lemmatized as *aborigine* where they occur in this text. *OALD3* lists the American *bleachers* as plural-only, therefore *bleachers* A13:1780 is lemmatized as *bleachers*, but the form in *bleacher-type seats* A08:0160 is lemmatized as *bleacher*.

In harmony with its *OALD3* entry the word *data* is lemmatized as *data* whatever its context (although *datum* occurs as a singular noun in the Corpus).

§ 2.53   Irregular comparatives and superlatives such as *further*, *eldest* are referred in the lemma field to absolute forms such as *far*, *old*. However, the group of comparative adjectives wordtagged JBR (§ 3.73), such as *inner*, *upper*, are treated as their own base forms. The words *more*, *most* (and words in -*most*), *less*, *least* are treated as their own base forms.

§ 2.54   Special problems arise with proper names that normally occur in the plural only, since here the authority of a dictionary does not help to determine whether singular forms exist. In the case of *West Indies* it is clear that *Indies* has no singular. In the case of sports-team names, found in contexts such as *Chuck Klein of the Phillies* A13:1320, *the Pittsburgh Steelers* A14:0230, the situation is more obscure: the names are undoubtedly most commonly used as plurals, but it is uncertain whether singular counterparts are occasionally used to denote team members (and, if so, it is unclear what the orthography of the singular form should be in the case of *Phillies*). The SUSANNE decision was to treat all these names as plural-only words, shown in the lemma field as *Indies, Phillies, Steelers*.[14]

CAPITALIZATION

§ 2.55   For non-proper words, *OALD3* is treated as authoritative on the issue whether a word contains an inherent initial capital and, in particular, whether the capitalized form of a word should be regarded as a distinct lexical item from the non-capitalized form and should therefore retain its capital in the lemma field. Thus, *OALD3* lists **Miss** and **miss** (as in *Miss Kelly* versus *Good morning, miss*) as separate subentries, hence *Miss* as a prefix within a personal name retains its capital in the lemma field.

§ 2.56   With foreign borrowings not listed in the dictionary, the orthographic rules of the source language determine the base form. Thus the word *gegenschein* in the sequence (italics/roman as in original):

Zodiacal light and the *gegenschein* give some evidence . . . J07:1260

---

[14] Where a team name is the plural of a common noun, by the SUSANNE rules on proper names (§ 3.20) the word is analysed as exemplifying that common noun and hence the problem discussed above does not arise: the team-name *Orioles* is lemmatized as *oriole*. This principle extends to the form *Sox* in e.g. *Chicago White Sox* A11:1860, since *sox* as a variant spelling of *socks* is not restricted in American usage to proper names: therefore *Sox* is lemmatized as *sock*.

is lemmatized as *Gegenschein,* since German orthography requires nouns to be capitalized (and this rule will sometimes be followed when the word is used in English).

§ 2.57   In the case of proper names wordtagged as such by the restrictive SUSANNE rules (§ 3.18 ff.), presence or absence of capitals in the lemma field depends on usage within English. Elements such as *de, la, von, van* may occur either capitalized or in lower case within European personal names; etymologically *de* and *De* are the "same word", but as part of a name within an English text *de* and *De* are treated as distinct words, each its own base form. In American English, foreign-derived names often include typography that violates the rules of the source language, e.g. *SanAntonio* without internal word-space as a surname at A05:1760; the lemma field reproduces the American English usage as it stands.

ORTHOGRAPHIC STANDARDIZATION

§ 2.58   Many differences between text forms and base forms of words in the SUSANNE Corpus arise from the fact that the text is American while the dictionary used to define standard orthographic forms is British. Thus text words such as *altho flavored defense plowing* are lemmatized as *although flavour defence plough.* However, American/British spelling contrasts are shown only when they appear as a consequence of the process of referring forms to dictionary headwords. Distinctive American inflexion patterns, such as *traveled, traveling* for British *travelled, travelling,* are not marked in any way; and where American/British lexical differences go beyond orthography, the form in the lemma field is based on the American form in the text even if this is not listed in *OALD3* — e.g. *aluminum anyways batters councilman sidewise* for British *aluminium anyway batsmen councillor sideways* are lemmatized as *aluminum anyways batter councilman sidewise.*[15]

§ 2.59   Another frequent type of orthographic standardization relates to written representations of non-standard pronunciations. Thus e.g. *onct, 'pache, somethin',* (Australian pidgin) *fella,* (Southern US Negro) *sho' massuh* are lemmatized as *once, Apache, something, fellow, sure master* respectively. The imitation of a German accent in *Zthere iss no mod'n F-french Musik* G28.101 is lemmatized *there be no modern French music.* But when non-standard wordforms differ from their standard equivalents with

---

[15] The words *advisor* J22:0810, *rator* J02:1110 are lemmatized as *adviser, rater,* though there is room for debate whether *-or* and *-er* should be regarded as alternative spellings of the same suffix.

respect to features other than pronunciation, these features are retained in the lemma field: thus *hisself* N11:0740, *howsomever* N09:0630, *Looky* (for "look!", N09:0700) are lemmatized as *hisself howsomever looky*. Drawing the relevant distinction is sometimes difficult. For instance, *doc* is lemmatized as *doc* rather than *doctor*, but *cap'n* as *captain*, (Australian pidgin) *tabac* G04:1670 as *tobacco*.

§ 2.60   A further source of word-field/lemma-field contrasts is the fact that *OALD3* uses a larger character-set than the Brown Corpus from which SUSANNE text forms are derived. The Brown Corpus includes no diacritics other than umlaut/diaeresis (§ 2.31), whereas *OALD3* includes the full range of French, German, and Spanish diacritics on words which commonly retain them when borrowed into English: thus for instance the word which appears as *detente* in the word field at A04:1220 (and which may have been printed as *detente* or as *détente* in the original publication from which the Brown Corpus was compiled) is assigned the base form *d<eacute>tente* in the SUSANNE lemma field.

§ 2.61   There are naturally also many text-form/dictionary-form contrasts with respect to hyphenation versus writing of compounds solid or as separate words. For instance, the corpus forms *infrared bumblebees parimutuels payrolls farfetched* are lemmatized as *infra<hyphen>red bumble<hyphen>bee pari<hyphen>mutuel pay<hyphen>roll far<hyphen>fetched*, while conversely *tattle-tale over-all to-day* are lemmatized as *tattletale overall today*. The decision whether to split a continuous sequence of characters across multiple SUSANNE lines is made in terms of principles discussed in §§ 2.33 ff., and does not take dictionary usage into account; but the result sometimes is that SUSANNE treats as a single word an item which is listed in *OALD3* as a multi-word phrase. In such cases the public entity *<blank>* is used to represent word-space in the lemma field. Thus *shortcuts* A09:0090 is the plural of the *OALD3* subentry **short cut**, and *all-out* appears hyphenated at A04:1540 (and is treated as a single word by the rules of § 2.37 — if split, the phrase would rank as a "grammatical idiom"), but corresponds to the *OALD3* subentry **all out**; the base forms are shown as *short<blank>cut*, *all<blank>out*.[16] On the other hand, in the rare cases where a phrase is written as separate words in the text but appears hyphenated in *OALD3* (e.g. *willy nilly* G17:0940, *point blank* N04:1390, in *OALD3* as **willy-nilly**, **point-blank**), the lemma field does not show the dictionary punctuation (each of the SUSANNE words *willy* and

---

[16] In the sequence *old agrarian who mutters "yassuhs"* G08:1030 the form *yassuhs* is used as the plural of a Southern US Negro pronunciation of the phrase standardly written *yes, sir*: in this case the lemma field contains comma as well as *<blank>*.

nilly stands unchanged in the lemma field, corresponding to the parts of the *OALD3* headword on either side of its hyphen).

The word-segmentation rules of § 2.36 cause a prefix such as the *pro* of *pro-Western* A04:1590 to be given a line of its own. The *OALD3* headword for such a prefix will normally (as in this case) end in a hyphen, **pro-**; therefore the base form is shown as *pro<hyphen>* even though in the word field the hyphen of *pro-Western* is placed on the following line.

§ 2.62   Where a vocabulary item does not appear in the dictionary, an appropriate base form is chosen in the light of common sense and by analogy with those forms that are listed. In such cases there is a presumption in favour of leaving the orthography of the text form unchanged, but this is overridden in cases where it is clear that the usage of the dictionary in matters such as hyphenation is systematically different from the usage exemplified by the text form. For instance, the word *quarterback* does not occur in *OALD3*, but the analogous word *half-back* occurs hyphenated, and hyphens are regularly used in comparable compounds in *OALD3*; therefore the text form *quarterback* is assigned the base form *quarter<hyphen>back*.

§ 2.63   *OALD3* often lists alternative orthographic forms for a headword. Ideally, irrespective of the form occurring in the text the SUSANNE base form should always reflect the primary variant (which is taken to be the first variant, where alternatives are listed at the head of a single dictionary article, or the variant shown at the head of an article to which other variants are cross-referred). Thus the text forms *pixies, regime, role* are assigned the base forms *pixy, r<eacute>gime, role*, because *OALD3* heads the respective articles with the variant-lists **pixy, pixie; régime, regime; role, rôle.** Unfortunately, the effort required to identify all such cases was beyond the resources available to the SUSANNE project, and there are many cases in the Corpus where the base form is one listed in *OALD3* as a secondary variant. Thus *indorsed* A09:0940 is assigned the base form *indorse*, and *program* stands as its own base form, although *OALD3* identifies *indorse, program* as secondary variants of *endorse, programme*.[17]

A similar problem is that *OALD3* includes a few non-standard wordforms as headwords; thus, in the sequence *rubbin' agin that thar little ticklebrush* N13:1380 the form *agin* is not lemmatized as *against* because the variant form *agin* does occur as an *OALD3* headword.

---

[17] The nature of the algorithm used to generate base forms in the SUSANNE lemma field meant that uninflected versions of text forms were not identified as secondary variants if they differed from primary variants with respect to their alphabetic characters, unless both variants would have yielded the same inflected form (as in the case of *pixies* from either *pixy* or *pixie*).

§ 2.64   Enclitics such as +*n't*, +*'s*, +*'ve* are assigned full base forms such as *not*, *has* or *is* (according to context), *have*. (The form +*'ll* is assumed always to represent *will* rather than the much less frequent *shall*.) On the other hand, conventional short by-forms of words are not referred to their formal, longer equivalents: the forenames *Mike*, *Liz* stand as base forms rather than being replaced by *Michael*, *Elizabeth*, the noun *auto* stands as a base form in the sense "automobile". (We have seen that formal abbreviations, marked A or S in the status field, are not given lemma-field entries.) The company name *Plee-Zing, Inc.* A20:1790 is evidently coined in order to coincide in sound with *pleasing*, but as a name *Plee-Zing* is the correct, conventional form and stands unaltered in the lemma field.

§ 2.65   Some non-standard spellings represent purely idiosyncratic variations: *shu-tt up-pp* N09:0090 is lemmatized as *shut up*, and the interjection *Aah* N09:0240, which does not occur in *OALD3*, is lemmatized as *ah*, which does.

§ 2.66   The lemma field cannot in general be used to determine the correct forms corresponding to misprinted forms (marked E in the status field) in the original texts. In many E lines, the lemma field does contain the correct version of the misprinted word. But the fact that the lemma field shows uninflected versions of inflected forms means that that is not always so; cf. the occurrence of *alloted* for *allotted* at A06:1680, where the base form *allot* does nothing to reveal the nature of the misprint. Not all misprints are localized within single text words, so it would be impractical to correct them via fields in individual records. Users wishing to establish normalized versions of SUSANNE texts should refer to the list of misprints in the documentation file which accompanies the Corpus.

SENSE CODES[18]

§ 2.67   Of those words which are assigned base forms according to the criteria specified at § 2.47 above, a subset are also assigned numerical sense codes, showing which of their alternative dictionary senses is intended in the context. The concept of sense-coding is inapplicable to some words that are given base forms, particularly proper names; and furthermore, while sense-coding might be applied to closed-class words, this did not seem particularly desirable. Words like *have* or *if* tend to have extensive ranges of numbered

---

[18] The following sections §§ 2.67–74 define a coding scheme which, as explained in Ch. 1, is not applied in current SUSANNE releases. The material is included here to enable this book to retain its value as a reference if future Corpus releases include sense codes; it may also serve a useful purpose currently as an outline of the issues arising in the development of a coding system of this sort.

senses in dictionaries, the distinctions between which are very complex and sometimes rather arbitrary. It would be extremely difficult, and might not be very useful, to specify which sense is relevant to occurrences of such words. The SUSANNE sense-coding system is intended to distinguish between senses of open-class words, where the alternatives tend to be few and relatively clear-cut.

Specifically, the SUSANNE sense-coding system is intended to apply to all and only those words for which a base form is assigned and which, in addition, have a wordtag beginning with the characters J..., N... (but not NP...), VV..., or RR... (but not RRQ...) — that is, adjectives, common nouns, main verbs, and general adverbs. These words should have a numerical sense code suffixed after an underline character to the base form in the lemma field, according to a system described below: if the word is unambiguous, the code is 0 (zero), otherwise (apart from certain special cases) the code is a sequence of one or more numerals separated by stops. For those words which are assigned a base form but are outside the sense-codable class, the base form appears in the dictionary field without a suffix.

§ **2.68** Occasional words (e.g. *agglutinating, unhitched*) fall within the sense-codable class but cannot be coded because the relevant vocabulary item happens to be missing from the dictionary on which the coding scheme is based. These cases are indicated by a question mark suffixed to the base form: *agglutinate_?, unhitch_?*.

§ **2.69** The sense-coding system relates to the structure of entries in *LDOCE*, so we begin by describing this.

LDOCE treats uses of a given word as different parts of speech in separate articles, whose headwords are distinguished on the page by numerical superscripts. Thus adjectival uses of *open* have an article headed **open**[1], verbal uses have an article headed **open**[2], and nominal uses (e.g. *life in the open*) have an article headed **open**[3]. In some cases of homonymy separate articles with differently superscripted headwords are provided also for uses representing a single part of speech, thus *ear* as the organ of hearing has an article **ear**[1] while *ear* as ear of corn has an article **ear**[2].

A single article is divided into subsenses, normally labelled by bold numerals; in the special case of phrasal verbs (e.g. *open out*) the phrase itself appears in bold as a heading following the various numbered subsenses for the verb not followed by a particle, and in some cases a phrasal verb is itself given alternative senses listed after bold numerals.

The treatment of phrasal verbs is one way in which multi-word units are recognized by the *LDOCE* structure. There are two other ways: some headwords contain more than one orthographic word (e.g. **open-heart surgery, open verdict** — these are separate articles from the articles **open¹, open², open³**); and a numbered subentry within an article may define, not a sense of the headword itself, but a phrase containing the headword — in this case the phrase is printed in bold immediately after the subsense number.

Thus the logical structure of some of the *LDOCE* contents relating to the word *open* might be diagrammed as follows:

open¹ *adjective*
  1 not shut . . .
  2 not surrounded by walls . . .
  . . .
  13 with open arms in a very friendly way . . .
open² *verb*
  1 to (cause to) become open . . .
  2 to (cause to) spread or unfold . . .
  . . .
  8 open someone's eyes (to) to make someone know or understand . . .
  open into/onto sthg *phrasal verb* to provide a means of entering . . .
  open out *phrasal verb* to speak more freely . . .
  open up *phrasal verb*
    1 to make possible the development of . . .
    2 to open a door . . .
    3 to speak more freely . . .
open³ *noun*
  . . .
open-air *adjective*
  . . .
open-heart surgery *noun*
  a medical operation in which . . .
  . . .
open verdict *noun*
  a decision that records . . .
  . . .

An example of a one-word *LDOCE* headword lacking a superscript (because it can only act as a single part of speech) is:

opera *noun*
  1 a musical play . . .
  2 such musical plays as a form of art . . .

A case where the headword has neither superscript nor multiple subsenses is:

opiate *noun*
a sleep-producing drug . . .

§ 2.70 In order to construct a SUSANNE sense code for a particular use of a word, the *LDOCE* article which covers the use is treated as a tree whose root node is labelled with the superscript numeral on the headword of the article; a headword with no superscript is deemed to have zero as superscript. Lower nodes are labelled either with numerals (in the case of numbered senses), or with the word or words following the verb, in the case of a subentry for a phrasal verb. (Where a phrasal verb is followed by more than one particle, as in **look down on** under **look**, the node-label includes the public entity *<blank>* in place of the space: *down<blank>on*. Where a phrasal verb heading includes material additional to the verb and particle(s), only the particle(s) are relevant for the node-label: the label corresponding to the subentry **open into/onto sthg** is *into/onto*.) Then the sense code for an individual use is created by listing the labels of the nodes on the path through the tree which leads to the relevant sense, separating nodes by stops. The dictionary field for *opened* "caused to spread or unfold" would contain *open_2.2*; that for *opened* in *opened up* "spoke more freely" would contain *open_2.up.3*; that for *operas* "musical plays" would contain *opera_0.1*; the form *opiate_0* would appear in the lemma field for *opiates*.

§ 2.71 In a case where the word in the text is found in the dictionary, but it is impossible to relate the use in the text to any of the dictionary senses, a question mark occurs in place of the last node-label in the list. Thus *rebound* occurs as a malapropism for *redound* in the sequence *It can only rebound to Mr. Hughes' discredit . . .* A06:0670. The text word *rebound* can be identified as *LDOCE*'s entry **rebound¹**, verb (as opposed to **rebound²**, noun), but this entry naturally includes no sense corresponding to "redound", so *rebound_1.?* appears as the sense code.[19] (The same system is available for cases where a word has acquired a novel sense not yet recorded by the dictionary, but in practice this mechanism is hardly ever used since novel senses can almost always be identified as extensions of established, listed senses.)

---

[19] If a word *xyz* has only one dictionary entry, hence no superscript numeral on the headword, and the part of speech matches the text usage but all the senses listed are wrong, the code would be *xyz_0.?*; if it is clear that *xyz* is used in the text not only in a different sense but as a different part of speech from any *xyz* dictionary entry, then the sense code would be *xyz_?* (the same as if the wordform did not appear in the dictionary at all).

§ **2.72** Where a usage in the Corpus corresponds to an *LDOCE* article headed by more than one orthographic word, e.g. *open verdict*, the dictionary codes for the individual words in the SUSANNE file lead to the *LDOCE* article for the multi-word phrase, rather than to articles for the individual words. (Both words in the phrase *open verdict* are arguably used in standard senses — e.g. *open* is used in sense **open_1.5**, "not completely decided or answered"; but sense-coding indicates a relatively specific usage, if this is listed in *LDOCE*, in preference to the more general usages from which it is made up.) Likewise when a hyphenated text word such as *wine-glass* is split over multiple SUSANNE lines, the individual dictionary codes lead to the *LDOCE* entry or subentry for the compound. In these cases there is a clash between the base form derived from *OALD3* by the rules of §§ 2.48–66, and the form relevant for locating the applicable sense in *LDOCE*. This clash is resolved by including, in the sense-code part of the dictionary field for the first sense-codable SUSANNE word, the complete *LDOCE* headword, separated by a colon from the part of the lemma field which gives the *OALD3*-derived base form for the individual SUSANNE word, and followed by a zero or other numerical indication of *LDOCE* subsense; for the other sense-codable SUSANNE words in the expression, the sense-code part of the lemma field contains the character > followed by the reference number (omitting the first four bytes) of the line on which the *LDOCE* headword appears. Thus:

reference field	word field	lemma field
X12:5670b	many	many
X12:5670c	open	open:open<blank>verdict_0
X12:5670d	verdicts	verdict>5670c
X12:5670e	resulted	result_1
X13:0460e	the	the
X13:0460f	wine	wine:wineglass_0.1
X13:0460g	+<hyphen>	–
X13:0460h	+glasses	glass>0460f

When a numbered subsense of an *LDOCE* headword is a multi-word expression incorporating that headword (e.g. **open_1.13** is the phrase *with open arms*), the line corresponding to the headword has the numerical sense code, and the lines for the other sense-codable words of the expression use the >... system to point to the line corresponding to the headword:

```
X04:2160c  welcomed  welcome_2.2
X04:2160d  with      with
X04:2160e  open      open_1.13
X04:2160f  arms      arm>2160e
```

§ 2.73 There will sometimes be clashes between the *OALD3* derived base form of a word and the form appropriate for identifying an *LDOCE* sense that do not have to do with expressions being split over multiple SUSANNE lines. For instance, *LDOCE* has separate headwords **liberalism** (wide understanding and advanced opinions) and **Liberalism** (aims and beliefs of the Liberal party), while *OALD3* lists only a single headword **liberalism.** If the only spelling in the lemma field were the *OALD3* **liberalism,** it would be impossible for sense-coding to indicate that a text word was used in the sense of the capitalized *LDOCE* headword. Such clashes are resolved by the technique of including the *LDOCE* form of the headword separated by a colon from the *OALD3* base form. In general, whenever an *LDOCE* sense needs to be indicated by citing an *LDOCE* headword which is different in form from the *OALD3*-derived base form on the line in question, the *LDOCE* headword is suffixed to the *OALD3*-derived base form after a colon. Thus:

word field	lemma field
liberalism	liberalism_0
of	of
outlook	outlook_0.3
voters	voter_0.2
rejected	reject_1.1
Liberalism	liberalism:Liberalism_0

§ 2.74 To sum up: lemma-field entries of the following structures (where *xyz* stands for the base form of some word) have the meanings indicated:

–	the contents of the word field are not the kind of item appropriately assigned a base form;
xyz	the word *xyz* is not the kind of word to which sense-coding applies (e.g. a closed-class word, or a proper name);

xyz_?	the word *xyz* is the kind of word to which sense-coding applies, but no code can be identified because *xyz* is not in *LDOCE*;
xyz_0	the word *xyz* is the kind of word to which sense-coding applies, and is unambiguous;
xyz_3.2	the word *xyz* is the kind of word to which sense-coding applies, and in the context it bears sense 2 of *LDOCE* entry **xyz**^{3};
xyz_2.?	the word *xyz* is the kind of word to which sense-coding applies, it represents *LDOCE* entry **xyz**^{2}, but it is used in a sense clearly different from any sense listed in that entry;
xyz:xyz<blank>pq<blank>abcd_0.1	the word *xyz* is part of a multi-word expression representing sense 1 of an *LDOCE* article headed **xyz pq abcd**;
xyz>9999a	the word *xyz* is part of a multi-word expression whose place in *LDOCE* is identified in the lemma field of line 9999a;
xyz:xyzw_1.2	the text word represents sense 2 of a headword given as **xyzw**^{1} in *LDOCE*, but the *OALD3* orthography for the same vocabulary item is **xyz**.

Citation of Examples

§ 2.75 The present work contains many analysed examples, normally taken either from the SUSANNE or Lancaster-Leeds analysed corpora, illustrating the various annotations defined. The conventions used in such citations require brief explanation. The SUSANNE annotation scheme is rather complicated, and the conventions described here have been chosen in order to enable relevant aspects of the annotation to be displayed clearly, without overwhelming the reader with more details than he can reasonably absorb.

§ 2.76   The italic v. roman contrast is used to distinguish elements of the text being analysed (including elements represented by entity names within angle brackets) from analytic annotations, such as wordtags, tagmatags, and square brackets marking tagma boundaries. Bold type is used to pick out elements of quoted examples for special attention.

§ 2.77   Inevitably, authentic corpus examples illustrating a particular grammatical phenomenon often contain stretches of wording which are irrelevant to that phenomenon and would be confusing if included in the citation; the ellipsis mark "..." is used to show where such stretches have been omitted. Since there is no italic/roman contrast for ellipsis marks, an ellipsis mark occurring as part of the analysed text is represented in this book by the ISO entity name *<hellip>*.

§ 2.78   Similarly, SUSANNE analyses often comprise many levels of constituency, and it would be confusing to show all the labelled brackets that apply to a passage which is cited in order to illustrate its analysis at some particular level. Accordingly, cited analyses include only those aspects of the full SUSANNE annotation deemed relevant to the point at issue (other aspects of the annotation being omitted silently). Wherever a left bracket is shown, however, its corresponding right bracket will always be shown (and vice versa). Even if the example involves only the first few words of a long tagma, the remainder of the tagma will be indicated by an ellipsis mark preceding its right bracket.

§ 2.79   Many non-terminal nodes in SUSANNE parsetrees have labels including two categories of information separated by a colon (see § 4.21 below) — "formtags" representing surface grammatical properties before the colon, symbols standing for logical or functional properties after the colon. In Chapters 2 to 4, only the formtags are shown in cited examples even for tagmas whose labels also include logical annotation.[20] In Chapter 5, full node-labels are shown — if a node-label is printed without a logical-grammar extension in that chapter, this implies that it has none. (Chapter 5 often returns to the same examples whose surface annotation has been shown in

---

[20] Where it is occasionally necessary to deviate from this practice, a note drawing attention to the point is provided.

Chapter 4, in order to show how this is expanded to indicate the logical structure of the passages.) Except for the systematic omission of logical extensions in tagmatags cited before Chapter 5, node-labels are shown in full wherever they are shown at all.

§ 2.80 Non-terminal node-labels are printed immediately to the right of the opening bracket marking the beginning of the tagma to which they apply. Since it is guaranteed that brackets shown in a cited example balance, in a short citation it would be redundant to repeat the labels with the corresponding closing brackets and these are often left unlabelled. In long and complex cases it can sometimes be helpful to the reader to show which closing bracket balances a particular opening bracket, and this is done by repeating the tagmatag immediately to the left of the closing bracket.

§ 2.81 Where the wordtag of an individual word is indicated within an analysed example, this is done by placing the wordtag (in roman type) after the word (in italics) joined together by the underline character. The underline character has a further use in cited examples: where it is desirable to show explicitly that a sequence of orthographic words is analysed as a single "grammatical idiom" (§ 3.55), the words are printed with linking underlines, e.g. *up_to_date.* (Absence of underlines in a cited example does not imply that a sequence is *not* analysed as an idiom; often the idiomatic status of a short word-sequence will be entirely irrelevant to a point being made about the analysis of a longer sequence in which it occurs, in which case the idiomatic sequence will be printed normally.)

§ 2.82 So far as is practical, wording from the original texts is quoted in this work in its ordinary typographic form, using the original symbols (e.g. *ï, §*) rather than ISO entity names. Hyphenations, punctuation marks attached to adjacent words, etc. are printed continuously although split up by the SUSANNE word-segmentation rules, unless the analysis into separate units is relevant to the point being made with the example. Even where a sequence of characters printed continuously in the original text is interrupted in the citation by (labelled or unlabelled) brackets marking tagma boundaries, the continuity of the original is shown by printing italicized material immediately next to the outsides of the brackets, for instance:

He answered "Broxbourne".

could be represented as:

He answered "[Q [Nns Broxbourne]]".

as an alternative to:

He answered <ldquo> [Q [Nns +Broxbourne]] +<rdquo> +.

Nevertheless, whenever it is clearer to use the plus-sign notation to identify SUSANNE words which are printed continuously in the original text as separate items, or to use entity names for special symbols, this is done. Italic/roman and bold/plain contrasts in the original text are shown with <bital> . . . <eital> and <bbold> . . . <ebold>; roman in cited examples is reserved for elements of the annotation, and bold for directing the reader's attention to a particularly significant segment of the example. A full stop or a dash in a cited example will always be part of the original text rather than part of the annotation.

In examples quoted from the LOB Corpus, where LOB transcription rules normalize the occurrence of whitespace in a manner that seems unlikely to reflect usage in the original texts (for instance solidus between words is standardly shown in LOB with following but no preceding space, cf. *LCUM*, p. 25), the examples as shown in the present work incorporate a conjectural reconstruction of the original typography.

§ 2.83   In discussing the principles of annotation rather than quoting specific examples it is sometimes convenient to use a notation representing any inflected form of a given verb; the base form of the verb written in capitals is used for this purpose. Thus "clause beginning with relative pronoun + *BE*" covers clauses beginning *who is, who are, which was*, etc.

§ 2.84   Examples taken from the Brown or LOB Corpora (commonly, from the SUSANNE and Lancaster-Leeds analysed subsets of these) are followed by references to their Brown or LOB locations, by text- and line-number. Unfortunately, Brown and LOB texts do not have distinctive filenames: A01, A02, etc. can refer either to Brown or to LOB texts. Rather than adding distinguishing prefixes to keep the American and British sources apart, this document uses the convention of separating text- from line-number with a colon for Brown but with a full stop for LOB. This distinction is reinforced by a contrast in the system of line-numbering used in the respective corpora. Brown line-numbers normally increment in tens (§ 2.6) and therefore consist of four digits. LOB lines, on the other hand, are numbered continuously and reach only into the hundreds. Therefore a three-figure line-number indicates a LOB source, a four-figure line-number indicates a Brown source: the first line of the first Brown text is cited as "A01:0010", the first line of the first LOB text as "A01.001".[21]

---

[21] In the LOB Corpus itself, low line-numbers are shown as "1", "20", etc., but references to LOB locations in the present work add leading zeros to make line-numbers up to three digits.

An example more than a few words long will commonly stretch over two or more Brown or LOB lines. The reference in the present work specifies the corpus line on which the quoted text material begins.

Occasional examples are quoted from authentic sources other than the Brown or LOB Corpora, in which case the sources are specified in whatever format is appropriate to their nature, whether book, newspaper, etc. Examples quoted with no reference to a source (as well as some quoted from other technical publications on English grammar) have been invented, either by the present author and his research team or by the authors of the cited publications. Invented examples are sometimes useful in order to provide clear, uncluttered illustrations of a specific analytic issue, but such examples should be treated with the caution appropriate when linguists rely on "native speaker's intuition" rather than observation.

Text Corrections

§ 2.85   Like any other printed material, the texts from which the Brown Corpus derives contain a proportion of misprints, and normally these are logged in the Brown Manual; the errors are reproduced uncorrected in the Brown Corpus. Inevitably, further errors were introduced into the text during the creation of successive versions of the electronic Brown Corpus, such as the "Bergen I" version of Brown which was used as the primary source for the SUSANNE word fields.

The SUSANNE Corpus aims to reflect the incidence of errors found in real-life written English, and therefore to reproduce those errors which stem from the original texts while correcting errors introduced in the corpus-construction process. Accordingly, whenever the Bergen I text seemed erroneous the SUSANNE team checked (sometimes directly, but in most cases through W. Nelson Francis) whether the error reflects the original source. If so, the error is preserved in the SUSANNE Corpus (flagged by an E in the status field), otherwise the original text is restored. Where errors are original, wordtagging and grammatical analysis are applied to the erroneous text as best they can be by analogy with correct forms (cf. § 4.26 ff.). From Release 3 onwards of SUSANNE, the documentation file contains a detailed listing of all errors found (of either type).

It is of course all too possible that the task of creating the SUSANNE Corpus may have introduced new errors in the word field, and that some errors in Bergen I which were not original have been allowed to stand by oversight. Users who discover errors not logged in the documentation file are encouraged to bring these to the author's attention for correction in subsequent releases.

□ 3 □
WORD CLASSES

The Principles of Wordtagging

§ **3.1**   This chapter lists the system of wordtags used in SUSANNE wordtag fields, and explains how choices between alternative wordtags are made in debatable cases. The principles by which text is segmented into taggable "words" were stated in §§ 2.33–45.

§ **3.2**   Although the system of wordtags used is referred to as the "SUSANNE wordtag set", because it is being published for the first time in connection with this Corpus, it was developed for more general purposes by a research team that has been executing other projects in addition to the creation of the SUSANNE Corpus. (The fact that the wordtag system is not designed specifically for the SUSANNE Corpus is demonstrated for instance by the fact that a few of its elements are applicable more to British than to American text.) The tagset is intended to apply to a broad spectrum of general texts in modern written English of either national standard variety. (The same research team has also developed extensions of the tagset for tagging transcriptions of spoken English; this scheme, which is less fully worked out than the scheme of wordtags for written English, is described in Chapter 6.) The SUSANNE tagset contains some resources for annotating technical material and archaic or substandard forms of English, and is suitable for tagging text in which limited amounts of these phenomena occur (as is true of the Brown Corpus), though not for tagging heavily technical material or texts which are written entirely in archaic language.

Unitary Wordtags versus Grammatical Features

§ **3.3**   A first point to be made about the SUSANNE word-classification scheme is that it involves unitary tags: a SUSANNE wordtag is a string of characters which is intended as a single atomic symbol, not as shorthand for a set of grammatical features. Naturally, since there are several hundred wordtags, it is more convenient to assign them character-strings which have some mnemonic value, rather than randomly selected combinations of characters; and this has the consequence that sets of tags for words having some common grammatical property do often have a character in common. For instance, the characters "1" and "2" are used in numerous tags for singular and plural words respectively. But this is a matter merely of practical convenience; it does not imply that there is some specific set of binary- or multiple-valued grammatical features underlying the tagset, such that any individual wordtag can be completely translated into a distribution of values over the various features.

§ 3.4   The point needs to be made, because this aspect of the SUSANNE parsing scheme has proved (unexpectedly, from the author's point of view) to be quite controversial. A number of linguists, on first encountering the SUSANNE scheme, have either presupposed that the wordtags were meant as shorthand for bundles of grammatical feature-values, or have expressed the view that words *ought* to be classified in terms of features.

§ 3.5   The SUSANNE philosophy is that unitary wordtags are preferable to sets of features, because they impose fewer prior assumptions about what sorts of difference between words are grammatically important. The contrast between singular and plural certainly is a grammatically significant feature, governing concord within noun phrases and between noun phrases and verbs; and it is the kind of feature which fits in well with the concept of word classes as bundles of feature-values, since it crosscuts many other grammatical features (the singular/plural contrast is found in nouns and in pronouns, in common nouns and in proper names, and so on). On the other hand, consider the range of names and abbreviated names such as *Hampshire, Hants., OH, Sussex, Conn.*: these represent a class which also has grammatical significance, being words which typically occur as the last word of a postal address, but a theorist proposing a set of features for the classification of vocabulary would not typically think of proposing a feature "final in addresses" — it does not crosscut a range of other grammatical features, it applies just to one small set of geographical proper names. If one insists on classifying words in terms of feature-values, this is likely to lead to word classes of the latter kind being overlooked, whether or not they are in fact grammatically important: almost all one's attention will be focused on the crosscutting features. That would be strategically quite undesirable, because the crosscutting features tend in any case to receive more than their fair share of attention from linguistic theorists for independent reasons: they tend to be the features which recur in numerous languages and may plausibly be related to psychological theories of language universals, whereas classes of words such as "address-final names" tend to be obviously culture-specific. It may well be that in some absolute sense the class of "plural nouns" is *more* significant grammatically than the class of "address-final names"; but in the current state of linguistic theorizing there is no danger of the former class being overlooked, whereas the latter class easily might be. It would be unfortunate to adopt notational conventions which reinforce this bias unnecessarily.

§ 3.6 Furthermore, classifying words in terms of crosscutting features creates a pressure towards equating similar features that occur in different word-types. We talk about words as being "singular" or "plural", implying that plurality means the same thing in whatever kind of word we find it; but of course that is not really so. Most obviously, for a possessive pronoun to be plural (e.g. *our* v. *my*) has nothing at all to do with verb agreement. But, more subtly, there is, for instance, the fact that nouns which are borrowed from classical or foreign languages and retain their original inflexion patterns tend to have etymological plurals which in English are treated as to varying degrees ambiguous in number. Probably most writers nowadays would give *data* a singular verb; some treat *automata* or *graffiti* as singular, others as plural, whereas no one would write a singular verb after *automatons* (and the form *graffito* is hardly found in English, so *graffitos* also does not occur). Again, a "plural" noun is commonly one which, as head of a subject noun phrase, requires a plural verb; but English also has the phenomenon of plural titles which require plural verbs when modifying singular heads (*the Misses Smith are here*), cf. § 3.43. Or, as another example, consider the conflicts created in the number system by the use of the royal *we*. If a monarch says "We shall allow ourself an hour's rest after luncheon", should *ourself* be called singular or plural? Various SUSANNE wordtags contain the character "2" as a mnemonic device for "plural" without any implication that "plural" means the same thing in each case; but classification by grammatical features would employ a pair of features SINGULAR and PLURAL (or +SINGULAR and −SINGULAR) which would have to be defined as carrying some constant meaning throughout the spectrum of vocabulary to which they applied.

§ 3.7 True, *any* method of classifying words involves neglecting some individual differences in order to group sets of words together; the SUSANNE wordtagging system does not in fact distinguish non-English plural forms from English plurals (cf. § 3.35). But the feature-value approach forces one to override the peculiarities of individual words to a greater degree than does the system of unitary wordtags, and it carries a tacit implication of scientific validity, whereas the more straightforward unitary wordtag system purports to be nothing more than the rough and ready practical convenience which is all any word-classifying system can be in reality. The feature-value approach does not seem suitable for an empirically based annotation scheme which aims to represent a language as it actually is rather than as a theorist might suppose it to be. (The present author has been told by Mitchell Marcus, who is directing another contemporary programme of English grammatical annotation, that he likewise prefers unitary wordtags to bundles of grammatical feature-values.)

Background to the SUSANNE Wordtag Set

§ 3.8   The SUSANNE wordtag set was developed from the "Lancaster" tagset of *CAE*, appendix B, which was the most adequate tagset available at the outset of work on the SUSANNE Corpus. The SUSANNE tagset is in a number of respects more detailed than the Lancaster set, and it is more tightly defined. The tabulation in *CAE*, appendix B, leaves many questions unanswered about the application of the Lancaster tags and their relation to the tags of the Tagged LOB Corpus and other tagsets; and research on usage in the Tagged LOB Corpus, the two versions of the "CLAWS" automatic wordtagging system described in *CAE*, and related material revealed a number of unacknowledged conflicts between wordtagging principles. (Designing the SUSANNE tagset involved producing a table far more detailed than that of *CAE*, appendix B, of correlations between wordtagging practice in various sources.) Since the Lancaster tagset has achieved some degree of recognition as a published standard, however, the SUSANNE tagset is explicitly designed as an extension of it. Where SUSANNE tags involve finer differentiations among word classes than are found in the Lancaster system, these are marked by adding lower-case differentiating letters to Lancaster tags (the Lancaster tagset makes no use of lower-case letters). With lower-case letters removed, SUSANNE wordtags are normally identical to Lancaster tags, and most exceptions involve only trivial character-substitutions made for the sake of computational tractability (the dollar sign used in the Lancaster tagset to indicate the feature "genitive" is replaced by G, the ampersand which occurs in two Lancaster tags is dropped, and punctuation marks are given alphabetical tags beginning with Y: thus all

SUSANNE wordtags consist wholly of alphanumeric characters). There are just a handful of cases where tags from the Lancaster list have been abandoned because it seemed inappropriate to treat the class of words they covered as a significant category, or new basic tags have been created.

§ 3.9   This decision to retain a visible relationship between SUSANNE and Lancaster wordtags has led to some minor illogicalities in the character-sequences used. For instance: in general, Lancaster tags of the form XY, XZ represent special cases of the word class indicated by the letter X. . ., with the residue of general cases tagged XX. Thus the letter I. . . is used for prepositions, so the bulk of prepositions are tagged II, but *of*, *with*, which have special syntactic properties, are tagged respectively IO, IW. The preposition *by* is given a distinctive tag in the SUSANNE but not in the Lancaster tagset; because its Lancaster tag is II, it is given the SUSANNE tag IIb rather than IB (which would have been the logical allocation if the Lancaster tags had been treated as open to revision). Or again, in the Lancaster system the tag MF is used for fractions, such as *two-thirds* or $\frac{2}{3}$; the SUSANNE system adds a lower-case letter to make a more specific tag MFn for fractions written digitally, but because the SUSANNE analytic scheme treats elements joined by hyphens as separately tagged words it has no use for the more general tag MF. The fact that SUSANNE wordtags are unitary symbols, whose internal structure has mnemonic value only, means that this degree of illogicality should be of little practical consequence.

§ 3.10   Each SUSANNE wordtag is related to a specific Lancaster wordtag; but, because the development of the SUSANNE system has entailed resolution of conflicts between inconsistent tagging principles (as already mentioned) and introduction of new principles, the classes of words and of word-uses covered by corresponding tags in the two systems do not always coincide. Sometimes they are very different. The present work specifies the SUSANNE system as precisely as possible, but does not go into detail on the ways in which this diverges from the Lancaster system and other earlier word-tagging systems.

§ 3.11   The purpose of the SUSANNE wordtag set is to establish a range of categories which offer a predictable label for any use of any word occurring in standard written English (segmented in accordance with the rules of §§ 2.33–45), and which differentiate words whenever they are importantly different from the point of view of grammatical parsing. That is, the intention is that text to be analysed by an automatic parser could be replaced by the corresponding strings of wordtags and the parser would still have almost all the information useful for executing its task, in so far as its parsing algorithm was based on grammar.[1] (An automatic parser may work partly by reasoning about the meaning and/or pragmatics of input texts, but SUSANNE wordtags relate only to grammar — though the borderline between grammar and semantics is of course debatable, and no claim is made that the SUSANNE wordtag system has drawn it in exactly the "right" place.)

§ 3.12   Over the history of the corpus-linguistics tradition of which SUSANNE is one of the latest fruits, concepts of what count as relevant grammatical distinctions for wordtagging purposes have continually developed. The Tagged Brown and Tagged LOB Corpora, for instance, were produced at a time when approaches to corpus annotation had not yet moved on from word classification to higher-level grammatical analysis, so the tagsets of these resources embody conventional linguistic categories which (particularly in the Tagged LOB case) are documented with outstanding precision, but which are not specially adapted to the task of automatic parsing. The Lancaster tagset added extra distinctions relevant for establishing the surface grammatical structure of texts; the reason for distinguishing *of* and *with* from other prepositions, for instance, is that *with* has a special use in connection with a particular syntactic construction (the W clause, cf. § 4.366) and that *of* phrases, unlike other prepositional phrases, almost always function as noun postmodifiers rather than clause adjuncts. Now that the SUSANNE Corpus incorporates analyses of deep as well as surface grammar, new word categories are brought into focus: thus, with respect to surface parsing, *by* is just one preposition among many, but in the context of deep parsing *by* phrases play a special role vis-à-vis the passive construction and for that reason the SUSANNE tagset assigns *by* a unique wordtag.

§ 3.13   In principle, as suggested above, there is probably no end to the grammatical distinctions one can draw between words. Very many words have some unique or near-unique grammatical behaviour which could at least occasionally be relevant for parsing. The SUSANNE wordtag set involves judgements about which distinctions are likely to be relevant frequently enough to be worth encoding, in the sense that there is a real likelihood that they might be exploited by the kind of system that one can envisage being produced in the current state of parsing technology.

§ 3.14   Furthermore, assignment of tags to words in context

---

[1] One category of information relevant for parsing that is not recorded in SUSANNE wordtags is presence of word-initial capitals.

itself requires linguistic analysis, and judgements are needed about how "analytical" the tags should be. Wordtagging could be done by a trivial dictionary-lookup algorithm, if the tagset included single tags with meanings like "modal-verb-or-singular-noun", for *can*: but any reasonable system will treat *can* as a grammatically ambiguous word, so that a computer-usable lexicon will include (at least) two candidate tags for it and context must be used to select the appropriate tag for a particular token of *can*. This is a case on which everyone would agree; but in many other cases there are real questions about how much grammatical disambiguation should be built into the wordtag system. For instance, all English verbs but one (*be*) use the same forms for infinitive as for non-third-person singular present tense; and the great majority of English verbs use the same forms for past tense and past participle. The SUSANNE tagset treats a form like *believe* as grammatically unambiguous but a form like *believed* as grammatically ambiguous: that is, it provides a single "uninflected verb" tag to cover both infinitive and present tense forms of verbs other than *be*, but it does not include a generalized tag for past-tense-or-past-participle, so that tagging a token of *believed* always requires analysis of context. Alternative wordtag systems could well differ from the SUSANNE system on either of these points; they might systematically require uninflected verbs to be marked as infinitive or present tense, or they might provide a generalized "past verb" tag for verbs which do not differentiate past participle from past tense. As compared with its predecessors, the SUSANNE system has tended to reduce the analyticity of tags by creating special tags for words with unusual usage-ranges rather than covering their diverse uses with combinations of common tags; thus the problems of locating the correct tag for a word-use are reduced.

§ 3.15   In all these cases where judgement is needed to fix the details of the wordtag system, no claim is made that the judgements embodied in the SUSANNE system are always "correct" — if indeed the concept of correctness applies. As with other aspects of the SUSANNE analytic scheme, the claim is only that the published system of categories has been developed through application to a substantial body of real-life language, so that many hidden problems in analysts' initial ideas about word classification have been shown up and resolved.

§ 3.16   Each "word" assigned a line of its own by §§ 2.33 ff. is given a wordtag, including items such as punctuation marks, prefixes and suffixes, etc. The tags provided for some of these items are less grammatically refined than those for words in the ordinary sense. For instance, §§ 4.539 ff. discuss the fact that the hyphen in English has a number of very different grammatical roles, but all hyphens are wordtagged YH. Any separately tagged prefix or suffix is tagged FB or FA respectively, without differentiation between, say, a suffix such as *-like* which forms adjectives and a suffix such as *-wards* which forms adverbs. (The possibility of giving affixes more differentiated wordtags, showing their typical grammatical functions as well as their affix status, was investigated by the SUSANNE team, but was rejected since it appears that affixes typically have too diverse a range of functions for this approach to be practical.)

§ **3.17**   The SUSANNE wordtag set is presented in § 3.73 as a list with brief definitions; the principles by which boundaries are drawn between logically adjacent tags are made precise in §§ 3.74 ff. The tagging of nouns in particular involves some novel principles, and these are presented at this point since the relevant sections of the wordtag list cannot be understood without them.

Wordtags for Proper Names

§ **3.18**   In the first place, the SUSANNE Corpus differs markedly from its predecessors in its approach to the tagging of proper names.

§ **3.19**   A proper name is a linguistic form which refers in a particular manner — without entering into questions of philosophical logic, one can say that the link between linguistic form and entity referred to is a matter of arbitrary convention, independent of word-sense, in the case of proper names. The category of English grammatical forms which refer is the category of noun phrases, and proper names are one type of noun phrase. Some proper names are one-word phrases (*London, Aristotle*), but others consist of more than one word (*Mr John Smith, New Jersey*). A noun phrase which picks out a referent via the arbitrary relationship characteristic of proper naming may also include words understood in their ordinary sense rather than as names (*that idiot John Smith*; *John Smith, who joined us yesterday*), but in such a noun phrase the boundary between the "proper name proper" and the non-proper elements is not always clear. In *the Lebanon* or *John of Gaunt*, are the modifying elements *the, of Gaunt* part of the names headed by *Lebanon, John* or not? TLCUM, p. 57, gives the examples *North West Norway* v. *East Germany*, where the latter phrase, referring to what was at the time a sovereign state, is as a whole regarded as an "established name" while the former is not (though the head word *Norway* clearly is); but just what degree of "separateness" does a territorial division have to have before a conventional reference to it ranks as an established name — what about *South America*, for instance, which is a conventional name for a geographically rather well-defined territory, but one that does not coincide with a political unit?

§ 3.20   In the SUSANNE Corpus, the property of functioning as a proper name is treated as a property of noun phrases rather than of individual words. In a SUSANNE parsetree, a noun-phrase node consisting of a proper name (with or without non-proper modifying elements) has the subcategory symbol "n" suffixed to the symbol "N" which stands for "noun phrase"; since this subcategory symbol identifies the location of a proper name without defining its boundaries, the problems just mentioned are avoided. (On the issue of what counts as a proper name for the purpose of tagging noun-phrase nodes, see under Nn in §§ 4.139 ff.)

A proper-name noun-phrase node may dominate a word which is itself given a proper-noun wordtag (a wordtag beginning NP...), but this will not necessarily be the case. A word is tagged as a proper noun if the word is inherently a proper noun (that is, the wordform has no other function, or is a merely accidental homograph of some non-proper word — *Swat* as a district of Pakistan is given a proper-noun wordtag although it happens to be spelled like the English verb *swat*); but many ordinary (non-proper) words are used as proper names, and in such cases the wordtag will reflect the word's ordinary use — the fact of functioning in context as a proper name will be shown at phrasetag rather than wordtag level. The town of *Flagstaff*, Arizona, has a common noun for its name, so an occurrence of the name, e.g. in *Flagstaff is his home town*, will be analysed as a proper noun phrase (Nn...) dominating a single terminal node having the common-noun tag NN1c.[2]

§ 3.21   Previous approaches to wordtagging in corpus linguistics have tended to define the category "proper noun" more broadly, to include all words used as names whether they also have non-proper uses or not. This is a natural policy in the case of a "tagged corpus", which provides only word classifications but no representations of higher levels of grammatical structure, since in such a corpus there is no other way of marking the important fact that a word or group of words is functioning as a name. In an analysed corpus

---

[2] A word which is "inherently a proper noun", with an NP... wordtag, may function as an uncountable rather than countable noun. For instance *Persil* (a proprietary name of a washing powder) will be tagged NP1x (and a noun phrase headed by *Persil* will be tagmatagged as a proper noun phrase, cf. § 4.145).

such as SUSANNE, on the other hand, the noun-phrase node is logically the primary point for indication of proper-name function. If this is done, it would be redundant also to use proper-noun tags automatically for all words dominated by proper-name phrase nodes. The SUSANNE wordtagging policy is more informative.

It is also convenient for another reason, having to do with the subclassification of nouns that are inherently proper. Where words are inherently proper names, it is desirable to classify them into more specific groups: for automatic parsing it will be useful to know, for instance, that *Helen* is a feminine forename (and hence pronominalized as *she*, able to form a proper-name phrase either alone or preceding another name but not commonly as the last word of a multi-word name, etc.) or that *Switzerland* is a country name (and hence unlikely to be followed by further names within an address, for instance). The SUSANNE wordtagging system provides a number of subcategories for proper names. However, such a system becomes very ill defined if subcategories are made to depend on the referent of a name in context, because of the way that entities of one category are frequently named after entities of other categories. A college may be called, say, *Greenwood College* because it is located in a town or area called *Greenwood*, and this name in turn may derive from the surname of a man who founded the town or who was commemorated by its foundation; and in contexts where the reference to a college is taken for granted, the single word *Greenwood* may be used rather than *Greenwood College* for the institution also. Thus the same name would be simultaneously a surname, a place-name, and the name of an institution, and it can be quite difficult to make sense of the task of assigning a specific token of such a name in context to one category rather than another.

§ 3.22   The SUSANNE approach to tagging proper nouns introduces a degree of fixity by making tags depend in general not on the referents of name tokens in context but on the original bearers of the names. If *Greenwood* was originally the surname of an eminent colonist who founded a town named after himself, and a college later established in that town was given the name of the town and hence also of the person, then *Greenwood* will be tagged NP1s (singular surname) whether it is used in context as a surname, a place-name, or an institution name.

§ 3.23   This system was adopted because it eliminates the need to choose answers to numerous pseudo-questions in tagging proper names, and because it harmonizes with the general SUSANNE wordtagging principle that as far as is reasonable wordtags should depend on word-type rather than on word-token. But it also gives an additional rationale for the policy of restricting proper-noun tags to "inherently proper" nouns. If *Greenwood* in *Greenwood College* is tagged as a surname because the college derives its name from a person called *Greenwood*, then it is logical that a town like *Flagstaff* which derives its name from a common object should have that name tagged as a common noun.

§ 3.24   There is one important exception to the principle that name words are tagged in accordance with the categories of their original bearers. Many personal forenames and surnames derive from other uses, whether as non-proper words (for instance the forename *Prudence* derives from a common noun, the surname *White* from an adjective) or from non-personal proper names (thus *York*, *France*, *Calder* all occur as surnames but derive from names of a town, a country, and a river respectively). Because the category of personal names is extremely significant for practical purposes, and the relationship between personal names and the things from which they derive is normally remote and non-significant, the SUSANNE rule is that a personal name is always tagged as such even if it is identical to a word of some other category: an entity named after a person is given a personal-name wordtag, but a person named after a non-personal entity is also given a personal-name wordtag.

§ 3.25   Since common words used as proper names, e.g. *Flagstaff*, are tagged as common words, logically it might seem to follow that proper names used as common words, e.g. *Airedale* as a breed of dog, ought to be tagged as proper names. But SUSANNE wordtagging follows a different logic, according to which any word (or word-use) listed in a published dictionary as a common word is tagged as a common word even if it is capitalized and identical to a proper name. (This unsymmetrical treatment is justified by the fact that dictionaries offer quasi-complete lists of common-word uses, whereas there do not exist even near-complete listings of proper names of diverse categories.) The SUSANNE Corpus takes *OALD3* as the authoritative dictionary for this purpose: thus, since *Airedale* "large rough-coated terrier" is listed in *OALD3* as a common noun, it will be tagged NN1c (countable singular common noun) in *He was walking his Airedale* (though as NP1g, singular geographical proper name, when used as the name of a valley, as in *Our house overlooked Airedale*). On the other hand, *OALD3* has no entries for *Labrador*, *Garibaldi*, so these words will be tagged respectively NP1g and NP1s (surname) even in e.g. *His Labrador has a passion for Garibaldi biscuits*. If the SUSANNE Corpus had used a larger dictionary, either or both of *Labrador*, *Garibaldi* might be tagged as common nouns in this context; any application of the SUSANNE scheme as an analytic standard must specify the dictionary used for this purpose (cf. § 3.76).[3]

§ 3.26   The SUSANNE wordtags for proper names are:

NP1s   surname
NP1m   masculine forename
NP1f   feminine forename
NP1i   initial of personal name, e.g. *W.* or *G.* in *W.G. Grace*
NP1c   country name
NP1p   "province" name: name of US state, English county, etc., except where this is a transferred use of a name for another category (cf. § 3.128)
NP1g   other singular geographical proper name, e.g. *Adriatic America Sherwood*[4]
NP1j   organization name, e.g. *Unilever Kiwanis*[5] *CIA* (cf. § 3.53)
NP1z   "code name" functioning as countable noun, e.g. *1-11, GTi, PDP11/70*
NP1x   miscellaneous singular proper name, e.g. *Parthenon Persil*
NPD1   name of day of week, e.g. *Sunday*
NPM1   month name, e.g. *October*

§ 3.27   Each of the above NP... tags except NP1i has a counterpart wordtag in which 1 is replaced by 2, for the corresponding plural name (e.g. the emphasized word in *the **Robinsons** are here* is NP2s) and for names of the same category which occur only in the plural, e.g. *Philippines* NP2c, *Antilles* NP2g. In some cases the plural form will be used only in connection with applications of the name to entities of categories different from its original bearer (for

---

[3] Occasionally a word listed in the dictionary only as a proper name may be used in a text as a common word, with lower-case initial. Thus *OALD3* lists *Capitol* only with capital C, as the name of a specific building, but the SUSANNE Corpus contains the phrase *the state capitol* A10:0750. Since dictionaries do not in general aim to list proper names, the authority of the dictionary is not used in order to assign an NP... tag to an apparent common word, but only (as in the *Airedale* case) to assign a "common" tag to an apparent proper name: *capitol* is tagged NN1c as a common noun. To summarize: any word used as a personal name is given an NP... wordtag, but otherwise a word-use has an NP... tag only if it is printed as a proper name, with initial capital, *and* is an "inherent" proper name not having an earlier common use, *and* is not used in a way listed in the dictionary as a "common" usage (such as *Airedale* for a dog).

[4] "Geographical" embraces "selenographical", etc.; thus *Mare Imbrium* is tagged NNL1cb NP1g. The words *Heaven* and *Hell*, whether or not capitalized, are treated as common nouns wordtagged NN1c. The word *Maplecrest* occurs as a street name in *1409 SW Maplecrest Dr[ive]*. A10:0450: although transparently compounded from common nouns, as a single typographic word this seems to have been invented for use as a proper name and is accordingly tagged NP1g.

[5] Non-American readers should be aware that *Kiwanis* is a singular name, not the plural of a word **Kiwani*.

instance the Falkland Islands are named after Viscount Falkland, but the phrase *the Falklands* refers only to the islands); such cases are wordtagged by reference to the category of the original bearer of the singular name, thus *Falklands* NP2s.

Wordtags for Common Nouns

§ 3.28   For common nouns, the basic tagging principle is that the tag should as far as possible represent the *range* of uses available to the noun, rather than the particular use relevant to a specific context. The set of common-noun tags can best be defined in terms of eight usage categories, which we shall symbolize with capital letters as follows:

M   uncountable ("mass")
C   countable singular
P   plural
J   descriptive head of organization name
L   descriptive head of place-name
S   noun of style or title
T   time noun
U   unit

§ 3.29   The uses symbolized M, C, P are defined in terms of the structural possibilities within noun phrases headed by the respective noun: thus a C normally requires a determiner, which may be *a/an*, an M noun can normally be preceded by *much*, a P noun by *many*. Almost any noun normally used in an M sense can on occasion be used in a C sense or vice versa: *she performed with a vitality not often seen; so much rust there's not much car left*. But these are fairly clearly derivative uses: *vitality* and *car* are basically uncountable and countable respectively, whereas e.g. *illness* is a noun for which both M and C uses are normal. Secondary, "derivative" M and C uses of nouns are ignored for wordtagging purposes.

§ 3.30   Verb agreement is not criterial for distinguishing P from C and M uses, since singular collective nouns may take plural verbs: in *the crowd were arguing among themselves*, the word *crowd* is classified as a C noun. (The SUSANNE wordtagging system does not distinguish collective from non-collective nouns.) Not all P nouns are morphologically marked (*sheep, police*), and occasionally a noun having plural morphology has a C or M use (*a brick works*).

§ 3.31   The categories J, L, S, T, U are defined in detail below.

§ **3.32**   Any (unabbreviated) common noun has at least one of the uses symbolized M, C, and P. A minority of common nouns have one (very occasionally, more than one) of the uses symbolized J, L, S, T, U. The SUSANNE wordtag for a common noun shows which combination of the usage categories is available to the noun in various contexts.

§ **3.33**   Each combination of the three usage categories M, C, P has a distinctive wordtag, thus:

M	NN1u	e.g. *snow Buddhism*
C	NN1c	e.g. *clock crowd Buddhist*
P	NN2	e.g. *clocks trousers Germans police British* (e.g. in *all the British have been eliminated*)
M+C	NN1n	e.g. *illness German* (cf. *a good German, German is an easy language*)
M+P	NNu	e.g. *measles bowls data French* (cf. *the French cook well, French is difficult*)
C+P	NNc	e.g. *sheep species people Swiss* (cf. *a Swiss, three Swiss*)
M+C+P	NNn	e.g. *fish* (*a fish, three fish, a piece of fish*) *Chinese* (*a Chinese, three Chinese, Chinese is tonal*)

§ **3.34**   Nouns ending in *-ics* although morphologically plural are either invariably or commonly syntactically singular in English, for reasons to do with the grammar of the Greek neuter plurals on which they are calqued. Special tags are provided for these words: NN1ux for the majority of cases which have only the M use (*athletics thermodynamics*), NNux for cases which also have the P use (e.g. *mechanics* — cf. *to study mechanics, both our mechanics are sick*).[6]

§ **3.35**   Nouns in *-ics* apart, where classical neuter plural nouns are borrowed into English there is a tendency to reinterpret them as singular uncountable nouns (since the *-a* suffix is not in itself decisive). In the case of *data* this tendency is so well established that the word is tagged NNu, and it would be highly pedantic not to tag *agenda* as NN1c; these tagging decisions override the *OALD3* entries, which classify *data* as plural and give an ad hoc statement for *agenda*. In other cases usage is various, and tagging conforms to *OALD3* where this has a relevant entry (e.g. *paraphernalia* NN1u)

---

[6] Some writers treat even the former group of *-ics* words as syntactically plural; cf. *The economics of ... were presented by Mr. John Nix* E29.077. For such writers the contrast between NN1ux and NNux tags corresponds to no grammatical difference; but SUSANNE wordtagging reflects the usage of the majority of writers for whom the grammar of *-ics* words correlates with their meanings.

and otherwise to etymology, i.e. NN2 for classical neuter plurals not listed in *OALD3*.

Common Nouns with Special Uses

§ **3.36** If a common noun has one of the "special uses" symbolized J, L, S, T, U, e.g. *road* which has the L use (it commonly occurs as the head of a place-name, e.g. *Abbey Road*), it will normally also have one or more of the general uses M, C, P (*road* is a C noun).[7] The exceptions are abbreviations: *Rd* occurs *only* as the head of a place-name phrase, i.e. it has the L but not the C use. These alternative possibilities are reflected in SUSANNE wordtagging: *road* (or *Road*) is tagged NNL1c, the "L" in the tag marking the possibility of L usage and the "c" marking the possibility of C usage, whereas *Rd* is tagged NNL. The occurrence of e.g. L within a common-noun tag such as NNL1c does not mean that a particular instance of a word with that tag is acting as head of a place-name, but only that the word can be used in that way. For instance, *square* is tagged NNL1c because of names such as *Berkeley Square*, and consequently it is given that same tag in a context such as *inversely proportional to the square of the distance* J06:1780.[8] But the range of alternative wordtags for words having special uses does not cover every logically possible combination of M, C, P, and the special uses, since many combinations are never found in practice.

§ **3.37** The structure of a tag such as NNL1c, where L use is indicated by a capital, C use is indicated by a lower-case letter, and a digit indicates absence of P use, is not the most logically straightforward way of symbolizing the relevant usage range. This is a consequence of the fact that the SUSANNE wordtagging system has emerged from a long process of evolving increasingly subtle tagsets, and the present system deliberately retains a visible relationship with its predecessors rather than abandoning them and starting from scratch.

§ **3.38** We now survey the "special-use" categories in detail.

---

[7] Use as a "nominal number", e.g. *dozen thousand million* as contrasted with more adjective-like numbers such as *three twenty*, might be included as another "special use"; nominal numbers are wordtagged NNOc, but are not discussed further here.

[8] Since abbreviations such as *Rd* are given tags showing that they can only occur within proper names, one might expect that the corresponding words written in full with lower-case initials, e.g. *road*, ought to be given tags showing that they cannot be part of proper names. However, some publications (both in Britain and in the USA) in fact systematically print place-names in the forms exemplified in *at 229 West Pratt street* A19:0800 or *slewed into Greenwich-avenue* N22.033. This is undoubtedly a minority style; nevertheless, SUSANNE practice is to tag both wordforms alike.

ORGANIZATION NOUNS

§ 3.39 The J use of a common noun refers to cases where the meaning of the noun is a kind of organization and the noun is used as the head word in the name of organizations of that kind. Thus *Board* in the name *National Coal Board* has the J use, although *Coal* in the newer name for the same organization, *British Coal*, does not have the J use, because the noun *coal* does not mean a kind of organization. A J use will not normally have quantifiers or an indefinite article; it may take the definite article, by largely arbitrary convention. The name headed by a J word may take a singular or plural verb regardless of the morphology of the J word.

§ 3.40 Except for abbreviations, any noun with a J use will also have either a C or (very rarely) a P use. Senses occurring in the C use will usually include a collective sense (i.e. one apt to take a plural verb). There may be a more or less unrelated M use, e.g. *company* has the M sense "being together with another or others".

SUSANNE wordtags are:

J only	NNJ	e.g.	*Corp Bros*
J+C	NNJ1c	e.g.	*club committee institute*
J+P	NNJ2	e.g.	*associates*
J+M+C	NNJ1n	e.g.	*company organization society*

PLACE NOUNS

§ 3.41 The L use of a common noun refers to cases where the meaning of the noun is a topographical feature and the noun is used as the head word in a place-name, although the name will often in practice be applied to an entity of a different category from the feature to which the noun refers — *Hill* has the L use in *Murray Hill, N.J.*, though this is normally used as the name of a town rather than a hill. Nouns with L uses resemble those with J uses with respect to co-occurrence with determiners, etc. A special complication is that certain L words, e.g. *Mount*, are often placed at the beginning rather than the end of names (*Mount Everest*). Wordtags are:

L only (singular, plural, or neutral)	NNL	e.g.	*Rd Mts Is*
L only, with tendency to begin name	NNLb	e.g.	*Costa Mt*
L+C	NNL1c	e.g.	*road island city*

L+C, with tendency to begin name	NNL1cb	e.g. *camp lake mount*
L+P	NNL2	e.g. *buildings mountains springs* (cf. *Alice Springs*)
L+M+C	NNL1n	e.g. *drive water green*
L+C+P	NNLc	e.g. *barracks links works*

NOUNS OF STYLE OR TITLE

§ 3.42 An S term is a status-indicating item which either accompanies one or more individual names within the full title of a person (e.g. *Dr Jones*) or is used to address a person of appropriate status (e.g. *Ma'am*), or both (e.g. *sir*, as vocative and as in *Sir Francis Drake*). Most unabbreviated S items also have a C use which may describe the title holder or be more or less distantly related in sense (*he is a doctor, the governor of a motor, the madam of a brothel*); a few unabbreviated items (e.g. *justice*) have an M use. Plurals of S+C or S+C+M items themselves occur, infrequently, in the S use (*Senators Smith and Jones*).

§ 3.43 Certain S items are plural not in the sense that they also have the P use, but in the sense that a title including them denotes more than one person: e.g. *Messrs*. The analogous distinction among J and L nouns (e.g. *Rd* v. *Mts*) is not marked in the SUSANNE word-tag set; but in the case of personal titles reference to one v. more than one individual is grammatically important, and separate tags are provided. Other S items (e.g. *Rev*) are adjectival, being abbreviations of adjectives and often being preceded by *the* and/or followed by another S item within a title.

§ 3.44 Furthermore, while most S items precede individual names within a title, certain S items (e.g. *Jr, BA*) follow the individual name. (Abbreviations for party affiliations, e.g. *Dem, D, R, Lab*, are included here.) Many of these items also have the C use (*He got his PhD in 1990*), and in some cases the C use is commoner than the S use (the British abbreviation *MP* for *Member of Parliament* occurs frequently in the LOB Corpus in constructions such as *to meet an MP* but never as in *David Curry, MP*).

§ 3.45 The SUSANNE wordtags for S nouns are:

| S only, singular | NNS | e.g. *Mr Mrs Miss Dr Dom Mme Gen Sen Sir Missy Ma'am Sire Mister* |
| S only, plural | NNSS | e.g. *Messrs Mmes Mesdames Sirs* |

S only, adjectival	NNSj	e.g. *Rev Very_Rev Hon Rt_Hon*[9]
S+C	NNS1c	e.g. *doctor miss madam minister prince queen*[10]
S+C+M	NNS1n	e.g. *justice*
S+P	NNS2	plurals of all NNS1c and NNS1n words, e.g. *doctors*
S item following name, with or without C use	NNSA	e.g. *Jr Sr Jun Sen Esq Bart BA PhD MP QC VC Dem Lab*

TIME NOUNS

§ 3.46   Nouns for *time* are grammatically distinctive because noun phrases headed by time nouns very commonly function adverbially, to indicate either duration (*he waited an hour*) or point (*she is getting married this week*). Almost all time nouns can form phrases functioning adverbially in combination with *this*, *that*, and some also with *last*, *next*, *yesterday*, *tomorrow*. The SUSANNE wordtags are:

NNT1h   for names of holidays and seasons, e.g. *Christmas Boxing_Day Hallowe'en summer*, most of which form phrases functioning adverbially with *last* and *next*

NNT1c   for other time nouns that can head noun phrases functioning adverbially, e.g. *hour day night morning afternoon evening week year century* and the noun *time* itself

NNT1m   for point-of-time nouns, which cannot head noun phrases having an adverbial function, e.g. *noon midnight midyear*

The borderline between common and proper nouns is logically vague in the area of names of holidays, months, etc.; the SUSANNE word-tagging scheme allots NP... tags to the seven day names (NPD1) and the twelve month names (NPM1) but NNT... tags to all other time names.

§ 3.47   Since the distinctions between different types of time noun phrase with adverbial function relate almost entirely to phrases

---

[9] The full form *reverend*, though listed as an adjective in *OALD3*, is scarcely ever used in English other than capitalized in the S use; therefore, as a special case, *Reverend* in the S use is tagged NNSj like its abbreviation. The full form *Honourable* on the other hand is tagged as an adjective even when functioning in the S use.

[10] Since *Miss* as in *Miss Smith* is treated as a separate word from *miss* as in *thank you, miss*, or *a saucy miss* (cf. § 2.55), the former is tagged NNS but the latter NNS1c.

headed by singular time nouns, the plurals of all NNT. . . nouns are indiscriminately tagged NNT2.

UNIT NOUNS

§ 3.48   A U use is a use of a unit of measurement, whether written in full (*inch, kilogramme*) or abbreviated either alphabetically or symbolically (*in* or *<Prime>* for *inch(es)*), as head of a noun phrase denoting a measured quantity. Words occurring in this use are grammatically distinctive notably through their association with numerals. The wordtags are:

U only (singular, plural, or neutral)	NNU	e.g. *in ins kg <Prime>* standing for *inch(es)*
U+C	NNU1c	e.g. *inch kilogram(me)*
U+P	NNU2	e.g. *inches*
U+M+C	NNU1n	e.g. *metre* (note M use as poetic metre)
U+C+P	NNUc	e.g. *hertz yen*
U+M+C+P	NNUn	e.g. *horsepower*

together with the special cases:

NNUb   unit symbol which precedes numeral, e.g. *$*
NNUp   *% percent per_cent*[11]

§ 3.49   Abbreviations of units of time are given U rather than T tags: *hr, secs* both NNU; and units of time written in full are given NNU. . . tags if they never have the behaviour specified above for NNT. . . words, e.g. *microseconds* J04:1630 is NNU2. The words *Fahrenheit Celsius Kelvin*, written in full with initial capitals, are tagged NP1s rather than being given NNU. . . tags (and *centigrade* written in full is RAj).[12] Note however that other units derived from surnames are properly spelled with lower-case initials (e.g. *ampere hertz newton*), and these unit names are given NNU. . . tags.[13] GMT for *Greenwich Mean Time*, and similar timezone abbreviations, are NP1x.

---

[11] The emphasized sequence in *adsorbed water (about 0.3 wt %)* J04:1790 is analysed as an NNUp= idiom.

[12] The abbreviations *°F °C °K* are treated as NNU words (or NNU= idioms if written with space after the degree symbol).

[13] If a unit name derived from a surname and properly spelled with lower-case initial occurs capitalized in a text, whether as a solecism or, say, within an all-capitals stretch of text, it is tagged NNU. . . despite the capital.

COMBINATIONS OF SPECIAL USES

§ 3.50   It is normal for a common noun which has one of the "special uses" symbolized J, L, S, T, U also to have M, C, or P uses to which none of the special-use symbols apply; we have seen that the wordtags containing J, L, S, T, U characters also cover the "general" uses. Much more rarely, the usage-range of a noun includes more than one of the special uses. In such cases, where the different special uses relate to sharply distinct senses of the word, alternative tags are used according to context. But such cases are few; the only examples identified by the SUSANNE team are:

bank	NNJ1c NNL1c
Co	NNJ NNLb
Corp	NNJ NNS
court	NNJ1c (law court) NNL1c (space enclosed by buildings)
Dr	NNL NNS
quarter	NNL1c (division of a town) NNT1c (3-month period) NNU1c (unit of weight)
spring	NNL1c NNT1h
springs	NNL2 NNT2
St	NNL NNS NNU
yard	NNL1c NNU1c
yards	NNL2 NNU2

In these cases it would be arbitrary to choose one or the other of the special-use tags to cover senses to which no special-use tag relates; so, exceptionally, ordinary tags not containing the special-use letters are applied to the remaining senses of the above words. Thus *spring* as "jump", "device for absorbing shocks", or "elasticity", and *quarter* as "one fourth", "mercy to an enemy", etc., are both NN1n.

J VERSUS L USES

§ 3.51   Because organizations commonly have fixed sites, there are very many words which might be regarded as falling on the border between NNJ. . . and NNL. . . — consider e.g. *St John's College is wealthy* v. *I walked through St John's College.* But these cases are allocated either J or L tags according to the perceived primary sense of the word: *college* is tagged NNJ1n because the geographical site sense is regarded as derivative from the reference to an organization, whereas *hospital, museum* are tagged NNL1c because a hospital or museum is deemed to be primarily a site rather than an institution (such things can be units within organizations which as a whole have another function). Likewise *church* is tagged NNJ1n but *chapel* NNL1c, because *chapel* sometimes refers to a building subsidiary to a larger organization, e.g. a chapel of ease or a college chapel, whereas a church (whether a parish church or the Roman Catholic Church) is always associated with an organization, although the word often refers to the principal building maintained by such an organization.

§ 3.52   It would be difficult to maintain that SUSANNE allocations to NNJ...v. NNL...tags are always "correct". To some extent the primary reference of these borderline words may be a subjective matter (a medical professional might think of *hospital* as primarily a J rather than L word), and in general this seems to be one of the many areas where the taxonomic task requires a sharp division to be imposed on a natural continuum. However, the approach adopted seems preferable to the alternative of allowing words such as *college* to take either J or L tags according to context, since this would necessitate far more numerous arbitrary decisions. Artificial divisions would have to be imposed on the lexical continuum in two places rather than one (between J-only and J-or-L words, and between the latter and L-only words), and instances of J-or-L words would have to be given one tag or the other although context would often provide no reason for choosing between the two.

§ 3.53   The criteria for deciding whether an entity is an "organization" for the purpose of applying NNJ...tags are also used to decide whether an intrinsically proper noun should be tagged NP1j.

§ 3.54   In addition to the categories of common noun surveyed here, there is a small number of additional tags for specialized types of common noun, e.g. NNb for nouns which are only normally used as premodifiers rather than heads (for instance *trouser*, as in *a trouser button*). These tags are shown in the general list of wordtags in § 3.73 below.

Idioms

§ 3.55   Certain sequences of two or more words are analysed in the SUSANNE Corpus as grammatical "idioms" in a manner first specified in *CAE* (e.g. p. 40): although appearing on separate Corpus lines they are treated as grammatically equivalent to single words. For instance, in *his ideas are very up to date*, the three words *up to date* are seen as jointly equivalent to an adjective. If such a sequence is equivalent to a word tagged, say, XY, then the individual words of the sequence are tagged XY21 XY22 (in the case of a two-word sequence), XY31 XY32 XY33 (for a three-word sequence), etc., and the sequence as a whole is immediately dominated by a node tagmatagged XY=.[14]

§ 3.56   A few wordtags are represented exclusively by idioms: for instance, CSk covers just *as_if*, *as_though*, that is to say these sequences when functioning as subordinating conjunctions are wordtagged CSk21 CSk22 below a node tagged CSk=, but no individual word is ever tagged CSk. (It goes without saying that words which jointly function as an idiom may happen to occur adjacently in other functions, and then they are not idiomtagged; for instance *in all* is tagged as an adverb idiom, RR=, in *From the terraces — eighteen in all — broad flights of steps descend* G05:1120, but as two separate words II DBa in *simultaneous pressures in all three vessels* J12:1330.)

§ 3.57   Grammatical idioms are distinct from "semantic idioms", of which the phrase *kick the bucket*, meaning "die", is a clear (if well-worn) example. The meaning of this phrase is entirely unpredictable from the meanings of its component words, but the phrase is not *grammatically* idiosyncratic: transitive verb followed by object noun phrase is a very usual construction, and this phrase occurs in environments similar to those in which other, non-idiomatic examples of the construction are found (*John kicked the bucket / John ate an apple / John knew the answer...*). When linguists in general talk about "idioms" they most commonly mean semantic idioms. In the SUSANNE Corpus semantic idioms are identified to some extent via the lemma field (cf. § 2.72), but they have no relevance for wordtagging or parsecoding. In the SUSANNE parsing scheme the term "idiom" is used in a technical sense referring exclusively to grammatical idioms.

§ 3.58   Idioms equivalent to closed-class wordtags are exhaustively listed together with the single-word representatives of the respective tags in the listings in § 3.73 below; the idioms are shown with underline characters in place of spaces between their component words. The closed-class lists (not preceded by "e.g." or followed by "etc.") are intended as exhaustive, though exhaustiveness is more difficult to guarantee in the case of idioms than in the case of single-word representatives of closed-class wordtags; it is likely for instance that the class of expressions of the form *in* + noun + preposition having a claim to grammatical-idiom status, such as *in favour of*, might be expanded beyond those shown in the II list.

---

[14] Although single digits occur also within independent wordtags, a sequence of two digits at the end of a wordtag occurs only in derived tags for idiom-components.

§ 3.59   The SUSANNE scheme also recognizes idioms equivalent to open-class wordtags. However, deciding when a sequence of words is sufficiently idiosyncratic grammatically to count as an open-class idiom is one of the less well-defined aspects of the SUSANNE analytic scheme. The SUSANNE team inherited lists of open-class idioms, together with a tradition of idiom tagging practice, from the body of corpus research described in *CAE* and from CUVOALD86. But in the case of open-class idioms fixed lists are not adequate to define idiom status (there will always be further examples, e.g. out-of-the-way foreign phrases, that are not on a list but have as much title to be counted as idioms as the items that are listed); and as the SUSANNE Corpus was constructed it proved desirable to modify some of the inherited principles in this area. It is not possible to throw the burden of decision on to a published dictionary, as is done in the case of choice between alternative open-class wordtags: grammatical-idiom status is not a category that is systematically coded in *OALD3* or other published dictionaries. Therefore, for the bulk of open-class wordtags, the most that is possible here is to identify the general considerations that lead to a phrase being given idiom status in the SUSANNE scheme, and to list those open-class idioms which happen to occur in the SUSANNE Corpus. Regrettably, this does not settle all the questions that arise about idiomatic or non-idiomatic status of phrases not found in the Corpus.

§ 3.60   The wordtag RR (adverb) has an intermediate status with respect to grammatical idioms. RR is certainly an open class for words, but the idiomtag RR= (which is used more frequently than other open-class idiomtags) seems to apply to a more limited, predictable range of phrases than, say, NN1c=, whose potential members are endlessly diverse. Therefore it may be useful to list the phrases for which the SUSANNE team have identified the RR= tag as applicable; but this list is not regarded as closed.

§ 3.61   In general, a word-sequence is tagged as an idiom if it is not liable to be interrupted by material inserted between its words (discontinuous sequences are never analysed as idioms), is uninflectable (the phrase *see to it*, as in *Clr. Brook saw to it that certain minimum standards were conformed with* A30.053, is syntactically as well as semantically idiosyncratic, but is not classed as an idiom because it inflects as *sees to it*, *saw to it*, etc.), and if one of the following applies:

• a multi-word phrase other than a proper name (unabbreviated proper names are not tagged as idioms, cf. § 3.117) made up of words which have other uses in the language but which are grouped in a non-productive fashion (the internal structure of the phrase does not generalize to other examples, and/or the behaviour of the phrase is not as predicted from its internal structure[15]): *at_all, thank_you*.[16] Very often, phrases classed as idioms fit into grammatical slots, the other potential occupants of which are almost all single words (most of the forms which can replace *in lieu of* are one-word prepositions), though this is not necessary (*up to date* is classed as an idiom equivalent to an adjective, but many multi-word adjective phrases can fill the same slots that may be filled by single adjectives).

- a set phrase in which one or more words are either non-English or, though English, have no independent use other than within certain set phrases: *charnel_house, cheval_glass, decree_nisi, de_facto, et_al*.
- a set phrase which would commonly be hyphenated but occurs sporadically written as separate words: *Vice_President*. (By § 2.37, the hyphenated variant would be analysed as a single word.[17])
- an acronym or abbreviation which is written with spaces but might alternatively be written solid: *B. & O.* (for *Baltimore & Ohio* [*Railway*]), *N. J.* (for *New Jersey*).
- a "code name" or the like which contains internal space(s) but where the elements separated by spaces have no generally understood independent reference: *F230 XFV* (a British car registration mark), *LA6 3AN* (a post-code).

§ 3.62   The fact that part of a phrase is elided by co-ordination reduction or similar processes when it is repeated does not prevent the full phrase from being recognized as an idiom: *in_terms_of* is analysed as an idiom where it occurs in the sequence *to be regarded in terms of the quality of service rendered rather than of the quantity of time expended* J24:1280, although it is reduced in the comparison clause to *of*.

---

[15] Although in general the SUSANNE scheme does not reckon to mark "semantic idioms" (see above), it is probably true that semantic unpredictability of phrases has sometimes influenced their analysis as idioms: for instance *by the way* is analysed as RR= although with respect to grammatical structure it is a normal prepositional phrase.

[16] The non-productivity requirement is not invoked to prevent preposition + noun + *of* sequences such as *in place of* from being recognized as idioms, although a number of them allow *of* + personal pronoun to be replaced by possessive pronoun: *in his place*.

[17] Likewise a compound word which is normally written solid but occurs sporadically with internal word-space will be treated as an idiom in the latter case, e.g. the use of *on to* as equivalent to *onto* in *The boy came on to the porch* N01:0440.

§ **3.63** Phrases to which the RR= tag applies, and idioms belonging to other open classes that are actually found in the SUSANNE Corpus, are listed in § 3.73.

The Wordtags Listed

§ **3.64** Each SUSANNE wordtag begins with two or more capital letters, and consists wholly of capitals, digits, and lower-case letters. The wordtag set for words given independent wordtags (i.e. not analysed as components of idioms) is listed below. (The only other wordtags are tags for the component words of idioms, derived by suffixing pairs of digits to tags in the list below.)

§ **3.65** Some wordtags (e.g. NN1c for singular countable noun) stand for open classes of words, others (e.g. RRQV for *wh-. . .-ever* adverb) stand for closed, listable classes. Open-class tags are illustrated via representative examples, preceded by "e.g." (or followed by "etc." if no definition precedes the examples); "e.g." is also used in a few cases where the extension of the tag membership is obvious, as with "e.g. *October*" under the tag NPM1 for month names. Where the indicators "e.g." and "etc." are lacking, the list of examples is intended as essentially exhaustive, omitting only variants such as reduced, informal, or non-standard pronunciations (e.g. *-n't* for *not*, *o'* for *of*, *ai-* for any of *am are is have has* in the form *ain't*), and capitalized forms and alternative spellings (e.g. *organization* implies *Organization ORGANIZATION organisation* etc.). In a few cases of closed but large classes, the wordlists are given at the end of the list of tags. Written abbreviations, e.g. *cm* for *centimetre*, often have grammatical privileges of occurrence which differ from those of their unabbreviated counterparts, and are assigned distinct wordtags in consequence; in cases where the tag definitions do not imply a distinctive tag for an abbreviation, it can be assumed to be tagged like the respective full form. In practice the lists of closed-class words include all relevant words which actually occur in the SUSANNE Corpus, and aim for exhaustiveness also with respect to words not found in the Corpus, but inevitably there will be occasional items in the latter category that have been overlooked.

§ **3.66** Hyphenated words are included in the lists where these are treated by the word-segmentation rules (cf. § 2.37) as single word-tagged units.

§ **3.67** Archaic and non-standard forms and uses are not listed explicitly. The SUSANNE approach is to wordtag them by analogy with the most grammatically similar forms of modern standard English. This sometimes implies that a word in an archaic use receives a wordtag different from any that is applied to the same word in its modern standard uses. For instance, the word *mine* in *mine host* is tagged APPGi1, but in modern standard English this tag applies exclusively to *my*; in *a friend of mine*, *the pen is mine*, the word *mine* is tagged PPGi1. In one variety of non-standard speech, *them* replaces *those* (e.g. *them people*), and in this usage *them* is tagged DD2a rather than PPHO2.

§ **3.68** The archaic pronouns *thou* and its derivatives (*thine*, *thyself*, etc.) and *ye* are wordtagged like the corresponding *you* forms (with no distinction in wordtagging between *thou*, *thee*, or *ye*); -(*e*)*st* forms of verbs (*hast, goest*) are tagged as uninflected base forms (*have, go*); -(*e*)*th* forms (*hath, goeth*) are tagged as modern third-person singular forms (*has, goes*).

§ **3.69** Where a word listed under a closed-class tag also has one or more alternative closed-class tags, these are shown after the symbol "≠"; the definitions in the entries for the respective tags should make clear how the various uses of the word are allocated between the tags. Open-class alternatives for closed-class tags are shown only where it might otherwise be supposed that the closed-class tag is intended to cover the open-class usage. Thus, under ICSt for *until, till*, there is no mention of the tags NN1c, VV0t for *till* in a shop, *till* the soil, since these are mere accidental homographs and no reader would imagine that the ICSt tag was intended to cover them; under RRT for single-word superlative adverb, including *worst* as in *the worst-dressed woman*, the alternative tags JJT (as in *my worst performance*) and NN1u (as in *the worst of the storm is over*) are specified, but VV0t is omitted since it is obvious that *worst* must be tagged as a verb in e.g. *to worst his enemy*. (Alternative tags are also omitted in cases such as AT1 for "indefinite article" where the word *a* can alternatively be an algebraic variable, tagged FOx, or a letter of the alphabet, tagged ZZ1, as in *'Descendant' is spelled with an a*.)

§ **3.70** Specific tag-definitions override general ones. Thus the existence of the tag JJs for "adjective in -*most*" implies that the tag JJ for "general adjective" will not be used for an adjective such as *topmost* which fits the definition of JJs; since NNOc covers a small finite set of number words such as *hundred*, those words are not given the more general tag MC "cardinal number"; MCy for "year name" overrides MCn for "cardinal numeral written in digits".

§ **3.71** In the definitions, certain terms are used with special meanings:

- "qualifier" means adverb modifying adjective or adverb;
- "interrogative" includes exclamatory uses — e.g. *how* in *how easy it is* counts as "interrogative" for wordtag definitions;
- "pre-co-ordinator" means the first of paired co-ordination markers, e.g. *both* in *both . . . and . . .* , *neither* in *neither . . . nor . . .*;[18]
- the terms "preposition", "prepositional use" are applied only to uses where a specific prepositional complement is either overtly present or logically retrievable — in a phrase such as *John walked in*, the word *in* is classified as an adverbial rather than prepositional use.

§ 3.72 The sequence of tags in the listing is determined by an alphabetical ordering in which lower-case letters precede digits and digits precede capital letters; this is intended to maximize the chance of related tags appearing adjacently.

§ 3.73 When a word occurs in the following lists either written solid or hyphenated, an occasional use with internal space is tagged as a grammatical idiom (see § 3.61); thus *some one*, e. g. are respectively tagged PN121 PN122, REX21 REX22.

APPGf	*her* as possessive ≠ PPHO1f
APPGh1	*its*
APPGh2	*their*
APPGi1	*my* as possessive
APPGi2	*our*
APPGm	*his* except as pronoun ≠ PPGm
APPGy	*your*
AT	*the* (whether as determiner or introducing the correlative construction of *CGEL*, p. 1111)
ATn	*no* as determiner or qualifier ≠ UH
AT1	indefinite article *a an*
AT1e	*every*
BTO	*in_order* introducing infinitive
CC	co-ordinating conjunction: *and and/or as_well_as plus & solidus character* ≠ *plus* IIm NN1c, solidus IIp YD[19]
CCn	*nor*
CCr	*or*
CCB	*but* as co-ordinating conjunction ≠ ICSx RR (cf. § 4.222)

[18] An item may be analysed as a pre-co-ordinator only when introducing a co-ordination; the phrase *not only* is not treated as an LE= in *Yet it is not only Europe the play refers to*. G12:1580.

[19] On the tagging of the solidus character, see n. 28 below.

CS	subordinating conjunction (see list at end)
CSf	*for* as conjunction ≠ IF
CSg	*though* as subordinating conjunction ≠ RR
CSi	*if*
CSk	*as_if as_though*
CSn	*when* as subordinating conjunction (i.e. equivalent to "at the time at which") ≠ RRQq RRQr
CSr	*where* as subordinating conjunction (i.e. equivalent to "at the place at which") ≠ RRQq RRQr
CSA	*as* as subordinating conjunction or as preposition in comparative sense ≠ IIa RGa
CSN	*than* in all uses
CST	*that* as subordinating conjunction, including in its use in introducing relative clauses; non-standard *as_how* (as in *I don't know as how I can*) ≠ *that* DD1a
CSW	*whether* in all uses
DAg	*own* as part of a genitive construction ≠ VV0v
DAr	*former latter* in all uses
DAy	*same selfsame*
DAz	*such* in all uses
DA1	*much little* ≠ *little* JJ
DA2	*many few* in all uses
DA2q	*several*
DA2R	*fewer*
DA2T	*fewest*
DAR	*more less* in all uses except *less* II
DAT	*most least* in all uses
DBa	*all* as determiner or pronoun[20] ≠ NN1c RR FB
DBh	*half* as determiner or pronoun[21] ≠ NN1c RR
DB2	*both* as determiner or pronoun ≠ LE RR
DD	*yon yonder* as determiner, *somesuch the_rest* ≠ *yon* RR, *yonder* RR
DDf	*enough* as pronoun or pre- or postmodifying a noun ≠ RGAf RRe
DDi	*some* as determiner or pronoun ≠ RGi
DDo	*a_lot*
DDy	*any* as determiner or pronoun ≠ RRy
DD1a	*that* as determiner, demonstrative pronoun, or qualifier (e.g. *that slowly*) ≠ CST

---

[20] The words *all half* are tagged NN1c when used with a determiner, replaceable by e.g. *quarter* (*he gave his all, more than a half*), but as DB... when used nominally without a determiner, replaceable by e.g. *a quarter* (*all/half of them*).
[21] See n. 20 above.

DD1b	*a_bit*
DD1e	*either* as determiner or pronoun ≠ LEe RR
DD1i	*this* in all uses including as qualifier (e.g. *this big*)
DD1n	*neither* as determiner or pronoun ≠ LEn RR
DD1q	*another each one_and_the_same*, as determiner or pronoun ≠ *each* RAq
DD1t	*a_little*
DD2	*a_few a_good_few a_good_many a_great_many*
DD2a	*those*
DD2i	*these*
DDQ	*what*
DDQq	*which* in interrogative uses ≠ DDQr
DDQr	*which* in relative uses ≠ DDQq
DDQGq	*whose* in interrogative uses ≠ DDQGr
DDQGr	*whose* in relative uses ≠ DDQGq
DDQV	*whichever whatever whichsoever whatsoever no_matter_which no_matter_what* ≠ *whatever* RAn, *whatsoever* RAn
EX	existential *there* ≠ RLh UH
FA	suffix (if separately wordtagged, e.g. because linked to stem by hyphen)[22]
FB	prefix (if separately wordtagged, e.g. because linked to stem by hyphen)[23]
FD	distorted word — used only in analysing speech, cf. § 6.17
FO	indeterminate formula[24]
FOc	formula or acronym for chemical substance, molecule, or subatomic particle, e.g. H_2SO_4 TNT DDT ^{14}C C-14 α (as in *α-particle*) etc.
FOp	London postal district, British post-code, American "Zip code": W.C.2, LA6 3AN, 06520, 06520-1911, etc. (Since occurrence of a space is a sufficient condition for recognition of a word-boundary, a British post-code such as *LA6 3AN* is treated as two words dominated by a node tagged FOp=, but an American Zip code including extension such as *06520-1911* is

[22] By § 2.36, affixes linked to stems by hyphens are tagged FA or FB irrespective of whether they are listed as affixes in *OALD3*.

[23] See n. 22 above.

[24] Because the Brown Corpus replaces segments of text identified as "formulae" (cf. § 2.20) by single conventional symbols, these are treated in the SUSANNE Corpus as single "words" which are given the generalized tag FO, except where the context makes it clear that a more specific tag such as FOx or FOqx applies. The tag FO would not be used in analysing original texts.

treated as a single word rather than split on either side of the hyphen.)

FOqc   chemical equation, when analysed as a single word (cf. § 2.42)

FOqx   algebraic equation, when analysed as a single word (cf. § 2.42)

FOr   road name (*M6 B6480 I-95* etc.)

FOs   registration/reference/serial/model number (contrast NP1z below)

FOt   telephone number (not including any exchange name spelled out in full). As in the case of FOp, a complex telephone number written with internal spaces is analysed as a tagma tagged FOt=, but where the components are linked by hyphens the whole is treated as a single word.

FOx   algebraic expression with nominal as opposed to equative function (*a*, π or *pi*, *dy/dx*, etc.)[25]

FW   foreign word not capable of being allocated a more specific tag by reference to its English context, e.g. because it occurs in an extended foreign sentence, or in a title grammatically independent of the context

FWg   biological Latin name of genus or other rank higher than species (e.g. *Equus Umbelliferae*)[26]

FWs   biological Latin species (or lower-rank) name (e.g. *sapiens officinale*)[27]

GG   Germanic genitive inflexion: +'s, or +' after plural stem and certain other stems ending in -s

ICS   *considering notwithstanding* ≠ *considering* VVGt RR, *notwithstanding* RR

ICSk   *like* as preposition, subordinating conjunction, or in the relative use described in § 4.312 ≠ FA JB NN1c VV0t

ICSt   *after before ere since until till* as preposition (with complement) or subordinating conjunction ≠ *after* RR FB, *before* RR, *since* RAa RR

---

[25] Algebraic expressions are regarded as either equative (FOqx) or nominal (FOx); the emphasized expression in *being a (1,1) curve* J21:0800 is more adjectival than nominal in its context, but in SUSANNE terms it is an FOx rather than an FOqx.

[26] Where a biological name is also used as the ordinary English name for a plant or animal, e.g. *nasturtium zebra*, the FW... tags are reserved for uses marked by special typography (italics, capitalization) or use of a full binomial designation, and other uses are given NN... tags.

[27] See n. 26 above.

ICSx	*but except save* as preposition or subordinating conjunction ≠ *but* CCB RR, *except* VV0t, *save* NN1c VV0v
IF	*for* as preposition ≠ CSf
II	preposition, including prepositional use of word that can function either as preposition or as adverb; see list at end
IIa	*as* used non-comparatively as preposition ≠ CSA RGa (The *as* of a construction such as *describe X as Y*, where Y is an adjective rather than a noun phrase, will be CSA rather than IIa.)
IIb	*by* as preposition ≠ RL
IIg	*aged* as pseudo-preposition ≠ JJ VVDv VVNv
IIp	*per*, solidus character representing "per" (as in *15 counts/minute*) ≠ solidus CC YD[28]
IIt	*to* as preposition ≠ TO RL
IIx	mathematical infix operator ("+", ">", "=", etc.)
IO	*of*
IW	*with* in all uses, *without* as preposition, *what_with* ≠ *without* RR
JA	adjective used only predicatively, e.g. *ablaze alone infra_dig unable*
JB	adjective used only attributively, e.g. *chief entire future inverse major planetary so_called undersea very* (as in *the very thing*)
JBo	*other* in all uses
JBy	*only* as adjective (*the only thing*) ≠ RRx
JBR	*inner lesser nether outer upper* ≠ *upper* NN1c
JBT	*utmost uttermost* ≠ NN1c in both cases
JJ	general adjective, e.g. *blue, Jewish*
JJh	pseudo-adjective formed by suffixing *-ed* to the last word of a nominal compound, e.g. *bellied* in *pot-*

[28] When unmistakably representing "per" (as in *ft / sec²*) the solidus is wordtagged IIp; when it can equally well or more easily be taken as representing "and" or "or" (e.g. *reading / language arts achievement, speed / accuracy tradeoff, a rural / suburban area*) it is wordtagged CC; used in grammatically looser constructions, e.g. to add a limiting element to a title (*UC / Berkeley, Vice President / Academic Affairs*) or to separate independent elements in displayed text, as in:

Television Week / C. Gerald Fraser
Sunday / May 22
Sunday / continued

it is wordtagged YD. Cf. § 4.238. On changing patterns in the use of the solidus, see Weber (1983).

bellied; where an adjective is formed by suffixing *-ed* to an independent noun, not part of a compound, e.g. *mustachioed*, the word is tagged JJ rather than JJh.

JJj   abbreviated adjective appended to organization name to identify its legal status: *Ltd Inc Pty* and counterparts in other jurisdictions (but not *plc*, which abbreviates a noun phrase and is tagged NN1c)

JJs   adjective in *-most*, other than *utmost uttermost*, namely *backmost easternmost foremost furthermost hindmost inmost innermost lowermost midmost nethermost northernmost outermost outmost rearmost southernmost topmost upmost uppermost westernmost* ≠ *foremost* RR, *midmost* RR, *uppermost* RR

JJR   comparative adjective, including *elder further*

JJT   superlative adjective, including *eldest furthest*

LE   *both not_only* as pre-co-ordinator ≠ *both* DB2

LEe   *either* as pre-co-ordinator ≠ DD1e RR

LEn   *neither* as pre-co-ordinator ≠ DD1n RR

MC   cardinal numeral from *zero* upwards, spelled out; includes *umpteen*

MCb   "labels" used for cross-reference within and between texts, comprising combinations of digits, letters, and/or non-alphanumeric characters, e.g. *(a) 1990b 1a IIc (1990).*[29]

MCd   numeral including decimal point

MCe   number containing a non-decimal separator, other than a time-of-day expression, e.g. *4:11* or *4.11* for "four years eleven months" or "chapter 4 verse 11", *3/4/93* or *3.4.93* for "3rd of April 1993" or "4th of March 1993". A numeral containing both decimal and non-decimal separators is MCe rather than MCd: *1.12.2* for "1 minute 12.2 seconds". (See further § 4.270.)

MCn   cardinal numeral written in digits (including numeral acting as ordinal but not overtly marked as such,

---

[29] Brackets are included as part of an MCb only when they are not serving their ordinary function of marking the insertion of an interpolation into continuous text. Thus, when the brackets act as part of the name of a reference, as in *see also (c)*, they count as part of an MCb; and when the reference is set off typographically by devices other than brackets, as in *the jury recommended that:* <bminhd> *(1)* <eminhd> *Four additional* ... A01:0580, again the brackets form part of an MCb; but where brackets are used to interpolate a reference into a sequence in which it has no grammatical role (e.g. *Smith wrote (1950) that* ...), the brackets are treated as separate wordtagged segments. "Labels" in the sense defined here are tagged MCb only when they consist of combinations of characters not having a more specific wordtag; thus, a single letter used as a label is wordtagged ZZ1, a number will be wordtagged e.g. MCn, MC1n, MCr, MCy as appropriate.

e.g. in *February* **28,** and including combinations of integer and fraction, e.g. *1<frac12>,* and negative numbers, e.g. *–78*)

MCo	*0* written as digit
MCr	roman numeral (from *I* upwards)
MCs	integer written digitally with leading zero (e.g. *007*)
MCy	year name written digitally, in full or with apostrophe, e.g *1987* or *'91.* (In a case like *1939–45* the full year name *1939* is tagged MCy, but the truncated form *45* is tagged MCn: a two-digit number without apostrophe would be given the MCy tag only if the style of the text made this a normal way of abbreviating dates written in isolation, or when referring to a year of the first century.)
MC1	*one* as numeral, spelled out, including uses as in *one of the major items,* or as placeholder head of noun phrase (*a large one*) ≠ PN1o
MC1n	*1* written as digit, including use as ordinal (e.g. *February 1*)
MC2	plural of cardinal, spelled out (*ones twos tens* etc.), including use of *ones* as placeholder head of noun phrase ≠ *fives* NNu
MC2n	plural of cardinal written in digits (*1s 2s 10s 10's* etc.)
MC2r	roman numeral pluralized
MC2y	plural of year name, e.g. *1960s*
MD	ordinal form (*third fourth* etc.) whether used as ordinal adjective or adverb or as fraction; includes *umpteenth nth,* but not *half quarter,* which are fractions but not ordinals — *half* is DBh NN1c RR, *quarter* (cf. § 3.50) is NNL1c NNT1c NNU1c
MDn	ordinal numeral written digitally (*1st 2nd 100th* etc.)
MDo	*first second* ≠ *second* NNT1c VV0t
MDt	*next last* ≠ *last* NN1c VV0i
MFn	fraction written digitally, e.g. *2/3* $\frac{2}{3}$
ND1	direction: *north N southeast* etc.
NNa	time of day written digitally, e.g. *10:30 10.30 1030*
NNb	attributive common noun, e.g. *scissor trouser pincer*
NNc	C+P noun, e.g. *sheep species people Swiss* (cf. *a Swiss, three Swiss*)
NNm	singular abbreviation normally followed by a numeral functioning as a proper name, e.g. *Fig. No. p. § #* (for "number")

NNmm	plural of NNm abbreviation, e.g. *Figs. Nos. pp. §§*
NNn	M+C+P noun, e.g. *fish* (*a fish, three fish, a piece of fish*) *Chinese* (*a Chinese, three Chinese, Chinese is tonal*)
NNp	time of day written digitally in 24-hour notation from 13.00 on, e.g. *13:30 1330*
NNu	M+P noun, e.g. *data measles bowls French* (cf. *the French cook well, French is difficult*)
NNux	M+P noun in *-ics*, e.g. *mechanics*
NN1c	C noun, e.g. *clock crowd Buddhist*
NN1m	noun beginning *mid-* other than time noun, e.g. *midstream midfield*
NN1n	M+C noun, e.g. *illness German* (cf. *a good German, German is an easy language*)
NN1u	M noun, e.g. *snow Buddhism*
NN1ux	M noun in *-ics*, e.g. *athletics thermodynamics*
NN2	P noun, e.g. *clocks trousers Germans police British*; also includes plurals of various items whose singulars have more specific, or non-noun, tags: numbers tagged NNOc, ordinals, fractions (e.g. *hundreds thirds fifths*), adjectives used as nouns and pluralized (e.g. *detergent actives* J05:1570), cited words (as in e.g. *ifs and buts*), currency symbols (as in e.g. *Save \$\$\$s!*), pluralized F... words (e.g. in *the x's cancel out*), also *others todays yesterdays.*
NNJ	J-only item (singular or plural), e.g. *Corp Bros*
NNJ1c	J+C noun, e.g. *club committee institute*
NNJ1n	J+M+C noun, e.g. *company organization society*
NNJ2	J+P noun, e.g. *associates*
NNL	L-only item (singular plural or neutral), e.g. *Rd Is Mts*
NNLb	L-only noun with tendency to precede the specific name, e.g. *Costa Mt*
NNLc	L+C+P noun, e.g. *barracks links works*
NNL1c	L+C noun, e.g. *road island city*
NNL1cb	L+C noun with tendency to precede the specific name, e.g. *camp lake mount*
NNL1n	L+M+C noun, e.g. *drive water green*
NNL2	L+P noun, e.g. *buildings mountains springs*
NNOc	*dozen score gross hundred thousand million billion trillion* (etc.) *zillion*
NNOn	abbreviated NNOc word, ambiguous between singular and plural, e.g. *m* for *million(s)*
NNS	S-only item, singular, e.g. *Mr Mrs Miss Dr Dom Mme Gen Sen Sir Missy Ma'am Sire Mister*

NNSj	S-only adjectival item, e.g. *Rev Very_Rev Hon Rt_Hon*
NNS1c	S+C noun, e.g. *doctor miss madam minister prince queen*
NNS1n	S+M+C noun, e.g. *justice*
NNS2	S+P noun, e.g. *doctors misses madams ministers princes queens justices*
NNSA	S item following name, with or without C use, e.g. *Jr Sr Jun Sen Esq Bart BA PhD MP QC VC Dem Lab*
NNSS	S-only item, plural, e.g. *Messrs Mmes Mesdames Sirs*
NNT1c	singular time noun that can head a noun phrase functioning adverbially (other than NNT1h), e.g. *hour day night morning afternoon evening week year century time*
NNT1h	name of holiday or season, e.g. *Christmas Boxing_Day Hallowe'en summer*
NNT1m	point-of-time noun, which cannot head a noun phrase functioning adverbially, e.g. *noon midnight midyear*
NNT2	plural of any NNT1... noun
NNU	U-only item (singular, plural, or neutral), e.g. *in ins kg <Prime>* standing for "inch(es)"
NNUb	unit symbol which precedes numeral, e.g. *$*
NNUc	U+C+P noun, e.g. *hertz yen*
NNUn	U+M+C+P noun, e.g. *horsepower*
NNUp	*% percent per_cent*
NNU1c	U+C noun, e.g. *inch kilogram(me)*
NNU1n	U+M+C noun, e.g. *metre*
NNU2	U+P noun, e.g. *inches*
NP1c	country name
NP1f	feminine forename
NP1g	miscellaneous singular geographical proper name, e.g. *Adriatic America Sherwood*
NP1i	initial of personal name, e.g. *W.* or *G.* in *W.G. Grace*
NP1j	organization name, e.g. *Unilever Kiwanis CIA*
NP1m	masculine forename
NP1p	"province" name: name of US state, English county, etc.
NP1s	surname
NP1t	town name (covering city, town, suburb, village, etc.)
NP1x	miscellaneous singular proper name, e.g. *Parthenon Persil*
NP1z	"code name" (acronym or arbitrary alphanumeric expression) functioning as countable noun, liable to take plural inflexion and/or indefinite article, e.g. *1-11, GTi,*

PDP11/70. Contrast FOs for an alphanumeric code not integrated into the grammatical system in these ways;[30] and note that an acronym or alphanumeric code which functions as an uncountable noun, or as another part of speech, is tagged as such: *PMT* for "pre-menstrual tension" NN1u, *A1* (as "first class") JJ.

NP2c	plural country name, as in *the **Philippines**, the two **Koreas***
NP2f	plural feminine forename
NP2g	miscellaneous plural geographical proper name, e.g. *Alps Americas Antilles*
NP2j	plural organization name, as in *up there with the **ICI**'s and **Unilevers***
NP2m	plural masculine forename, as in *both **Geoffreys***
NP2p	plural "province" name, e.g. *Carolinas*
NP2s	plural surname, as in *the **Robinsons***; includes company names formed by adding -s without apostrophe to a surname, e.g. *Woolworths Dresbachs*, even if these are historically genitive singulars
NP2t	plural town name
NP2x	miscellaneous plural proper name
NP2z	pluralized form of "code name" functioning as countable noun, e.g. *1-11's PDP11/70s*
NPD	abbreviated day of the week, e.g. *Tues*
NPD1	day of the week, e.g. *Tuesday*
NPD2	plural of day of week, e.g. *Tuesdays*
NPM	abbreviated month name, e.g. *Oct*
NPM1	month name, e.g. *October*
NPM2	plural of month name, e.g. *Octobers*
PN	*none* in all uses
PN1	*anybody anyone anything everybody everyone everything naught nobody no_one nothing somebody someone something* ≠ *nobody* NN1c
PN1o	*one* as impersonal pronoun ≠ MC1
PN1z	*so* as a pro-form, for instance in the *do so* construction ≠ RGz RRz
PNQOq	interrogative *whom* ≠ PNQOr
PNQOr	relative *whom* ≠ PNQOq

[30] This contrast between FOs and NP1z means that, rather illogically, a code name which functions as a proper noun is not given an NP... tag (thus *R101*, the serial number of a famous airship, would be tagged FOs), whereas a code name that functions as a countable common noun is tagged NP1z.

PNQSq	interrogative *who* ≠ PNQSr
PNQSr	relative *who* ≠ PNQSq
PNQVG	*no_matter_whose whosever*
PNQVO	*no_matter_whom whomever*
PNQVS	*no_matter_who whoever whosoever*
PNX1	*oneself*
PPGf	*hers*
PPGh2	*theirs*
PPGi1	*mine* as pronoun
PPGi2	*ours*
PPGm	*his* as pronoun ≠ APPGm
PPGy	*yours*
PPH1	*it*
PPHO1f	*her* as pronoun ≠ APPGf
PPHO1m	*him*
PPHO2	*them*
PPHS1f	*she*
PPHS1m	*he*
PPHS2	*they*
PPIO1	*me*
PPIO2	*us*
PPIS1	*I* as personal pronoun
PPIS2	*we*
PPX1f	*herself*
PPX1h	*itself*
PPX1i	*myself*
PPX1m	*himself*
PPX1y	*yourself*
PPX2h	*themselves each_other one_another*
PPX2i	*ourselves*, royal *ourself*
PPX2y	*yourselves*
PPY	*you*
RAa	*ago, since* as synonym for *ago* ≠ *since* ICSt RR
RAb	A.D. *Anno_Domini* and counterparts used in pre-date position in other calendars
RAc	co-ordination-closing element, e.g. *etc f* or *ff* (for "following") *respectively and_so_on et_al*
RAe	*else* in all uses
RAh	*am* (for *ante meridiem*) *pm o'clock*
RAi	*inst ult* etc.
RAj	postnominal adjective, e.g. *designate centigrade elect galore politic* (as in *body politic*)
RAn	*whatever whatsoever*, after negative or non-assertive

	(any...) nominal head ≠ *whatever* DDQV, *whatso-ever* DDQV
RAp	*per_annum pa per_diem* etc.
RAq	*apiece,* distributive uses of *each* (as in *they are charging $10 each for the tickets*) ≠ *each* DD1q
RAx	mathematical postfix operator, e.g. *!* for factorial
RAy	*B.C.* and counterparts following dates in other calendars
RAz	*or_so* as in *fifty or so*
REX	apposition-introducing element: *for_example for_instance namely eg ie that_is viz* (but not *such_as,* which is II=)
RG	qualifier having no other adverbial use, e.g. *very jolly mighty stark* (≠ *jolly* JJ, *mighty* JJ, *stark* JJ), *far_from* as in *was far_from impressive* A12:0350 ≠ *far_from* II
RGa	*as* as qualifier ≠ CSA IIa
RGb	*quite* as qualifier or before article (e.g. *quite a good idea*) ≠ RR
RGf	*too* as qualifier ≠ RR
RGi	*about around circa getting_on_for over some* (as in *some thirty*) *under up_to* used with quantity or number[31] ≠ *about* II RPK, *around* II RL, *over* FB II RP, *some* DDi, *under* FB II RL, *up_to* II
RGr	*rather* as qualifier or before article (e.g. *rather a good idea*), *more_of* before article (e.g. *more of an agricultural nation* N04:0470) ≠ *rather* RRR
RGz	*so* as qualifier ≠ RRz PN1z
RGA	*indeed* as qualifier (commonly following head) ≠ RR
RGAf	*enough* as qualifier ≠ DDf RRe
RGQq	*how* as qualifier ≠ RRQq RRQr
RGQV	*however no_matter_how* as qualifiers ≠ *however* RR RRQV, *no_matter_how* RRQV
RL	adverb of place or direction (see list at end)
RLe	*elsewhere*
RLh	*here; there* as adverb of place ≠ *there* EX UH
RLn	*downstairs upstairs* ≠ JJ NN1u in both cases
RLw	*somewhere someplace anywhere anyplace everywhere nowhere*
RP	adverbial uses of *across down in off on out over*

---

[31] Words having this use which also function as general adverbs, e.g. *approximately roughly,* are tagged RR and not RGi.

	through up ≠ II in each case; ≠ *down* JB NNL1n VV0t, *off* FB JB, *out* JB VV0t, *over* FB JB NN1c RGi, *through* JB, *up* FB VV0v
RPK	*about* in adverbial and catenative (*about to . . .*) uses ≠ II RGi
RR	general adverb, e.g. *fast skilfully*; RL. . . and RP. . . tags count as more specific than RR. . . , hence a word having an RL. . . or RP. . . tag is never also given an RR. . . tag, but a word may have both RR. . . and RA. . . or RG. . . tags for different uses
RRe	*enough* as clause adverb ≠ DDf RGAf
RRf	*far* as adverb ≠ JJ
RRg	*long* as adverb ≠ JJ
RRs	*otherwise yet*
RRx	*only* as adverb ≠ JBy
RRy	*any* as qualifier with comparative ≠ DDy
RRz	*so* introducing main clause or clause of purpose or result (including as in *so as to . . .*), or as adverb of manner or degree ≠ RGz PN1z
RRQq	interrogative *wh-* adverb: *how when whence where whereabouts whither why* ≠ *how* RGQq RRQr, *when* CSn RRQr, *whence* RRQr, *where* CSr RRQr, *whereabouts* NN2, *whither* RRQr, *why* RRQr UH
RRQr	relative *wh-* adverb (having overt antecedent — not "fused" relative, § 4.318, cf. CS CSn CSr): *when whence where whereat whereby wherein whereof whereon whereupon wherewith whither why* ≠ *how* RGQq RRQq, *when* CSn RRQq, *whence* RRQq, *where* CSr RRQq, *whereat* CS, *whereupon* CS, *whither* RRQq, *why* RRQq
RRQV	*wh-. . .-ever* adverb: *however no_matter_how no_matter_when no_matter_where no_matter_why whencesoever whenever wheresoever wherever whithersoever* ≠ *however* RGQV RR, *no_matter_how* RGQV
RRR	single-word comparative adverb other than *more less*: *better closer deeper earlier farther faster further harder higher later longer louder lower nearer nigher oftener quicker rather safer slower sooner wider worse* ≠ JJR for all but *oftener rather sooner*; ≠ *nearer* II, *nigher* II, *rather* RGr, *worse* NN1u
RRT	single-word superlative adverb other than *most least*: *best brightest closest deepest earliest farthest fastest*

	furthest hardest highest latest longest loudest lowest nearest nighest soonest widest worst ≠ JJT for all but soonest; ≠ *nearest* II, *nighest* II, *worst* NN1u
RT	*again hereafter overnight* ≠ *hereafter* NN1c, *overnight* JB
RTn	*then*
RTo	*now* ≠ CS
RTt	*today tomorrow tonight yesterday*
TO	infinitival *to* ≠ IIt RL
UH	interjection, e.g. *blimey hello please well yes* On the application of the UH tag, see §§ 4.449 ff.

In analysing spoken English, the UH tag is replaced by a range of more refined U. . . tags; cf. § 6.31.

VB0	*be*
VBDR	*were*
VBDZ	*was*
VBG	*being* ≠ NN1n
VBM	*am*
VBN	*been*
VBR	*are*
VBZ	*is*
VD0	*do*
VDD	*did*
VDG	*doing*
VDN	*done*
VDZ	*does*
VH0	*have*
VHD	*had* as past tense ≠ VHN
VHG	*having*
VHN	*had* as past participle ≠ VHD
VHZ	*has*
VMd	modal, past form: *could might should would*
VMo	modal, present form: *can dare may must need shall will* ≠ *dare* VV0v,[32] *need* VV0t
VMK	*ought used* as modal catenative ≠ *used* JJ VVDt VVNt

Tags beginning VV. . . are used for non-modal verbs other than forms of *be do have*, which are always given VB. . ., VD. . ., or VH. . . tags whether used as main or auxiliary verbs

---

[32] *Dare, need* are categorized as VMo only when occurring as leading verb of a verbal group, followed by further base-form verb(s) without *to*, e.g. *I dare say* . . ., *you needn't think* . . . . In *she wouldn't dare ask her father* . . . N10:0380, *dare* is tagged VV0v and *ask* is treated as initiating a new clause.

VV0i	base form of intransitive verb
VV0t	base form of transitive verb
VV0v	base form of verb having transitive and intransitive uses
VVDi	past-tense form of intransitive verb
VVDt	past-tense form of transitive verb
VVDv	past-tense form of verb having transitive and intransitive uses
VVGi	present participle of intransitive verb
VVGt	present participle of transitive verb
VVGv	present participle of verb having transitive and intransitive uses
VVGK	*going* as catenative (in *BE going to*) ≠ JJ NN1n VVGi
VVNi	past participle of intransitive verb
VVNt	past participle of transitive verb
VVNv	past participle of verb having transitive and intransitive uses
VVNK	*bound* as catenative (in *BE bound to*) ≠ JJ NN1c VV0v VVDv VVNv
VVZi	third-person singular form of intransitive verb
VVZt	third-person singular form of transitive verb
VVZv	third-person singular form of verb having transitive and intransitive uses
XX	*not*
YB	text division of paragraph or higher rank, not having a heading: *<majbrk> <minbrk>* (§ 2.21)
YBL	beginning of heading: *<bmajhd> <bminhd>* (§ 2.21)
YBR	end of heading: *<emajhd> <eminhd>* (§ 2.21)
YC	comma
YD	dash (em-dash or larger), solidus character ≠ solidus CC IIp[33]
YE	ellipsis mark (three dots)
YF	full stop (American "period")
YG	logical position of transformationally moved/deleted item
YH	hyphen or en-dash
YIL	opening (single or double) inverted comma(s)
YIR	closing (single or double) inverted comma(s)
YM	filled pause — used only in analysing speech, cf. § 6.22
YN	colon
YND	colon-dash :-
YO	bullet, pilcrow, or other special symbol visually marking a text division[34]

[33] On the tagging of the solidus character, see n. 28 above.
[34] The various "centred rules" discussed in Ch. 2 n. 5 above are wordtagged YO.

YP   silent pause — used only in analysing speech, cf. § 6.22
YPL   opening bracket (round, **square**, etc.)
YPR   closing bracket (round, **square**, etc.)
YQ   question mark
YR   interruption point — used only in analysing speech, cf. § 6.37
YS   semicolon
YTL   begin italics/bold-face, cf. § 2.22
YTR   end italics/bold-face, cf. § 2.22
YX   exclamation mark
ZZ1   singular letter of the (**roman** or other) alphabet (including names of letters **spelled** out, e.g. *Eta, aleph, ell* for L) ≠ FOx
ZZ2   letter of the alphabet **with** plural inflexion (including spelled-out cases, e.g. in *a mayor's chain of esses*)

Membership of Large Closed Word Classes

CS

according_as albeit although as_long_as because but_that considering_that even_if even_though except_that forasmuch_as inasmuch_as in_case in_order_that in_so_far_as in_that lest now now_that once other_than provided provided_that providing providing_that seeing seeing_that unless whereas whereat whereupon while whilst ≠ *now* RTo, *once* RR, *other_than* II, *whereupon* RRQr

The sequence *so that*, which might have been taken as CS=, is not analysed as an idiom.

II

abaft aboard about above according_to across afore against ahead_of à_la alias along alongside along_with amid amidst among amongst anent apart_from à_propos around as_against as_between as_for as_from aside_from as_of as_opposed_to as_regards as_to astride at athwart atop away_from back_of bar barring because_of behind below beneath beside besides between betwixt beyond but_for by_means_of by_reason_of by_virtue_of by_way_of concerning contrary_to despite down due during ex except_for excepting excepting_for failing far_from[35] *following for_fear_of from given in in_accordance_with in_accord_with in_aid_of in_back_of*

---

[35] As in e.g. *far from really being retired* A05:1210.

in_behalf_of in_between in_case_of in_charge_of including
in_common_with in_comparison_with in_conjunction_with
in_connection_with in_contact_with in_course_of in_defence_of
in_excess_of in_face_of in_favour_of in_for in_front_of
in_keeping_with in_lieu_of in_line_with in_need_of in_place_of
in_possession_of in_quest_of in_regard_to in_respect_of in_return_for
in_search_of inside in_spite_of instead_of inter in_terms_of into
in_touch_with in_view_of irrespective_of less let_alone mid minus
near nearer nearer_to nearest nearest_to near_to next_door_to
next_to[36] *nigh nigher nighest off off_of on on_behalf_of on_board*
on_the_part_of onto on_top_of opposite other_than out out_of
out_of_touch_with outside over owing_to past pending plus prior_to
pro qua re regarding respecting round sans save_for subject_to
subsequent_to such_as thanks_to through throughout times
together_with touching toward towards under underneath unlike
unto up upon up_against up_to[37] *versus via vice vis_à_vis wanting*
within with_regard_to with_respect_to worth

Of these items, the following are alternatively tagged RL: *abaft*
aboard above along alongside around astride behind below beneath
between beyond by forth in_between inside near nigh on_board
opposite outside past round throughout to under underneath within;
and each item listed under RP above is also on the II list. Other
alternative tags are: *about* RGi RPK, *above* JB, *afore* RR, *against*
RR, *alias* NN1c, *à_propos* JA RR, *around* RGi, *athwart* RR, *behind*
NN1c, *beneath* JJ, *besides* RR, *betwixt* RR, *beyond* NN1u, *down*
JB NNL1n VV0t, *due* JJ NN1c RR, *ex* FB, *far_from* RG, *following*
RA, *in_between* JJ, *inside* JJ NN1c, *less* DAR, *mid* JJ, *minus* NN1c,
near JB RL, *nearer* JJR RRR, *nearest* JJT RRT, *nigher* RRR, *nighest*
RRT, *off* FB JB, *opposite* JJ NN1c, *other_than* CS, *out* JB VV0t,
outside JJ NN1c, *over* FB JB NN1c RGi, *past* JJ NN1c VVNv,
pending JJ, *plus* CC NN1c, *pro* FB NN1c RR JJ, *re* FB NN1c *round*
JJ NN1n VV0v, *through* JB, *under* FB RGi, *underneath* NN1u, *unlike*
JJ, *up* FB VV0v, *up_to* RGi, *vis_à_vis* RR, *worth* JA NN1u.

The sequences *all over, due to, regardless of,* which might have
been taken as II=, are not analysed as idioms (*all over* is grammatically parallel to *all down, all through,* etc.; *due to* can be interrupted, e.g. *due largely to; regardless of* has grammatical parallels).

RL

aback abaft abed aboard above abroad afar afield afore aft aground
ahead aloft along alongside amidships apart around ashore aside

---

[36] Not as in *next to last*, which is [Jh *next* [P *to last*]].
[37] In the sense "as far/much as".

astern astride asunder away awry back backstage behind below beneath beside between beyond by crossways downhill downriver downstage downstream downtown downwards downwind eastward(s) forward forwards headlong hence hither home in_between indoors inland inshore inside interstage leeward left lengthways midway nationwide near nearby next_door nigh northward(s) offshore offside offstage on_board opposite out_back outdoors out_of_doors outside overboard overhead overland overseas past right round sidelong sideways southward(s) thence thither throughout to to_and_fro together under underfoot underground underneath underwater underway upcountry uphill upright upriver upside_down upstage upstream uptown upwards upwind westward(s) windward within without

See under II above for a list of words which have both II and RL tags. The following RL words are alternatively tagged JB: *away back backstage downriver downstage downtown eastward inland near next_door offshore offstage overhead overseas sidelong sideways upriver upside_down upstage upstream uptown upwards westward windward*; and the following are alternatively tagged JJ: *aft downhill downstream downwind forward headlong inshore interstage left lengthways nationwide offside overland right underground underwater upcountry uphill upright upwind*. Other alternative tags: *aground* JA, *aside* NN1c, *awry* JA, *home* NN1c VV0i, *left* NN1u, *midway* RR JA, *offside* NN1u, *outback* NN1c, *overhead* NN1c, *underground* NN1c, *upright* NN1c, *upstage* VV0t, *windward* NN1u, *without* IW.

The sequences *over here, over there*, which might have been taken as RL=, are not analysed as idioms.

RR= Idioms

This list is regarded as open to extension:

all_but all_right as_good_as as_it_were as_usual as_well as_yet at_all at_best at_first at_large at_last at_least at_length at_long_last at_most at_once at_random at_that at_the_most at_worst au_fond by_and_large by_the_way de_facto de_jure en_clair en_famille en_masse en_route even_so ever_so ex_officio far_from for_certain for_ever for_good for_once for_sure from_time_to_time half_way in_all in_brief in_common in_effect in_fact in_full in_general in_loco_parentis in_particular in_private in_public in_short in_situ inter_alia in_the_main in_toto in_vain inside_out ipso_facto kind_of more_than[38] *mutatis_mutandis nem_con no_doubt nolens_volens none_the_less of_a_sudden of_course of_late once_again once_more out_of_the_way par_excellence pari_passu per_se point_blank prima_facie pro_forma pro_rata pro_tem pro_tempore sine_die so_much_as*[39] *somehow_or_other sort_of sotto_voce sub_rosa time_and_again tout_ensemble ultra_vires upside_down vice_versa viva_voce willy_nilly*

≠ *all_right* JA=, *de_facto* JJ=, *de_jure* JJ=, *ex_officio* JJ=, *out_of_the_way* JJ=, *prima_facie* JJ=, *pro_forma* JJ=, *ultra_vires* JJ=, *viva_voce* JJ=

The sequence *in addition*, which might have been regarded as RR=, is not treated as an idiom, being related to *in addition to* which is not treated as an II= idiom.

Open-Class Idioms Occurring in the SUSANNE Corpus

This list does not include RR= idioms, which are on the border between open and closed classes (§ 3.60):

JJ=	*ad_hoc de_facto*
NN1c=	*coup_d'etat open_sesame status_quo zur_khaneh*
NN1u=	*D._C.* (for *direct current*)
NN2=	*sho'_nufs vasa_vasorum*
NNS=	*Atty._Gen. Lt._Gov.*
NNS1c=	*attorney_general*[40]
NNT1h=	*Mardi_Gras*
NNU=	*<deg>_K*
NNUp=	*wt_%*
NP1c=	*U._S.*
NP1j=	*B._&_O.*
NP1p=	*D._C.* (for *District of Columbia*)
NP1t=	*N._Y.*
RAc=	*and_so_forth and_so_on et_al*
RAp=	*per_diem*
UH=	*thank_you*

[38] As in *have more than doubled* A04:1930.

[39] As in *... before she* [Vcd *could* [R *so_much_as*] *lift*] *the receiver* N11.112.

[40] In principle this phrase has a potential plural, *attorneys general*, which would normally prevent it being considered an idiom. However, if the phrase were not treated as an idiom, there would be a difficulty in tagging its words: the phrase as a whole has the S use, but *attorney* alone does not (certainly not in a British context, nor so far as we know in an American context). Therefore *attorney_general* is treated as NNS1c=, *attorneys_general* if it ever occurred would be NNS2=, while *attorney* in other environments is NN1c.

Boundaries between Wordtags

DICTIONARY DEPENDENCE

§ 3.74   Because English has simple inflexional morphology and somewhat anarchical syntax, words are frequently indeterminate with respect to membership of open grammatical classes (noun, verb, adjective, adverb). The tagging of the LOB Corpus involved defining boundaries between open classes in great detail (*TLCUM*, pp. 30 ff.), rendering issues about assigning word-tokens to parts of speech determinate to an extent that is probably unprecedented in English linguistics. The creators of the Tagged LOB Corpus did the discipline a great service in this way, and the SUSANNE project in particular has benefited greatly from their work.

Nevertheless, the SUSANNE approach to open-class wordtagging varies from the Tagged LOB approach in one fundamental respect. For SUSANNE, the range of open-class wordtags available for a given word is limited to those which correspond to the parts of speech listed for the word in a specific published dictionary, namely *OALD3* (in its electronic version CUVOALD86, Mitton 1986). General rules for choosing between open-class wordtags in debatable cases are required only where the dictionary identifies a word as representing alternative parts of speech, both or all of which are arguably compatible with the context. The Tagged LOB Corpus project on the other hand made no explicit or implicit reference to a published dictionary.

§ 3.75   There are several reasons for this policy difference, some of which are purely practical. The Tagged LOB Corpus was created at a time when electronic versions of published dictionaries were not widely available; now they are, and the task of wordtagging a sizeable corpus is greatly eased by using one. But there are also reasons of principle why basing open-class wordtagging on a published dictionary is desirable.[41] An overriding consideration in evolving the SUSANNE analytic scheme, as discussed in Chapter 1, has been that it is more important for the analysis assigned to any language example always to be certain and predictable than for it

---

[41] The dictionary has no role with respect to defining membership of closed-class tags; these wordlists are stated within the present chapter as part of the definition of the SUSANNE analytic scheme, and the system of closed-class wordtags is far more detailed than the grammatical classification of *OALD3* or any other published dictionary. Thus for instance *offshore* is listed above as taking either of the wordtags RL or JB, though *OALD3* lists *off-shore* as an adjective only. Furthermore, if this chapter assigns a particular word to an open-class category in a way which contradicts the *OALD3* classification, the assignment here should prevail (but no instance of this is known).

always to be theoretically unimpeachable. Relating wordtagging to the authority of a specified dictionary is a good way to increase analytic predictability, since even rules as detailed as those of *TLCUM* leave many issues to be decided by the analyst's judgement (as the creators of the Tagged LOB Corpus were well aware — cf. comments such as "There definitely is no clear borderline between -*ed* adjectives and verb forms", "no claim can be made for complete consistency in the distinction between adjective and noun in attributive position", *TLCUM* pp. 34, 64). Furthermore, giving a dictionary authority over the range of candidate tags for words leads to considerable simplification of the rules needed to decide the residual problems of choice in context between the alternative classifications offered by the dictionary.

§ 3.76   The SUSANNE use of *OALD3* for this purpose does not imply any claim that the part-of-speech information given in this publication is always perfectly sound and consistent. There certainly are individual instances where the grammatical information given for one word is oddly divergent from what is said about another apparently similar word. To take one example: the nominal use of the word *running* to denote the activity of running is given a separate uncountable-noun entry in *OALD3*, and consequently the word is given a noun wordtag e.g. at A12:1020; yet many other present participles which seem equally well established in English as names of activities (e.g. *swimming*) are given no noun entries in the dictionary, and accordingly are tagged in SUSANNE as verb participles when functioning nominally. But what matters for SUSANNE purposes is that the dictionary offers a publicly accessible standard. If the resources invested in compiling a major published dictionary do not succeed in producing a totally consistent pattern of grammatical classification, it is hardly likely that an individual academic research project could hope to do better.

It is also not suggested that English-language grammatical annotation for NLP purposes ought to be based on this particular edition of this particular dictionary; the SUSANNE project chose *OALD3* for practical reasons of availability. But it would seem necessary for any rigorous NLP grammatical annotation scheme to treat some particular dictionary as authoritative on the issue of open-class tags for individual words, and to specify which dictionary is used as part of the definition of the analytic scheme. SUSANNE allots this status to *OALD3*, "second-guessing" its statements about open-class words only in occasional cases of straightforward misprints (as when *OALD3* categorizes *semi-* as a "*prep*[*osition*]" rather than a "*pref*[*ix*]").

§ 3.77 The part-of-speech indicators shown in *OALD3* (or other published dictionaries) are of course far from isomorphic with the SUSANNE wordtag set. *OALD3* uses a much smaller set of traditional part-of-speech names represented in abbreviated form, such as "*adj*", "*n*". But, although the Tagged LOB tagset, like the SUSANNE tagset, consists of categories much more numerous and refined than these, *TLCUM* makes it clear that the bulk of word-tagging problems which its complex rules are intended to resolve are problems as between the broad classes denoted by traditional part-of-speech names. If one knows that a particular word-token is to be tagged as, say, an adjective rather than a noun, then it tends to be a straightforward matter to decide which tag beginning J. . . from the Tagged LOB or SUSANNE tagsets is appropriate; it is the choice between adjective and noun which is more likely to be difficult to decide, and this choice will often be settled by the fact that the dictionary offers only one of these categories for the word (either in general, or for the sense which the word bears in context).

The dictionary is used to select between sets of wordtags corresponding to different traditional parts of speech, e.g. noun, adjective. It is not used to choose between alternative SUSANNE wordtags each associated with a single traditional part of speech, because the distinctions between SUSANNE wordtags are more refined than the dictionary grammar codes.

§ 3.78 Although in general the SUSANNE wordtags are more refined than the *OALD3* classification, occasionally *OALD3* includes an unusual ad hoc grammatical characterization of an individual word; for instance *clad* is identified as "old *p[ast] p[article]* of *clothe*". SUSANNE equates such descriptions with the nearest standard *OALD3* classification; thus *clad* takes the SUSANNE wordtag VVNt.[42]

§ 3.79 The fact that SUSANNE was wordtagged using CUVOALD86 rather than using *OALD3* directly is relevant particularly to the subclassification of nouns and verbs. The SUSANNE team modified the CUVOALD86 file for their purposes in various ways, for instance adding information about "special uses" of nouns; but the grouping of word-senses into entries, and the information about C and M uses of nouns, was left largely unchanged.[43] (The

---

[42] Likewise *swollen* is classified as "*pp* of *swell*, esp as *adj*"; this is taken to imply that *swollen* when functioning adjectivally is to be tagged JJ rather than VVNv. Such ad hoc classifications are not frequent enough to create significant difficulties for the SUSANNE approach to wordtagging.

[43] In a few cases SUSANNE wordtagging of nouns intentionally conflicts with the subclassification implied by CUVOALD86. This applies in the case of certain nouns which are singular in form but have plural uses, such as *people*, where the CUVOALD86 classification

statements in § 3.29 about what count as C or M usage represent the rationale used when decisions about countable/uncountable status had to be made by the SUSANNE team because a word was not found in *OALD3*, and harmonize with apparent practice in that dictionary; for instance *OALD3* appears to treat absence of determiner in phrases like *go to church* as criterial for categorizing a noun as having an "uncountable" use.) CUVOALD86 tends to group all uses of an orthographic form into a single entry, distinguishing senses only when they correspond e.g. to distinct pronunciations. For instance, *bridge* as structure (which has C and L uses) and *bridge* as card-game (which has the M use) are included in a single entry in CUVOALD86, although etymologically unrelated; and consequently all noun uses of *bridge* in the SUSANNE Corpus are tagged NNL1n as representing a noun having C+M+L uses. If the Corpus had been tagged using a differently structured dictionary (for instance the printed *OALD3* itself, which divides *bridge* into separate entries), *bridge* as structure would be tagged NNL1c and *bridge* as game would be tagged NN1u, and in general there would be many more NN...c and NN...u and fewer NN...n tags. Similar remarks apply to the categorization of verbs as transitive, intransitive, or both-transitive-and-intransitive, where the information has been reproduced from CUVOALD86 without modification beyond occasional corrections of apparent errors in that file.[44] Any wordtagging standard based on a published dictionary needs not only to identify the dictionary but to make clear how the tags relate to the structure of entries in that dictionary.

§ 3.80 There is a related issue about whether wordtagging is intended to relate to the total range of grammatical behaviours available to a word in either American or British English, or whether text representing one national variety is tagged in terms of the behaviour of words in that variety only. Consider, for instance, the wordtags NNLb and NNL1cb for L nouns which, when acting as

---

seems inappropriate, and also to certain "special-use" nouns. Among time nouns given SUSANNE NNT... wordtags, *OALD3* distinguishes between countable-only and both-countable-and-uncountable words (*night* v. *day* are respective examples), which suggests that SUSANNE ought to make a distinction between NNT1c and NNT1n. However, the basis of the *OALD3* distinction in this area is somewhat questionable (and the relationship between the information in CUVOALD86 and the printed *OALD3* is unclear), so that it did not seem worthwhile to add to the SUSANNE wordtag-set, and all these words are tagged NNT1c (there is no tag NNT1n). Some NNJ... words, e.g. *opposition*, are shown as uncountable-only in *OALD3*, however the J use (as in the political sense of "the Opposition") is intrinsically a countable use so that it would seem contradictory to coin a tag NNJ1u, and these words are tagged NNJ1n.

[44] Since *born* (as opposed to *borne*) is listed in *OALD3* as past participle only for transitive uses of *bear*, *born* is tagged VVNt although *bear* is tagged VV0v.

head of a place-name, tend to begin rather than ending the name. There are a number of L nouns, for instance *river, county*, which exhibit this special behaviour in British but not American English (cf. *River Thames* v. *Hudson River, County Durham* v. *Yoknapatawpha County*). Because *OALD3* covers both British and American standard varieties of English, the policy of the SUSANNE Corpus is to make wordtagging reflect the total range of word behaviours in both national varieties, so *river* and *county* are tagged NNL1cb. Again, the general point is that an explicit wordtagging standard should identify the particular spectrum of national or other dialects which wordtag assignments are intended to reflect.

§ 3.81   Where an open-class word found in a text is missing from the dictionary (and in the case of *OALD3* this is a quite rare occurrence, cf. Sampson 1989*b*), it is usually easy to deduce from the information given under analogous headwords how the dictionary would classify the missing word if it were included. Likewise, where an open-class word exhibits a grammatical usage which is not listed in the dictionary because it represents a variety of English outside the range which the dictionary sets out to cover (an example would be the Northern English use of *happen* as an adverb equivalent to standard English *perhaps*, not listed in *OALD3*, which does not aim to cover regional dialects), or because it represents a usage developed too recently to have been included in *OALD3* (e.g. the verbal use of *author* as in *to author a software package*), the rule about restricting candidate tags to those implied by the dictionary is suspended and the wordtag is chosen by analogy with equivalent uses in the standard language of the *OALD3* period.[45]

§ 3.82   Occasional difficulties can arise where a non-English word not listed in the dictionary is integrated into an English context (so that it calls for a wordtag more specific than FW), but represents a grammatical class having no English parallel — e.g. the Latin ablative noun in *he was born <bital> anno <eital> 1753*. Such cases will be tagged by analogy with the nearest similar English word class; in this example the ablative is functionally somewhat akin to an English preposition, therefore *anno* would be tagged II.

---

[45] SUSANNE examples would be the use of *ordinary* as a noun denoting an American local-government office-holder, e.g. at A01:0430 (*OALD3* does not list a noun use for *ordinary*, probably because the use is regional even in the USA); the use in substandard American English as adverbs of words which in standard British usage can be only adjectives and are classified accordingly in *OALD3*, e.g. *you wouldn't talk so **tough*** N12:0970; the solecism *atune* G07:1840 for "in tune" or "attuned", which is tagged JA; or the use as an adverb, tagged RL, of the Australian word *outback* in the sequence *an Australian friend who had lived "outback" for years* G04:0760, which seems to represent an American writer's misunderstanding of a term which in Australian English is a noun or adjective only.

§ 3.83 Minor aspects of wordtagging are occasionally affected by the SUSANNE word-segmentation rules. Thus *re-set* A01:0290 is listed in *OALD3* as a transitive verb, but the SUSANNE rules concerning hyphenation cause it to be divided into three SUSANNE words, *re* +<*hyphen*> +*set*, the last of which corresponds to *OALD3 set*, which is listed as both transitive and intransitive. Therefore +*set* is wordtagged VV0v rather than VV0t.

§ 3.84 In some cases the role allotted to *OALD3* in determining available wordtags means that SUSANNE wordtagging systematically conflicts with that of the Tagged LOB Corpus. It is worth drawing detailed comparisons between wordtagging practices in the SUSANNE and Tagged LOB Corpora, because the wordtagging of the latter, as described in *TLCUM*, set a standard that is unrivalled in English-language corpus linguistics.

§ 3.85 For instance, in the Tagged LOB Corpus words which are morphologically (past or present) participles occurring as premodifiers within noun phrases are regularly tagged as adjectives; *TLCUM*, pp. 32, 35, explicitly contrasts e.g. *the observed data* J32.055, *so many sitting targets* A23.098, where the emphasized words are tagged as adjectives, with *the headfirst downward swimming observed in the field* J06.092, *a man sitting opposite her* N17.082, where the same words are tagged as verb participles. In SUSANNE terms no possibility arises of tagging *observed* or *sitting* as adjectives in any context. *Observed* is given in *OALD3* only as the past participle (or past tense) of the verb *observe*; *sitting* is either the present participle of *sit*, or a noun, but the definitions make it clear that the former rather than latter use is the one relevant in both examples quoted.[46] Thus both instances of *observed* receive the SUSANNE tag VVNv, and both instances of *sitting* receive the SUSANNE tag VVGv. Again, *TLCUM* appeals to the same rule in choosing adjectival tagging of *mentioned* in *the above mentioned bodies* B10.215 versus verbal tagging in *the work mentioned in Chapter XVII* G02.062. *OALD3* offers both verb and adjective tags for *mentioned* but reserves the latter specifically for the compounds *above-mentioned, below-mentioned*, so that in this case the SUSANNE tagging will agree with Tagged LOB but without appealing to a rule about premodifying v. postmodifying positions.

---

[46] Strictly, of course, *observed* being an inflected form does not occur as an *OALD3* headword at all. When we say that a given wordform is assigned by *OALD3* to a given grammatical class or classes, what this means is that *OALD3* headwords together with knowledge of English inflexion patterns jointly imply the class(es) for the word. SUSANNE wordtagging exploited the version of the CUVOALD86 file which includes inflected forms of *OALD3* headwords explicitly.

§ **3.86** Words having past-participle endings offer a good case-study in the contrast between Tagged LOB and SUSANNE approaches to wordtagging, since *TLCUM* recognizes this area as a specially problematic one. By *TLCUM* rules, pp. 30–4, words which are morphologically past participles are normally tagged as adjectives when acting as noun premodifiers or as heads of noun phrases (e.g. in *the aged and the maimed*); following a form of *BE* they are tagged as adjectives if *BE* is interpreted as copula but as verbs (i.e. as VVN..., in SUSANNE terms) if the construction is interpreted as passive; and numerous criteria are cited for choosing between these possibilities. Using *OALD3*, the great majority of cases quoted by *TLCUM* must be given VVN... tags. (VVD... tags are of course also compatible with the dictionary but are normally straightforwardly excluded by the context, though see below.) The word *aged* can be tagged VVNv or JJ (or, in special contexts, IIg), but the body of the dictionary definition explicitly associates the phrase *the aged* with the tag JJ. In another *TLCUM* example, *her firstborn*, *OALD3* implies JJ or NNc for *firstborn*, and if the noun classification is ever to be applicable, as *OALD3* says it is, it must clearly be the one chosen when the word heads a noun phrase.

Where an ...*ed* form begins with a prefix that does not apply to the corresponding base form, e.g. *unexpected, downtrodden* (there are no verbs **unexpect, *downtread*), VVN... tags are excluded and by SUSANNE rules, as by *TLCUM* rules, the tag must be JJ. Negatives in *un-* are one of the few categories of word which are frequently missing from *OALD3* even when common in the language (Sampson 1989*b*: 32), but this will create a wordtagging problem for *-ed* words only in cases where a verb in *un-* does exist: e.g. *unlocked* will appropriately be tagged VVNv as derived from *unlock*, but neither *unlock* nor *unlocked* is listed in *OALD3*. The set of *un-* verbs is rather small and clear-cut, so it is reasonable to say that a VVN... tag will be available for an *un-*...*ed* word whenever a corresponding *un-* verb is known by the analyst to exist, and that in such cases a JJ tag will be considered as an alternative only if *OALD3* explicitly lists an adjective sense of the *un-*...*ed* word (e.g. *undone* appears in the dictionary both as adjective and as past participle, in different senses); where there is no *un-* verb, an *un-*...*ed* form must be an adjective.[47]

§ **3.87** Apart from the special case of *un-* words, in five pages

---

[47] Thus in sequences such as *I felt exposed, unprotected,...* N13.134, or *a charged particle will tend to stick to an uncharged surface* J05:1050, while the pairs of *-ed* words "feel" entirely parallel to one another, *exposed* and *charged* must be tagged VVN... but *unprotected* and *uncharged* JJ.

of *TLCUM* there appear to be only four examples — namely *surprised pleased worried involved* — where *OALD3* does not prima facie specify an unambiguous wordtag. By *TLCUM* rules, *surprised pleased worried* are tagged as verbs when preceding *by* phrases, but as adjectives when preceding "prepositions which typically occur after adjectives", the examples quoted being *surprised at, pleased with, worried about. TLCUM* tags *involved* as a verb in the phrase BE *involved in*, though as an adjective in e.g. *too involved and tortuous. OALD3* permits both VVN... and JJ tags for *surprised pleased worried*, and the definition bodies include *surprised at, pleased with, worried about* examples for the verb as well as adjective subentries; *involved* in the BE *involved in* sense is shown both as a form of *involve* and as an adjective. That is, in these cases *OALD3* in effect classifies particular senses of inflected forms redundantly, both as separate words and also under the stems from which they are derived. The natural rule in such cases is to say that the SUSANNE tagging standard reflects the part of speech assigned by *OALD3* to the more specific subentry for the inflected form rather than that assigned to the general entry for the stem, in which case the *surprised at, pleased with, worried about* examples, and both uses of *involved*, are all tagged JJ. There remains a question about the tagging of *surprised pleased worried* where not followed by the special prepositions shown in *OALD3*; here it does become appropriate to invoke the general rule given in *TLCUM*, that if BE followed by an *-ed* word has a "dynamic" sense, as in *A ewe will abort if it is worried*, the construction is regarded as passive and the *-ed* word is tagged as a verbal past participle, while if the construction has a stative sense, as in *John was worried and fidgety*, the construction is seen as copular and the *-ed* word is an adjective. Undoubtedly it is also true, as asserted by *TLCUM* in a more specialized rule, that presence of a *by* phrase will push an analyst towards the passive interpretation. But this is now a semantic issue about the general conceptual difference between copular and passive constructions in English (discussed with respect to the SUSANNE analytic scheme in §§ 4.335–6), not a technical matter about choosing tags for individual words in terms of detailed properties of surrounding words. Arguably, the detailed rules specified in *TLCUM* have more to do with defining a wordtagging algorithm enabling a system with no access to an electronic dictionary to generate appropriate tags automatically, than with defining a target standard against which the output of an automatic tagger is to be judged. And when the use of a published dictionary reduces the class of problematic tagging decisions to such a small proportion, it becomes appropriate for those residual problems to be settled in terms of general semantic concepts rather than in terms of highly detailed and specific contextual criteria.

§ 3.88   As well as many cases where *TLCUM* treats -*ed* words as potentially ambiguous between verb past-participle and adjective tagging, there are also a lesser number of cases where *TLCUM* identifies such words as ambiguous between past-participle and past-tense tags. Two examples quoted (*TLCUM*, p. 30) are:

> "You **heard** what happened to Appleton after the meeting?" I said. <minbrk> "Yeah," he said. N06.036
>
> "But I've just been extremely clumsy, trying to find my way around. **Knocked** something over and **turned** the whole room into a shambles, apparently." P09.152

In the first case, the question might be an informal elliptical version of *Have you heard* . . . , or it might represent a statement converted into a question by intonation rather than syntactic rearrangement. In the second case it is clear that there has been ellipsis, and the issue is whether the notional unelided sentence began *I have knocked* . . . or simply *I knocked*. . . . In each case the former alternative implies VVN. . . , the latter alternative VVD. . . tagging for the words underlined.

But this is a rather different sort of wordtag ambiguity from the past participle v. adjective ambiguity discussed above. There, the assumption was that the passages of English concerned were in themselves clear and unambiguous, and the problem was to decide how best to fit particular unequivocal word-uses into a set of theoretical pigeon-holes. Here the problem is rather than the texts are genuinely ambiguous. If we decide on a particular interpretation, the choice of VVN. . . or VVD. . . tags is immediately settled. A scheme of analytic categories cannot be expected to resolve actual ambiguities in language, which must be done by corpus analysts using the same multifarious intellectual resources which speakers apply in real life (including, when necessary, guesswork); cf. §§ 4.31 ff.

§ 3.89   The only other problematic wordtag boundary identified by *TLCUM* in connection with -*ed* words concerns past participle versus subordinating conjunction in the case of the word *provided* and the phrases *provided that, granted that*. (The *TLCUM* decision is to use CS, CS= for *provided, provided_that* as subordinating conjunctions, but to tag *granted that* as a verbal past participle — VVNt in SUSANNE terms — followed by *that* as CS.) Since "subordinating conjunction" is a closed class, both SUSANNE and

TLCUM analytic schemes resolve these questions via explicit listing, and the SUSANNE scheme conforms to the *TLCUM* precedent in each of the three cases.[48]

§ 3.90   Thus the decision to treat a published dictionary as authoritative for open-class wordtagging means that an area — the treatment of words in *-ed* — which for the Tagged LOB project was particularly problematic, requiring the statement of a large number of special rules, in the SUSANNE approach is handled entirely by a few general principles about relating dictionary definitions to wordtags and about the conceptual distinction between passive and copular constructions.

§ 3.91   It is true that this decision means placing oneself in the hands of dictionary compilers whose grammatical classification practices are not a matter of public record, and thus forfeiting any ambition to achieve a "scientifically perfect" system of wordtagging. But although (or possibly to some extent because) the compilation of major commercially published dictionaries is not executed in the manner of an exercise in academic scientific research, it yields results which are of a higher quality than an academic research project could hope to achieve in practice. Any inconsistencies that do exist in dictionary word classification are far outweighed by the certainty that derives from appeal to a publicly accessible authority.

§ 3.92   Two areas where the appeal to the dictionary does not resolve wordtagging problems are abbreviations and proper names.

ABBREVIATIONS

§ 3.93   The dictionary cannot be used to tag abbreviations, because *OALD3* while including a list of abbreviations in its endmatter does not assign them grammatical parts of speech; although, by § 3.65, an abbreviation standing for a single word will receive the same tag as that word unless the abbreviation has distinctive grammatical behaviour, this principle does not settle cases where an abbreviation stands for a multi-word phrase, or for a non-English word having no close English grammatical equivalent.

In order to exemplify the kinds of problem that arise in wordtagging abbreviations, and the solutions adopted by the SUSANNE scheme, we now examine the difficult cases encountered in wordtagging the set of common abbreviations included in CUVOALD92

---

[48] *TLCUM* (p. 130 n. 29) adopts a special treatment for *given* as in . . . *but given fine weather, another crop could still be gathered* G19.178; for *OALD3*, *given* here is simply a past participle, so for SUSANNE *given* is wordtagged VVNv (and the sequence *given fine weather* is tagmatagged Tn, cf. § 4.347).

(no abbreviations were included in CUVOALD86). About 350 of the entries in CUVOALD92 are abbreviations; for most of them the appropriate wordtags (or alternative wordtags, in the case of character-sequences which can stand for different words in diverse contexts) are straightforwardly identifiable, but about thirty cases merit individual discussion.

In each case the word or phrase which the abbreviation is taken to represent is stated; in some contexts the same character-string may be used to represent other words or phrases, in which case the wordtag specified here will not necessarily apply.

§ **3.94** Although personal titles standardly receive NNS. . . tags, abbreviations such as *PM* for *Prime Minister*, *VP* for *Vice-President*, or *DG* for *Director-General* do not seem to occur in the definitive NNS. . . environments (one does not standardly write *PM Major* or *VP Quayle*, nor address a Vice-President as "*VP*"), hence these abbreviations are tagged NN1c. Conversely, *SS* for *steam ship* and *USS* for *United States Ship* do standardly occur prefixed to proper names, but since the resulting expressions do not denote persons NNS. . . is again inapplicable and NN1c is used.

§ **3.95** The abbreviations *eta* and *etd* (*estimated time of arrival/departure*), though standing for phrases headed by the word *time*, do not exhibit the special grammatical behaviour of NNT. . . words and are tagged NN1c.

§ **3.96** *HP* can stand for *horse power* or *hire purchase*; the former is a unit noun, so since individual nouns are not given both "special-use" and "general noun" tags (§ 3.36) *HP* is tagged NNU in either case. Likewise *MC* is tagged NNSA whether standing for *Military Cross* (which exhibits the special NNSA behaviour) or *Master of Ceremonies* (which does not). However, *PC* is tagged NNS as *Police Constable* but NNSA as *Privy Councillor*, since these titles are respectively prefixed and suffixed to personal names and there is no rule forbidding both tags from applying to the same character-string. (*PC* in the sense *politically correct* would be JJ.)

§ **3.97** The word *idem* (not an abbreviation, though listed as such in CUVOALD92) is a pronoun, though no English pronoun is synonymous; it is tagged PN1. The abbreviations *ibid loc_cit op_cit* (for *ibidem, locus citatus, opus citatum*) function in English as place adverbs and are tagged RL: since these forms abbreviate Latin words it is convenient to ignore the grammatical properties of the full forms and tag in terms of the behaviour in English of the abbreviations. On the other hand, *Anon* and *approx* retain a close psychological link for English-speakers with the full forms *anonymous*, *approximately*, and the decision was accordingly made to tag them

JJ, RR, like the latter words, although the abbreviations have specialized grammatical behaviour (*Anon* is used to represent an author's name when the true name is unknown, *approx* is used with numerical material) which might arguably justify an NP. . . tag or the tag RGi respectively. But *LP* for *long playing* has been used more commonly in phrases like *an LP* rather than like *an LP record*, so it is tagged NN1c which is appropriate to both of these uses, rather than being given an adjective tag as the full form might suggest.

§ 3.98   *Cantab, Oxon* are tagged RAj when standing for *Cantabrigiensis, Oxoniensis,* as in *J.K. Smith, MA (Cantab)*, but *Oxon* is NP1p when abbreviating *Oxfordshire*.

§ 3.99   When acronyms function as proper names it is usually easy to select an appropriate NP1. . . tag. Thus *BVM* for *Beata Virgo Maria* is NP1f, since *Maria* would be so tagged. *V_and_A* for *Victoria and Albert [Museum]* is NP1x= — we have seen (§§ 3.51, 3.53) that a museum is not an "organization" for the purpose of applying the NP1j or NNJ. . . tags. *GATT* (*General Agreement on Tariffs and Trade*) is NP1x. *SALT* stands for *Strategic Arms Limitation Talks,* so one might expect it to be tagged NP2x; however, in practice it seemed always to be used (when current) in contexts such as *the SALT talks,* therefore it is instead tagged JB. The string *SOS* (historically not an acronym, though often supposed to stand for *save our souls*) is tagged NP1z.

§ 3.100   When an acronym stands for words that do not form a phrase with head and modifiers, but, say, a whole clause, it is impossible to tag in terms of the tag appropriate to the head word, and one must choose a tag in terms of the functioning of the acronym in the contexts in which it is used. If the acronym represents an imperative or optative clause, it can be tagged VV0i; this tag is used for *PTO* (*please turn over*), *qv* (*quod vide*), *RIP* (*requiescat in pace*). However, *QED* abbreviates a declarative clause, *quod erat demonstrandum,* and is thus not grammatically equivalent to a verb alone (English declarative clauses need subject as well as verb), therefore *QED* is tagged UH. And *DIY* (*do it yourself*), *PAYE* (*pay as you earn*), though they look like commands when spelled out, function as descriptions of an activity and a tax-collection system, and are tagged NN1u.

§ 3.101   *COD* (*cash on delivery*) and *lbw* (*leg before wicket*) normally function adverbially and are tagged RR.

§ 3.102   A difficult acronym to tag is *HM*, standing for either *Her Majesty* or *Her Majesty's* (or, during other reigns, *His Majesty('s)*). In the non-genitive use, as in *HM the Queen, HM Queen Elizabeth II,* the tag NNS fits reasonably well (though few other NNS words can be followed by *the*). In the genitive use, it sometimes appears to form part of a title (e.g. *HM Inspector of Taxes*), but is often prefixed to non-personal terms (*HM Government*, *HM Prison*), functioning to change them from common nouns into proper names. No wordtag seems adequately to capture this behaviour; when standing for *Her Majesty's*, *HM* is tagged JB as a pis aller.

PERSONAL NAMES

§ 3.103   The tags NP1s (surname), NP1m and NP1f (male and female forenames), and NP1i (initial) are used for personal names, with pluralized forms of personal names being tagged NP2s NP2m NP2f respectively. NP1m and NP1f include names from classical and other cultures to which the forename/surname distinction does not apply: *Plato Isaiah* NP1m, *Ariadne* NP1f.[49] Forenames which are ambiguous with respect to sex, e.g. *Hilary* or *Evelyn*, or forenames from non-European cultures which do not always use distinctive forenames for the two sexes, are tagged by reference to the sex of their bearer (in *Hilary can be a boy's or a girl's name*, the tag would be NP1m in line with the general English-language convention that male is the "unmarked" sex). NP1s includes European noble or royal "dynastic" names which are not strictly surnames, such as *Bourbon* or *Ferrers* (Lord Ferrers's surname is Shirley), unless these are preceded by *of*: an *of*-phrase within a noble title, e.g. *of Clarendon* in *Earl of Clarendon*, is wordtagged and parsed as it would be in other contexts, ignoring the fact that it forms part of a personal name.[50] Non-English prefixes such as *de van von* within personal names are tagged NP1s: thus *Ludwig van Beethoven* is wordtagged NP1m NP1s NP1s (and no higher-level analysis is recognized within such a sequence).

§ 3.104   The term "forename" in the definitions of NP1m and NP1f refers to names bestowed on an individual, as opposed to inherited family surnames. In some cultures, e.g. in East Asia, "forenames" follow surnames and are commonly quoted in that order even when the name is used in an English context: the names *Mao Tse-tung, Nguyen van Lam* are respectively tagged NP1s NP1m, NP1s NP1m NP1m. Americans make heavy use of what are etymologically surnames as male forenames (*Brooks Creighton*

---

[49] Roman nomina and cognomina (e.g. *Lucretius, Caesar*) are both NP1s.

[50] A case such as *Safavids* G05:0140, referring via the *-id* suffix to the descendants of an individual royal ancestor, Saifu, is treated as a common noun: no individual bore *Safavid* as a name.

Heywood Mayer Munroe Richardson Sheldon and many others occur in the SUSANNE Corpus in contexts which make their function as forenames unmistakable); in this use such names are tagged NP1m rather than NP1s.

§ 3.105   As explained in § 3.24, the SUSANNE rule is that a person is treated as the "original bearer" of his names; thus a girl's name *Prudence White* is tagged NP1f NP1s, not NN1u JJ. This contrasts with the general SUSANNE practice for wordtagging names, which is to trace back through a chain of entities named after one another until reaching either the first entity to bear the name (if it was coined as a name), or a non-proper use of the word, where-upon the tag appropriate to this original use is applied to subse-quent bearers of the name. In effect, the personal-name rule means that the process of constructing such chains backwards from a taggable instance of a name halts if it reaches a person.

§ 3.106   For this purpose one must be precise about what counts as a person, and what counts as a name.

§ 3.107   "Persons" are not restricted to human beings: a god's name (e.g. *Zeus Kali*), the name of an animal presented in human terms in a children's story, or the name of an extraterrestrial alien in science fiction will be tagged NP1m or NP1f as appropriate.[51] On the other hand animal names in normal circumstances are not treated as personal names: the racehorse *Foinaven* was named after a mountain, so this name is tagged NP1g. As a test of whether an entity named in a text is sufficiently person-like for the rule about personal names to apply, one can go by the use of *who* rather than *which* as relative pronoun.[52]

§ 3.108   The name *God* is treated as a capitalized version of the common noun *god*, and both variants are tagged NNS1c.

§ 3.109   There is a cline between formal names of persons, and descriptive epithets not perceived or tagged as names; the border-line lies in the area of nicknames. The presumption is in favour of tagging nicknames as personal names, unless they are either signalled as nicknames by the use of inverted commas or brackets (*Merry* JJ in *"Merry" Sanders*), or are intrinsically implausible as "official" names, thus *Banjo_NN1n Ferguson* N15:0120; in *Lludd Silver-hand* (a Welsh mythical personage, J62.044) *Lludd* is tagged NP1m but *Silver-hand* is analysed as an appositional noun phrase divided into three words tagged NN1u YH NN1c. (An overtly

---

[51] In the case of sexless extraterrestrials one goes by the use of *he* or *she*; failing these cues the tag is NP1m.

[52] The criterion of *he/she* versus *it* would not be satisfactory in view of the use of the former for animals and *she* for ships, etc.

marked nickname will have an NP1m/f tag, if its only use is as a name: *Nobby* NP1m in *"Nobby" Clarke*. An informal distorted form of a forename, e.g. *Sally* for *Sarah*, will always be tagged as a forename.) A difficult case is *Red*: this is not a standard forename and sounds like a nickname referring to hair colour, yet it is usually printed without inverted commas in the name of the well-known fire engineer Red Adair, and it seems not impossible that it could be a name used for formal purposes. Therefore SUSANNE uses the NP1m tag in e.g. *The seventh man was Red Hogan, a wiry little puncher* ... N10:0950, though JJ in *between Reps. V.E. (Red) Berry and Joe Ratcliff* A02:0550.

FOREIGN NAMES

§ 3.110   The SUSANNE analytic scheme applies to the English language, and in general it treats words of foreign languages as meaningless symbols to be tagged by reference to their use in English. This means that, in the case of (non-personal) foreign names, the process of tracing their use back to an "original bearer" is limited to that portion of their total history since they were used in English. For instance, the name of the French town Tours means "towers" in French, and doubtless the town took its name from this sense; but, if so, the word's change of status from plural common noun to proper name of a town was a transaction that occurred outside the English-speaking community: the name *Tours* is wordtagged NP1t, whereas for instance *Plains*, Georgia, is tagged NNL2 since the development from common- to proper-noun status took place "within English". In the case of BATON ROUGE, LA. A08:1180, it happens that both of the French words *baton* and *rouge* have been separately borrowed into English with senses related to their respective French meanings "stick" and "red"; but the conversion of the phrase *baton rouge* "red stick" into a place-name was clearly a French-language transaction, so the town name is tagged NP1t NP1t.

§ 3.111   Similarly, although the renowned Florentine family name *Medici* is in Italian a plural noun, the SUSANNE system tags it as an ordinary singular surname, NP1s — the name *Catherine de' Medici* would be tagged NP1f NP1s NP1s. (In support of such an approach, note that English-speakers are liable to refer to this family as *the Medicis*.)

§ 3.112   Places which to an English-speaker are transparently named after people are given personal-name tags, irrespective of whether the use as a place-name was implemented by English-speakers or others — *St Louis*, Missouri, was named by Frenchmen but the tags are NNS NP1m. Because of their very frequent occurrence in place-names of the English-speaking world (and cf. *Santa Claus*) the words *San Santa* are deemed to count as NNS words like English *St*, so that the towns *San Jose*, *Santa Barbara* for instance are tagged NNS NP1m, NNS NP1f. On the other hand *Los Angeles* (Spanish "The Angels") is treated as a meaningless town name tagged NP1t NP1t. In the case of *Santa Cruz* (Spanish "Holy Cross"), exceptionally *Santa* does not translate "saint" and *Cruz* is not a personal name; the SUSANNE approach avoids delving into facts internal to other languages, so in this case it gives *Santa* the normal tag and treats *Cruz* as a town name, thus the tags are NNS NP1t. And note the case *St Petersburg* NNS NP1t, where the prefix remains separate but the saint's name has been merged with the *burg* element to yield a single word that is only a town rather than a personal name.

§ 3.113 Where names derive from languages associated with cultures that are alien to the English-speaking community, the boundaries around English are drawn relatively tightly for purposes of halting the process of tracing names back to original bearers. This is often relevant in the case of names derived from Amerindian languages. In the case of *Narragansett Electric Co.* A24:0750, for instance, the word *Narragansett* is one which occurs in many names associated with the Rhode Island area, and the application to a company is manifestly a derived use. SUSANNE wordtagging assumes that the original use of this name within English was as the name of Narragansett Bay, hence it is tagged NP1g in this use and in derived uses such as the company name. The bay in turn took its name from the Narraganset Indians (standardly spelled with a single *t*), now extinct or near-extinct. But it would be difficult to use this Amerindian ethnic reference as the basis for selecting a SUSANNE wordtag, because of ignorance about exactly what it applied to. The problem is not that the SUSANNE team in particular are ignorant in this area (although that is true), but that — regrettable though this may be — the English-speaking community in general tends to be largely ignorant of the nature of Amerindian sociopolitical groupings or institutions. Amerindian names with ethnic reference are probably perceived by the average English-speaker as terms, usually uninflectable, for tribe members, grammatically equivalent to *Swiss*. In some cases this may be so, but other cases are in reality more complex. *Iroquois*, for instance, refers to a confederation of six tribes, and was coined by French-speakers by adding the French adjectival suffix *-ois* to what is believed to be an imitation of a phrase frequently used for ritual purposes by members of the confederation. It would be very impractical to have to choose SUSANNE wordtags by reference to ethnological considerations of that order. Accordingly, except where the primary use of an Amerindian name in English is widely perceived, in areas of the English-speaking world distant from the homeland of the group in question, to be reference to an ethnic group (e.g. *Iroquois Sioux Cheyenne*) — in which case the name is tagged NNc or JJ depending on context, like *Swiss* — the SUSANNE approach is to tag the name by reference to the first entity within the cultural horizons of the English-speaking world to which the name was given. Names deriving from other exotic languages are treated similarly.

§ 3.114   Consider, as a difficult case of a contrasting type, the name *Israel*. To a present-day English-speaker this is primarily the name of a country; it also occurs, rarely, as a male forename (cf. the character Israel Hands in *Treasure Island*). But if one asks where the State of Israel ultimately derives its name from, the answer is clear: it comes from the occasion when God, appearing incognito in human form, wrestled with Jacob and then announced "Thy name shall be called no more Jacob, but Israel" (Genesis 32: 28) — meaning something like "God struggles". The ancient people and land of Israel were notionally Jacob's descendants and the territory inhabited by them, and the chain of developments whereby an Old Testament patriarch's name became the name of a twentieth-century State can hardly be regarded as foreign to the English-speaking world — indeed some of the people involved in creating the State of Israel in the 1940s were native speakers of English. Therefore, although the names of most countries are tagged NP1c, *Israel* must be tagged NP1m. (Fortunately, very few name tags will depend on circumstances as remote and exceptional as this.) It might of course be that modern scholarly research casts doubt on the historical reality of an individual called Jacob/Israel, but even if he can be proved to be mythical this would not be regarded as relevant for SUSANNE wordtagging, which is not intended to depend on specialist research in non-linguistic fields. For the English-speaking community in general, Genesis provides the "standard account" of the origin of the name *Israel*, hence this is what governs the tag assigned to all uses of that name.

§ 3.115   Difficulties can arise in tagging foreign names because of non-English grammar. The name *Pathet Lao* occurs in texts A04 and A07, referring to a Laotian political faction. Here *Lao* means "Laotian" and follows the noun in accordance with Laotian word-order rules; but it seems that the indigenous form *Lao* is quite often used within English texts as an alternative to *Laotian*, hence it is tagged as a meaningful word despite the non-English word-order, and *Pathet Lao* is NP1j JJ (rather than NP1j NP1j).

§ 3.116   It is fair to say that the SUSANNE approach to word-tagging non-English names, assuming as it does detailed knowledge of aspects of the cultural inheritance of the English-speaking world, such as the Bible, but no knowledge at all of independent cultures, and ignoring the meanings of non-proper words whenever these happen to belong to languages other than English, embodies a kind of Anglocentrism which may strike some as dated, even objectionable. But, although Anglocentrism as a general sociopolitical stance may be undesirable, as the basis of an analytical scheme for the English language it is appropriate and inevitable. The languages of the world are diverse, and each must be analysed in its own terms. Alternatives to the "Anglocentric" approach described here would repeatedly require words derived from other languages but found in English texts to be forced into an analytical framework in which they did not fit. It is that, surely, which would constitute a real failure of respect for other cultures.

MULTI-WORD NAMES

§ 3.117   A multi-word name is not tagged as an "idiom" (although see § 3.124), even if some or all of the words composing it have no other use: *Nova Scotia* NP1p NP1p, *Procol Harum* (a pop group) NP1j NP1j, *Pepsi-Cola* NP1x YH NN1u. Although etymologically the *Nova* of *Nova Scotia* is identical to the common noun *nova* in astronomy, as words of English the two are unrelated homographs — the name did not develop from the astronomical use or vice versa, both English uses were separately derived from Latin; on the other hand the name *Pepsi-Cola* was modelled on the analogy of *Coca-Cola*, formed from two common nouns for plants with edible leaves and nuts (and, since *Cola* at least is a recognizable word within *Pepsi-Cola*, the hyphenation is split).

§ 3.118   Where a derivational affix applies to one word of a multi-word name, the orthographic words are each tagged "in their own right" despite the fact that this conflicts with the logical structure of the phrase (cf. § 2.45): *a New Yorker* AT1 JJ NN1c, *Sri Lankan* NP1c JJ.

PROPER NAMES EMBEDDED IN FOREIGN WORDING

§ 3.119   The words of an extended foreign-language quotation, title, etc., are tagged FW, but if they include a proper name this will be tagged as it would be when occurring in an English-language context, provided the name might appear in the same form in a passage of English: . . . *entitled* <bital> les_FW *mystères*_FW *d'*_FW +*Isis*_NP1f <eital> +, . . . G44.095.

A foreign name which would normally be replaced in English by a conventional equivalent is tagged FW in its foreign form: a clear case occurs in the passage:

> the first act of <bital> Il Barbiere di Siviglia <eital> G43.184

where *Siviglia* is the Italian name for the Spanish town called *Seville* in English and *Sevilla* in Spanish. More debatable are cases of place-names within stretches of foreign wording which have distinct English equivalents but where the native rather than the Anglicized form is sometimes used in English (in recent decades it has become increasingly usual to retain native forms of place-names within English), e.g. *Lyon* for the French town whose English name is *Lyons*. In such cases the choice between FW and NP. . . must be made in terms of a judgement about how normal it would be in practice to find the form occurring in English.

ABBREVIATED NAMES

§ 3.120   An abbreviated proper name will often have a proper-name tag (because the abbreviation has no other use) while the unabbreviated name is tagged as a non-proper word. An example is the abbreviation *El* in *the El project, the El track* A09:0260, A09:0420, referring to the Frankford Elevated Railway. Written in full, *Elevated* in *Elevated Railway* is tagged VVNt, but *El* cannot act as a past participle and is tagged NP1j.[53]

§ 3.121   A subtler example is *the A's* A11:1350 for *the Athletics*, a Kansas City baseball team. The word *athletics* is tagged NN1ux, as an *-ics* noun having only the (singular) M use; *the Athletics* referring to a team represents a pluralization of the adjective *athletic*, hence it is tagged NN2, and this tag also applies to the abbreviation *A's*.

§ 3.122   Like any other name, an abbreviated name is tagged by reference to its original bearer even if it has become better known in a transferred use. Thus *ASDIC* is widely known as the name of a type of submarine-detection equipment and is used as such in:

---

[53] Contrast *A&M*, standing for *Agricultural and Mechanical* in the names of many American colleges: this can be used informally as the head of a naming expression, as in *A&M has the best defense against passes* A12:1780, but it can equally be used descriptively, as in *these institutions having previously been A&M colleges* G17:1670, hence *A&M* is tagged JB in all environments.

*The spy ring also was particularly interested in ASDIC, the under-
water equipment for detecting submarines . . .* A20:1020

— but the original use of *ASDIC* was as an acronym for the Allied
Submarine Detection Investigation Committee, hence *ASDIC* is
wordtagged NP1j as the name of a committee even in the context
quoted.

§ **3.123** The rule of § 3.65, according to which abbreviations
not displaying distinctive grammatical behaviour receive the same
tags as the corresponding full forms, sometimes yields counterintuitive
results. In *the twenty-first annual K. of C. Games* A11:1700 the
abbreviation *K. of C.* stands for *Knights of Columbus,* and is tagged
NNS2 IO NP1i (and parsed as including a prepositional phrase).
The word *C.* is an initial representing a personal name, hence falls
under the definition of NP1i. However, *K.* does not regularly represent *Knights* other than in this phrase, so there is no independent
basis for assigning a wordtag to this abbreviation: it must be tagged
NNS2, although it is quite unusual for a single initial letter to be
tagged as a plural.

§ **3.124** Acronyms represent the sole exception to the rule that
multi-word names are tagged as sequences of separate words rather
than as grammatical idioms. English typographical practice varies
very freely between omitting and including spaces in acronyms such
as *US, U.S., U. S.* for *United States;* the SUSANNE Corpus includes
both forms *B.&O., B. & O.* for *Baltimore & Ohio (Railroad)* within
one text (A19). Accordingly, although presence of a space is a sufficient condition for splitting a form across multiple Corpus lines,
so that *B. & O.,* with spaces, is treated as three taggable words,
whenever such an acronym is of a kind which might alternatively
within standard typographical conventions be written solid, the
version with spaces is treated as a grammatical idiom: *B. & O.* is
tagmatagged NP1j=, with the individual words tagged NP1j31
NP1j32 NP1j33 (*&* is not tagged CC within an acronym treated as
an idiom). Likewise *US, U.S.* are NP1c (whether used in nominal or
adjectival contexts), and *U. S.* is NP1c= (whereas *United States*
written in full is tagmatagged as a plural proper noun phrase, Nnp).
But *&* and some other special symbols are the only words liable to
occur in full in acronyms written solid. The option of tagging *K. of
C.* (see above) as an idiom does not exist, since it would be quite
unconventional to write such an abbreviation solid as **KofC.*[54]

---

[54] *IOU* is tagged NN1c, and if written with spaces would be tagmatagged NN1c=. Even
a publication which includes abbreviatory stops is unlikely to distinguish the *I,* as an entire
word, from the *O* as an initial or the *U* as a phonetic imitation.

COUNTRIES AND PROVINCES

§ 3.125 The tag NP1c applies to names of countries: territories which are sovereign States, or which are perceived to be the homes of individual nations. Thus e.g. *USSR Ukraine Tibet UK Scotland England* are all tagged NP1c. We have seen that by the general SUSANNE nametagging rules *Israel* is tagged NP1m rather than NP1c, and similarly the African State *Niger*, being named after a river, is tagged NP1g; but most "countries" in the ordinary sense will take NP1c. Note that e.g. *China Turkey* are NP1c, since the common nouns *china turkey* derive from the country names rather than *vice versa*. *America* was originally the name of a continent, and the colloquial use to refer to the United States of America in particular is derivative from this, hence *America* is NP1g in either use.

§ 3.126 Sovereignty is a very slippery concept — the range of sovereign States in the world has changed greatly during the years of the SUSANNE project; and the application of the tag NP1c is not intended to depend on fine judgements about political status. Within the British Isles, for instance, Guernsey and the Isle of Man enjoy a considerable measure of independence, whereas England as part of the UK has none at all; nevertheless English-speakers regard England, but not Man or Guernsey, as a "country", and accordingly *England* is NP1c but *Man*[55] (or the acronym *I.o.M.*) and *Guernsey* are NP1p, as "provinces" of the British Isles.[56] Texas was an independent republic from 1836 to 1845, but from the viewpoint of a present-day English-speaker the overwhelming majority of associations with the place-name *Texas* are with Texas as a state of the USA, therefore *Texas* is tagged NP1p (even in the context of a historical reference to the Republic of Texas). At the time of writing it is debatable whether the member States of the European Community (now European Union) ought to be regarded as having surrendered their sovereignty to the supranational body, and in fifty years' time it may well be that the acronym *EU* for *European Union* will naturally be tagged NP1c, but with respect to current perceptions in the English-speaking world the European Community or European Union is an organization composed of separate countries, and *EC, EU* are tagged NP1j.

---

[55] The name of the Isle of Man has no etymological connection with *man* as human being.

[56] An attempt to render objective the criteria for "country" status might run as follows: association with a distinct nation, or full political sovereignty, are each sufficient conditions, and if neither obtains then the political dependence must be on a distant rather than adjacent State, and the territory must be at least comparable in area with an average European State. This would yield NP1c tags for e.g. *Singapore* or *Nauru*, and would have made e.g. *Kenya Nigeria Burma* NP1c even without decolonization, but leaves e.g. *Hong Kong* as NP1p NP1p.

To summarize: since place-names are tagged by reference to their original bearer, any territory name which was derived from the name of some other kind of entity is tagged by reference to that entity; but, where the first English use of the name was to refer to the territory, it is given an NP... subcategory by reference to the status chiefly associated with that territory by English-speakers at the present time (irrespective of whether the text reference is contemporary or historical).

Where a current political unit coincides with a territory which forms a natural geographical unit, such as an island or archipelago, and has a name which can be seen as naming either the political or the geographical unit, the "political" wordtags apply: *Philippines* is NP2c, *Wight* NP1p, rather than ...g in either case.

§ 3.127 A problem arises with extinct territory names, particularly those dating from periods before the concept of the nation-state was established, such as *Judea*. Such names will normally be tagged as miscellaneous geographical names, NP1g.

§ 3.128 The tag NP1p, "province", was created primarily in order to provide a distinctive classification for the grammatically significant class of words that are liable to appear (commonly in abbreviated form) following a town name after a comma, to give a more specific indication of location, for instance in a postal address: *Cleveland, OH*; *Malvern, Worcs.* (cf. § 3.5). Thus names tagged NP1p will normally be recognized territorial divisions of the next-lower "rank" below countries; but the tag is used for territory names which are suffixed to town names in the way described whether or not they are of this rank (an NP1p will not necessarily correspond to a political subdivision at all, thus *L.I.* for *Long Island* is NP1p). Paradigm cases of NP1p words will be names of US states and UK (pre- and post-1974) counties, in so far as the rule on tagging by original bearer does not imply a different tag for individual cases (for instance the state of *Ohio* and the post-1974 English county of *Avon* are named after rivers and accordingly are tagged NP1g). Even when a "province" name written in full takes a tag other than NP1p, its conventional abbreviation will normally be used exclusively to refer to the province and hence will be tagged NP1p — thus *New Mexico* is JJ NP1c, but *N.M.* or *NM* is NP1p.[57] Occasionally more than one "rank" of territorial divisions may appropriately be given the NP1p tag; for instance a letter to the Channel Islands might be addressed either to, say, *St Peter Port, Guernsey*,

---

[57] A special case is the occasional use of *N.Y.* to refer to New York City rather than State. Since there is no particular reason to regard either use of the abbreviation as derived from the other use, *N.Y.* is tagged either NP1p or NP1t according to its reference in context.

or to *St Peter Port, Guernsey, C.I.,* where both *Guernsey* and *C.I.* (for *Channel Islands*) are tagged NP1p.

§ 3.129   As a case-study in how the SUSANNE rules for tagging proper names work out in practice, we now examine the tagging of the names of the states of the USA, a set of names which recur frequently in the SUSANNE Corpus.

§ 3.130   Where a name was coined to refer to the territory in question, or has no other reference in English, the tag is straight-forwardly NP1p. This applies to *Arizona Columbia* (in *District of Columbia*) *Florida Georgia Idaho Indiana Louisiana Maryland Montana Nebraska Oklahoma Oregon Pennsylvania Texas Vermont Virginia*; and *North Carolina, South Carolina, West Virginia* are ND1 NP1p.

§ 3.131   A number of states are named after rivers (some of whose names in turn derive from Amerindian ethnic references, see § 3.113) and their names are accordingly tagged NP1g: *Alabama Arkansas Colorado Connecticut Illinois Iowa Kansas Minnesota Mississippi Missouri Ohio Tennessee Wisconsin*. NP1g tags relate to other geographical features in the cases of *Alaska* (peninsula), *Hawaii* (island), *Kentucky* (plain), *Massachusetts* (bay), *Michigan* (lake), *Utah* (lake), *Wyoming* (valley).

§ 3.132   In the case of *California* it is debatable whether the name should be regarded as originally applying to the territory, or to the peninsula forming the present-day Mexican state of Baja California, but SUSANNE practice is to tag *California* NP1p. *Maine* is named after a province of France, and is thus NP1p by derivation. *Nevada* takes its name from the Sierra Nevada (Spanish "snowy range"), but *Nevada* as a separate name can stand only for the state rather than the range and is again NP1p.

§ 3.133   *New Hampshire, New Jersey, New Mexico, New York* are respectively JJ NP1p (Hampshire, English county), JJ NP1p (Jersey, semi-autonomous Channel Island), JJ NP1c (Mexico, sovereign State), and JJ NP1t (York, English city). *Rhode Island* is named after a small island within the state (and this island in turn derives its name from Rhodes in Greece, but the name without *-s* appears to be used in English only for the American reference), thus *Rhode Island* is NP1g NNL1c.

§ 3.134   *Dakota* is a problematic case. The word means "confederated", and described the Sioux Confederation, but the general approach to Amerindian names discourages one from taking this into account. There was a Dakota River, renamed the James River, but it is not clear whether the territory was named after the river or vice versa, or whether both were separately named after the Amerindian reference. The SUSANNE choice is to tag *North Dakota, South Dakota* ND1 NP1p.

§ 3.135 Finally, *Delaware* is named after Thomas West, 3rd/ 12th Baron De La Warr or Delaware, i.e. this name is a noble dynastic name, and *Washington* is named after George Washington; hence these two names are tagged NP1s. (George Washington's family derived their surname from the village of Washington in co. Durham, but by § 3.24 this has no relevance for wordtagging.)

§ 3.136 Some readers may find it inappropriate or silly for an analytic scheme oriented towards the processing of modern English for information-technology purposes to depend so heavily in one area on issues relating to past history. (This feature of the SUSANNE scheme is particularly salient in connection with American English; in Britain it is true to a large extent that a place-name is only a place-name, but in recently colonized parts of the English-speaking world such as the USA it is very common for places to be named after people or things.) However, the SUSANNE team began their task assuming that the appropriate scheme for categorizing proper names would be by actual referent of the token in context: they found themselves driven to the alternative system described here, of tagging names by historical origin, because the more obvious approach proved unworkable in practice. Under the historical tagging system, there is normally a rather clear-cut answer to questions about the correct tagging of particular names, though in some cases it requires considerable enquiry to establish what that answer is. Under the system of tagging by current reference in context, it appeared that analysts were frequently put in the position of having to ask questions which have no correct answers even in principle. It is a cardinal axiom of the SUSANNE project that it is more important for a standard analytic scheme to prescribe a definite, unequivocal analysis for any particular linguistic form, than for the prescribed analysis always to be one which seems intuitively appealing.

§ 3.137 That said, the SUSANNE team cannot pretend that wordtags for names in the Corpus are invariably correct in terms of the SUSANNE scheme. In the case of names as important as those of the American states, it is worthwhile to put effort into establishing the correct tags, and reference books which enable this to be done are reasonably accessible. On the other hand, where a story in a small-town newspaper mentions some institution name or place-name of purely local interest, it would have needed resources far beyond those available to the SUSANNE project to discover what the true history of the name was. In such cases, analysts were instructed to guess whether the name was originally a surname, town name, etc., and to tag accordingly, using whatever clues were offered by the context together with general knowledge of American culture and history. (The researcher chiefly involved was herself North American.) Since the only ways that tagging of obscure names in the SUSANNE Corpus is likely to be exploited in practice are statistical, this limitation on the accuracy of the Corpus should not significantly affect its usefulness.

□ 4 □
SURFACE GRAMMAR

Grammatical versus Semantic Constituency

§ **4.1**   The rules for drawing trees and labelling their nodes which comprise the following chapters are designed, first, to yield analyses that are consistent and as uncontroversial as possible from a linguistic point of view; as a secondary matter, within the range of alternatives allowable (given the differences of opinion that exist among English linguists), the scheme chooses analyses that do not cause unnecessary difficulties for the kinds of corpus-based natural language processing techniques with which the scheme's creators have also been involved.

§ **4.2**   Certain general principles follow.

§ **4.3**   Where grammar and sense or pragmatics suggest alternative analyses of a sequence, the SUSANNE scheme tends to follow the former, despite the fact that the semantic analysis may be embodied in spoken stress patterns and phonetic reductions, some of which are reflected orthographically; and where the intended sense of an expression used figuratively suggests a grammatical analysis different from that of its literal sense, the SUSANNE analysis normally follows the literal sense.

§ **4.4**   For instance, the figurative turn of phrase *he's pushing fifty* means that he is near fifty; thinking of the intended meaning of the words one might take *pushing fifty* as a tagma parallel to the prepositional phrase *near fifty*, and phonetically the item *+'s* groups with *he* rather than with *pushing*. In terms of the grammar of its literal interpretation, though, the sequence is parallel to *he is eating porage*; the SUSANNE scheme treats *+'s pushing*, not *he's* or *pushing fifty*, as a tagma (*+'s pushing* is classed as a verb group, V). Some further examples:

> *provided it* [*+'s not*] *too cold* A39.183 — not *it's* [*not too cold*]
> *It is* [R *all*] [J *very well*] [Ti *to scoff at . . .*] G34.163 — not
>   *It is* [*all very well*] . . .
> *Yet they* [Vde *didn't do*] [R *at_all*] [R *badly*]. E17.050 — no
>   attempt to register *not at all* as a logical unit

That will [Vsep *wasn't made*] [Fa *until after I'd gone away*]!
L22.163 — no attempt to register *not until* as a logical unit
Clr. Brook [Vd *saw*] [P *to it*] [Fn *that certain minimum standards were conformed with*] A30.053 — the sequence *saw to
it*, which is treated as separate words rather than as an idiom
(cf. § 3.61), is not treated as a logical unit

§ 4.5   With prepositional verbs, the preposition is associated with
a following nominal element, logically the object of the verb, within
a prepositional-phrase tagma:

I came [P *across* [Ns *a praying mantis on a blackberry leaf*] P]
E07.066 — not ... [*came across*] ...
... *it is only common sense to look* [P *after it*] *properly* E03.044
— not ... [*look after*] ...

With phrasal verbs, the particle is parsed as an adverb phrase, IC
of the clause:

He [Vdc *could always turn*] [R *on*] [Ns *the charm*] L01.014 —
not ... [*turn on*] ... (nor ... [*on the charm*] ...)

(For the distinction between "prepositional verbs" such as *look after*
and "phrasal verbs" such as *turn on*, cf. the particle-postposing
diagnostic: *he turned it on* v. **he looked them after*.)
§ 4.6   The idiomatic construction *come/go/try and* Verb is analysed as co-ordinated clauses:

... *I want* [Ti *to try* [Ti+ *and find properties that don't concern
me directly*]]. E11.155
"[S *I might go* [S+ *and see Pete*]]." K25.194
He said he hoped [Fn *I'd come* [Fn+ *and take a look at her*] *when
he got her all proper and laid out* Fn]. G10.163

§ 4.7   A polite request of the form *Could you please tell me* ...
F12.121 is tagged as an interrogative clause, not an imperative
clause.
§ 4.8   Some respects in which the surface-grammar annotation
scheme fails to represent the semantics of English constructions are
made up for by the logical-grammar annotation system to be set out
in Chapter 5. But the cases described above are chosen as ones
where the SUSANNE scheme as a whole represents only the grammatical structure of English, rather than its sense. Any linguistic
annotation scheme must have its limits, and this is one for the present scheme.

§ 4.9 Where some linguists would see a construction as produced by concatenation while others see it as produced by recursion, the SUSANNE scheme adopts the former approach; for instance *Two sprightly elderly ladies* C09.190 is parsed as a noun phrase with four ICs, rather than as:

[*Two* [*sprightly* [*elderly* [*ladies*]]]]

(The type of analysis preferred by the SUSANNE scheme is described by Winograd (1983: 198) as characteristic of transition-network models of natural language, as opposed to production-rule models.) Thus, in a SUSANNE tagma with more than two ICs, one can think of the sequence of constituents as grouping always towards the head — that is, for most constructions, to the right; if a pair of constituents before the end of a sequence having its head at the right grouped together logically, they would be given a node of their own and would thus form a single IC of the higher tagma. Similarly, where a construction involves multiple postmodifiers following a head, these are understood as grouping to the left; in:

a lot of [*guys* [*I know*] [*who have moved past the 2-score-year milestone*]] A13:1100

the SUSANNE analysis includes no structure formally marking the fact that the first relative clause coheres more closely with *guys* than does the second.

§ 4.10 The preference for concatenation rather than recursion does not mean that analyses in which a node has the same formal category label as one of its own daughter nodes are never allowed. In some cases such "endocentric" analyses are the only reasonable way to represent the situation. For instance, there are cases of adverbial clause, Fa, consisting of subordinating conjunction followed by adverbial clause:

The men remained at their homesteads [Fa *except* [Fa *when they were required for military service* ...]] J22.039
The heel ... *remaining in contact with the floor,* [Fa *until* [Fa *after the second step is positioned*]]. E13.187

and cases of prepositional phrase, P, consisting of preposition followed by prepositional phrase:

to sell direct to the public on [Np *certain conditions,* [P *such_as_II= [P *after a proper introduction by a retailer*]]] F41.158
practically no new houses have been built for letting [P *except* [Pb *by public bodies*]] ... E28.062

But there is a presumption against this situation. Where the analysis of a linguistic form is debatable, that structure is chosen which avoids the need to posit like-formtagged mother and head daughter. Thus, in a sequence such as *a far more terrible price* G74.024 one might see *far more terrible* as an adjective phrase consisting of an adjective phrase *more terrible* modified by *far* (note that *more terrible* could be replaced by *higher*); but the SUSANNE scheme treats *far more terrible* as a phrase with three ICs. Or again, in the phrase:

all but a tiny minority of their military advisers J57.176

there are in principle three conceivable constituency structures:

1. [*all* [*but a tiny minority* [*of their military advisers*]]]
2. [[*all* [*but a tiny minority*]] *of their military advisers*]
3. [*all* [*but a tiny minority*] [*of their military advisers*]]

Structure (1) is taken to be excluded on semantic grounds (what is meant is not "all persons, excluding a few military advisers", but rather "all military advisers, excluding a few"). Structures (2) and (3) are both semantically reasonable; but (2) involves positing a determiner phrase *all but a tiny minority* which would be an IC of the larger determiner phrase including all nine words. Therefore the SUSANNE analysis is (3), in which sister prepositional phrases each modify the head determiner *all*. The concatenative analysis is used even in cases where one modifier belongs with the head as a fixed formula while another is attached by a productive construction:

... [Nns+ *and Joan* [Po *of Arc*] [P *on a gilded statue,* ...]] L20.134

§ **4.11**   Likewise, one or more sentence-adverbial elements at the beginning of a sentence are treated as ICs of the main clause (S), rather than as left sisters of nested S nodes:

[S [R *Consequently*], [P *at the end of April 1835*], [Nns *Anglesey*] ... [Vd *arrived*] [P *within hailing distance of the great Hahnemann himself* S]. G06.096

— not: [S [R *Consequently*], [S [P *at the end* ...], [S *Anglesey* ... *arrived* ... S] S] S].

Paragraph Division

§ **4.12**   Any text is treated as a series of "paragraphs" separated by "headings". A "paragraph" normally coincides with an ordinary typographic paragraph; a "heading" may consist of actual verbal material, or may be merely a typographic paragraph-division (symbolized

<*minbrk*> in the SUSANNE word field). The structure of each paragraph or heading is a labelled tree with a unique root node, and with a leaf node, labelled with a wordtag, for each SUSANNE word or "ghost" (the term used for the structural element marking the logical position of a constituent which has been shifted elsewhere, or deleted, in the surface grammatical structure, cf. §§ 5.4 ff.) — that is, a leaf node for each line of the Corpus. There will commonly be many intermediate labelled nodes.

§ 4.13 The usual approach within the linguistic tradition is to assign trees to individual sentences rather than to paragraphs. For SUSANNE purposes this would be impractical. The texts contain many cases where a sequence of two or more grammatically and typographically independent sentences is included as a direct quotation within a higher sentence; that is, in general sentence units are organized not sequentially but hierarchically. Also, boundaries between sentences are not always clear-cut in practice. SUSANNE analyses must often impose decisions in cases where the true structure is intrinsically vague, but it would be unfortunate for an issue as fundamental as the placement of boundaries between successive parsetrees to depend on grammatical choices which are often blurred.

§ 4.14 Accordingly, the text segments which are assigned individual parsetrees in the SUSANNE Corpus normally correspond to paragraphs in the typographic sense. Specifically, the text segments to be assigned parsetrees are determined as follows: a major or minor break symbol (cf. § 2.21) is given a one-leaf tree of its own, and a pair of begin-heading and end-heading symbols (ibid.) are treated as the first and last leaves of a tree dominating the heading, with the consequence that passages preceding and following a break or heading are assigned to separate trees; except that no boundary between trees is created in a position which divides a single sentence. Individual sentence structures are never divided between trees; and no further segmentation is introduced beyond what is required by the occurrence of break and heading-boundary symbols.

§ 4.15 The root node of a SUSANNE tree is labelled O, or Oh if the tree dominates a heading or break symbol.

§ 4.16 In texts consisting of moderately long paragraphs, tree structures immediately below O nodes will be relatively broad and flat by comparison with structures found lower in trees: an O will have a daughter sequence such as:

S YF S YF S YF S YF S YF

— where S represents the category "main clause" (including clauses subordinate to it, i.e. in effect "sentence"), and YF is the full-stop wordtag.

§ **4.17** An Oh root, on the other hand, will commonly dominate either a single daughter wordtagged YB, in the case of a text break without a heading, or, in the case of a heading, a sequence of three daughters of which the first and last will be labelled with the wordtags YBL, YBR, and the second will carry a wordtag or grammatical category label such as N (noun phrase) indicating the overall grammatical category of the heading, and will dominate a subtree giving the internal structure of the heading. There is no requirement that words forming a heading must be analysed as a single tagma (cf. § 4.394), but most commonly headings do comprise sequences analysed by SUSANNE rules as single tagmas.

§ **4.18** The formtags O, Oh appear only on root nodes of SUSANNE parsetrees. The rule in § 4.14 requiring single grammatical sentences always to be contained within single parsetrees means that in complex prose styles there may sometimes be typographic paragraph-breaks, and/or elements categorized in the Brown Corpus as "headings", medially within the text material dominated by a single tree. In such a case the *<minbrk>* symbol or heading is dominated by a node labelled I (interpolation) rather than Oh. Thus, consider the following passage:

> [S *On other matters, the jury recommended* [Fn% [Fn%& *that:* [I *<bminhd>* (1)_MCb *<eminhd>* I] *Four additional deputies be employed at the Fulton County Jail* [Fn%+ *and "a doctor, medical intern or extern be employed for night and weekend duty at the jail"* Fn%+] Fn%&]. [Fn– [I *<bminhd>* (2)_MCb *<eminhd>* I] *Fulton legislators "work with city officials to pass enabling legislation that will permit the establishment of a fair and equitable" pension plan for city employes* Fn–] Fn%] S]. A01:0580

The sequences headed *(1)* and *(2)* are all grammatically part of the nominal clause introduced by *that*, which is object of the verb *recommended*. Accordingly, the whole of the material displayed above is assigned a single parsetree analysing it as one main clause (S) followed by the closing full stop, with the S node dominating a series of daughters among which the last, labelled Fn (nominal clause), dominates everything from *that:* to *employes* and has the full stop which immediately precedes the second heading as one of its own daughters. Again, in the following passage the typographic sentence introduced by *Yes* is grammatically part of the preceding sentence, so is parsed as part of the same O tagma, with the intervening typographic paragraph-break analysed as an I:

[S+ *But there surely can be no doubt about the slender southpaw* *belonging* [P *with the all-time great lefthanders in the game's* *history.* [I <minbrk>] Yes_UH, [P@ *with Bob Grove, Carl* *Hubbell,* . . . *et al* P@] P] S+]. A13:1150

If a passage of direct speech is introduced by quoting material such as *X stated:* followed by multiple typographic paragraphs, the question whether the quoted material as a whole should be regarded as grammatically subordinate to the quoting clause is likely not to have a very clear-cut answer, and the decision is made by reference to punctuation. If the sequence of quoted paragraphs are as a whole surrounded by a single pair of inverted commas, then the material between opening and closing inverted commas is analysed as a Q (direct quotation) within which the typographic paragraph-breaks are I's (cf. § 4.428). If on the other hand the successive paragraphs of such a quotation each have their own opening and closing inverted commas, they will be treated as separate Q's, of which only the first is analysed as subordinate to the *X stated* clause:

[O [S *X stated:* "[Q S YF S YF S YF]" S] O] [Oh <minbrk> Oh] [O "[Q S YF S YF]" O] [Oh <minbrk> Oh] [O "[Q S YF S YF S YF]" O]

(For the case where successive quoted paragraphs are introduced but not terminated by inverted commas, see § 4.412.)

For texts embodying particularly elaborate formatting conventions, perhaps including some legal prose, the SUSANNE approach under which paragraphs are sequential items, with occasional subordinate paragraph-breaks and headings being analysed as "interpolations", would probably not be adequate. Such texts might demand an analytic scheme which recognized a concept of paragraphs nested within paragraphs. However, the Brown and LOB Corpora do not offer suitable test-beds for a scheme elaborated along these lines. For the genres of written material represented in these resources, the approach defined here works, and a subtler scheme might force the analyst to answer a series of pseudo-questions.

§ 4.19 The fact that typographic paragraph-breaks can sometimes be included within the material dominated by a single parsetree, and that most headings and paragraph-breaks are given parsetrees of their own, means that the choice of the term "paragraph" to refer to the stretches of Corpus text associated with individual parsetrees is not an altogether happy one. But it seems unlikely that any simple term could be found which was thoroughly suitable for this rather disparate class of text segments; and most of the segments dominated by O rather than Oh roots will in fact coincide with paragraphs in the ordinary typographic sense. The term has the merit of reminding the reader that in the SUSANNE analytic scheme, contrary to what is otherwise a near-universal practice in linguistics, stretches of text assigned single parsetrees will standardly comprise a number of independent grammatical sentences.

§ 4.20   Although most "paragraphs" with O roots will coincide with typographic paragraphs, it should be noted that the first and last SUSANNE paragraph of each text will commonly *not* amount to a full typographic paragraph. This is an unavoidable consequence of the way the original Brown Corpus was constructed. Beginning and end points for excerpting Brown texts from books and other sources were chosen by locating the nearest sentence boundary to a randomly selected word, ignoring the question of whether this was also a paragraph boundary. In some cases the sentence boundary will by chance have been a paragraph boundary also, but this information was not always included in the Brown Corpus (cf. § 2.21) and cannot be included in the SUSANNE Corpus when it is not recorded in Brown. Any use of the SUSANNE Corpus for research on paragraph structure would need to discard the first "paragraph" of each text, where this has a root labelled O rather than Oh, and the last paragraph of every text.[1]

Node-Labels

§ 4.21   A leaf node is always labelled with one of the wordtags listed in § 3.73, or with an idiomtag formed by suffixing a pair of digits to one of those tags. A non-terminal node-label has a tag containing up to three types of information: a *formtag*, a *functiontag*, and an *index*, in that order. In a label containing a formtag and one or both of the other two elements, a colon separates the formtag from the other elements (and colons are used for no other purpose in SUSANNE node-labels). A functiontag is always a single alphabetic character, and an index is a sequence of three digits. Restrictions on valid combinations of elements within a node-label mean that complex labels can always be unambiguously decomposed into their elements: if a non-terminal node-label contains no colon, then it is a formtag unless it fits one of the two patterns *addd* or *ddd*

---

[1] This point may also apply internally to some of the Category A texts, which, because newspaper reports are often less than 2,000 words long, consist of sets of passages representing separate reports. (Details on the boundaries between successive extracts are included in the information about sources of individual texts given in *BCUM*.)

(*a* = alphabetic character, *d* = digit), in which case it consists of functiontag + index, or index alone, respectively. No node-label may consist solely of a functiontag.

§ 4.22   A formtag identifies the internal properties of the word or tagma associated with the node bearing the tag. Formtags are classified into *wordtags*, which occur on leaf nodes, and *tagmatags*, which occur as the formtag element within non-terminal node-labels. Wordtags were discussed in Chapter 3; the system of tagmatags will be discussed in detail in the remainder of the present chapter.

Functiontags and indices relate to logical as opposed to surface grammar. The system for annotating logical grammar is defined in detail in Chapter 5, but it will be convenient to give a very brief sketch here. The SUSANNE scheme assumes that logical grammar can be specified in terms of roles (e.g. subject, time adjunct) which constituents play within tagmas. In many cases (e.g. most constituents of phrases) the formal nature of a constituent itself sufficiently identifies its logical role within its tagma, and in these cases the constituent label includes nothing more than a formtag. In other cases, the logical role is shown by supplementing the formtag with a functiontag, drawn from a list given in § 5.19 below. Furthermore, in cases the set of constituents having logical roles in a tagma is not identical to the set of that tagma's surface constituents, and such disparities are indicated by means of so-called *ghost* and *guest* nodes. When an item playing a logical role in a tagma is not physically realized within that tagma, it is represented there by a terminal node associated with no verbal material, labelled with a special wordtag YG, and immediately dominated by a one-daughter non-terminal node whose label lacks a formtag: a "ghost node". If an item occurs in surface grammar as a constituent of a tagma within which it plays no logical role, it is functiontagged as "surface subject" or "surface object" if it plays one of these grammatical roles, and otherwise is treated as a "guest node", indicated by a special functiontag :G. Pairs of identical index numbers are used to show which ghost constituents correspond to which guest or other *full* (non-ghost) constituents; and, where appropriate, ghost nodes also carry functiontags showing the logical role of the missing items within the tagmas to which they logically belong.[2]

---

[2] The term *trace* is used by some theoretical linguists in more or less the same sense as the SUSANNE term "ghost node". However, when documentation accompanying the initial release of the SUSANNE Corpus used the term "trace" in order to avoid unnecessary multiplication of technical terms, this was perceived as committing the SUSANNE analytic scheme to a specific theoretical position within the spectrum of rival linguistic theories. No such theoretical commitment is intended (cf. § 5.3); so it has seemed best in the present work to retain the "ghost" and "guest" terminology which was actually used by the SUSANNE team.

Included Adverbials

§ 4.23 Although the general treatment of discontinuous and dislocated grammatical elements is left to Chapter 5, one particular point merits explanation at this stage. It is a characteristic of English that elements functioning adverbially have great freedom of movement and are often inserted within other tagmas. The SUSANNE scheme accordingly allows an adverbial element to be parsed as an IC of any tagma within which it occurs medially; when the adverbial element is logically a sister (or aunt, etc.) rather than daughter of the tagma within which it occurs, the logical-annotation system will show this, but the point relevant here is that the SUSANNE scheme prefers, other things being equal, to analyse an adverbial element as having been moved into the middle of a tagma to which it does not logically belong, than to treat that tagma as discontinuous, having part of itself broken off and shifted to the far side of the adverbial element. (This point relates only to adverbials which are medial within a higher tagma — there would be no purpose in counter-logically attaching an adverbial element to another tagma as first or last daughter, since no discontinuity would thereby be avoided.[3]) For the purposes of this principle, an "element functioning adverbially" may be an adverb or adverb phrase, but may equally be a prepositional phrase, an adverbial clause, a present-participle clause, the word *not*, or indeed any constituent fulfilling an adverbial function (in terms of Chapter 5, an "adjunct" function), irrespective of whether it belongs to a formal category which regularly fulfils such functions. Some examples of "included adverbials" are:

[Vf *have* [R *long since*] *segregated*] G17:1790
[Vip *to* [R *first*] *be given*] A01:1450
[Vgfb *having* [R *previously*] *been*] G17:1670
. . . *it would be* [Jh *subject* [P *like the brain*] *to the law of* . . .
Jh] D14.079

---

[3] There is one ad hoc exception to the rule that an adverbial is not included as a daughter of a logically separate tagma to which it is adjacent: if an adverbial is adjacent to one conjunct of a co-ordination, and applies only to that conjunct rather than to the entire co-ordination, it is parsed as within the co-ordination — which means that if the co-ordination as a whole is immediately followed by an adverbial applying to its last conjunct, this is treated as an included adverbial within the co-ordination despite not being medial to it:

. . . *embraced* [N [NN1u& <bital> *kunst* <eital> [NN1u+ *and* <bital> *list* <eital>]], [Ds+ *and much else*] [R *besides*] N] J35.046

— *besides* is logically a sister to *and much else*, and is therefore treated as a daughter of the N co-ordination. This special and unsatisfactory rule is linked to the considerations discussed at §§ 5.112 ff. below.

[Vfp *have been,* [P *following conquest*], *ruled*] G01:1430
[Jh *apt* [Pb *by nature*] *to be impersonal . . .*] G22:1270

§ 4.24 A tagma may include adverbials at more than one point:

[Vfp *have* [R *also*] *been* [R *recently*] *discussed*] J05.047

and more than one adverbial may be included at a single point:

Handel, Mendelssohn and Gounod [Vwp *were* [R *all*]
[P *in their turn*] *astonished* — [Vn+ *and,* [Tg *being human*],
delighted Vn+] — Vwp] *by the adoration . . .* A17.061

(in this example, *all* and *in their turn* are separately included within
the Vwp, and *being human* is an included adverbial within the Vn+).

§ 4.25 The rule of § 4.23 included a ceteris paribus clause,
because it is not invoked in order artificially to represent a logical
tagma as continuous, if it is clear that part of the tagma has been
dislocated (perhaps in order to postpone a "heavy" element, or
because an afterthought by the writer has produced an appositional
element too late to be adjacent to its antecedent), even though the
only element separating the parts of the logical tagma may happen
to be an adverbial:

. . . had [Np *many acquaintances*] [P *in the Chinese quarter*],
[Np@ *friends from the war days*] P12.122
Is there [Ns *anything*] [P *in your book*] [Fr *that people haven't
said about me . . .*] P19.191
. . . contributing [Ns *a couple of pounds*] [P *to the family exchequer*] — [Fr *some of which she invariably borrowed
back . . .*] P27.086

That is: if an adverbial divides a tagma into two segments, of which
the segment following the adverbial is a single constituent of a kind
which is commonly postposed, then the "included-adverbial" analysis is not used and the following constituent is treated by the
logical-annotation system as having been shifted; but if what follows the adverbial consists of more than one constituent, or if it is
a single constituent which is not of a type that in general one
expects to find postposed, then the included-adverbial analysis is the
preferred solution.

Misprints, Solecisms, and Non-Standard Language

§ 4.26 The SUSANNE scheme is intended to apply to anything
that actually occurs in written English, which means that it must

often be applied to material including misprints or non-standard usage; it is no part of the analyst's job to correct these. The scheme does not include specific components for representing linguistic forms as substandard; such forms are annotated as best they can be by analogy with the analyses appropriate to related standard usage. It is not realistic to hope that rules can be laid down for annotating such cases which will yield analyses that are as predictable as the analyses of standard English examples.

§ 4.27 In the case of elements of the annotation scheme which have formal definitions, the items appearing on the page will be given the annotations appropriate to what actually appears rather than to what "should have" appeared; where aspects of the annotation scheme are defined largely in conceptual rather than purely formal terms, the analyst will use his judgement about what type of construction is intended in order to guide the choice of annotation for what appears. For instance, in the case:

> *The evidence suggest that . . .* E06.087

the relevant wordtags have rather formal definitions, therefore *evidence* and *suggest* are tagged respectively as singular noun and uninflected form of verb, ignoring the fact that *suggest* should almost certainly have read *suggests*. On the other hand, when choosing a category for the entire clause, the logic of the sequence is more relevant; the clause is tagged as an S (main clause), since it is manifestly a statement, rather than as Tb (complementizerless nonfinite subordinate clause) — a Tb can occur independently, e.g. as an exclamation (*Damn you*), but this case is not one of that kind.

Where a word is misprinted so that it coincides with a different word, e.g. *or* printed as *of*, the wordtag for the word as printed will be used; if the misprint gives no existing word (e.g. *or* printed as *ar*), the analyst will use his judgement to decide what word was intended and tag the misprint accordingly.

§ 4.28 The analysis of non-standard forms will often be affected by the analyst's judgement as to whether they result from unintentional misprints or accurately reflect the writer's (non-standard) intention. In the former case, annotation reflecting what actually appears rather than what should have appeared is confined as low in the parsetree as possible; in the latter case, annotations determined by what actually appears may be found at higher points. Consider, for instance, the sequence:

> *. . . would cost the employers between £25 to £30 million a year.*
> A27.012

In carefully edited writing, *to* here would read *and*. If *to* were taken as a simple misprint for *and*, then it would be given one of the wordtags appropriate to *to* (IIt, since this fits the context better than TO or RL), but in all other respects the sequence would be analysed as a co-ordination — it would appear as a normal co-ordinate structure except that a preposition appears where normally a co-ordinating conjunction appears. However, since *to* and *and* are not alphabetically similar, it seems unlikely that one was accidentally misprinted for the other, and more likely that the writer intended the wording that appears. Consequently *to* is not only wordtagged as a preposition but is treated as introducing a prepositional phrase, P, and the whole is analysed as if it had read *from £25 to £30 million*; for this writer, it seems, *between* is not required to take as complement a form denoting both or all boundaries of the location referred to. Or compare the passage:

> ... *it would be right for Britain to make a formal application .. for negotiations with a view to joining the Community.* A06.129

where two stops, rather than the standard three, are used as an ellipsis mark. The SUSANNE scheme has no wordtag for a single word consisting of two stops, but if the lack of a third stop were seen as a misprint then the sequence of two stops would be treated as one word tagged YE, as if there had been three stops. However, it seems possible that the writer, unusually, deliberately chose to use just two stops to indicate an ellipsis (as is conventional in the programming language Pascal); therefore the stops are treated as a sequence of two separate full-stop "words", each tagged YF, and each, non-standardly, occurring as a medial IC of the Ns tagma headed by *application*.

§ 4.29   Also, where a passage is well formed and meaningful as an example of standard English, but in context it appears that the intended meaning is different because the passage embodies non-standard conventions, the annotation reflects the writer's intended analysis rather than the alternative standard analysis. Consider: *the conflict which a century ago insured national unity over fragmentation* G02:0650. In standard usage the word *over* in this context would have to be a paraphrase of "concerning", "with respect to", so that the phrase *over fragmentation* would either be a postmodifier of *unity* or an adjunct of Respect as an IC of the relative clause. In context, however, it seems more likely that for this writer *over* is being used as a paraphrase of "rather than", "instead of", which makes the phrase a Modality adjunct within the relative clause; the latter annotation is adopted. (This example relates to the logical-rather than surface-annotation scheme, but is included here because the issue of how to deal with non-standard usage is predominantly a matter affecting the surface scheme.)

§ 4.30   Non-standard usage is often not simply idiosyncratic but reflects established linguistic conventions, which happen not to be the conventions of standard English — e.g. informal substandard grammar, telegraphic style in diaries — and in such cases there is normally no difficulty in analysing the material as it stands. Thus:

'Ten-thirty be all right?' K01.019
"Where you goin', son?" K25.188
At last slept and lay in till 7.30. G12.121

are treated as containing main clauses which happen to lack finite verbs (in the first two cases), and subject (in the last case):

'[S? [M *Ten-thirty*] [Vjb *be*] [J *all_right*] S?]?'
"[S? [Rq *Where*] [Ny *you*] [Vg *goin'*] S?], [Ns" *son*]?"
[S [R *At_last*] [Vd *slept*] [S+ *and lay in till 7.30*] S].

Where it is difficult to judge whether a non-standard form is an accidental misprint or represents the writer's intention, the presumption is in favour of the latter.

Ambiguity

§ 4.31   Linguistic forms are often ambiguous. The SUSANNE scheme contains no notation for representing ambiguity explicitly; it requires the analyst to select one possible sense for a form and represent that. Since ambiguity (that is, the possibility of two or more explicitly incompatible interpretations, as opposed to vagueness, where there may be only one interpretation of a linguistic form but this is compatible with a wide range of states of affairs) is not normally intended by writer or speaker, for most purposes this approach seems appropriate. There are of course some kinds of linguistic behaviour (puns, according to Empson poetry) which consciously exploit ambiguity, and the SUSANNE scheme may appear unsatisfactory in connection with research on these genres.

§ 4.32   In the construction of the SUSANNE Corpus, analysts were asked to represent in their annotation whichever interpretation of an ambiguous form seemed initially most plausible, even if fuller consideration might suggest that it was not in fact the intended interpretation — the rationale being partly that resource limitations militated against a more careful policy, and partly that it is more reasonable to hope that probabilistic language-analysis systems might succeed in simulating human readers' "snap" interpretations of text, which are presumably based on fairly superficial cues, than that they would successfully identify subsequent interpretations based on subtle reasoning — therefore, if the Corpus is to be used in order to generate statistical information for this purpose, it ought to reflect the former category of interpretations. An example (from LOB rather than the SUSANNE Corpus) is:

> *It is convenient to classify wholesale merchants, according to the extent of the sales territory . . .* F41.029

At a hasty initial reading, the comma appears to mark the right boundary of the infinitival clause beginning *to classify*, so that the prepositional phrase *according_to the extent . . .* would be an IC of the main clause. Further consideration suggests that the *according_to* phrase makes sense only as a basis for classification, i.e. that the phrase is within the infinitival clause. But the kinds of automatic parsing routines being investigated alongside the SUSANNE research programme, while possibly able to make deductions from commas to clause boundaries, would certainly not be capable of using the individual meaning of the verb *classify* and the prepositional idiom *according_to* to decide constituency.

§ 4.33   However, whether or not the principle stated for choosing among alternative annotations for ambiguous examples is a judicious one, it cannot be claimed that the analyses of the SUSANNE Corpus as eventually released conform to it consistently. The processes by which the Corpus was developed over a period of years were so complex, involving many reconsiderations of particular passages for a variety of reasons, that in some cases the resulting analyses depend on careful reasoning while in other cases they do represent snap reactions, and the proportions of the two types of case are unknown.

§ 4.34   A point that is worth making, though, is that even when alternative structural analyses are available for a stretch of text, the difference between the alternatives appears impressionistically to be pragmatically significant less often than the theoretical-linguistics tradition might lead one to expect. Cases such as the following are not infrequent:

> *. . . he prepared his supper and ate it beside the fire in the living-room, . . .* L04.060
> *Bongo was whining from the kitchen where he had been put to bed for the night.* N16.164

He had not disturbed nature, except close to the house where
there were gravelled walks . . . N03.036

Structurally these passages involve the well-known problem of level
of attachment of a postmodifying phrase. Does the prepositional
phrase *in the living-room* describe the fire, so that it should be
included within the noun phrase headed by *fire*, or is it a second
Place adjunct, sister of the phrase *beside the fire*, both of which are
ICs of the *ate* clause and specify where the eating occurred? Syntactically there is a clear difference, but pragmatically the two interpretations amount to much the same. Likewise, the *where* clause in
the second example might be a relative clause modifying *kitchen*, or
an adverbial clause acting as a Place adjunct IC of the main clause;
similarly the *where* clause of the third example, which must be a
relative clause, may modify *house* or *close*. (It is unusual for a relative clause to have an adjective as its antecedent, but if the passage
read *close by, where there were . . .* , this analysis would be unmistakable.) The SUSANNE scheme, and, it is believed, any other
system of grammatical analysis, would treat these as genuine structural ambiguities, making contrasting annotations available; contrasting analyses must be available, since by varying the wording
one can construct examples in which alternative structures correspond to significantly different meanings. (Compare the *Bongo*
example with, say, *Bongo was waiting for the dawn when he was*
executed — on one interpretation he was to be executed at dawn,
on the other he was still waiting for dawn to arrive at the time of
his execution.) Yet, in each of the authentic cases quoted, the substance of what is being said is unaffected by the structural decision.
A similar structural ambiguity can occur at the beginning rather
than end of a clause:

Their offering last night differed little from their earlier act . . .
C04.080

— *last night* may postmodify *offering*, or may be a Time adjunct
in the clause. In this case the analysis which treats *last night* as a
clause IC would entail a rather unusual ordering (a Time adjunct
would more normally occur either as first or as last element of the
clause than between its subject and verb), so there is a motive for
choosing the noun-postmodifier analysis; but either analysis would
describe the same non-linguistic reality.

§ 4.35   Of course, there are also cases in authentic material where
structural ambiguity corresponds to genuinely significant differences,
but this phenomenon does not seem as salient in practice as it sometimes is in theoretical discourse.

§ 4.36 In some cases, the scheme makes alternative structures available which, it would seem, could hardly ever or never correspond to a real difference of meaning. Thus, the grammatical phenomenon of "Whiz Deletion" allows a relative clause to be reduced by the omission of the relative pronoun and verb *BE* — in a sequence such as *the man now at the starting gate is the Czech competitor* there is no way of understanding *now at the starting gate* other than as a reduced form of *who is now at the starting gate*, and thus as a postmodifying tagma within the *man* phrase. Likewise, in a sequence like *charming as always, James made her feel at home immediately*, there is no alternative to regarding *charming as always* as a clause IC, effectively a reduced form of something like *being charming* . . . or *since he was charming* . . . . But, given that the language provides both of these two patterns of reduction, it would be artificial for the parsing scheme to fail to offer alternative analyses in cases such as:

> *Bentham, intent on widening and improving recruitment to the Civil Service, was characteristically interested in examinations.* J36.059
> *. . . the sea-wall, houseless, manless, goes marching down the coast . . .* F26.072
> *"You look after yourself, son," said Dad lighting one of his hand-rolled cigarettes and leaning back . . .* K25.190

— the adjective phrases *intent on . . .* and *houseless, manless*, and the present-participle clause *lighting one of . . .*, can in each case be taken either as a reduced appositive relative modifying the preceding noun, or as a clause adjunct (*being intent . . .*, *being houseless . . .*, or *lighting . . .* without reduction). Yet it is not clear that this structural contrast will ever correspond to a difference of meaning. In such cases the SUSANNE scheme attempts to avoid positing distinctions without a difference by offering general principles for choice; thus, the SUSANNE approach prefers flat to many-layered parsetrees, other things being equal, and this gives a motive for preferring the clause-adjunct rather than noun-postmodifier analysis in each of the above cases. But it is not possible to make such principles yield decisions for every case. For instance, an example rather similar to the above is:

> *It was certainly an exciting offer, far more attractive than going back to London.* P08.084

Here the parallel with the premodifier *exciting* makes it more natural to opt for the treatment according to which the adjective phrase *far more attractive than* . . . postmodifies *offer*: the statement assumes "given" information *it was an* . . . *offer* and gives two pieces of "new" information, *exciting* and *far more attractive than* . . . . There will be other examples where the choice between reduced-postmodifier and clause-adjunct analyses is too evenly balanced to do more than make a random decision; and there may be other types of semantically non-significant structural ambiguity for which general principles of choice cannot be found. The SUSANNE parsing scheme attempts to minimize situations in which alternative analyses are equally defensible, but cannot wholly eliminate them.

§ 4.37   Another point about structural ambiguity in authentic usage is that where a passage is ambiguous and the ambiguity makes a genuine pragmatic difference, it is by no means always true that a competent native speaker can tell which interpretation is intended. Often this will require highly fallible guesswork about the aspect of reality being described. Consider the case:

> . . . *to provide ingots of zone-refined aluminium containing additions of various elements, which were then rolled to sheet for determination of recrystallisation temperatures.* J77.025

Grammatically, the antecedent of the *which were* . . . clause could be *ingots, additions,* or *elements.* The author's guess is that the first of these is the intended antecedent, but this guess depends on surmises about the nature of an industrial process which is far removed from his experience, and his conception of which might prove very naïve if brought into confrontation with the reality. The author has published work elsewhere (Sampson 1987a) which suggests that in authentic usage ambiguity may be commoner than readers usually realize, and that readers are less good at resolving it correctly than some versions of theoretical linguistics assume.

§ 4.38   In sum, there is a woolliness about the logical structure of natural language, which may do something to excuse the fact that resolution of structural ambiguity has not received as much attention as it might in connection with the SUSANNE Corpus.

The Formtags Listed

§ 4.39   Every terminal and non-terminal parsetree node, apart from ghost nodes immediately dominating YG wordtags, has a label including a formtag. The shape of a parsetree is defined in terms of a hierarchy of formtag ranks:

1. wordrank formtags (begin with two capital letters; formtags of all other ranks begin with one capital and contain no further capitals)
2. phrasetags (begin with one of: V N J R P D M G)
3. clausetags (begin with one of: S F T W A Z L)
4. rootrank formtags (begin with one of: O Q I)

§ 4.40 We have seen that the root of a parsetree is always labelled with a rootrank formtag; and any leaf node is labelled with a wordtag, which is a wordrank formtag. However, wordrank and rootrank formtags do not invariably label leaf nodes and root nodes respectively. For instance, an "idiomtag" (§ 3.55), such as RR= for *by_the_way*, is a wordrank formtag, but labels a non-terminal node; other kinds of non-terminal wordrank formtag are introduced below. Conversely, "Q" representing "quotation" is a rootrank formtag but does not occur on root nodes: a Q node will be the root of a direct quotation included as a subtree within the tree representing a larger text sequence, thus the Q node will be dominated, often by a node representing a clause containing a verb of quoting. Other rootrank formtags can occur in non-root positions, in ways identified below. However, the classification of formtags into four ranks is relevant for the rules which control the overall structure of the labelled tree assigned to a text by the SUSANNE scheme.

§ 4.41 A summary listing of the tagmatags is as follows.

For phrasetags, the fundamental classification is into categories represented by single capital letters: "verb group" (V), "adverb phrase" (R), and the other main categories are defined independently of their subcategories. Lower-case subcategory letters are then added in whatever combinations are justified by the properties of a particular phrase; a main phrase-category letter may be followed by none, one, or several subcategory letters, e.g. the verb group *cannot be* is formtagged Vceb, since it begins with a modal, is negative, and ends with *BE*. Multiple subcategory letters after a capital-letter phrase category appear in the order shown below.

Among clauserank and rootrank formtags, on the other hand, capital + lower-case character combinations are best regarded as unitary tags (the clausetags beginning F. . . share that letter because each category is normally headed by a finite verb, but it is more straightforward to define categories of adverbial clause, relative clause, etc., than to state a general definition of "F. . . clause" and add individual criteria for types of finite clause). Multiple lower-case letters do not co-occur with a rootrank or clauserank capital-letter category symbol.

PHRASETAGS

V   verb group

    Vo   operator
    Vr   remainder
    Vm V beginning with *am*
    Va   V beginning with *are*
    Vs   V beginning with *was*
    Vz   V beginning with other 3rd singular verb
    Vw V beginning with *were*
    Vj   V beginning with *be*
    Vd   V beginning with past tense
    Vi   infinitival V
    Vg   V beginning with present participle
    Vn   V beginning with past participle
    Vc   V beginning with modal
    Vk   V containing emphatic *DO*
    Ve   negative V
    Vf   perfective V
    Vu   progressive V
    Vp   passive V
    Vb   V ending with *BE*
    Vx   V lacking main verb
    Vt   catenative V

N   noun phrase

    Nq   *wh-* N
    Nv   *wh. . .ever* N
    Ne   *I/me* as whole or head
    Ny   *you* as whole or head
    Ni   *it* as whole or head
    Nj   adjectival head
    Nu   unit of measurement as head
    Nn   proper name
    Na   marked as subject
    No   marked as non-subject
    Ns   marked as singular
    Np   marked as plural

J   adjective phrase

    Jq   *wh-* J
    Jv   *wh. . .ever* J
    Jx   measured absolute J

Jr   measured comparative J
Jh   "heavy" (postmodified) J

R adverb phrase

    Rq   *wh-* R
    Rv   *wh...ever* R
    Rx   measured absolute R
    Rr   measured comparative R
    Rs   adverb conducive to asyndeton
    Rw   quasi-nominal adverb

P prepositional phrase

    Po   *of* phrase
    Pb   *by* phrase
    Pq   *wh-* P
    Pv   *wh...ever* P

D determiner phrase

    Dq   *wh-* D
    Dv   *wh...ever* D
    Ds   marked as singular
    Dp   marked as plural

M numeral phrase

    Ms   M headed by *one*

G genitive phrase

    Gq   *wh-* G
    Gv   *wh...ever* G

CLAUSETAGS

S   main clause
Ss   embedded quoting clause
Fa   adverbial clause
Fn   nominal clause
Fr   relative clause
Ff   fused relative
Fc   comparative clause
Tg   present-participle clause
Tn   past-participle clause
Ti   infinitival clause
Tf   *for-to* clause
Tb   bare non-finite clause

Tq   infinitival relative clause
W   *with* clause
A   special *as* clause
Z   reduced ("Whiz-Deleted") relative
L   miscellaneous verbless clause

ROOTRANK FORMTAGS

O   paragraph
Oh   heading
Ot   title
Q   quotation
I   interpolation
Iq   tag question
Iu   technical reference

NON-ALPHANUMERIC FORMTAG SUFFIXES

§ 4.42   A non-alphanumeric character may be suffixed to a wordtag or tagmatag to create another tagmatag of the same rank, as follows.

After clausetags:

?   interrogative
*   imperative
%   subjunctive

after clausetags or phrasetags:

!   exclamation
"   vocative

after wordtags:

=   grammatical idiom

Other non-alphanumeric suffixes are used to display the structure of co-ordinate constructions, which in the SUSANNE scheme are assimilated to subordinate constructions (§§ 4.462 ff.); thus *the heat and the dust* N13:0490 is given the structure [*the heat* [*and the dust*]], with *and the dust* called a "subordinate conjunct" within the entire co-ordination.

After any formtags (including wordtags):

+   subordinate conjunct introduced by conjunction
–   subordinate conjunct not introduced by conjunction

& co-ordinate structure acting as first conjunct within a higher
co-ordination

after any tagmatags (but not wordtags):

@ appositional element

§ **4.43** The only way in which more than one non-alphanumeric
suffix can apply to a single formtag is when there are two suffixes,
one drawn from the set + – & @ relating to co-ordination and
apposition, and the other not from this set; in that case the symbol
relating to co-ordination/apposition is placed after the other non-
alphanumeric symbol.

§ **4.44** Certain unsuffixed wordtags can occur as non-terminal
formtags when accompanied by functiontags, see § 5.111.

§ **4.45** The status of the different symbols found in formtags
varies, and in particular there is a distinction worth noting between
lower-case subcategory symbols found with rootrank tags and clausetags, on the one hand, and those found with phrasetags on the
other. In general, clause subcategories (and rootrank subcategories,
but in their case the point is too obvious to be worth dwelling on)
are functional classifications, which often have to be selected by
reference to the meaning as well as the overt grammatical features
of the clause in question; whereas the phrase subcategories, except
in special cases, represent only properties that are overtly marked
within the relevant phrase. For instance, in *The report that John was
writing is unsatisfactory*, the subordinate clause is tagged Fr, relative clause, although in terms of its surface properties it cannot be
distinguished from Fn, nominal clause, as in *The report that the
Germans have invaded is alarming*. On the other hand, the subject
noun phrase in *the cow is dead* is formtagged Ns, singular noun
phrase, because the word *cow* can be only singular, not plural, but
the corresponding phrase in *the sheep is dead* will be formtagged
just N, noun phrase, without indication of singular or plural because
within the phrase itself the matter is indeterminate.

§ **4.46** In this sense the terminological distinction made within
the SUSANNE scheme between "formtags" and "functiontags" is
arguably misleading. In reality there is a gradient among grammatical features between those which relate more to surface form and
those which relate more to meaning or logic; some of the elements
of SUSANNE "formtags" are more functional than purely formal,
and this tends to apply more to the higher-ranking than to the
lower-ranking "formtags". (Even this is far from being an absolute
rule: thus the phrase subcategories Vo and Vr, and Vf, Vu, Vp,
represent logical as much as formal distinctions.)

§ **4.47** From the point of view of automatic parsing, one way to look at this is that clause subcategory letters represent part of the information that a successful automatic parser ought to include in its output, whereas many phrase subcategories represent the SUSANNE team's guesses as to what mechanically ascertainable features of the phrases are likely to be helpful as inputs to routines determining parser output, and might be missing from that output without the performance of the parser being regarded as thereby inferior. The set of phrase subcategories detailed here is simply the current result of a long history in which some subcategories used previously (e.g. a distinction among noun phrases between those headed by countable and uncountable nouns) have been eliminated as not worth keeping, while other subcategories not at first thought of have been added. The SUSANNE team believe that the list of phrase subcategories that happens to have survived this process includes everything that a successful parsing system ought to identify in this area, and various additional things, but a different list of additional things might be equally defensible.

Tree Structure

§ **4.48** Detailed definitions of the various tagmatags listed will be given below. This range of tagmatags can only be used, of course, provided that one is able to assign to a given text a parsetree of a particular shape, having nodes which require to be labelled. The SUSANNE parsing scheme relies on the fact that linguists share a tacit ability to group words and phrases into constituents in many uncontroversial cases. There are plenty of individual debatable issues about the shape of parsetrees, and explicit rules are laid down in later sections for dealing with these issues; but the SUSANNE scheme does not attempt to state explicit formal rules to replace linguists' intuitive grasp of constituency structure in straightforward cases. To do that would be to solve a large part of the problem of automatic parsing, which is not the purpose of this document.

§ **4.49** However, even when the overall constituency structure of a text is clear and uncontroversial, there is little consensus among linguists about how many "layers" of intermediate nodes should occur between root and leaves. In particular, there is considerable vagueness in the literature of the discipline about when, if at all, it is appropriate to posit "singulary-branching" nodes (mother nodes with a single daughter). Transformational grammarians, for instance, have quite reasonably tended to neglect such questions because the amount of layering in a parsetree, as opposed to its general shape, will commonly not affect the application of transformational rules. However, research which is directed to analysing authentically occurring language samples rather than plotting a theoretical boundary between well-formed and ill-formed word-sequences must commit itself to specifying this aspect of the structure of the target outputs it aims to produce as well as other aspects. Furthermore, statistical research which depends mainly on information about immediate constituency (relationships between mother and daughter nodes) is particularly dependent on consistent decisions about depth of layering.

§ 4.50   The SUSANNE scheme includes rules which are designed to ensure that the structure of any text is made adequately explicit, while limiting the proliferation of layers of nodes. These rules are rather complex to state, but have proved reasonably easy to apply in practice. They depend on the concept of tagmatag rank, and run as follows.

§ 4.51   Any sequence of more than one word and/or lower-level tagma which, to a human analyst, recognizably coheres as a unit will be given a node of its own, subject to the proviso of § 4.9 about endocentric constructions being treated as constructed by concatenation rather than recursion. (Detailed rules about individual categories settle cases where there is room for doubt about whether some sequence counts as a tagma.)

§ 4.52   Any constituent functioning as a clause will be given a clausetag, even if it consists only of a single word.

§ 4.53   A minority of clauses, including main clauses, are verbless (all cases of Z and L are verbless, and other clause categories sometimes lack a verb). Apart from these cases, any clause will contain a V (verb group) as its head IC. Any V will be head of a clause (except that what is logically one multi-word V may be split, e.g. by subject-auxiliary inversion as in *Does the mountain listen?* N08:1630, into disjoint sequences tagged Vo and Vr — in such a case both V elements will be ICs of the same clause tagma, and the Vo will be considered its head). With one exception stated in § 4.56 below, any verb word that occurs in a clause other than as (part or all of) its head V or a Vr will be analysed as (part or all of) a V heading a subordinate clause within the higher clause. Thus, within the Ti clause *to see powerful enough scattering experiments performed* J09.091, the Vi *to see* is head of the clause, so *performed* must be analysed as constituting a clause of its own (tagged Tn) subordinate to the Ti:

[Ti [Vi *to see*] [Np *powerful enough scattering experiments*]
[Tn [Vn *performed_VVNv*]]]

§ 4.54 Any verb word occurring within a phrase other than a
V is treated as (part or all of) a V heading a clause subordinate to
that phrase; thus *scattering* in the example just quoted is analysed as
a Vg forming the whole of a Tg premodifying the noun *experiments*
— the Np is analysed as:

[Np [Jh *powerful enough*] [Tg [Vg *scattering_VVGv*]] *experiments*]

Likewise in *a depressing experience,* since *depressing* is listed in
OALD3 as a VVG and not as an adjective, this word must be
analysed as a one-word Vg constituting a one-daughter Tg premodifying the noun. In the noun phrase *the 20 situations investigated*
J10.090, the VVNt *investigated* is a one-word Vn daughter of a
one-word Tn postmodifying *situations* (the Tn node will also
dominate a ghost node identifying the logical relationship between
investigated and *situations*).

§ 4.55 There will never be an intermediate node between a clause
node and its head V. Thus, although a Tf (*for-to* clause) will normally
contain a subsequence formally identical to a Ti (infinitival clause),
the latter subsequence will not be treated as a separate Ti tagma:

Arranging [Tf *for* [Np *ministerial graduates*] [Vi *to spend*]
[Np *from 6–12 months*] [P *as apprentices*] . . . Tf]
A10:1730

In the sequence:

. . . *the problem facing the selectors at this moment,* [W *with
Conroy* **injured** [W+ *and two other likely candidates . . . not
available*]]. A08.160

the emphasized word is a Vn but not a Tn, since it is the head of
a W clause.

§ 4.56 The exception to the rule that all words wordtagged as
verbs must belong to V tagmas acting as heads of clauses or as Vr's
is that an *uninflected* verb form may occur as head or whole of an
N (noun phrase), in which case no V or clause node is inserted
between wordtag and N node. This is particularly common in the
case of nominal uses of phrasal verbs, e.g.:

a [Ns *drive_VV0v* +<*hyphen*>_YH +*in_RP*] *theater in Seekonk*
A05:0350
two girls were missing at [Ns *call_VV0v over_RP*]

[Ns *an*_AT1 *Indian*_JJ *take*_VV0v +<*hyphen*>_YH +*away*_RL][4]
[Np+ *and lay*_VV0v +<*hyphen*>_YH +*offs*_NN2] A19:0030

— since the presence of the particle removes any temptation to reclassify the verb as a noun at the wordtag level even in cases where such a tagging would be allowed by the dictionary. But the exception can also apply with other verbs:

he caused [Ns *the fumble*_VV0v *that set up our touchdown*] A12:0800
in [Np *foster*_VV0t *homes*_NN2] A01:0320
Sally's pa was coming out best on [Ns *the haggle*_VV0i] N13:0150
With [Ns *a bellow*_VV0v] *Carmer lunged at him.* N14:0660
during [Ns *a drift scan*_VV0v *across the moon* . . .] J01:1670
[Ns *a shear*_VV0t *field* [P *with a height of* . . .] . . .] J03:0740

Such forms, when occurring in positions requiring tagmatags (§ 4.59), are always tagmatagged N. . . , not e.g. J in cases where they modify nouns (as in the *drive-in* example). In some of these cases one might intuitively think that the word tagged as a verb (e.g. *bellow, scan*) is a normal noun, but by the "dictionary test" these words cannot be given noun tags.

§ 4.57   Any IC of a clause, even if consisting of only one word, will be tagmatagged, unless it belongs to a class of words which cannot be analysed as one-word tagmas because they never head multi-word tagmas and hence have no corresponding tagmatag. Thus the sentence *There are drinks here* receives the analysis:

[S *There*_EX [Vab *are*_VBR] [Np *drinks*_NN2]
  [R *here*_RLh] S]

— existential *there*, wordtagged EX, has no corresponding tagmatag (there is no category of phrase whose typical head is *there*_EX), therefore the EX wordtag node is directly dominated by the S node, but each of the other words is analysed as a one-word phrase: the verb is a verb group, the noun is a noun phrase, the adverb is an adverb phrase.

§ 4.58   The class of wordtags which can be directly dominated by clause nodes are (with "XY. . ." for "any wordtag beginning XY"): BTO, C. . . , EX, FA, FB, FOqc, FOqx, FW (but FWg and FWs below a clause node are one-word N's), LE. . . , UH, XX,

---

[4] Although the hyphen shows that the sequence *take-away* coheres more closely than the noun phrase as a whole, the rule (§ 4.9) that association where unmarked is towards the head means that it is not necessary to give *take-away* a node of its own within the noun phrase, as it is in the *drive-in* case.

Y. . . ; together with I. . . words when introducing subordinate clauses, e.g. *until*_ICSt introducing an adverbial clause, *for*_IF introducing a *for-to* clause.

§ 4.59 An IC of a phrase or rootrank tagma, on the other hand, will be tagmatagged only if one of the following applies:

- the IC consists of more than one word or tagma and/or is itself a clause;
- the applicable phrasetag would be Nn. . . (proper name, cf. § 4.140) or a tag ending in the suffix " (vocative) or ! (exclamation);
- the IC is an item (such as an included adverbial, §§ 4.23 ff.) which has been shifted to its surface position from a logical position as daughter of some other tagma;
- the IC is one which under the logical-grammar annotation system is assigned an index marking it as co-referential with some other element in the parsetree, cf. § 5.9.

§ 4.60 Otherwise the phrase node or rootrank node will directly dominate a wordrank node. Thus a one-word noun phrase is not given an N. . . node when it occurs as complement within a prepositional phrase:

[P *from*_II *growers*_NN2] F41.008 — not [P *from*_II
[Np *growers*_NN2]]

a single adjective is not parsed as an adjective phrase, J, in attributive position (i.e. as a noun-phrase IC), though it is parsed as a J in attributive position (i.e. as a clause IC):

[Ns *a green*_JJ *purse*] F04.030 v. *had been painted* [J *green*_JJ]
L23.185

a heading consisting of one-word tagma(s) other than verbs will involve no nodes intermediate between root and leaves:

[Oh <bmajhd> 1._MCb INTRODUCTION_NN1n <emajhd> Oh]
J01:0010

§ 4.61 When a rootrank formtag occurs at a non-root position in a parsetree, normally it will be directly attached as one daughter of a clause or phrase node having further daughters; the only case where singulary branching will occur immediately above a rootrank node is that an Ot node will standardly be dominated by an Nn node (cf. §§ 4.396–7 below).

§ 4.62 If the foregoing rules leave any room for doubt about the level at which a given tagma is to be analysed, it receives the highest-rank tag applicable, together with any other tags below this that may be implied by the interaction of this rule with the earlier rules. Thus, in a sequence such as *For there were (remember) three further questions* . . . , the interpolation *remember* is a one-word verb group, V, but is simultaneously an imperative main clause, S*, a tag which outranks V and which requires a V below it; hence the analysis is:

    . . . *were (*[I [S* [V remember_VV0v]]]*) three* . . .

Singulary branching is not allowed by the SUSANNE scheme other than when it is explicitly required by the above rules, or by a certain rule (see § 4.483) requiring singulary branching in the analysis of some co-ordinations.

The Treatment of Punctuation

§ 4.63   As we saw in §§ 2.36 ff., most individual punctuation marks are treated as separate "words" having their own leaf nodes in a SUSANNE parsetree, bearing wordtags beginning with the letter Y. . . , as are also typographic shift indicators such as *<bital>*, *<ebold>*.

§ 4.64   When a punctuation mark (such as comma or bracket) marks the boundary of a tagma, it is parsed as the sister (rather than first or last daughter) of that tagma. Among other consequences of this rule, sentence-closing punctuation marks such as full stop or question mark are treated as sisters of the nodes dominating the wording of the sentences.

§ 4.65   Where a punctuation mark can equally well be regarded as marking the boundary of superordinate or subordinate tagmas, it is treated as bounding the former; i.e. punctuation marks are attached as high in the parsetree as possible. For instance, in the sequence:

> *While never minimising the immensity of her work, it lifted the saintly halo* . . . C01.008

the comma simultaneously marks the end of the noun phrase *her work*, the prepositional phrase *of her work*, the larger noun phrase *the immensity of her work*, and the adverbial clause *While never minimising the immensity of her work*: it is parsed as bounding the last of these, i.e. as an IC of the whole sentence.

§ 4.66   Some punctuation marks (e.g. all brackets, probably a majority of dashes, many commas) occur in balanced pairs, marking either boundary of a tagma. (Inverted commas also occur in this way but are a rather special case, discussed in more detail below.)

Where punctuation marks are paired in this way, the parsing wherever possible makes the members of the pair sisters (that is, ICs of the same higher tagma). Thus, in:

> ... [W *with* [Np *two piano concertos* [P *by Alan Rawsthorne and Prokofiev*] ([Nns@ [G *each composer's*] *No. 1* [P *in the medium*] Nns@]) Np] *to enliven both halves* ... C03.063

— the left bracket is necessarily part of the plural noun phrase (Np) headed by *concertos*, since the parenthetic sequence is included appositionally within that phrase, and since the left bracket must be part of the Np because medial in it, the right bracket (which occurs at the end of the Np) is also treated as a daughter of the Np rather than attached higher to the W clause which dominates the phrase. In other words, where it is clear that punctuation marks occur in a paired fashion, the rule that they should be analysed as sisters takes precedence over the rule by which punctuation marks are attached as high as possible. (However, the rule about analysing paired marks as sisters can itself be overridden by other principles, as will be seen below.)

§ 4.67	In some cases, usually with commas, it is unclear whether the punctuation mark occurs as half of a balanced pair or as a "singleton" independently of other punctuation. If the meaning of the sentence, and the norms of orthography, leave this issue genuinely open, then it is settled in terms of the principle of attachment as high as possible. Thus, consider:

> [S *There are* [Np *two main Societies, for England and Scotland respectively*], [S+ *and they exist* ...]] F41.105

— here the second comma might equally well be seen either as balancing the first comma in order to "bracket off" the *for* phrase, or as marking the boundary between conjoined clauses. The former choice would make the second comma a daughter of the *societies* noun phrase while the latter choice makes it an IC of the S node dominating the noun phrase; since both interpretations are available and the latter leads to higher attachment of the comma, it is preferred.

§ 4.68	Often, though, decisions about comma placement can be made in terms of more specific considerations. Thus, in the examples:

> [Ns *A shudder,* [Jh *more mental than physical*],] *ran through him,* ... M01.002
>
> ... [Fa *when* [Ns *one of the clerks in the reception desk* — [Ns@ *a young educated Malay*] — Ns] *came up to him* Fa]. P12.125

[Fa *When they said charming things to us* — [Fn?@ *how grateful they were for our company, how pleased to have found us such a nice house* Fn?@] — Fa] *we could not meet their eyes.* K22.134

— the second of each pair of punctuation marks is taken as balancing the first, and consequently as the last daughter of the tagma which ends at that point, rather than sister of that tagma and daughter of the higher tagma dominating the following material, because the second mark would not normally be expected to occur if the tagma bounded by the pair of marks were absent: English orthography does not usually tolerate a comma between subject and predicate, or a dash between adverbial clause and main clause. That is, we rarely encounter sequences such as:

A shudder, ran through him
when one of the clerks in the reception desk — *came up . . .*
When they said charming things to us — *we could not meet their eyes.*

and consequently the marks are only satisfactorily explained as paired bounding marks surrounding the extra tagmas.

§ 4.69 Since there is a degree of looseness about English orthographic practice, these rules are not always wholly straightforward to apply. Consider for instance the case:

On Poverty Flat, which was a comparatively level stretch of gravelly ground that had once been part of the lake bed, Orestus Hancock had had erected . . . N03.032

The treatment of the second comma is debatable, since introductory prepositional phrases are sometimes separated from the remainder of a sentence by a comma. However, were the relative clause absent, the sequence *On Poverty Flat, Orestus Hancock had had erected . . .* might seem a little less likely than the corresponding sequence without a comma; whereas appositive relative clauses are quite standardly surrounded by paired commas. So on the balance of probability the parsing to be adopted is:

On [Nns *Poverty Flat,* [Fr *which was a . . . lake bed*],] *Orestus . . .*

§ 4.70 Consider a relatively complex case:

With a vigour and authority which delighted old Parliamentary friends and foes alike, the Earl of Avon, the former Sir Anthony Eden, in his maiden speech in the House of Lords last night, gave a warning . . . A05.121

Here it is clear that the comma following *alike* is an IC of the main clause, bounding the *with* phrase; the comma after *Avon* must be an IC of the noun phrase headed by *Earl*, and marks the left boundary of the phrase *the former Sir Anthony Eden* which is attached in apposition to the *Earl* phrase; and the comma after *night* must be an IC of the main clause, marking the right boundary of the prepositional phrase *in his maiden speech* . . . . The difficult decision concerns the comma after *Eden*. A comma would be required here in order to balance the comma after *Avon*, bracketing off the appositional phrase, even if the following prepositional phrase were absent; but by the same token, even if the appositional . . . *Eden* phrase were absent, the comma concerned would be needed to balance the comma after *night*, bracketing off the prepositional phrase. Since the one comma, after *Eden*, is simultaneously part of two balanced comma-pairs, the choice of placement in the tree is made in the way that attaches it as high as possible: the comma after *night* is higher than the comma after *Avon*, so the comma after *Eden* is parsed as balancing the comma after *night*:

[S [P *With a vigour . . . alike*], [Nns *the Earl of Avon*, [Nns@ *the former Sir Anthony Eden*]], [P *in his maiden speech . . . last night*], *gave a warning . . .* S]

§ 4.71 Although the principle that balanced punctuation marks should be parsed as sisters overrides the principle that punctuation marks should be attached as high as possible, in cases where the respective principles yield unambiguous but inconsistent placements, the balancing principle is in turn limited by the principle that appropriate parsing of verbal material takes precedence over appropriate parsing of punctuation, where these conflict. For instance, brackets are obviously a category of mark which very clearly occur in balanced pairs; but in practice brackets do not always surround one or more integral tagmas, e.g.:

adjustment to (the prospect of) ageing and retirement F02.193

In such a case, the requirement that the verbal material should be parsed appropriately makes it impossible to attach the brackets as sisters, so each is independently attached as high in the tree as possible.

§ 4.72 Likewise, the principle that verbal material should be parsed appropriately overrides the principle that boundary-marking punctuation marks are treated as sisters of the tagmas they bound, in a case like:

[S? *Is it not the existing organism that determines the use and quality of the new material introduced +?* [S?+ *and how could this be, except on the principle of transmission of quality*] S]? D14.064

— a question mark normally bounds a sentence, but the first of the two question marks in this sequence is internal to a compound main clause, being followed by lower-case *and*, and this question mark must therefore be attached as daughter of the main clause.

§ 4.73 Although full stop, question mark, and exclamation mark are normally used to bound sentences, the choice between these marks is sometimes made in terms of the properties of a subordinate tagma at the end of the sentence, rather than the properties of the entire sentence. This does not affect the placement of the punctuation mark; if, for instance, a declarative sentence ends with an indirect question followed by a question mark, the question mark is still taken as bounding the entire declarative sentence:

[S* *Go through his pockets,* [Iq [S? *will you*] Iq] S*]? N14:0720
[S *Upon this, we have to ask* [Fn? *if the life of a dog is not in the same category*]]? D14.105

§ 4.74 When an ellipsis mark occurs at a point where a sentence-final punctuation mark is expected, and no other sentence-final punctuation mark is adjacent to it, it is analysed as a sentence-bounding item, outside the S:

[S *End* <bbold> *Gene Raesz* <ebold> ... *was back working out with* <bbold> *Rice* <ebold> *Monday, and* <bbold> *John Nichols* <ebold>, *sophomore guard, moved back into action after a week's idleness with an ankle injury* S] <hellip> [S *The* <bbold> *Texas Aggies* <ebold> *got a day off* ... S] <hellip> ... A12:1150

(Here and in the following passage the reader should bear in mind that an ellipsis mark from the original text is represented as <hellip>, while three stops indicate that the quotation in the present work omits material from the original text.) Likewise, when an ellipsis mark occurs at the beginning or end of a quoted sequence to indicate that the text being quoted continues before or after the material excerpted, then provided the quoted sequence can be parsed as one or more complete tagmas the ellipsis mark is treated as their sister:

... *Thomas Griffith* ... *wrote:* "[Q +<hellip> [S *most of what was different about it (the Deep South) I found myself unsympathetic to* S] <hellip> Q]". G01:0550

Otherwise, for instance if the ellipsis mark occurs at the end of a complete sentence but with a full stop following it (that is, four stops occur in sequence), or if it occurs at the beginning of a non-quoted sentence, it is placed as high as possible within the tagma to which it is adjacent, e.g. last or first daughter of an S.

§ 4.75 A dash or ellipsis mark is sometimes used to indicate that a tagma has been prematurely terminated; in such a case, the incomplete tagma will often be final in its sentence, but the dash or ellipsis mark is treated as part of the incomplete tagma rather than as a sentence-final punctuation mark:

> [S *I've got enough money for a completely new outfit* [S+ *and* — S+] S]" P29.104
> [Q ... [S *I just can't take any chances on getting her pregnant,* [S+ *and* [Fa *if we were sleeping together* Fa] <hellip> S+] S] Q]" N01:1590

In the P29 case the analyst's assumption is that the incomplete element was to have been a co-ordinate clause (alternatively, one might equally guess that *and* was to have introduced something else that the speaker has enough money for, in which case the sequence *and* followed by dash would be parsed as N+ within the *outfit* N). Contrast these examples with:

> [S "[Q [Nns *Granville*] — Q]" *she said at last, shakily.* P25.067
> [S *They walked* . . . , [S+ *and went over the problem* [R *endlessly,* [RT&@ *again and again and again*] R] S+] <hellip> S]. F18.180
> [S *We can love Eisenhower the man,* [Fa *even if we considered him a mediocre president*] <hellip> [S+ *but there is nothing left of the Republican Party* . . .]]. A06:0180

— in the P25 case there is no basis for guessing what kind of tagma has been interrupted, so here the dash is treated as an IC of the Q. In the F18 case, semantically the ellipsis mark might be seen as tied to the phrase *endlessly, again and again and again,* but grammatically that phrase and the S+ clause containing it are complete, so the ellipsis mark is attached as high as possible, to the S tagma; since the original contains a sequence of four stops, the fourth is analysed as a sentence-closing full stop outside the S. (Many publishers make no distinction between "ellipsis followed by full stop" and "ellipsis only", printing both as three stops — if the F18 passage had been printed that way, the ellipsis mark would have been parsed as sister to the S tagma.[5]) The ellipsis mark in the A06 example may

---

[5] The situation turns out to be more complicated than at first appeared: there are alternative versions of the LOB Corpus in circulation which have differing numbers of stops (three v. four) at this point in text F18. The author surmises that the three-stop version is corrupt.

be intended to suggest that the *even if* clause is incomplete, but it may equally be used merely to link conjoined main clauses, as an alternative to colon or semicolon; since the former is not clearly the case, the latter is the default analysis.

§ 4.76   On the parsing of punctuation marks terminating direct quotations (Q tagmas), see § 4.414.

§ 4.77   Where inverted commas are used other than to bound a Q tagma — perhaps marking wording that is quoted but which has been integrated into the quoting sentence rather than functioning nominally within it as a Q element does, or as "scare quotes" which identify wording as needing special consideration rather as quoted from a separate source — it is particularly common for them to be placed typographically in positions which conflict with the principle that balanced punctuation marks ought to be sisters. (The same is true with other punctuation marks which can function similarly to inverted commas, such as dashes and typographic-shift elements, wordtagged YT.... .) For instance, when a closing inverted comma occurs adjacent to another punctuation mark, one common publisher's convention is to place the other punctuation mark before the closing inverted comma irrespective, in cases where inverted commas mark quotation, of whether that other punctuation mark occurs in the original text.[6] Thus we find sequences such as:

> [S *The urge came from a conference of activists of Nkrumah's*
> *Convention Party* "[P *after powerful addresses by*
> [Nn *Comrades Krobo Edusei,* [Nns– *Tawia Adamafio*],"
> [Np+ *and others*] Nn] P] S]. A02.076
> [S? *What does he mean* [Pb *by* "*death* Pb] S?]?" D14.154

Consequently the rule is that pairs of inverted commas and other items functioning similarly are parsed as sisters only when this can be done without violence not only to the structure appropriate to the verbal material but also that appropriate to other punctuation marks. In the former example above, the wording makes it clear that the material from *Comrades* to *others* is a compound noun phrase, therefore the two inverted commas cannot be sisters, and each is independently placed as high as possible (the opening inverted comma is not made first daughter of the prepositional phrase in order to be "closer" to the closing inverted comma: since it is impossible for them to be daughters of the same mother node, their relationship is ignored and the opening inverted comma becomes an IC of the sentence node). In the latter example, a question mark is

---

[6] One publisher has defended this convention to the present author as the only practical policy to deal with the fact that few writers can be relied on to check details of punctuation in their sources.

a sentence-bounding punctuation mark, therefore should be outside the S? tagma; consequently the closing punctuation mark must also be outside the S?.

§ 4.78   However, where the wording and other punctuation does allow inverted commas to be parsed as sisters, this is done:

> *In Takoradi,* [Ns *a "limited state* [Po *of emergency* Po]" Ns] *was declared* . . . A02.080
> . . . *and Vol. 5 which also includes* [Nns "[Ot *Les bergers* Ot]," [Pb *by his one-time pupil Olivier Messaien* Pb] Nns]. C10.204

— in the former example, the closing inverted comma is included within rather than outside the noun phrase, and in the latter example the opening inverted comma is within rather than outside the noun phrase, despite the fact that the alternative placement would put them higher in the tree.

The Formtags in Detail

The formtags are now defined in detail, in the order in which they were listed above. (For non-terminal wordrank formtags, see §§ 3.55, 4.482 ff., 5.111.)

PHRASETAGS

§ 4.79   Phrase-subcategory symbols are written in a phrasetag in a conventional order reflecting the order in which the corresponding features are marked within a generalized case of the corresponding phrase. This order corresponds to the order in which the subcategories are listed, under § 4.41 above and under the main phrase-category headings below. Under each main phrase-category heading below (in the case of those main categories for which subcategories are defined), a list of subcategories is shown in a form which uses semicolons to group subcategories into mutually exclusive sets, thus if the subcategories for an X phrase are listed as "a b c; d; e f", this means that at most one of a, b, or c can occur, at most one of e or f can occur, and whichever subcategories occur are written in the order shown.

§ 4.80   The ordering of subcategory letters is never distinctive; a particular lower-case letter always means the same thing after a given capital letter. But a lower-case letter can have different meanings after different main phrase-category letters, for instance p means "plural" after N (noun phrase) but "passive" after V (verb group).

For convenience, the present work often writes e.g. "the subcategory Np" to mean "the subcategory symbolized p of the main category symbolized N".

V Verb Group

§ 4.81 A verb group is a sequence of auxiliary and main verbs.[7] The term "verb group" rather than "verb phrase" is used to in order to remind users of the scheme that a V in this scheme is different from a Chomskyan "verb phrase", which also includes objects, predicate complements, etc. The SUSANNE scheme recognizes no tagma equivalent to "verb phrase" in that sense; a subject + verb + direct-object clause is treated by the SUSANNE scheme as having three separate ICs. As explained in § 4.23 above, a verb group will often contain an element functioning adverbially, if this is medial within the sequence of auxiliary and main verbs; the logical-grammar annotation system of Chapter 5 will represent this as an insertion into the sequence. (The word *not*, though sometimes regarded as an adverb, is treated both logically and at the surface as part of a verb group which contains it.) On the other hand (cf. § 4.5) the particle of a phrasal verb, which may be adjacent to but not medial in the verb sequence, is not parsed as part of the V but as a separate one-word phrase.

§ 4.82 Examples of V (in some cases containing included adverbials) are the emphasized sequences in:

*They **believe** that* . . . G01:1720
*which **are**,* [R *often*] [P *in a dramatic preconscious*
    breakthrough], ***reactivated** by* . . . J24:0860
*a thick substance that **could be sensed** but never identified,* . . .
    N08:1400
*we **are*** [R *probably*] ***not** much more afraid* . . . G11:0550
*an important **moderating** influence* G07:0460
*how **to*** [R *merely*] **go** *through the motions* A13:1240
*Palmer **has** such an inherent sense* . . . A14:1530
*The religion **supports, re-enforces, reaffirms, and maintains** the*
    fundamental values. J23:0920
*Holding the pistol **concealed**, he walked* . . . N03:0500

---

[7] The term *main verb* in this work always means "the verb of a clause which identifies the type of action, state, etc. indicated by the clause, and which is modified by any auxiliary verbs accompanying it"; it does *not* mean "the verb which is inflected to agree with the subject". A "main verb" is thus the last, not the first, verb of a verb group. The term *leading verb* is used for the first verb of a verb group, which in a finite clause agrees with the subject.

§ 4.83   There are a number of verbs in English with a "quasi-auxiliary" status, which occur in place of the *BE* of the standard expressions of progressive and passive and carry some semantic force of their own in addition to their grammatical function. Thus *BE* of the passive may be replaced by *GET* or *BECOME*; *BE* of the progressive may be replaced by *KEEP, GO, COME*. The SUSANNE scheme does not recognize these quasi-auxiliary constructions as occurring within a V; any quasi-auxiliary verb introduces a non-finite clause. (Compare the way, § 4.336 below, that the scheme does not treat the *is risen* of *Christ is risen from the dead* as a V with non-standard representation of perfective aspect, but analyses the sequence as *Christ* [Vzb *is*] [Tn [Vn *risen*] *from the dead*].) Examples of sequences with quasi-auxiliaries are:

He [Vd *kept*] [Tg [Vg *watching*] *me*] . . . L15.072
She [Vd *went*] [Tg [Vg *striding*] *briskly towards the chief's hut* Tg]. K09.171
. . . *are liable* [Ti [Vi *to get*] [Tn [Vn *hung*] [R *up*]] [Ti+ *and pull their stifles*] Ti]. E15.037
What are you trying to do? [S [V *Get*] [Tn [Vn *thrown*] [R *out*]]]? N18:1080
It then [Vd *became*] [Tn [Vn *caught*] [R *up*] [P *in* . . .]] J40.104
. . . *to forget her own problems by* [Tg [Vg *becoming*] [Tn [Vn *absorbed*] [P *in those of* . . .]]] P23.044
He merely [Vd *became*] [Tn [Vn *victimized*] *by a form of athletics* . . .] A14:1150

When this analysis creates ambiguities about which clause a modifying element following the participle belongs to, it is assigned to the lower clause:

. . . *the sea-wall* . . . [Vz *goes*] [Tg [Vg *marching*] [P *down the coast*] [P *for a dozen lonely miles*]]. F26.072 — P phrases not placed in *goes* clause
He [Vd *came*] [Tg [Vg *hurrying*] [R *out*]]. K09.117 — *out* not placed in *came* clause

§ 4.84   Some of these "quasi-auxiliary" constructions are given a special annotation in the logical-grammar annotation scheme: cf. §§ 5.199 ff.

V subcategories

§ 4.85   The lower-case subcategory symbols for V are:

o r; m a s z w j d i g n; c k; e; f; u; p; b; x t

When the definition of a V subcategory refers to the "first verb" of a verb group, this means "first verb" and not "first word". Thus, the first word of a Vj, a Vi, etc. will often be *not* (as in some of the examples given below); and the first verb of any V may be preceded by punctuation or typographic-shift "words".

Vo, Vr   operator, remainder
§ 4.86   When the verb group of a clause is split by a movement rule into two discontinuous segments, often (but not exclusively) by subject-auxiliary inversion in an interrogative or "subjunctive" form, the portion containing the first auxiliary is labelled Vo and the remainder Vr (together with any other applicable subcategories). Insertion of an adverbial element within a V (§ 4.23 above) does not count as splitting it into two segments.

> [Vo *Have*] *we* [Vrnu *been putting*] *our money on the wrong horses?* J42.179
> [Vo *Do*] *they* [Vr *quarrel*]? F14.073
> [Vodc *Would*] *it* [Vreb *not be*] *possible* ... B16.124
> ... *Why* [Vode *didn't*] *you* [Vr *go*] *there"?* N01:0910
> [Voc *Will*] *advances in human sciences* [Vr *help*] *us* ...? G11:0080
> [Vozb *Is*] *anything* [Vrgp *being done*] *to increase our margin of safety?* G03:0040
> [Fa [Vod *Had*] *there* [Vrnb *been*] *time enough* Fa], *there could* ... G19.106
> ... *never before* [Vod *had*] *such tremendous innovations* ... [Vrnp *been contemplated*]. A30.060

§ 4.87   The additional subcategory symbols written with Vo or Vr are all and only those justified by the contents of the respective V-partial taken separately. Thus neither V-partial will be labelled p for passive if the *BE* of the passive is in the Vo and the past participle in the Vr:

> *Only where the issues were posed so as to cause doubt and confusion* [Vowb *were*] *positions* [Vrn *lost*]. B06.127

— and likewise a Vr whose first verb is a participle will be given the g or n subcategory even if the logical, undivided V is a Vu or Vf rather than a Vg or Vn (cf. the *had* ... *been contemplated* example quoted above — as a continuous phrase, *had been contemplated* would be formtagged Vdfp with no n subcategory symbol). A Vo which ends with *BE* will be labelled Vb even though *BE* is not the main verb of the logical V (cf. the *hampered* ... example below).

§ 4.88 Where a negative verb group is split leaving just the word *not* as the "remainder", this is not analysed as a Vr (and consequently receives no phrasetag):

[S? [Vsb *Was*] [Ni *it*] *not*_XX [J *possible*], ...] N08:0590

§ 4.89 Vr may precede Vo, as in:[8]

[Vrg *Seeking*] *this two-year term* [Voab *are*] *James Culbertson, ... and Theodore W. Heitschmidt.* A10:1120
[Vrg *Opposing*] *him* [Vosb *was*] *the French Admiral* ... G01.010
the continuing growth of the building society movement,
 [Vrn *hampered*] *though it* [Vozb *has been*] *by limited available funds, indicates* ... E28.063

§ 4.90 The Vo and Vr subcategories are used only when partial V tagmas are sisters, so that when a Vo is completed separately in separate conjuncts only the completion within the main conjunct will be labelled Vr:

 ... [S+ *or* [Voab *are*] *we just* [Vrg *pursuing*] *an agreeable ritual* [S+ *and* [Vg *maintaining*] *our own reputations* ...]]? D11.035
 "[S? *Then,* [Voce *won't*] *you* [Vr *come*] [S+ *and* [V *see*] *it all*]]?" K08.107

Vm   am *phrase*
§ 4.91 First verb of V is wordtagged VBM:

I [Vmb *am*] *probably the only one* ... G06:1260
I [Vmu *+'m waiting*] *to see* ... L05.076

Va   are *phrase*
§ 4.92 First verb of V is wordtagged VBR:

hydrophobic (oleophilic) substances ... [Vab *are*] *more at home in the center of a micelle* J05:1381
we [Vaeb *are* [R *probably*] *not*] *much more afraid* ... G11:0550
SIXTY-SEVEN living units [Vaup *are being added*] *to the 165-unit Harbor View Apartments* A19:1870

Vs   was *phrase*
§ 4.93 First verb of V is wordtagged VBDZ (whether as first- or third-person form):

---

[8] With hindsight it might have been preferable not to use the Vo/Vr system for such cases, but to use the logical-annotation scheme of Ch. 5 to treat the main verb as shifted leftwards out of the verb group: the division of a complex verb group between Vo and Vr is quite different in these cases from a case of subject-auxiliary inversion (**Has it been hampered** ... ?).

the season [Vsb *was*] *at its peak* J10:0860
"Old Crip [Vsex *was +n't*]*", retorted Cobb* N14:1090
I [Vsp *was shown*], *instead, a batch . . .* N06:0470

Vz   third-person singular verb group

§ 4.94   First verb of V has third-person singular inflexion (including *is*, but not *was*):

<bmajhd> HOUSE [Vz THROWS] WILD <emajhd> A11:0160
The Philadelphia Transportation Co. [Vzu *is investigating*] *the part . . .* A09:0130
[Voz *Has*] *the agrarian tradition* [Vrn *become*] *such an addiction . . . ?* G08:0620

Vw   were *phrase*

§ 4.95   First verb of V is *were*:

You [Vwb *were*] *right* N14:0840
technical details [Vwep *were not* [R *fully*] *worked*] *out* A01:1460
"[Vowb *were*] *I* [Vrn *arraigned*] *at the bar, . . ."* G07:1590

Vj   be *phrase*

§ 4.96   First verb of V is the infinitive form *be*, not preceded by *to*. A Vj will commonly occur in an imperative — hence "j", from "jubeo" — but it can alternatively appear in a subjunctive clause, or in a Tb (§ 4.361).

"[Vjb *Be*] *careful, McLish"!* N03:0370
. . . advised . . . that "large supermarkets, . . . [Vjep *not be allowed*] *to do business" on Sunday.* A05:0880
demands that the right to secede [Vjp *be put*] *into the Constitution* G10:0680
whether they [Vjb *be*] *airplanes, . . .* J08:1760

The subcategory Vj is never included in a Vr tagma:

[Vodc *Should*] *there* [Vrb *be*] *evidence they are shirking, . . .* A05:0720

Vd   past-tense verb group

§ 4.97   First verb of V is a past-tense form of a verb other than BE. "Past tense" includes modal forms wordtagged VMd, but not *ought*, nor *used* when wordtagged VMK.

these two offices [Vdcp *should be combined*] A01:0210
Budd [Vdf *had thought*] *up* N01:0290

Dewey Lawrence... [Vd *sounded*] *the opposition keynote*
    A02:0210
One of the first things... [Vdcb *would be*] *to organize*...
    A05:0440
What [Vod *did*] *you* [Vr *mean*] *by*...? N09:0780

Vi   infinitival phrase

§ **4.98**   First verb of V is an infinitive (i.e. a base form preceded by
to). The word *to* is treated as part of the Vi; material "splitting the
infinitive" will normally be analysed as an "included adverbial"
within the Vi.

It appears [Ti [Vib *to be*] *one of intense dislike,*...] G01:0500
Sometimes it was [Ti [Vi *to skirt*] *a gulley*]. G04:0170
...*seemed* [Ti [Vifp *to have been carved*] *from*...] G04:1370
Carmer himself was nowhere [Ti [Vip *to be seen*] Ti]. N14:0470
notice would have [Ti [Vip *to* [R *first*] *be given*] *that*... Ti]
    A01:1450

§ **4.99**   An infinitival phrase reduced to the word *to* alone is still
a Vi:

I shall be delighted [Ti [Vix *to*]]. P07.077

Vg   present-participle phrase

§ **4.100**   First verb of V is a present participle.

orgone energy [Tg [Vg *flowing*] *through the body*...] G13:0190
In [Tg *so* [Vg *doing*]] *he*... J24:0650
[Tg *these institutions* [Vgfb *having* [R *previously*] *been*] A&M
    colleges] G17:1670
employees [Tg [Vge *not belonging*] *to unions*] A19:0110
[Tg [Vgf *Having persisted*] *too long*...] N08:0690

Vn   past-participle phrase

§ **4.101**   First verb of V is a past participle. The structure of English verb groups implies that the past participle will normally be the
only word in a Vn, other than a Vrn... or a reduced tagma.

a leg injury [Tn [Vn *suffered*] *in the Raiders' 38-7 loss*...]
    A12:1120
if people were [Tn [R *better*] [Vn *informed*] [P *on this
    question*] Tn],... A02:0600
Yet [Vod *had*] *he* [Vrne *not visited*] *the girl* N14:1220

[Fn *that . . . religion . . .* [Vzf *has* [R *often*] *supported* Vzf]
[Fn+ *or* [Vnp *been identified*] [P *with*] Fn+] *other
groupings . . .* Fn] J23:1720

Vc modal phrase
§ 4.102 First verb of V is wordtagged VM. . . , or is *had* in its quasi-
modal use with a comparative or superlative adverb such as *better,
best, rather*:

One [Vc *must include*] *the preparation . . .* J08:1850
No more [Vodc *could*] *he* [Vr *defend*] *himself* N09:1480
They [Vcu *can be going*] *along, . . .* A12:1520
his gift for color and imagery [Vcfp *must have been* [R *greatly*]
stimulated] *by . . .* G18:0320
A searching question, which the writer [Vdc *had* [R *better*] *ask*]
himself D11.037

Vk emphatic verb group
§ 4.103 A Vk is a verb group whose first verb is a form of *DO*
which is not grammatically required as a consequence of negation,
subject-auxiliary inversion, or deletion of main verb, and which
accordingly may represent emphasis. Thus:

they [Vk *do challenge*] *the worker's skill* J24:0880
Some forms of capitalism [Vk *do* [R *indeed*] *work*] G22:0840
I never [Vdk *did miss*] *one* A12:0300
It [Vzk *does,* [A *as in type I*], *supply*] *the hilar lymph nodes, . . .*
J12:0100

but:

they [Ve *don't challenge*] . . .
[Vo *do*] *they* [Vr *challenge*] . . .
. . . it aroused a new vitality in the younger poets, as [Vdx *did*]
Byron's <bital> *Childe Harold* <eital>. G18:0370

§ 4.104 In a V whose main verb is *HAVE*, negation and subject-
auxiliary inversion do not make *DO* insertion mandatory, since forms
such as *hasn't, have you . . . ?* followed by a noun phrase (with or
without *got* inserted) are possible ways of questioning or negating
a *HAVE* clause. But (to different extents in Britain and America)
these are stylistically marked alternatives to constructions with *DO*
(*doesn't have, do you have . . . ?*), and there is no presumption that
DO in these latter forms represents emphasis. A negative or interrogative V is never given the Vk subcategory.

Ve   negative verb group

§ **4.105**   V contains a word wordtagged XX, i.e. *not* or *+n't*. Other negative words, such as *never*, are not marked in the analysis by the Ve symbol.

> *and* [Vze *does not rely*] *only on . . .* J22:0110
> *We* [Vef *haven't slept*] *together* N01:1610
> [Voce *Can't*] *you just* [Vr *see*] *the headline . . .* A09:0540
> *if one kind* [Vzp *is charged*] *and the other* [Vzex *is not*] , . . . J05:1030
> *which* [Vefb *have not* [R *always*] *been*] *its trademark* J22:1900

§ **4.106**   When *not* occurs adjacent to a V, but is in construction with the element on its other side and would yield a non-standard verb group if taken as part of the V, it is not included within the V. This situation is particularly common with *not . . . but . . .* sequences (on which see §§ 4.535 ff. below):

> *prompt us* [Ti [Vi *to ask*] [Fn? *not why it happens when it does* [Fn?+ *but why it does not happen more often* Fn?+] Fn?] Ti][9] G74.173
> *routine catering, which* [Vd *demanded*] [N *not_only brains and skill, but common sense . . .*] E31.186
> *I* [Vf *have decided*] [Ti [Vie *not to marry*] *Group Captain Townsend*] F18.191

Vf   perfective phrase

§ **4.107**   V contains *HAVE* followed by a past participle, marking perfective aspect. A V is labelled Vf only if it explicitly contains both of these two elements (cf. § 4.109).

> *. . . as soon as we* [Vf *+'ve had*] *chuck".* N10:0810
> [Vefp *have not* [R *previously*] *been published*] J01:1550
> *What* [Vodc *would*] *you* [Vrf *have done*] *in . . .* N04:0180

Vu   progressive phrase

§ **4.108**   V contains *BE* followed by a present participle, marking progressive aspect. A V is labelled Vu only if it explicitly contains both of these two elements (cf. § 4.109).

---

[9] *Ask not* can occur as a tagma in English, but it is archaic or stylistically highly marked: *Lovers lying two and two* / [Ve *Ask not*] *whom they sleep beside* (Housman). The G74 example given above, however, is grammatically standard taken as a whole; the rule requires the negative particle *not* to be grouped into a V that would be stylistically uncharacteristic of the text.

who [Vau *are approaching*] *at night* G11:1100
...*the GOP* [Vzu *is "Campaigning*] *on the carcass of Eisen-
hower Republicanism"*. A06:0040
seem [Ti [Viu *to be contenting*] *themselves with* ...] G08:0670
They [Vweu *weren't sleeping*], *of course* ... N05:1060
which [Vf *have had* [Vau+ *and are having*]] *enormous consequences* G02:0520

Vp   passive phrase

§ **4.109**   V contains *BE* followed by a past participle, marking
passive voice:

Jones [Vcp *will be chosen*] *the Republican Party's nominee*
A06:0740
what [Vzp *is deemed*] *essential* G22:1380
the need of [Tg [Vgp *being linked*] *with* ...] J23:0350
the only man in history [Ti [Vip *to be* [R *unanimously*] *elected*]
President Ti] G07:0530

A V is labelled Vp only if it explicitly contains both of these two
elements. Thus e.g. the reduced V conjunct in:

...*polychrome ware* [Vsep *was not only imported* [Vn+ *but
indeed made*]] *during a very short period,* ... J67.145

is labelled Vn+, not Vp+. Likewise:

[S ... [Vap *are inherited*] [Pb *by the new material*], [S− [Vn
taken] [R *up*] [Pb *by them*]], ...] D14.071

Vb   verb group ending in BE

§ **4.110**   Last verb of V is a form of *BE* (but not other copular
verbs such as *BECOME, SEEM*). The Vb subcategory applies both
to verb groups containing *BE* as main verb, and to verb groups in
which *BE* is an auxiliary that is not followed by a main verb,
because of subject-auxiliary inversion or because the main verb is
understood. (Thus the subcategories Vb and Vx can co-occur.)

Mr. Martinelli [Vzfb *has,* [P *in recent weeks*], *been*] *of the opinion
that* ... A05:1400
Let <bital> *Q* <eital> [Tb [Vjb *be*] *a nonsingular quadric surface* ... Tb] J21:0110
seemed [Ti [Vifb *to have been*] *amenable to prayer or ritual* Ti]
G11:0630
nor [Voab *are*] *we* [Vrn *given*] *to emotional outbursts* G01:0640

... [Voseb *was not*] *America* [Vrn *founded*] *by rugged indi-*
vidualists . . . ? G22:0430

... *it* [Vcp *can be changed*]; *it* [Vzfbx *has been*], *many times.*
G17:0410

Vx   *V lacking main verb*

§ **4.111**   Vx is used for elliptical verb groups in which auxiliary
verb(s) are not followed by a main verb, as in:

I have heard many say that they are content to earn a half or a
third as much [Fc *as they* [Vdcx *could*] *up North*] G01:1820
those who [Vfp *have been reconstructed*] *and those who* [Vex *have*
+n't] G01:0850
it [Vdcf *would have ended*] *in states like Virginia years before it*
[Vdx *did*]. G01:1230

§ **4.112**   Vx covers cases where the verb is elided from an infinitive
phrase, e.g.:

How could he exert authority . . . [A *as he had* [Ti [Vix *to*]]] —
if he knuckled under to this small-town clown? N09:1320

§ **4.113**   If the last verb of a V is *BE*, *DO*, or *HAVE* functioning
as a main verb, with no further verb understood, Vx does not
apply:

And they [Vd *had*] *almost everything they needed* N05:1250

§ **4.114**   The x subcategory symbol is not included in a Vo tag,
since a Vo necessarily lacks a main verb.

Vt   *catenative V*

§ **4.115**   V whose main verb is wordtagged VMK, VVGK, or
VVNK, i.e. *ought used going bound* functioning as a catenative verb.

The church's ability to change her methods [Vzut *is*
going_VVGK] *to determine her ability to . . .* A10:1640
I [Vct *used_VMK*] *to work on a ranch.* N01:1100
that [Vct *ought_VMK*] *never to have left his neck.* N06:0280
one [Vzpt *is bound_VVNK*] [Ti *to ask the question sooner or*
later] C01.150

Further potential V subcategories

§ **4.116**   In addition to the V subcategories listed above, it might
increase the usefulness of the Corpus if one were to adopt further
subcategories showing whether the main verb of the verb group is

intransitive, transitive, transitive-or-intransitive, or is the verb *DO* or the verb *HAVE*; the existing scheme marks only lack of main verb or *BE* as main verb, but these additional subcategories could be derived more or less mechanically from the wordtags dominated by a V node, and would place the information in a position where it could be exploited by a context-free natural-language analysis system. At present the SUSANNE Corpus does not embody such additional subcategories.

N   Noun Phrase

§ 4.117   A phrase headed by, or consisting wholly of, a noun or pronoun is categorized as N; so too are phrases headed by or consisting of various other word-types, when such phrases fulfil the central grammatical functions of pronouns and phrases headed by nouns, such as acting as subject or object of a clause. Thus, in . . . *as the rich still supplied* . . . G01.117, *rich* is an adjective head of a noun phrase; the two bracketed sequences in *typed on the envelope by a battered old machine that had a piece missing from* [*the "L"*] [*and a badly worn and unaligned "E"*] L18.118 are noun phrases whose heads are ZZ1 words. An N may be headed by an FO. . . (other than an FOq. . .), or by an FWg or FWs — though the head word of an N will not normally carry the simple FW "foreign word" tag, since a foreign word whose role within an English passage is sufficiently clear to be treated as heading an N will be given a more specific wordtag, such as a noun wordtag, by analogy with English words that it resembles functionally. Some "core" examples of N are the emphasized phrases in:

> In normal use **weights are hung** . . . J03:0050
> put **his mouth** to the ground G04:0320
> **Gov. Vandiver is expected** . . . A01:1190
> **Vital secrets** . . . , of **the entire United States navy's still-building nuclear sub fleet**, *were stolen* . . . A20:0010
> has been undergoing **this phenomenal modernization** [Fr **that is so disappointing to the curious Yankee**], . . . G08:1520
> . . . uses **time-honored focused casework techniques** [Po **of specific emotional support, clarification, and anticipatory guidance** Po]. J24:0800

§ 4.118   A tagma may rank as an N although its head is quite unnounlike, if the rest of its structure and its function are noun-phrase-like; cf.:

since [N [Tn *ordered*] *"up" and "down"*] *implies a larger unit cell* J04:0990

— *up* and *down* are both wordtagged RP.

§ **4.119** However, a phrase even if fulfilling a typical noun-phrase role, such as clause subject, and having internal structure otherwise typical of a noun phrase, will not be categorized as N if its head is a determiner, a numeral, or a genitive word, since the alternative categories D, M, G are provided for such cases (see below).[10] An MCe word is phrasetagged N if representing a date (§ 4.512), e.g. *25.12.1992* or *3/4/93*, but as M otherwise.

§ **4.120** English has a number of idiomatic expressions which include unmodified singular count nouns used without reference to their literal meanings: *take place, give rise to, . . .* These expressions, although grammatically non-standard, do not meet the conditions for "grammatical-idiom" status, and they are given no special treatment in the SUSANNE scheme; the nouns are analysed as N's:

An entire change . . . [Vz *takes*] [Ns *place*] *in the interval.* D14.011
This [Vz *gives*] [Ns *rise*] [P *to an oxygen deficiency in the final product and to . . .*]. J70.083

In cases like *take hold of . . .* , the *of* phrase is interpreted as a post-modifier within the Ns (since this would be the logical analysis if the phrase were intended literally).

§ **4.121** Pronouns wordtagged PN1, e.g. *something, anything,* are commonly followed by adjectives, determiners, or adverbs; in such sequences the PN1 word is regarded as the head, hence the whole phrase is an N:

. . . there must be [Ns *something wrong*] *between her daughter and son-in-law.* K05.070
. . . there was [Ns *something immoral*] *about going to the theatre . . .* K16.053
. . . I would like to say [Ns *something more*] *about it.* E26.018
. . . do [Ns *anything else*] E11.161

§ **4.122** The word *one* as an impersonal pronoun is wordtagged PN1o and tagmatagged Ns, although a phrase headed by it in any other use is an M phrase:

when [Ns *one*] *remembers that . . .* F22.033

---

[10] An exception is that an N may have, say, a numeral as surface head if, logically, this modifies an "understood" noun which has been deleted through co-ordination reduction; cf. § 4.493.

§ 4.123 The word *so* used as a pro-form is treated as a pronoun, wordtagged PN1z, and tagmatagged Ns:

...*I have seen them do* [Ns *so*]. F40.133
Admission price was low; [Ns *so*] *was the annual subscription.*
  G30.139
this need not be [Ns *so*]. F41.021
... *if that was the white man's custom,* ... [Ns *so*] *be it.* K29.081
... *if they* [Ns *so*] *wish* ... H21.067
... *if* [Ns *so*] *the drill has been incorrectly ground.* E03.151
... *as if the poor fellow had rocks in his head,* [Ns *so*] *the verger*
  described afterwards. P01.164

— except that various phrases including *so* are idiomtagged, for instance:

[Rx [Ns *a week or_so_RAz=*] *ago*] C04.081
... *the question of why this river is* [J *so_called_JB=*].[11] E09.119

§ 4.124 The sequence *more so* is not treated as a tagma, e.g. in:

... *it* [Vdcb *would have been*] [D *more*] [Ns *so*]. G09.091

§ 4.125 An N may begin with *not*, when this word cannot conveniently be treated as part of a Ve (cf. § 4.437):

...*showed* [Ns *not the slightest sign* [Po *of fatigue*]]. K02.028
Nothing moved: [N@ *not a child,* [Ns– *not a rooster*]]. K09.115
— here, the "@" shows that the *not* sequence is logically in apposition to *Nothing*; the logical grammar notation of Chapter 5 will represent the N@ tagma as moved out of the phrase headed by *Nothing*

§ 4.126 The word *quite* introducing an N, wordtagged RGb, is included within the N:

... *if the nucleus* [Vweb *were not*] [Ns *quite a point*], ... J09.088

§ 4.127 An N may often include a postmodifying adverb:

... *one's answer to* [Nns *question (1) above_RL*] J34.020
For [Np *several years past_RL*] A25.177 — contrast this example with *the world over,* § 4.235 below

---

[11] This is a case where a Corpus usage contradicts an implied claim made by the wordtagging; the idiom *so_called* is listed as a JB=, "used only attributively", but in this case it is used predicatively. Sporadic inconsistencies like this are the norm in authentic language usage, of course; the occurrence of one such example does not constitute a sufficient reason to change the wordtagging.

But an apposition-introducing (REX) element such as *for_example* is not part of the N it "introduces" even when it follows rather than preceding the N:

> ... *there are* [Np *things specially addressed to the remnant then back in the land* — [Nnp@ *verses 9-17*], [R *for_instance_*REX=] — Np] *yet the main drift* ... D11.053

§ 4.128 An N is not commonly postmodified by another N, other than an appositional element (for which see §§ 4.500 ff.); but in *all costs in excess of* [Nu *$20* [Ns *a patient*]] A03:1120 the phrase *a patient* is interchangeable with *per patient* which as a P would be a clear postmodifier, so the analysis is as shown. Likewise [Ns *the first time* [Fr *we've been ahead*] [Ns *this season*]] A12:0720, where *this season* while formally a noun phrase is functionally a time adverbial and hence a normal postmodifier.

N subcategories

§ 4.129 The category N takes the following subcategory symbols:

q v; e y i j u; n; a o; s p.[12]

§ 4.130 The subcategories q (*wh-*...) and v (*wh*...*ever*) are common to all the phrase categories N, J, R, P, D, G. They are "reverse-inherited" from daughter node to mother node in a parsetree: that is, if, say, a noun phrase is tagmatagged Nq because it contains a *wh-* word, e.g. *what stage*, then a P having that noun phrase as an IC will be tagged Pq: [Pq *At* [Nqs *what stage*]] G11:0230. Reverse inheritance applies to each node moving upwards through a tree until the first node having a tagmatag to which the q or v subcategory is inapplicable. Thus:

> [Pq *After* [Nqp [Dqp *how many*] *generations*]] G17:1230
> [Pq *as* [Nqs *a result* [Poq *of which*]]] A42.153

— but:

> [Np *welfare states,* [Fr [Nqs *the organizing principle* [Poq *of which*] Nqs] *is collective responsibility* ... Fr] Np] G02:1110
> — the Fr node prevents the Np from being labelled Nqp

In a highly formal sequence of the type:

---

[12] On p. 209 the sections dealing with subcategory Nu have been placed after the material on Nn.

Harvey . . . was described in <bital> Pharmacopoeia Londinensis <eital>, on the Committee dealing with which he had been serving, as . . . G02.028

— the phrase [Ns *the Committee* [Tg [Vg *dealing*] [Pq *with which*]]] is not given the q subcategory: among the ICs of the N, the constituent which contains the *wh-* word is a Tg, which cannot itself carry the q subcategory.

Nq wh- *noun phrase*
§ 4.131 An Nq is a noun phrase which begins with a *wh-* word (but not including *wh. . .ever* words — see Nv below) or consists of a *wh-* pronoun, or which has a Pq or Dq as an IC:

who
what voices G17:0930
whose ambitions J22:0050
both [Poq *of whom*] C16.085
[Dqs *how much*] *help* H25.152

Nv wh. . .ever *noun phrase*
§ 4.132 An Nv is an N which consists of or begins with a *wh. . .ever* word or equivalent idiom (e.g. *no_matter_which*) — such words bear wordtags containing the characters . . .QV. . . — or which has as an IC a Pv or Dv:

[Nva *whoever*]
[Pv *in* [Nvs *whichever direction*]] G52.109
[Nvp *whatever steps of planning*] A10:0520
[Nvp [Dvp *however many*] *years*] H25.173

Ne first person singular
§ 4.133 The words *I, me* (together with phrases having these words as head) are tagged respectively Nea, Neo. Multi-word Ne phrases are exemplified by:

[Nea *I myself*] *was fond of him* N18:0720
will have forgotten [Neo *me — * [Ns@ *his own father*]] N10:0630

Ny you
§ 4.134 *You* (or another word tagged PPY) as a complete N, or an N having a PPY as head, is tagged Ny. Examples of multi-word Ny phrases are:

kill [Ny *you* [N+ *and your people*]] . . . N04:0190
[Ny" *You* [J *cheap, no good, two-timing*] *bitch*]*!* N18:1550
which [Ny *ye yourselves*] *have sown* G17:1040

Ni   it

§ **4.135**   Ni is used for any case of *it* (whether referential or merely introductory, as in *It was generally agreed that the subject was important*... A10:0690), together with phrases having *it* as head, as in:

> *about* [Ni *it* (Nns@ *the Deep South*])] G01:0570

§ **4.136**   The subcategories Ne, Ny, Ni are not used for reflexive pronouns *myself, yourselves, itself*, etc., which are tagged Nos or Nop depending whether they are singular or plural.

Nj   N with adjective head

§ **4.137**   Nj is used for an N whose head is any J... word, i.e. an adjective in absolute, comparative, or superlative form, or an MD... word (ordinal numeral), or a past participle functioning as an adjective (parsed as [Tn [Vn VVN...]]). The chief reason for assigning such N's a special subcategory is that they can often govern plural verbs without themselves containing plural morphology. Examples of Nj occur in:

> ... *as* [Nj *the rich*] *still supplied the traditional revenues*...
>   G01.117
> [Nj+ *and the older* [Po *of those buildings*...]] D02.052
> ... *32 per 1,000* — [Nj@ *the lowest recorded*] A13.220
> [Nj *The first*] *showed a mother*... A26.179
> *the consent of* [Nj *the* [Tn [Vn *governed*]]] G17:0490
> "[Q [S *It seems anything but nonsense to our enemies*], [Nj" *my
>   dearest*]. Q]" K13.032
> [Njs *a woolly-headed, humble old agrarian* [Fr *who mutters*...]]
>   G08:1030

§ **4.138**   Nj is not used where an understood head noun has been deleted by co-ordination reduction:

> ... [P *not_only to* [N *my physical* [P+ *but also to* [N *my spiritual*] P+] *wellbeing* N] P] N06:1610

Nn   proper name

§ **4.139**   The subcategory Nn marks an N which, as a whole or in part (the part to include at least the head constituent), is a proper name. Thus *John* as a one-word N, or *John Smith*, are given the Nn subcategory, and so is *young John*, or *that man John you were talking about*; on the other hand the N's *John's car*, or *the girl with John*, are not given the subcategory Nn since their heads are not part of a name (though each of these N's dominates structure which includes a lower Nn for *John*).

§ **4.140** Proper names are an exception to the general rule (§§ 4.59–60) which prohibits singulary-branching phrase nodes as daughters of non-clause nodes. Any proper name is given an Nn node, even if that node has a single daughter and is itself the daughter of a phrase or rootrank node — unless the higher node is itself an Nn node, in which case the normal rule applies and a "name within a name" is recognized only where the subordinate name constituent has more than one daughter (or unless the name is embedded in non-English text — *Isis*_NP1f will not take an Nn. . . node within the title *les mystères d'Isis* quoted within the G44 example discussed in § 3.119 above, since foreign wording is deemed to be impervious to grammatical analysis). Thus, in *the girl with John*, the NP1m node for *John* has an Nns node above it, although this node in turn is dominated by the P node for *with John*; on the other hand, in *the Bradford Alhambra* (name of a theatre in Bradford), the NP1t *Bradford* is not dominated by a singulary Nn node because all three words are dominated by an Nn node whose head is *Alhambra*. In *the Wootton Bassett Odeon*, the two-word town name *Wootton Bassett* has an Nn node below the Nn node for the four-word phrase headed by *Odeon*.

§ **4.141** Where co-ordinations of one-word names meet the requirements for wordlevel co-ordination (§§ 4.484 ff.), they are given a word-co-ordination tag and the individual conjuncts are not given separate Nn nodes; the issue of whether or not the co-ordination has a singulary Nn node above it depends on whether or not the next-higher node is an Nn, as in the rule of the previous paragraph. Thus, *the Romney Hythe and Dymchurch Light Railway* is as a whole dominated by a node tagged Nns; within this tagma, *Romney Hythe and Dymchurch* is dominated by an NP1t& node, and no singulary Nn node is inserted above this because the node for the entire tagma has the Nn subcategory. Where only the subordinate conjunct(s) of a wordlevel co-ordination are proper names, no Nn node will appear: [Na [PPHS1m& *He* [NP1m+ *and Dean*]] Na] N03:0050, [P *between* [NN2& *liberals* [NP2s+ *and Bourbons*]] P] G01:0090.

§ **4.142** The subcategory Nn signifies that a (one-word or multiword) phrase is functioning as a proper name; its applicability by no means depends on the word(s) of the name having NP. . . wordtags, which signify, roughly speaking (cf. § 3.20), that a word is a name by origin. *Long Island* as the name of an island belonging to New York state, for instance, is functionally a clear proper name and would be tagged Nns, but the words *Long* and *Island* are tagged respectively JJ, NNL1c: they are ordinary non-proper descriptive terms (and accurately describe the island in question).

§ 4.143   There is a cline between proper names which are composed of NP... words, and phrases which identify unique referents by means of descriptive use of ordinary words. Syntactically we find a tendency for clear cases of proper names to lack determiners (unless the names are plural, e.g. *the Orkneys*), but this is not a reliable rule: proper names may be preceded by *the* either as an exceptional case (*the Lebanon* regularly takes *the* although other country names do not), or as members of an open-ended category of names (*the Wrekin*, a hill in Shropshire, or *the Maelstrom*, a Norwegian whirlpool, exemplify a large class of one-word topographical names that standardly take *the*).

§ 4.144   The SUSANNE scheme uses a broad concept of "proper name" for the purpose of applying the Nn subcategory; according to this concept, proper names include not only cases like those already quoted but also cases like *the Queen, Parliament, the President* (in an American context, meaning the President of the United States), *the Navy* (meaning the Royal Navy, the US Navy, etc. depending on context), even though these phrases are composed of non-proper words which identify the referent of the phrase via their ordinary sense. We have seen that the senses of the words *Long Island* also apply to the referent of that phrase, although the phrase is unquestionably a proper name. Admittedly examples like *Long Island* versus *the Queen* are not on all fours: many islands are long but not all long islands are called *Long Island*, whereas any queen will be referred to as *the Queen* in a suitable context (e.g. within her kingdom and during her reign). However, it would be difficult to use this consideration in order to control the application of the Nn subcategory, because there are too many obscure intermediate cases. The National Coal Board, which ran the British coal-mining industry after nationalization in 1947, had a descriptive name and was the only candidate in British minds for referent of the phrase *National Coal Board* — in these respects the phrase resembles *the Queen* — yet the name must have been arbitrary, like *Long Island*, since it has subsequently been changed to *British Coal*. The *British School of Motoring* is the only driving school with branches nation-wide; does this make the phrase a descriptive one, like *the Queen*, and if so would it lose that status if a competitor arose? The SUSANNE scheme avoids entanglement in such conundrums by making application of the Nn subcategory depend largely on typography rather than on logical status.

§ **4.145** Specifically, the SUSANNE scheme assigns the sub-category Nn to any N whose principal words are required to be given word-initial capitals, in order to mark proper-name status, by a recognized authority on typographical practice. The authority used is Hart's Rules, 39th edition.[13] This implies Nn for a broad range of descriptive names such as *the Queen, the President* (in a context making reference to a particular president clear, e.g. President of the USA, of Magdalen College, Oxford, etc.), *the Bishop* (but not e.g. in *when he became bishop*), *the Thames Estuary* (but not *the estuary of the Thames*), as well as for terms such as trade names which are commonly used in contexts that show them not to be logically singular, e.g. *a (Ford) Cortina, a Concorde, Persil* (washing powder).[14] The word *God*, wordtagged NNS1c, justifies Nn on a phrase it heads when used as the name of the unique Supreme Being, but not when used as a common noun even if capitalized: ... *like* [Ns *a God upon earth*] G06.067; *Heaven, Hell* (wordtagged NN1c) are treated analogously.

§ **4.146** Hart's Rules are distributed widely, and we shall not reproduce the relevant pages here. But a number of special considerations must be mentioned which affect the implications of Hart's Rules for the use of Nn in particular cases.

§ **4.147** First, Nn is used by reference to whether a word or phrase *ought* to be capitalized by the Rules, not whether it actually is capitalized in the text under analysis; but this proviso tends in practice to operate in one direction only — it is common for a capitalized N not to be tagged Nn, but very unusual for an N written in lower case to be given the Nn subcategory. The initial letter of a word may be capitalized for many reasons, some of which have nothing to do with proper-name status — for instance it may be the first word of a sentence, or may occur in a passage written in all-capitals; and some writers are given to using initial capitals other than as prescribed by Hart's Rules in diverse and unsystematic ways. Therefore, if a word appears capitalized in a text, before applying Nn one must ask whether the section of Hart's

---

[13] *Hart's Rules for Compositors and Readers at the University Press Oxford* (Oxford University Press, 39th edn., 1983): see pp. 8–14.

[14] If one asks what criterion distinguishes the class of name-like words and phrases for which Hart's Rules, along with typographical practice more generally, require capitals, the answer seems to lie not in a single criterion but in a compromise between at least two criteria which do not always coincide: a referring phrase is more likely to be regarded as a name if its wording is arbitrary rather than descriptive, and if the referent is unique rather than one of a class. (Cf. § 4.159 below.) It is because proper-name status depends on a mixture of considerations that the SUSANNE scheme has to invoke established typographical authority in order to define the boundaries of Nn rather than attempting to state a set of principles independently.

Rules relating to proper names requires the capital. On the other hand, where a descriptive word or phrase is recognized by the Rules as a capitalizable proper name, there will commonly be a lower-case counterpart which is equally legitimate according to the Rules and which has a more general meaning. Hart's Rules capitalize *the Army*, as the title of a particular organization (in a UK context, the British Army), but of course they also admit *the army*, as a purely descriptive phrase. (A use of the phrase *the army* may in context refer to the British Army, but it does so by indicating, as it were, "the thing which is an army", while *the Army* indicates "the thing which is called 'the Army' ".) If a name is arbitrary rather than descriptive, Hart's Rules will not recognize a valid lower-case usage unless the name has been borrowed for a separate meaning (e.g. *boycott sandwich*); but arbitrary proper names will very rarely occur uncapitalized in texts (the American poet's name *e.e. cummings* is an extremely unusual exception). Thus, if a word or phrase is not capitalized, it is normally safe to assume that the Nn tag does not apply.

§ **4.148** Where a word is capitalized not in order to mark the word itself as a proper name but because it is derived from a proper name, the capital does not in itself justify Nn for an N containing the word. Thus *Londoner, American* meaning a person from London or a citizen of the USA are in no sense proper names, and an N headed by these words would not be tagged Nn.

§ **4.149** However, such a word can of course be used as (the whole or part of) a name of a category that would be capitalized irrespective of the word's derivation. For instance, *Ulsterman* meaning a man from Ulster is not a proper name, but as the name of a boat train connecting with a ferry to Northern Ireland it is one. In such cases, where capitalization would occur for independent reasons, the test of whether an N is enough of a proper name to justify the Nn subcategory must be whether names of similar entities that are not derived from proper names are capitalized. For instance, *Golden Arrow* was the name of a boat train for France, and is capitalized although derived from non-proper words; therefore both this and *Ulsterman* are tagged Nn as train names.

§ **4.150** A problem arises in connection with the clause in Hart's Rules enjoining capitalization for "Parties, denominations, and organizations, *and their members*" (op. cit. 10; our italics). There is a very vague borderline between e.g. *a Londoner*, which involves a straightforward common noun that happens to derive from a proper noun, and e.g. *a Marxist* or *a Calvinist*, which refer to a member of a political party or movement, and a religious denomination, whose names are derived from proper names. For that matter, one might hold that *a Catholic* is capitalized at least in part because the term is "derived" in an extended sense from the proper name *Catholic Church*, although the word *Catholic* within this name itself stems from the non-proper adjective *catholic*. In order to achieve a clear-cut practice, the SUSANNE scheme applies the Nn subcategory to names of "parties, denominations, and organizations", but *not* to words or phrases denoting their members.

This is an across-the-board modification of Hart's Rules for purposes of applying the Nn subcategory, and is invoked even in cases where a capitalized word for a member of a group or organization does not derive from a name for the group/organization itself. For instance, the word *Jew* does not derive from a name for the community of Jews,[15] but a noun phrase headed by *Jew* is not tagged Nn. In the case of *the Sioux* (an Amerindian nation), *the Miami Orioles* (a baseball team), the name for the group is simply the plural of the term for the group members, seen collectively. By the rule quoted, *a Sioux, an Oriole* are not tagged Nn, and neither are *the Sioux, the Miami Orioles*.

Although names of "parties, denominations" etc. are given Nn tags, words such as *Communism* which refer to abstract movements or principles rather than concrete social organizations are not tagged Nn.

§ 4.151   A proper name borrowed unchanged as a common noun, listed as such in the relevant dictionary (cf. § 3.25 re *Labrador, Garibaldi*), does not justify the Nn subcategory. Names of languages, e.g. *French, Malayalam*, are tagged Nn.

§ 4.152   The Nn subcategory requires only the "principal words" of an N to be capitalizable under Hart's Rules; obviously lower-case words such as *the, of* do not prevent phrases like *the Queen, the Church of England* from being tagged Nn. In the great majority of cases, the head word of an Nn will be among the capitalized words; but this is not absolutely necessary. Hart's Rules capitalize "Proper names of periods of time", but alongside examples such as *Old Stone Age, Iron Age*, is listed *Palaeozoic era*, with small *e*. The example is not discussed further; we take it that the entire phrase *Palaeozoic era* (not just the word *Palaeozoic* alone) is being cited as a capitalizable phrase — and is thus a phrase to be tagged Nn within the SUSANNE scheme — and that the reason for writing a capital only on the first word is that *palaeozoic* is so much longer and more

---

[15] Ultimately the word derives from a personal name, *Judah*, but it seems questionable whether this fact would be perceived as relevant to English typographic practice.

specific than *era* that the compiler of Hart's Rules did not regard the latter as a "principal word" within the phrase.

§ **4.153** Because all principal words of a capitalizable phrase will be capitalized, not just the head word, it will sometimes be difficult to know whether a modifying word is capitalized "in its own right" or only because of its position within a larger phrase. Here the guide must be how the same word is treated in different contexts. Thus, the phrase *the Queen of Spades* is clearly Nn as a whole; one might reasonably suggest that *Spades*, as the name of one of four unique suits in the playing-card system, should itself be regarded as a proper name, but in a context such as *He made five tricks in spades* a capital would not be usual on *spades* and nothing in Hart's Rules would require it, so the word is not treated as an Nn in *the Queen of Spades*. A phrase describing a unique referent which might be Nn by Hart's Rules if occurring in isolation will not be Nn if modifying a clear proper name: [Nns [Ns *Secretary of Labor*] *Arthur Golderg*] A10:0940, [Nns *Charles E. Raymond,* [Ns@ *District Attorney*]] A10:0020 (cf. [Nns *The Secretary of Labor*] *announced . . .* , [Nns *The District Attorney*] *said . . .*).

When a proper name refers to a model or marque of a manufactured item, it is often followed by the generic description of the item in lower case: *He had been carrying* [Nn *an Enfield rifle and . . .*] N03:0020. There is a subtle distinction between e.g. *. . . which contain* [Nnp *Polaris missiles*] G03:0080 (*Polaris* is the name of a type of missile) and *. . . in contact with* [Np *the* [Nns *Polaris*] *subs*] G03:1180 (submarines which carry Polaris missiles — *Polaris* is not the name of a model of submarine).

For phrases including day-of-week or month names see § 4.513.

§ **4.154** When the head of an N is an alphanumeric "code word" or a conventional abbreviation, rather than an ordinary word, e.g. *B-52* (type of aircraft), *P45* (Inland Revenue form), *MW* for *megawatt*, *H-bomb* for *hydrogen bomb*, the use of capitals is normally dictated by the set form of the word (and hence such words are not discussed in Hart's Rules, since they require no decision from a copy-editor). In these cases the use or non-use of Nn depends on whether analogous ordinary words in similar contexts would be capitalized. Thus, aircraft types such as *Spitfire, Concorde,* are specifically listed in the Rules as capitalizable, so *a B-52* will take Nn. On the other hand, the name of a form such as the tax form *P45* does not seem close to any of the classes identified in Hart's rubrics, so *a P45* will not be Nn; and the full forms abbreviated *MW, H-bomb,* are not capitalized, so N's headed by the abbreviations are not Nn.

§ **4.155**   Phrases such as *Type B, page 211* are tagged Nn in line with Hart's Rules, whether capitalized or not:

> *in* [Nnp *Figs* [M *10a* [P *to 10d*]]] J74.201 — the MCb words are not themselves treated as Nn items
> *on* [Nns *clause 8,* [Fr *which concerns* . . .]] A11.190

— and this is extended to make e.g. *No. 6, §§20-22* Nn's; but a word such as *B, 211, IIa* functioning as a name in itself, not preceded by a word such as *page, type,* which might in principle be capitalized, is not tagged Nn. An algebraic variable is not Nn.

§ **4.156**   In the case of biological names for genera, species, etc. (used as biological names wordtagged FW. . ., cf. the footnotes to these wordtags in § 3.73), capitalization is determined independently of Hart's Rules by the international authorities on nomenclature, and the SUSANNE use of Nn conforms to the logic of the international systems — that is, names or abbreviations for ranks higher than species are capitalized and regarded as proper names, those for species and lower ranks are not normally capitalized and are not regarded as proper names. Thus a reference to *Equus, Equus caballus,* or *E. caballus* would be tagmatagged Nn, but an N headed by *caballus* would not be Nn.

§ **4.157**   A noun phrase consisting of an NNS. . . word without an accompanying name, whether the NNS. . . word is capitalized or not and whether it is used referentially or vocatively, is not given an Nn. . . tagmatag:

> *Leaning forward in her chair,* [Ns *Gran*_NNS1c] *nearsightedly scrutinized* . . . N13:1360
> *what would have happened* [P *to Missy*_NNS] *if* . . . N04:0440
> *"Yes* [Ns" *sir*_NNS]*"* N12:0230

§ **4.158**   For the treatment of book titles and similar items, see §§ 4.395 ff.

§ **4.159**   It cannot be claimed that the use of a compositor's manual always yields a fully logical boundary between proper and non-proper noun phrases, because written capitalization is sometimes used to represent specificity of reference in a relative rather than absolute fashion. Thus SUSANNE text J07, on astronomy, consistently capitalizes *Earth* but not *sun*, in sequences like:

> . . . *causes the dust to spiral into the sun in times much shorter than the age of the Earth.* J07:0040

Both words are being used to denote individual bodies of our solar system, so arguably they have exactly equal claims to be given the

Nn subcategory. However, while Hart's Rules do not make explicit recommendations for these particular words, the usage illustrated is in the spirit of those rules: *Earth* needs a capital to distinguish it from the substance *earth*, whereas *sun* standardly refers to a unique heavenly body. In this case the SUSANNE analyses conform to the capitalization practice found in the text, i.e. Nns for *the Earth* but Ns for *the sun*. It may be that a criterion for applying the Nn subcategory can be devised that gives a more logical boundary to the concept "proper name" than does our criterion based on Hart's Rules; in the mean time, however, our criterion is preferable to leaving the issue to be settled in terms of individual analysts' intuitions about the concept.

§ **4.160**   As an example of the use of Nn in a complex example, consider the following example:

> *The jury praised the administration and operation of the Atlanta Police Department, the Fulton Tax Commissioner's Office, the Bellwood and Alpharetta prison farms, Grady Hospital and the Fulton Health Department.* A01:0640

The co-ordination of names is tagged as follows:

[Nn *the Atlanta Police Department,*
[Nns– [G [Nns *the Fulton Tax Commissioner*] +'s] *Office*],
[Np– *the* [Nn [NP1t& *Bellwood* [NP1t+ *and Alpharetta*]]] *prison farms*],
[Nns– *Grady Hospital*]
[Nns+ *and the Fulton Health Department*]]

Atlanta, Fulton, and *Grady* are not given Nn nodes, being one-word proper names which are ICs of larger Nn tagmas. Each of the institutions mentioned other than the prison farms has a capitalized head noun; and it is quite plausible that a typographic contrast between e.g. *the Fulton Health Department* and *the Alpharetta prison farm* might correspond to a logical difference between the two re-ferring expressions, akin to the difference discussed above between *the Army* and *the army*. Accordingly, the typographical contrast in the text is allowed to decide the application or non-application of the Nn subcategory. Since this means that the *prison farms* conjunct is not an Nn, there must be an Nn node above the wordlevel co-ordination *Bellwood and Alpharetta* (had the conjunct ended *Prison Farms*, it would have been tagged Nnp–, and no intermediate Nn node would have been inserted below this Nnp– node and above the NP1t& node). The top node is given the Nn subcategory because the phrase *the Atlanta Police Department* is a proper name (cf. § 4.468).

§ **4.161**   Grammatical structure within a proper name is recognized only if the markers establishing it are English; thus:

The [NP1s& *Baltimore* [NP1g+ *and Ohio*]] *Railroad* A19:0010
[Nns *Sir*_NNS *Iain*_NP1m *Moncrieffe*_NP1s [Po *of* [Ns *that Ilk*_NN1n]]]

but:

[Nns *Sonji*_NP1f *Van*_NP1s *der*_NP1s *Merwe*_NP1s] K23.144
[Nns *Charles*_NP1m *de*_NP1s *Gaulle*_NP1s]
[Ns *a*_AT1 [Nn *Romeo*_NP1m *y*_FW *Julieta*_FW]
   *cigar*_NN1c]

— all without internal structure, except that the trade name *Romeo y Julieta* is recognized as an (unanalysed) name tagma within its English-language context. (Foreign "grammatical words" occurring within names, such as *de la y*, are tagged as unanalysed foreign words when components of a non-personal name some of whose words receiving "meaningful" tags, and as names when occurring within personal names, ignoring in either case their meanings in the languages from which they come.)

In the case of an acronym such as *B. & O.* for *Baltimore and Ohio*, since by § 3.124 the sequence is tagged as a grammatical idiom, the subsequence *& O.* cannot be analysed as a subordinate conjunct even though *&* is an English symbol.

Nu   unit noun phrase
§ **4.162**   A noun phrase whose head is an NNU. . . (but not NNO. . . or NNT. . .) word or idiom.

an estimated mass of [Nu 25 *g*] J07:1360
the temperature range of [Nu [M 77 +<hyphen> +294] M]
   +<deg>K_NNU] J04:1720
It cost us [Nu [M *a hundred thousand*] *dollars*_NNU2 [Ns+ *and*
   [Np *thirty days*] *lost time* Ns+] Nu] N07:1740

§ **4.163**   The u subcategory is assigned mechanically, irrespective of whether the NNU. . . word is used in its measure sense: e.g. *she was already on* [Nup *her feet*] N05:0520.

Na, No   noun phrase marked as subject or as non-subject
§ **4.164**   An Na or No is normally a first- or third-person pronoun, occasionally with modifying elements. For instance *he she we* are

tagged Nas or Nap as appropriate, while *him her us* are tagged Nos
or Nop; and *I*, *me* are tagged Nea, Neo respectively. Examples of
multi-word Na or No phrases are:

[Na *He* [Ns+ *or his deputy*] [Ms+ *or one of* [Np *their seven
    assistants,* [Z *all full colonels*], Np] Ms+] Na] *mans the heart
    of the command post . . .* G03:1270
Once indeed [Nas *He* [Fr *who was the "truth" as well as the
    "way," and the "life,"*] Nas] *was in her midst . . .* D11.060
for [No *myself* [Np+ *and my fellow-employees*]] G22:1750

§ 4.165   The word *whom* is tagged Nqo:

This remarkable man of medicine, [Fr [Nqo *whom*] [Nns *Sir
    Francis Burdett*] *described . . .*] G06.066

— but *who* is tagged simply Nq rather than Nqa, since it can be
used in either subject or non-subject position:

A Texas halfback [Nq *who*] *doesn't even know . . .* A12:0010
"How many people know [Nq *who*] *they are"?* N07:1090
discussing what I wanted to see and [Nq *who*] *I wanted to meet
    in Leningrad.* G49.029
a shy, diffident Englishman [Nq *who*] *they had seen on the Queen
    Mary.* B05.035

§ 4.166   An N consisting of any reflexive pronoun (wordtagged
PPX. . .), including *each_other, one_another*, is tagged No:

he established [Nos *himself*] *as . . .* A19:1530
. . . to size [Nop *each_other*] *up.* A31.069
Maybe [Fa *if the marshal hears this* [Nos *himself*]], *it'll make
    a difference.* N12:1730

— this applies even in exceptional cases where a reflexive pronoun
functions as subject, as in:

Each side proceeds on the assumption [Fn *that* [Nos *itself*] *loves
    peace, but the other side consists of warmongers*]. G75.034

§ 4.167   In a compound N containing subordinate N conjunct(s),
the main conjunct is given Na or No subcategories if that conjunct
is marked as subject or as non-subject (irrespective of whether a
subordinate conjunct has the same or the opposite marking), but
not if a subordinate conjunct alone is so marked; thus:

[Na *he* [Nns+ *and Beatrice*]] J39.098

— but:

[N *My Uncle* [Nea+ *and I*]] N18:0280
[Na *she* [Nos+ *and him*]]

Ns, Np noun phrase marked as singular/plural
§ **4.168** An N is assigned one of the subcategory symbols s or p if it is internally marked as belonging to one or the other number, either by virtue of the head word having a . . .1. . . or . . .2. . . wordtag or being tagged NNS, NNm, or NNSS, NNmm, or through premodification by a . . .1. . . or . . .2. . . determiner or numeral word, or a Ds, Dp, or Ms phrase: thus *his shoe, this sheep, one sheep* are Ns while *his shoes, many sheep, very few sheep* are Np; *my sheep* is N without s or p, and so is *two sheep* (number words above *one* do not contain . . .2. . . in their wordtags, and are not infallible guides to the grammatical number of the noun they modify). Not all word-tags containing digits 1 or 2 are relevant for the subcategories Ns, Np, of course: the contrast between APPGi1 and APPGi2 relates to the number of possessor rather than possessed, and the digits of idiomtags serve a quite different purpose.

The fact that a head is modified by a co-ordination, or by a singular or plural modifier other than a determiner or numeral, is in itself irrelevant to the application of the Ns, Np subcategories:

[Ns *an* [Np *eight months*] *period*] A08:1550
of [Ns [JJ& *personal and divine*] *wisdom*] J35.051

§ **4.169** The Ns subcategory is also used in the case of an N whose head is a Tg (see § 4.340):

. . . *without* [Ns *the* [Tg *fullbacking*] *of a top star, Jack Spikes*]
A12:1440

§ **4.170** For the use of Ns/Np above wordlevel co-ordinations, see § 4.490 below.

§ **4.171** Appropriate premodifiers may justify the s or p sub-category for an N whose head is not a noun or pronoun:

[Njs *A third*_MD, [Ms@ *one of at least equal and perhaps even greater importance*], Njs] G02:0660
[Np *These three* <bital> *d*_FOx <eital>] *form* . . . J21.025

§ **4.172** Neither s nor p is included in the case of phrases contain-ing contradictory indications of number:

. . . *is recorded as* [Nu *a full three feet*] J23.073
. . . *with* [N *an additional two persons*] H09.043

In:

a [Jx [Ns *twenty year*] *old*] *law student* G06:1650

the modifying phrase of the Jx is tagged Ns because *year* is singular, and *twenty* (as explained above) is not relevant for Ns v. Np.

§ 4.173   A compound N, having a plus-tagged or minus-tagged IC, is never marked s; it is marked p only if each conjunct is plural (cf. § 4.468).

§ 4.174   The subcategories Ne, first person singular, and Ni, *it*, are taken to imply singular number, so s would be redundant and is not included: *I me it* are tagmatagged Nea Neo Ni, not Neas Neos Nis.

§ 4.175   The semantic singularity of nouns such as *trousers scissors* is ignored by the SUSANNE scheme; N's headed by such words are both morphologically plural and govern plural verbs, and are formtagged Np. Conversely, the SUSANNE scheme provides no special classification for collective nouns such as *herd crowd committee*, and N's headed by such nouns are formtagged Ns (although in British English they frequently govern plural verbs). Proper names which are formally plural are formtagged Nnp even if used to denote singular referents, e.g. *the United States*, or *Highlands* as an abbreviation for *the Highlands Oil & Gas Company* at N09:1040.

§ 4.176   Because the SUSANNE scheme has no category of collective nouns, phrases of the form *a number, a couple, a group, a number/couple* of Np, etc. are all tagged Ns (though this is not helpful with respect to verb agreement phenomena):

[Ns *quite a number* [Po *of* [Np *lame hounds*]]] E15.031
[Ns+ *and a large number* [Po *of* [Np *other similar computations*]]] J80.098
After contributing [Ns *a couple* [Po *of pounds*]] *to the family exchequer . . .* P27.086

§ 4.177   A phrase of the form "*none_PN of* Y" is given the Ns subcategory if Y is an element marked as singular (e.g. it is itself an Ns, or is a word such as *this* with a . . .1. . . wordtag), but is not given the Np subcategory even if Y is marked as plural: usage differs on verb agreement in such cases.

she felt [N *no jealousy* [Ns+ *and none of the hate she had resolved to bear for her sister*]] K17.186
. . . [N *almost none* [Po *of the writers*]] *has forsaken . . .* G08:0190
there are [N *none* [Po *of the modern aids to navigation*]] *on board* A40.120

J Adjective Phrase

§ 4.178   A tagma headed by an adjective (JJ...) or ordinal numeral (MD...), or by a Tn or Tg that is modified by elements not forming part of the Tn or Tg, is a J. Some "core" examples would be:

what is [J *expedient*] *at the time* A06:1410
Kid Boyd was [J *unusually silent*], ...   N07:0510
...*tend to be* [Jh *bigger than the first ones*], ...   J10:0710
a [J *relatively immense*] *degree* J12:0670
a [J *fairly* [Tn [Vn *modernized*]]] *urban sector* J22:0450
if the interpretation is [J *too* [Tg [Vg *threatening*]]], ...   J24:1640
...*ranks* [J *fourth_MD*] *in Southwest Conference scoring*...
     A12:0020

§ 4.179   According to *OALD3* and general usage manuals, the ordinal *first* is grammatically ambiguous as between adjective and adverb functions, but the ordinals *second* upwards are only adjectives, not adverbs. SUSANNE tags ordinals MDo or MD in either adjectival or adverbial uses; but an occasional adverbial use of an ordinal from *second* upwards will be phrasetagged J (the function-tagging system of Chapter 5 will show its logical role), whereas phrases consisting of or headed by *first* will be phrasetagged either J or R depending on function in context:

[J *Second*], *it would be much easier*...   K14.158
[R *First* [Po *of all*]] [Np *simple part-songs*]: [S@ *I found*...]
     G04.041

§ 4.180   A frequent problem in deciding constituency in connection with J phrases occurs where an adjective is followed by a prepositional phrase or a clause (often a Ti) which may be seen either as a postmodifier within the J or as a sister of the J.

§ 4.181   This issue cannot be considered independently of the functiontagging system of Chapter 5. In essence, if a tagma following a predicative adjective or equivalent item can be seen as fulfilling one of the "adjunct" roles discussed there with respect to the containing clause, it will be treated as sister of the adjective and allotted that role; if it can be seen only as completing the sense of the predicative adjective, it will be treated as a postmodifier of the adjective. The presumption is in favour of treating the following item as sister rather than daughter of the J in cases of doubt.

§ 4.182   Thus we have the analysis:

no two are [J *alike*] [P *in specification or sound*], ...   C10.190

— the P is an adjunct of Respect (its complete tagging including functiontag is "P:r"), giving information (which might have been omitted) about the respect in which the remainder of the proposition holds; but:

> *The number of nuclei is* [Jh *dependent* [P *upon the physical and chemical properties of . . .* P] Jh]. J08.071

— here *dependent* refers to an inherently relational concept, so that it would be scarcely meaningful to call something *dependent* without saying what on, and none of the logical adjunct categories closely fits the *upon* phrase.

§ 4.183 Situations where the semantic relationship between adjective and P in predicative position clearly justifies the analysis that places the P within the J include the following:

- the preposition of the P is *by* and the material preceding it resembles a passive verb group except that the word morphologically akin to a past participle must instead be wordtagged as an adjective:

  > . . . *ought to be* [Jh *unaffected* [Pb *by the condition of the body*]] D14.090 — *unaffected* must be JJ rather than VVN. . . , because there is no verb *unaffect

- the P is the logical completion of a modifier of degree preceding the adjective — see § 4.330
- an *of* phrase following a superlative defines the domain to which it relates:

  > [Jh *Eldest* [Po *of the seven*]] G07:0370

§ 4.184 When an adjective of cognitive attitude is followed by an *of* phrase or an Fn representing the object to which the attitude is directed, the latter tagma will be treated as postmodifying the adjective:

> [L [R *Obviously*] [Jh *conscious* [Po *of the fierce and widespread resentment over the U.S. Polaris base in Britain*]]], *Mr. Gaitskell said . . .* A04.111
>
> . . . *one had been* [Jh *unaware* [Po *of the really decisive act*]]. G11:0740
>
> *He closed his eyes,* [Jh *ashamed* [Po *of his tears*]]. N02:0330
>
> *He was* [Jh *proud* [Po *of his accomplishments*], [Jh– *proud* [Po *of his job*]], [Jh– *proud* [Fn *that Donald Kruger and his associates trusted him*] Jh–] Jh]. N07:1510
>
> *Delius was* [Jh *quite aware* [Fn *that his music was enjoying a vogue . . .*]] A17.063

§ 4.185 In *due to . . .* , *regardless of . . .* sequences, the P's post-modify the adjectives. There is a special problem with these phrases, in that while *due* and *regardless* are clear adjectives, the phrases they introduce commonly function adverbially:

> *Probably* [Jh *due* [P *to his rather squalid surroundings as a child*]], *Frank is one of the most extravagant . . .* E11.185
> *It is* [Jh *due* [P *to his financial and untiring help*]] [Fn *that the band is . . .*] E12.172 — in this case it is because the Jh phrase counts as adverbial that the *that* clause is formtagged Fn (cf. § 4.308)
> *. . . everyone is presented to them,* [Jh *regardless* [Po *of title, age or sex*]]. F08.125

It might seem tempting to regard *due to, regardless of* as II= idioms; however, it is quite normal for *due to*, at least, to be interrupted (e.g. *due largely to*), which rules the idiom analysis out. Accordingly they are treated as adjective + preposition sequences introducing J phrases; the functiontagging system of Chapter 5 will show that these J's, exceptionally, fulfil roles typical of adverbs.[16]

§ 4.186 In the example:

> *His chest was* [Jh *curiously* [JJ& *high and sharp*] [P *like a pigeon's*]]. K06.080

the *like* phrase does not cohere particularly closely, semantically, with the co-ordination of adjectives, but it must nevertheless be analysed as within the Jh, since it fits none of the logical adjunct categories.

§ 4.187 Where a clause has been grammatically reduced to a phrase headed by an adjective, a following tagma which might have been treated as an adjunct in the full clause must instead be regarded as postmodifying the adjective:

> [Ns *an offence* [Jh *punishable* [P *with imprisonment*]]] A02.083

— in a clause such as *which is punished with imprisonment* the *with* phrase would be an adjunct of Manner, but there is no possibility of treating it as other than an adjective postmodifier in the actual example. (If one regarded the sequence as a Z reduced from *which is punishable with imprisonment*, the *with* phrase would not be regarded as a Manner adjunct in such a clause, hence would still be an adjective postmodifier; and, since this implies that the clause has

---

[16] It is in any case not so very unusual for a J to function adverbially. Cf. for instance:

[J *True*], *St John's was on the outskirts of Farlingham . . . , but . . .* P03.032

been reduced to just one constituent, it cannot be formtagged Z —
cf. § 4.372 — but must be regarded as a J phrase, not a clause.)

§ **4.188**   A Ti following an adjective is commonly treated as a
postmodifier, only rarely filling an adjunct role:

> *They were* [Jh *happy* [Ti *to do the job voluntarily*]]. F20.211
> ... *he will be* [Jh *well advised* [Ti *not to publish them* ...]]
> B09.159
> *But he seems* [Jh *willing* [Ti *to listen a lot*]]. F03.030
> *Hanson* ... *was* [Jh *annoyed* [Ti *to find Freeman following him*]].
> N05.051

— though compare:

> ... *it's* [J *almost certain*] [Ti *to disappear*] F31.134

which is a surface representation of a logical structure along the
lines of "[*it to disappear*] *is almost certain*": for a full explanation
of how this structure is analysed, see § 5.64.

§ **4.189**   A reduced Fa is regularly parsed as a postmodifier after
an adjective:

> *The parties of* <bital> *guerre à outrance* <eital> *dwindled to*
> [Np [Jh *impotent* [Fa *if vociferous*]] *cliques*] *at Bordeaux*
> *and Versailles,* ... J57.180
> *the* [Jh *common,* [Fa *though not_XX* [J *universal*]],] *belief*
> J58.196

§ **4.190**   But in some cases a clause following an adjective will
be its sister, even though closely connected to it semantically, for
instance the *sorting* clause fits the Manner adjunct category (cf. the
carving in a road example at § 5.148 below) in:

> *Cortés was* [J *busy*] [Tg *subduing the Aztecs*] G70.159
> *Neutral or inversion meteorological conditions are* [J *necessary*]
> [Tf *for a cloud to travel along the surface*]. J08:0480 — the
> Tf is a Contingency adjunct
> [S [L [J *Poor*] [Fa *where they had once been rich*], ... L], *the*
> *rebels who would not surrender in spirit drew comfort from* ...
> G01:1130 — the verbless clause (L) is a reduction of a sequence
> something like *although they were poor where they had*
> *once* ... , which contains no temptation to group the adjective
> into a single J constituent with the *where* clause

Of course, often an adjective and a clause happen to occur consecutively without having a close semantic relationship, so that it is
obvious that they do not belong together as a single tagma:

the Kennedy administration would be held [J *responsible*] [Fa *if the outcome in Laos was . . .*] A04:1130

§ 4.191   *Enough* following an adjective is treated as a post-modifier (wordtagged RGAf) within a J:

[Fa *if the coffee is too weak* [Fa+ *or the tea too strong*] [Fa+ *or* [Ds *either of them*] *not* [Jh *hot enough*]]] E26.026

J subcategories

§ 4.192   Subcategory symbols for J are: q; v; x r; h. On the reverse inheritance of Jq and Jv, cf. § 4.130.

Jq   wh- adjective phrase
§ 4.193   An adjective phrase in which the head is modified by a *wh-* word (but not a *wh. . .ever* word, see Jv below):

"No telling [Jq *how good*] *this horse is*" N03:0810
[Jq *How effective*] *have Kennedy administration first foreign policy decisions been . . . ?* A04:0960

Jv   wh. . .ever adjective phrase
§ 4.194   An adjective phrase in which the head is modified by a *wh. . .ever* word (or idiom wordtagged similarly):

[Jv *however bad*] *I may be* G17:0180
[Jv *no_matter_how high*] *a purpose that may be* B15:0400

Jx   measured absolute adjective phrase
§ 4.195   An adjective phrase whose head is an adjective in absolute rather than comparative form, or is a Tn, and is premodified by a measure expression. A qualifier, such as *very*, or an interrogative adverb (*how*), does not count as a measure expression in this context; a determiner such as *this*, which refers implicitly to a measurement, does count as such.

[Jx [Nup *several centimetres*] *long*] J15.205
[Jx [Nup *about* [M *one and a half*] *feet*] *square and . . .*] G03:1520
[Jx *this big*] M02.022
They looked [Jx [Ns *a good deal*] *alike*], . . . N01:0680
The [Jx [N *15* +<hyphen> +*year*] +<hyphen> +<old>] *adopted son of . . .* A19:1120

§ 4.196   The word *so* does not count as a measure expression:

. . . *my love for* [Nns *Georgie*, [J *so* [JJ& *tender and sensuous and gay*]]]. K15.041

Jr   measured comparative adjective phrase

§ 4.197   A Jr is a tagma akin to a Jx except that the head is a comparative adjective (either an *-er* form, or a *more/less* + JJ phrase):

[Jrh [Np *almost two years*] *later* [P *than that of . . .*]] D11.006
a [Jr *much smaller*] *area* F41.036
[Jr [R [M *several thousand*] +<hyphen> +*fold*] *more toxic*]
  J08:1130

§ 4.198   Although e.g. *how long, so quiet* do not count as Jx tagmas, [Dqs *how much*] *longer*, [Ds *so much*] *quieter* are tagged Jr. *No* as in *no better* justifies the Jr subcategory.

§ 4.199   The SUSANNE parsing scheme recognizes no internal grouping in premodified periphrastic-comparative sequences such as:

[Jr *much more important*] P08.136
[Jr *far less severe*] G55.014
. . . seems [Jrh *far more meaningful* [P *than most of the noise generated by the big concert aggregations*] Jrh]. C08:0730

— the scheme makes a structural contrast between e.g. [Ns [D *much more*] *trouble*] and [Jr *much more troublesome*]: the latter wording has obvious parallels with the former but this is offset by the fact that *more troublesome* is grammatically equivalent to a one-word adjective in *-er*.

§ 4.200   The subcategory Jr is used for the "correlative" *the . . . the . . .* construction of *CGEL*, p. 1111 (the construction which translates into German with *je . . . desto . . .*), if either or both of the correlated elements are functioning adjectivally rather than ad-verbially (if they are adverbial, see § 4.230 below). The *je . . .* half of the correlation is as a whole treated as an Fc which is introduced by a Jr and which modifies another Jr corresponding to the *desto . . .* half; thus:

[Jr [Fc [Jr *the wider*] [Ns *the wheelbase*] [Vzb *is*] Fc], *the more satisfactory* Jr] *is the performance*

The word *the* is the "measure expression" justifying the Jr formtag in either case. Authentic examples of this construction are:

[Jr [Fc [Jr *the more* [Tn *highly placed*] Jr] *they are —
that_is*_REX=, [Fc@ [D *the more*] *they know* Fc@] — Fc] *the
more concerned* Jr] *they have become.* G03:0390
. . . the non-diagonal <bital> d_{ij} <eital> *being* [Jr *the smaller* [Fc
[Rr *the better*] [Ns *the waviness of* $\Omega_{<bital>}$<eital>] [Vzp *is re-tained*] Fc] Jr] J80.110

(In the G03 case, since there is no SUSANNE subcategory Dr the r subcategory does not appear on *the more they know*.)

Jh "heavy" (postmodified) adjective phrase
§ 4.201 A J phrase which includes modifying material following the head; "modifying material" for this purpose does not cover subordinate conjuncts or appositional elements,[17] or non-verbal material such as punctuation. Where the head of a J is a Tn, the J takes the h subcategory if there is material following the Vn of the Tn, whether this material is inside or outside the Tn tagma.

> *a concept* [Jh *analogous to the principle of internal responsibility*] G02:1130
> *for* [Jh *long enough*] *times* J07:0660
> [Jh *as rigid* [P *as black statuary*]] G04:0020
> *he was* [Jh *too* [Tn *exhausted*] [Ti *to stay awake*]] N01:0120
> *was* [Jh *so* [Tg *overwhelming*] [Fc *that . . . Matilda could not speak at all*] Jh] N13:0450
> *. . . will become* [Jh *so* [Tn [Vn *decimated*] [Pb *by war, famine and self destruction*] Tn] [Fc *that . . .*] Jh] D12.081

R Adverb Phrase

§ 4.202 Normally an R will be a phrasetagged adverb, or a phrase whose head word is an adverb. Some core examples:

> *naturally*
> [R *As early* [P *as 1913*]] J12:1220
> *could* [R *very well*] *seek* A08:1590

The words *when* and *where* constitute Rq (§ 4.224) tagmas even if wordtagged CSn or CSr, introducing antecedentless clauses identifying times or places (see the examples in § 4.291).[18]

§ 4.203 Direction names such as *south* are invariably wordtagged ND1, but are given R rather than N phrasetags when heading phrases with adverb-phrase-like structure or occurring as one-word phrases in adverbial rather than nominal functions:

---

[17] Except that, if a subordinate conjunct or appositional element in a J co-ordination is itself a Jh, the main conjunct will also be tagged Jh.

[18] It is arguably an illogicality in the SUSANNE scheme that *when*_CSn and *where*_CSr are tagmatagged as *wh*- phrases, whereas *that*_CST introducing a relative clause is not treated as a relative pronoun (§ 5.79). It might be preferable not to recognize the wordtags CSn, CSr, but to extend the use of the tag RRQr to cover these uses of *when* and *where*. But the analyses of the SUSANNE Corpus follow the rule in the text.

to go [R *west*] *through the narrow river valley* N15:0540

[Ns *the 1½-story brick home* [P *in the Franklin Manor section*], [Rx [Nup *15 miles*] *south* [Po *of here*] Rx] [P *on the bay*] Ns] A19:1230

Dirion found [Ns *a large war party*] [R *south of us*]. N04:0050

[Nn *the* <bital> *Mar Tenebroso* <eital>, [Nns+ *or "Sea of Darkness"*] [R *south of Cape Nun*] Nn] J58.197

[Ns *a 520-acre tract* [R *west* [Po *of Stage 1 Residential*]]] A09:1260

— *contrast* [Np *several cities* [P *to* [Ns *the north*]]] A19:0890.

§ **4.204**   When a superlative is morphologically ambiguous between adjective and adverb and the context is not clear-cut, the presumption is in favour of wordtagging as an adverb and tagmatagging as R:

The photographers apparently came off [R *worst*] *in the encounters . . .* G54.183

Her history blazoned before our eyes [N *the bravery of Wallace,* [Nn– *Bruce and his indomitable spider*], [Nns– *Bannockburn*], [Nns– *Mary Queen of Scots*] [Nns+ *and* [R *best* [Po *of all*]], *Bonnie Prince Charlie* Nns+] N], . . . G22.041

§ **4.205**   An adverb phrase, like any other element functioning adverbially, may always be included within any tagma in which it occurs medially (cf. § 4.23); but it is often difficult to decide whether an adverb phrase is a sister or a daughter of a tagma to which it is adjacent. Such problems are particularly frequent when an adverb or adverb phrase precedes a prepositional phrase, or a clause.

§ **4.206**   When an adverb or adverb phrase precedes a P, the two elements are taken as sisters, unless the adverb phrase would make no sense without the following P, or is understood as modifying the preposition of the P (cf. § 4.242) — in these cases the adverb element is treated as first IC of the P and therefore, if a single word, is not dominated by an R phrasetag. Thus:

[P *down*_RP *on* [*the field*]] C14:0320

Trouble ain't easy to dodge [P *out*_RP *in* [Ns *this country*]] N04:0580

[Ns *the squalid* [Nns *La Ruche*] *building* [P *way over in* [Ns *the 15th arrondissement*]]] J66.129

— *down, out, over* can only be understood if taken with the following words; or:

. . . as though his mind were [P *far*_RR *beyond reality*]. N21.060

. . . [P [R *close up*] *behind her*] N16.163

[P *just*_RR *before nightfall,* [Rx@ *two hours late*]] A11:1300
[Np *our embassies* [P *all*_RR *over* [Ns *the world*] P] Np] B09.216

— *far, close up, just, all* specify "to what extent beyond/behind/
before/over", and are thus logically analogous to [P [Np *three
minutes*] *from the end*], cf. § 4.242. But compare:

> ... *until South Africa actually becomes a Republic* [R *later*]
> [P *in the year*]. B01.010
> [S [R *Early*] [P *in April*], *Sabena Belgian World Airlines
> brought* ... S]. E21.109
> ... *sent to* [Ns *her husband* [Z [Rx *four hundred miles away*]
> [P *in the Colony's prison*]]] K23.145
> *one woman who went* [R *up*_RP] [P *to the ticket window*] ...
> A29.101
> *It's* [R *here*] [P *in my pocket*]". N10:1490
> *Tom Horn was soon* [R *back*] [P *at work*], ... N11:0580

— *later, four hundred miles away,* etc. do not specify "how far in
the year/prison, etc."; and similarly, though in this case an N
functioning adverbially is involved in place of a P:

> ... *can be expected* [R *late*] [Ns *next summer*]. A11:1270

The P in the sequences above is not taken as postmodifying the
adverb or adverb phrase.[19]

§ 4.207   In cases where the semantic relationship between adverb
and prepositional phrases is unclear, the presumption is in favour
of the analysis which treats them as sisters.

§ 4.208   Phrases such as *in here, over here, out there* are treated
as single R tagmas (the words are tagged RP RLh respectively); and
compare:

> *I floated* [Rw *right*_RR *up*_RP *here*_RLh] *on a cloud* N13:1330
> *to drop one* [Rxw *way*_NNL1n *up*_RP *there*_RLh] A14:1520
> [Rxw [NNL1n& *way, way*] *back*_RL *there*_RLh] N13:1290
> [R *up*_RP *North*_ND1] G01:1830

and, in view of the parallel between *here* and *this way*:

> [Ns *Over*_RP *this way*]! N14:1500

§ 4.209   When an adverb phrase follows a P it will not be included
within the P, except for certain special cases discussed separately:

> ... *one is* ... *ignored* [P *from then*] [R *onwards*]. F16.164

---

[19] In ... *his horse would be close to where he was hiding.* N12:0320, *close* is wordtagged
JJ, and the emphasized sequence is a Jh tagma.

§ **4.210**   When an adverb phrase is followed by a clause, as in the case of adverb phrase before P, the adverb element will be included as first daughter of the following element if the former makes no sense without the latter:

[Fa [R *back_RL*] *when I was a lad*]

— and, if there is prima-facie unclarity about whether it is daughter or sister to the clause, there are also two special cases in which the adverb phrase is treated as first daughter of the clause. One case is described in § 4.304 below, where the adverb phrase functions analogously to a measure noun phrase as modifier of the subordinating conjunction of an Fa. The other is where the clause is a subjectless Ti: the consciously maintained sanction against "split infinitives" frequently leads to adverbs that logically belong within a Ti being preposed before its Vi:

I don't want [Ti [R *ever*] [Vi *to see*] *either of you again*]. L21.153
... which eventually tend [Ti [R *largely*] [Vi *to hide*] *the Old Way* Ti]. G08:1790
[Ns *an up to date guarantee of access,* [Ti [R *perhaps*] [Vip *to be supervised*] *by a commission . . .* Ti] Ns] B02.044

and cf. also the pattern:

Carmer himself was [Ti [Rw *nowhere*] [Vip *to be seen*] Ti]. N14:0470

§ **4.211**   In other cases, an adverb phrase immediately before a finite or non-finite subordinate clause is treated as its sister:

But no doubt his 45 years are now catching up with him, [R *particularly*] [Tg *bearing in mind the tremendous pace at which he lives*], . . . E11.161
some think his position unassailable [R *simply*] [Fa *because there is no one else in sight . . .*] A03.085
. . . [R *especially*] [Fa *when it peters out . . .*] E15.027
. . . they do not leave me entirely, [R *even*] [W *with the spring brightness of Hyde Park to delight my eyes*]. N26.075
"You must come and take a look round the grounds of the Manor House one day, [R *that_is_REX=*] [Fa *if you would care to do so*]." P07.071

§ **4.212**   Considerations of the functiontagging of the adverb phrase (cf. Chapter 5) may make it clear that it is an adjunct of the verb of the subordinate clause: usually this is obvious and no doubt would arise, but consider:

> *... the simple ruse we employed succeeded handsomely, thereby*
> *confirming the theory ...* L24.021

— this might prima facie seem comparable to the examples above, but *thereby* can be only a Manner adjunct to *confirming*, and hence must be a daughter of the Tg headed by that word.

§ **4.213** Certain adverbs, notably *even* and *only*, seem frequently to bind more tightly than others to an element following them. In a few cases the SUSANNE parsing scheme recognizes this by treating the adverb together with the following word as an idiom: *even_if, even_though* are tagged CS=, *even_so* is tagged RR=. In other cases no special treatment is provided. Thus, in sequences such as:

> *This was brought about **only to a limited extent** by ...* J42.140
> *is removed by **even the best detergent formulation** in a single wash.*
> J05:0590

there might seem to be a case for treating the emphasized sequences as tagmas, in which the adverb modifies the following P or N. However, there is a continuous cline between these adverbs and others which behave more independently (for instance, *just* is somewhat akin to *even* and *only* in this respect but its propensity to bind seems less strong); and it is not always true that *even* and *only* bind closely, so for instance the emphasized sequences clearly do not form logical units in:

> *It's **only possible** in certain cases.* L16.088
> *She **even had** [Ti to modify the very speech that she used] ...*
> J22.047
> *... the effect through apparent size **only occurs** if the difference*
> *... is optimal* J25.083

It is therefore difficult to state a hard and fast rule about the parsing of sequences containing *even* or *only*. The general SUSANNE approach is to discount their special propensity for close binding and, normally, to attach them to the tree at a relatively high level. This gives analyses such as:

> *This* [Vsp *was brought*] [R *about*] [R *only*] [P *to a limited*
> *extent*] *by ...*
> [P *by* [R *even*] [Np *the best detergent formulation*]] — *even*
> parsed as included adverbial, not part of Np
> *It's* [R *only*] [J *possible*] [P *in certain cases*].
> *She* [R *even*] [Vd *had*] [Ti *to modify the very speech that she*
> *used ...*]

... [Ns *the effect through apparent size*] [R *only*] [Vz *occurs*]
[Fa *if the difference . . . is optimal*]

and cf.:

[R *Only*] [Ns *the mistaken idea that it will be a wrench*] *has
held them back.* F21.023

[R *Only*] [Ns *an outcast*] *is free.* M06.065

... *this was* [R *only*] [J *slight*]. E25.164

[R *Even*] [Np *recorded cha cha chas*] *were played during the
interval* ... E22.129

A second class [Vz *covers*] [R *only*] [Np *specific parts or regions*
...] F41.034

This policy has aroused considerable rancour, [R *even*] [Fa *when
the shop takes only part* ...] F41.163

[Fa *If* [R *only*] [Np *all those foreign outsiders*] *could grasp* ...]
A18.092 — not [*if only*]

[Dp *any* [Po *of the politicians*] *(*[R *even*] [Nns@ *President Kennedy*
]*)* ...] A18.094 — *even* treated as included adverbial introducing appositional element

That goal [Vsb *was*] [R *just*] [Ns *the tonic Wolves needed*], ...
A22.139 — not [*just the tonic*]

... [Vd *knew*] [R *just*] [Ff *what I was after*] E14.010

Pinturischio . . . shot up to them, [R *only*] [Ti [Vip *to be
steadied*] [R *again*] Ti]. A32.019

Some plain tapered legs have the taper [P *on the two inner faces*]
[R *only*], ... E02.033

... *you commence* [Ti [Vi *to rise*] [P *in the body*] [R *only*]].
E13.186

and some [R *even*] [Vfp *have been known*] [Ti *to* ...] C08.155

Faulkner culminates the Southern legend [R *perhaps*] [R *more
masterfully than it has ever been . . . done*]. G08:1640

§ **4.214** A sequence of *only* (or similar adverb) + numeral +
noun will normally be treated as three ICs — the adverb and numeral
will not be grouped as a tagma:

... *for most verbs* [Np *only* [MC1& *one or two*] *entries*] J33.009

There were [Np *only two blast furnaces*] *in Nord* J55.146

... *England scored* [Np *just three goals*], *losing to South Africa*
... A08.157

[Np *Only 19 people*] *died from polio* ... A13.227

She weighs [Nu *only 60 lb*] *but can carry* ... E04.069

[Ns *At_least one F.H.A. member*] B10.182

Such an adverb can of course form a tagma with a following numeral if the numeral functions nominally, with noun "understood":

> ...; *of those <bital> d <eital> that pass through a <bital> g <eital> which is not a ray* [Ms *only one*] *belongs to ℱ,...* J21.036

and cf.:

> *Degree of physical mobility is* [Ms *only one* [Po *of a number of interdependent social factors*...]]. J30.136
> [Ms *At_least one* [Po *of the propositions*]] *must be incorrect.* B09.166

§ **4.215** *Even* forms a tagma with a following comparative:

> *Stoker David Banks from Sheerness did* [R *even better*] <hellip> *making seven trips as skipper*... F23.140
> *Stokes*... *has* [Ns *an* [J *even stronger*] *case against the league's present contract*...] A07.143
> [Np [J [D *Even more*] *complex* [Tn+ *and* [R *obviously*] [R *cortically*] [Vn *induced*] Tn+] J] *forms of emotional arousal* Np]... J17:0080

§ **4.216** *Just* forms a tagma with a following sequence introduced by *as, how, so,* or *such*:

> ... *he realised* [Fn? [Jq *just how remarkable*] *the woman was to look at* Fn?],... L20.044
> *In* [Ns *just such a manner*] *there now showed itself*... M03.109
> *the Russians were* [Jh *just as* [Tn *surprised*] [P *as anyone else*] Jh]... B20.065

§ **4.217** Whenever one of the words *all both each* follows rather than precedes the item to which, logically, it applies, whether it follows immediately or with other wording intervening, it is given an adverbial wordtag (RR in the case of *all, both*, RAq for *each*) and parsed as an R phrase, sister rather than daughter of its logical head:

> *When the three were charged* [Nap *they*] [R *all*] *denied the offence.* A43.033
> *"I'll shore be needing* [Ny *ye*] [R *both*] *on the pull out o' the canyon".* N13:1680
> ... [Nn *the Spanish War, the two World Wars, and the Korean War*] [R *all*] *served to overcome*... G01:1520
> [Ns *the forest*] *would accept* [Nop *them*] [R *all*] N08:0860
> *"Then, won't you come and see* [Ni *it*] [R *all*]?" K08.107
> [Nap *They*] [R *both*] *died that night.* P15.154

[Nn *The* [NN1c& MONARCH *and* RENOWN]] [R *each*] *had
a thermostatically controlled boiling burner* ... E25.166
[Nn *Handel, Mendelssohn and Gounod*] *were* [R *all*] [P *in their
turn*] *astonished* ... A17.061
... *when* [Ds *this*] *was* [R *all*] [R *over*] N08:0920 — *all over*
not a tagma
To do this [Ny *you and your wife*] [Vc *will* [R *both*] *have*] *to
give up your pension* H20.055

§ **4.218**　Likewise *alone* is not grouped into a single tagma with
a preceding noun phrase:

a world [Tn *created* [P *for us*] [R *alone*] [P *out_of* ...]] L12.018

§ **4.219**　Words such as *about, circa, c, nearly, over, roughly* —
words tagged RGi and others functioning similarly — preceding a
sequence of numeral and measure are analysed as forming a three-
IC tagma without internal grouping:

[M *an upper one* [Z [Nu *about 30 cm*] [P *in depth*] Z], [Fr *in
which* ...], [Ms+ *and a lower one* ... Ms+] M] J06.049
deaths of [Np *babies* [Jx [Ns *under a week*] *old*]] A13.219
[Nu *nearly 3 per_cent._*NNUp= [Po *of the £34 million issue*]]
A25.076
[Rx [Nus *about a half* +<hyphen> +*mile*] *off*] N11:0790
[Jx [Np *about seven* +<hyphen> +*stories*] *high*] A08:0320
[Nu *only about 2* +<prime>] J01:1470 — that is, ... *about 2′* for
"two feet"; cf. § 4.214 above for treatment of *only*
at [Nup *about* [M *eight hundred*] *feet*] N15:0690

— and by extension of this principle there is no internal structure
within the phrases introduced by such words in:

It was ... *at* [Ns *about this stage*] *that* ... G54.180
He told [Np *some 350 persons*] *that* ... A10:0140
A glimpse of [Np [MC& *three or four*] *vague figures,
at_the_most_*RR= Np]. N06:0100

In the N06 example, the standard ordering has been modified by
postposing the adverb idiom *at_the_most*, but since it remains adjacent to the Np tagma of which it is logically a daughter, it is
parsed as part of that tagma (§ 5.7).
　§ **4.220**　*Never yet* is not grouped as a tagma, thus in:

Jerusalem [Vzfb *has* [R *never*] [Rs *yet*] *been*] *worthy of* ...
D11.064

each word is treated as a separate included adverbial.

§ **4.221**   An R may include diverse modifying elements:

expenditures should be cut [R *sufficiently* [Ti *to make the tax reduction possible*...]] J43.148
...*mounted* [R *slightly forward*_RL [Po *of the head of the jib*]] H06.175

§ **4.222**   There is no way of analysing the use of *but* as in *So great a man could not but understand, too, that*... G10:1490 which is both faithful to the logic of the construction and consistent with other aspects of the parsing scheme. Since the construction is marginal in modern English, the SUSANNE analysis opts to distort its logic, wordtagging *but* as RR rather than as ICSx and parsing the sequence as:

[Ns [J *So great*] *a man*] [Vdce *could not* [R *but*] *understand*]...

— with *but* treated as an included adverbial within a single verb group.

R   subcategories

§ **4.223**   Subcategories for R are: q v; x r; s; w. On the reverse-inheritance of Rq and Rv, cf. § 4.130.

Rq   wh- adverb phrase
§ **4.224**   Adverb phrase beginning with a *wh-* (but not *wh*...*ever*, see Rv) word:

when
how completely E01.052
[Rq *Where else*] *would he get it?* N14:0860

Rv   wh...*ever adverb phrase*
§ **4.225**   Adverb phrase beginning with a *wh*...*ever* word (or idiom wordtagged similarly):

[Fn+ *and that West Germany might well fall in with this,* [Rv *however reluctantly*]]. B02.046
[Jv [Rv *no_matter_how well*] *intentioned*] *one may be* G32:0080

Rx   measured absolute adverb phrase
§ **4.226**   Adverb phrase containing a gradable adverb in its absolute form, premodified by a measure expression:

The last scrip issue was [Rx [Np *seven years*] *ago*]. A25.171
charges [Rx [Np *many £s_NN2*] *extra*] *for early settlement* . . .
   B10.182

[Rx [D *no more* [P *than a mile*]] *away*] N02:1510

§ 4.227   Rx includes "postpositional" constructions, as in:

*But laughter at obscene jokes has (it would appear) the same
sound* [Rx [Ns *the world*] *over_RP*]. G77.051

§ 4.228   The word *so* modifying an adverb is not counted as a
measure expression justifying the Rx subcategory (and in general
the bounds to what counts as a "measure expression" for Rx agree
with those for Jx):

[R *so darkly*] K15.036
[R *so long* [Fc *as the Soviet Union has them*]] A04.107
. . . *were recognized* [R *as long ago* [P *as the eighteen-eighties* [Fr
   *where it was the custom to stuff pillows and mattresses with
   pine-shavings* . . .]]]. F06.063

On the constituency structure in the F06 example, cf. § 4.325.

Rr   measured comparative adverb phrase
§ 4.229   An R consisting of a comparative adverb premodified by
a measure expression (again using "measure expression" in the same
way as in the case of Jr):

[Rr [Np *Five minutes*] *later*] N07:0360
his thoughts [Rr *once more*] *on Kitty* L04.061
[Rr *no longer*] *concerned with* . . . J34.022

§ 4.230   Rr is used for the "correlative" construction (cf. § 4.200
above), where one or both correlated items function adverbially, as
in:

[Rr [Fc [Rr *The sooner*] [Nap *they*] [V *get*] [Rw *here*] Fc], *the
   better* Rr] *I shall like it*

or:

[Rr [Fc [Rr *The sooner*] *it is* [Fn *that they get here*] Fc], *the better*
   Rr] *I shall like it.*

An authentic example:

[Rr [Fc [Jr *The smaller*] [Ns *the particle*] Fc] *the further* Rr] *it
   will travel* . . . J08:0540

Also compare:

> *He went prone on his stomach,* [Rr *the better* [Ti *to pursue his examination*] Rr]. N09:0290

Rs   adverb conducive to asyndeton

§ 4.231   The subcategory Rs is used for a word tagged RRs, RRz, or RTn, when occurring as the whole of a clause IC and hence requiring a phrasetag; the words in question are *otherwise then yet,* and *so* when not a qualifier or pronoun. The reason for phrasetagging these words distinctively is that they behave somewhat like co-ordinating conjunctions, so that they often introduce clauses which in the SUSANNE scheme are formtagged S–.

§ 4.232   The Rs subcategory is not used in a case where one of the relevant words is preceded and/or followed by modifying material:

> [S [Rw *Then,* [Rw+ *and only then*]], [W *with the Jacksons and Dan as their true guests of honor*], *did the Harrows take time . . .* N13:0600

Rw   quasi-nominal adverb

§ 4.233   A phrase consisting of or headed by one of the words *here there now then anywhere elsewhere nowhere somewhere* (wordtagged as an adverb, e.g. not *there_EX*) is given the subcategory Rw. The reason for tagging these adverbs distinctively is that it is rather usual for them to occur in noun-like rather than adverb-like environments, for instance:

> *. . . we left* [Rw *here*] *for a flat . . .* F14.141
> *Here in* [Ns *the God-forsaken place,* [Ns@ *the westerly end* [Po *of nowhere*],]] *. . .* N09:0400

Examples of multi-word Rw's include:

> [Rw *Every* [RTo& *now and then*]] *he'd look down the table at Nelly, . . .* [20] P18.161
> "[S? *What do you mean —* [Rw@ *not now*] S?]?" N17.171

P   Prepositional Phrase

§ 4.234   By far the commonest type of P consists of a preposition followed by an N, D, or M.

---

[20] For a phrase to be headed by a "wordlevel co-ordination" having word X as its main constituent counts as the phrase being headed by word X, for the purposes of applying subcategory symbols that depend on the identity of the head word.

to [Ns *the earth*] G04:0070
behind [D *any of these tree-clumps*] G04:0530
in [M *a hundred*] A05:0330

Since P is a phrase category, a one-word N, D, or M within a P will
not be phrasetagged, unless an N node is required to carry the Nn
subcategory — cf. § 4.140: [P *in water*_NN1u], [P *for*
[Nns *Victor*_NP1m]].

§ 4.235   On occasion, the complement of a preposition is something other than an N, D, or M; for instance it may be a genitive:

this favourite bar [Po *of* [G *Granville's*]] P25.115
experiences [Po *of* [G *my own*]] G22:1680

or another P (see the examples quoted in § 4.10 above).

§ 4.236   A P may lack any overt complement, because the logical complement has been removed by a grammatical movement rule
(in this case the logical-grammar annotation system will represent
the missing complement by a "ghost node"):

jumping from the chair [Fr *she sat* [P *in*]] (Leigh Hunt)
[Ns *a magical cavern,* [Tn [Vn *presided*] [P *over*] [Pb *by the
    Mistress of the Copper Mountain*] Tn] Ns] C05.102
Much as they had [Ti *to look forward* [P *to*] Ti], ... N13:0380
I don't know what you're [P *up_to*_II=], ... N12:0810

§ 4.237   It is common for the complement of a P to be a Tg, e.g.:

[P *Because_of* [Tg [Ns *its important game with Arkansas*] *coming
    up Saturday*]], <bbold> *Baylor* <ebold> *worked out* ...
    A12:1130
... *kept him* [P *from* [Tg *reaching inside his coat for his gun*]].
    N10:1230

and this analysis is used even where the introductory word is one
which has uses as a subordinating conjunction as well as prepositional uses, so that analysis as a finite clause might in principle be
considered:

[P *Before*_ICSt [Tg *leaving for India*]], *Curzon came* ... G08.082
Consumer spending edged down in April [P *after*_ICSt [Tg *rising
    for two consecutive months* Tg] P], ... A28:1740
We think this is a lesser risk, however, [P *than*_CSN [Tg *having
    a pupil* [Tb *get to a corner and forget how to get round it,* ...
    Tb] Tg] P]. E13.095

— such sequences are not parsed as [Fa *before* [Vg *leaving*] ...],
etc.

§ 4.238 The solidus ("slash") is wordtagged IIp and begins a P when unmistakably representing *per*:

> *the units being* [Nu *kg* [P +/ [Nu +sq. *mm.*] P] Nu]; [S@ *English eyes would have preferred* [Nup *tons* [P +/ [Nu +sq. *in.*] P] Nup] S@] J77.041

— contrast this with *true stress/strain curves* J77.037, where the curves may be graphs of stress "against" strain but where the phrase can equally be read as "stress and strain": in such a case the solidus is wordtagged CC:

> [Np *true* [NN1n& *stress* [NN1n+ +/ +*strain*]] *curves*] J77.037

§ 4.239 A P will not normally include a postmodifier after the N (or other) complement:

> ... *were* [P *much like ordinary folk*] [Ti *to look at*]; ... G21.032
> *I was* [P *in time*] [Ti *to hear the charge,* ...] G23.054

— the Ti's are not analysed as daughters of the P nodes.

§ 4.240 The word *like* in its prepositional use, wordtagged ICSk, introduces a sequence tagmatagged P even in a case such as:

> *the* ... *movements seem* [P *like* [Np *facets of one personality*]];
> ... G42.066

— where a P introduced by a different preposition could scarcely occur as complement of a copular verb.

§ 4.241 For P following comparative *as*, see §§ 4.321–2 below.

Premodified P

§ 4.242 A P phrase may include a measure expression preceding the head, as may an Fa clause (§ 4.304 below). The rationale is the same in both cases: logically, such an expression might best be seen as modifying the preposition (in the P case) or the conjunction (in the Fa case), rather than the entire clause or phrase; but the SUSANNE scheme has no category of phrase consisting of an II... or CS... word together with a modifier, so instead these measure expressions are treated as immediate constituents of the Fa or P tagma.

> [P [Np *Three minutes*] *from* [Ns *the end*]] *a typical bit of Woosnam Soccer technique laid on* ... A22.142
> ... *should be prepared* [P [Ns *at_least_*RR= *a fortnight*] *before Christmas*] E20.126
> ... *given* [P [D *not less* [P *than four weeks*]] *before the date* ...]. J48.016

§ **4.243**   A "measure expression" for the purpose of this rule may be e.g. an adverb or determiner standing for an amount (it covers a wider range of expressions than those criterial for the subcategories Jx/r, Rx/r):

> [P *All through* [Np *the centuries*]] D11.104
> ... *goes* [P *far beyond* [Ns *anything that was realized* ...]]; ... D11.055
> ... *hammered a long home run* [P *deep into* [Ns *the corner of* ...]] A13:1770
> "*The path will be* [P *more_DAR like_ICSk* [Ns *a river*] P]." L11.213

§ **4.244**   Contrast, however, the sequence:

> *But, for more than twenty years before the passing of the new Act, the second object had* ... J50.040

If the word *for* were missing, *more than twenty years* would be treated as a measure expression premodifying the *before* P. With *for*, however, *more* becomes the head of a D complement within a P introduced by *for*, so that the P introduced by *before* is treated as a postmodifier:

> [P *for* [D *more* [P *than* [Np *twenty years* [P *before the passing* ...]]]]]

§ **4.245**   Where an adverbial element preceding a P cannot be seen as specifying "how far" or "how much" the preposition applies, the adverbial is parsed as sister rather than daughter of the P (cf. § 4.206). Thus:

> ... *whether,* [P *at all events*] [P *in his dreams*], *Issigonis hadn't visualized a flat-four* ... E16.044

— logically speaking *at all events* seems to "modify" *in his dreams*, but clearly it does not specify "how far in", and therefore it is not treated as a daughter of the *in* phrase.

§ **4.246**   On the analogy of *out there*, which is treated as a single R phrase (§ 4.208), a sequence like *Out in the center of the circle* N13:1070 is treated as a single P phrase with *Out* premodifying the preposition *in*. But the R is sister of the P in the example:

> ... *joined them* [R *out there*] [P *in the circle*]. N13:1130

P   subcategories

§ **4.247**   Subcategories for P are: o b; q v. On the reverse-inheritance of Pq and Pv, cf. § 4.130.

Po of phrase
§ 4.248 Preposition of the P is *of*. The reason to give such phrases a special symbol is that *of* phrases have a much lower propensity than other prepositional phrases to occur as clause ICs.

[Dp *many* [Po *of yesterday's Southerners*]] G08:0830
I've had [D *enough* [Po *of you*]] N05:0900
the intentional use [Po *of living microorganisms or their toxic products*] [P *for the purpose* [Po *of destroying or reducing the military effectiveness* [Po *of man*] Po] P] J08:0010

Where a quantity phrase having the structure "Measure-Term *of* Noun-Phrase" is postmodified, the presumption is in favour of attaching the postmodifier to the measure term rather than to the subordinate noun phrase:

[Ns@ *a body* [Po *of* [Ns *legal principle*]] [Fr *which by and large was made up of . . .* Fr] Ns@] G02:0100
a reduction in [Ns *the number* [Po *of* [Np *forest fires*]] [P *in the state*] Ns] A06:1190

Logically, however, *of persons* must modify *thousands* rather than *hundreds* in:

[Np *hundreds* [Po *of* [Np *thousands* [Po *of persons*]]]] *will mass along this thoroughfare . . .* A08:0190

Pb by phrase
§ 4.249 Preposition of the P is *by*. This subcategory provides a special annotation for phrases which are candidates to be understood as agents in passive constructions.

[Pb *by* [Dp *those of Jackson Pollock*]] G09:1030
[Pb *by* [Ff *what must have seemed an illusion:* [Ns@ *a great garden . . .*]]] G05:0050
[Pb *by implication*] A20:0020

Pq wh- prepositional phrase
§ 4.250 P whose complement is a *wh-* word (but not a *wh. . .ever* word, see Pv below), or a phrase itself having the "q" subcategory:

[Pq@ *with what*]? N09:0660
[Pq *in* [Nqp *which cases*]] J09:1600
[Pq *After* [Nqp [Dqp *how many*] *generations*]] G17:1230

Pv wh. . .ever *prepositional phrase*
§ 4.251 Defined as Pq, but reading "*wh. . .ever* word" for "*wh-*word", and "v" for "q", in the definition:

[Pv *in* [Nvs *whichever direction*]] *it operates* G52.109

D   Determiner Phrase

§ 4.252 A phrase headed by a determiner, wordtagged D. . . (other than *whose*, for which see § 4.277), whether in premodifying position or as a clause IC.

> . . . *a useful corrective to* [Np [Dp *so many*] *nostalgic pictures of a "quaint" old-fashioned France*]. C14.088
> [Np [D *no less* [P *than fifty-two*]] *works*] J02.012
> *given* [P [D *not less* [P *than four weeks*]] *before the date. . .*] J48.016 — note the analysis used for such a sequence: the scheme does not treat *not less than four* as a D tagma premodifying *weeks*
> *Since 1939* [Np [D *practically no*] *new houses*] *have been built. . .* E28.062
> [Ns [D *more* [P *than enough*]] *land*] J22.035 — again, not [D *more* [P *than enough land*]]
> . . . *have helped* [Dp *so many*] [Ti *to achieve those titles*]. D05.093
> [D *Such_DAz*] *was the power of voyeurism in this case.* G56.024
> . . . *one can spread one's wings* [Ds *a_little_DD1t=*] *and forget* . . . E19.071
> . . . *the total. . . was* [Dp *75 fewer* [Fc *than in the previous December quarter*]], . . . A13.222

§ 4.253 The word *more*, wordtagged DAR, as a clause IC (or head of a clause IC) always takes a D tagmatag whether functioning nominally (*I ran more (of the race) than you*) or adverbially (*you ought to run more*, i.e. do more running) — these uses will be distinguished via the functiontagging system of Chapter 5.

§ 4.254 It is frequently difficult to decide whether to group a determiner together with adjacent elements as a tagma, and as usual the tendency of the SUSANNE scheme is to refrain from doing so in borderline cases. Thus the emphasized word-sequences do not form tagmas in the examples:

> [Np *the many* retail Co-operatives, which . . .] F41.106
> [Ns *no such* thing as . . .] D14.083
> [Nus– *half a gill* of Orange Curaçao] E19.043
> *for* [Np the *next few* months] P08.086

[Ns **Not every** case who comes before you] *is* ... L23.015
he realised, however, as [Np **not all** *Zionists*] *did* ... G15.153
And he did **little else** *until he scored another fine goal* ... A22.179

and *as much* does not constitute a tagma, for instance in:

She spent [Ds *twice as much* [Fc *as he saved*]] P22.034

— a sequence like *twice as much* is regarded as parallel to *twice as good, far less severe*, cf. § 4.199. Likewise *far too much* are three daughters of a D in:

these stones dominate [Ds *far too much*] E10.143

§ **4.255** On the other hand *any more, one more, two more*, etc. are treated as D tagmas, with *more* taken as head:

We shouldn't have [Ns [D *any more*] *trouble*] ... L16.090
... *send* [Np [D *any more*] *anonymous messages about me*] ... L21.155
[Ns [Ds *One more*] *demonstration* [Po *of* ...]] B04.083
... *to be* [D *nothing more* [P *than that*]] N10:0890

and *more* is premodified by a multi-word tagma in:

... *may cost* [D [Ds *as much* [P *as £4 per ton*] Ds] *more* [P *than average coal*] D]. J42.143

§ **4.256** A Ti following *enough* is treated as a modifier:

... [Ns+ *and* [R *perhaps*] *evidence* [D *enough* [Ti *to have brought a killer to book in modern times*] D] Ns+]. F04.042

§ **4.257** The sequence *the same* premodifying a noun is not analysed as a tagma. The SUSANNE scheme treats adverbs and adverbial elements preceding *the same* as daughters of the phrase in which *the* and *same* are modifiers, if they modify *same*:

[Ns *Exactly the same sort* [Po *of thing*]] *is being said in America.* G75.031
... *are* [D *much the same* [P *as those used by Fornasetti* ...]] E05.081
It was [P *for* [Ns *precisely the same reason*] P] *that* ... J37.082

(one might see a sequence like *Exactly the same sort* ... as a transformational modification of [Ns *the* [J *exactly same*] *sort* ...], but nothing in the SUSANNE surface or logical annotation represents it as such). Contrast:

> *The technique of cutting sections was* [R *essentially*] [D *the same
>   as that described by Coons . . .*] J16:0220
> *. . . politicians in the state are* "[R *all*] [D *the same*]" A07:0520

— the J16 example could not be seen as deriving from a sequence . . .
the essentially same . . . ; and *all* in the A07 case modifies *politicians,*
cf. § 4.217.

D   subcategories

§ **4.258**   The category D has subcategories: q v; s p. On the reverse-
inheritance of Dq and Dv, cf. § 4.130.

Dq   wh- determiner phrase
§ **4.259**   A D which consists of or has as an IC a word with a
. . .Q. . . (but not . . .QV. . .) wordtag:

which
[Dqs *each* [Poq *of which*]] J10:1230
[Dqp *how*_RGQq *many* [Po *of us oldsters*]] G17:0440

Dv   wh. . .ever determiner phrase
§ **4.260**   A D which consists of or has as an IC a word with a
. . .QV. . . wordtag:

[Nvs [Dvs *however much*] [NN1n& *force or pressure*]] P22.116
[Ff [Dv *whatever*] *might be lying . . . on the floor below*]
    N06:0760

Ds   singular determiner phrase
§ **4.261**   A D consisting of or headed by a D. . .1. . . word, or
postmodified by a singular Po (see § 4.263 below, and see § 4.490
for wordlevel determiner co-ordinations):

another
. . . vary [Ds *very little*] *from society to society* G77.041

Dp   plural determiner phrase
§ **4.262**   A D consisting of or headed by a D. . .2. . . word, or
postmodified by a plural Po (see § 4.263 below):

these
[Dp *A_few*_DD2=] *sat alone . . .* G25.072
[Np [Dp *so many*] *affairs of the heart*] N18:0580

§ **4.263**   A determiner phrase of the form "DX *of* Y", where DX is
a non-interrogative determiner word which is not inherently singular

or plural (the wordtag does not include . . .1. . . or . . .2. . .), such as *some most all any plenty a_lot the_rest*, is tagged Ds or Dp if the complement (Y) of *of* is marked as singular or plural (for instance, if Y is an Ns or Np, or a single word with a . . .1. . . or . . .2. . . wordtag):

> . . . *than have* [Dp *some* [Po *of their more conventional contemporaries*]] . . . R05.125
> [Dp+ *or any* [Po *of* [Np *the film stars* . . .]]] A18.094
> [Dp *most* [Po *of* [Np *the difficulties which* . . .]]] E14.016
> [Ds *most* [Po *of* [Ns *their emphasis*]]] A04.114
> [Dp *the_rest* [Po *of* [Np *the Dog River stamps*]]] E09.118

The phrase [D *Plenty of people*] L02.025 is not given the Dp subcategory; to an English-speaker the phrase is clearly plural, but *people* is wordtagged NNc as having both singular and plural uses.

§ 4.264   When the DX of a "DX *of* Y" construction is a determiner which is itself marked as singular or plural (wordtagged D. . .1. . . or D. . .2. . .), the subcategories Ds and Dp are applied by reference to this word rather than to the properties of the Y element; and if the DX is an interrogative determiner such as *which*, neither Ds nor Dp is assigned irrespective of the properties of the Y element:

> [Dq *which* [Po *of your readers*]] *would* . . . B27.172
> [Ds *each* [Po *of the 12 District Councils*]] H23.149
> [Dp *both* [Po *of these picturesque tales*]] F06.083
> *flirting with* [Ds *either* [Po *of them*]]. P13.192

M   Numeral Phrase

§ 4.265   A phrase headed by a cardinal number, wordtagged MC. . ., MF. . ., or NNO. . . (but not by an ordinal, wordtagged MD. . ., and not an expression representing a date, cf. §§ 4.119, 4.512), whether modifying a nominal element or functioning nominally in a clause.

> . . . *would run* [M *1 billion* [D+ *or more*]] *in the first year,* . . . A03:0980
> . . . *by* [Ns *a* [M *4* [P *to 3*] M] *vote*], . . . A10:0880
> *In* [M *four* [Po *of his nine previous seasons*]] A13:1400
> *to* [M [G *Baylor's*] *126*] A12:1760
> . . . *from a wholesaler carrying one commodity group to one with* [M *several hundred*] F41.061
> *a right balance between* [M *the two*] . . . G10:1610

If this doesn't work out, [M *the three* [Po *of you*]] *barricade
yourself in the house* . . . N03:0270
and made [M *26* [P *in a row*]] *at one time.* A12:0290

§ **4.266**   Multi-word numbers are tagmas which modify the units
counted as heads:

with [Np [M *a thousand*] *foes*] G05:1640
[Np *About* [M *a dozen*] *animals*] *were held* . . . N03:0210
[Np [M *a_few*_DD2= *hundred thousand*] *persons* Np] A08:0340
would produce [Nup [M *17 million*] *dollars*] . . . A02:0100
[Ns *a* [Nu <*dollar*> [M *+60 million*]] *bond issue* [Ti *to under-
write the program*]] A06:1650 — i.e. *a $60 million bond
issue* . . .

§ **4.267**   In sequences of the form Number + Preposition +
Number, the analysis is as in:

[Np [M *nine* [P *out_of ten*]] *men* [Fr *who* . . .]] F21.021
. . . [Nj *the first young*] *emerge,* [Np@ [M *four* [P *to eight*]] *small
daughters that begin to play* . . .]. J10:0650

— not e.g.: [M *nine* [P *out_of* [Np *ten men* . . .]]]. (This rule is
not contradicted by the analysis of *four of his nine previous seasons*
shown in § 4.265, where the preposition is not immediately followed by the second number.)

§ **4.268**   Fractions are wordtagged as nouns when spelled out,
e.g. *half*_NN1c, but as cardinal numerals when written digitally,
e.g. $\frac{1}{2}$_MFn. An expression including a whole number and a fraction will have the fractional part tagmatagged N. . .+ (on the use of
the plus sign, cf. § 4.465 below) when spelled out, although written
digitally the same number will be a single word wordtagged MCn,
and tagmatagged M in a situation requiring a phrasetag:

   . . . *came to office* [Rx [Np [M *three* [Ns+ *and a half*]] *years*]
   ago]. A03.094
   . . . *Penguins rose* [Nu *10$\frac{1}{2}$*_MCn *+d.*_NNU] [P *to* [Nu *20*_MCn
   *+s.*_NNU [Nu– *4$\frac{1}{2}$*_MCn *+d*_NNU]] P].[21] A16.049
   . . . *suggests that* [Ns *almost a quarter* [Po *of the dwellings occupied
   today*], [M@ *some*_RGi *3$\frac{2}{3}$*_MCn *million*_NNOc M@], Ns]
   were built before 1880. J47.008

---

[21] The abbreviations *s.*, *d.* represent the units "shillings", "pence" of Britain's pre-1970
currency.

— no internal constituency is recognized in sequences such as *almost a quarter . . . , some 3⅔ million,* where the multi-word number is the head of its phrase (contrast § 4.219).

§ **4.269** In time-of-day expressions, the terms *am, pm, o'clock,* wordtagged RAh, are treated as postmodifiers within M phrases:

[P *at* [M *nine o'clock*]] N24.055
[P *at* [M *nine a.m.*]] [R *precisely*] N04.043
in [Ns *tomorrow's* [M *8 P.M.*] *contest*] A11:1030
[M *Twelve o'clock*] *level.* N15:0950

§ **4.270** A special wordtag MCe is provided for numerals including non-decimal separators, e.g. *4.11* or *4:11* for "four years eleven months" or "chapter 4 verse 11". However, such a number is treated as a single word only provided its parts do not themselves contain structure of a type normally recognized by the SUSANNE system. Thus e.g. *4.11-13* for "chapter 4, verses 11 to 13" will be analysed as:

[M *4*_MCn +._YF [M@ *11* +<*hyphen*> +*13*_MCn M@] M] (cf. § 4.541)

and *4:11, 12* for "chapter 4, verses 11 and 12" as:

[M *4*_MCn +:_YN [MCn& *11* +, [MCn– *12*]]]

— because *11-13* is recognizably an M tagma and *11, 12* a wordlevel co-ordination, the separator between these phrases and the preceding number must itself be a separate word.

M   subcategory

Ms   numeral phrase headed by one
§ **4.271** The only subcategory defined for M is Ms, for a numeral phrase whose head is the number one (spelled out or written digitally, whether as an arabic or roman numeral), and which does not contain a subordinate conjunct (so that e.g. [M *one* [Ns+ *and a half*]], [M *one* [J+ *or the other*]] are not tagged Ms, cf. § 4.490):

Maxwell's paradox was not [Ms *the only one* [Tn *raised*]]. J18.171
[Ms *one* [Po *of* [Nnp *the few Churchills* [Fr *she liked*]]]] F24.053

§ **4.272** The word *one* used as a placeholder for a head noun in a noun phrase, as in *a red one,* is given the same MC1 wordtag as numeral *one,* and accordingly such a phrase is tagmatagged Ms:

and [Ms *that one* — [G@ *Mr Wesker's*] —] *was . . .* A19.104

G Genitive Phrase

§ 4.273   A phrase whose head has the Germanic genitive inflexion
(which under the SUSANNE scheme is always treated as a separate
word, +'s or +', wordtagged GG — see § 2.35), or is a possessive
pronoun (irrespective of whether the phrase is functioning as a
genitive modifier or nominally):

> [Ns [G [Ns *his master*] +'s] *voice*]
> *eyes . . . lidless as* [G [Ns *a lizard*] +'s], . . . N07:1590
> *could see* [N [G [Nns *Max*] +'s] *loose grin* [Np+ *and* [G [Nnp
>   *the Burnsides*] +'] *glowering faces*]] N13:0010
> *Was it* [G [Ns *the dog*] +'s]? D14.115
> *But tonight was* [G *mine*_PPGi1]. L12.031

§ 4.274   When it is unclear semantically whether a determiner
preceding a genitive should be understood as within or outside the
G, it is treated as inside it:

> [Ns [G [Ns *A wholesale merchant*]'s] *business*] *cannot be . . .*
>   F41.170
> [Ns [G [Ns *the council*] +'s] *resolution*] *said* A05:0830

(not e.g. [*a* [G *wholesale merchant's*] *business*]).

§ 4.275   The word *own*, wordtagged DAg, groups with a preceding genitive as a G tagma:

> [Ns [G *his own*] *briefcase key*] R02.080
> *of* [Ns [G *our own*] [Tg *doing*]] G11:1010
> *. . . make the best* [Po *of* [Np [G *their own*] *lives* Np] Po]. B19.009
> *to* [Ns [G *one* +'s *own*] *state*] G07:1650

G subcategories
§ 4.276   The category G has the subcategories Gq, Gv. On the
reverse-inheritance of these subcategories, cf. § 4.130.

Gq wh- genitive phrase
§ 4.277   The word *whose*, when occurring in an environment
requiring a phrasetag, is tagged Gq:

> [Gq *Whose*_DDQGq] *is this?*

Gv wh. . .ever genitive phrase
§ 4.278   A word or idiom tagged PNQVG, when occurring in an
environment requiring a phrasetag, is tagged Gv:

> [Fa [Gv *no_matter_whose*_PNQVG] *it is*], . . .

CLAUSETAGS

A clausetag consists of a capital letter followed in some cases by a single lower-case subcategory letter; various non-alphanumeric suffix symbols apply.

S Main Clause

§ 4.279 A sequence which is typographically an independent sentence, normally beginning with a capital letter and (unless quoted) immediately followed by a full stop, question mark, or exclamation mark, and which is grammatically a "complete sentence", is formtagged S; and a main clause conjoined with a typographically independent sentence, e.g. linked by comma and co-ordinating conjunction, or by semicolon, whether complete or having undergone the reduction phenomena standardly associated with co-ordination, is formtagged S+ or S−.

[S *Morgan nodded*]. N01:0860

[S *Stengel will receive the Ben Epstein Good Guy Award*]. A14:0450

[S *It is interesting* [Fn *that a 1:1 correspondence can be established between the lines of two such pencils, so that in a sense a unique image can actually be assigned to each tangent* Fn] S]. J21:0410

[S [P *With the dominance of the sympathetic division of the hypothalamus*], *the opposite changes occur*]. J17:0630

"[S *I don't understand*]", . . . N18:1310

"Yeah. [S *See you*]", *Donovan said* . . . N15:0280

[S "[Q [S? *Who's in there*]]"? *Black called fearfully* S]. N12:1620

[S *He nodded* [S+ *and, going into the bedroom, brought a needle, thread, and scissors* S+] S]. N01:1520

[S *A fly would crawl down the bulging forehead, into the socket of the eye,* [S− *walk along the man's lashes and across the wet surface of the eyeball* S−], [S+ *and the eye did not blink* S+] S]. G04:1220

[S *She got to her feet,* [S− *staggered* S−], [S+ *and almost fell* S+] S]. N01:1280

[S *Lobularity is extremely well developed in type I;* [S− *absent in type II* S−]; [S− *imperfectly developed in type III* S−] S]. J12:1680

[S *The top of the sample was nearly flat* [S+ *and* [Ns *the bottom*] [J *hemispherical*] S+] S]. J04:1910

[S *Their consequences are irrelevant* — [S+ *or there are no consequences at all* S+] S]. G09:1540

[L *Not* [Fn *that her mother knew what had happened* Fn], [S+ *but they could speculate upon it* S+] L]. N10:0290

On the occasional occurrence of S. . . tagmas in subordinate positions other than as conjuncts, see § 4.305. On sentential apposition, see §§ 4.526 ff.

§ 4.280   A sequence which is typographically separate from its environment, beginning with capital letter, having sentence-final punctuation after it, and not linked grammatically to the surrounding wording, but which internally is less than a complete main clause, is formtagged in terms of its internal constituency, e.g. as a noun phrase or an "L" (verbless clause, §§ 4.374 ff.), not as S:

[Nns *Chapter 7*]. M01.011 — a chapter heading
[Nns <bbold> [Ot *Family Jewels* Ot] <ebold> [Pb *BY PETRU DUMITRIU*], [Nns@ *Collins*], [Nu@ *21s*] Nns]. C09.183
[Np *Noisy surfaces,* [L+ *but* [Ns *the right kind of noise*] [P *behind them*] L+] Np]. C10.205
[L [Ns *A nice boy*] [R *of course*]]. M04.033
[L [Jh *Foremost among these*], [R *of_course*], [Nns *Adolf Hitler's famed "Eagle's Nest"*, [Ns@ *that stupendous piece of engineering•leading up to the Alpine boudoir where so much mischief had been hatched for all the world*]] L]. G05.060
[Tg+ *And Morfydd Owen* [Vg *waving*], *unkissed, from the window*]. M04.039
[Tg *The heel of the foot* [Vg *remaining*] *in contact with the floor, until after the second step is positioned*]. E13.187
'[Q [S *I had a different impression;* [S– *I rather thought he was goading him* S–] S]. Q]' <minbrk> '[Q [Ti [Vi *To abstain*] Ti]? Q]' <minbrk> K03.041
[Fa *Until quite suddenly . . . he realised that it had become a different kind of love*]. N25.067
[L [Nns *Paris*] [P *in the spring*] L]*!* [W *With mist rising from the Seine in the early morning* [W+ *and the cafes gaily spilling out across the pavements in the midday sunshine*]]. P20.016
[L [R *So far*] [J *so good*] — [S+ *but this conclusion applies . . .*] L]. J18.191
[L *All gentry characters unpleasant,* [L– *all peasant ones unattractive*], [L+ *but the whole enjoyable once difficult beginning surmounted* L+] L]. C09.187
[L [R *Sometimes*] [Np *pleasant but moving experiences*] [L+ *and* [R *sometimes*] [J *very disheartening*] L+] L]. K10.129

§ 4.281   However, where a main clause is reduced by omitting the leading verb of a multi-verb group, informally, as in the *See you* example quoted in § 4.279 above, or as a matter of telegraphic style (e.g. in newspaper headlines), the clause is analysed as an S rather than e.g. a Tn, Tg, or Tb:

[Oh [S [Nns *GOP*] [Vn *RESTRAINED*]] S] Oh] A04:1010
[Oh <bbold> [S [Vn *MADE*] [R *UP*] [Pb *BY GRANT*]] S] <ebold> Oh] A11.197
[Oh [S [Ns *MERGER*] [Vn *PROPOSED*]] S] Oh] A01:0210

§ **4.282** In deciding whether a given word boundary is also a sentence boundary, it is of course necessary to take into account that some stops are markers of abbreviation, and that capitals occur for many reasons other than starting a sentence. Obviously the word boundary within . . . *Mr. Brown* . . . would not usually be a sentence boundary. There are also cases, however, where typography provides genuinely conflicting cues to sentence-boundary status. For instance, a sequence ending with punctuation which is usually sentence-internal may be followed by a sequence beginning with a word that is capitalized for no reason other than to mark initial position in a major tagma. Thus, one common American publisher's convention capitalizes any word following a colon irrespective of whether the word would in other respects be seen as beginning a separate sentence:

> *To Rickards, . . . it was an old story: His plane was being hijacked . . . .* A42:0670

Conversely, a usually sentence-final punctuation mark will sometimes occur medially in a logical tagma, without following capitalization, as in:

> *But in 1897, alas! there was no fingerprint bureau, . . .* F04.043
> *"Had you rested there!" said the Queen, "I should have been too well satisfied. But . . .* K20.099
> *. . . we may have grown accustomed to asking only — where is it this time? which service? what rank of officer? and have they taken over the radio station?* G74.043

The SUSANNE principle is that in cases of conflicting typographic cues, unless it is clear from the wording that a grammatical boundary exists, the elements either side of the debatable boundary are taken to belong to a common tagma. The analyses of the above examples are:

> [S *To Rickards, . . . it was an old story:* [S@ *His plane was . . .*]] S].
> [S . . . [P *in 1897*], *alas*_UH +*!*_YX *there*_EX [Vsb *was*] [Ns *no fingerprint bureau*] . . . S]

"[Q [S [Fa *Had you rested there*] +!_YX +<rdquo> [Ss *said the Queen*], "[Nea *I*] [Vdcfp *should have been* [R *too well*] *satisfied*] S]. . . . Q]"

[S . . . [P *to* [Tg *asking* [R *only*] —_YD [S? *where is it this time* +?_YQ [Nqs– *which service*] +?_YQ [Nqs *what rank . . .*] +?_YQ [S?+ *and have they taken over . . .* S?+] S?] Tg] P] . . . S]?

In the A42 example the *hijacked* clause is in "sentential apposition" (§ 4.526) within the *it was* clause. The interjection *alas* and its exclamation mark are ICs of the surrounding sentence in the F04 example, as is the exclamation mark in the K20 example. In the G74 example, the second, third, and fourth questions are subordinate to the first question by the rules for analysing co-ordinations (§§ 4.462 ff.), which forces the first, second, and third question marks to be daughters of the S?, but the last question mark is a sister of the entire S (by § 4.73).

§ **4.283** Sometimes typography unambiguously implies a sentence boundary (by means of full stop or similar punctuation, followed by initial capitalization) at a point which divides what appears grammatically to be a single sentence (that is, a single S, or other tagma directly dominated by a rootrank node). The analysis in such a case depends on where the typographic boundary falls in relation to the structure that would be attributable to the complete sentence. If the typographic boundary separates what would be ICs of that sentence, then the SUSANNE analysis follows the typography and treats the separate typographic sequences as independent daughters of the rootrank node. This is particularly common in the case of typographic sentences beginning with co-ordinating conjunctions, which are formtagged S+ but not linked to preceding clauses (as . . .+-tagged elements normally are, cf. §§ 4.462 ff.):

"[Q [S *We remain for it*]. [S+ *But the Tories never were*]. Q]" A01.193

[O [S *Mr. Nixon, for his part, would oppose intervention in Cuba without specific provocation* S]. [S+ *But he did recommend that President Kennedy state clearly that if Communist countries shipped any further arms to Cuba that it would not be tolerated* S+]. O] A04:1250

In general there is no presumption against analyses in which S+ clauses are immediately dominated by rootrank nodes rather than by superordinate S's:

<minbrk> [O <bbold> [S+ *And that brought the figure to a record £2,415,000,000* S+]. <ebold> O] <minbrk> A06.202

<minbrk> [O [S+ *AND to all this theatrical richness, the poor darling dodos can only squeak "kitchen sink" and "dustbin" drama*]. [S *In fact, only one play in the last few years has had a dustbin in it,* ...]. ... O] A19.100

"[Q [S [Fa *If you prefer to stick here in this dreary place* Fa] — [I [S+ *and you know just how dull and forsaken it is after the season's over* S+] I] — *that's your look-out* S]. [S+ *But I must say I think it's rather mean of you,* ... S+]. ... Q]" P05.056

But the same rule also applies e.g. when a typographic sentence boundary splits one complement or adjunct IC from the remainder of a main clause:

"[Q [S [Nas *I*] [Vmu +*'m leaving*] S]. [R *Now*]. Q]"

[O [S *Even in the very area where the shooting had been done, cattle were still disappearing*]. [Fa *For less than a dozen miles from the unplowed land of the dead man lived* ... *a blatant and defiant rustler named Fred Powell* Fa]. O] N11:0650

[O [S *Dumont spoke on the merit of having an open primary*]. [S *He then launched into* [Fn? *what the issues should be in the campaign* Fn?] S]. [N *State aid to schools, the continuance of railroad passenger service,* ... *and making New Jersey attractive to new industry*]. O] A06:0340 — by § 4.527, if the full stop after *campaign* were a colon, the *State aid* ... N would be an appositional IC of the *launched* S

On the other hand, if the typographic sentence boundary divides what would be a subordinate tagma within the unified sentence, then the analysis overrides the typography and keeps the subordinate tagma as a unit:

[S *He might say or do* [Ns *something foolish.* [Ns@ *Something all of them would regret* Ns@] Ns] S]. N03:0420

[L? [Dq *What*] [Fa *if the President himself* ... *"goes ape"?* [Fa+ *Or singlehandedly decided to reverse national policy and* ... Fa+] Fa] L?]? G03:0960

— in the N03 example, the second *something* phrase is in apposition within the first; in the G03 example, a co-ordination of adverbial clauses crosses a typographic sentence boundary. And compare:

[S *Sets of slides were then shown to illustrate* [Ns *the effect* [Po *of:-* X Po] Ns] S]. J03.026

— where the material which appears at "X" is a series of indented paragraphs preceded by numbered headings and containing several complete typographic sentences each. In the case "[Q [Ns+ *But this goddamn climate.* [S@ *It's for carabao not airplanes* S@] Ns+] Q]". N15:0250, the second typographic sentence is included within the first because the Ns+, although a root IC here, represents a grammatical category which is normally subordinate within a full sentence. (If the full stop after *climate* were a comma, the S@ below Ns+ structure would be clearly mandatory by § 4.525 below.)

§ 4.284   In the sequence:

> *A final class of exceptional lines is identifiable from the following*
> *considerations: Since no two generators* . . . J21:0620

the text following the colon continues for many separate typographic sentences, with no clear boundary to the material that is intended as expanding "the following considerations"; this phrase is used more to create a general logical link between the preceding statement and the following passage than to name a specific proposition-set. Consequently the colon is taken as marking the end of an independent sentence (the colon being analysed as sister to the preceding S), and *Since* begins a new S tagma not subordinate to the preceding S. In terms of § 4.282, this is taken as a case where the wording makes clear the existence of a grammatical boundary.

§ 4.285   A formula logically equivalent to a proposition, word-tagged FOq. . . , will always be analysed as heading a clause, even if the clause contains no further material; and a clause headed by a formula will be formtagged S unless introduced by wording implying an F. . . clausetag. Thus:

> . . . *is given by* [S <formul>_FOqx [Fr *where* χ *is the angle of*
> *extinction*] S]. J03:1100
> *it follows from* [Ns *the formula* [S@ <formul>_FOqx] Ns] *that* . . .
> J21:0350
> . . . *states* [Fn *that* <formul>_FOqx +, [Fr *where q is the prob-*
> *ability that* . . . Fr] Fn]. J03:1670
> *a molecular susceptibility of* [N <formul>_FO +, [Fr *where*
> <formul>_FOqx Fr] N]. J04:1370

Ss   embedded quoting clause

§ 4.286   An Ss is a clause of quoting, embedded within a constituent of the direct quotation which is logically its object, as in:

> "[Q *I could use some help*", [Ss *Morgan said finally*], "*but I can't*
> *afford to pay you anything. I guess you'd better go on in the*
> *morning* Q]". N01:1060

The use of this tag depends on the SUSANNE system for representing logical grammar, and a detailed statement of its use is therefore deferred to §§ 5.93 ff.

F... Finite Subordinate Clause

§ 4.287 A clause labelled with an F... formtag includes the subordinating conjunction introducing it (if any). Normally, an F... clause will contain a verb group beginning with a finite verb; in certain special cases sequences are identified as reduced F... clauses by reference to their introductory conjunction although they lack finite verb groups — such cases are discussed under the specific F... headings below. All F... formtags include a lower-case subcategory symbol.

Fa adverbial clause

§ 4.288 The most usual type of Fa is a clause introduced by a subordinating conjunction (wordtagged CS... or ICS...), such as *although, though, while, because, if* (in most cases, though see § 4.306), *as_if, as_though,* etc.

[Fa *if these procedures are applied more often*] J17:1300
[Fa *because it teaches us something useful to know about ourselves*] G12:0140
[Fa *Once we get over the mountains*] N04:0360
[Fa *although Pamela, now, in her new frame of mind, was careful not to pretend too much assurance*] N08:0150
[Fa *unless he was told*] N14:1260
[Fa *until it is either acquired by another proprietor* [Fa+ *or the government decides to drop it*]] G22:1470
... *treated him* [Fa% *as_if_CSk= he were of their own age*]. G16.161
His eyes were staring at me wildly [Fa *as_if_CSk= he'd not hesitate to do me an injury...*]]. L15.065
... *occasionally she saw lights and heard traffic* [Fa *as_though_CSk= they were passing through villages or towns*]. P04.045

§ 4.289 The word *now* has a CS use:

However, [Fa *now_CS I <bital> have <eital> found out*] *it makes it easier to say this.* L21.152

§ 4.290 *Whether* introduces an Fa when it is equivalent to "no matter whether":

This is equally true [Fa *whether the production is on our own farms or those overseas*]. H10.068

— in other cases *whether* introduces an Fn?, § 4.305.

§ 4.291 Clauses introduced by *wh-* adverbs such as *where, when,* are Fa's when they function adverbially rather than as relatives or interrogatives, e.g.:

The victim was beaten [Fa [Rq *when_CSn*] *he attempted to stop the bandit* Fa]. A19:0270

"But you want a job [Tn *guaranteed* [Fa [Rq *when_CSn*] *you return* Fa] Tn]" G06:1660

"You must play it [Fa [Rq *where_CSr*] *it lies*]". A14:1630

Subordinate clauses introduced by such words may alternatively be categorized as Fn?, Fr, or Ff (§§ 4.305, 4.313, 4.318).

§ 4.292 Clauses and reduced clauses introduced by *-ever* phrases are Fa when they are concessive:

whatever the reason (is)
however strongly you may feel
[Fa [Rv *However long*] *we stayed in bed every day*], *we had to get up at last* ... K22.131
[Fa [Rv *No_matter_how_RRQV=*] *they are formulated*], *a large number of organic actives are simply not suitable* ... J05:0440

or frequentative:

whoever you ask
the same right must be conceded to each remaining state [Fa *whenever it saw fit to secede*] G10:1090

For the other kind of clause introduced by *-ever* phrases, see § 4.318.

§ 4.293 The word *or* is invariably parsed as a co-ordinating conjunction even when it could be paraphrased "since otherwise", hence the *or* clause is not an Fa but an Fn+ in:

I thought [Fn *you must have some Scandinavian blood,* [Fn+ *or_CCr you wouldn't be sitting there* ...]] N15.156

(despite the fact that the passage does not mean that the speaker thought one or the other must be the case).

§ 4.294 Another type of Fa places what is logically the complement of the clause in initial position, preceding the subordinating conjunction if there is one; cf. the E28 example quoted in § 4.89 above, or:

[Fa [Vrn [VVNt& *Distorted,* [VVNt– *stunted*]]] *as*_CSA
[Ni *it*] [Vcb *may be*] [Pb *by the wear and tear of modern
life*] Fa] *the original form is still traceable . . .* J52.057
*There can hardly be much fear, however, of a reduced distribu-
tion,* [Fa [J *so strong*] [Vzb *is*] [Ns *the company's financial
position*] Fa]. A25.176
[Fa [J *Important*] *as*_CSA [Np *these differences*] [Vab *are*] Fa],
they should not obscure . . . J17:0780

§ **4.295**　This construction has an American variant in which the
predicative adjective is qualified by *as*:

[S [Fa [Jh *As*_RGa *different physically*] *as*_CSA [Nns *the tall,
angular Jefferson*] [Vsb *was*] [P *from the chubby, rotund
Adams*] Fa], *the seven were striking individualists* S]. G07:1000

§ **4.296**　Similarly an adverbial element may be moved from its
logical position to the beginning of an Fa:

And so I would only touch upon it now, ([Fa [Ds *much*] *as*_CSA
[Nea *I*] [Vf *have* [R *long*] *wanted*] [Ti *to write a book about
it*] Fa]). G10:0190 — the clause is seen as derived from *I long
much have wanted . . .* , though such a sequence would be
unnatural as it stands (§ 5.117)

§ **4.297**　Where this construction involves splitting a verb group
into two parts, the Vr, unusually, precedes the Vo ("Vo" is defined
as the part of the verb group containing the finite verb). Although
the conjunction in such a construction is often the word *as*, these
sequences are always classified as Fa rather than as A clauses.

§ **4.298**　Another special type of Fa is the "subjunctive" construction exemplified by:

[Fa [Vod *Had*] [Ns *an exact solution of this problem*] [Vrnp *been
carried*] +<hyphen> [R *out*] Fa] *there would have been . . .* [22]
J76.015
. . . what it would have been [Fa [Vod *had*] [Nas *he*] [Vrnp *been
brought*] [R *up*] [P *at the plough*] Fa] D14.029
*begins the formation of a new individuality by means of new
impressions,* [Fa [Vodc *should*] [Ns *his power to receive new
impressions*] [Vrefp *not have been destroyed*] [P *by the ca-
lamity*] Fa]. D14.037

---

[22] The original typography hyphenates the verb and particle of a phrasal-verb
sequence, . . . *been carried-out . . .* , as not infrequently happens. Irrespective of the hyphen,
the verb belongs with the preceding auxiliary in a V tagma; the hyphen is treated as a clause
IC.

Even the officer in charge, [Fa% [Vjb *be*] [Ni *it*] [N *a captain*
... [Ns+ *or a general*] N] Fa%], *is restrained by monitoring.*
G20:1040

(Only the last of these examples is given the subjunctive formtag
suffix "%", cf. §§ 4.390-1, since only this example has a verb
group beginning with a form which fails to agree with the subject
if taken as an indicative.) A rather different case occurs in the
sequence:

*But let a "stroke" affect the brain . . . , the person's individuality
vanishes.* D14.034

Here the imperative *let* clause functions pragmatically as an Fa (it
paraphrases "if a stroke affects..."). However, this use of an
imperative to represent a condition is most commonly (although not
in this particular case) linked to the following consequence clause
by a co-ordinating conjunction (*give them an inch and they take a
mile*); it would be very odd to treat a structure of that sort as
linking a subordinate with a main clause. Accordingly, the pragmatics is ignored and such a sequence is treated as a co-ordination of
imperative with indicative main clauses (which, in the case quoted
above, happens to be an asyndetic co-ordination):

[S*+ *But* [V *let*] [Ns *a "stroke"*] [Tb [V *affect*] . . .] . . . , [S–
the person's individuality vanishes S–] S*+].

§ 4.299   Reduced Fa's occur, beginning with a subordinating
conjunction but lacking a finite verb:

I shall . . . pay you back myself, [Fa *if* [J *necessary*]]. L21.154
What this amounts to, [Fa *if* [J *true*]], *is . . .* A03:0170
[Fa [Rq *When*] [J *necessary*]], *we should . . .* J22:0280
. . . it becomes a perilous anachronism [Fa [Rq *when*]
   [Vn *adopted*] [P *on a world-wide basis*] Fa]. G02:1620
. . . staggering forward, a half-filled bottle upraised [Fa [CSk= *as_if*]
   [Vi *to strike*]]. N14:0630
[Fa *Whether* [Np [NNL2& *flats or shops or restaurants*]]], *there
   is a marked individuality.* E22.125
He kicked several [Fa *while* [Vg *playing*] [P *at Stamford High
   School*]], . . . A12:0260

— and examples like the last quoted, which can be seen as reduced
from *while he was playing . . .* , are used as a precedent for a similar
analysis in cases such as:

... *even the Communists, who number millions in France,*
[Fa *although officially* [Vg *opposing*] *him during the last
referendum* ... Fa], *are* ... B08.138
... *Jack Fisher* ... *held the A's scoreless* [Fa *while* [Vg *yielding*]
[Np *three scattered hits*] Fa]. A11:0080
[Fa *After* [Vg *reading*] [Ns *his statement discharging the 23d
ward case* Ns] Fa], *Karns told* ... A03:0710

(even though, in these latter cases, expansions into sequences with
finite verbs would not preserve the participles — they would run
they opposed, he yielded, he read rather than *they were opposing,*
etc.). Such sequences are not analysed as containing internal non-
finite clauses: one does not parse [Fa *when* [Tn *adopted on a world-
wide basis*]], [Fa *although* [Tg *officially opposing him* ...]].

§ 4.300   Also analysed as Fa's, though these cases are harder to
see as reduced versions of clauses containing finite verbs, are adjective or adverb postmodifiers consisting of subordinating conjunction followed by another adjective or adverb element; see the
examples at § 4.189, or:

[S+ *and* [Fa *if* [Ns *so*]], *she has succeeded admirably*]. P12.032

— this use of *so* is formtagged as a noun phrase but is functiontagged
as a Manner adjunct, § 5.154.

§ 4.301   Words tagged ICS ... , e.g. *till, after,* can introduce either prepositional phrases or adverbial clauses. When the complement of an ICS... word is a straightforwardly nominal element or
a full clause with finite verb respectively, the choice of P v. Fa for
the tagma introduced by the word is clear. When the complement
is some other kind of tagma or tagma-sequence, the presumption is
that the construction introduced by the ICS... word is a reduced
Fa; cf. the *After reading his statement* example in § 4.299, or:

... *we took the episode without a smile* [Fa *till* [R *afterwards*]].
G04.010
... *consumption was maintained* [Fa *except* [P *in families with
more than one child* ...]]. H04.110
... *there were no objections at the College of Physicians to
Harvey's new ideas* [Fa *except* [P *on_the_part_of Dr James
Primrose* ...]] G02.021

§ 4.302   Clauses tagged Fa do not invariably function adverbially;
sometimes they act as complements of copular verbs. This is particularly frequent with *as_if, as_though*:

it was [Fa *as_though the Corsican belonged spiritually to another species*] N23.049

One felt [Fa *as_though one hadn't arrived anywhere*]. P03.031

Well, that looked [Fa *as_if it had been a near miss*]. L13.038

But it didn't seem [Fa% *as_if there were a garden boy*]. L13.039

§ 4.303 The sequence of words *as if* are not invariably a CSk idiom; they can be separate subordinating conjunctions:

. . . the syllabus has been essentially [D *the same* [Fc *as* [Fa *if the pupils were to become candidates . . .*]]] H03.087

§ 4.304 Subordinating conjunctions that introduce Fa's are sometimes premodified by measure expressions, which can be N's (often unit noun phrases, i.e. Nu's), or adverbs indicating degree or measurement. The SUSANNE scheme has no category of phrase headed by CS. . . words; the measure expression in these cases is parsed as first daughter of the Fa:

They began their discussions . . . [Fa [Np *two hours*] *after Mr. Kennedy flew in*]. A28.035

The two men met . . . [Fa [R *shortly*] *after President Kennedy flew in . . .*]. A31.070

. . . signed [P *on March 11 —* [Fa@ [Ns *nearly a month*] *before hostilities began*] *—*] G10:0620

. . . to happen [Fa [R *just*] *after the fish had risen . . .*] E06.092

This construction represents an exception to the general rule (§§ 4.210–11) that a finite subordinate clause does not begin with an adverb.

Fn   nominal clause

§ 4.305 An Fn is normally a declarative-sentence-like sequence introduced by *that* or by no special element, or an indirect question introduced by a *wh-* word:

He knew [Fn *that* [Ns *anything a brainy little lady like her had to say*] *would be plumb important, as well as pleasin' to the ear* Fn], *. . .* N09:0130

[Ns *the important fact* [Fn *that fundamental alterations in conditioned reactions occur in a variety of states . . .*]] J17:1430

I'm [Jh *well aware* [Fn *that you've got a pedigree as long as my leg,* [Fn+ *and that I don't amount to anything*]]]. N09:0030

Patrolman James F. Simms said [Fn *he started in pursuit when he saw . . .* Fn]. A20:1810

DAN MORGAN TOLD HIMSELF [Fn *HE WOULD FORGET Ann Turner*]. N01:0010

... *asked* [Fn% *that the cost of 'antiseptic diaper service' be made a tax deductible expense*]. J44.156

You asked me [Fn? *whether I knew the man*] *and I told you* ... L02.011

they reveal [Fn? *what they hate*], ... G13:0950

It is difficult to be certain [Fn? *how the administration views that $28 million*], ... A08:1550

For the "?" suffix in the tag Fn?, see § 4.379.

An Fn will not include subject-auxiliary inversion. *CGEL*, p. 1051, notes that subject-auxiliary inversion may occur in a clear subordinate clause, e.g. *The problem is* **who can we get to replace her**; in SUSANNE terms the emphasized sequence will be tagged S?, not Fn?. (See e.g. the G74 example quoted in § 4.282.)

§ 4.306   *If* introduces an Fn rather than an Fa when it stands at the beginning of an indirect question, synonymous with *whether*, and also when it introduces an extraposed finite clause similar in function to a *for-to* clause:

He wanted to know [Fn? *if my father had beaten me* [Fn?+ *or my mother had run away from home*] *to give me an unhappy childhood* Fn?]. G12:1370

Perhaps it would be helpful [Fn *if I were to say something* ...] H21.084

It would have been acceptable to all concerned [Fn *if John had stepped into Fort Blockhouse clad in plain-clothes* ...], ... N04.044

§ 4.307   A *that* clause in which each verb valency slot is filled, postmodifying a noun denoting a fact, speech-act, etc., is Fn rather than Fr:

She gave [Ns *no sign* [Fn *that she had even heard him*]]. K11.147

§ 4.308   The *that* clause of a cleft construction is Fn when the focused element is adverbial, e.g.:

It is [P *within the framework provided by them*] [Fn *that idiosyncratic preferences operate*]. J30.148

It was [Ti *in_order to cater for the needs of* ...] [Fn *that Gresham's College was founded* ...]. J37.074

It was [Rsw *then*] [Fn *that she noticed Michael*]. P28.178

it's usually [P *under* [R *just*] *those conditions*] [Fn *that help is called for*]. F22.035 — *just* treated as included adverbial within P

It is [Fa *because there is not only darkness but also light*] [Fn *that our situation becomes inexplicable*]. G12:1060

— for cases where the focused element is nominal, see § 4.315.

§ **4.309**   On the borderline between Fn and Q, see §§ 4.406 ff.

§ **4.310**   Reduced indirect questions lacking a finite verb sometimes occur, e.g.:

> *Legislators always get restless for a special session* ([I [S [Fn?
> *whether* [P *for the companionship or the $22.50 per diem*] Fn?]
> *is not certain* S] I]) *and* . . . A08:0890
>
> *The room has been tidied: I wonder* [Fn? [Nq *who*] [Pb *by*]].
> . . . *regardless* [Po *of* [Fn? [Jq *how trying*] [Np *the circumstances*
>]]] N05:1090
>
> *A* new *question asked* [P *about housing tenure,* [Fn?@ *whether
> the accommodation* . . . *was held by them as owner-occupiers;*
> [Fn– *occupied in connection with employment* . . .]; [Fn?–
> *rented from a Council* . . . *or a private landlord* ([**Fn?**– [Fa *if
> so*], *whether* [Tn *furnished* [J+ *or unfurnished*]] **Fn?**–]) Fn?–];
> [Fn?+ *or occupied on some other terms*] Fn?@] P]. H01.047

Fr   relative clause

§ **4.311**   An Fr is a tagma which modifies an antecedent by presenting a proposition with a gap in its logical structure (sometimes
represented by a relative pronoun), implying that the antecedent fills
the gap. The SUSANNE parsing scheme does not distinguish between "restrictive" relative clauses, which help to identify the antecedent, and "appositive" relative clauses which give new information
about an antecedent supposed to be already identified.

> . . . *the* <bital>k<eital>*th order complex of* [Np *lines* [Fr *which meet
> g*]]. J21:0270
>
> [Dp *those* [Fr *who use none or only part of the hospital-care
> credit*]] A03:1100
>
> [Ns *the role* [Po *of advisor and guide*] [Fr *which at an earlier
> stage foreign experts assumed in dealing with the central gov-
> ernments* Fr] Ns] J22:0800
>
> . . . *ordered* [Np *their own tests,* [Fr *which are in progress at
> Massachusetts Institute of Technology* Fr] Np] A12:1800
>
> [Ns *a committee* [Fr *that included James A. Farley, Bernard Gimbel
> and Clint Blume* Fr] Ns] A14:0580
>
> [S?+ *But do the plays deal with* [Np *the same facets* [Po *of ex-
> perience*] [Fr *religion must also deal with* Fr] Np] S?+]?
> G12:1330
>
> *It is* [Ns *nothing* [Fr *you can put your fingers on*] Ns] . . .
> N18:0700

§ 4.312   An Fr may be introduced by *like_ICSk*:

I've got [Ns *a queer feeling,* [Fr *like_ICSk I always get when
something sensational's going to happen*]]. M03.025

or by *so_RRz*, in the substandard construction:

I have [Ns *a way* [Fr [R *so*] *we can carry on without his suspecting us*]] N18:1120

§ 4.313   An Fr may be introduced by a *wh*- adverb rather than
pronoun; the subordinate clauses are Fr rather than Fa in:

... *in* [Ns *the clothing trade,* [Fr [Rq *where*] *he sometimes acts
as a speculator* ...]]. F41.087
till [M *1768,* [Fr [Rq *when*] *they were delivered* ...]] J37.080
... *record the Ommeganck of* [M *1615,* [Fr [Rq *when*] *the
Infanta Isabella* ... *had succeeded in shooting the popinjay at
the first attempt*]]. J63.077
After all, there was [Ns *no reason* [Fr [Rq *why*] *he should come
here*]]. N21.025
On [Nnp *Fridays,* [Ns@ *the day* [Fr [Rq *when*] *many Persians
relax with poetry,* ... Fr] Ns@] Nnp], ...   G05:0430

§ 4.314   Likewise, in an Fr with zero relative pronoun or introduced by *that*, the antecedent may fill a "when", "where", "how",
or "why" slot rather than a "who" or "what" slot:

... *that Zuck had been followed* [Ns *the day* [Fr *he ordered a
music-box from a store on Fifth Avenue*] Ns]. L12.064
at [Ns *precisely the time* [Fr *that the nation-state attained its highest
number (approximately 100)* Fr] Ns] G02:1570
The reason [Fr *we subtract the correction term* <formul>] *is
that* ... J19.203

In this last case, note that if an explicit connective were included it
would most probably be *that*; there is a subtle distinction between:

[Ns *the reason* [Fr *that_CST we subtract the correction term* ...]]

and

[Ns *the fact* [Fn *that_CST we subtract the correction term* ...]]

— in the former, the "purpose" slot in the subordinate clause is
represented by a fronted relative pronoun, while in the latter the
subtraction is not thought of as having a purpose, but is introduced
by *that* as a subordinating conjunction; thus the clauses are verbally
identical although the first has a missing valency slot and the latter
does not.

§ **4.315** In a cleft construction whose focused element is nominal rather than adverbial (for which see § 4.324), the subordinate clause is formtagged as Fr rather than Fn (but as sister, not daughter, of the focused element — the Fr is analysed as an extraposed postmodifier of the *it*, as discussed in § 5.77):

> ... *in steeplechasers it is* [Ns *the influence of the mare*] [Fr *which predominates*]. A23.148

In the similar construction with *there*, however, the Fr is treated as postmodifying the postposed subject:

> *There's* [Ns *nothing* [Fr *he likes more than to frighten the Party*]]. K03.044

§ **4.316** The antecedent of an Fr may be an entire clause, representing a state of affairs or the like, in which case the Fr ("propositional relative clause") is an IC of the clause rather than of an N. (On the logical annotation for such cases, see § 5.198.) Thus:

> [S *They all occurred during my service with the Trinity House,* [Fr *which is not altogether surprising when one remembers* ...]]. F22.032

§ **4.317** An Fr must have some explicit verbal material that can be treated as its antecedent. An antecedentless relative clause is form-tagged Ff (see the following section).

Ff fused relative

§ **4.318** A relative clause lacking an explicit antecedent and functioning as a nominal element is formtagged Ff. The categories Ff and Fn? are often formally indistinguishable, but they differ semantically (an Ff is not an indirect question) and distributionally (Ff's are common, but Fn?'s rare, in subject position). In some cases, furthermore, there are formal cues: a *wh...ever* word or phrase can begin an Ff but not an Fn?; *who* and *which* commonly begin Fn?'s but not Ff's.

> ... *share with each other* [Ff [Nvs *whatever light*] *God has given them*] B03.055
> *Is there no such thing as* ... *forgetting* [Ff [Dq *what*] *one has learnt*]? D14.083
> ... *climbed the stairs, to* [Ff [Rq *where*] *Thomas was waiting*]. K17.060
> ... , *good use being made of activity methods and of* [Ff [Nvp *whatever ancillary aids*] *were available*]. H03.095

The others put on [Np [Np *old coats or ducking jackets*],
[Ff@ [Dv *whichever*] *they carried behind their saddle
cantles* Ff@] Np]. N10:0870
And that was [Ff [Rq *when_CSn*] *Mort and I came into the
picture*]. L06.087
... *to do exactly* [Ff [Dq *what*] *they wanted*], [Fa [Rq *how*] *they
wanted*]. G48.123

— in the G48 example, the *how* clause functions adverbially rather
than nominally within the *to do* clause, and it is not capable of
expansion into an Fr preceded by an explicit antecedent, so it must
be Fa rather than Ff. In the L06 example, on the other hand, the
when clause is Ff rather than Fa since it could be expanded into a
sequence such as [Ns *the time* [Fr *when Mort and I came* ...]].
(Although it is possible for an Fa to act as complement of a copular
verb, cf. § 4.302, such a complement is parsed as Fa only if no
other analysis is available for it.)

Fc comparative clause
§ 4.319 A clause formtagged Fc is normally introduced by one of
the conjunctions *than, that* (in a construction *so ... that ...* or *such
... that ...*), or *as* (in *as ... as ..., so ... as ...* ,[23] *such ... as ...* ,
or *the same ... as ...*). Constructions of these kinds have an Fc as
their last IC (in the case of *as ... as ...*, the second *as* introduces
an Fc); the material preceding the Fc is not grouped together as a
single tagma. Some examples of Fc are:

Barton's voice was [Jh *rougher* [Fc *than Dill had ever heard it*]].
N07:1190
[Jh *so tipsy* [Fc *that it seemed unlikely he was bothering to note
anything or anyone about him* Fc] Jh] N14:0310
But the ball developed [Ns *such a crazy spin* [Fc *that Leslie could
not cope with it*]]. A22.137 — *such* modifies the whole phrase
a crazy spin, not just the adjective *crazy* for which the corre-
sponding qualifier would be *so*
[R *as soon* [Fc *as possible*]] A19:0850
[Jh *as safe* [Fc *as we should be*] [P *from such a disaster*]]
G03:0030
Error produces strife [R *just as certainly* [Fc *as truth produces
peace*]]. D11.097
[Jh *so fastidious* [P *in its growth requirements*] [Fc *as* [Vi *to make*]
[Ns *production on a militarily significant scale*] [J *improb-
able*] Fc] Jh]. J08:1270

---

[23] But for *so as ...*, with no wording between *so* and *as*, see § 4.368.

... *to recover* [R *so far* [Fc *as* [Ti *to be inclined to take another lover*, ...]]]. C08.155

§ 4.320   In the case of the category Fc it is common to find reduced clauses lacking a finite verb, e.g:

... *he was more puzzled* [Fc *than* [R *ever*]]. N01:0320
... *shown* [R *so well* [Fc *as* [P *during the promenade at the Khaju bridge*]]]. G05:0860
... *should be met* [P *from voluntary donations*] [R *rather* [Fc *than* [P *from rates compulsorily levied*]]]. A14.025

§ 4.321   After *as_CSA* or *than_CSN* an Fc may be reduced to just a tagma functioning nominally. (*As* is never wordtagged as a preposition, IIa, when used in a comparative sense.) In such a case, the reduced tagma will normally be formtagged P rather than Fc, despite the CS... wordtag:

[Jh *as popular* [P *as* [Np *football coupons*]]] A19.213
You know this stuff [R *better* [P *than me*]] M05.123
... [D *little more* [P *than* [Ns *the amount which* ... *the Chancellor may have to spare* — [Nu@ *just over £100m*]] P] D]. B07.154
spaces of [Np [D *more* [P *than three*]] *dimensions*] J21:0090
[Np *nine greater alcoves* [Jh *as frescoed and capacious* [P *as_CSA* [Np *church apses*]]]] G05:0990 — position of the reduced tagma within a phrase creates no presumption about the logical role of *church apses* in an underlying clause

§ 4.322   The Fc analysis will be used even in such cases, though, if the underlying clause status of the reduced element is made obvious by use of nominative pronoun, or by the fact that the logical role of the nominal element contrasts with what would be expected from its position. Thus:

No man was [Jh *more sensitive* [Fc *than* [Nas *he*]] [P *to the changing moods of the House of Commons*] Jh]. G31.176 — contrast *than me* in the M05 example in the previous section, where the connection with the meaning "than I know it" is so attenuated that the object form of the pronoun is used
some having gained [D *more* [Fc *than* [Np *others*]]] G02:1510 — the D phrase is in object position but *others* is understood as a subject, making the derivation from *than others gained* clear
to "*pursue* [Ns *the study of the law*], [R *rather* [Fc *than* [Ns *the gain of it*]]]" G07:1230 — the *than* sequence is not sub-

ordinate to *the study of the law* but occurs within a separate clause IC, bringing into focus the fact that it is a reduced form of a separate clause in which the *gain* phrase is direct object

... *are held* [R *more tenaciously*] [P *in the Tidewater*] [Fc *than* [Nns *the Piedmont*] Fc]; ... G01:1000 — *the Piedmont* has no explicit preposition but in context is clearly functioning as a Place adjunct

§ **4.323** If what follows *as* or *than* is a non-finite clause, it will have its own T... node:

... *is* [Jh *more important* [Fc *than* [Tg *aiding them economically*]]] A10:0100

First, whether ... *the school need do* [D *more* [Fc *than* [Tb *provide an environment in which* ...]]]. G47.116

§ **4.324** A sequence *different than* ..., which occurs in American English although regarded as solecistic, is analysed using the Fc category when *than* has a non-nominal complement:

might be [Jh *different* [P *in the dog*] [Fc *than* [P *in the horse*]]] J12:0640

§ **4.325** In a sequence ending with an Fc, it can be debatable whether the Fc should be seen as modifying the immediately preceding word, or as a dislocated modifier of an element premodifying that word. For instance, in a sequence *so extremely cold that the pipes froze*, one might argue that the logical structure is [[*so extremely that the pipes froze*] *cold*]; but the SUSANNE approach is not to postulate dislocation in such cases:

[Jh *so extremely cold* [Fc *that the pipes froze*]]

... *eating* [Ns *the same food* [Fc *as* [Ns *a person of light complexion*]]] D14.055

The smell is [Jh *sexual,* [Ns+ *but so powerfully so*_PN1z [Fc *that a civilized nose must deny it*]]]. G04:1500

— an Fc is treated as dislocated only in cases such as:

to resemble [R *more nearly*] [Ns *the performance of a rain dance*] [Fc *than the carrying out of an experiment in physics*]. G11:1200

the second education [R *as quickly*] [Vd *disappeared*] [Fc *as the first*], ... D14.043

... *to function* [D *more*] [P *in other departments*] [Fc *than I have been able to do in the past*]. E11.154

... he [Vdc *would* [R *still*] [R *rather*] *sing*] [Fc *than* [V *do*]
[Ns *anything else*]]. E11.161

where the *nearly, quickly, more* phrases do not modify the following phrases but rather the pairs of phrases are sister ICs of a clause;
and, in the last case, *rather... than do anything else* is logically a
sister of *would sing*. On the full analysis of these and similar cases,
see § 5.90.

§ 4.326   In a case where deletion of repeated material has
occurred, as in:

... approaches [Rr *much more closely*] [P *to countercurrent*
[Fc *than* [P *to crossflow*] Fc] *conditions* P]. J07.065

— the deletion is analysed as occurring from the Fc, and the element to which the Fc is compared is made complete: in this example,
the single surface token of *conditions* is made part of the P *to
countercurrent... conditions*, rather than the sequence being analysed as [P *to countercurrent*] [Fc *than to crossflow conditions*].[24]

§ 4.327   *That* introducing an Fc can be elided, as in:

... it would happen [R *so fast* [Fc *people would think it took
place overnight* Fc] R]. N04:0340

§ 4.328   A *so... that...* sequence is not analysed using the Fc
category in a case such as:

Gillian's arrest [Vsp *was* [R *so_RRz*] *contrived*] [Fn *that Mrs.
Wynter would be with him at the time*];... L24.024

— here *so* is paraphrased "in such a way" rather than "to such an
extent"; the logical annotation scheme will treat the Fn as having
been dislocated out of the R headed by *so*.

§ 4.329   On Fc's in "correlative" constructions, see §§ 4.200,
4.230.

§ 4.330   The principle that sequences drawing comparisons are
given the structure:

[attribution of characteristic [standard of comparison]]

is extended to expressions of comparison which do not employ an
Fc; thus:

It was always [Jh *too big* [P *for the centre of the room*]], ...
K08.104

---

[24] The remarks at § 4.199 about a sequence such as *much + more/less + adjective* being
analysed as a three-constituent J phrase, without grouping of the first two elements, applies
equally when the third element is an adverb as in *much more closely*.

— and again dislocation is not posited in a case such as:

> ... *is* [Ns *too big an undertaking* [Tf *for him to adopt it*]]
> <hellip>. E16.049

T... Non-finite Subordinate Clause

§ **4.331** As in the case of F..., every instance of a T... formtag includes a lower-case subcategory symbol.

§ **4.332** When a clause with a non-finite verb as head is introduced by a subordinating conjunction that normally introduces a finite clause, the whole is treated as a reduced Fa and the Tg tag is not used: cf. various examples discussed in § 4.299. (However, for *whether to* ..., see § 4.356.)

§ **4.333** Where a present-participle or past-participle clause occurs following a higher clause having a transitive verb, with the logical subject of the lower clause intervening, the logical subject is analysed as a daughter of the higher clause in surface structure (for the logical annotation, see §§ 5.54 ff., especially § 5.57). On the other hand, when such a clause preceded by its logical subject occurs other than following a transitive verb — for instance, when the sequence follows a preposition — then the logical subject is included as a daughter of the lower clause. Thus:

> ... *when he first sees* [Np *light machine-guns*] [Tg *being assembled*], ... K09.112
> *Father Felix had seen* [Ns *the platoon*] [Tg *marching by the mission*]. K09.116
> ... *you'll get* [Ns *your pretty self*] [Tn *squashed flat*]! K11.146
> ... *to hear* [Ns *someone*] [Tg *running towards them*]. F11.112
> *The means of setting* [Np *talks*] [Tg *going*] *are clear enough* ...
> B02.019

but:

> ... *the melancholy* [Po *of* [Tg [Ns *a tempest*] *subsiding*]], ...
> K12.158
> ... *the only sound was* [Po *of* [Tg [Np *iron tyres*] *grinding down into the gritty dust*]]. N14.143
> *I cannot say that I have ever known* [Po *of* [Tg [Ns *a young lady*] *dying of love*]]. C08.152

§ **4.334** However, there is a subtle semantic distinction between either of these two constructions, and the alternative constructions in which the non-finite clause acts as a postmodifier of the nominal element:

> ... *the beam bears* [Ns *the weight-stamp of George III* [Tg *obliterating a number of older marks*]]. F09.093
> *It has* [Ns *a hull* [Tn *patterned on that of the United States navy's Nautilus,* ... Tn] Ns]. A20:0070

When the nominal element is the direct object of the higher clause and the verb of that clause is one which cannot take a complement clause, only this latter analysis is possible. Thus, in the *weight-stamp* example, *bear* meaning "carry" cannot take a complement clause (although if *bear* were interpretable as "tolerate" in this environment the alternative analysis would be a possibility). In other cases the decision must be made in terms of whether it is the thing denoted by the noun phrase, or the action denoted by the clause, which is intended as the object of the higher verb or preposition, and this decision is frequently not easy — several of the examples quoted in § 4.333 might reasonably have been given the alternative analysis.

§ **4.335** Another delicate semantic distinction arises where a participle occurs in predicative position following part of the verb *BE*. Here a choice must be made between analysing the participle as head of a Tg or Tn, on the one hand, or treating the *BE* + participle sequence as a progressive or passive verb group on the other. Thus, in *the knives which are now well rounded by wear* F09.091, the choice is between the analyses:

> ... [Fr *which* [Vab *are*] *now* [Tn *well* [Vn *rounded*] *by wear*]]
> ... [Fr *which* [Vap *are* [Rw *now*] [R *well*] *rounded*] *by wear*]

In such cases, the T... analysis goes with a "static" interpretation, the analysis which treats *BE* + participle as a V goes with a "dynamic" interpretation. Thus, in the example quoted, the Tn analysis is chosen because from the context it is clear that the knives are being described as now in a state resulting from rounding action over a long period in the past; the Vp analysis would imply that the knives are at the present moment being rounded. Likewise:

> ... *they* [Vwb *were*] [Jh [Tn *relieved*] [Ti *to hear* ...]] F11.112

— *relieved*, though by the "dictionary test" a verb past participle, seems interchangeable in context with adjectives such as *glad*, *happy*, and there is little sense that this is a passive expression of something that might be expressed actively as *hearing* ... *relieved them*. Likewise, compare *The house* [Vsb *was*] [Tn *sold*] *when I enquired about it* v. *The house* [Vsp *was sold*] *last week*. Or compare the following pairs of examples, quoted in *TLCUM*:[25]

> *. . . all her movements* [Vwb *were*] [Tn *limited* [J+ *and painful*]]. F31.024
> *. . . the powers contained in the Trustee Act* [Vwb *were*] [J *far too* [Tn *limited*]]. J50.054

versus

> *. . . the intake* [Vcp *will* [R *still*] *be* [R *strictly*] *limited*]. B18.094
> *I doubt very much whether the word* [Vcp *can be limited*] *to this meaning . . .* F27.185

And contrast:

> *This* [Vzb *is*] [Tg *disturbing*], *for . . .* D10.167

with

> *It is, of course, this aspect of the matter that* [Vzu *is disturbing*] *the Home Secretary*. B17.060

§ 4.336 When the past participle of a *BE* + past-participle sequence is understood intransitively, there is no possibility of interpreting the sequence as a passive construction, so the past participle must head a Tn:

> *The Lord* [Vzb *is*] [Tn [Vn *risen*]] [R *indeed*] (Luke 24: 34)
> *It* [Vsb *was*] [Tn [Vn *turned*] [R *away*]], . . . K06.083 — in context it is clear that this does not mean "someone had turned it away"
> *Suddenly my reflexes* [Vab *are*] [Tn [Vn *gone*]]. A13:0990

— or, with normal word-order disturbed by topicalization:

> [Tn [Vn *Gone*]] [Vzb *is*] *the realist décor; . . .* C05.108

§ 4.337 Although in principle the issue of Vb + T. . . versus Vn/Vu analyses arises with respect both to past participles and to present participles, in practice the difficult decisions usually relate to past participles, because of a characteristic of the reference dictionary, *OALD3*: whereas this rarely gives a separate adjective listing for a

---

[25] *TLCUM* uses these examples to contrast adjectival and verbal analyses, since the Tagged LOB Corpus frequently tags morphological participles as adjectives although the SUSANNE dictionary test often requires them to be tagged as verbal participles whatever the context: thus a sequence treated by the SUSANNE scheme as *BE* + Tn (rather than as Vp) will typically be treated as *BE* + adjective in the Tagged LOB Corpus.

past participle having a stative sense, it usually does so for a present participle with a comparable function — *boring, striking, surprising, tiring*, etc. are all listed as adjectives. The word *disturbing* used in one pair of examples above is unusual in being a present participle regularly used adjectivally but not listed in *OALD3* as an adjective.

Tg   present participle clause
§ 4.338   Clause with Vg head:

[Np *seven cases* [Tg [Vg *involving*] *35 persons*]] A03:0620
Britain began [Tg [Vg *designing*] *the ship*] *in 1956*... A20:0710
Clearly, any line... *will be transformed into* [Ns *the entire pencil*
   [Tg [Vg *having*] *the image of the second intersection of <bital>*
   l <eital> and <bital> Q <eital> as vertex [Tg+ *and* [Vg *lying*]
   in the plane determined by...] Tg] Ns]. J21:0720
guilt about [Tg [Vgef *not having attended*] *his funeral*] J24:0200
[Tg *Apparently* [Vg *sensing*] *this,* [Tg+ *and* [Vg *realizing*] *that*
   it gave him an advantage Tg+] Tg], *Jess became bold.* N12:0940
Barton turned away, [Tg *his eyes* [Vg *falling*] *upon Rankin beside*
   his horse]. N07:0570
Each mode is believed to have a specific attribute — [Tg *one*
   [Vg *inducing*] *pleasure,* [Tg- *another generosity*],
   [Tg- *another love*], [R *and_so_on_RAc=*] Tg],... G05:1580

§ 4.339   There is a gradient, among tagmas having a Vg as head, from clauses to noun phrases; cf. *GCE*, p. 133. The SUSANNE scheme divides that gradient between *GCE* examples [5] and [6]. A tagma headed by a Vg will always be a Tg (unless the Vg is regarded as a reduced finite V — see §§ 4.281, 4.492); but if modifiers of the types found in examples [1] to [5] occur — namely, adjective (rather than adverb); postmodifying *of* phrase, or other prepositional phrase that would be inappropriate within a finite clause; or premodifying determiner (but not genitive phrase) — these are analysed as sisters of the Tg node, and daughters of an Ns headed by the Tg. Elements which would be equally grammatically appropriate in a finite clause, e.g. adverb modifiers, objects (even if preceding the participle), are analysed as within the Tg. Thus (examples taken from *GCE*, pp. 133–4):

[Ns *The* [Tg [Vg *painting*]] [Po *of Brown*]] *is as skilful as that*
   of Gainsborough.
[Ns *Brown's deft* [Tg [Vg *painting*]] [Po *of his daughter*]] *is*
   a delight to watch.

but:

> [Tg [Nns *Brown*] [R *deftly*] [Vg *painting*] [Ns *his daughter*]]
> *is a delight to watch.*
> [Tg [G *Brown's*] [R *deftly*] [Vg *painting*] [Ns *his daughter*]]
> *is a delight to watch.*
> [Tg *Painting his daughter*], *Brown noticed that his hand was*
> *shaking.*
> [Tg *Brown painting his daughter that day*], *I decided to go for*
> *a walk.*
> [Ns *The man* [Tg *painting the girl*]] *is Brown.*
> [Ns *The* [Tg [R *silently*] [Vg *painting*]] *man*] *is Brown.*

Corpus examples in which the Tg heads an Ns include:

> *too deeply moved by* [Ns *this* [Tg [Vg *romanticizing*]]]; ...
> G08:1320
> ... *is concerned with* "[Ns *the* [Tg [Vg *becoming*]], [Ns@ *the*
> *process of realization*] Ns]", *but* ... G09:0970
> ... *took a swipe at* [Ns [G *the State Welfare Department's*]
> [Tg [Vg *handling*]] [Po *of federal funds*...]]. A01:0300
> ... *that* [Ns *the* [Tg [Vg *winding*] [R *up*] Tg] Ns] *should be*
> *done*... H05.150
> [Ns *The* [Tg [Vg *smoothing*] [R *out*] Tg] [Po *of income tax rates*],
> [P *without any special concept of*... P], Ns] *would mean*...
> B07.142

In the case:

> [Ns [Tg [Ns *Hard-surface*] [Vg *cleaning*] Tg] [P *in household*
> *application*] Ns] *is represented by*... J05:0200

the placing of object before participle does not in itself make the Tg
an Ns, but the wording of the postmodifying prepositional phrase
is naturally interpreted as a restrictive modifier of a nominal element, rather than as a verb adjunct. If the sequence ran *Surface*
cleaning is represented by..., then *Surface cleaning* would be a
Tg but not an Ns; and in *Surface cleaning for lengthy periods is*
represented... the emphasized sequence would be a Tg but not an
Ns, with *for lengthy periods* an adjunct P within the Tg.

§ 4.340 Where a Tg functioning as a complement within a higher
clause is postmodified by a nominal conjunct or by a relative clause,
this is within an Ns headed by the Tg:

> ... *and the need for* [N [Tg *strengthening conventional*
> *forces* Tg] [Ns+ *as_well_as the maintenance of the nuclear*
> *deterrent* Ns+] N]. A04:0660

[Ns [Tg <bital> [Vg *Distinguishing*] <eital> [Np *cases*] Tg], [Fr
which consists in giving reasons why a rule . . . Fr], Ns] [Vzp
is [R *often*] *conceived*] *to be an indication that . . .* J49.030

— the J49 example is not a "propositional relative clause" in the
sense of § 4.316: within the *is often conceived* clause, *Distinguishing cases* is a referring expression, and as fit to be an ordinary
Fr antecedent as a noun-headed N would be.

§ 4.341   Where the subject of a Tg is represented by a genitive
phrase as an alternative to the commoner construction with an
accusative noun phrase, the genitive will always be a daughter of
the Tg, though when the subject is a noun phrase, if the Tg is the
logical object of its containing clause the subject is treated as occurring in the higher clause in surface structure (cf. §§ 5.54 ff.):

I dislike [Tg *Brown's painting his daughter*].
I dislike [Nns *Brown*] [Tg *painting his daughter*].
I watched [Nns *Brown*] [Tg *painting his daughter*].

A premodifying genitive is parsed as outside the Tg if it is a mandatory genitive which cannot be replaced by a non-genitive N; thus:

Soon after that Pete staged [Ns *his* [Tg *drowning*]]. L01.016 —
no possibility of * *. . . staged him(self) drowning*
. . . changes that have affected the Negro have been [N *his* [Tg
moving up, row by row, in the busses]; [Ns– *his* [Tg *requesting, and often getting, higher wages . . .*]]] G08:0840 —
no possibility of **him moving up . . . , *him requesting . . .*

— contrast:

. . . the positive arguments for [Tg [G *their*] [Vgp *being composed*] *for gentle ears*] F27.082
he was excited about [Tg [G *his son's*] [Vgf *having received*] *the
Prix de Rome in archaeology*] G06:1500

(*them being composed . . .* , *his son having received* could equally
occur).

§ 4.342   When a Tg occurs as N postmodifier it will normally
lack an overt subject, and the antecedent will be understood as
implied subject of the Tg; cf. *the man painting the girl*, above. However, a Tg including an explicit subject can occur as an N postmodifier:

[Np *three distinguished historians (*[Tg [Ms *one*] [Vg *specializ-
ing*] [P *in the European Middle Ages*], [Tg– *one in American
history*], [Tg+ *and one in the Far East*]]*)* Np] G17:0280

Tn past-participle clause

§ 4.343 The category Tn includes two main types of clause headed by a past participle.

§ 4.344 The commoner type is a clause lacking an overt subject, and usually functioning adjectivally, e.g.:

> ... *with* [Ns *a certainty* [Po *of architectonic design*] [Tn [R *still*] [Vn *denied*] [P *to Brown*] Tn] Ns] ... C07.132
> [Ns *the mark* [Tn *set by Helen Shipley* ... *in the National A.A.U. meet in Columbus, Ohio* Tn] Ns] A11:1760
> [Ns *A beacon* [Tn [Vn *seen*] [P *on the shore*] Tn] Ns] *becomes* ... C07.148
> ... *who would like* [Ti *to see* [Ni *it (the resolution)*] [Tn [Vn *passed*] Tn] Ti]". A01:1610
> *Visibility continued* [Ti *to be* [Tn [Vn *limited*] Tn] Ti], ... N15:0780

§ 4.345 If this type of Tn includes a noun phrase preceding the participle, this will normally be playing some role other than subject, e.g.:

> [Ns *an initial state* [Tn [Ns *a long way*] [Vn *removed*] [P *from the more typical states in equilibrium*]]] J18.186

— here *a long way* premodifies the Vn as a Degree adjunct, analogous to the measure expression in a Jx tagma (§ 4.195).

§ 4.346 The past participle in a sequence of the kind ... *HAVE/ GET X VERBed* is treated as heading a Tn of this type; even if the participle is reordered so as to be adjacent to the preceding verb, it is not grouped with it into a single V:

> *He patted the eye* [Fr *Joel* [Vdf *had had*] [Tn [Vn *blackened*] *in a fight* ... Tn] Fr]. K15:0600

(if one *had* were absent here, the SUSANNE scheme would recognize a structural contrast between *Joel* [Vdf *had blackened*] ... , i.e. he had done it, and *Joel* [Vd *had*] [Tn [Vn *blackened*] ...], i.e. he had it done).

§ 4.347 The second type of Tn are "absolute" constructions: clauses including a subject and functioning in a way comparable to the Latin ablative absolute, as a concise equivalent of an adverbial clause:

> [Tn [Ns *This*] [Vn *done*] Tn], *she contemplated with dismay* ... P23.040

Here, the guests arrive in ghost-like yachts, [Tn [Np *the wildly
flapping white sails*] [Vn *slashed*] [Pb *by the glaring beacon
of a lighthouse*] Tn]. C02.049
Mary sat down in the desk chair, [Tn [Ns *her back*] [Vn *turned*]
[P *to Dora May's gaze*] Tn], *while . . .* L05.079

§ 4.348 Where a clause headed by a past participle is introduced
by a subordinating conjunction which standardly introduces a finite
clause, the whole is treated as a reduced Fa and the formtag Tn is
not used (cf. § 4.299).

Ti   infinitival clause
§ 4.349 A clause having an infinitival verb group as head:

[Ti *To accomplish this*] *would necessitate . . .* A10:1630
And I want [Ti *to sing jazz*]. A39.122
. . . was [Nj *the first* [Ti *to hit four at home*]] A13:1300
[Ns *the only way* [Ti *to deal with Southerners who oppose integration* Ti] Ns] *is . . .* G01:0690
Nevertheless, impulses still exist among the ruling elite [Ti *to
rationalize* [Ti+ *and thus to perpetuate*] *the need for central-
ized and authoritarian practices* Ti]. J22:1540
. . . proved [Ns *man enough* [Ti *to say this publicly —* [Ti– *to give
his foe the benefit of the fact that . . .* Ti–] Ti] Ns]. G10:1470

§ 4.350 A Ti does not include the subject of the verb. If the
logical subject appears before the infinitive, it is parsed as a sister
rather than daughter of the Ti:

I want [Ny *you*] [Ti *to marry me*], . . . K21.131
She did not want [Nop *them*] [Ti *to worry about her*]. K05.134
Douglass found [N <formul>] [Ti *to be trigonal, . . .*]. J04:0530

For infinitival clauses this is an absolute rule, unlike in the case of
participial clauses, § 4.333 above, where a logical subject may be
sister or daughter depending on grammatical environment.
§ 4.351 However, the Vi is not necessarily the first constituent
of a Ti — cf. § 4.210.
§ 4.352 The idiom *in_order*_BTO= occurs within a Ti, as left
sister of the Vi:

[Ti *in_order* [Vi *to prevent*] *law suits and other misunderstandings about what actually happened at their meetings*] A19:0700

§ 4.353 Any infinitive phrase (Vi) will be head of a separate
clause, which will be formtagged Ti (unless it is a Tf or Tq, see

below). However tightly an infinitive is bound, semantically, to a preceding verb, it requires a clause node of its own:

> *Rhode Island* [Vzut *is going*] [Ti *to examine its Sunday sales law . . .*]. A05:0480
> *Curt Adams* [Vz *wants*] [Ti *to see her*] N12:0110
> *One* [Vze *does not have*] [Ti *to look for distress*]. G12:1440

§ 4.354 An infinitival clause may be reduced to just the word *to*; cf. the example quoted in § 4.99.

§ 4.355 Where a Ti acts as a standard of comparison in a sequence such as:

> [R *too rapidly* [Ti [Vip *to be measured*] [Pb *by the techniques used in the previous investigations*]]] J12.115

the Ti is parsed, as shown, as the last daughter of a tagma headed by the dimension of comparison, on the analogy of the treatment of Fc clauses (§ 4.330 above).

§ 4.356 An infinitival indirect question is formtagged Ti? (for the "?" suffix see § 4.379):

> *. . . knows* [Ti? [Nqs *exactly which step*] *to take next in the course of . . .* Ti?] N08:0250
> *. . . in choosing* [Ti? [Rq *how far*] [Vi *to observe or disregard*] [P *in any particular set of circumstances*] [Np *the sentiments, obligations and expectations which . . .*] Ti?] J30.144
> *the right to decide independently* [Ti? *whether to continue or end it*] G10:1180

This construction is to be distinguished from the infinitival relative clause (Tq, § 4.365).

Tf *for-to clause*

§ 4.357 A clause with infinitive head and introduced by *for*. There are two types of Tf clause. The commoner type acts as a postmodifier in a noun phrase or similar tagma and, like a relative clause, contains a logical "gap" corresponding to the antecedent:

> *— and that would be* [D *a lot* [Tf *for* [D *a lot of people*] [Vi *to swallow*] [R *all*] [R *at_once*]]] B02.050
> *. . . there is* [Ds *little* [Tf *for* [Nns *the West*] [Vi *to do*] Tf] *except stand firm* Ds]. B02.052
> *. . . there was not* [Ns *space enough* [Tn *left*] [Tf *for* [Neo *me*] [Vi *to refer*] [P *to Lilla Kunvari's sculpture, . . .*]]]. J66.125

(In connection with the J66 example, note that the treatment of phrases containing an Fc, § 4.319 above, suggests by analogy that a sequence *enough remaining space* [*for me to . . .*] should be treated as a four-constituent N phrase, the first and third words being attached directly to the N node, *remaining* attached as a Tg, and the fourth constituent being the Tf. The fact that — for differ-ent reasons — *enough* and *left* appear after rather than before the head in the actual example does not affect the constituency.)

§ 4.358   The other type of Tf has no logical gap, and functions nominally:

> *It just remains* [Tf *for* [Ns *the afterbirth*] [Vi *to come*]
> [R *away*] Tf]. F32.140
> [Tf For [Ns *the present Government*] [Vi *to ignore*] [Ns *this aspect*
> *of the situation*] Tf] *is* [Ti *to create its own opposition*
> . . . Ti], . . . B09.075

§ 4.359   In a Tf of either type there will be a sequence *for* + nominal element which in other circumstances might be parsed as a P, and a sequence including the Vi which in other circumstances might be parsed as a Ti; but within a Tf these respective sequences are not recognized as tagmas — the word *for* and the Vi are ICs of the Tf node.

§ 4.360   In a sequence such as *As we waited for the film to begin . . .* G49.179, the word *for* can be regarded as doing double duty, serving both as a preposition marking the "case" of the fol-lowing element (which in this instance is a clause, but might equally be a noun phrase, as in *He waited for an answer but none came.* N27.193), and also as the element introducing the Tf construction. (Classical transformational grammar treats the single preposition as being derived from a sequence of two underlying occurrences of *for* by a rule of Preposition Deletion.) The SUSANNE scheme treats the surface preposition in such a case as belonging to the Tf clause:

> [*As we waited* [Tf *for the film to begin*]]

Tb   bare non-finite clause

§ 4.361   A subordinate clause whose leading verb is a base form without the infinitival marker *to*. Most Tb clauses are complements within higher clauses whose verbs are either verbs of perception or else verbs relating to causation such as *let, have, make.*

> . . . *would have* [Nop *us*] [Tb [V *run*] [Np *risks greater than the*
> *West ought to run . . .*] B02.028
> . . . *who reluctantly lets* [Nos *him*] [Tb [V *go*]]. C05.105

...*I heard* [Ny *you*] [Tb [V *cry*]]. N18.183
[S [S& *Then she heard* [Ns *the soldier*] [Tb [V *shout*]:
'[Q [S* *Fall out*]! ... Q]' [S+ *and* [Ns *the Colonel*] [Tb [V *add*],
[P *in their language*], '[Q [S*+ *And don't waste any time about
it*]! Q]' S+] S&] [S+ *and* ...] S]. K14.013
I have known [Ns *a producer*] [Tb [V *refuse*] *a commission
because of* ...] G43.079
...*I think I* <bital> *have* <eital> *got something that helps*
[Neo *me*] [Tb [V *size*] *a thing up pretty well*]. L23.014
...*letting himself* [Tb [Vjp *be browbeaten*] *by a woman* Tb].
N05:1080

§ **4.362**   The underlying subject of a Tb, like that of a Ti, is treated as sister rather than daughter of the clause, as shown above. In special cases that subject may be missing:

Arthur heard [Tb [V *tell*] *of this*] ... J62.052

§ **4.363**   The *had better Verb* construction is analysed using the Tb category:

...*You* [Vd +'*d*] [R *better*] [Tb [V *sleep*]]". N01:1580

§ **4.364**   Tb is used only where the absence of an inflected verb conforms to a convention of standard English, not where such a verb has been elided in informal speech, telegraphic style, etc.; thus the clauses in the K01 and K25 examples quoted in § 4.30 above are tagged S? rather than Tb.

Tq   infinitival relative clause
§ **4.365**   Clause functioning as relative and having Vi head:

This is [Ns *a good time* [Po *of year*] [Tq [Pq *at which*] [Vi *to
lay*] [Ns *turf*] Tq] Ns]. E08.108
...*laying* [Np *the foundations* [Tq [Pq *on which*] [Vi *to win*]
[Ns *the next election*] Tq] Np]. A03.087

W   *With* Clause

§ **4.366**   A non-finite or reduced (verbless) clause introduced by a word tagged IW (*with, without*, or *what_with*). W clauses act both as postnominal modifiers (*with* X Y Z semantically equivalent to *who/which has* X Y Z), and as adverbial ICs of a higher clause (*with* X Y Z equivalent to *since* X *is/was* Y Z or the like). Thus:

[Ms@ *one* [W *with* [Ns *blood*] [P *all over it*], [Ns@ *Arbuckle's blood*] W] Ms@] N12:0860

The thought [Fn *that I might have to leave the Army in 1941,* [W *with* [Ns *the war*] [R *only*] [R *half*] [Vn *fought*]],] *was unbearable.* G09.154

and [W *without* [Ns *the direct light of the sun*] [Ti *to act as compass*] W], *Pamela could no longer be positive of her direction.* N08:1040 — the *to act...* sequence is a Ti, despite § 4.55: the sequence would be a subordinate Ti within a main clause *Pamela had* [Ns *the direct light of the sun*] [Ti *to act as compass*].

...go on to [Rw *somewhere else* [W *with* [D *vastly more*] [Ti *to offer*] *...*]]. P03.035

[W *With* [Ns *my ballpoint*] [P *in my hand*] [W+ *and* [Np *my thoughts*] [Vn *arrayed*] W+] W], *my greater morbidities shrink back ...* N26.074

And so it was over the weekend [W *what_with 40-year-old Warren Spahn pitching his no-hit masterpiece against the Giants* [W+ *and the Giants' Willie Mays retaliating with a record-tying 4-homer spree Sunday* W+] W]. A13:1030

§ 4.367 If a tagma is to be categorized as W it is essential that what follows the IW word itself consists of more than one constituent; otherwise the tagma will be categorized as P. This is particularly relevant in the case of the nominal-postmodifier type of W, where it can be difficult to decide whether or not the material following *with* consists of sister constituents or of one constituent itself containing a postmodifier. Thus, contrast *one* [W *with blood all over it . . .*], above, with:

[Ns *a beige box* [P *with a bright red door*], *. . .*] G03:1520

He was [Po *of short, stocky, powerful build*], [P *with* [N *fiercely curling black hair* [Np+ *and eyes which immediately apprehended the essential things around him* Np+] N] P]. G16.163

In the case of clause-adverbial W's, the meaning of *with* will often be crucial in deciding whether or not the material following *with* should be grouped as a single postmodified tagma (in which case *with* introduces a P rather than a W) or as independent ICs of a W: the P analysis is appropriate when *with* has one of its ordinary prepositional meanings (accompaniment, instrument), the W analysis is appropriate when *with* is more naturally paraphrased "because X is Y", "in circumstances where X is Y", or the like. So for instance W is used for *with the war only half fought*, above (= "in

circumstances where the war was only half fought"), but not for a
case such as:

> *The Dallas Texans were back home Monday* [P *with* [Ns *their third
> victory in four American Football League starts* — [Ns@ *a 19-
> 12 triumph . . .*] Ns] P] — *but . . .* A12:1260 (*with* meta-
> phorically equivalent to "accompanied by")

Where the word *without* is followed by a present participle, particularly one lacking an overt subject, the analysis will normally be
as in:

> *we can only keep adding to our ritual* [P *without* [Tg *daring to
> abandon any part of it*]], . . . G11:1070
> *. . . to ride in and rack their broncs* [P *without* [Tg [Ns *any
> particular attention*] [Vgp *being paid*] [Nop *them*] Tg] P].
> N14:0040

A Special *As* Clause

§ 4.368 Certain clauses or reduced clauses introduced by *as* are
formtagged A. Although some *as* clauses are similar in internal
structure to clauses introduced by other subordinating conjunctions,
other *as* clauses have structures which are found only with this
particular word. The occurrence of these unusual structures is what
justifies the use of a special formtag. However, the range of structures found in clauses with other conjunctions is too diverse to
define A simply as "an *as* clause with internal structure that could
not occur with another conjunction" — such a definition would be
too vague. Accordingly, an A is defined as any clause introduced by
as, wordtagged CSA, for which both of the following conditions
hold:

- the clause is not the last part of an *as . . . as . . .* or *so . . . as . . .*
  comparison — in which case it will be formtagged Fc (see
  examples in § 4.319); but *so as* without intervening wording
  does introduce an A clause, see below;
- the word *as* is not interpretable as "because", "while", "when"
  — in which case the clause will be formtagged Fa:

> *the Birds were to end their victory drought* [Fa *as they coasted
> along with a 3-to-0 advantage*]. A11:0050 (misprint corrected)
> [Fa *As we began to converse in the lounge of his Fifth Avenue
> hotel*], *his restlessness . . . became immediately apparent.*
> G06:0150

This, however, can only be considered approximate, [Fa *as the diameter of the pulley was increased by the build-up of tape* [Fa+ *and the tape was occasionally removed from the pulley during the runs* Fa+] Fa]. J03:0150

If these conditions are met, the clause is formtagged A whether or not its internal structure resembles that of subordinate clauses introduced by other conjunctions. (For subordinate clauses in which the subordinating conjunction is preceded by a complement, see § 4.294 above.)

Some examples are:

... the unit may thus be considered [A *as* [Vg *comprising*] *several cross-flow sections, ...*] J07.063

[A *As befits a queen*], *a bumblebee female is rather choosy ...* J10:0460

... I did not feel [A *as I had felt before*]. N13.134

... the rhythm and ritual they have adopted [A *as uniquely their own*], ... G13:0570

... the faintest change in colour of the <bital> *Clinistix* <eital> *was taken* [A *as* [J *positive*]]. J14.151

One diplomat described the tenor of Secretary of State Dean Rusk's speeches [A *as* "[J *inconclusive*]"]. A04:0320

Taylor (1956) regards recorded cases of recovery after submersion for more than 7 or 8 minutes [A *as* [J *wholly unreliable*]] *unless this has been intermittent ...* J16.165

and cut transversely [R *so* [A *as* [Vi *to separate*] *the various protein bands* A] R]. J09:1160

She must be cautious [R *so* [A *as* [Vie *not to alert*] *the scheming forest* A] R]. N08:0190

It may be that [A *just as* [P *with FAE due to retinal size*]], *the effect through apparent size only occurs ...* J25.082

... understands by "soul" [A *as* [J *distinct from "spirit"*]] D14.136

She would return this symbol to the mountain, [A *as one pours seed back into the soil every Spring* <hellip> [A+ *or as ancient fertility cults demand annual human sacrifice* A+] A]. N08:0350

§ 4.369   An A may function in a manner akin to a relative clause:

to depict [Np *not the concrete objects of his experience* [Np+ *but their essences* [A *as revealed in abstractions ...*]]] G09:0540

the "threshold", [A *as the conventional forces strengthening is called*], *will prove ...* A04:0670

He, therefore, at [Ns *the same time* [A *as he sent Cranbrook his copy of the telegram* A] Ns], *sent also a copy to Beaconsfield at Hughenden* . . . J59.009

Some of the earlier episodes have [Np *touches* [Po *of the supernatural*], [A *as suited to the legendary background*]]. G18:1660

Asked which institution most needs correction, I would say [Ns *the corporation* [A *as it exists in America today*]]. G22:0390

the limiting supportive tissue septa [A *as* [P *in Type I*]] J12:0020

. . . *the distinction between* [Np *Roman Catholics* [Np+ *and Papishes,* [A *as she termed them*]]]. G46.107

§ 4.370 An A containing the logical "gap" typical of standard relative clauses may be attached to a higher clause as a "propositional relative" (cf. § 5.198):

[A *As is well known*], *detergent actives belong* . . . J05:1250

The short poems grouped at the end of the volume as "Thoughts in Loneliness" is, [A *as Professor Böök indicated*], *in sharp contrast* . . . G18:0610 (*is* an error for *are*)

[Fn *that* ε *does not increase linearly with* τ *for a given* <bital> C_J <eital> *value* ([A *as might be implied by a glance at equation (11)* A]) *due to* . . . Fn] J74.194

§ 4.371 The idiomatic phrase (not classed as a "grammatical idiom") *as such* is analysed as Fa, not A:

[Fa *As*_CSA [D *such*_DAz]], *it gives a set of average relationships* . . . J44.159

Z Reduced ("Whiz-Deleted") Relative Clause

§ 4.372 A modifying element in a nominal tagma is formtagged Z if it is seen as a reduced relative clause from which the relative pronoun and a finite part of the verb *BE* have been omitted (provided that what remains is more than one constituent — a relative clause reduced to just, say, a Tn will be formtagged Tn, not Z). Classical transformational grammar had a transformational rule often called "Whiz Deletion" which removed these elements of a relative clause. For instance:

. . . [N *his pupil and successor,* [Nns@ *Marcel Dupré* Nns@], [Z [Nos *himself*] [P *in his seventies* [Ns+ *and a pioneer of organ records*]] Z], N] *has re-recorded it* . . . C10.195

for [Np *educational purposes* ([Z *not*_XX [R *necessarily*] [Po *of the formal type*] Z]) Np] G22:1410

[Np *orders* [Z [R *only*] [Jh *sufficient* [Ti *to cover his sales*] Jh] Z] Np] F41.092

... *for the potential energy to be stationary:*
   [N@ <*formul*> [I <*minbrk*> I] [Z [Rq *whence*]: [N <*formul*> N]
   [I <*minbrk*> I] [Tg *being the deflection*...] Z] N@]. J76.011

... *is then often operated as* [Ns *an ancillary concern* ([Z [R *generally*] [Ns *a subsidiary company*] Z]) Ns], *perhaps under a different name.* F41.147

[Nns *Sir Patrick* ([Z [Rw *now*] [Ns *Lord Justice*] Z]) *Devlin*]
   G57.035

The example:

[Np *firms* [Z [P *with an annual turnover of* £$\frac{1}{2}$*m.*]
   [R *each*] Z] Np] G72.181

must be analysed using the Z tag rather than treating the wording following *firms* as a W or a P. By § 4.217, *each* is a separate R phrase applying to *firms* (hence not part of a P introduced by *with*); an analysis [W *with* [Ns *an annual turnover*...] [R *each*] W] would imply a nonsensical meaning something like "since an annual turnover ... was each".

§ **4.373**   The fact that a Z is a reduced relative clause implies that a Z tagma will normally follow the head it modifies; but this is not an absolute requirement. In the G57 example in the previous section, the Z must presumably be regarded as modifying *Devlin* (the sequence could be paraphrased "Sir Patrick Devlin, who is now Lord Justice Devlin"). This case is debatable, since in general modifier–head relationships are not clear-cut as between forenames and surnames (historically a surname would have been regarded as postmodifying a forename, but it is doubtful whether that fact is of more than antiquarian relevance to the grammar of current English in which surnames are often used alone and most people have multiple forenames). But the Z formtag is also extended to cover cases such as the following, where the tagma in question is indisputably in premodifying position:

the [Z [R *already*] [J *extremely short*]] <*formul*> *interlayer distance*... J04:0790

In terms of classical transformational grammar such a tagma would be derived from a standard relative clause which has undergone both Whiz Deletion and Preposing; usually a relative clause will not be Preposed unless it has been reduced to just a single J constituent (in which case the formtag Z will not be used), but where a multi-constituent reduced relative is preposed, as here, it receives the form-tag Z despite its surface position.

L   Miscellaneous Verbless Clause

§ 4.374   A tagma functioning as a clause, lacking a finite or non-finite verb, and not belonging to one of the more specific verbless-clause categories (Z, or reduced types of F..., W, or A) is form-tagged L. Like a Z, an L is required to comprise more than one IC.[26]

§ 4.375   Since the category L is defined negatively, it inevitably comprises a diversity of constructions. One type of L can be re-garded as a Tg from which the word *being* has been deleted:

[S [L [Nns *The Luger*] [J *ready*] L], *he walked slowly back* ...]
L03.056

a number of other topics, [L [P *among them*] [Np *the Atlanta
and Fulton County purchasing departments which* ... Np] L]
A01:0170

*Already the troops dug in on the ancient ramparts sweltered from
the heat of burning buildings* — [L [Ns *the smoke*] [Jh *so dense*
[Fc *even dispatch riders groped through the town on foot*
...]] L] F23.043

... *should be left to rest in peace,* [L [R *forever*] [J *dead*]
[Tn+ *and (*[I *let us fervently hope* I]*) [R *forever*] [Vn *done*]
[P *with*] Tn+] L]". G08:1370

suspended drops of [Ns *cyclohexanol phthalate (*[L [Ns *viscosity*]
[Nup *155 poises*] L]*) Ns] J03:1490

§ 4.376   Other cases of L are multi-constituent clauses from which verbs are omitted conventionally, either because they are written in "telegraphese" style (e.g. newspaper headlines), for instance:

[Oh [L [Ns *Nuclear cloud*] [P *over Siberia*] [P *after
blast*] L] Oh]
[Oh [L [Ns *Litter man*] [Ti [Vi *to appeal*]] L] Oh][27] (both
examples from *The Times*, 1993.04.08)

---

[26] One of the minimum of two ICs may be a co-ordinating conjunction, where it is clear that the tagma this introduces is not the other constituent but a larger construction of which parts are elided:

<minbrk> "[Q [L+ *But* [P *after a time away from you* P] L+] <hellip> Q]". <minbrk>
N10:0560

— the word *But* introduces a clause, only the opening phrase of which is actually uttered.

[27] Since the "full" wording *Litter man is to appeal* would be analysed as [S [Ns *Litter man*] [Vzb *is*] [Ti *to appeal*] S] (cf. § 5.199), *to appeal* remains a subordinate clause within the telegraphese version which is therefore regarded as lacking a verb of its own.

or because they constitute stock formulae or turns of phrase in which verbs are usually omitted:

... '[L@ [Ns *Happy New Year*] [P *to you*] [R *all*] L@]'. E12.165
They walked [L [Ns *hand*] [P *in hand*] L] *under the trees* ... F18.180
They are supplied, [L [Ns *a batch*] [P *at a time*] L], *by a secret source* ... G03:1590

§ 4.377   Other L clauses again belong to no clear general class:

he recalled [Ns *Sir Gabriel Gulliver's guess* [P *at* [Ns *Astarte Oakes's background* Ns] P]: [L@ [Np *the ponies and the spaniels*] [P *in decay*], [Tg+ *and a garden boy beginning to feel entitled to a rise in wages*] L@] Ns]. L13.035
[S *He decided to go and make some tactful enquiries in the Chinese quarter;* [L– *not_XX* [Fn *that he expected to find Hyacinth there*], [S+ *but someone might have seen her*] L–] S].[28] P12.120
I mean you can't imagine the Christian martyrs twisting and shrieking, no matter how bad it felt, [N@ *the fire* [I *you know*], [Tg+ *or a lion munching*], [L+ *or* [Np *arrows*] [Fa *where it hurts most*] L+] N@]. M03.028

§ 4.378   In the sequence *At least a dozen men, some armed, are never far away* ... G03:1390, one might think of *some armed* as a reduced version of [*some of whom*] *are armed* and hence as a candidate for the formtag Z. However, for Z it is required that the whole clause-IC containing the relative pronoun should be missing — that is, the presence of *some* in this case prevents the tagma being formtagged Z. Instead *some armed* is analysed as an L functioning as an Absolute adjunct (§ 5.190) within the clause:

[Np *At least a dozen men* Np], [L [D *some*] [Tn *armed*] L], *are never* ...

Interrogative, Imperative, and Subjunctive Clauses

? *interrogative clause*

§ 4.379   A direct or indirect question clause, marked as such by subject-auxiliary inversion and/or by the use of a *wh-* word in an interrogative rather than relative sense, takes "?" as a suffix immediately following the alphabetic clause formtag, e.g. S?, Fn?, Ti?:

---

[28] Here, *not that* ... is regarded as a reduced version of *it was not that* ....

"[S? *How many is that* S?], [Nns" *Jim*]"? A14:1360

"[S? *Does this make it any easier*], [Ns" *coward*]"? N12:1040

[S? *Is there a different reality behind the facade* S?]? G02:1880

[S *My future lay solely with the hall,* [S?– *yet what did I know about the hall at this point* S?–] S]? N06:0920

[Rw! *Now*], [S? *are you going to take me* [S?+ *or am I supposed to walk* S?+] S?]"? N09:0600

... *I don't savvy* [Fn? *why you'd go off* [Fn+ *and leave your jobs*] *in the first place* Fn?]". N01:1640

When I went for my interview with the director I saw [Fn? [Rq *why*]]. N06:1230

... *will depend* [P *on* [Fn? *what happens as a result* ...], [P+ *and* [R *also*] [R *of_course*] *on* [Fn? *how long the cold war remains cold* Fn?] P+] P]. G12:1660

... *to decide independently* [Ti? *whether to continue or end it*]. G10:1180

... *not more than one person in a hundred would know* [Ti? *what to do* [Ti?+ *or where to go*] *in the event of an enemy attack*]. A05:0330

[Tb? [Rq *Why*], [P *in the first place*], [V *call*] [Nos *himself*] [Ns *a liberal*] [Fa *if he is against* <bital> *laissez-faire* <eital> ... Fa] Tb?]? G01:0430

§ 4.380 An "indirect question" is not necessarily interrogative in function. *CGEL*, p. 1051, points out that there is a gradient

from the request for an answer to a question (as in [*She asked me who would look after the baby*]) through uncertainty about the answer (as in *I'm not sure who will look after the baby*), certainty about the answer (*It's obvious who will look after the baby*), expressions of other mental states or processes about the answer (*I found out who will look after the baby, It's irrelevant who will look after the baby*), and informing about the answer (*I told you who would look after the baby*). In all instances a question is explicitly or implicitly raised ...

Accordingly, in all cases the SUSANNE scheme includes the ? suffix on the subordinate clause formtag.

§ 4.381 However, an *if* clause whose function is similar to a *for-to* clause is not given the ? suffix (see the H21 and N04 examples at § 4.306).

§ 4.382 An Fa can take the ? suffix:

She could not scream, [Fa? *for* ... *who would hear,* [Fa?– *who would listen*]]? N08:1610

— but the fact that an Fa begins with *whether*, in the sense "no matter whether", does not justify the suffix:

> the <bital> Pax Britannica <eital> of the nineteenth century, [Fa *whether* [W *with the British navy ruling the seas* [W+ *or with the City of London ruling world finance*]] Fa], *was strictly* ... G02:0270

§ 4.383   The fact that a clause closes with a tag question does not lead the containing clause to be given the ? suffix, though the Iq (tag question) node itself will dominate an S? node (see § 4.424).

§ 4.384   A clause which "underlyingly" involves subject-auxiliary inversion is given the ? suffix even if the inversion is obscured by elision of the Vo, as in the examples *Ten-thirty be all right?* and *Where you goin', son?* discussed at § 4.30 above.

§ 4.385   An "echo question", containing a *wh-* word without subject-auxiliary inversion, will be given the ? suffix:

> [S? *You paid* [Dq *how much*] S?]?
> "[Q [S? *Must have been* [Nq *who*] S?]? Q]" *Max prompted.* L07.056

§ 4.386   On the other hand a clause containing no interrogative grammar is not given the ? suffix merely because it is used as a question, followed typographically by a question mark (and possibly corresponds to a spoken form that would be marked as a question by intonation):

> "[Q [S *You bought it* S] Q]"? N05:0260
> "[Q [Rw! *Here*], [Nns" *Idje*], [S *you fella like tabac*] Q]"? G04:1660

And only clausetags may take the ? suffix — the queried phrases and words are not given tagmatags with the ? suffix in:

> "[Q [Ns *A year*], [Nns" *Luis*]? *Five*_MC +? *Ten*_MC +? [S? *How long should I wait*] Q]"? N10:0570
> "[Q [Nqs *What luck*], [Nns" *Cobb*] Q]"? *he said swiftly.* N14:0380
> [S "[Q [Pb *By* [Tg *telling him you are making passes at me* Tg] Pb] Q]"? *she said incredulously* S]. N18:1130

A form such as *Who?* as an independent utterance would be analysed: [Q *Who*_PNQSq +?_YQ Q].

* *imperative clause*

§ 4.387   A clause grammatically marked as imperative, by occurring as a main clause without a subject and having a leading verb in base form, is given an asterisk suffix. It follows that the only symbol that will precede * is "S".

[S* *Now turn around so I can see your face*]". N12:0780

[S* *To see this, consider a general pencil of lines containing a general secant of G*]. J21:0970

[S "[Q [S* [R *Never*] [V *mind*] S*] Q]", *she said sternly* S]. N05:0360

[S* *Note that the mass scale is one to two orders of magnitude greater . . .*] J07:1540

[S* *Count* [Ff *what you've got there*] S*], . . . N14:0860

§ **4.388** A sentence like [Nns" *Todman*], [S *you take the one on the left*]. N15:1120 is pragmatically an imperative but contains no explicit grammatical marker of imperative status, therefore the asterisk suffix is not used. If a clause is not otherwise marked as imperative, it will not be given the asterisk suffix merely because of the occurrence of *will you* (rather than *do you*) as a tag question:

[S *You go ahead,* [Iq [S? *will you*]]]

§ **4.389** Non-second-person imperatives, using *let,* are analysed as S* clauses containing Tb clauses:

[S* [V *Let*] [Nop *us*] [Tb *look in on one of these nerve centers — SAC at Omaha —* [Tb+ *and see what must still happen . . .* Tb+] Tb] S*]. G03:1220

. . . [S* [V *let*] [Nop +'*s*] [Tb *try to go under this stuff*] S*]. N15:0570

"[S* [V *Let*] [Neo *me*] [Tb [V *go*]]]." N21.161

% subjunctive clause

§ **4.390** A main or subordinate clause which in other respects appears to be a finite clause is given the suffix % to its clausetag if it is explicitly marked as subjunctive by having as its leading verb the form *be,* or the base form of another non-modal verb (or the form *were*) when the nature of the clause subject would normally require the third-person singular inflexion (or the form *was*):

the requirement [Fn% *that each return* [Vjp *be notarized*]] A02:0820

demanding [Fn% *that the viewer* [V *respond*] *to it in his own never-predictable way*] G12:0870

The same delivery vehicles — [Fa% *whether they* [Vjb *be*] *airplanes, submarines or guided missiles*] *— should be usable.* J08:1750

. . . I should most surely have joined the group that day [Fa%
[Vowb *were*] *I* [Vrge *not working*] *on a project of my own*
Fa%]. K26.179

There may be other 1961 state committee retirements [Fa% [V
come] *April 18*], *but . . .*[29] A06:1850

[S% *LONG* [V *LIVE*] *TOBACCO ROAD*]. G08:0010

§ **4.391** If the subject of a clause is not third person singular
and the leading verb is not *be*, the % suffix is not used, because
subjunctive status is not overtly marked; thus, in *I ordered that John
go home and that his parents accompany him*, from the context there
is little doubt that *accompany* would fail to inflect even if *parents*
were replaced by *parent*, but since after *parents* the form *accompany*
is unmarked, the *accompany* clause does not take the % suffix:

I ordered [Fn% *that John go home* [Fn+ *and that his parents
accompany him*]]

The % symbol is not used where an uninflected form is the leading
verb of a clause merely because a preceding inflected form has been
elided (as in the K01 and K25 examples discussed at § 4.30).

ROOTRANK FORMTAGS

O   *paragraph*
§ **4.392** On the concept "paragraph" as applied in the SUSANNE
scheme, see §§ 4.12 ff.

Oh   *heading*
§ **4.393** With respect to the SUSANNE Corpus, the decision that
a particular character-string in a text counts as a "heading" rather
than as part of the running text was already made by the compilers
of the Brown Corpus, on criteria which are not explicitly stated in
BCUM, probably because they are felt to be too obvious to need
spelling out. It may be that in some circumstances in written English
the distinction between headings and running text is blurred, but
the present work has no contribution to make on the issue.

The typographical "centred rules" discussed in the footnote to
§ 2.18 are in all but one case analysed within the Brown Corpus as
constituting "major headings"; SUSANNE regularizes this analysis
so that each such symbol occurs in a parsetree of the form:

---

[29] The colloquial use of *come* as in *she will be 21 come May* is included by *OALD3* among
the verb uses (rather than listed separately as a prepositional use), so a sequence introduced
by *come* in this use is an Fa.

[Oh <*bmajhd*> <*cruleN*>_YO <*emajhd*> Oh]

§ 4.394 Commonly, an Oh containing verbal material (i.e. not consisting solely of the items <*majbrk*> or <*minbrk*>) will consist of a single N or S tagma surrounded by begin- and end-heading markers. A heading in "telegraphese" style consisting of a clause from which essential elements have been omitted can still be parsed as having a single daughter between the YBL/YBR markers, if the remaining elements recognizably cohere grammatically into, say, an L or an N. But where what is typographically a single heading contains grammatically disconnected elements, these will be separate daughters of the Oh node:

[Oh <*bminhd*> 2.2_MCe <*bital*> [Ns *The Recovery of lead-210 tracer from solution*] +._YF <*eital*> <*eminhd*> Oh] J04.044
[Oh <*bminhd*> [Nns *VIENNA*] +,_YC [N *Jan. 9*] <*eminhd*> Oh] A03.005

Where a heading is begun and ended with inverted commas or typographical-shift markers, these will as normal be sisters rather than daughters of the material they surround, and accordingly will be daughters of the Oh node.

Ot title

§ 4.395 The term "title" here refers to a word or word-sequence used as the name of a book, play, or other artistic work, or of a ship, locomotive, racehorse, public house, etc., rather than to words or phrases such as *Earl*, *Chief Inspector*, in their basic use as specifying the status of persons. Thus, the emphasized sequence is a "title" for present purposes in *Jill is working behind the bar at the Duke of Denver* but not in *A wrinkle furrowed the brow of the Duke of Denver*. Furthermore, the special treatment of "titles" discussed below is not used for words when they appear at the head or foot of a piece of writing which they name; in this case they are counted as "headings", like picture captions or typographically distinct phrases used to introduce and to break up newspaper articles. "Titles" for the purposes of this section are forms functioning logically as proper names within surrounding text.

A chief reason for providing special parsing rules for titles as defined here is that, frequently, the internal grammar of the name of one of the kinds of entity listed above (as opposed, for instance, to a personal name) is at variance with the grammatical environment in which it occurs. For instance, there is a pub in Ipswich called "The Case is Altered" — grammatically a main clause but functionally a name. A commoner type of example is as in:

> *When his famous <bital> The Green Hat <eital> appeared,...*
> G30.122

— where *The Green Hat* (title of a novel by Michael Arlen) has the internal structure of a complete Ns beginning with a determiner, but is embedded as head within a larger Ns having its own determiner *his*.

The SUSANNE scheme treats "titles" as follows:

§ **4.396**   In the case of a title which is a single word (or idiom) tagged NP1x (NP1x=) because of its title status, e.g. *Deuteronomy* (though not e.g. *Joshua, Psalms, Hebrews* which are also titles of books of the Bible but which have wordtags other than NP1x), no special annotation rules apply. A title whether or not tagged NP1x will be immediately dominated by an Nn... phrasetag, like any other proper name (for a title this will commonly be Nns, but cf. for instance [Nn *Deuteronomy*_NP1x [Np+ *and other books*]]).

§ **4.397**   In other cases, the material (whether one word or tagma, or possibly more than one[30]) which forms the title is given a node with the rootrank label Ot. Below the Ot node, the material of the title is parsed in terms of its internal structure, ignoring the surrounding material outside the Ot (with which it will normally have no grammatical relationships). With respect to the surrounding text, the Ot node is treated as equivalent to an NP1x wordtag (and thus is normally dominated by an Nns node) — except that, since "Ot" is not a wordtag, an Ot node will not take part in wordlevel co-ordination, so:

> *a mating of* [Nn [Ot [Ns *Better Self*]] [Nns+ *and* [Ot [J *Rosy Fingered*]]]] A11:1550

— not [Nn [Ot *Better Self* [Ot+ *and Rosy Fingered*]]]. Thus the earlier example is analysed:

> *... [Nns his famous <bital> [Ot [Ns The Green Hat Ns] Ot] <eital> Nns] ...*

Inverted commas or typographic-shift markers will normally be sisters rather than daughters of the Ot node, and daughters of the Nn... node above the Ot node. Since title status is itself a reason for capitalization, capitals within an Ot constituent will not justify use of the Nn... subcategory for an element that would not count as Nn... apart from its occurrence within or as the whole of a title.

---

[30] A title might contain more than one IC; for instance, *VIENNA, Jan. 9* (§ 4.394) could conceivably occur as a book title as well as a heading. But such cases will be few. A title such as *Around the World in Eighty Days* would be a single L, since it is clearly a reduction of a single clause such as *Travelling around the world in eighty days.*

§ **4.398** The wording dominated by an Ot node will not necessarily be identical to the official title of e.g. a publication. One common divergence relates to the definite article: *The* is often omitted, when grammatically inappropriate in context, from the name of a publication whose official title includes it. For instance, a leading British daily paper is called *The Times* — this (apart from the italics) is how the name appears on its masthead, in its logo, etc. — but one would be much more likely to encounter the phrase *a Times editorial* than *a The Times editorial*. And even where *The* or *the* does appear, it may belong grammatically to the context rather than to the title: in *The Times building was* ... the word *The* occurs as modifying *building*, not as part of the name *The Times*. (A subject noun phrase headed by *building* as a count noun requires a determiner, whereas a noun phrase premodifying a noun will normally lack one.) Thus the respective sequences are analysed:

[Nns [Ot [Np *The Times*]]] *was* ...
[Ns *a* [Nns [Ot *Times*_NNT2]]] *editorial*]
[Ns *The* [Nns [Ot *Times*_NNT2]]] *building*] *was* ...

Conversely, if a writer prefixes a title by *the* but shows via lower case, placement of typographic shifts, etc., that this word is not part of the title, then *the* will be within the Nn. . . but outside the Ot.

§ **4.399** To be labelled Ot, a word or word-sequence must with respect to its environment be equivalent to an NP1x, i.e. must function as a singular proper name. Thus, no Ot node occurs in the analysis of:

I hadn't anything to read and I finished [Nnp *all the Scottish Fields* [P *in the lounge*]] *on Sunday* ... L11.182

The reference is to a magazine entitled *Scottish Field*, but since it is pluralized (to indicate various numbers of the magazine) there is no constituent equivalent to an NP1x. (On the other hand, the tagma headed by *Scottish Fields*, as a whole, does meet the criterion for the Nn. . . subcategory.) *Scottish Fields* in this context is quite different from *The Times* as a newspaper title, which is internally a plural noun phrase but as a title functions as a singular name (*The Times has* — not *have* — *a new editor*).

§ **4.400** The decision whether or not to use an Ot node in the analysis of a proper name is made primarily in terms of the kind of entity denoted by the name. With the types of entity listed in § 4.395, the presumption is that Ot will appear (unless the name is an NP1x word or NP1x= idiom). With names of persons, places, or pet animals, on the other hand, the presumption is that there will be no Ot, because such names commonly conform to standard patterns which are integrated into their grammatical environment in English (or, in the case of foreign names, consist of words which with respect to English function exclusively as names and receive NP. . . wordtags, cf. § 3.110). The presumption in favour of the Ot analysis in the case of the former types of entity may be overridden, in the case of a name which denotes such an entity but verges on being a description of its referent, and is regarded as a proper name only because it is capitalized and conventionally used as the name of the referent:

> *On Christmas Day they visited* [Nns *the Last Inn, Hengoed*], *and made a collection . . .* E12.169

— the pub in question is probably called "the Last Inn" because it is or once was the last inn on the road through Hengoed. (*Hengoed* is included within the Nns as appositional to the pub name.) The phrase *the Chinese Book of Changes* is not analysed as forming an Ot, because there is ambiguity about whether it should be regarded as a description or a title, in:

> *. . . the oracles of* [Nns *the* <bital> [Ot *I Ching*] <eital>, [Nns@ *the Chinese Book* [Po *of Changes*]]] G09:0790

Names for entities of the latter kinds (persons, places, pet animals), however, will never be given an Ot analysis even in occasional cases where such names are grammatically very unusual. The Devon village of *Westward Ho!* is possibly the only place-name in the English-speaking world which includes an exclamation mark, but it will be analysed as [Nns *Westward*_RL *Ho*_UH +!_YX], without Ot. (This particular name derives from the title of a novel, but as the name of a village it is analysed as shown. It is only with respect to wordtags that the analysis of a name depends on the original bearer of the name.)

§ 4.401   The above rules have the consequence that elements of the annotation scheme such as functiontags, co-ordination markers, and indices usually appear in logically appropriate positions even in complex cases, such as (giving the full logical annotation to be defined in Chapter 5):

> [S [Nn:s101 [G *Hemingway's*] "[Ot [S [Ns:s *The Sun*] [R:m *Also*]
> [Vz *Rises*] S] Ot]" [Nns+ *and* "[Ot [Ns *A Farewell* [P *to*
> *Arms*]]]" Nns+], [Fr [Dq:s101 *which*] . . . Fr] Nn:s101] . . . S]
> [S [Nns:s103 <bital> [Ot [Ns:105 *The Spy* [Fr [Nq:s105 *Who*]
> *Came in from the Cold*]]] <eital>, [Fr [Dq:s103 *which*] *is* . . .]
> Nns:s103 . . .]

§ 4.402 A foreign title, if not consisting of a single NP1x word or idiom, will have FW wordtags directly below the Ot node. A following translation will be appositional at the Nns level. Thus:

[Nns [Ot *Die*_FW *Jungfrau*_FW *von*_FW *Orleans*_NP1t Ot] ([Nns@ [Ot [Ns *The Maid* [Po *of* [Nns *Orleans*]]] Ot] Nns@]) Nns]

§ 4.403 Material such as publication information following a book title is also treated as appositional below the Nns. Where a title includes a subtitle, the latter is not given a separate Ot node; it is treated as in apposition to the main title, below a single Ot:

... *the spectator will stand or sag in front of the picture* [W *with* [Nns <bital> [Ot [Ns *The Visual Experience:* [Ns@ *An Intro- duction to Art* Ns@] Ns] Ot] <eital> Nns] *pressing down on his mind* ... W]. G45.093

§ 4.404 Some examples of sequences including titles, which in some cases require Ot in their analysis and in other cases do not:

... *as reported in* [Nns *the* <bital> [Ot [Ns [Nns *Sheffield*] *Guardian* Ns] Ot] <eital> Nns] *in March* ... G03.030
I came back in "luxury" on [Nns *the* <bital> [Ot [Nns *Queen Mary*] Ot] <eital> Nns]. G10.101 — *the Queen Mary* has the phrasetag Nns below the Ot because *Queen Mary* is the pro- per name of a person, and has the same phrasetag above the Ot because *Queen Mary* is the proper name of a ship
[Nns *The Bible*_NN1c] *says* ... D14.108 — by the "dictionary test" *Bible* is a common noun
[Nns <bital> [Ot [Nns [G [Nns *Little Arthur*] +*'s* G] *England* Nns] Ot] <eital> Nns] *brought us good King Alfred and Harold after a page or two of blue-painted Britons* ... G22.045
... *a new Conservative booklet* [Tn *called* [Nns <bital> [Ot [S [Ns *The Record*] [Vz *Speaks*] S] Ot] <eital>] Tn] [Fr *which outlines* ...] A03.092
... *the Rabbinic dictum* ([Iu [Nns [Ot [Np *Ethics of the Fathers*] Ot], [M@ *V, 23* M@] Nns] Iu]) *that a man should* ... J65.113
[Nns *His* <bital> [Ot [Np *Elements of Reconstruction* Np] Ot] <eital> +, [P *with an introduction by Viscount Milner*], Nns] *appeared in* [Nns [Ot [Np *The Times*]]] *during* ... G13.130
... *performances of* [Nn *Puccini's* <bital> [Ot [Nns *Manon*_NP1f *Lescaut*_NP1s Nns] Ot] <eital> [Nns+ *and* [G *de Falla's*] <bital> [Ot *La*_FW *Vida*_FW *Breve*_FW Ot] <eital> Nns+] Nn]. G06:0600

... *in this language are written* [Nnp *the four Vedas*_NP2x, [Np@ *the holy writings of the Brahmans* Np@], [Np@ *the oldest literary works* [Po *of these people* Po], [Np@ <bital> *circa* <eital> *10,000 years* Np@] Np@] Nnp]. F19.191

The chilling horror of "[Nns [Ot [Nns *Malachias*_NP1m Nns] Ot] Nns]" *is due* ... C02.029

[Oh <bbold> [Ns [Nns *Bible*_NN1c] *study* — [Nns@ [Ot [Nns *Zechariah*_NP1m] Ot] Nns@] Ns] <ebold> Oh] D11.002

[Np <bital> [G [Nns [Ot *Sceptre*_NN1c Ot] Nns] +'s G] <eital> *recent successes* Np] *have led* ... E18.062 — "Sceptre" was a yacht. Note no phrasetag between a single common noun and an Ot node. Since the genitive ending attached to the yacht's name is included within the domain of italicization, the <bital> marker is placed outside the G tagma.

Apart from [Ns [G [Nns *Tchaikovsky*] +'s] [Nns <bital> [Ot [Nn [NP1m& *Romeo and Juliet*] Nn] Ot] <eital> Nns] *fantasy overture* Ns], *last night's Prom was* ... C03.061 — the name of the overture is *Romeo and Juliet*; it is standard, as here, to write the word *overture* itself after this title in lower case

the current issue of [Nns <bital> [Ot [NNL1c& *Road and Track*] Ot] <eital> Nns] E16.048 — again NNL1c& requires no phrasetag below a rootrank node

[Nn *Scene IV* [Po *of* [Nns *Act II* [Po *of* [Nns [G *Delius's* G] "[Ot [Nn *A Village* [NP1m& *Romeo and Juliet*] Nn] Ot] Nns] Po] Nns] Po]," [Ns– *Stravinsky's* "[Nns [Ot *Firebird*_NN1c Ot] Nns]" *suite* Ns–], [Nnp– *Borodin's* "*Polovtsian Dances* Nnp–]," Nn] ... G28.103 — the analysis assumes that *Polovtsian Dances* would standardly behave as a plural with respect to its context, e.g. *Borodin's "Polovtsian Dances" are* ... , hence does not take Ot

Progressive teachers will know of [N *the similar series* [Tn *titled* [Nn '[Ot [S *Sally Go Round The Moon* S] Ot]', [Nns+ *and* '[Ot [L [Np *Bells*] [P *Across The Meadow* P] L] Ot]' Nns+], Nn] Tn] [Fr *which seem to me* ... Fr] N] E24.151

[Nns <bbold> "[Ot [Ns *A Fair Cop*] Ot]," <ebold> [Z [Ns *the B B C Whitehall farce*] [Ns *last night*] Z], Nns] *looked like* ... C04.087

... *in the mode of life and death* ([Iu [Nns *Eccles*_NP1x [M@ *iii.19-20*] Nns] Iu]). D14.109 — *Eccles*, short for *Ecclesiastes*, name of a book of the Bible, is tagged NP1x so needs no Ot

... *as recorded in* [Nns [Ot *2*_MCn *Kings*_NNS2 Ot] [M@ *25* : [M@ [MCn& *25, 26*]]]]. D11.023 — *2 Kings* represents "The Second Book of Kings", another book of the Bible; in this abbreviated form it does not cohere as a tagma, hence both words are separately attached to the Ot node

Q   quotation

§ 4.405   Where a text contains direct speech, the quoted material (excluding surrounding items, such as inverted commas, serving to mark it as quoted) is analysed as it would be if it had occurred independently, not embedded within a quoting text, except that the node dominating a quotation is formtagged Q rather than O.[31] (A Q node will never be the root node of a SUSANNE parsetree — cf. § 4.413.) Structure below a Q node is analysed in the same way as if it had occurred under an O node.

§ 4.406   The category Q is used where a short or long quoted passage functions nominally within the quoting environment, acting logically as a sort of proper name for a piece of language. No Q node will appear where quoted wording is integrated into the surrounding sequence, so that this would read equally naturally if the inverted commas were missing. Thus, in:

> *The recent report of the Royal Commission on National Passenger Transportation in Canada says that "the general taxpayer and the public subsidise car travel by an estimated 1.8 cents per passenger kilometre".* (letter by T. Bendixson to the Editor of *The Times*, 1993.01.05)

— the word *that* preceding the quotation makes it part of a normal nominal clause within the quoting sentence, so the analysis will be:

> [S ... [Vz *says*] [Fn *that* <ldquo> [N *the general taxpayer and the public*] [V *subsidise*] ... <rdquo> Fn] S].

Without *that*, and with *says* followed by colon and/or with the first word of the quoted passage capitalized, the quotation would be a Q. If *that* did not appear before the section within inverted commas but there were no colon or initial capitalization in the quotation, the case would be debatable and would depend on the analyst's judgement about the general prose style of the publication: if *Times* Letters to the Editor normally do introduce quotations with colons, this suggests that there should be no Q in this case, but if writers of such letters rarely use the informal *that*-less Fn construction, that would argue in favour of introducing a Q node.

---

[31] Whereas the root node of an independent paragraph will consist of the letter O and nothing more, the label of the node dominating a quotation may contain more than simply the letter Q: for instance there will often be a logical functiontag marking the quotation as object of a quoting clause.

A case where the boundaries of a Q are marked by italicization rather than inverted commas is:

> ... *repeating* [Ns *the now often-used formula* [Po *of* <bital> [Q
> [S? *what was there to go wrong, after all* S?] Q] <eital> Po] Ns]?
> L09.142

Without inverted commas or typographic shifts, a colon alone will not justify treating what follows as a Q.

In a case like:

> [S *The hero ... is represented* [P *as* [Ns *a pilgrim* ... [Fr *who,* [Ti
> *to quote from Professor Böök again*], *"even in the pleasure
> gardens of Sardanapalus can not cease from his painful search
> after the meaning of life* Fr] Ns] P] S]. [S *He is driven back* ...
> S]". G18:0800

the fact that the quotation is integrated into the quoting text means that the quoted material does not fall within a single tagma at any level below the root, and no Q node is used.

§ 4.407   Quoted wording integrated into the surrounding material may be interrupted by non-quoted wording; if the degree of integration is such that the formtag Q is inapplicable, and the interrupting phrase would not be seen as a case of transformational dislocation if the inverted commas were absent, then nothing in the annotation will indicate the unity of the quoted passage:

> [S *The fact that homoeopathy utterly rejected the weapons com-
> monly used against disease ... ensured* [Fn *that 'every Apothe-
> cary',* [A *as Lord Ponsonby put it*], *'must be its determined foe*
> Fn] S].' G06.108

§ 4.408   The fact that the object of a verb of quoting or of propositional attitude precedes rather than following that verb does not in itself justify use of the Q analysis, if there are no orthographic cues implying direct quotation, despite the fact that one cannot see such a sequence as resulting from elision of a *that* complementizer:

> [S [Fn *It was Mrs. Kennedy who drew the crowds*], *said police*
> S]. A28.026
> [S [Fn *A WIFE led a perfectly blameless life* <hellip> *until she was
> "ensnared in the hire-purchase network* Fn]," *a court was told
> yesterday* S]. A12.209
> [S [Fn *Being at a cross-roads was unsettling*], *she also decided* S].
> P03.031

[S [Fn [Fa *If she was really in love with Stevie Hewitt*] *it was madness to go on worrying about her* Fn], *he told himself moodily*]. L04.061

In the A12 example here, the occurrence of an ellipsis mark in the newspaper report may suggest that the wording before the passage in inverted commas is intended as a more or less verbatim transcription of what was said in court, but this is not a standard indicator of direct speech status and the passage is treated as an indirect statement which includes some quoted words integrated into their environment. In the P03 example, note that the object of *decide* rarely comprises direct speech represented orthographically as such.

§ 4.409   For cases where direct speech is interrupted medially by a quoting clause, see § 5.93 ff. on Ss.

§ 4.410   In the absence of punctuation cues grammar alone will not normally justify using the Q formtag rather than analysing a sequence as indirect speech. No Q node appears in cases such as:

[S *He said* [S* *do it right away*]].

... *to tell me* [Fn *the sketch I had put in was not good enough 'for such a good Journal as mine* [S?+ *and would I improve it before going ashore*]]'. G12.124 — the S?+ tagma occurs within direct quotation but the quotation as a whole is integrated into the context and not analysed as a Q (§ 4.406); for the use of the tag S?+ rather than Fn?+, see § 4.305

§ 4.411   If modified, a Q may be head of a noun phrase (in which case the inverted commas surrounding the Q will be daughters of the N):

She tossed him [Ns *a pert* "[Q [S? *Who do you think you are*]? Q]" Ns]

— though more commonly a Q tagma will be an IC of the clause containing it.

It is an absolute rule that a Q node may not include the inverted commas or other marks delimiting the quotation (though it can include the logically redundant unbalanced inverted commas referred to at the end of § 4.412, and if interrupted by an I (§§ 4.415 ff.) or an Ss clause (§ 5.93) it will have the internal inverted commas showing the suspension and resumption of the quotation as its daughters). This has consequences for the analysis of sequences involving co-ordination or apposition of quotations. It is common for a Q to occur appositionally within a higher tagma of another category, with the inverted commas analysed as daughters of that tagma (cf. §§ 4.500 ff., 4.526 ff.):

> *to* [Ns *this anonymous folk poem:* "<bital> [Q@ [S +*They brought me news that Spring is in the plains . . .* S] Q@] <eital>" Ns] G05:1610
>
> . . . *wasted no time on* [Ns *a first notice:* [I <minbrk> I] <bital> [Q@ [S IF YOU DON'T LEAVE . . . S] Q@] <eital> Ns]. N11:1250
>
> [S *Professor Fredrik Böök . . . acclaims it* [A *as follows*]: "[Q@ [S +*In this we have the verse of . . .* S]. [S . . .]. . . . [S+ . . .] Q@]" S]. G18:0380

and a Q may be in apposition to a higher Q, where a direct quotation is broken off and continued afresh all within one pair of inverted commas (cf. §§ 4.522 ff.):

> . . . *would she mind speaking a little louder?* <minbrk> [O [S "[Q [S *I think you stink*], [Nns" *Tom Lord*]*!* [S *I think* [Fn *you're mean and hateful and stupid,* [Fn+ *and*] Fn] S] — [Q@ *louder*_RRR Q@] Q]"? *said Joyce* S]. N09:0150

But if a direct quotation is in apposition to another, each surrounded by its own inverted commas, or if direct quotations each with their own inverted commas are conjoined, one or all of the quotations must be analysed as N's headed by Q's in order to avoid the need to parse inverted commas, or unquoted conjunctions, as elements falling within a Q:

> [S+ . . . [Fa *when he said,* [N "[Q [S *They make a desert, and call it peace* S] Q]" ([N@ "[Q *Solitudinem faciunt, pacem appellant* Q]" N@] Fa] S+].) G17:0360
>
> *From the crowd were coming cries* [Po *of* [N "[Q [S *He's right*] Q]"*!* [N- "[Q [S *There must be a line* S] Q]" N-]*!* [N+ *and* "[Q *Bravo*_UH, [Nns" *Garry*], [S* *Continue*] Q]" N+] N] Po]*!* G47:0700

§ 4.412 Commonly a direct quotation will consist of just one sentence or lesser tagma, yielding a structure such as [Q [S . . .]] or [Q [N . . .]], and it is unusual for a direct quotation to amount to more than one typographic paragraph. On occasion, however, a speech may be recorded as a series of paragraphs surrounded as a whole by inverted commas and introduced by a quoting clause — in such a case the entire quotation is one Q, within which the <minbrk> symbols are I elements. That is, the overall structure is analysed along the lines:

[S . . . *said:* "[Q [S . . .]. [S . . .]. [I <*minbrk*>] [S . . .]. [S . . .].
[I <*minbrk*>] [S . . .]. [S . . .]. Q]" S]

If the second and subsequent typographic paragraphs are introduced by opening inverted commas, not balanced by closing inverted commas — which is one standard typographic convention — these opening inverted commas are treated as daughters of the Q node, right sisters of the I node dominating the preceding <*minbrk*>.

§ 4.413 A Q tagma is not necessarily introduced, or followed, by a quoting clause. A paragraph might consist of, or might include, a quotation marked as such by inverted commas but not introduced by any wording, in which case the structure will be:

[O "[Q . . .]" O]

(where the quotation is a separate paragraph in the text which includes it), or, say:

[O [S . . .]. "[Q . . .]" [S . . .]. . . . O]

(where the quotation is part of a paragraph). Thus:

[O [S '[Q [J *Excellent*] +!_YX]' *said Holmes* S] +._YF '[Q [J *Excellent*] +!_YX [S* *Pray continue*] +._YF Q]' O] (Conan Doyle, *The Return of Sherlock Holmes*)

Even when a paragraph consists wholly of a quotation, it is guaranteed that the O node will have daughter(s) other than the Q node: if there were no inverted commas or other marks of quotation, there would be no grammatical justification for treating the paragraph as a quotation. A single typographic paragraph might contain a succession of two or more quotations each with its own surrounding inverted commas, say representing different speakers' contributions to a dialogue; in that case the analysis would be along the lines:

[O "[Q . . .]" "[Q . . .]" . . . O]

§ 4.414 Where a direct quotation is terminated by a punctuation mark within the closing inverted comma(s) (or other typographical mark indicating boundary of quotation, e.g. <*eital*>),[32] the former mark is treated as within the Q (although not within an S

---

[32] Because of the normalization that was applied (as discussed in § 2.24) to punctuation in the Brown Corpus, from which the SUSANNE Corpus is derived, there are few cases of the type described here in the SUSANNE Corpus. With respect to English usage in general, however, it is a frequent situation.

dominated by the Q) even if it occurs only because the material is quoted (as in the case of the commas terminating the Q tagmas in the first two examples below, which serve only to link the quotations to the quoting clauses):

[S "[Q [S *That's her* S], Q]" *he said* S]. L07.111
[S "[Q [S *Maybe he'll stuff her and keep her* S], Q]" *I said, trying to introduce a lighter note.* G10.175
"[Q [Fa *Because I witnessed all the other wills she ever made* Fa], Q]" *Vera said simply.* L22.166
[S '[Q [S *These are <bital> Dienstgeheimnisse <eital>* S]! Q]' *Magda interrupted* S]. K10.131
[S "[Q [S? *What sort of boat is it* S?]? Q]" *I asked* S]. L07.105

On the other hand, where a direct quotation is terminated by a punctuation mark *outside* the closing inverted comma(s) or other indicator of quotation boundary, the Q tagma excludes both the boundary indicator and the following punctuation mark even if the nature of the latter is determined by the nature of the quotation:

[S "[Q [S *You <bital> are <eital> hurt* S] Q]"! *she breathed* S]. N03:0080
[S *He asked,* "[Q [S? *Could we have a drink* S?] Q]" S]? N01:0480

In view of the low weight given to inverted commas in determining structure where Q tagmas are not involved (§ 4.77) it is arguably illogical to make the boundaries of Q's depend wholly on inverted commas when present, but this is the SUSANNE rule.

I interpolation

§ 4.415   The formtag I is used for interpolations: material inserted into a structure which would be grammatically and semantically complete without it, and commonly marked off typographically by surrounding brackets, dashes, or commas. (The delimiting punctuation is parsed as outside the I constituent.) An I constituent will normally be the daughter of an S or other clause- or phrasetag: when a paragraph contains a series of sentences of which one happens as a whole to appear within brackets, this would simply be given an S node which, together with the brackets, would be daughters of the O node over the paragraph — grammatical relationships among O or Q ICs are too weak for a particular IC to rank as an interpolation on grammatical grounds. (However, if for instance a multi-sentence quotation is interrupted by material not part of the quotation — and not forming an embedded quoting clause, Ss, cf. §§ 5.93 ff. — then this will be given an I tag on semantic grounds.)

§ **4.416** Two special types of interpolation-like phenomenon, tag questions and technical references (e.g. bibliographical citations, references to illustrations, etc.), are given formtags derived from the interpolation tag, namely Iq and Iu respectively — see §§ 4.424–5, §§ 4.426 ff.

§ **4.417** Like O and Q, an I... node in itself carries no implication about the grammatical form of the material it dominates: this is shown entirely by the structure and labelling below the I... node, and very commonly an I... will have a single daughter labelled S.

§ **4.418** Some examples of I constituents are:

I was having lunch not long ago ([I [Np *apologies* [P *to N.V. Peale*]]]*) with three distinguished historians . . .* G17:0270

. . . people [Ve *do not,* [I [S *it is true*]], *stream* Ve] *into Chehel Sotun* G05:0440

But the landlady was terribly bossy — [I [S *they can be*] [S! *you know*] I] *— and kept hinting that we weren't married.* F14.142

§ **4.419** A paragraph boundary or heading interrupting a higher clause will be given an I node, cf. § 4.18. Where such I elements separate items in a list, an I consisting of a simple paragraph boundary will be attached as high in the tree as possible, but a heading marking the beginning of a list item will be treated as the first constituent of that item (cf. the placement of the heading *(2)* within the analysis of the A01 passage quoted in § 4.18 above), as will a punctuation mark introducing a list item:

A capsule view of proposed plans includes: [I <minbrk>] [Tg <mdash>_YD *Encouraging by every means . . . +.* [I <minbrk>] [Tg– <mdash>_YD *Engaging mature, experienced men to . . .*]. *. . .* Tg] A10:1660

§ **4.420** While enclosure in brackets suggests that an element is an interpolation, by no means everything appearing between brackets is given an I node. The use of the I analysis is a pis aller, invoked only when a sequence lacks cohesion with its context and cannot therefore be analysed as having a more specific relationship with it. Elements which are written in brackets often play standard grammatical roles in their contexts, and might have appeared without brackets. In such cases, no I node is used:

a girl child fetching, on marriage, [N *some ten head* [Po *of* [N *cattle* ([Tn *highly prized on both economic and religious grounds* Tn]) N] Po] N] *from the prospective bridegroom.* J22.054 — bracketed sequence is noun postmodifier

[N *315 lines <bital> g <eital>*] (*[Tg all three points on a <bital> g <eital> being <bital> m <eital>*]) [V *lie*] [P *on <bital> Q <eital>*], *while* . . . J21.021 — bracketed sequence is an Absolute adjunct

[Ns *This patient* ([Nns@ *R. I.* [Nn@ *No. 42050* Nn@] Nns@]), *aged 43 years* Ns], *was admitted* . . . J17.179 — bracketed sequence is an appositional attachment to a noun phrase

. . . [Ns *submersion in extremely cold water*] [Vdc *might* [P *on rare occasions*] *chill*] [Ns *the body*] [R *so rapidly that vital organs are protected from the effects of lack of oxygen*] ([A *as is now practised surgically*]), . . . J16.169 — bracketed sequence is an *as* clause acting as propositional relative (§ 4.370)

[S [Fa *If one of her progeny jumps well*], *they all do,* ([S+ *and* [Fa *if one jumps appallingly*] *they all do* S+]*!*), [J *regardless of the sire*] S]. A23.149 — bracketed sequence is a conjoined sentence, followed by an exclamation mark which in accordance with the principle of highest possible attachment is analysed as outside the S+ element

In the sequence:

. . . *which may be more closely defined* [P *as* ([Ns +*the assumption* [Po *of* +) [Ns *a universal <bital> subjective <eital> necessity in regard to* . . . Ns] Po] Ns] P]. J53.086

the bracketed segment does not even contain a whole tagma; the principle that priority is given to appropriate analysis of verbal material rather than punctuation in case of conflict means that the bracketing is ignored in parsing this case and the two brackets are attached at different levels in the tree.

§ 4.421   There are many borderline cases where it is hard to say whether a bracketed sequence is sufficiently grammatically cohesive with its context to be parsed without an I node. In:

. . . *desperation can set in if any of the following things have been forgotten:* [N@ *salt,* [Ns– *pepper*], [Ns– *mustard* ([I [Fa *when ham or sausages are served* Fa] I]) Ns–], [Ns– *soft sugar* ([P *for grapefruit or stewed fruit*]) Ns–] [Dp+ *or any of the requisite implements* Dp+] N@]. E26.027

the P following *soft sugar* is a normal type of noun postmodifier, hence is not treated as an I, but an Fa is not a usual noun postmodifier so the earlier parenthesis is so treated. On the other hand, in:

A young healthy human being feels the unity of body and mind' ([I [S+ *or rather,* [I [S *one might say* S] I], [Fa *since this is already*

metaphysical], <bital> *he cannot conceive their disunity* S+] I])
<eital> '[L *the one present in the other,* [Tg+ *the mind govern-
ing the body* . . . Tg+] L]; . . . J52.062

the fact that the parenthesis beginning *or rather* is both an unquoted
passage interrupting a direct quotation, and is enclosed within
brackets, are jointly taken as justifying the I parsing despite the fact
that the word *or* suggests a measure of grammatical coherence within
the context. (In an ordinary uninterpolated co-ordinate clause,
however, it would be unusual to include the word *he*, which tends
to confirm the rightness of the I analysis.) The phrase *one might say*
is in turn analysed as I within I (it cannot be treated as Ss, because
what "one might say" is only the words *following* this phrase —
not the whole parenthesis beginning *or*).

§ 4.422   Likewise, dashes surrounding a sequence suggest an I
tagma, but in many cases sequences surrounded by dashes are sufficiently cohesive with their context to be parsed otherwise:

   . . . *said* [Fn *that boarding schools* — [Fa *though there were exceptions* Fa] — *tended to be in the country in rating areas
   which were not wealthy* Fn]. A11.192
   . . . *the earnest desire* — [Fa% *be it in the civic field of duty or
   on the field of sport* Fa%] — *to 'play the game.'* A30.055
   [Ns *The economics of organic and water irrigation systems* — [Z
   [R *always*] [Ns *an important matter*] Z] — Ns] *were presented* . . . E29.077

In the A11 example, it would be more usual to place the Fa either
immediately after *that* or else at the end of the Fn, and the unusual
placement no doubt explains the use of dashes; but the Fa remains
a perfectly standard adjunct IC of the *tended* clause. In the A30
example, the *be it* clause is logically an IC of the infinitival *play*
clause, out of which it has been moved transformationally; this will
be shown via the logical grammar annotation system, and there is
no need to mark it as an interpolation. In the E29 case, the material
between dashes is clearly a "Whiz-Deleted" relative clause, Z.

§ 4.423   Although an I element is most commonly medial within
the tagma to which it is attached, an I may occur at beginning or
end of a tagma if typographical or logical considerations show that
an element having no grammatical relationship with the tagma is
intended to group with it:

   . . . *to a present value* [Tn *estimated by some as exceeding*
   $10,000,000 ([I [S <bital> +*we* <eital> *don't disclose financial
   figures to the public* S] I]) Tn]. G22:1860

Iq tag question

§ 4.424 Tag questions should arguably not be classified as a special case of "interpolations" — in English their structure is heavily dependent on that of the clause to which they are appended, and they are not normally enclosed in brackets. Nevertheless they are given the label Iq in the SUSANNE scheme for want of a more appropriate category. The standard type of tag question, a sequence such as *isn't it, do you*, etc., will be analysed as an Iq dominating a single daughter labelled S? which itself will have V and N daughters; the Iq will be a daughter of the clause to which the tag question is appended. Irrespective of whether or not the natural interpretation of the sentence including the tag question is interrogative, the S or other mother of the Iq will not take the ? suffix; any mood suffix it takes will depend on the grammatical structure of the main clause, ignoring the tag question. Thus:

[S *Having all the guns makes you a big man*, [Iq [S? [Vex *doesn't*] [Ni *it*] S?] Iq] S], [Nns" *Adams*]? N12:0960
[S* *Go through his pockets*, [Iq [S? [Vcx *will*] [Ny *you*]]]]? N14:0720
[S *You'll maybe be sick*, [Iq [S? *will you*]] S]? N24.051
[S *I don't think* [Fn *I have to tell you* [Ti *to keep your mouth shut*], [Iq [S? *do I*] Iq] Fn] S]? L10.172

— in the L10 case the Iq is an IC of the Fn, since the tag question concerns "whether I have to . . .", not "whether I think . . .".

§ 4.425 In dialogue, items other than verb + pronoun sequences can be used as tag questions, and Iq is used in these cases also:

[S *Maybe you could write it down for me*, [Iq *huh_UH*]]? N09:0230
[S *Maybe I should withdraw my advice* — [Iq *no_UH*]]"? N10:0670

Iu technical reference

§ 4.426 Iu is used for interpolated technical references, such as:

- bibliographical citations, which may include author name(s) as well as year and/or page number(s), or may include year/page number(s) alone appended to an author's name which has a grammatical role in the surrounding text;
- literature citations using conventional abbreviations such as *op_cit, ibid*;
- interpolated references to or labels for illustrations, examples, or items in a list.

§ **4.427** In a sequence of elements such as author's name, year, and page number in a Harvard-style bibliographical reference, later elements are treated as appositionally attached to earlier elements. Sequences of such references, if separated by punctuation but no conjunction within a single pair of brackets, are treated as concatenated rather than as forming a co-ordination structure.

§ **4.428** Iu is not used when a number or similar item occurs as (part of) the heading of a chapter, section, etc., since this is not an interruption:

[Oh *<bminhd>* 1._MCb [Ns *TRANSPIRATION COOLED ANODE WITH CARBON ANODE HOLDER* Ns] *<eminhd>* Oh] J02:1200

§ **4.429** Below an Iu, tagmas comprising multiple leaf nodes are parsed as normal (if the material dominated by the Iu node consists of multiple leaves all forming one phrase or clause, the Iu will be shown as having a single phrase or clause daughter).

[A *As* [Nns *Dolph*_NP1s ([Iu *<bbold>* 8_MCn *<ebold>* Iu]) Nns] *points out* A], . . . J20.003

[Nn [NP1s& *Knighting and Hinds*] ([Iu 1960_MCy Iu]) Nn] *showed* . . . J10.094

[Ns *The structure* [P *in* 38b_MCb], [Tn *suggested by* [Nns *Chomsky* ([Iu 1981:171_MCe Iu]) Nns] Tn] Ns], *does* . . . (*Language*, 68 (1992), 264)

. . . *according to the definition of this term* [P *in* [Nns *Chomsky* ([Iu 1986:3_MCe Iu]) Nns] P]. (*Language*, 68 (1992), 265)

Some previous investigations have shown that the exchanges . . . occurred relatively rapidly ([Iu [Nns *Treherne*_NP1s +,_YC 1961<bital>a<eital>_MCb Nns] Iu]) *and appeared to be* . . . J12.103

[A *As John Sinclair . . . points out* ([Iu *Sinclair*_NP1s 1982_MCy]) A], *the problem of data-capture . . . is becoming* . . . (*CAE*, p. 6)

. . . *as more and more evidence becomes available* ([Iu [Nns *Czaykowska-Higgins*_NP1s 1988_MCy Nns],_YC [Nns *Bethin*_NP1s 1989_MCy Nns] Iu]) *that* . . . (*Language*, 68 (1992), 303)

. . . *this type of comprehension task is known to be sensitive to pragmatic cues* ([Iu [Nn [NP1s& *Eisele* [NP1s+ *& Lust*] 1990_MCy Nn],_YC [Nns *Eisele*_NP1s 1988_MCy Nns] Iu]). (*Language*, 68 (1992), 342)

. . . [P *from Mars and Jupiter*] [P *at 3.15 cm*] [P *in 1956*] ([Iu [Nn [NP1s& *Mayer, McCullough, and Sloanaker*],

*1958<bital>a<eital>_MCb, <bital> b_ZZ1 <eital>, <bital>
c_ZZ1 <eital> Nn] Iu])*, *and . . .* J01:0750

. . . the complete intersection of <bital> Q <eital> with
[N *<bital> E <eital>* +, [Nj@ *the polar [*[Iu 4_MCn *]] of <bital> g
<eital>]]*. J21.025 — reference enclosed by square brackets
in the original

. . . separated into [Np *two areas (*[Iu [Nn [Nnp *donors P.J.*
[Nns+ *and R.S.*], [Nns@ *Fig. 1*] Nnp] [Nns+ *and E.M.,* [Nns@
Fig. 2] Nns+] Nn] Iu]*)* Np]. J09:1480

. . . other than [P *in* [N *the dog and cat*] *(*[Iu [[Nns *Miller, '13;
'25*] Iu]*)* P]. J12:0960 — two abbreviated dates, wordtagged
MCy, attached as appositional sisters (cf. §§ 4.500 ff.) to the
Nns

[S *There is* [Ns *(*[Iu 1_MC1n Iu]*) the body,* [Fr *which is the basis
of* [Ns *(*[Iu 2_MCn Iu]*) the life,* [Fr *which develops* [N *(*[Iu
3_MCn Iu]*) the spirit, or mind* N] Fr] Ns] Fr] Ns] S]. D14.139

. . . [Fa *until they become* [J *(*[Iu 1_MC1n Iu]*) tired,* [J+ *or (*[Iu
2_MCn Iu]*) more used to the disturbance* J+] J] Fa]. E06.090

[Np *two classes of alkaline products:* [Np@ *(*[Iu 1]*) the for-
mulations made expressly for machine dishwashers,* [Np+ *and
(*[Iu 2]*) the general-purpose cleaners . . .*]]] J05:0210

There are [N *(*[Iu a_ZZ1]*) the <bital> topography of the site
<eital> which influences drainage, surface run-off and the
chances of erosion, (*[I [S* *think of this in relation to the mass
of debris left after the retreat of the ice sheet* S*] I]*), *[Ns– *(*[Iu
b_ZZ1]*) the <bital> climate within the developing profile <eital>
— *[Ns@ *a composite of temperature, . . . and drainage*] Ns–]
N]. J03.019

§ 4.430 Where an Iu introduces a following item, as in the
latter examples, it is analysed as first daughter rather than sister of
that item; and as last sister when it is appended to the item to which
it refers:

. . . whether the hydrogen atoms are located [R *symmetrically (*[Iu
1_MC1n]*)* [R+ *or asymmetrically (*[Iu 3_MCn]*)* R+] R].
J04:1010

Also included in [Ns *Edmunds' account (*[Iu 1938_MCy Iu]*)* Ns]
is the first contribution . . . J11.103

§ 4.431 The formtag Iu is not used where the reference as a
whole plays a grammatical role in the surrounding text (in which
case brackets will often be treated as part of an MCb word rather
than as separately wordtagged items, cf. MCb in § 3.73):

<bital> Q <eital> consists, as explained [P *in* [3]_MCb]*, of* . . .
J21.021

Since I have made this case at much greater length [P *in* [N *my*
*[1983a]*_MCb N] P]*,* . . . (*British Journal for the Philosophy of*
Science, 36 (1985), 322)

[S [M [MCb& *(a)* [MCb+ *and (b)*]] M] *indirectly influence*
[Ns *(*[Iu *c_ZZ1*]*) <bital> the kind of vegetation <eital> which*
. . .] S]. J03.024

. . . *one of the most impressive and enduring insights* [Po *of*
[Nns *Chomsky 1965*]]*.* (*Language, 68* (1992), 264)

In the J03 example here, note the contrasting treatment of *(a) and*
(b) versus *(c)* in the same sentence: *(a) and (b)* is used here as a
nominal reference to topography and climate, introduced with those
symbols as labels in the immediately preceding sentence (which was
quoted at the end of § 4.429 above), so in the latter sentence *(a)*
and (b) is not an Iu, whereas *(c)*, occurring for the first time to label
a new topic, is one. In the last example, *1965* is treated as a one-
word M phrase in apposition within the Nns (and, because only one
word, not separately phrasetagged), rather than as an Iu, because
the passage is interpreted as referring to the insights of the book
"Chomsky 1965" (Noam Chomsky's *Aspects of the Theory of*
Syntax), rather than as referring to the insights of the man, with the
book cited in support of the allusion.

§ 4.432 Iu is also not used where the interpolated sequence has
more grammatical structure than a mere mention of an item or
items; such cases are tagged I rather than Iu:

The upper limit was determined by the difficulty of measuring the
characteristic anode surface temperature ([I [S* [V *see*]
[R *below*]]]*) since only a small region* . . . J02:1310

. . . *will be discussed later (*[I [S* [V *see*] [Nnp *pp. 1746–*
1748]]]*)*. J05:1770

. . . *this can only be defined in relation to internal entropy in-*
crease ([I [S* [V *cf._VV0t*] [Nns *Bartlett, 1956*] S*] I]*)*. J18.193

. . . *using optical techniques (*[Iu [Nns *Sinton, 1955, 1956,*] Iu]*;*
[I [S* *see also chap. 11* S*] I]*)*. J01:1300

§ 4.433 If a "label" or similar item functions as a "technical
reference" within a grammatical constituent but is printed as a
separate paragraph, then by § 4.18 the item together with its surrounding heading markers will be tagged I (rather than Iu) — see
the treatment of *(1), (2)* in the long example from A01 discussed in
that section.

§ 4.434 An Iu may include a word tagged REX:

> ... *which was derived from the variation in the infrared emission*
> *during eclipses* ([Iu e.g._REX +,_YC [Nns *Garstung*_NP1s +,_YC
> *1958*_MCy Nns] Iu]*). J01:0050
> ... *in the standard generative model* ([Iu e.g._REX [Nns
> *Gussmann*_NP1s *1980*_MCy Nns] Iu]*) inflectional yers were*
> *postulated* ... (*Language,* 68 (1992), 302)
> ([Iu e.g._REX [Nns *Carden*_NP1s *1986*_MCy Nns],_YC [Nns
> *O'Grady*_NP1s *et_al.*_RAc *1986*_MCy Nns] Iu]*) (*Language,*
> 68 (1992), 346)

§ 4.435 Iu is used only for technical and bibliographical references, involving numerical/literal codes or scholarly conventions such
as the idiom *loc_cit.* Structurally similar references, which may be
surrounded by brackets, of a non-technical kind will be analysed in
terms of apposition (see § 4.500):

> ... *the cast list of* [Nns <bbold> [Ot [Fa% [V *Come*] [Nns
> *September*] Fa%] Ot] <ebold> ([Nns@ *Odeon,* [Nns@
> *Leicester-square* Nns@] Nns@]*) Nns],* ... C06.116
> *At this point,* [Nns *Mr. Paul Williams* ([N@ *Cons.,* [Nns@ *Sun-*
> *derland* Nns@] N@]*) Nns] called out "Shame."* A06.132
> [Nns *Sir Humphrey Gilbert* ([M@ *1539-1583*]*)] proposed* ...
> J37.087

— in the J37 case, the dates are not codes identifying items such as
publications, but are used in their literal application as dates (of
birth and death).

Words Lacking Phrasetags

§ 4.436 Of the word classes listed in § 4.58 as having no corresponding phrase category, the grammar of two requires discussion
at this point (the analysis of the others is explained under various
headings elsewhere in this chapter).

THE WORD *NOT*

§ 4.437 There is a presumption in favour of grouping the word
not (or *-n't*), wordtagged XX, with adjacent words into a phrase
rather than analysing it as a clause IC.

§ 4.438 Thus, when subject-auxiliary inversion has created a
split between Vo and Vr, *not* will be treated as part of one of these
V-partials, provided it is adjacent:

[Vo *Do*] *we* [Vre *not derive*] *our idea of . . .* D14.155

— the fact that *not* binds most closely with *do*, logically speaking, is not a bar to grouping it with *derive* in surface structure. *Not* may be included as a premodifier in a variety of phrase-types, e.g.:

Lee, however, showed [Ns *not the slightest sign of fatigue*]. K02.028
Nothing moved: [N@ *not a child,* [Ns– *not a rooster*]]. K09.115
a [J *not unlikely*] *conclusion* A08:1590
[R *Not entirely*] [P *to* [Ns *my regret*]], *I was* . . . G05.050
looking [Tn [Tn& *flushed* [J+ *and very pretty*]], [P+ *but* [P *not in the least*] *like his mama*]] P18.162
[Rx [R *not long*] *ago*] G05:0740
"*I learned* [Ti? *how* [Vie *not to conduct*]]". G06:0390
. . . *he hurried that way,* [Tg [Vge *not remounting*] [Fa *till he was* . . .]] N14:1550 — the relationship between *not* and *till* does not justify excluding *not* from the V; compare the fact that, in *he did not remount till* . . . , the sequence *did not remount* would be a clear Ve tagma
"[Q [Rw *Not now*] Q]", *Wilson said.* N05:0830

§ 4.439 On the other hand *not* will not normally be first daughter of a subordinate clause (though a Ti may have *not* as its first word, if it begins with a Vie tagma in which the *not* precedes the *to* in order to avoid a split infinitive):

[S *Not_XX* [Fa *until they were on the level again* . . .] *did the girl speak.* N14.147
[Ns+ *and the humility* . . . [Ti [Vie *not to impose*] *himself upon another*]]. G12:0310

§ 4.440 The presumption in favour of grouping *not* with a following phrase does not require the analyst to create illogical structures in cases of co-ordination and similar phenomena; in . . . *she didn't want to talk to anyone, not even to Fergus,* . . . P11.115 it would be inappropriate to treat *not to Fergus* as a prepositional phrase (with *even* as an included adverbial) in apposition to *to anyone*, because this would yield a structure of the schematic form [S . . . *didn't* . . . [P . . . [P@ *not* . . .]]] in which the negative of *didn't* would appear to apply to both P's. In fact, *not even to Fergus* is a reduced counterpart of the main clause, from which the negation has been preserved although the subject, main verb, and part of its complement clause have been deleted; the analysis is:

... [S *she* [Ve *didn't want*] [Ti *to talk to anyone*], [S@ *not*_XX [R *even*] [P *to Fergus*]]]

§ **4.441**   On the linking of *not* to a preceding V, see § 4.106.

§ **4.442**   The words *why not*... are treated as two ICs of a clause, with the following V being a constituent of the same rather than a subordinate clause:

[S? [Rq *Why*] *not*_XX [V *collect*] *round you the odd few you loved,* [S+ *and*...]]? K28.061

[S? [Fa *If he attaches little importance to personal liberty*], [Rq *why*] *not*_XX [V *make*] *this known to the world*]? G01:0460

§ **4.443**   For *or not*, see § 4.491.

EXISTENTIAL THERE

§ **4.444**   Clauses containing *there*_EX are analysed as in the following examples. The material following the logical subject of such a clause is treated as an IC of the clause, rather than as a postmodifier of the logical subject; and, if this material begins with a verb, it is treated as a subordinate non-finite clause, not linked with the *BE* of the *there* clause in a Vo/Vr relationship:

*There*_EX [Vab *are*] [Np *several closely related inner functions*]. J23:0160

*There*_EX [Vab *are*] [Ns *plenty of fresh horses*] [R *halfway*] [P *at my place*]. N02:1250

... *there*_EX [Vwb *were*] [Np *200,000 Spaniards*...] [Tn *established in the New World*]. G70.163

I know [Fn *there*_EX [Vzb *+'s*] [Ns *a lot of rot*] [Tn *talked about a sixth sense and all that* Tn] Fn] L23.013

*While there*_EX [Vcb *may still be*] [Nnp *many Faulknerian Lucas Beauchamps*] [Tn *scattered through the rural South*],... G08:1060

On the logical annotation of existential *there* constructions, see § 5.71.

Exclamations and Vocatives

§ **4.445**   Items having an exclamatory or vocative force cut across the general structure of the SUSANNE parsing scheme in several ways. For a form to be a vocative or an exclamation is logically speaking a functional rather than a formal property, but exclamations and vocatives often occur in contexts where the SUSANNE scheme does not use functiontags (that is, not as ICs of clauses). An item functioning as an exclamation may be anything from an entire main clause, e.g.:

> ... *it was unpopular (*[S! *how many of us oldsters took up drinking in prohibition days,* [S@ *drinking was so gay, so fashionable, especially in the sophisticated Northeast* S@] S!]*!) and was repealed.* G17:0440

to a single word not tagged as a separate phrase. Some words — interjections — have an inherently exclamatory function, but many exclamations consist of ordinary words.

The SUSANNE treatment of these elements is as follows.

§ 4.446   So far as the boundaries between exclamations, vocatives, and interpolations are concerned:

§ 4.447   Words or short finite clauses (such as *I mean, you see*) inserted into speech or text in order to colour the pragmatic force of the utterance or maintain the interactive relationship between the parties to the discourse, rather than to add to its informative content, are regarded as exclamations or vocatives rather than interpolations. Thus:

> '[Q [S! *I say*],' [Ss *he said*], '[S *you know what is in their minds*], [S! *I suppose*]? [Nn *Lady Wade and my father*], [S! *I mean*]? Q]' K19.085
> '[Q [S *Otherwise,* [S! *you see*], *it pulls the pockets of one's trousers out of shape* S]. Q]' K16.128

— on the other hand, in a case like *It would be the trail up to Colorado, I figured.* N06.062, the past tense of *figured* makes it less like a conventional piece of "phatic communion" and more like a literal statement that this is what I figured, so the *It would be* clause is treated as a subordinate Fn, object of *figured* — cf. *one might say* in the J52 example in § 4.421.

§ 4.448   A form which constitutes a referring expression whose reference is the addressee of the surrounding text is a vocative rather than an exclamation, even in a case such as "[Q [Ny" *You cheap bitch*]]"! *I exclaimed.* N18:1540; but *Damn you* N12:0730 (where the reference to addressee is only one constituent of the tagma), or *My God* in *"My God, I'm shot"!* N11:0830, not addressed to the Deity, are exclamations, tagged Tb! and Nns! respectively.[33] (Contrast

---

[33] Expressions such as *damn it, damn you* are not to be thought of as imperative main clauses, tagged S*, lacking subjects because *you* as subject is "understood" in an imperative: note that one says *damn you* rather than **damn yourself* as would be expected if the expression were an imperative (cf. Quang 1969). Accordingly, we also parse: "[Q [Tb! *Thank God*], [S *it never was*], Q]" *Fritz said.* K13.169.

the latter example with *Please, **dear God**, make my pilots good, he prayed.* N15:1510, where the emphasized phrase is a vocative, tagged Nns".)

It follows that a vocative will normally be a form taking an N... phrasetag. The vocative status of such a form is marked by suffixing the symbol " to the phrasetag.

§ 4.449 Where an exclamation consists of a single word which is inherently an interjection, this is wordtagged UH. (On occasion a UH word may occur other than in an exclamation; e.g. the book title *The Last Hurrah* A07:0610 is analysed as an Ns headed by a UH.) The wordtag UH is not used, however, merely because a word is functioning as an exclamation: in *Hell, in a year or five* ... N10:0620, or *<bital> Now, <eital> Mis-ter McBride* N09:1360, the exclamations *Hell, Now* receive their normal wordtags (NN1c, RTo), which are in turn dominated by singulary-branching phrase nodes tagged Nns!, Rw! (§ 4.452). OALD3 is treated as authoritative for deciding whether a word originally belonging to another part of speech has a sufficiently established exclamatory use to be tagged UH; for instance, *well* though obviously derived from the adverb homograph is tagged UH as an interjection, because *OALD3* allots **well** a separate "*int[erjection]*" subentry. As special cases, the word *please* is tagged UH when used as a grammatically-isolated politeness marker, though OALD3 classifies this usage in historical terms as an imperative verb; *thank you* is treated as a UH= idiom; and the words *yes, no,* listed in OALD3 as "particles" rather than "interjections", are tagged UH:

"[Q *Please*_UH, *please*_UH [S* *help me*]! Q]" *she said urgently.*
N18.111
[S? [Vodc *Could*] [Ny *you*] *please*_UH [Vr *tell*] [Nos *me*] ... S?]
F12.121
"[Q *Yes*_UH, [Fa *for they deal with distress* Fa]. ... Q]" G12:1340
[S "[Q *Thank_you*_UH, [Ns" *my dear*] Q]", *he said* S]. N03:0100
(misprint corrected)

§ 4.450 Even a word which is listed as an interjection among other parts of speech in *OALD3* will be given a non-interjection wordtag when it occurs in a multi-word exclamation in a context which shows that it is playing a part within a grammatical structure: thus *damn* as a one-word exclamation is wordtagged UH, but the same word in the phrase *damn it* is given its non-interjection wordtag VV0t.

§ 4.451 Where an exclamation is represented in writing by a distorted or non-standard spelling of the word(s) from which it derives, such that the text form is unlikely to occur other than as an exclamation, this form is wordtagged UH notwithstanding the general rule that non-standard spellings are analysed by analogy with their standard equivalents. Thus *dammit* N04:0020, *Gawdamighty* N03:1550 are both UH, although UH would not occur in the analyses of the exclamations *damn it, God Almighty.*

§ 4.452   A single word tagged UH needs no further marker of exclamatory status. Any other word or tagma functioning as an exclamation is marked as such by suffixing the symbol ! to its tagmatag. Thus, in *"Now, hold on, damn it; ..."* N10:1350, *Now* is analysed as an Rw! phrase dominating a wordtag RTo, while *damn it* has the structure [Tb! [V *damn*_VV0t] [Ni *it*_PPH1]]. An exclamation written *my Gawd* would be analysed as [Ns! *My*_APPGi1 *Gawd*_UH]: the non-standard spelling leads to the UH tag for *Gawd*, but *my* establishes that the words form a noun phrase. Cf.:

[S+ *But,* [Pb! *by gosh*_UH], *I want him and I'm going to have him*]! N09:0510

[O *"*[Q [Nns" *Tom*] +!_YX [P! *For God's sake* P!] Q]*"* +!_YX O] N09:0690

§ 4.453   In a sequence such as:

I understand how you feel about the child <hellip> +*".* <minbrk> *"The hell you do".* N07:1180

the phrase *The hell* is analysed as an Ns! within a declarative S. Cf.:

"[S* *Just go* [Ns! *the hell*] *on*]*".* N09:0250

[S? [Dq *What*] [Ns! *the hell*] +*'s the matter ...*] N12:0590

"[S? [Rsw *Then*] [Rq *why*] [Np! *the blazes*] *did you say there was*]?*"* P14.144

§ 4.454   A main clause marked as subjunctive would commonly have exclamatory force; consequently it would be redundant to give such an exclamation the ! symbol in addition to the % symbol, and this is not done:

... and Gran Harrow exuberantly shouting [N *"*[Q [S% **Glory Be**] Q]*"* [N+ *and* *"*[Q *Hallelujah*_UH Q]*"* N+] N] *above their united chant ...* N13:0740

On the other hand an independent main clause will be tagged S! if it exhibits the characteristic exclamatory grammar exemplified by [S! [Nqs *What a spectacle*] *he was, ...*]. N13:0070.

§ 4.455   Rootrank formtags never themselves take ! or " suffixes, and where an exclamation or vocative is marked as such in the text by the occurrence of an exclamation mark (as part of the material under analysis, rather than as part of the notation system), the exclamation mark is not parsed as a part of the ... !-tagged or ..."-tagged form. Thus a paragraph consisting wholly of the sequence *Wonderful!* would be given the analysis [O [J! *Wonderful_JJ*] +!_YX].

§ 4.456   Furthermore, occurrence of an exclamation mark in the text is not itself taken as a sufficient reason to assign a tagmatag the ! suffix, if the structure and context of the tagma suggest that it is an ordinary declarative statement:

> *... leads also to an autonomic reversal: a stimulus acting sympathetically under control conditions elicits in this state of tuning a parasympathetic response!* J17:1220

— the clause following the colon is tagged S as a declarative clause, rather than S! as an exclamatory clause. In the sequence:

> [S *You* [Vdcb *should* — [I *smack*_NN1c +!_YX I] — *be* Vdcb] *ashamed of yourself* S]. N18:1570

the form *smack!* is a device to represent a physical smack interrupting a passage of direct speech; it is tagged as an interpolation, but does not appear to be in any sense an "exclamation". The paragraph [O [S "[Q [S? *How dare you* S?]! Q]" *she gasped* S]. O] P14.157 is analysed as shown: the quoted speech is grammatically an S? though pragmatically an exclamation and followed by exclamation mark rather than question mark in the text.

§ 4.457   In order that vocatives and exclamations should always be marked as such in the annotation, even one-word vocatives and exclamations (other than exclamations wordtagged UH) take tagmatags, irrespective of whether they are clause ICs or ICs of tagmas of other ranks (by § 4.458 they will often be ICs of rootrank tagmas). If a word has a use as an interjection, but belongs to a class of words for which no tagmatag is available to carry the ! suffix, it would be wordtagged UH irrespective of the dictionary classification. However, it is not clear that this latter rule will ever need to be invoked in practice. In a case such as:

> *She asked what he would do if he won. "If!" he responded scornfully.*

the word *If* is clearly a heavily reduced Fa, so the analysis would be [Q [Fa! *If*_CSi]!_YX Q]. In *My, you are tall!* the word *My* (listed by *OALD3* as a possessive pronoun even in this use) would be tagmatagged G! as an (incomplete) genitive phrase.

However, if a vocative or exclamation tagma contains co-ordination or apposition structure, the " or ! suffix will appear only on the complete tagma and not also on its subordinate elements:

"[Q [N! *Good morning* [Ns+ *and a happy new year* Ns+] N!], [Nn" *Dr Smith* [Nns+ *and Professor Jones* Nns+] Nn"]! Q]"

§ 4.458   Since exclamations and vocatives are not grammatically integrated into clause structures, a form or forms analysed as exclamations or vocatives will be treated as sister(s) rather than daughter(s) of a larger tagma to which it is (they are) adjacent:

"[Q *Good-bye*_UH +,_YC [Nns" *Dai*],_YC Q]" *said Morfydd,* . . . M04.036

"[Q *Yes*_UH, [Fa *for they deal with distress*]. [S *Some people object to this . . .* S]. . . . Q]" G12:1340

*Well*_UH, [S *really there is none at all*]. G12:1230

*Yes*_UH: [S [Fa *though not professional musicians*], *they were a music-loving family*]. G06:0250

"[Q [J! *All_right*_JA=] —_YD [S *you can take the lift down*], Q]" *said Hanson . . .* N05.054

"[Q *Oh*_UH [Ns" *darling*] —_YD [S *I feel so hopeless*]. [S *Sometimes I am afraid*]. Q]" K13.173

. . . *he said,* '[Q *Well*_UH [Nns" *Jim*] [S *I believe you,* [S− *I don't like it*] S] Q]'. L15.075

— and a typographic sentence consisting of a series of exclamations and/or vocatives will not be grouped as a tagma:

"[Q [J! *All_right*_JA=] +,_YC [Ns" *boy*] +,_YC [J! *All_right*_JA=]. [S *I'll make them ready . . .* S]. [S? *Will that do*]? Q]" N24.055

. . . [Nns! *God*], [S! *what a world you people live in* S!]". N04:0150

'[Q [S? *Are they*]? *Well*_UH +, *well*_UH +! Q]' *He waved . . .* K11.037

[O "[Q *Oh*_UH +,_YC *no*_UH [Nns" *Jimmy*] <hellip> Q]" [S *She was aghast at this*]. O] K18.094

§ 4.459   However, sometimes exclamations and vocatives will be medial within clause tagmas:

[S+ *But* [Jh! *honest* +<hyphen> [P +*to* +<hyphen> +*Betsy*]], *I've seed more hair than that on a piece o' bacon* S+] N13:1410

[S *I've got something to say to you,* [S+ *and* [Pb! *by God*] *you're going to listen* S+] S]. N09:0100

§ **4.460** A series of exclamation tagmas, interjection words, vocatives, and/or associated punctuation is not grouped as a tagma even if forming a standard sequence (e.g. *gee whiz*) and even if occurring medially in a clause:

> [Tb *Become a success with a disc* [S+ *and hey*_UH *presto*_UH +!_YX *You're a star* S+] <hellip> Tb]. C04.154
>
> '[Q *Oh*_UH [Nns! *my God*]! Q]' *said Celia, . . .* K28.085
>
> "[Q [Nns *Bismarck*]? *Oh*_UH *yes*_UH, [R *of_course*_RR=], [Ns *the Paris ambassador*]. Q]" K13.052
>
> . . . *people learned to say*: '[Q *Hello*_UH +, [Nns" *Willie*] +, *hello*_UH +, [Nns" *Helen*] +, [L [J *nice*] [Ti *to see you*] L] +, [Nns" *Helen*]. Q]' N12.143
>
> . . . *it was my own fault,* [Tg *dreaming of a knight in shining armour* [Tg+ *and thinking* [Fn *I'd found him in Gregory*] Tg+] — [S!@ *how funny that is* — [Nns! *Gregory* +!_YX [Nns@ *a new-style Sir Lancelot*] Nns!] +!_YX — [S@ *it's really terribly funny when you think about it* S@] S!@] Tg] — " P11.134

§ **4.461** Furthermore, such elements whether occurring singly or in sequence are not placed under interpolation ("I") nodes, even if surrounded by brackets (e.g. the example quoted in § 4.445); part of the function of the I formtag is to indicate that the material it dominates is grammatically disconnected from its environment, and that would be redundant with these forms.

Co-ordination and Apposition

§ **4.462** The treatment of co-ordination is probably the most non-standard aspect of the SUSANNE parsing scheme. Co-ordination is widely recognized (e.g. Dik 1968: 114–15) as a particularly knotty area of grammar from the viewpoint of various formal linguistic theories (for instance, theories which claim that most of the grammatical structure of a natural language can be defined by a finite set of context-free rules sometimes suggest that, exceptionally, extra machinery must be introduced to allow for co-ordinations of an indefinite number of conjuncts). The method of annotating co-ordinate structures embodied in the SUSANNE scheme, though unusual, is both practically convenient and, arguably, attractive from a theoretical point of view.

§ **4.463** The central innovation is that the conjuncts of a co-ordinate structure are not treated as occupying the same grammatical level. Instead, co-ordination is assimilated to subordination: the second and any subsequent conjuncts of a co-ordinate structure are treated as subordinate to the first, "main" conjunct. Because the *semantic* function of co-ordination is to represent a relationship of equivalence between two or more elements, linguists commonly assume that *grammatical* structure ought to reflect this equivalence. But this rests on an axiom about grammatical iconicity which is not self-evidently true, and which indeed is not accepted in relation to other areas of grammar. (Thus, plural forms are not required to contain more morphological elements than singular forms — in the case of English verbs they contain fewer.)

§ 4.464 A simple case of co-ordination is *the heat and the dust* N13:0490, which the SUSANNE scheme analyses as:

[N *the heat* [Ns+ *and the dust* Ns+] N]

In isolation, *the heat* would be an N (in fact an Ns), so the same sequence with a further item conjoined to it is also an N; within the co-ordination, *the heat* is not a tagma. As in the case of subordinate clauses, the conjunction is treated as part of the constituent it introduces. Punctuation, for instance comma, between conjuncts is parsed as belonging to the higher tagma.

§ 4.465 A "subordinate conjunct" (that is, each conjunct other than the first element of a co-ordination) is given its normal formtag, including all subcategory symbols that would apply to the form considered in isolation, followed by a plus sign if the conjunct is introduced by a co-ordinating conjunction, or by a minus sign if there is no such conjunction.

§ 4.466 Items in apposition are treated similarly to subordinate conjuncts, but with the symbol "@" in place of a minus sign; for details see §§ 4.500 ff.

§ 4.467 The symbols + – @ (and "&" discussed in § 4.475 below) follow all other characters within a formtag.

§ 4.468 The tagma comprising the entire co-ordination is tagged with the formtag that would be given to the first conjunct considered in isolation, again with all normal subcategory symbols, except that where the main conjunct belongs to a category (N, D, M) which can take the subcategory symbols "s" for "singular" or "p" for "plural", neither of these symbols is applied to the co-ordination unless the main conjunct and all subordinate conjunct(s) would independently be marked as plural, in which case the co-ordination node is given the "p" subcategory.[34] Thus:

---

[34] On Jh in co-ordinations, see the footnote to § 4.201.

to see [N *the moon* [Np+ *or displays of fireworks*]] G05:1010
useful [P *for* [N *the characterization* [Po *of many commercial
materials*] [Np+ *as_well_as_*CC= *theoretical studies*] N] P].
J03:0560
[N *the preparation* [Po *of soft drinks*] [Ns+ *and the* [Tg
processing] [Po *of* [N *milk* [Np+ *and milk products*] N] Po]
Ns+] N] J08:1850
[N *the child,* [Ns– *the dog*], [Ns– *the cat*] <hellip> [Ns+ *and even
the cheese* Ns+] N] N13:1120
[N *none_*PN [Ns+ *or only part*] [Po *of the hospital-care credit
Po*] N] A03:1110
[Np *the turbinates* [Po *of the nose*] [Np+ *and the cilia_*NN2 [Po
of [N *the trachea_*NN1c [Np+ *and larger bronchi_*NN2] N]
Po] Np+] Np] J08:0340
of [Np *the Yankees* [Np+ *and the local National Leaguers*]]
A14:0820
[S *One girl describes* [N *her past,* [Ns– *her succession* [Po *of broken
marriages*] Ns–], [Np– *the abortions she has had* Np–] N] [S+
and finally confesses [Fn *that she loves sex* [Fn+ *and sees no
reason why she must justify her passion* Fn+] Fn] S+] S].
G13:1100
[S *The third belief, in six points, emphasizes* [Ns *the Deity of the
Lord Jesus Christ* Ns], [S+ *and:* — *emphasizes* [N *the Virgin
birth* — [Ns– *the sinless life of Christ* Ns–] — [Np– *His
miracles* Np–] — [Ns– *His substitutionary work on the cross*
Ns–] — [Ns– *His bodily resurrection from the dead* Ns–] —
[Ns+ *and His exaltation to the right hand of God* Ns+] N] S+]
S]. A10:1330 (misprint corrected)
one [Po *of* [Ns [J *at_least_*RR= *equal* [J+ *and* [R *perhaps*] *even
greater* J+] J] *importance* Ns] Po] G02:0660
Tom Lord looked [J *almost insignificant,* [J– *almost contemptible*
J–] J]. N09:0410
No southern novelist has done for Atlanta or Birmingham [Ff *what
Herrick, Dreiser, and Farrell did for Chicago* [Ff+ *or Dos Passos
did for New York* Ff+] Ff] <hellip> G08:1580
Two thieves are crucified with Christ, [Tn *one saved* [Tn+ *and the
other damned* Tn+] Tn]. G12:1090
. . . *a so-called "cone-sphere" apparatus,* [Tg [Ns *the "cone"*] [Vgb
being] [Ns *a 2-liter Erlenmeyer flask*] [Tg+ *and* [Ns *the "sphere*
Ns],*" [Ns *a 2-liter round-bottom flask*] Tg+] Tg]. J09:0860

§ **4.469** The capital-letter category symbol on a subordinate
conjunct will commonly be the same as that on its main conjunct,

but this depends purely on the actual properties of the respective conjuncts; sometimes they will differ:

[R *orally* [P+ *or on paper*]] E24.156
... *of* [Ns *the life* [Tg *pertaining to it,* [Fr+ *or that may be conceived as pertaining to it* Fr+] Tg] Ns]. D14.165
such as [N *intoxication,* [Ns– *possession*], [Tg– *speaking with tongues*], [Ns– *inspiration*], [Ns– *insanity*], [Ns+ *and mystic vision*] N]. G69.162

The rule of § 4.468 against including the "singular" subcategory symbol on a constituent containing a subordinate conjunct applies even when the conjunct is of a category that does not affect the singular interpretation of the referent of the co-ordination:

It is [N *a lonely, rather desolate region,* [Jh+ *but full of legendary and historic associations*] N]. G18:0130
... *had revolved around her* [D *so much* [P+ *and for so long*] *that now he felt* ... D]. N01:0060

§ 4.470 On the occurrence of tagmas beginning with *And, But,* etc. immediately below rootrank nodes, see § 4.283.

§ 4.471 Since the SUSANNE parsing scheme normally avoids innovative or controversial analyses, it will be appropriate to offer a brief defence of its approach to co-ordination. One advantage, from the point of view of gathering statistical information on grammatical phenomena, is that it distinguishes notationally those elements which need to be treated separately while not differentiating elements best counted together. The distribution of a compound tagma of a given category will differ little, if at all, from that of the corresponding simple tagma. Plus and minus signs, on the other hand, mark tagmas which are distinctive both in the environments in which they occur (usually as non-initial ICs of tagmas of the same category) and with respect to their internal structure, since "subordinate conjuncts" are subject to various reduction phenomena (in transformational terms, Co-ordination Reduction and Gapping).

The SUSANNE team would also argue that its treatment of co-ordination is relatively plausible psychologically. The traditional approach, in which each conjunct of a co-ordination is analysed as a separate tagma all equally dominated by a node for the co-ordination itself, implies that, at the outset of a sequence which is destined to be a co-ordination, two separate constituent boundaries are established — despite the fact that the left-hand end of a co-ordination is normally not distinct in any overt way from the left-hand end of the corresponding simple, non-co-ordinate category.[35] From the hearer's point of view the traditional analysis is implausible because the hearer has no way of knowing, when a tagma begins, whether it is destined to be a co-ordination or not; from the speaker's point of view it is implausible because conjuncts which convert a simple into a compound tagma are often in fact afterthoughts, not planned when the tagma was embarked on. From the point of view of abstract analytic elegance the SUSANNE approach has the advantage of reducing structural complexity (co-ordinations are analysed with fewer nodes than on the traditional approach).

GROUPING OF CONJUNCTS

§ 4.472   In a sequence of several conjuncts, when the grammatical and typographical relationship between each conjunct and the one preceding is similar and the meaning of the sequence does not make a different grouping unmistakable, the structure is assumed to group to the right, i.e. to be of the form (as it would be expressed in ordinary logical notation):

$$(X \ \& \ (X \ \& \dots (X \ \& \ X) \dots))$$

Thus:

> [S *It also appears that* $\delta\varepsilon/\delta\alpha$ *increases as* α *increases,* [S+ *but this is only noticeable at the higher values of* <bital> C_J <eital>, [S+ *and for* <bital> C_J <eital> = 4.0, α = 20 deg, $\delta\varepsilon/\delta\alpha$ *is still less than 0.4 at the extended chord-line position* S+] S+] S]. J74.209

§ 4.473   This structure is regarded as the "unmarked" type of co-ordination, invoked when there is no clear evidence for other groupings of constituents. But frequently there is such evidence, either in the meaning of the sequence or from grammar and/or typography. For instance, the common device of including a conjunction before only the last of three or more conjuncts, separating the others by comma only, indicates "flat" co-ordination:

> ... *depends on* [N *the current,* [Ns– *the temperature in the arc column*], [Ns– *the anode material*], [Np+ *and the conditions in the anode sheath*] N]. J02:0290

§ 4.474   Flat co-ordination, in which a compound tagma includes two or more subordinate-conjunct constituents — i.e. (X & X

---

[35] It must be admitted that this same argument could be used against the SUSANNE analysis of genitive constructions, to which no obvious alternative is available.

& ... X) — is common. Less frequent are cases where a "main conjunct" is itself a co-ordination, i.e. the logical structure is:

((X & X) & X)

When this type of co-ordination does occur, the scheme assigns a structure of the form:

[X [X ... [X+ ...]]] [X+ ...]][36]

— that is, this case is treated as an exception to the general rule that the "main conjunct" of a co-ordination is not bracketed off as a separate tagma. It is necessary to make this exception if the parsing scheme is to mark the logical distinction between left-grouped and flat co-ordinations.

§ 4.475 Where the main conjunct belongs to a clause category, a left-grouped co-ordination within it is marked by suffixing the symbol "&" to its formtag; thus, if the outermost "X" in the schematic structure just shown were a clause category, it would be tagged:

[X [X& ... [X+ ...] X&] [X+ ...] X]

In principle it would be desirable to use the "&" notation for *all* cases of left-grouped co-ordination. Unfortunately the need for such a marking was appreciated at too late a stage in the SUSANNE project for it to be practical to make this modification in early releases of the SUSANNE Corpus.

§ 4.476 Examples of left-grouped co-ordination are:

[S [S& *The Australian and I were both wearing insect repellent* [S+ *and were not badly bothered by insects*] S&], [S+ *but my eyes watered ...*] S]. G04:1240

He does not know [Ti? [Ti?& *whether to look up* [Ti?+ *or look aside*] Ti?&], [Ti?– *to put his hands in his pockets* [Ti?+ *or to clench them at his side* Ti?+] Ti?–], [Ti?– *to cross the street,* [Ti?+ *or to continue on the same side* Ti?+] Ti?–] Ti?]. G11:1140

[S [S& *We may diligently observe the Lord's Supper on the first day of the week*], [S– *diligently preach the Gospel*], [S+ *or minister to the saints*] S&]; [S+ *but are we doing it with God Himself ... before us,* [S+ *or are we just ...* S+] S+] S]? D11.033

[S *Above, ... boys sing the ghazals of Hafiz and Saadi,* [Fa [Fa& *while* [P *at the very bottom,* [P@ *in the vaults*], P] *the toughs and blades of the city hoot* [Fa+ *and bang their drums* Fa+]

---

[36] In this generalized example both subordinate conjuncts are shown as "X+", but (depending on the nature of the wording) they may have tags of the form "X–", or "X@".

Fa&], [Fa– *drink arak*], [Fa– *play dice*], [Fa+ *and dance*] Fa]
S]. G05:1290

§ 4.477   A particular grouping of conjuncts may be implied in
the sense of a co-ordination, but it may also or alternatively be
manifested grammatically, for instance by degree of grammatical
reduction. Thus deletion of the subject in the second (but not third)
clause of the G04 example above makes its ((X & X) & X)
structure explicit; compare:

> [S *Arthur heard tell of this* [S+ *and he came into the North* [S+
> *and summoned to him Gwyn son of Nudd* S+] [S+ *and set free
> his noblemen from his prison* S+] S+] [S+ *and peace was made
> between Gwyn son of Nudd and Gwythyr son of Greidawl* S+]
> S]. J62.052
> [S [S& *She'd bought this place by then* [S+ *and had settled in*]
> S&] [S+ *and she asked us to come and see it* S+] S]. L06.099
> [S [S& *Lace became the servant of vanity* [S+ *and lent its rich
> decoration to robes and dresses*] S&] [S+ *and one thinks
> particularly of . . .* S+] S]. E01.022

§ 4.478   The tendency to introduce only the last of a series of subordinate conjuncts by *and* implies that there are two levels of co-
ordination in:

> *an arm which was* [Jh *swollen to enormous proportions* [Tg+ *and
> stinking,* [J+ *gangrenous*]]] N08.083
> [P *such_as* [N [NN1n& *conker* [NN1n– *calf*] [NN1n+ *and
> charcoal*] NN1n&], [N– *rocco* [Ns+ *and Russian violet*] N–]
> N][37] H30.013

§ 4.479   In other cases, variation in conjunctions may suggest a
special grouping, for instance *and* tends to bind conjuncts more tightly
than *but*, implying ((X & X) & (X & X)) structure in:

> [S *Inside, she was* [J [JJ& *untidy* [JJ+ *and grubby*] JJ&] [J+ *but
> roomy enough* [Tn+ *and well lit by two rows of good-sized
> windows* Tn+] J+] J] S]. L07.116

Likewise comma normally binds conjuncts more tightly than semicolon, thus:

---

[37] In these examples some of the co-ordinations are "wordlevel co-ordinations", cf.
§ 4.482 below.

[S *Her legs were* [N *the full, sexy kind,* [Jh– *full bodied like a rare wine* [Jh+ *and just as tantalizing to the appetite* Jh+] Jh–] N]; [S– *the calf was magnificent,* [S– *the ankle perfect* S–] S–] S]. N18:0400

But one common publisher's house style delimits the last conjunct of a flat co-ordination of three or more conjuncts by a conjunction and no punctuation mark, where previous conjuncts were preceded by commas — i.e.: *X, X and X.* And likewise comma-plus-conjunction seems to be equivalent to semicolon-without-conjunction, i.e. there is one flat three-part co-ordination, in:

The normal rise and fall in the Waltz basic amalgamation is: [L *Down as the first step in the bar is taken;* [S*– *commence to rise at the end of this step, as you take the second step*], [S*+ *and then* <bbold> *continue to rise as . . .* S*+] L]. E13.180

§ 4.480   In general, mechanical considerations about the identity of conjunctions or punctuation are not allowed to override the implications of the sense or wider grammatical issues in deciding how a co-ordination is intended to be grouped. For instance, in:

. . . similar workers [P *in* [N *local government,* [Np– *the health services*] N], [P+ *and at other universities*] P]. A14.013

the lack of conjunction before *the health services* might suggest that the entire P is a flat three-conjunct co-ordination, but this would imply an odd turn of phrase in which the preposition was deleted from the second but not the third of a series of conjoined prepositional phrases; rather than postulating such a structure the analysis shown is preferred.

§ 4.481   Where there is choice about how high in a parsetree co-ordination should be treated as occurring, it is made to occur as low as possible. Thus:

[S *I* [Vce *can't agree* [Vce+ *and won't agree*]]].

— although it would be normal for an S+ to be reduced, this sequence will not be parsed as:

[S *I* [Vce *can't agree*] [S+ *and* [Vce *won't agree*]]].

However, punctuation as well as wording is allowed to influence decisions about level of co-ordination; comma between conjuncts suggests co-ordination at a level higher than V, hence:

[S* [Ve *Don't run*], [S*+ *and* [Ve *don't dawdle*]]]!

WORDLEVEL CO-ORDINATION

§ 4.482   The logical conclusion of the principle that co-ordination is treated as occurring as low as possible is that it can occur between words rather than tagmas. The SUSANNE scheme recognizes wordlevel co-ordinations. The formtags for the subordinate conjuncts in a co-ordination of words are formed by adding plus or minus signs to the respective wordtags; the formtag for the entire co-ordination suffixes an ampersand to the wordtag of the first co-ordinated word. Thus:

> *collaboration* [P *between* [NN1u& *management* [NN2+ *and employees*]]] H23.117
>
> [S *I was quite unsympathetic to* [Np *his earlier surrealist figures,* [Tn [Vn [VVNt& *dismembered* [VVNv+ *and reassembled*]] Vn] Tn] Np], . . . S]. C07.134
>
> [Np *the* [ZZ1& *T* +<hyphen> [ZZ1+ *and I*]] +<hyphen> +*figures*] — i.e. *the T- and I-figures* J25.084
>
> . . . *performs the special services of* [Tg [N [NN1n& *tea* +<hyphen> [NN1n+ *and coffee*]] N] +<hyphen> [Vg +*blending*] [Ns+ *and* [NN1u& *cocoa* [NN1n+ *and chocolate*]] *production* Ns+] Tg] *for them.* F41.120

The formtag for a wordlevel co-ordination counts as a wordrank formtag, hence whether or not such a formtag is dominated by a phrasetag is settled in terms of the same rules as apply to individual words; for instance:

> [Ns *a* [JJ& *long* [JJ+ *and arduous*] JJ&] *walk* Ns]

but:

> *the walk was* [J [JJ& *long* [JJ+ *and arduous*] JJ&] J]

§ 4.483   Where a subordinate conjunct in a wordlevel co-ordination is not introduced by a conjunction, the wordtag node for the word will be immediately dominated by a singulary-branching node whose label suffixes a minus sign to the same wordtag:

> *a* [JJ& *careful*_JJ +, [JJ– *uninterrupted*_JJ] JJ&] *report* N07:0720
>
> . . . [Fa+ *or* [R [RR& *suddenly,* [RR– *coolly*] RR&] R] *decide to clobber the Russians* Fa+]? G03:0960
>
> . . . *to* [Ns *some creative writing pursuit* — [N@ [NN1n& *writing,* [NN1n– *painting*], [NN1u– *music*] NN1n&] N@] Ns]. G13:1020
>
> *by* [N *the* [NN1c& *cow* +,_YC [NNc– *sheep*] +,_YC [NN1n+ *and pig*] NN1c&] N] J12:1660

Tags for subordinate wordlevel conjuncts are not used outside co-
ordinations. In:

[O ... [Q ... [S ... *I'm* [J *awfully tired*] S] Q]". O] <minbrk>
[O [S "[Q [J+ *And hungry*] Q]", *he said* S]. ... O] N01:1310

the phrase *And hungry* (uttered by a new speaker) is J+, not JJ+.

§ 4.484 The circumstances in which wordlevel co-ordination is
recognized are narrowly limited. If any conjunct of a co-ordination
belongs to a rank higher than wordrank, then the co-ordination as
a whole is analysed as a co-ordination of tagmas even if most
conjuncts consist of only one word:

through a rite of [N *calisthenics,* [Ns– *dance*], [Ns– *chanted poetry*],
[Ns– *and music*]] G05:0530

(However, an idiom tag is a wordrank formtag, so an idiom can be
a conjunct of a wordlevel co-ordination, e.g.: ... *so many comics
bolted* [P [II& *in* [II+ *and out_of_*II=] II&] *holes* P] *so often*
C04.089.)

§ 4.485 Futhermore, although the tag of a wordlevel co-ordination
is itself of wordrank, a wordlevel co-ordination may not include a
wordlevel co-ordination as a conjunct:

... *the gaps between* [N [NN2& *rulers and subjects*],
[N– [NNL1c& *town and country*]],] *will widen;* ... J22:0030

§ 4.486 The option of wordlevel-co-ordination analysis is not
resorted to where it would do violence to the logical structure of a
co-ordination, for instance in context the complement of *to* in:

to [N *banks,* [N– *insurance*] [Np+ *and pipeline companies*]]
A02:0290

is intended as a flat three-conjunct co-ordination, the second conjunct
of which is a reduced form of *insurance companies* — this would
be contradicted by an analysis in which *insurance and pipeline* was
treated as a wordlevel co-ordination.

§ 4.487 The rule by which an adverbial element may interrupt
another tagma does not extend to interruption of wordlevel co-
ordinations. If a co-ordination is interrupted by an included adverbial, it must be analysed as a co-ordination of tagmas:

He seemed to make no effort [Vi *to speak* [V+ *or* [R *even*] *smile*]].
K06.086 — not [Vi *to* [VV0v& *speak or* [R *even*] *smile*]]
The right to leave legacies [Vdcp *should be* [R *substantially*]
reduced [Vn+ *and* [R *ultimately*] *eliminated* Vn+] Vdcp].
G22:1420

§ **4.488** Various other items which sometimes occur within ordin-ary co-ordinations, e.g. RAc words such as *respectively*, are also not permitted within wordlevel co-ordinations. The only elements which may occur within a wordlevel co-ordination are: the words or idi-oms deemed to be co-ordinated; co-ordinating conjunctions (but not the first element of a "double conjunction", § 4.534 below); punc-tuation marks; and typographical shifts (e.g. [ND1& *North* [ND1+ *<bital> and <eital> South*]] G17:0910). Any sequence which is a co-ordination but which contains at least one item not on this list must be treated as a co-ordination of tagmas:

> ... *of* [N *either_LEe ignorance* [Ns+ *or recklessness*]] D14.050
> ... *being* [M *0.20* [M+ *and 0.35*] *respectively_RAc*] J74.209

§ **4.489** The formtag for a wordlevel co-ordination is always the wordtag of the first co-ordinated word with an ampersand suf-fixed; subsequent conjuncts will often have formtags based on different, sometimes unrelated wordtags:

> [N *all the* [NN2& *bricks* [NN1n+ *and mortar*]] *but not the joists, ...*] R03.107
> *of* [Ns [JJ& *elementary,* [JJ– *secondary*], [JJ– *technical*] [NN1n+ *and university*] JJ&] *education* Ns] J36.062

§ **4.490** For purposes of applying the "singular" and "plural" subcategories to N, D, or M nodes a wordlevel co-ordination tag of the form ...1...& does not count as a singular or plural formtag, though ...2...& does count as a plural formtag:

> *a limited range of* [N [NN1n& *size and distance*] [Po *of the other figure*]] J25.090
> [Np [NN2& *plays, dramas or novels*] [Jh *too long for one evening and therefore continued for a number of weeks*]] J26.093
> ... *over* [Np [NN2& *methods,* [NNc– *means*] [NN2+ *and goals*]]]. A07:1170

§ **4.491** Since the negative particle alone has the wordtag XX, if *or not* conjoined with a word were analysed as a case of wordlevel co-ordination, it would imply a tag XX+ which would be unusual in that it could occur only within a main conjunct having a con-trasting tag. Rather than allowing this, the SUSANNE scheme dis-allows the formtag XX+, and requires any instance of *or not* to be analysed as a reduced phrase or clause:

> ... *he had imagined that,* [J *mad* [J+ *or not*]], *it was the custom of the white man.* K29.069

To me it'd be immaterial [Fn? *whether you'd retaliate* [Fn?+ *or not*]]. K07.095

... is faced at last with the necessity of doing something about it, [Fa *whether he likes it* [Fa+ *or not*]]. A21.132

... but they can hardly deny that, [Tn [Vn *exaggerated* [Vne+ *or not*] Vn] Tn], *the old panorama is dead.* G08:1320

[Fa *Whether* [R *historically*] [Ns *a fact*] [Fa+ *or not*] Fa], *the legend has...* G17:1070

REDUCED CONJUNCTS

§ 4.492 Commonly, the "subordinate conjuncts" in a co-ordination omit elements that can be understood by reference to the main conjunct. Thus plus- or minus-tagged tagmas will often consist of sequences that could not occur, even shorn of their introductory conjunction (if any), other than as subordinate conjuncts within a co-ordination:

[S *The walls were white-washed* [S+ *and* [Ns *the ceiling*] [Jh *innocent of any stain*]]]. P14.141

The latter clause is understood as *the ceiling was innocent of any stain,* by reference to the verb of the main conjunct. When a subordinate conjunct is reduced, it is given the formtag that would be appropriate to the hypothetical complete tagma from which it is deemed to be reduced (with as few elements reconstructed as necessary to yield a complete tagma); plus or minus sign is added as appropriate (and only those lower-case phrase-subcategory symbols are included which are justified by the actual contents of the reduced conjunct). A reduced clause conjunct will (as above) not be form-tagged L just because its verb is understood through co-ordination, and likewise in a co-ordination of main clauses where the V of the subordinate conjunct has its finite verb deleted, leaving a Vg or Vn, the conjunct will be labelled S+ (or S−), not Tg+, Tn+.

§ 4.493 A subordinate conjunct may be analysed as belonging to a given category despite lacking the element which is most essential to that category, outside co-ordination; for instance the essence of a Tg is to contain a Vg, but the Tg+ contains no Vg in:

[S *Three were doubles,* [Tg *Brooks Robinson getting a pair* [Tg+ *and* [Nns *Marv Breeding*] [Ms *one*] Tg+] Tg] S]. A11:0270

Furthermore, not just one but several elements may be "understood" in a subordinate conjunct:

She knew [Fn *that* [Nea *I*] [Vd *expected*] [Nns *John*] [Ti [Vi *to go*] [P *into the Army*]] [Fn+ *and* [Nns *Richard*] [P *into the Church*]]].

— here the minimal expansion of *Richard into the Church* that forms a tagma is *that I expected Richard to go into the Church,* in other words the conjunct quoted must be regarded as a reduced version of this.

Consider the cases:

That was just what she and Ian liked, but not when there was a maniac at large. N21.022

Others, badly wounded, gripped hands in manes, knees in bellies, held on as long as possible and then, weak from ghastly wounds, slipped . . . N04:1620

In the N21 example, the sequence *but not when . . .* is not a subordinate conjunct within a co-ordination of Fa's, and it would be difficult to regard the sequence as an Fa+ (a finite subordinate clause cannot normally begin with *not*, cf. § 4.439); therefore the analysis treats the sequence as a reduction of *but that was not what she and Ian liked when . . .* :

[S *That was just* [Ff *what she and Ian liked*], [S+ *but not*_XX [Fa *when . . .*]]].

In the N04 case, *hands in manes* and *knees in bellies* appear at first sight to form a close two-element co-ordination; but *hands in manes* is not a tagma (*hands* and *in manes* are separate daughters of the *gripped* clause); therefore *knees in bellies* cannot form a co-ordination with *hands in manes*, but rather must be understood as a reduction of *others gripped knees in bellies*, and the whole sequence is a four-element S co-ordination:

[S *Others . . . gripped hands in manes,* [S– [Np *knees*] [P *in bellies*]], [S– *held on as long as possible*] [S+ *and then . . . slipped . . .*]]

A subordinate conjunct is formtagged by reference to an understood element only if the corresponding element is explicitly present in the main conjunct. In:

there were . . . [Np *seven caesium units which were in clinical use,* [M@ *four* [P *in England*] [M+ *and three* [P *in North America*] M+] M@] Np]. J15.154

the phrase *caesium units* is understood in main as well as subordinate conjuncts, so these are tagged M@, M+ rather than Np@, Np+.

§ 4.494 Understood elements affect formtags only in connection with co-ordination. Compare the analysis of:

> ... *run the gamut* [P *from* [Np [J *very high*] [P *to* [J *very low*] P] *standards* Np] P]

— since no co-ordination is involved here, the fact that *standards* is understood after *low* is not invoked in order to tag the complement of *to* as N rather than J. Likewise, in the J15 example quoted in the preceding section, the main conjunct *four in England* is in apposition to the phrase headed by the noun *units* which is understood after *four*, but understood elements in appositional constructions do not influence the formtagging of those constructions.

§ 4.495 There is a presumption in favour of conjuncts of a co-ordination being identically or similarly formtagged. The possibility of labelling conjuncts in ways that reflect understood elements offers an alternative to postulating co-ordinations of grammatically dissimilar elements. For instance, in *Thus Faulkner reminds us, and wisely, that ...* G08:1800, the main conjunct contains no remotely R-like element to which *wisely* can be seen as conjoined, so the phrase is analysed as being all that is left of a reduced clause:

> [S *Thus Faulkner reminds us,* [S+ *and* [R *wisely*]], *that ...*]

Likewise cf.:

> ... [R *so* [Fc *that a line ... would roughly divide the Old South from the new,* [Fc+ *but* [P *with ... minority enclaves*]]]]. G01:1010

— logically the *with* phrase is co-ordinated not with the *from* phrase but with the entire preceding clause, so it is treated as itself an Fc+ reduced to nothing more than conjunction and P.

No hard-and-fast rules can be given to decide between co-ordination at a low level in the parsetree of formally dissimilar elements without postulation of understood material, and co-ordination at a higher level and/or with postulation of understood material of elements formtagged alike. This must depend on the analyst's "feel" for the level at which co-ordination occurs. It is justifiable to postulate a certain amount of understood material, or to represent the co-ordination at a higher level than necessary, if this allows the formtags of the conjoined elements to be much more similar than they would otherwise be. But similarity of formtagging here refers only to formtags which stand for elements that are similar in function. Thus phrases such as [NP1f& *Stella* [PPIS1+ *and I*]] F44.046, [NP1t& *Tucson* [NN1c+ *and Flagstaff*]] are treated as wordlevel co-ordinations rather than co-ordinations of noun phrases — the pairs of wordtags NP1m, PPIS1, and NP1t, NN1c are not very similar as strings of characters, but proper names and pronouns are functionally similar entities, and in the second case both words are functioning as proper names. Likewise, wordlevel co-ordination is recognized in:

> *by* [Np [JJ& *charitable* [JBo+ *and other*]] *organizations*] A11.191
> *of* [N *the* [NN1n& *business* [NN2+ *and policies*]] *of the industry*] H23.116

— the pairs of co-ordinated wordtags (JJ and JBo, NN1n and NN2), while not identical, are similar (both adjectives in one case, both nouns in the other); and the alternative analyses, namely [N *charitable* [N+ *and other*] *organizations*], [N *the business* [Np+ *and policies*] *of the industry*], would imply material understood in the subordinate conjuncts (*organizations, of the industry*) which is large relative to those conjuncts' overt contents.

§ **4.496** The contrast between wordlevel and phraselevel coordination will sometimes mark a logical distinction. Thus

> *a* [J *very* [JJ& *long* [JJ+ *and arduous*]]] *walk*

(in which *very* modifies both adjectives) contrasts with:

> *a* [J *very long* [J+ *and arduous*]] *walk*

(in which *very* modifies only *long*) — the principle of analysing coordination as low as possible implies that the latter analysis will not be used if *long and arduous* is a logical constituent.

§ **4.497** The main conjunct of a co-ordination does not necessarily entirely precede the subordinate conjuncts. Some material from a main conjunct may also occur after the subordinate conjuncts, as in:

> *an upsurge of interest in* [Np *the many formulations* [Np+ *and preventive adaptations*] *of brief treatment in social casework* Np] ... J24:1300
> [N *a limited* [Ns+ *or an all-out*] *war*] A04:1540
> [Tg *time and again stuffing* [Tg+ *and dragging* [P *on*]] *his pipe*] G06:0220
> *in* [Nns [Ns *late 19th* +<hyphen> [J+ *and early 20th* +<hyphen>] +*century*] *Rumania*][38] C09.185

---

[38] There would be no internal constituency in a phrase *late 19th-century*, which is a four-IC noun phrase; cf. § 4.543.

Such co-ordinations are analysed as shown rather than, for instance, as [*a limited* [*or an all-out war*]], [… *stuffing* [*and dragging* [P *on his pipe*]]]. A co-ordination will be analysed in such a way that the main conjunct, containing the first words of the co-ordination, is complete.[39] This will sometimes force a subordinate conjunct into a lower position than daughter within the main conjunct:

> … *neither having* [N *a formal education* [Jh *applicable* [P *to*, [Ns+ *or experience in*], [Tg *manufacturing or selling our type of articles*]]]]. G22:1830
>
> … [Fn *that they were addressed* [P *to* [Fn+ *and spoken* [Po *of*]] [Np *living men*]]] D14.131
>
> [S+ *But the South* [Vzp *is*, [S+ *and* [Vzfb *has been*] [P *for the past century*]], *engaged*] *in* … G08:0270
>
> *who has* [Ns *this special affinity* [P *for* [Fr+ *and* [Vz *champions*] Fr+] [N *the works of Bruckner and Mahler*] P] Ns] G06:1280
>
> *The transient solutions,* [Fr *which show* [Np *deviations* [P *from*, [Np+ *or short-period fluctuations about* Np+], [Np *the "growth equilibrium" paths*] P] Np] Fr], … J46.194 — *about* is not phrasetagged P as one-word daughter of a phrase, even though it is a reduced version of a multi-word P
>
> [S *Their intricately textured and symbolic relief sometimes appears* [J *positive*] [P *on* [Ns *the front*, [S− [J *negative*] [P *on* [N *the back*] P] S−] *surface* Ns] P] S]. C07.142 (the smallest tagma from which *negative on the back* can be seen as reduced is a conjoined main clause)

§ 4.498   Conversely, in some cases a subordinate conjunct may be dislocated to a position where it is not below the main conjunct at all (in these cases the logical-grammar annotation system will show the logical position of the subordinate conjunct, cf. § 5.87) — note that the rules for adding subcategory symbols to main conjuncts (§ 4.468 above) remain in force even if subordinate conjuncts are displaced, thus the *flask* phrase in the N24 example below is N rather than Ns in view of the conjoined Np+:

---

[39] Exceptionally, the grammar of the co-ordination may make this impossible. For instance, consider:

> *by political campaigns being waged* [P *not on* <bital> [Fn? *whether*] <eital> [P+ *but on* [Fn? <bital> *how much* <eital> *social legislation there should be*]]]. G02:0590

— there is no possibility of an analysis in which *whether* opens a well-formed indirect question, because *how much* has influenced the following word-order in a way that is incompatible with *whether*.

Mr. L. Smith ... *said that* [Np *many employed in public service*] *already had three weeks holiday* [Np+ *and* [R *also*] *many white collar workers* ..., *who were winning the day in negotiations with individual firms*]. A27.014

I'll take [N *a flask o' tea*] *wi' me, Mam,* [Np+ *and a few sand-wiches*]. N24.053

Note that [Np *squared lines* [Tg *marking* [N *the top member of the toe*]]] *are needed* [Ns+ *as_well_as the upper extent of the taper*], *and in this case* ... E02.037 — the Ns+ has been extracted from the *member* N

... *artists* [Fr *in whom* [R *only*] [R *recently*] *much interest has been taken,* [P+ *and then mainly by specialists*]]. J63.065

In principle the need to postulate such dislocations could often be avoided by instead analysing the subordinate conjunct as a tagma of a higher level that has been highly reduced: [S *I'll take a flask o' tea wi' me, Mam,* [S+ *and* [Np *a few sandwiches*]]]. But, particularly where the subordinate conjunct is the sort of "heavy" tagma which often is dislocated, the dislocation analysis, which does not require postulation of understood material, is preferred.

§ **4.499**   Sometimes, co-ordination forces a sequence to be treated as a tagma which would not otherwise be regarded as one under the parsing scheme (though this is a last-resort solution to be avoided whenever alternative analyses are available). Thus, consider:

The plot tells of a stone-cutter, Danila, loving a young girl, Katerina, and dissatisfied with his art. C05.100

Without the material from *and* onwards, *a stone-cutter* ... *loving a young girl* ... would be a Tg consisting of three ICs formtagged Ns, Vg, Ns (§ 4.333). On the other hand, without the material from *loving* onwards, the sequence *a stone-cutter dissatisfied with his art* would be [Ns *a stone-cutter* [Tn *dissatisfied* ...]]. To treat everything after *Danila,* as a Tg co-ordinated with a reduced Ns would do violence to the logic of the passage, which correlates two characteristics of the stonecutter. Therefore the most reasonable solution is to treat *loving a young girl* as a tagma, and to parse:

... *tells of* [Ns *a stone-cutter, Danila,* [Tg *loving a young girl, Katerina,* [Tn+ *and dissatisfied with his art*]]].

APPOSITION

§ **4.500**   Appositional elements are treated as postmodifiers and marked by suffixing the symbol "@" to their formtag. In terms of transformational grammar, an appositional element is commonly a relative clause from which everything but a noun phrase has been removed by Whiz Deletion; if any additional constituent (apart from an apposition-introducing word, wordtagged REX) has survived Whiz Deletion, the remains of the relative clause are formtagged as a Z clause rather than as an appositional item. Thus:

[Nns *Aaron McBride*, [Ns@ *field boss for the Highlands Oil & Gas Company*]] N09:0990
... *said* [Nns *Arnold*, [Ns@ *a man who knows the rules*]]. A14:1640
[Nj *The other*, [Ns@ *a shallow concave gradient (*[Iu *Fig. 1*]*)*], Nj] *was produced* ... J09:0850 (misprint corrected)

but e.g.:

[Nns *Aaron McBride*, [Z [R *currently*] [Ns *field boss for* ...] Z] Nns]

§ 4.501 In conformity with the general rule that one-word phrases are not phrasetagged within phrases, one-word appositional elements are not normally given tagmatags and hence are not identified as appositional:

[Nn *Smith and Jones, Florists*] — not [Nn ... [Np@ *Florists*]]

In view of the parallel between the formtag suffixes +, −, and @, and the fact that one-word subordinate conjunct phrases are regularly given minus-sign phrasetags within phrases, this point is with hindsight regrettable; it is hoped that apposition symbols may be applied comprehensively in a future release of the SUSANNE Corpus. If a one-word appositional element is given a tagmatag for some independent reason, e.g. because it is a proper name in apposition to a non-proper name, cf. § 4.140, then the "@" symbol is added to the tagmatag:

[Ns *a young girl*, [Nns@ *Katerina*]] C05.100

In ... *let's you and me go for a walk* ... N13:0030, the object of *let* is analysed as [Nop +'s_PPIO2 [PPY&@ *you* [PPIO1+ *and me*]]].

§ 4.502 An appositional element may precede and/or follow postmodifying elements of other kinds:

[Nns *Rep. Charles E. Hughes* [Po *of Sherman*], [Ns@ *sponsor of the bill*],] *said* ... A02:0270
Liston is [Nns *Bill Liston*, [Ns@ *baseball writer for the Boston Traveler*], [Fr *who quoted Jensen* ... Fr] Nns]. A13:0960

§ 4.503 While the term "apposition" is commonly used for a noun phrase in postmodifying position within a larger noun phrase, the SUSANNE scheme extends the concept and the "@" symbol to constructions involving other types of constituent but which are logically akin, in that the postmodifier in some sense elucidates the antecedent:

> *She thought him* [J *arrogant,* [Tg@ *despising everything not British*]], ... F24.051
> [O *BLWYDDYN NEWYDD DDA I CHWI I GYD (*[L@ *Happy New Year to you all* L@]*).* O] E12.165 — words of Welsh all wordtagged FW directly below the O node
> [S *His voice was* [P *like* [Nj *his black and pin-stripe*], [Ns@ *a grey superimposition of respectability over ... his own natural vowels* Ns@] P], ... S]. R03.097 — the Ns in apposition to the P
> ... *the response is* [Jh *proportional to the incident momentum of the particles,* [Ns@ *a relation deduced from laboratory results linearly extrapolated to meteoritic velocities* Ns@] Jh]. J07:1010

However, a Fn or Ti in postmodifying position within a noun phrase and not separated from the head by punctuation (*the fact that ...*, *his need to ...*), which might be seen as logically comparable to core cases of apposition, is never normally given the "@" suffix (because it would be very difficult to draw a boundary between cases which should and cases which should not have the suffix):

> [Ns *the obvious and frequent statement* [Fn *that science eliminated much of magic and superstition* Fn] Ns] G11:0760
> ... *to* [Ns *the effect* [Fn *that the* <bital> *Mayflower* <eital> *on its second voyage brought a cargo of Negro slaves* Fn] Ns]. G17:1060

Where a comma or other material divides the clause from the preceding noun, the "@" suffix is used:

> [Ns *the fact* [Fr *that Mr. Barnett denies*], *viz.*_REX, [Fn@ *that the mind is "subject to the law of atomic change," and depends* ... Fn@] Ns] D14.085

§ 4.504 Sometimes an appositional element is used as a grammatical peg on which to hang a further complex statement in the guise of a relative clause:

> *The extended family was always present,* [Fr *which helped greatly in the rearing of* [Np *children;* [Np@ *children* [Fr *that were of vital importance ...*] Np@] Np] Fr]. J22.049

— such cases are analysed as appositional, following the surface grammatical relationships, despite the complexity of the appositional element, and despite the punctuation.

§ 4.505 The SUSANNE scheme recognizes no structure of "wordlevel apposition" parallel to wordlevel co-ordination. Thus, in the sequences:

[Ns *a group ('block')* [Po *of villages*] [P *in the Nilokheri area . . .*]] G65.118

[Ns *the excitatory* [Tg [Vg *desynchronizing (alerting)* Vg] Tg] *effect on the EEG* Ns] J17:1410

the words *block, alerting* are attached directly to the higher Ns and Vg nodes respectively, without an intervening @-suffixed node. If the parsing scheme were revised to mark one-word appositional phrasetags below phrasetags, as suggested in § 4.529, *block* and *alerting* would be phrasetagged Ns@ and Vg@.

§ 4.506 Appositional elements tend to be set off from their heads by a comma or comparable punctuation mark. Thus, in:

[Ns [Ns *the French Admiral,* [Nns@ *Jean de Vienne*] Ns] — [N@ *a great sailor* [Ns+ *and an able strategist*] N@] Ns] G01.010

the comma before *Jean* makes it clear that the name is in apposition to *Admiral*; and the fact that the final N co-ordination is preceded by a "larger" punctuation mark than comma, namely the dash, suggests that the co-ordination is in apposition to the material before the dash as a whole, which accordingly is a single left-grouped tagma, cf. the note to § 4.474 (rather than the co-ordination being in apposition to *Jean de Vienne*, i.e. nested within a higher-level appositional item). Brackets surround an appositional element in:

[Ns *His hat (*[Ns@ *the cause of his baldness*]*?)] hung on a hook . . .* [40] N06:0260

Conversely the name is not seen as in apposition to the preceding description in:

of [Nns [Ns *American General*] *Maxwell Taylor,* [Ns@ *brilliant commander of that crack 101st U.S. Airborne Division*]][41] G05.056

---

[40] One might want to say that the appositional tagma here includes the question mark as well as the *cause* Ns, and hence that the apposition should be analysed as Z@ or L@ rather than Ns@. However, a sentence-closing punctuation mark such as the exclamation mark is not treated as a daughter of the clause it closes, so this analysis is not available.

[41] The analysis shown assumes a reading in which the individual is named as *Maxwell Taylor*, and described as an *American General*. The form is in fact ambiguous; if *General Maxwell Taylor* were regarded as the name, and *American* as a description, then there would be no tagma below the Nns and before the Ns@.

— where there is no comma. The presence of a determiner internal to the entire phrase would cause apposition to be postulated in [Ns *his old friend* [Nns@ *the Duke*]]. But no apposition is postulated in:

[Nns *his old friend Van Schaack*] G07:1530
[Nns *that little upstart Winston*] F24.053
[Ns *the interval May 3* [P *to June 19*], *1956*] J01:1570
[Np *the seven unknown deflections* [FOx& Δ_1, Δ_2, +<hellip> +, Δ_7]] J76.017

If the F24 example had read *that little upstart, Winston* the analysis would have been [Ns *that little upstart,* [Nns@ *Winston*]] (since one-word Nn's are recognized within phrases). But in the actual example, without comma, *Winston* is head of the four-word phrase, which is therefore as a whole an Nn and no internal structuring is postulated. In [Nns *Jackson, Mississippi*] no Nn@ tag is given to *Mississippi* because, although appositional, the phrase within which it occurs is itself an Nn (cf. § 4.140). Although, since apposition is not postulated, the head of the J01 example is the date (which in isolation would be tagged N, see § 4.512) and the head of the J77 example is the FOx&, the preceding nouns *interval, deflections* are used to justify the Ns, Np subcategories.

§ 4.507 When a definite description refers to a linguistic form, and consists of an example of that form preceded by *the word, the phrase*, or the like, the linguistic form is regarded as appositional whether or not picked out by inverted commas or italicization. Thus:

[Np+ *and the words* "[Ns@ *special delivery*]" Np+] L18.118
... *use* [Np *the terms* [N@ *'wholesale'* [Ns+ *or 'warehouse'*] N@] Np] *as a customer-catching device.* F41.154

and *wîsheit, Jew, mug* are regarded as single-word appositional elements in:

[Ns *the term* <bital> *wîsheit* <eital>] J35.046
[Ns *the name, "Jew,"*] D11.104
... [Ns *the word mug*] *meant the object which she held* ... G29.112

— though, because of the SUSANNE treatment of one-word appositions (§ 4.501 above), no "@" nodes occur in these latter cases.

§ 4.508 A word or idiom wordtagged REX, or another adverbial element which serves to introduce an apposition, is treated as sister of the appositional element it introduces (unless that element is a clause of a kind which could standardly include a Modality adjunct, § 5.157), thus:

[Np *all perennial weeds, i.e._REX* [Np@ *weeds such as docks, dandelions, . . .*]] E08.113

he reads [Np *mystery stories, in_particular_RR=* [Nns@ *Sir Arthur Conan Doyle*]]. G06:1470

. . . *at the expense of* [Np *the actors, especially_RR* [Nns@ *Currie* [Tg *playing a middle-aged matron with a large lop-sided bosom*]]]. L19.125

But [Np *investigations, notably_RR* [Np@ *those of the Rowntree Trust at Earswick (York), where on a large estate it was found . . .* Np@], Np] *have shown . . .* H22.100

. . . *which satisfy* [Ns *the stricter definition of renal glycosuria, i.e._REX +,* [Ns@ *the constant passage of glucose in the urine . . .*]]. J14.142

. . . *being* [Ns *the deflection* [Po *of* [S *<bital> x <eital> = 0*], *that_is_REX= +,* [P@ *at the load*] Po] Ns]. J76.015

He had been the inventor of [Np *curious gadgets, for_example_REX=* [Ns@ *a new stirrup which was adopted by cavalry regiments*]]. G11.114

but —

[S* *Note that the mass scale is one to two orders of magnitude greater than some previously used;* [S@ *for_example_REX=, Jacchia (1948) derived a scale of . . .* S@] S*]. J07:1540

Because of this rule and the rule (§ 4.501) that one-word appositional elements within phrasetags are not marked, there is no internal structure in the phrase headed by *gold* in:

A system of [Np [Ns *"gold_NN1u"* — *actually yellow* — Ns] *phones* Np] G03:1050

The adjective *yellow* is a one-word appositional phrase, and the adverb *actually* is its one-word sister.

§ 4.509 When a sequence of appositional elements follow one another, there is a (rebuttable) presumption in favour of each being in apposition to the immediately preceding item (cf. § 4.472), rather than two or more being sisters within an earlier item. Cf.:

[Ns *the man at the centre of the crisis,* [Nns@ *Herr Willy Brandt,* [N@ *Mayor of West Berlin* [Ns+ *and a strong candidate for the Chancellorship of Western Germany*]]]] A21.127

However, where it is clear either in terms of grammar and typography or in terms of meaning that appositional elements are to be
understood as sisters, they are parsed as such; cf. the *Jean de Vienne*
example quoted in § 4.506, or:

> [Nns *Almighty God*, [Ns@ *Father of our Lord Jesus Christ*], [Ns@
> *Maker of all things*], [Ns@ *Judge of all men*] Nns] (Book of
> Common Prayer)
> ... *in this language are written* [Nnp *the four Vedas*_NP2x, [Np@
> *the holy writings of the Brahmans*], [Np@ *the oldest literary
> works* [Po *of these people*], [Np@ <bital> *circa* <eital> *10,000
> years*]]]. F19.191

§ **4.510**   Referring expressions consisting of sequences of phrases,
normally comma'd off from one another, in which each names an
element of the one next to it are treated as appositional constructions. Such expressions may proceed from large to small or from
small to large:

> ... *on* [Nns *page 27,* [Nns@ *paragraph 63*],] B09.173
> [Nns <bital> *P.O. Box* <eital> *121,* [M@ <minbrk> *301,* <bital>
> [Nns@ *Glossop Road,* [Nns@ <minbrk> *Sheffield* <eital> *10*
> Nns@] Nns@] M@] Nns][42] B10.221

And the scheme assimilates to this construction phrases such as
those in:

> [Nns *Mr. Godber,* [Nns@ *Minister of State,* [Nns@ *Foreign Office*
>]],] *said earlier* ... A05.115
> [Nns <bbold> [Ot *A Man On The Roof*] <ebold> [Pb *BY
> KATHLEEN SULLY*], [Nns@ *Peter Davies*], [Nu@ *15s.*]]
> C09.189 — the publisher's name and price are sister apposi-
> tional elements
> <minbrk> [Nns —_YD *Elspeth Huxley,* [Nns@ <bital> [Ot [Np
> *The Flame Trees of Thika* Np] Ot] <eital> Nns@] Nns].[43]
> G71.180

§ **4.511**   In a case such as *Mr. Marcus Lipton (Lab., Brixton)*
A27.125 it is arguable that the party and constituency names should
be treated as sisters each in apposition to the personal name, since
party and constituency are independent classifications of members
of parliament; however, it is also possible to see the phrase as meaning

---

[42] The <minbrk> elements marking breaks between address-lines are included within the
lines they introduce by the rule of § 4.419.
[43] The initial dash is included within the Nns by the rule of § 4.419.

that Mr Lipton is a Labour member and, among Labour members, the one for Brixton, so the presumption in favour of right-branching apposition leads to the analysis:

[Nns *Mr. Marcus Lipton (*[N@ *Lab.,* [Nns@ *Brixton*] N@]*)* Nns]

§ 4.512   A special treatment is used for dates. When written in day/month/year order the general rule above would make month + year an appositional element (and year a one-word apposition within that), whereas logically the month/day/year order (where a comma is normally found before the year) would be given some different treatment. To avoid this pointless variation, the SUSANNE scheme simply treats dates containing at least two of the three elements day-of-month number, month name or number, and year number, written in any order, and whether or not including commas, as N's composed of sequences of words without any intermediate structure:

of [N *10 October 1959*], . . . J41.123
starting [N *April 1, 1963*]. A15.045
by [N *May 19*], . . . A07.149
In [N *July 1960*] *the new Group received . . .* H27.179
[N *25.12.1992_MCe*]
[N *27_MCn vii_MCr 1944_MCy*]

This also covers e.g.:

[Ns *the end of the current fiscal year* [N@ *next Aug. 31*]]
   A02:0120
on [N *Nov. 15,* [Ns@ *the same date as . . .*]]. A10:0920

§ 4.513   A day-of-week name or a month name alone is an Nn; and these names are treated as justifying the Nn subcategory for phrases such as:

[Nns *last June*] A14:0910
[Nns *Tuesday night*] A01:0890
[Nns *last Saturday night*] A12:0120
[Nnp *two more Sunday afternoons when the situation will arise*]
   A13:1580

In a date including both day-of-week name and one or more of the three elements day of month, month, and year, the latter are treated as an N in apposition to the Nn:

[Nns *Saturday,* [N@ *Oct. 21*]] A12:1100
[Nns *Saturday afternoon,* [N@ *Jan. 7*]] A20:0600

§ 4.514 Measurements made up of a sequence of pairings of a number with a unit of decreasing size are treated as "flat" co-ordinations rather than as appositional constructions:

[Nup *two pounds* [Nup– *four ounces*]]
[Nu £ +23 [Nu– *18* +s.] [Nu– *9* +d.]] A16.046

The meaning of the whole in cases like these is the quantity comprising the sum of the parts; the logical relationship is quite different from the cases at § 4.517 above.

ASYNDETIC CO-ORDINATION

§ 4.515 Co-ordination includes structures lacking any co-ordinating conjunctions:

> *I felt* [Tn [Vn *exposed*], [J– *unprotected*], [Jh– *somehow afraid of what might happen*]]. N13.134
> [S *I came;* [S– *I saw*]; [S– *I conquered*]].
> ... *widespread contamination of* [Np *kitchens,* [Np– *restaurants*], [Np– *food stores*], [Np– *hospitals*], *etc_RAc Np*].[44] J08:0580
> [S *The former comprise analeptic and psychoactive drugs,* [S– *the latter the tranquilizers* S–] S]. J17:0740
> [S *He wiped his lips with a sleeve,* [S– [Rsw *then*] *stared at Clayton in a childish kind of wonder* S–] S]. N02:0210
> [Fa *If he is the child of nothingness,* [Fa– *if he is the predestined victim of an age of atomic wars* Fa–] Fa], *then* ... G13:0790
> *Was it not possible, after all,* [Fn *that the forest was in league with her and her child* <hellip> [Fn– *that its sympathy lay with the Culvers*] <hellip> [Fn– *that she had erred in failing to understand this* Fn–] Fn]? N08:0590
> ... *suggests* [Fn *that banks when offering personal loans have* [N *no paper work,* [Ns– *no* [Tg [Vg [VVGt& *collecting and recording*]] Tg] *of monthly instalments* Ns–] N] [Fn+ *and do not have to make provision* ...]]. B10.186

(The last example is a special case: probably the writer omitted *and* before *no collecting* ... because he thought of the object of *suggests* as a three-way co-ordination of the type "X, Y, and Z" — it is normal in such a case for a conjunction to appear only before the last conjunct. But it cannot grammatically be analysed as a flat three-way co-ordination, unless it were treated as a co-ordination of

---

[44] A classicist might argue that a co-ordination ending with *etc* cannot be described as lacking a co-ordinating conjunction, but in the SUSANNE scheme *etc* is wordtagged RAc, not CC. ...

Fn's in which the middle conjunct had been reduced all the way down to an object N — the presumption against avoidable postulation of understood material rules this out; if it is a co-ordination of two Fn's in which the first conjunct contains a co-ordination of N's, then the latter is asyndetic.)

§ 4.516 When functionally similar elements occur in sequence there are subtle borderlines between asyndetic co-ordination, apposition, and non-conjoined concatenation. It has proved extremely difficult to find rules which reliably specify predictable and satisfactory choices of analysis in this area.

§ 4.517 In the case of adjectives or other elements in attributive position within a noun phrase, if they are co-ordinated (with or without conjunctions) each is understood as separately modifying the head noun, but when concatenated each is understood as modifying the phrase formed by the following adjective(s) together with the noun. In this situation apposition does not normally occur, and will be recognized only if typographic cues such as brackets make it unmistakable. The distinction between asyndetic co-ordination and concatenation tends to correlate with presence v. absence of commas between the elements; thus, cf.:

[Ns *their* [JJ& *faint,* [NN1u– *silver*]] *light*] M03.023

— meaning light which is both faint and silver, versus:

[Ns *a high_*JJ *positive_*JJ *normal_*JJ *pressure*] J03:0250

— which is most naturally interpreted as "high as positive normal pressures go" rather than as "both high and positive".

Since presence v. absence of intervening punctuation seems to be a fairly good objective indicator of a semantic distinction which is often elusive, in this situation (sequences of attributive elements) the SUSANNE scheme treats the punctuation cue as decisive; thus no co-ordination, only concatenation, is recognized in:

[Np *the grey_*JJ *heady_*JJ *airs* [Po *of Bloomsbury*]] K26.024
[Ns *a concentrated_*JJ *comprehensive_*JJ *survey* [Po *of a life work*]] C01.018

— despite the fact that semantically the paraphrases "grey and heady", "concentrated and comprehensive" might seem reasonable in these cases.

Another case where elements linked by commas will regularly be analysed as co-ordinated is that of postmodifying prepositional phrases; thus the scheme recognizes co-ordination in:

... the dust [Po *of fake security,* [Po– *of the fake friend of the family*]], ... R03.102

but would treat postmodifying P's as concatenated when not separated by punctuation, e.g. in:

the dust [P *on the floor*] [P *by the cooker*]

(assuming that *by the cooker* is not seen as postmodifying *floor*, which in this example is implausible).

§ 4.518 In other cases, for instance with sequences of clause adjuncts, punctuation is little help in drawing the structural distinction because if the sequence is replaced by a single element it will nevertheless often be surrounded by commas. Take for instance the example:

... they could find what they were seeking to the west, at a place called Cale, 'where F25.065

Even were *to the west* missing, there could well be a comma before *at a place ....* . Should this passage be interpreted as "to the west, and furthermore at a place called Cale, ..." (asyndetic co-ordination), as "to the west, more specifically at a place called Cale, ..." (apposition), or should the two indications of place be seen as disconnected concatenated elements, as will often be appropriate when adjuncts fulfil different logical roles? — in a case like:

In Edinburgh, during the winter, the east wind can be bitter.

there is little reason to think of the Place and Time adjuncts as anything other than separate ICs of the clause (and either might be followed by a comma if the other were missing).

When clause ICs fill complement roles such as direct object (§ 5.15), the concatenation solution is not available: the logical annotation system forbids a clause from having more than one complement of any single category (§ 5.18). Thus, in the N13 example quoted in § 4.515, or in the case:

... the god Anubis, represented [P *as a jackal or wolf,* [R *sometimes*] [P– *as a human figure with a jackal's or dog's head* P–] P]. E09.122

the choice lies between seeing the elements following *felt* or *represented* as asyndetically co-ordinated, and seeing the later elements as attached in apposition to their predecessors (so that, in either case, all these elements form a single tagma taking the "predicate complement of subject" functiontag). Co-ordination is semantically a relationship between independent elements, whereas apposition is a construction in which the second element makes the first element clearer or more specific; in these examples the choice goes in favour of co-ordination — in the E09 case representation as a human figure is obviously an alternative to representation as a jackal or wolf, not a more precise description of the same thing,[45] and in the N13 case the three elements following *felt* appear to be independent characterizations of the writer's feeling, not in a general/specific relationship with one another (though it cannot be claimed that the distinction is very clear in this case).

In order to reduce to some extent the number of underdetermined analytic decisions to be made, we can extend to clause adjuncts the approach which is imposed on clause complements by the rule against multiple complements of the same category. There is no SUSANNE rule against a clause containing more than one adjunct of a given category and clauses will often contain, say, two Place adjuncts not adjacent to one another; but we can say that whenever a clause contains a sequence of tagmas which are adjacent (that is, separated by nothing more than punctuation or other elements which may interrupt co-ordinations) and which by the logical-annotation system of Chapter 5 would receive the same functiontag, whether a complement or adjunct tag, then the analysis is required to treat them either as co-ordinated or as linked appositionally (unless in a particular case it is clear that both of these analyses are semantically unreasonable). It will often be easier to make the distinction between co-ordination and apposition in terms of semantics than to find semantic grounds for choosing between either of these analyses and concatenation.

Thus, in the F25 example above, *at a place called Cale...* manifestly makes the preceding general phrase *to the west* more precise, hence this example will be analysed as an appositional construction:

> ... *they could find what they were seeking* [P *to the west,* [P@ *at a place called Cale, 'where* ... P@] P]. F25.065

Likewise *no farther* specifies *down to* ..., both being Place adjuncts, in:

> *A saw cut is made at the upper toe line* [R *exactly*] [P *down to the taper line,* [R@ *no farther* R@] P]. E02.040

On the other hand the relationship between successive Direction adjuncts is clearly one of co-ordination rather than specification in:

---

[45] On the treatment of *sometimes* in this example see §§ 5.118 ff.

[S *His eyes flicked* ... [P *to the rank badges on his right sleeve,* [Rsw *then*] [P– *back* [R *again*] *to his rifle bolt* P–] P] S]. N19.192 — *back* included within the P– in accordance with § 4.246, *again* an included adverbial

And cf. the co-ordinated Absolute adjuncts (§§ 5.187 ff.) in:

[S [L *Demure one moment,* [L– *hard and decisive the next* L–] L], *she caught* ... S]. C01.016

[S [Jh *MORE mature than either,* [P– *with a certainty of architectonic design still denied to Brown* P–] Jh], *F.E. McWilliam held me longest* ... S]. C07.132

... *drawled a journalist,* [Tg *his elbows sprawling over the canteen table,* [Tg– *his pencil doodling among his shorthand notes* Tg–] Tg]. M02.014

When clause ICs would take different functiontags (e.g. the example quoted in § 4.14 above, which begins with Contingency and Time adjuncts), or in the case of sequences of modifying elements within phrases other than the cases discussed earlier of attributive elements and postmodifying prepositional phrases, the presumption will be in favour of concatenation unless there is clear evidence implying apposition or co-ordination (for instance, brackets are often used to indicate apposition, and of course a co-ordinating conjunction requires an analysis in terms of co-ordination irrespective of the properties of the elements co-ordinated — cf. § 5.107). Thus sequences of relative clauses will normally be analysed as concatenated; or consider:

she was [Ns *the same girl, miserable*_JJ, *shy*_JJ, [Fr *who had sat at* ...]] P02.022 — not [JJ& *miserable, shy*], nor [J *miserable,* [J– *shy*], [Fr– *who* ...]]

§ 4.519   The foregoing is one of the most difficult areas of the SUSANNE scheme; unfortunately, it is certainly not the case either that the rules given here yield a definite solution for every authentic example, or that current releases of the Corpus always conform to the rules where their implications are clear.

§ 4.520   Clauses introduced by Rs adverbs (cf. § 4.231) are in some ways intermediate between subordinate and co-ordinate clauses (cf. *GCE*, p. 555). Semantically they resemble Fa's, but they resemble co-ordinate clauses in being incapable of preceding the clause to which they are attached, and in permitting elision of a shared subject. They are sometimes prefixed by a co-ordinating conjunction. The SUSANNE scheme treats clauses introduced by Rs adverbs as subordinate conjuncts:

He missed the 1955 season because of an operation on the ailing knee, [S– [Rsw then] played 77 minutes in 1956 S–]. A12:0330

[S [S& There is one exception . . . , [S+ and that is that fluids can relax by flowing into fields of lower rates of shear S+] S&], [S– [Rs so] the statement should be modified . . . S–] S]. J03:0980

"[Q [S As an independent American I considered all who were not for us . . . as against us, [S*– [Rs yet] be assured that . . . S*–] S] Q]". G07:1555

[S We must believe we have the ability to affect our own destinies: [S?– [Rs otherwise] why try anything S?–] S]? G22:0260

[S The times were discouraging [S+ and [Rs yet] at Southam . . . an Allotments Association had been successful . . . S+] S]. G11.077

If a clause introduced by an Rs is the main clause of a typographically independent sentence, however, it is not artificially treated as conjoined to a preceding sentence:

[S Say the power-drill makers, [Fn 75 per cent of major breakdowns can be traced to neglect of the carbon-brush gear Fn] S].
[S [Rs So] it pays to carry out regular inspection . . .]. E03.047
<minbrk> [O [L [Rs So] to this year's European Championships, when Poland omitted some of their stars in favour of younger men L]. O] <minbrk> [O [S [Rs Yet] they didn't . . .]. . . . O] E17.048

[S We are already committed to establishing man's supremacy over nature and everywhere on earth, not merely in the limited social-political-economical context we are fond of today S]. [S [Rs Otherwise], we go on endlessly trying to draw the line, . . . S]. G22:0190

§ 4.521   An issue arises with the American number construction exemplified by *conducted one hundred fifty concerts* G06:0080, where British usage requires *and* between the *hundred* and the lower figure (and American usage has this as an optional alternative, e.g. *conduct only* [M *one hundred* [M+ *and twenty*]] *concerts* G06:0130). Since the latter phrase is analysed as shown, strict logic might suggest that in the previous turn of phrase without *and*, the word *fifty* should be analysed as an M– phrase. However, since a number of the pattern *one hundred fifty* does not standardly contain even a comma to suggest co-ordination, it is in fact treated as one three-IC M phrase, without internal tagmatagging. (On the other hand, a phrase such as [M *two thousand,* [M– *one hundred fifty*]] would be analysed as shown, since this numeral construction usually does include a comma.)

CHANGES OF TACK, AND REPEATED CONSTITUENTS

§ 4.522 In informal dialogue we sometimes find cases where a
clause or smaller construction is interrupted and the speaker says
something which grammatically does not continue the material before
the interruption; often this is indicated typographically by a dash.
In general the SUSANNE scheme parses the "new" sequence as in
apposition to the "broken-off" sequence, as in:

> ... [Fa *when I* — [S?@ *what is it*]]?

§ 4.523 A frequent case is that the break precedes a repetition
just of the last word, sometimes representing the speaker overcome
by emotion, and here the repeated unit will be in apposition to the
phrase consisting of or containing that word (and if the repeated
unit is only one word, the result is that an appositional phrase node
will normally not be created):

> "[S [Nea *I* — *I*] *just wanted* — [S@ *people sometimes like to be
> alone together* — *please*_UH [S*@ *try to understand*]]]."
> P14.145
> "[Q [Ny" *You* — [Ny@ *you polecat*]]*!* Q]" *she screeched*, ...
> L01.114
> "[Q *Well,* [S? *what do you do nights,* ...]? [Ns *The secret life
> of* [Nns *Matthew Helm*] <hellip> [Nns@ *Helm*]]? Q]" *she said.*
> N15.151

In the N15 example, the name is repeated after the ellipsis mark because the speaker is about to query it. The second *Helm* is in apposition to the *secret life* Ns — it is not attached to the Nns *Matthew
Helm*, because the second, questioning *Helm* represents a change of
tack from the entire *secret life* Ns, uttered in assertive mode.

§ 4.524 The item before the interruption to which the following
material is placed in apposition must be a tagma; thus in:

> ... *he* [Vdfp *had been 'convulsed,* [Vn@ [R *absolutely*] *con-
> vulsed* Vn@] Vdfp] *with grief'.* G07.076
> [Fa *If* <hellip> [Fa@ <bital> *if* <eital> *they're Japs* Fa@] Fa].
> N15:1140

one might be inclined to see *absolutely convulsed* as attached to the
single word *convulsed* in the G07 example, and the italicized *if* as
the only word needing to be analysed as appositional in the N15
example; but the lowest tagma node to which *absolutely convulsed*
can be attached is the Vdfp node, and since subordinating conjunctions have no phrasetags the second example can only be treated as
an Fa in apposition to a broken-off Fa.

When apposition is used to represent spoken interruption in this way, the presumption is that the sequence in apposition is more likely to be complete than the material to which it is attached (unlike the practice in the case of co-ordination, § 4.497). Thus the N15 example is analysed as shown, rather than with the second *if* as a one-word Fa@ embedded within a complete Fa.

§ 4.525 A different sort of repetition (often using a pronoun rather than echoing the original phrase, and sometimes separated by a comma rather than a dash) occurs when a speaker establishes a topic and then goes on to make a grammatically complete comment about the topic. Here the comment sequence (commonly an S) is treated as appositional to the topic phrase (commonly an N); nothing in the analysis shows the logical relationship between the topic and the phrase within the comment sequence that refers back to the topic. (As stated in Chapter 1, the SUSANNE scheme does not in general mark co-reference.) Thus:

"[Ns *This girl you have been telling me about* — [S@ *she is the one <hellip>*]]?" P15.155
[Nns *Sharon,* [S@ *she's cooked in a restaurant*]]. N01:1110
<minbrk> [Ns '[Q *Mon ami Packe,* Q]' [S@ *the phrase recurs throughout the writings of Count Henri Patrick Marie Russell-Killough* S@] Ns]. G33.159 — since it has a clause in apposition to it, the Q tagma heads an Ns as discussed in § 4.411
[Ti *To find a form that accommodates the mess,* [S@ *that is the task of the artist now* S@] Ti]". G12:0830
[Np *The relations* — [S! *you know*] — [S@ *they want to know where ...*]]. K10.127
[N [N *Water,* [Ns– *air*], [Ns– *fruit*], [Ns– *poetry*], [Ns– *music*], [Ns– *the human form*] N] — [S@ *these things are important ...*] N]. G05:0620

SENTENTIAL APPOSITION

§ 4.526 There is a construction — commonly, but by no means invariably, marked by colon or dash — in which a clause is followed by a tagma which in some sense redeems an IOU issued by the clause. In such cases the latter tagma is treated as appositional to the clause:

[S *As the New South snowballs toward further urbanization, it becomes more and more homogeneous with the North* — [Ns@ *a tendency which Willard Thorp terms "Yankeefication", as evidenced ...* Ns@] S]. G08:0330

[S *One thing was certain* — [S@ *his method was effective* ...]].
N11:1520

[S *It took me a moment to realize what was odd about that
panel:* [S@ *there was a gimbaled compass welded to it,* ... S@]
S]. G04:0860

In the following example:

[S *The Constitution of the Southern "Confederation" differed
from that of the Federal Union only in two important respects:*
[S@ *It openly, defiantly, recognized slavery* — *an institution
which the Southerners of 1787* ... *found so impossible to
reconcile with freedom that they carefully avoided mentioning
the word in the Federal Constitution* S@] S]. [S *They recognized that slavery was a moral issue* <sentence continues for
five lines> S]. [S *The other important difference between the
two Constitutions was* ... S]. G10:0690

— logically speaking both the *recognized* clause and the later sentence beginning *The other* jointly redeem the IOU issued by ...
differed ... *in two important respects*; but the former alone can
reasonably be taken as *grammatically* subordinate to the *differed*
clause, so the analysis is as shown.

§ 4.527 Where an indirect question is followed by its own answer, the answer is treated as in apposition to the clause introducing the indirect question, as in:

[S *There was* [Ns *no doubt* [Fn? *where they had gone*] Ns], [R@
downstream, [P@ *to Sheila's home* ... P@] R@] S]. K17.064

[S *This confession serves* [Ti *to make clear in part* [Fn? *what is
behind this sexual revolution* Fn?]: [N@ *the craving for sen-
sation* ... N@] Ti] S]. G13:1180

— the appositional elements are subordinated to the S and to the
Ti respectively, rather than to the Fn?'s.

§ 4.528 On the other hand the concept of sentential apposition
does not apply when the material following the colon is a dislocated
element which is logically part of an earlier tagma, as in the E26
example quoted in § 4.421 above, where the *salt* ... sequence has
been extracted from a logical position in apposition to *the following
things*, and will be marked as such by the logical-annotation system
of Chapter 5.

§ 4.529 When the tagma in "sentential apposition" is itself a
clause, there is a subtle distinction between this construction and
sentential co-ordination, which is frequently marked by semicolon
rather than co-ordinating conjunction. Compare:

[S *Then she told me what I had feared:* [S@ *we were trapped*]].

with:

[S *Then she told me what I had feared;* [S– *my heart sank*]].

Commonly, sentential apposition is marked by colon or dash, while sentential co-ordination is marked by comma or semicolon; and this orthographic difference can be used as a diagnostic if the semantic relationship is unclear. (Also, if the latter sequence omits elements which are recoverable by comparison with the former sequence, this again points towards co-ordination rather than sentential apposition; however, Co-ordination Reduction and Gapping are not common when clauses are linked by punctuation of higher rank than comma.) Thus the dash is taken as diagnostic of apposition rather than co-ordination in:

[S *So too are the merry jingles, nursery rhymes, limericks and sing-song skipping snatches* — [S@ *these by their very beat or homely humour are quickly memorised*]]. E24.148

But in some cases this orthographic regularity will be clearly violated and then the scheme parses according to meaning rather than punctuation. For instance, where semicolons link statement with question or question with imperative, a co-ordinate analysis is semantically unreasonable:

[S* *Take the colour of the eye and the colour of the hair;* [S?@ *how does he account for* ... S?@] S*]? D14.056

"[S *He killed Tom* — [S?@ *do you understand that* S?@] S]"? N02:1300

And an appositional rather than co-ordinate analysis is semantically more appropriate despite semicolon in:

[S+ *or maybe she liked men old enough to be her father;* [S@ *some women with father fixations do*]]. N18:0770

Conversely, the semantic relationship seems to be co-ordination rather than "redemption of IOU", despite the colon, in:

[S *This was brought about only to a limited extent by closing pits:* [S– *mainly, it appears, by the closing of uneconomic seams within mines*]]. J42.140

§ 4.530 Although a verbless subordinate conjunct clause in a compound S will be formtagged S+ or S– rather than L (that is, the lack of verb will be treated as a consequence of co-ordination reduction rather than as inherent to the clause), there is no objection to an L in sentential apposition:

[S+ *But there were three deaths from diphtheria* — [L@ [N *none*]
[P *in the previous period*]]]. A13.228
[S *Everything is splendid* — [L@ [R *never*] [R *better*]]]. K05.066

§ 4.531 A quotation which is introduced via a clause that does
not contain a verb of quoting is analysed as Q@:

[S *He swung round to the other men* — "[Q@ [S *We can catch*
him easy]! [S *There are plenty of fresh horses . . .*]. . . . Q@]"
S]. N02:1240

§ 4.532 Sentential apposition may be medial rather than final in
the higher clause. The L must be in apposition to the higher S as
a whole, rather than just to the N *a big kick*, because it contains
clause ICs other than the verb object, in:

[S *Although he never gets to play while the clock is running, he*
gets [Ns *a big kick*] — [L@ [Dp *several*] [Nns *every Saturday*],
[R *in fact*]] — [P *out_of football*]]. A12:0040

CO-ORDINATION-CLOSING ELEMENTS

§ 4.533 Elements such as *respectively, etc* (wordtagged RAc) are
treated as daughters of the co-ordinations they terminate. (Since a
wordlevel co-ordination may not include an adverb, it follows that
co-ordinations of single words closed by an RAc word must be
parsed as phraselevel co-ordination.)

. . . *pieces of* [N *string,* [Ns– *paper*], *etc*], . . . J23.069
— *by* [Nn [Ot *Gay Light* Ot] [Nns+ *and* [Ot *Erin's Pride* Ot] Nns+]
respectively Nn] A23.152 (the Ot's are racehorse names)
. . . *to manifest themselves in* [N *paint,* [Ns– *clay*], *etc.*], *with a*
maximum of freedom . . . G47.118
. . . *charge up to* [Nup $VC_2/(C_1+C_2)$ [N+ *and* $VC_1/(C_1+C_2)$] *volts*
respectively] J69.148 — the use of *respectively* means that the
co-ordination cannot be a wordlevel FOx& construction; since
and $VC_1/(C_1+C_2)$ must be treated as an N+ in any case, and
such a tagma will standardly be grammatically reduced, it is
better, as here, to treat the phrase as reduced from *and* $VC_1/$
(C_1+C_2) *volts* than to treat $VC_2/(C_1+C_2)$ *and* $VC_1/(C_1+C_2)$ as an
N co-ordination premodifying *volts*, which would require *re-*
spectively to be analysed as dislocated out of the co-ordination
. . . *being* [M 0.20 [M+ *and* 0.35] *respectively*]. J74.209
. . . *for* [Nn *England* [Nns+ *and* Scotland] *respectively*], . . .
F41.105

DOUBLE CONJUNCTIONS

§ 4.534 "Double conjunctions" are pairs of words such as *either
... or ... , both ... and ...* , the first of which has an LE... wordtag
(except in the case of *not ... but ...* , see below). Provided an
LE... word is contiguous to the co-ordination it introduces, it is
parsed as a daughter of the main conjunct. (For cases where the first
conjunction has been moved elsewhere, see §§ 5.87, 5.111.)

[Nn *Neither Miss Charlotte* [Nns+ *nor Gregory*]] *were welcome
... P11.112*

... the total destruction of [Ns *music,* [N *both manuscript* [Tn+
and printed]],] *...* J68.148

at [Np *five castles,* [Tn *either built by Edward I,* [Tn– *occupied
by the English for a limited period*], [Fr+ *or where the deposits
are related to building periods of the structure*] Tn] Np].[46]
J67.133

in [Ns *this hour* [Po *both of "national peril"* [Po+ *and of "national
opportunity"*]]] G07:0050

... [Fa *for not_only_LE= did they ensure continuity ...* , [Fa+ *but
they were also economically profitable, ...*]]. J22.051

[S *He not_only_LE= felt his need of her* [S+ *but was equally aware
of ...*]]. L04.064

... that they [Vc *will either_LEe modernize* [V+ *or democratize*] Vc] *their societies.*[47] J22:0690 (misprint corrected)

§ 4.535 Although *not* is always wordtagged XX rather than
LE..., the double conjunction *not ... but ...* (with *but* translating
German *sondern* rather than *aber*) is analysed like other double
conjunctions whenever *not* is in construction with the main conjunct;
see the examples at § 4.106 above, or:

... to meet [Np *Russians* ([N@ *not intellectuals,* [N+ *but common folk*]]) *who took a contrary view*]. A26.054

... most of them have bathed [R *before*], [R *not once* [Np+ *but
ten times*]], [P *within the last half-hour*]. E15.152

... it bears [Ns *the imprint* [Po *not,* [A *as the blurb says*], *of major
literature,* [Po+ *but of a major* <bital> *littérateur* <eital>] Po]
Ns]. C09.176 — the A a propositional relative, § 5.198

---

[46] The logic of the co-ordination is as shown, although in good style the word *either*
should not introduce a three-way co-ordination.

[47] Here *modernize or democratize* cannot be analysed as wordlevel co-ordination: if it
were, *either* would be adjacent to the co-ordination and by the above rule should be included
within it, but by § 4.488 *either* may not be included within a wordlevel co-ordination.

... that he should come back [J [J *not voluble* [J+ *but silent*] J],
[J– *not beautiful* [Tn+ *but defaced*] J–], [P– *not in obloquy*
[W+ *but with his praises ringing* W+] P–] J]*!* G07.072

However, if *not* is adjacent to a sequence of verbs with which it
forms a normal Ve phrase it will be included in such a phrase, and
in such cases it is not regarded as having been dislocated from the
main conjunct which logically it introduces:

... these branches of knowledge [Vwep *were not appraised*]
[R [RR& *objectively,* [RR+ *but socially*]]]. J35.043
... the majority [Vde *did not come*] [P *from Warminster itself*
[P+ *but from Maiden Bradley and Mere*]]. J11.100
... it [Vzeb *is not*] [Ns *the Old Country*] [Fr *on which they model
themselves*], [Nns+ *but the New Jones*]. R01.070
He says life [Vzeb *is not*] [N *the <bital> result <eital> of organisation,* [Ns+ *but a principle that operates through organisation*]]. D14.103
Beethoven [Vde *did not say*] [Fn *that Handel was* [N *the greatest
<bital> Künstler <eital>* [Ns+ *but the greatest <bital> Komponist
<eital>*] [Fr *that had lived*]] Fn],... G42.062

And the *not* of a *not ... but ...* construction will also not be regarded as part of the co-ordination, at surface or logical analytic
levels, if it modifies an adverbial (other than *only — not_only* is
recognized as an LE= idiom):

to be treated [R *not just*] [R *descriptively,* [P+ *but in ways which
produce criticism ...*]] G60.013
[L [R:m *Not* 210] [N:e *a breeze* [R:G210 *exactly*], [Ns+:211 *but
a pocket of icy air that* s211 *settled ...*] N:e] L]. N08:1370

The annotation of the N08 example is given in full, including logical
notations which show among other things that *Not exactly* groups
as a tagma at the logical level, with *exactly* displaced into the N
tagma [*a breeze ... but a pocket ...*]. This latter example should
be contrasted with:

[Ns:o123 *a vision* [Po *of life*] [Z s123 m125 [Jh:e *not* [R:G125
indeed] *identical with his* [Jh+ *but somewhat comparable in
scope* Jh+] Jh:e] Z] Ns:o123] G34.165

— where *not indeed* is not an adverbial phrase in which *not* modifies
indeed: the modification relationship is the other way round, *indeed*
applies to the negated sequence *not ... identical with ...* , so *indeed*
is treated as logically a sister of the J co-ordination beginning with
not (as indicated by the 125 indices).

§ 4.536 A double conjunction with *but* as second element may on occasion have a negative word other than *not* or *not_only* as first element:

> ... [Fa *because according to the theory the body* [Vzb *is*] [R *never*] [J *alive*], [Fa+ *but only* [Vn *inhabited*] [Pb *by the real invisible man*, ...]]]. D14.173

In such cases, where the "pre-co-ordinator" is not an LE. . . or XX word, it is parsed as it would be if no co-ordination were involved, for instance in a case where *never* was adjacent to the main conjunct it would not be joined to it as its daughter.

§ 4.537 However, even in such a case the parsing of the conjuncts may be affected. Double conjunctions require a co-ordination to be analysed as two-way, so that if there are more than two conjuncts the analysis must postulate co-ordination of co-ordinate tagmas:

> *And he could no longer think* [Po [Po *of face-saving*, [Po– *of honor*]], [Po+ *but only of escape*] Po]. N09:1500

§ 4.538 Sequences of the form *not X but Y* do not invariably represent double conjunctions. In the following example, *but* would translate into German as *aber*, not as *sondern*. However, the parsing is no different in this case from what it would have been if the construction were a case of true double conjunctions; *not* is part of the P, not because it is a pre-co-ordinator, but because *not* in general standardly groups together with the item following it (§ 4.437):

> [Np *Londoners* [P *not in* [Ns *housing need*], [Fr+ *but whose departure from London may be assumed to release accommodation there* Fr+], P] Np] H07.189

The Analysis of Hyphenations

§ 4.539 Most hyphenated words are divided by the SUSANNE scheme into separately tagged units, as discussed in §§ 2.36 ff. This has the advantage that a hyphen can be shown as linking items some of which may be tagmas with internal word-spaces, as in:

> *data for* [Ns *a* [Ns *force* +<hyphen> [Ns +*rate of shear*] Ns] *graph* Ns] *can be obtained.* J03:0100
>
> [Nns *the* [Nns *Class* +<hyphen> +*D*] [Nns [Nns *New York*] +<hyphen> +*Pennsylvania* Nns] *League* Nns] A11:1060

and internal structure can be recognized within a hyphenated sequence, as in:

the [Ns [M *2* +\<hyphen> +*score*] +\<hyphen> +*year*] *milestone*
A13:1100

a [Tn *sealed*] [J [Ns *X* +\<hyphen> +*ray*] +\<hyphen>
+*proof*_FA J] *"unique device"* G03:1590

§ 4.540 Often, the function of hyphenation in English is to link
two or more words into a unit which as a whole functions like a
single word rather than a phrase. The form *X-ray-proof* in the G03
example above, for instance, could readily be replaced by an individual adjective but hardly by an adjective phrase consisting of
more than one typographic word. Likewise, in *at* [Np [N *oil-water*]
interfaces] J05:1470 the hyphenation *oil-water* might be replaced
by a single noun but not by a normal noun phrase beginning with
a determiner. However, since these hyphenations are by the rules of
§§ 2.36 ff. multi-word tagmas, they are given tagmatags rather than
wordtags: *X-ray-proof* is tagged J, *oil-water* is tagged Ns.[48] The
tagmatag is chosen in terms of the categories of the words hyphenated: the reason for hyphenating *oil-water* is to create a form
suitable to act as a noun premodifier, so that functionally *oil-water*
is arguably more like an adjective than a noun, but it consists of
nouns and is therefore tagged as a noun phrase.

This can lead to unusual grammatical configurations, particularly
when the head word of a hyphenation is a verb. For instance, in:

[Nas *He*] [Vd *side*_NN1n +\<hyphen>_YH +*stepped*_VVDv Vd]
[Ns *her blow*] . . . N05:0960

a noun + verb combination *side-step* is converted by hyphenation
into the equivalent of a unitary verb; the SUSANNE analysis includes the noun as a daughter of the verb group.

§ 4.541 Hyphenations differ in the extent to which they have
grammatical force. In *the 2-score-year milestone* the hyphens serve
merely to mark the fact that the words they link form a tagma
within the larger tagma headed by *milestone*; one could not replace
the hyphens by alphabetic words. In *the Mason-Dixon line* the
hyphens might be seen as standing for *and*. In:

one that beat Anson, 3-0, in a 1953 district game A12:0270

the hyphen has a prepositional force — it might be replaced by *to*;
and in the *force-rate of shear* example above the hyphen could again
be seen as prepositional, though a likelier explicit translation would

---

[48] The SUSANNE team experimented with the concept of adding a suffix to wordtags to
form tagmatags meaning "hyphenated word grammatically equivalent to a single word of
class X", but this proved to create larger analytic problems than the approach described here.

be *against*. Often, it is difficult to specify which of these roles a hyphen should be seen as playing. In *The September-October term jury* A01:0070 the hyphen could be translated as either *to* or *and*. In:

> *whether they prefer* [N *the* [M 6-3-3 ([Ns@ *junior high school*]) M] *system* [Ns+ *or the* [M 8-4] *system* Ns+] N]. A10:0890

the hyphens could reasonably either be translated *and* or regarded as merely devices linking elements of tagmas.

Because of these indeterminacies, the SUSANNE scheme does not recognize structure internal to hyphenated sequences except where the nature of the words implies structure independent of the hyphenation. Thus *the 2-score-year milestone* is analysed as shown in § 4.539, because the sequence of words would have that structure whether or not the hyphens were included — the hyphens merely make it easier for the reader to work out the writer's intended logic. But where a hyphen arguably represents a preposition or a conjunction, it is not treated as initiating a P or . . .+ tagma:

> [Ns *the experimentally determined* [Nns *Curie* +<hyphen> +*Weiss*] *constant*] J04:0110
> *a* [Tg [Vg *stabilizing* +<hyphen> +*conserving*]] *function* J23:1780
> *one that beat Anson,* [M 3 +<hyphen> +0], *in* . . .
> [Ns *The* [Ns [Nns *September* +<hyphen> +*October*] *term*] *jury*]
> *the* [M 6 +<hyphen> +3 +<hyphen> +3 ([Ns@ *junior high school*]) M] *system*
> (*see* [Nnp *pp.* [M 1746 +<hyphen> +1748 M] Nnp]) J05:1780
> *This links with* [Np [G *the company's*] *Caravelle schedules* [Nns *London* +<hyphen> +*Brussels* [L+ *and* [R *onwards*] [P *from Athens*] [P *to various points in the Middle East*] L+] Nns] Np]. E21.111 — *where* London-Brussels *stands for* London *to* Brussels

and even (where the interpretation of hyphen as *to* is unmistakable):

> *to spend* [Np [P *from* [M 6 +<hyphen> +12] P] *months* Np] *as apprentices* A10:1730

In these cases the hyphen is intrinsic to the grammar, that is the words would not form normal tagmas if written with spaces instead of hyphens: in such cases the tagmatag for the hyphenation is made to depend on the head word of the hyphenation (the first word, if the hyphenation represents *and* or a preposition), thus *Curie-Weiss* is an Nns because *Curie* alone would be an Nns, *1746-1748* is an M because *1746* alone, if phrasetagged, would be an M, etc. (If the hyphen in *Curie-Weiss* were replaced by *and*, the entire co-ordination would not be given the Ns subcategory, cf. § 4.173; but no such rule applies when a hyphen occurs instead of *and*.)

Where hyphens link prefixes or suffixes to stems, the hyphens are "non-intrinsic" (a prefix or suffix implies structure independently of typographic symbolization of that structure by a hyphen), and the hyphenated sequence is formtagged in terms of the grammatical nature of the sequence — thus the emphasized subsequence in *an inter-species comparison* J12:0580 is tagmatagged P, even though *inter* as a prefix is wordtagged FB rather than II (§ 3.16).

§ 4.542   When the dash is used to link words, it is always grammatically intrinsic (that is, it functions similarly to the hyphen of *beat Anson, 3-0* rather than to the hyphens of *the 2-score-year milestone*), therefore words linked by dashes are similarly analysed as lacking internal structure: [Nns *the* [M *1939* +— +*45*] *War*] is not treated as containing [+— +*45*] as a tagma. The solidus, on the other hand, tends to be used with more specific grammatical force than hyphen or dash, and is therefore given contrasting wordtags in different grammatical functions (see the footnote to tag IIp in § 3.73, and see § 4.238); when wordtagged IIp or CC the solidus is analysed as introducing a P or . . .+ tagma respectively, like alphabetic prepositions or conjunctions, but when wordtagged YD it is analysed in the same way as a dash or a "grammatically intrinsic" hyphen.

§ 4.543   When "non-intrinsic" hyphens are used to show that a sequence of words coheres tightly with respect to the surrounding wording, the hyphenation need not be treated as a SUSANNE tagma if the principle of § 4.9 about ICs of a construction grouping towards the head would imply such tight coherence in any case. Thus, in *a regular "Hoe-Down"* N13:0700 that principle implies that *Hoe*_NN1c and *Down*_RP cohere more closely than the pair of words do with *regular* or *a*, so the hyphen merely reinforces the default cohesion assumption and the whole phrase is an Ns without internal structure. (Contrast *the 2-score-year milestone*, where the hyphens function to show a violation of the default assumption that *year milestone* is the most cohesive word-pair.) Furthermore, the cohesion implied by the hyphenation may conflict with general SUSANNE rules on the recognition of constituency. For instance, in *Even the non-church members* J23:1010 the hyphen appears to link the prefix *non-* with the phrase *church members*; but in SUSANNE terms *church members* would not be a tagma within *the church* *members*, so the actual phrase is analysed as a five-IC tagma [Np *the non +<hyphen> +church members*] without internal structure.[49]

§ 4.544   As pointed out in § 2.45, even when hyphenations are split into separate words it occasionally remains impossible to assign the logically appropriate structure. Thus, logically, the structure of *two ex-National Football Leaguers* A12:1350 appears to be *two* [[*ex* – [*National Football League*]] *ers*], but since *Leaguers* is a single SUSANNE word the sequence *ex +<hyphen> +National Football Leaguers* is treated as a five-daughter Np, without internal structure. In *only six hits in 46 at-bats for a .130 batting average* A13:0780, the prepositional phrase *at bat* has been turned into the equivalent of a noun by hyphenation, and pluralized, so SUSANNE treats *46 at +<hyphen> +bats* as a four-IC Np. A more complex case is:

> *this brief discussion of* [Np [J *neo-*_FB +, [J– *paleocortical*_JJ], [J+ *and cortico*_FB +<hyphen> +*hypothalamic*_JJ J+] J] *relations* Np] J17:0330

— where there is no possibility of showing that *neo-* is logically prefixed to *-cortical*, since the latter does not occur as a separate word.

---

[49] The tagma in fact has more than five ICs, since the wording quoted here is followed in the source text by an appositional element: this is not relevant to the point under discussion.

□ 5 □
LOGICAL GRAMMAR

§ 5.1   It is generally accepted by linguists and philosophers of logic that the surface or formal grammatical structure of natural-language texts does not correlate perfectly with the logic of the texts. Sentences have a "logical grammar" or "underlying grammar" (linguists such as Noam Chomsky have used the phrase "deep structure" in the same or a closely related sense) which clashes in some respects with the surface grammar of the sentences. The term "functional grammar" is also used in contrast to "formal grammar".

The SUSANNE parsing scheme aims to reflect the logical (or functional) as well as the surface or formal grammar of English text.

§ 5.2   Theoretical linguists have differed widely from one another on the question of how large the differences between surface and logical structure are. One group of linguists influential during the 1960s and 1970s advocated the psychological reality of extremely "abstract" underlying structures — that is, ones having a great deal of internal complexity not reflected at all in the surface grammar of the relevant texts. D. T. Langendoen's 1969 textbook *The Study of Syntax*, for instance, argued (Langendoen 1969: 101) that the apparently simple sentence *Claude is a man* has a logical structure comprising one main and five subordinate clauses. But this surprising complexity did not reflect previously unnoticed aspects of the meaning of the four-word sentence; rather, it represented one theoretical view about the most adequate way to represent the meaning of the sentence as generally understood.

§ 5.3   The SUSANNE parsing scheme aims to express logical aspects of sentence meaning in as straightforward and perspicuous a manner as possible, avoiding issues of psycholinguistic theory as not its proper concern; so this scheme deliberately refrains from postulating abstract logical structures akin to Langendoen's (without thereby implying that such abstract structures are wrong in their own terms). The SUSANNE project was initiated at a time when the system of surface-structure notation described in Chapter 4 was already well established; the SUSANNE scheme adopted, as one of its guiding principles, the decision that logical grammar should be expressed only by adding material to these surface-structure parsetrees, without changing their hierarchical shape in any way. In particular, no underlying clauses were to be postulated in addition to the clauses recognized by the surface-structure analysis. The SUSANNE team believe that an annotation scheme conforming to this principle is adequate to express all those factors which are generally accepted as characterizing logical grammar but not explicitly expressed in surface structure.[1]

According to one point of view, there are no pretheoretical truths about the logical grammar of English; in order to describe the logical structure of a language sample, one must first choose one among competing theories of grammar, and then state such facts as appear if one contemplates the sample through the spectacles provided by that theory — these facts possibly having no identifiable equivalents in terms of a different theory. The SUSANNE team explicitly believe that this point of view is mistaken, and that to a large extent (although certainly not completely, see e.g. § 5.21 below) alternative grammatical theories offer alternative formalisms for describing a common set of facts. Debates between proponents of different theories are motivated by the theoretical-linguistic goal of "explanatory adequacy" (Chomsky 1964: ch. 2); but if, as in the present work, one's goal is limited to "observational adequacy", the debates lose their significance. In the case of a clause such as *they wanted to vote* A08:0360, for instance, it is uncontroversial that the people doing the voting would have to be the same as the people feeling the wish, if the latter were to be satisfied. Any system for representing logical grammar must have some means of expressing that fact; different techniques could be devised; and for present purposes any reasonably clear method is as good as any other.

§ 5.4 The formal or surface-grammar analyses described in Chapter 4 are supplemented in two ways in order to enable SUSANNE analyses to encode logical and functional as well as formal, surface-grammar properties. Extra nodes dominating no wording ("ghost nodes") are added to the parsetrees to represent the logical position of elements that have been moved or deleted in surface structure; and extra classes of symbol are added to the

---

[1] While linguists such as Langendoen have held that an adequate theory of logical grammar needs to be extremely abstract, the philosopher of logic Richard Montague (see e.g. Thomason 1974) at the other extreme seems, so far as the present author understands his work, to have held a view according to which surface and logical grammar are more or less identical. The SUSANNE scheme represents a practically convenient middle way, lacking theoretical pretensions, between these alternatives.

labels of ordinary constituents and ghosts, in order to represent logical properties of the respective constituents. (The term *full constituent* is used for a node which dominates one or more text words, in contrast to ghost nodes.)

The symbols added to node-labels in order to mark logical structure are of two categories. Numbers, called "indices", mark the relationship between nodes marked grammatically as counterparts, such as a ghost and the corresponding full surface constituent. Thus indices commonly occur in pairs; but we shall see that there are circumstances in which three or more nodes can share a common index. Alphabetic symbols ("functiontags") mark the logical roles played by the various complement and adjunct constituents within a clause. As we saw in § 4.22, the complete label of a SUSANNE parse node may include all three components — formtag, functiontag, index — or in different circumstances may lack one or two of the three components.

A ghost node never has a formtag; all other nodes have formtags. When a node-label comprises a functiontag and/or an index in addition to a formtag, the formtag is written first and is separated by a colon from the additional components; when functiontag (always a single letter) and index (always three digits) both occur, functiontag precedes index. Thus a complex node-label can be unambiguously decomposed into its components. For instance, the label "Nns:S103" contains a formtag Nns, a functiontag S, and an index 103. Within the sequence of parsetrees for a single 2,000-word SUSANNE text, sets of nodes requiring indices are numbered from 101 upwards; different node-sets within a single text have different indices, but there is no significance in the number assigned to a particular set of nodes, and the sequence of index numbers used through a text contains gaps and cases where later items are indexed with lower numbers than earlier items.[2]

§ 5.5 Ghost nodes are inserted whenever one of a well-defined range of grammatical phenomena, identified below, either deletes the whole of an element that plays a logical role within a tagma, or causes the element to appear in surface structure as a daughter of a tagma other than the one which is logically its mother. For instance, in a case of Extraposition from NP, such as *a performer will appear shortly who is dressing now*, the Fr *who is dressing now* is logically a daughter of the N headed by *performer* but has been

---

[2] The logical-grammar annotation scheme has been applied only to the material of the SUSANNE Corpus; hence, when examples in this work are invented or taken from other sources, such as the Lancaster-Leeds Treebank, arbitrary index numbers such as 123 are created as needed for the purposes of illustrating the annotation system.

shifted out of that N, so that at the surface the Fr is a daughter of
the S headed by *will appear*; accordingly a ghost node is inserted as
an additional daughter of the N *a performer*, and an index number
is used to mark the relationship between this ghost node, and the
Fr node dominating *who is dressing now*:

[S [Ns:s *A performer* 123] [Vc *will appear*] [R:t *shortly*] [Fr:G123
who is dressing now] S].

The Fr in this case is functiontagged :G, "guest", because *as a
constituent of the S tagma* it has no grammatical role. (When a
shifted constituent is the surface subject or object of the tagma
within which it physically appears, the functiontags :S, :O respectively are used.) The functiontags :s and :t show that *A performer*
and *shortly* have the respective roles of logical subject and Time
adjunct within the S tagma. The ghost daughter of the Ns is represented by the index number 123 (which has no accompanying
functiontag — as will be discussed in §§ 5.11 ff., ICs of phrases are
not normally functiontagged).

The index system in fact applies in a second way to the above
example. The relation between a relative pronoun and its antecedent
is one of the grammatical relationships which indices are used to
represent (§§ 5.74 ff.), and *who* is a relative pronoun having the
performer Ns as antecedent. A more complete representation of the
SUSANNE annotation of the example will be:

[S [Ns:s125 *A performer* 123] [Vc *will appear*] [R:t *shortly*]
[Fr:G123 [Nq:s125 *who*] *is dressing now*] S].

— *who* is shown to have the *performer* phrase as its antecedent,
and to be logical subject of the *is dressing* clause. (The full annotation will also label *is dressing* as a Vzu phrase, and will label *now*
Rw:t as a Time adjunct within the relative clause.)

A ghost node is marked in the wordtag field as YG, and its word
field contains a hyphen, representing absence of any overt verbal
material. On the conventions deciding where in the sequence of
daughters of a tagma a ghost is placed, see §§ 5.112 ff. below.

§ 5.6   The ghost system is *not* used, because it is not needed in
order to express the facts, in cases where grammatical movement
merely reorders the ICs of one tagma. If, for instance, the logical
object of a clause is placed at its beginning, whether obligatorily by
Wh-Fronting (*What does he want?*) or optionally by Topicalization
(*Strawberries I love*), then the extended node-labelling system alone,
as we shall see, adequately represents the logical relationships between the clause ICs, and the SUSANNE analytic scheme makes no

assumptions about the surface ordering having been derived from a different underlying linear order. SUSANNE grammatical analyses are expressed entirely in terms of node-labels and hierarchical relationships between nodes; left-to-right ordering of nodes, where this is not determined by the ordering of text words dominated by the respective nodes, has no significance.

§ 5.7 When the ghost system is used to mark a case where a constituent has been moved out of the tagma to which it logically belongs, if the surface position of that constituent is adjacent to a tagma boundary there will be alternative possibilities concerning the "level" at which it will be attached to the surface-structure tree. For instance, in the example of § 5.5, rather than analysing the Fr tagma as a daughter of the S node, it might in theory be represented as a daughter of the R tagma headed by *shortly* — but this would clearly be a highly unnatural analysis. Choice of placement for a displaced constituent is not always as clear as this, so it is desirable to adopt a general rule. The SUSANNE rule is that displaced elements are made daughters of the lowest possible tagma which also dominates the corresponding ghost node. Thus, in the previous example, the Fr cannot be made a daughter of the *shortly* R, because the ghost corresponding to the Fr does not occur within that R. In the case:

... [Np *his two allusions* ... [P *to* [Nn *Sallaert* [Nns+ *and Van Alsloot*], [Np@ *artists* [Fr *in whom* [R:m *only*] [R:t *recently* 234] *much interest has been taken,* [P+:G234 *and* [Rsw:t *then*] [R:m *mainly*] *by specialists* P+] Fr] Np@] Nn]]]. J63.063

the postposed P+ could be made a daughter of the Fr, of the *artists* Np@, or of one of the higher tagmas dominating the Np@, but since it is logically conjoined to the R headed by *recently* it is made a daughter of the Fr which immediately dominates that R. (The functiontag :m on *mainly* marks it as a Modality adjunct, § 5.153 below.) In:

[S *It was* [Ns:e135 *a* [J *terrible* 136] *thing* [Ti:G136 *to do* o135] Ns] S]. N04:0560

the Ti is placed within the Ns, because this dominates the J from which it is extracted. (The o135 ghost shows that the *thing* noun phrase is antecedent of the logical object of the Ti clause.)

As a more complex case, consider e.g. *It seems to follow that by and large an antagonism exists* ... J17:0130. A conventional description of the grammar of this example would say that, logically, the Fn *that by and large an antagonism exists* ... is subject of *to follow*, and that the clause headed by *to follow* is itself subject of *seems*; the word *It* would be inserted, and the surface word-order achieved, by a combination of the transformational processes of Raising to Subject and Extraposition (see §§ 5.64, 5.70 below). This implies a partial analysis [S [Ni:S *It*] *seems* [Ti:s ... *to follow* ...] ... S] (where :s marks the *follow* clause as logical subject of *seems*, and :S marks *It* as its surface subject); but where is the Fn *that by and large an antagonism exists* ... to be placed in the parsetree? The intuitive response might be that it should go inside the S but outside the Ti, with the Ti having a ghost indexed to it:

> [S [Ni:S *It*] *seems* [Ti:s s123 *to follow*] [Fn:G123 *that by and large an antagonism exists* ...] S]

— where "s123" represents a ghost node showing the logical position of the Fn and marking that clause as logical subject of *follow*. This analysis might seem to be supported by the possibility of inserting an adverb such as *therefore*, which logically belongs to the *seems* clause, between the Ti and the Fn:

> [S [Ni:S *It*] *seems* [Ti:s s123 *to follow*] [R:m *therefore*] [Fn:G123 *that by and large an antagonism exists* ...] S]

However, the analysis shown for the sentence without *therefore* violates the rule that a dislocated element must be placed in the lowest possible tagma which dominates its ghost; since the Fn is adjacent to the Ti clause which contains its ghost, it could be included within that clause (in which case the dislocation involves merely left-to-right ordering among daughters of a single tagma, and no ghost is needed) — so the correct SUSANNE analysis is:

> [S [Ni:S *It*] *seems* [Ti:s *to follow* [Fn:s *that by and large an antagonism exists* ...] Ti:s] S]

The alternative sequence including *therefore* does not in fact constitute evidence against this analysis, since *therefore* can be treated as an included adverbial moved out of the *seems* clause into the Ti; the SUSANNE scheme always prefers to treat an adverbial element as dislocated, if by doing so it can achieve a better analysis of the remaining elements of a sequence (§ 4.23). In other words, the analysis of that hypothetical sentence would be:

> [S [Ni:S *It*] *seems* m123 [Ti:s *to follow* [R:G123 *therefore*] [Fn:s *that by and large an antagonism exists* ...] Ti:s] S]

— where "m123" is a ghost node showing the logical position and role of *therefore*.

§ 5.8   Relationships between surface and logical grammar are discussed in this chapter in terms of the "dynamic" metaphors of classical transformational grammar theory, according to which a sentence begins with a specific logical or underlying structure which is then deformed by a succession of tree-reshaping operations into a different surface structure. The concrete quality of this framework makes for clarity of exposition, and even today it is probably the most widely familiar approach to the issues under discussion. But nothing in the SUSANNE analytic scheme is intended to imply a preference as between dynamic theories and more recent, static grammatical theories according to which the diverse grammatical properties of a sentence correspond to different aspects of a single complex structure. Indeed SUSANNE parsetrees themselves include logical and surface grammar within a single structure. As already said, the SUSANNE scheme deliberately avoids representing "facts" which are meaningful only within particular versions of grammatical theory. For instance, some versions of classical transformational theory describe a constituent which appears at the surface in a clause much higher than that of its logical position (e.g. the *What* of *What did John say Margaret thought Basil wanted her to do?*) as having been raised via a series of steps each crossing a single clause boundary (cf. Chomsky 1976: 92–3); but the SUSANNE scheme indicates only the two end-points of such a process.

§ 5.9   In situations where the index system is used to relate co-referential items, each of such a pair of items is given a non-terminal node of its own to bear the index even if one of them is a one-word phrase IC of a higher phrase, which would not normally receive a separate phrase node; and the label of such a node will include formtag as well as index. On the other hand, where one of the items related by indices is a subordinate conjunct preceded by a conjunction, the conjunction is treated as part of the indexed constituent, and the material introduced by the conjunction is not given a separate node of its own. Both these points are illustrated by the analysis of:

Hughes would not comment on [Np *tax reforms* [Np+:173 *or other issues* [Fr [Pq:u *in* [Dq:173 *which*]] *the Republican candidates are involved*]]]. A06:1730

— the antecedent of the relative is the Np+ *or other issues . . .* , within which *other issues . . .* is not a constituent; the relative pronoun *which* is given a Dq node within the P *in which*, so that the Dq node can have the index 173 attached to it in order to mark it as having the *issues* phrase as its antecedent. A one-word G is given a separate index-bearing node below a phrase node in:

... [Np@:155 *long, domed, chalk-white rooms with daises of turquoise tile,* [Tn [Np:S [G:155 *their*] *end walls* Np:S] *cut through to the orchards and the sky by open arches* Tn] Np@:155]. G05:0560

§ 5.10   As already said in § 4.46, the SUSANNE distinction between "formtags" and "functiontags" is not always drawn in a logically compelling fashion. There are many aspects of the formtag system which might more easily be seen as relating to logical function than to surface grammatical form: for instance the classification of a *wh-* clause such as *when they met* by reference to context as either an indirect question or an adverbial clause is really a functional classification, but is expressed via the formtagging system (Fn v. Fa). This blurring of general analytic categories is an inevitable consequence of the way that the SUSANNE analytic scheme evolved from simple beginnings over many years. While it might be possible to rationalize the "form"/"function" distinction to some extent if the existing notation were discarded and a new scheme designed from scratch, it seems doubtful whether any adequate analytic scheme could entirely disentangle function from form.

The Functiontag System

§ 5.11   Before giving full details of the use of ghosts and indices by listing the individual grammatical phenomena that they are used to mark, we now survey the range of functiontags used.

§ 5.12   Functiontags are assigned to all ICs (whether full constituents or ghost nodes) of *clauses*, with the following exceptions:

- constituents belonging to the formal categories V..., I..., or Ss;
- constituents which are word- rather than tagmatagged, such as existential *there*, or punctuation marks;
- constituents whose formtag includes one of the symbols + – @ &, showing them to be conjoined or in apposition to a higher tagma or to be a left-grouped co-ordination within a co-ordination;
- constituents whose formtag includes one of the symbols ! ", showing them to be exclamations or vocatives.

Even an item from this list will be functiontagged :G, "guest", if it has been moved into its surface position below a clause node from a different tagma in which it plays a logical role (in practice this occurs with the second and third of the four classes of exception).

§ 5.13   The rationale of the exceptions listed in § 5.12 is that in these cases the formtag alone identifies the function of the constituent within its tagma, making functiontagging redundant; a V within a clause must be its head, for example (and in the case of Vo, Vr, the Vo item must be head and Vr its displaced modifier). In other cases functiontags are needed to show the logic of the clause. (Arguably some punctuation marks play a variety of roles within clauses which could in principle be distinguished by functiontagging; but the concept of integrating punctuation into parsetrees is itself so novel that the SUSANNE team have made no attempt to evolve an analysis of punctuation functions.)

§ 5.14   ICs of phrases and of wordrank and rootrank tagmas are not functiontagged, with certain limited exceptions (see § 5.22 on the functiontag :G, and § 5.120). Within phrases, there is usually little to be said about functional differentiation of ICs beyond the fact that one IC is head and the others are "modifiers" or "dependents" — if, for instance, a dependent element within a tagma formtagged as a noun phrase is itself formtagged as a determiner, then there is really nothing further to say about its relationship to the head of the noun phrase. Likewise the formtagging of a wordrank tagma as an idiom or a wordlevel co-ordination implies the roles of its constituents. When a rootrank tagma has multiple daughters, these are best regarded logically as forming a simple chain rather than as bearing specific functional relations to one another.

One circumstance in which there is potentially more to say about phrase-IC functions beyond identification of the head IC is where the phrase is a nominalized clause. In the classic example *the shooting of the hunters was terrible*, one might wish to mark *(of) the hunters* as logical subject or logical object of *shooting* in order to resolve the ambiguity. The SUSANNE scheme does not do this. If the surface parsing rules of Chapter 4 imply that a nominalization is to be formtagged as a phrase rather than a clause (as is so in this case: *the shooting of the hunters* is an N rather than a Tg by the rules of § 4.339), then functiontags are not assigned to its ICs.

§ 5.15   The majority of specific categories recognized by the SUSANNE functiontag system can be grouped under two broad classes which go by various names in the literature; the terms used here are *complements* and *adjuncts*. (Other terms used for approximately the same distinction are *actant* and *circonstant* (Tesnière 1965: 102 ff.), or *argument* and *modifier* (Dowty 1982: 89; Gazdar *et al.* 1985: 128); see also Matthews 1981: ch. 6; Somers 1987: 12–18.) Complements are relatively tightly bound to the verb of a clause, adjuncts relate to it more loosely: in the generative tradition which postulates a "VP" constituent intermediate between verb group and entire clause, complements (other than the subject) would be within the VP, adjuncts outside it.

§ 5.16   The distinction is, admittedly, not always easy to draw. Complements are often realized formally by noun phrases, adjuncts by adverb-like elements such as adverbs themselves, adverbial phrases, prepositional phrases, or adverbial clauses; but there is no absolute rule about this — a noun phrase may have an adjunct function, a prepositional phrase may be a complement. Some writers suggest that complements are items whose existence is necessarily entailed by the identity of the verb (so that they are "understood" in cases where they are not physically realized in a clause), whereas adjuncts are "optional extras" (thus e.g. *John gave £20* assumes that the hearer can mentally expand the wording into, say, *John gave £20 to the Amnesty appeal*, whereas e.g. *John opened the door* does not in the same way assume an unspoken instrument phrase, say *John opened the door with a spare key* — John may simply have pushed the door open without using any instrument). On the other hand, Joan Bresnan (1982: 167) argues that this "entailment test" for distinguishing complements from adjuncts is unworkable: she sees the significant difference as being that a clause may have no more than one complement of a given category, whereas it can have multiple adjuncts, not co-ordinated together, of the same category.[3] Gazdar *et al.* add the criterion that the semantic force of an adjunct is independent of context, whereas the interpretation of a complement depends on the other constituents of the clause (thus the indirect object represents the one who acquires legal title in *leave John a legacy*, but the one to whose attention something comes in *send John his instructions*); and that the possibility or otherwise of inserting an adjunct in a clause is predictable from the meaning of the adjunct and of the clause, whereas individual verbs allow or disallow particular types of complement in unpredictable ways.

§ 5.17   The SUSANNE analytic scheme reduces the room for doubt between these two classes by recognizing only a narrow range of complement categories, so that a constituent is classified as an adjunct unless it ranks as a complement on virtually all the criteria

---

[3] Bresnan illustrates multiple locative, temporal, and manner adjuncts via the example:

Fred deftly [Manner] *handed a toy to the baby by reaching behind his back* [Manner] *over lunch* [Temp] *at noon* [Temp] *in a restaurant* [Loc] *last Sunday* [Temp] *in Back Bay* [Loc] *without interrupting the discussion* [Manner].

She contrasts the ungrammaticality of multiple agent phrases in **She was admired by him by the President* with the alleged acceptability of multiple *by*-phrases expressing location, in *She was sitting by him by the President*. But these judgements are fine-drawn; encountered from a corpus-linguistics perspective, the last example has a contrived air.

mentioned above. For instance, while most locative phrases are clearly adjuncts, certain uses of locatives (e.g. *He keeps his whisky **in the sideboard***) might be categorized as complements by some of the above criteria, but the SUSANNE scheme follows *CGEL*, p. 52, in treating all locatives as adjuncts: thus *in the sideboard* in the above invented example, or the R in *Estimates . . . have ranged* [R:p *as high as $200,000*]. A09:0040 and the P in *to get all the allied cars* [P:p *back on the track . . .*]. A04:0260, are functiontagged as Place adjuncts rather than predicate complements. Instrumental *with* phrases are often regarded as complements, but the SUSANNE scheme assimilates them to Manner adjuncts. The emphasized element in a construction of the type *her shoes had mud **on them***, or (British) *had mud **on***, is a Place adjunct rather than a complement.

§ 5.18 In choosing a functiontag for a particular constituent, the definitions of the individual complement and adjunct tags, below, are treated as criterial; the discussion here of the general contrast between complements and adjuncts is indicative only. However, it is a rule of the SUSANNE scheme that each complement type (other than :G) may be instantiated at most once in a clause, whereas clauses may include multiple adjuncts of the same type; this rule will sometimes force constituents to be analysed as adjuncts rather than complements.

§ 5.19 The functiontags are as follows:

COMPLEMENTS

:s logical subject
:o logical direct object
:i indirect object
:u prepositional object
:e predicate complement of subject
:j predicate complement of object
:a agent of passive
:S surface but not logical subject
:O surface but not logical object
:G "guest" constituent

ADJUNCTS

:p place
:q direction
:t time
:h manner or degree

:m modality
:c contingency
:r respect
:w comitative
:k benefactive
:b absolute

:n particle of phrasal verb
:x propositional relative clause
:z complement of catenative

Since a functiontag in the SUSANNE scheme almost always appears preceded by a colon, in this work references to particular functiontags are made in the form ":s", ":O", ":m", using the colon as a convenient device to identify the letter as a tag of a particular category.[4]

Complement Categories

§ 5.20   The complement tagging system assumes the widely understood concepts of "logical subject", "logical object", "surface subject", and "surface object". For instance, in the clause *but no satisfactory explanation seems to have been offered* J71.076, the Ns *no satisfactory explanation* is the surface subject of *seems* but the logical object of *offered*; the logical subject of *seems* is the clause *(no satisfactory explanation) to have been offered*, and *offered* has no logical subject or surface object. The SUSANNE team have no special insights to offer into the meanings of the terms "logical subject", "surface object", etc.; they claim about these categories only that, in most instances, they and other analysts all seem to know one when they see one. Certain debatable cases will be discussed explicitly in the following pages.

§ 5.21   A number of linguists, notably Charles Fillmore (Fillmore 1968) and his followers, have argued that these categories can be defined in terms of a range of more fundamental, semantically significant "case" categories. At an early stage in the process of constructing the SUSANNE Corpus, it was intended to tag complements in terms of a version of case theory. The team surveyed various published versions of the theory, ranging from Fillmore's original article to Starosta (1988), and selected Stockwell *et al.* (1973)

---

[4] The only situation in which a functiontag appears in the SUSANNE annotation not preceded by a colon is when it applies to a ghost node.

as the most fully elaborated attempt to apply a system of cases to the variety of clause-types found in English; the team attempted to extrapolate from Stockwell *et al.*'s examples to the range of clauses in the SUSANNE Corpus. Unfortunately, despite strenuous and protracted efforts, it proved impractical to develop the Stockwell *et al.* system into a scheme sufficiently comprehensive and precise to offer predictable, consistent labels for the very diverse complement functions found in authentic data. It may of course be that the difficulty stemmed from inadequate work on the part of the SUSANNE team, but the team themselves (who began with considerable enthusiasm for the case concept and respect for Stockwell *et al.*'s implementation of it) became convinced that they had "tested to destruction" the hypothesis that a small finite set of case relationships can be defined so as to cover in a predictable manner the diverse logical complement relationships contracted by different verbs and other predicate words. Consequently the SUSANNE complement tagging scheme limits itself to the perhaps less informative, but more straightforward traditional concepts of subject and object.

SUBJECTS, OBJECTS, AND "GUESTS"

§ 5.22   A clause constituent (full or ghost) is given the :s or :o functiontag if it is the logical subject or direct object of its clause, respectively, provided that it does not occupy the converse surface role in the same clause. A constituent is given the :S or :O tag if it is the surface subject or surface direct object of its clause but does not play the corresponding logical role in the same clause. A ghost node is given the functiontag corresponding to the logical role of the corresponding item in the clause containing the ghost, that is a lower-case functiontag, except that if the clause containing the ghost is passive and the ghost represents the passive subject then it is functiontagged :S, not :o or :i.[5] When an item has been moved into a tagma where it does not logically belong, without becoming its

---

[5] It may seem illogical to use an upper-case, "derived role" functiontag for ghosts representing subjects of passive clauses, while lower-case "logical role" functiontags are used for all other ghosts. But the alternative of functiontagging passive-subject ghosts :o or :i leads to annotations which analysts (and therefore probably also users) find highly unnatural. With hindsight, it might have been preferable for the scheme to treat the passive as a logically basic rather than derived construction and to use some additional lower-case functiontag for "subject of passive clause", reserving :S for "item acting as surface subject of a clause but having no logical role in that clause", and :s for "logical subject of active clause". However, the distinction between the new functiontag and :s might equally be found unnatural, given the close relationship in English between passive constructions and active *BE* + adjective constructions. A third possibility would be to use two lower-case functiontags for "logical subject of clause having *BE* as leading verb" — including passive subjects — versus "logical subject of clause having another leading verb". But this would move the SUSANNE scheme some way away from the consensus view of English grammar.

surface subject or object, it is given the :G functiontag; the :G tag is used on any element which is marked by the SUSANNE scheme as shifted under a node which is not logically its mother, even if this is a position where functiontags are not otherwise used — see e.g. the discussion of Negative Transportation, § 5.100 below.

§ 5.23   Where the subject of a Tg is represented by a genitive phrase, this is functiontagged :s or :S —

> *I dislike* [Tg:o [G:s *Brown's*] *painting his daughter*].
> *... the positive arguments for* [Tg [G:S *their*] *being composed for gentle ears*] F27.082

§ 5.24   The functiontag :o covers the noun phrases in idiomatic constructions as discussed in § 4.120, e.g. *take place*, which lack many characteristics of normal direct objects (they cannot be passivized, and cannot be expanded with determiners or adjectives); in general, as we have seen, the SUSANNE analytic scheme annotates idiomatic expressions as if they were intended literally.

§ 5.25   A direct or indirect object will not normally be preceded by a preposition. For indirect objects, this is criterial (§ 5.27 below). Occasionally a prepositional phrase may be recognized as a direct object, if it follows a transitive verb and fills a semantic role that would more commonly be filled by an N or equivalent: e.g. *to spend* [P:o *between six months and a year*].

§ 5.26   The concept of surface subject is not dependent on the overt existence of a verb: reduced clauses in which verbs are "understood", and even verbless clauses in which it would be quite unnatural to supply a verb, can contain constituents functiontagged :s or :S. In a case such as [W *with the village as her ostensible destination*] N08:0130, *the village* is logical subject, :s (and the *as* phrase is predicate complement of subject, :e), although the use of *as* virtually precludes any possibility of inserting a verb. In [W *with Miller and Rankin added to the escape party*] N07:0380, the phrase *Miller and Rankin* is surface subject of a reduced passive construction that could be expanded to *being added*, hence this co-ordination is tagged Nn:S.

INDIRECT OBJECT

§ 5.27   The functiontag :i is used for an indirect object in the narrow sense of a noun phrase not preceded by a preposition, standing after the verb in addition to an (overt or understood) direct object, and representing the "recipient" or similar role; the tag :i is not used for noun phrases preceded by *to* or *for*. This means that while the emphasized constituents in *I gave **Mary** the book, I threw **him** a stick*, are both tagged :i, those in the close paraphrases *I gave*

*a book **to Mary**, I threw a stick **to him*** are not; the former is tagged
as a prepositional object, the latter as an adjunct of Direction.

I can't afford [Ti:o *to pay* [Ny:i *you*] *anything*]. N01:1070
Perhaps this is [Ff:e *what gives* [Ns:i *the aborigine*] *his odd air
of dignity* Ff:e]. G04:0680
the victim may do a pirouette, sit down, or offer [Ns:i *his as-
sailant*] *a fork and spoon.* G09:1520

Indirect objects, functiontagged :i, include addressees of verbs of
saying, etc., with the direct or indirect speech treated as direct object:

I told [Nos:i *him*] [Fn:o *that he would get his teeth kicked in by
the dancers . . .*]. G43.176
to convince [Ns:i *the recipient*] [Fn:o *that he is getting the real
thing*] G03:1690
He promised [Np:i *nearly 200 Democratic county committee
members*] *at the meeting . . . :* "[Q:o *When I come back . . .*
Q:o]". A06:1360
[S "[Q:o *. . . and who else would have told him* Q:o]"? [Nas:s
he] *asked* [Nos:i *himself*] S]. N14:1250

§ 5.28   In a clause with a single prepositionless "object", this is
functiontagged either :o or :i depending on meaning; the SUSANNE
analytic scheme does not follow the usage described in *CGEL*,
p. 727 n. [a], whereby a single object is always called "direct object". Thus the emphasized constituents in the examples:

*Bob is teaching **the older children**.*
*You can pay **me** instead.*

are given the SUSANNE functiontag :i rather than :o.

AGENT

§ 5.29   The functiontag :a is used for the special case of *by* phrases
representing agents (logical subjects) of passive constructions; thus,
in a passive clause, the surface subject is functiontagged :S and the
logical subject, if it appears, is tagged :a.

has been experimentally investigated in detail [Pb:a *by Maecker*]
J02:0360
an artificial lake . . . , [Tn *fed* [Pb:a *by a half dozen springs that
popped out of the ground above the hillside orchard* Pb:a] Tn]
N05:1530
. . . every time a portion of the old ones are paid off [Pb:a *by tax
authorities*]. A01:1330

§ 5.30 The :a functiontag is also used for cases where the notional subject of a passive verb is marked by *of* rather than *by*, e.g.:

> *a body of legal principle* [Fr *which by and large was made up* [Po:a *of what Western nations could do...*]] G02:0100
>
> *...a board* [Tn *composed* [Po:a *of the governor... and chief justice of the Texas Supreme Court*]] A02:0460

§ 5.31 When a subordinate clause functions as an Agent, it may take no distinctive agent-marking preposition:

> [Nas:S *He*] [Vsp *was annoyed*] [Ti:a *to learn that the train would be delayed*].
>
> *I looked up,* [Tn:b *somehow* [Vn *startled*] [Fn:a *that he had been unable to follow the wistful trend of my mind*]]. P15.150

(on the fact that no subject is reconstructed for the Tn in the P15 example, see § 5.192).

PREPOSITIONAL OBJECT

§ 5.32 The functiontag :u is used in the case of "prepositional verbs", e.g. *look for* meaning "seek" or *talk to* (American *talk with*) meaning "address", where what is logically an object of the verb occurs within a prepositional phrase whose preposition is determined by the verb rather than chosen for its individual sense. It covers all cases of prepositional phrases which would be classified as either direct or indirect objects if the preposition were lacking, hence (as we have seen) *to Mary* is :u in *I gave the book to Mary*. A clause containing a :u element will normally be paraphrasable by a clause in which the same element appears as an :i or :o (either through alternation between *to/for* phrase and true indirect object, or by substitution of verbs as in the case of *look for ~ seek*, or, in a case such as *it suffered from a variety of sores* G04:1040, without change of verb). Thus (cf. *CGEL*, p. 741 n. [c]) in *I have found a place for Mrs Jones*, the phrase *for Mrs Jones* is functiontagged :u because the clause could be paraphrased *I have found Mrs Jones a place*; on the other hand, in *I have found a place for the magnolia tree*, the phrase *for the magnolia tree* cannot be replaced by an indirect object (**I have found the magnolia tree a place*), so it is functiontagged :k (Benefactive, § 5.184) rather than :u.[6]

---

[6] Some analysts might argue that the phrase *for the magnolia tree* requires no functiontag because it should be seen as a postmodifier *of place*; but *CGEL* regards it as an IC of the clause, and other examples given the :k functiontag are unquestionably clause ICs.

giving rise to local heat fluxes . . . J02:0180
It is presumed that this negative head was associated *with some
    geometric factor of the assembly,* . . . J03:0440
He was thinking *of Rittenhouse and how he had left him there,* . . .
    N02:0040
of White House aids in Washington [Fr *with whom he talked by
    telephone*] A03:0250
. . . *and have had* [Tn:j *imposed upon them*] social and economic
    controls they dislike. G01:1440

§ 5.33   The functiontag :u covers the "experiencer" in constructions such as *it seems dreadful to me, it seems to me that* . . . (for
the analysis of other components of *seem*-type constructions, see
§ 5.64), together with *to* + reflexive phrases in constructions such
as:

John said to himself . . .
I think to myself "What a wonderful world".
Clyde Miller was crying softly to himself, . . . N07:0480

Similarly the emphasized phrase is :u in *these things are important
to Persians* G05:0620, with BE rather than SEEM; there is a fine
borderline between this use of the :u functiontag and the use of the
Respect functiontag discussed under § 5.173.

§ 5.34   The functiontag :u is used in cases of *feel like* meaning
"want":

"*Or maybe you just don't feel* [P:u *like a cigar*]"? N09:0580

§ 5.35   In a sequence such as *to make use of such words*
G01:0310, *use* is :o (cf. the discussion of *take place*, § 5.24), and
the Po *of such words* is :u — cf. *He let* [Tb:o *go*] [Po:u *of the shirt*],
. . . N12:1540. In . . . *are tripping over their feet* A06:1430 the
emphasized phrase is P:u.

§ 5.36   Where the preposition of a prepositional verb has been
deleted before a Tf, as in *he waited* [Tf *for the curtain to rise*] (cf.
§ 4.360), the Tf is functiontagged :u despite the fact that the one
preposition occurring at the surface is included within the Tf rather
than in the higher clause.

PREDICATE COMPLEMENTS

§ 5.37   The functiontags :e, :j are used for constituents (commonly adjective or noun phrases) which are predicated of the (logical
or surface) subject or object of their clause respectively — thus the
emphasized elements of *John is angry, my father is the managing*

director, John *was elected* **acting chairman** would be functiontagged
:e, those of *I painted the door* **green,** *we elected John* **acting chairman** would be functiontagged :j.

> *we must be* [J:e *extraordinarily patient*] A10:0300
>
> *Properly mindful of* [Np:131 <*bital*> *all* <*eital*> *the cultures* [Z s131
> [P:e *in existence*] *today throughout the world* Z] Np:131], . . .
> G22:0320
>
> *The only exception to this is* [Np:e *certain bees* [Fr *that have
> become* [Np:e *parasites*]]]. J10:0320
>
> *The Yankee triumph made Ralph Houk* [Ns:j *only the third man
> to lead a team to both a pennant and . . .*]. A13:1830
>
> [Ns:s *The fact that . . .*] *made* [Ns:o *the conflict*] [J:j *grimmer,*
> [Jr+ *and the greater*]]. G10:1330
>
> *He saw them* [Tn:j *ambushed,* [Tn– *strewn in the postures of the
> broken and the dying*]]. N02:0830
>
> . . . *that these animals are* [Ff:e [Dq:o *what*] *we call* [Np:j
> *"queens",* [Np@ *young females that have mated . . .*]]].
> J10:0070

When a predicate complement is a non-finite clause, no ghost node
is inserted in it to mark the identity of its subject with the subject
or object of the higher clause — for instance the Tn *ambushed . . .*
in the N02 example above does not contain an :S ghost indexed to
them.

§ 5.38   When a clause containing an :e or :j constituent has
contrasting surface and logical subjects or objects respectively, the
logical subject (object) is the one of which the :e (:j) item is predicated:

> [Ns:S167 *land reform*] *is* [J:e *likely*] [Ti:s s167 *to be politically
> disruptive*] J22:1040

— the clause does not assert that land reform is likely, but that (if
it occurs) its being politically disruptive is likely. Where a clause
contains no full constituent functiontagged as logical or surface
subject (object), an :e (:j) element may be predicated of an element
which is represented by a ghost node carrying the appropriate
functiontag:

> *to* [Nns:199 *Prince Souvanna Phouma,* [Fr [Nqo:G199
> *whom*] [Ni:s *it*] *felt* [Fn:o s199 *was* [Jh:e *too trusting of
> Communists*] Fn:o] Fr] Nns:199] A04:1660
>
> *in* [Ns:197 *the balance* [Fr *they believed* o197 [Jh:j *essential to
> the sovereignty of the citizen*] Fr] Ns:197] G10:1570
>
> *from* [Ns:243 *the sympathy* [Fr *they felt* o243 [Tn:j *extended to
> them by the mother country*]]] G01:1150

— or an :e or :j element may be predicated of an element which is "understood" and by SUSANNE rules not represented even by a ghost node:

> *He is not interested in* [Tg *being named* [Ns:e *a full-time director*]]. A05:0080

(for the lack of ghost subject in the Tg clause here, see § 5.55).

§ 5.39   The need to recognize a functiontag :j is one consequence of the SUSANNE principle (§ 5.3) whereby logical analyses are not permitted to postulate extra clauses not present in surface structure; a more "abstract" analysis might represent :j constituents as subject complements within lower clauses that are deleted at the surface.

§ 5.40   The complement in a copular clause will in some cases be an item which could equally well occur, in the same sense, as an adjunct in a transitive or intransitive clause. For instance *here* is in ordinary grammatical parlance the "complement" of *is* in *John is here*, but is an adjunct in *We overtook the other car here*. In keeping with the general SUSANNE principle of drawing a relatively tight border round the class of items receiving complement rather than adjunct functiontags, items are given :e or :j tags only if they are not capable of occurring in the relevant sense as adjuncts in transitive or intransitive clauses. That is, the adverb *here* in *John is here* is functiontagged as a Place adjunct, :p, rather than as a predicate complement, although the adjective *present* in the close paraphrase *John is present* is functiontagged :e. In *Heating is by individual gas-fired, forced warm air systems.* A19:1940 the *by*-phrase is tagged as a Manner adjunct, :h, although again it would commonly be described as the complement of *is*;[7] on the other hand, no functiontag other than :e is plausible for ... *the theory is in excellent agreement with experiment.* J04:0310. In:

> *If they avoid the use of the pungent, outlawed four-letter word* [Ni:s *it*] *is* [Fa:c *because it is taboo; it is sacred*]. G13:0370

the *because* clause is functiontagged :c rather than :e. On the other hand, the *of* phrase can be only :e (no adjunct category applies) in:

> *Mr. Martinelli has, in recent weeks, been* [Po:e *of the opinion that . . .*] A05:1400

---

[7] The distinction drawn here between complement and adjunct elements following BE relates to the discussion in *TLCUM*, p. 76, of choice between adjective and adverb wordtags for words following BE. Arguably, however, *TLCUM* relies too much on the test of whether BE can be replaced by exclusively copular verbs such as *SEEM*, *LOOK*. Note that *present* is an indisputable adjective in *John is present*, yet one cannot say **John looks present*, **John seems present*.

§ 5.41   A predicate complement may be an independent clause,
if this functions as a complement:

[S *Yet the question remains, as before:* [S?:e *is the Soviet govern-*
ment interested chiefly in sealing off East Germany and . . .]]?
B02.037 — cf. § 4.305 on subject-auxiliary inversion requiring
the tag S?

[S *The normal rise and fall in the Waltz basic amalgamation is:*
[L:e [R:q *Down*] [Fa:t *as the first step in the bar is taken*];
[S*− *commence to rise at the end of this step, as you take the*
second step], [S*+ *and then* <bbold> *continue to rise as the*
feet close on the third step <ebold>] L:e] S]. E13.180

§ 5.42   In the case of a non-copular verb, the :e or :j functiontags
are used whenever the interpretation of a constituent as predicated
of subject or object contrasts with a hypothetical interpretation as
modifying the verb or the proposition as a whole. Thus, in *The*
common codes . . . bind the devotees together J23:1480, the adverb
together is one that would commonly be functiontagged :w,
Comitative, but in this case binding is not an act which is carried
out communally but one which results in the devotees being together, hence the adverb is functiontagged :j. Conversely, in:

historically peoples have clung [R:w *together*] [P:e *as more or*
less coherent cultural units] J23:1670

the R is functionagged :w, but the *as* phrase here is functiontagged
:e because it denotes not how they clung but what their clinging
formed them into. In:

. . . seek to trim it [R:n *down*] [P:j *to a more streamlined and*
workable unit]. A11:1200

the P is functiontagged :j (trimming is not a movement that arrives at
a unit, but an activity that changes the object into such). Likewise:

[Np:S *fractions from the column*] *were concentrated by negative*
pressure dialysis [P:e *to volumes of 1 ml or less*], . . . J09:1290
setting the lantern [P:j *to* [Tg *swaying*]], . . . N12:1380

In *I could have mistaken it* **for my Aunt** N18:1480 the *for* phrase
is functiontagged :j.

§ 5.43   The word *as* often introduces phrases or clauses given
the :e or :j functiontags. In *Using his hands* **as a trumpet** N04:0080,
the emphasized P does not modify an independent proposition that
he used his hands, rather the word *using* implies that his hands were
a trumpet, so the tag is P:j; likewise in the case:

Vandiver likely will mention [Ns:o *the $100 million highway bond issue* . . .] [P:j *as his first priority item*]. A01:1200

An A clause is A:j in:

Washington castigated [Ns:o *his critic, General Conway,*] [A:j *as* [Vgb *being*] [Jh:e *capable of "all the meanness of intrigue* . . ."] A:j]. G07:1080

In [Nas:s *he*] *established* [Nos:o *himself*] [P:j *as one of the guiding spirits* . . .] A19:1530, the reflexive pronoun implies that subject and object are identical but the P is given the :j functiontag because the *establish* . . . *as* construction in general implies that the *as* phrase applies to the object.

§ 5.44   An A:e contains a J:e in a case like:

mass trials have been upheld [A:e *as* [J:e *proper*]] *in other courts* . . . A10:1800

§ 5.45   Furthermore the :e or :j functiontag applies to the preposed predicate phrase in the American construction exemplified by:

[Fa:c [Jh:e As_RGa *different physically* 140] *as the tall, angular Jefferson was* [P:G140 *from the chubby, rotund Adams*] Fa:c], *the seven were striking individualists.* G07:1000

§ 5.46   An Fa acting as complement of a copular verb, as in the examples quoted in § 4.302, will normally be functiontagged :e (though in the case of the *seem* example see § 5.65 below).

§ 5.47   On occasion a constituent functiontagged :j will be complement of a prepositional object, functiontagged :u —

to think [P:u *of the nation*] [A:j *as* [J:e *representative of* . . .]] G02:1340

§ 5.48   The functiontag :e covers cases such as *he weighs* [Nu:e *ten stone*], where the complement cannot be regarded as an object (for instance the clause cannot be passivized). On the other hand, in a case like *These Seven Founders constituted an intellectual and social elite* G07:0920, while *constituted* means much the same as a true copular verb such as *became*, grammatically it is transitive — one can write e.g. *the elite was constituted of a few elder statesmen* — so the *elite* phrase in the G07 example is tagged Ns:o.

§ 5.49   The functiontag :e also has a use as "default" functiontag in constructions which are too grammatically reduced for the standard concepts of subject, object, etc. to be applicable. This is particularly common within Fc clauses, which like other clauses require their ICs to be functiontagged, but which are frequently verbless:

> *to occupy* [Np:o [Jh *general,* [R *rather* [Fc *than*
> [J:e *special*]]],] *positions . . .*] J04:0850
> *. . . was* [Jh:e *more surprising* [Fc *than* [J:e *unpleasant*]]].
> G04:1460
> *. . . to accept a de facto cease-fire in Laos,* [R:m *rather*
> [Fc *than* [Tb:e *continue to insist on a verification of the*
> *cease-fire . . .*]]] A04:0850

And, apart from Fc cases, cf. the G02 example in § 5.47 above, or:

> [Np [Jh *impotent* [Fa *if* [J:e *vociferous*]]] *cliques . . .*] J57.181

In "correlative" Fc's lacking a verb, e.g. [Rr:h [Fc [Jr:e *The*
smaller] [Ns:s *the particle*] Fc] *the further* Rr:h] *it will travel . . .*
J08:0540, the ICs of the Fc will commonly be :s and :e as shown.

§ 5.50   However, where the grammatical relationship of a constituent to the elided verb of a reduced clause remains clear, the
appropriate functiontag is used:

> *to "pursue* [Ns:o *the study of the law*], [R:m *rather* [Fc *than*
> [Ns:o *the gain of it*]]]"* G07:1230

In examples such as:

> [Fa:c *if* [J:e *necessary*]] L21.154
> [L [Ns:e *No wonder*] [Fn:s *Melissa responded . . .*] L]. N08:0570

the :e functiontag is appropriate, not as "default" functiontag, but
because the clauses are clearly reduced from *If it is necessary, It was*
no wonder that Melissa responded . . . .

§ 5.51   Q tagmas are given the functiontags :e, :j in cases such
as:

> [S "[Q:e *They're Japs. They're Japs*]", *came* [Ns:s *a high-pitched*
> *voice*] S]. N15:1310
> [S "[Q:e *Over this way! He ain't gone far*]"! [Ns:s *a harsh*
> *cry*] *floated to him across the brush* S]. N14:1500
> [S <bital> [Q:j *Die Frist ist um, und wiederum verstrichen sind*
> *sieben Jahr,* Q:j] <eital> [Nns:s *the Maestro*] *quoted* <bital>
> [Nns:o *The Flying Dutchman*], <eital> *as he told . . .* G06:0010
> [S "[Q:G190 *Yeah_UH,* [S *I can see that*] Q:G190]", [Ns:S189
> *the friend*] *was forced* [Ti:o s189 *to agree* e190] S]. N11:1090
> [S "[Q:e *Take a ride on this one*]", [Nns:s *Brooks Robinson*]
> *greeted* [Nns:o *Hansen*] *as . . .* S]. A11:1210

§ 5.52   Another example of :e as "default functiontag" is exemplified by the analysis of:

> [S [A:m *As Lipton puts it*]: "[Q:e [S *The Eros is felt . . . in the*
> *mutual metaphysical orgasms*]. [S *The magic circle is, in fact,*
> *a symbol of and preparation for the metaphysical orgasm* S]
> Q:e]" S]. G13:1590

The quoted material contains two sentences which must be given a
Q node to unite them into a single quoted "paragraph", and these
occur within a quoting S containing a premodifying *as* clause.
Normally the part of an S excluding a subordinate clause would not
be treated as a single tagma, so there is no appropriate functiontag
available for it; hence the default tag :e is used in this case.

Logical/Surface Disparities

§ 5.53   We now give an (exhaustive) statement of the range of
grammatical phenomena in connection with which the SUSANNE
scheme uses indices and/or functiontags to mark divergences between
logical and surface grammatical structure. The policies summarized
in this statement were arrived at by trawling through standard works
on English transformational grammar in order to identify cases where
the linguistic consensus has perceived contrasts between surface and
logical grammar (the works chiefly consulted were Burt (1971),
Stockwell, Schachter, and Partee (1973), Akmajian and Heny
(1975)), and ensuring that the SUSANNE notation scheme adequately represented the relevant facts either via the index and
functiontag mechanisms or otherwise. Where examples quoted below
are not identified as authentic, they are in many cases taken from
these works.

   In many cases where classical transformational theory postulated transformational rules, no special notation is called for in
the SUSANNE scheme. For instance, the works cited include a
Complementizer Placement rule which inserts either *that, for . . . to,*
or *'s . . . ing* where a subordinate clause has a nominal role within
a higher clause; but formal analysis already shows which of these
alternatives occurs in a particular case, and there is no advantage
for SUSANNE purposes in a notation representing the sentence as
it would putatively have been "before" a complementizer was inserted. Or again, a rule of Modifier Shift has been postulated in
order to derive noun phrases containing premodifying adjectives
from structures having the same canonical linear sequence as cases

where a head noun is postmodified by relative clauses, Jh phrases, etc.; since the SUSANNE analytic scheme is not concerned with the task of designing a set of production rules to "generate" the spectrum of actually occurring constructions, there is no motive to introduce notation implying that one of these orderings is derived at an underlying level from the other.

The contrasts between logical and surface structure which are shown in the SUSANNE scheme are as follows.

EQUI-NP DELETION AND RAISING TO OBJECT

§ 5.54 Where a Ti, Tg, or Tb has an ascertainable logical subject which occurs as an overt complement in a higher clause, it is represented by a ghost linked by an index to its antecedent:

[Nns:s123 *John*] *wanted* [Ti:o s123 *to go*]

[Ns:s123 *One wife*] *wanted* [Ti:o s123 *to name* [Ns:o *her baby daughter*] [Nns:j *Rowena — Ophelia — Elvira — Cardetta — Osberga*] — [P:r *after the ships . . .*] Ti:o]. F18.058

[Nns:s123 *Sam*] *would have liked* [Ti:o s123 *to have complained to the management*]*!* N10.124

[Fa *if* [Nas:s123 *he*] *wanted* [Ti:o s123 *to rise* [Ti:q s123 *to be head of his department*]] Fa][8] D16.066

[Nnp:s129 *The United States*] *must plan* [Ti:o s129 *to absorb the exported goods . . .*] A10:0350

[Nns:s *John*] *wanted* [Nns:O123 *Mary*] [Ti:o s123 *to go*]

[Nap:s *They*] *wanted* [Ns:O123 *prayer*] [Ti:o s123 *to be extemporary and unfettered*]. D05.190

. . . and [Np:s *many people in the country*] *would like* [Ns:O123 *that unity*] [Ti:o S123 *to be made* [J:e *apparent*]], *. . .* B12.187

[Ds:S123 *This*] *is expected* [Ti:o s123 *eventually to replace the Fiat G-91, and the F 104 Starfighter, . . .*]. A03.212 — on the functiontagging of the Ti, see § 5.67

[Nns:s *John*] *forced* [Nns:O123 *Mary*] [Ti:o s123 *to go*]

[Ns:s *An injury*] *forced* [Nns:O119 *Skorich*] [Ti:o s119 *to quit after the 1948 season*] A14:0230

[Nns:s123 *John*] *likes* [Tg:o s123 *eating* [Np:o *strawberries*]]

[Nas:s123 *he*] *disliked* [Tg:o S123 [Vgp *being ignored*]], *. . .* L17.108

---

[8] In this example, the inner Ti is functiontagged :q, Direction, since *rise* is seen as logically followed by a prepositional *to* which is deleted at the surface before infinitival *to* (cf. § 5.134 below).

Let [Neo:O123 *me*] [Tb:o s123 *go*] — but no subject is recon-
structed for *go* in the *let go of* construction mentioned in § 5.35
letting [Ns:O148 *the smoke*] [Tb:o s148 *lie* [J:e *warm and
soothing*] ... Tb:o] N07:0770
[S* *let* [Nop:O127 *+'s*] [Tb:o s127 *try* [Ti:o s127 *to go under
this stuff*] Tb:o] S*] N15:0570
[Nn:S129 *Skinny Brown and Hoyt Wilhelm* ...] [Vap *are slated*]
[Ti:o s129 *to oppose* [Np:o *the American League champions*] ...
Ti:o]. A11:1010 — again see § 5.67 for the Ti functiontagging
[Ns:s *A tabulation of these features*] *permits* [Np:O181 *the lungs*]
[Ti:o S181 *to be grouped* ...]. J12:1630
[Ti:c *to allow* [Ns:O153 *the captain*] [Ti:o s153 *to elaborate* ...]]
A20:0680
[Nas:s *he*] *told* [Nns:O151 *Jones*] [Ti:o s151 *to wash up*]
N01:1160
That's [Ff:e *why* [Np:s *the British*] *never got* [Np:O117 *the tribes*]
[Ti:o s117 *to fight for the King*] Ff:e]. N04:0210

§ 5.55　However, where the logical subject of a non-finite clause is
logically non-specific, as in ***Eating people*** *is wrong*, or even as in *It
is wrong **to kill oneself*** (where the reflexive object implies an underlying non-specific subject pronoun *one* but this does not otherwise
occur in the sentence) or where the logical subject corresponds to
you which has been deleted in an imperative higher clause, or to a
constituent that has been elided from the higher clause for some
other reason, no logical subject is represented in SUSANNE notation:[9]

Certainly, the mere fact of [Tg *failing* [Ti:o *to demonstrate them
...]] does not conclusively deny their existence* ... J12:1470
[S* *Try* [Ti:o *to find these Feds*] S*]. N03:0780
[S *Don't like* [Ti:o *to bother no one*] *unless we have to,* ...].
N09:1160 — the pronoun *I* informally elided before *don't*

And where the non-finite clause is introduced by a catenative construction such as *be going to* ... , *be about to* ... , the subject of
that clause — which will be identical with the subject of the higher
clause — is not indicated.[10]

---

[9] In the case of *help* + Tb constructions, compare:

a "shack-up" partner who will help [Tb:o *support them*] G13:1350 — no logical subject
within the Tb

— with:

This combined experience ... *has helped* [Neo:O263 *me*] [Tb:o s263 *do things* ...].
G22:1770

[10] On the treatment of "catenative" constructions, see §§ 5.199 ff.

§ 5.56 An item raised to surface object position may become surface subject if the higher clause is passivized — note the treatment of:

[Ns:S124 *the exchange of inactive chlorine . . .*] *was found* [Ti:o s124 *to be the most satisfactory*]. J06:0490 — on the functiontagging of the Ti, see § 5.67

§ 5.57 Raising to Object is not recognized where the lower clause is a Tn, since such a sequence is often quasi-adjectival. Sequences such as:

They keep [Np:o *their wings and feet*] [Tn:j *pressed tightly against their bodies*], . . . J10:0050
. . . and have had [Tn:j *imposed upon them*] [Np:o263 *social and economic controls they dislike*]. G01:1440

are analysed as shown, with no logical subject reconstructed within the Tn.

§ 5.58 Furthermore, no underlying subject is reconstructed where the verb of the higher clause has been nominalized:

he made [Ns:o *no attempt* [Ti *to get in touch with . . .*]] A07:0250

— or where a Tg is complement of a *without* P, as in the G11 example quoted in § 4.367 above.

§ 5.59 There is a special case of Raising to Object where the lower clause (logically) and the element raised out of it (at the surface) are objects of a prepositional rather than an ordinary transitive verb, e.g. *No cow thief could count on a jury of his sympathetic peers to free him any longer.* N11:1340, and such a case is analysed as:

. . . could count [P:u *on* [Ns:G210 *a jury of . . .*] [Ti s210 *to free him*] P:u] *any longer*

§ 5.60 The antecedent of a Raised subject may be deleted from the immediately higher clause under identity with a constituent of another clause, in which case the index will link the logical subject with this latter item:

[S *They expected greater things from him . . .* , [S+ *and* [Nap:s146 *they*] *were* [J:e *disappointed.* [Tn+ *And* [Vn *determined* Vn] [Ti:o s146 *not to show it*] Tn+] J:e] S+] S]. N05:1080

— *to be determined to X* is treated as a passivization of *to determine Y* [*Y to X*], as in:

[Nap:s104 *they*] [Vab *are*] [Tn:e *determined* [Ti:o s104 *not to tame...*]] G13:0330

§ 5.61 Classical transformational grammar makes a further logical distinction between two of the constructions discussed above: *John forced Mary to go* and *John wanted Mary to go* would be seen as differing in the logical roles attributable to *Mary*. In the *wanted* case, *Mary* would have a logical role only in the subordinate clause, being turned into surface direct object of *wanted* by the "Raising to Object" transformation; in the *forced* case, *Mary* would be seen as having logical roles in both subordinate *and* main clauses, and the *Mary* which is logically the subject of *go* is deleted (because of its identity with the *Mary* in the main clause) by the "Equi-NP Deletion" transformation. Semantically, it might be said that *John forced Mary to go* is about something being forced on Mary, but *John wanted Mary to go* is not about Mary being wanted.

This distinction could be reflected in SUSANNE notation by preserving the analysis shown above for the *wanted* case, but replacing [Nns:O123 *Mary*] in the *forced* case by [Nns:i123 *Mary*]. That might be a large extension of the traditional concept of "indirect object". But in any case the SUSANNE scheme does not recognize the logical distinction just outlined, since this breaks down in more realistically complex cases. For instance, *allow* would standardly be categorized as a *force*-type rather than *want*-type verb, and it is true that *John allowed Mary to go* is about something being allowed to Mary; but *carelessness allows accidents to happen* is not about something being allowed to accidents, and *the police did not allow the suspect to be interviewed by the press* might be either about something not being allowed to the suspect or about something not being allowed to the press. The SUSANNE parsing scheme assumes that these differences should be attributed to the meanings of the individual vocabulary items, rather than to different logical forms. (Cf. Sag and Pollard 1991.) Even *the thing* [Fr *that moves* [Np:O185 *men*] [Ti:o s185 *to sacrifice their lives*] Fr] G10:1500 is analysed as shown, with *men to sacrifice their lives* as the logical direct object of *moves*. The analysis for the *police* example quoted above will be:

[N:s *the police*] *did not allow* [Ns:O123 *the suspect*] [Ti:o S123 *to be interviewed* [P:a *by the press*]]

This decision does have the awkward consequence that the person taught plays a contrasting logical role in pairs of examples such as:

his mother taught [Nos:O117 *him*] [Ti:o s117 *to play the piano*] G06:0260
his mother taught [Nos:i *him*] [Ns:o *Italian*]

— if Raising to Object were distinguished from Equi-NP Deletion as suggested above, *him* would be :i in both cases. But this is regarded as a lesser drawback in the scheme.

§ **5.62** Passive subjects which have been moved elsewhere are an exception to the general rule that only the logical and surface end-points of transformational movements are marked: the surface subject of a passive construction is in general shown only at its surface position, not at its putative logical position as direct or indirect object elsewhere in the same clause tagma, and if a passive subject is then shifted into another clause the positions marked for that item by the notation will be intermediate and final positions rather than initial and final positions. Cf. §§ 5.22, 5.67.

§ **5.63** Where the subordinate clause in a *force*-type construction is understood, as in *She made me* for *She made me do it*, the item that would be functiontagged :O in the full construction is still functiontagged :O in the reduced version, despite the lack of a sister :o element:

[Nas:s *She*] *made* [Neo:O *me*].

In the simple clause *his mother taught him*, the pronoun *him* would normally be functiontagged :i because it is most natural to interpret the understood object as an N rather than a clause (whatever the thing taught); but in *his mother told him*, *him* would be functiontagged :O if the understood object were a clause (e.g. *to tidy his room*), but *him* would be functiontagged :i if the understood object were a N (e.g. *the family secret*).

RAISING TO SUBJECT

§ **5.64** Where a verb such as *seem* takes a clause complement, the logical subject of this clause, and the fact that the complement as a whole is logically the subject of the higher verb, are both indicated:

[Nns:S1 *John*] *seems* [Ti:s s123 *to be* [J:e *ill*]]
But [Nns:S115 *Mr. Buckley*] *seems* [Ti:s s115 [Vif *to have assumed*] [Fn:o *he would…*] Ti:s] A07:0350
… [Ds:S203 *this*] *seems* [Ti:s S203 t205 [Vip *to be* [R:G205 *rarely*] *encountered*] *in educational circles* Ti:s]. G01:0760
… [Ni:S123 *it*]*'s* [J:e *almost certain*] [Ti:s s123 *to disappear*]. F31.134
It was [Ns:e159 *the only thing* [P *about her*] [Fr *that was* [Jx:e *the least bit hard*] [Ti:s *to remember* o159] Fr] Ns:e159]. N05:1460
it teaches [Nop:i *us*] [Ns:o109 *something* [Z [J:e *useful*] [Ti:s *to know* o109] Z] [P *about ourselves*] Ns:o109] G12:0140

[Fa:c [J:e *Difficult*] *though* [Ns:S123 *such research*] *may be* [Ti:s *to plan and execute* o123] Fa:c], *it should* . . . J32.180

§ 5.65   Since the SUSANNE scheme never postulates underlying clauses where these have been reduced at the surface to single phrases (see § 5.3 above), the analysis of *the Berlin situation seems more stable* A05.064 (which classical transformational theory would again derive from a structure along the lines [[*the Berlin situation BE stable*] *SEEM*]) is simply:

[Ns:s *the Berlin situation*] *seems* [J:e *more stable*]

— *the Berlin situation* is here treated as logical (as well as surface) subject of *seems*. And no Raising to Subject has occurred in:

[S+ *But* [Ni:S123 *it*] [Vde *didn't seem*] [Fa:s *as_if there were* [Ns:s *a garden boy*] Fa:s] S+]. L13.039 — cf. § 5.70

or in the hypothetical alternative:

[S+ *But there_EX didn't seem* [Ti:s *to be* [Ns:s *a garden boy*]] S+] — cf. § 5.72

PASSIVE

§ 5.66   As already noted, the surface subject of a passive clause is functiontagged :S, whether logical direct or indirect object; the logical subject, if present, is functiontagged :a. (We saw in Chapter 4 that the passive status of the V is shown by the formtag symbol p.) The :S tag does not show whether the surface subject is logically direct or indirect object (as in *she was taken to Rome, she was given lunch* respectively); however, the relatively infrequent cases where passive subjects are logical indirect objects are commonly revealed by the presence in the same clause of a separate direct object, functiontagged :o, as in some of the following examples.

[Nns:S *John*] [Vsp *was attacked*].
[Nns:S *John*] [Vsp *was attacked*] [P:a *by a swarm of bees*].
[Nas:S *She*] [Vsp *was taken*] [P:q *to Rome*].
instances [Fr *where* [Np:S *the general mores*] h119 [Vdfp *had been* [R:G119 *radically*] *changed*] [P:h *with "deliberate speed* . . .] Fr] G17:0310
[Ns:S225 *The son of a wealthy Evanston executive*] [Vsp *was fined*] [Nu:h *$100*] *yesterday* . . . A20:1720
[O [S *The plan does not cover doctor bills* S]. [S [Nap:S *They*] t181 [Vdcp *would* [R:G181 *still*] *be paid*] [Pb:a *by the patient*] S]. O] A03:1270

[Ns:S159 *A bond issue which would have provided* ...] [Vsp *was defeated*] [Pb:a *by district voters*] [P:t *in January*]. A10:0850

[Nas:S *She*] [Vsp *was given*] [Ns:o *lunch*].

[Nas:S *he*] [Vsp *was awarded*] [Nus:o *the university's degree in law*] A19:1500

[Ns:S123 *Such grassland as had to be temporarily retained*] [Vsp *was given*] [Ns:o *a dressing of some 7 cwt. per acre of potassic supers* ...]. E36.020

in a sense [Ns:S *a unique image*] m133 [Vcp *can* [R:G133 *actually*] *be assigned*] [P:u *to each tangent*] J21:0430

[Nns:S123 *John*] [Vsp *was told*] [Ti:o s123 *to mend* [Np:o *his ways*]].

"[Q <bbold> [S [Nas:S123 *I*]] [Vcep *cannot be told*] [Ti:o s123 *to sit down*] <ebold> [Pb:a *by the Prime Minister*] S]. Q]" A06.103

[S [Fn:o *Several defendants in the Summerdale police burglary trial made statements* ... Fn:o], [Nns:S *Judge James B. Parsons*] [Vsp *was told*] *in Criminal court yesterday.* A03:0010

§ 5.67   Apart from the case described in § 5.66, a passive clause will contain a constituent functiontagged :o if some other grammatical process makes an element which is not the logical object of the main verb into the surface subject of the clause. This can happen when the logical object is a subordinate clause whose subject is Raised to Object and made surface subject of the higher clause by passivization (cf. the A03 and A11 examples of § 5.54, and the example of § 5.56), or when a passive subject is displaced by Extraposition (§ 5.70), e.g.:

[Ni:S *It*] m169 [Vdcp *should* [R:G169 *also*] *be recognized*] [Fn:o *that the problem of rural tenancy cannot be solved by administrative decrees alone*]. J22:1050

§ 5.68   The idiosyncratic construction exemplified by:

[Ns:s *everybody*] *is* [Tn:e *agreed* [Fn:o *that we need* ...]] A10:0570

is analysed as shown, and not with *BE agreed* as a Vp.

§ 5.69   Where in telegraphic style a Vp is reduced to a Vn, its subject is still functiontagged S:

[Oh <bmajhd> [S [Ns:S *MERGER*] [Vn *PROPOSED*] S] <emajhd> Oh] A01:0210

EXTRAPOSITION

§ 5.70 The epenthetic *it* of Extraposition is treated as surface subject, thus:

[Ni:S *It*] *is* [J:e *clear*] [Fn:s *that we must leave*].
[Ni:S *It*] *is* [J:e *true*] [Fn:s *that New England . . . was dedicated to education from the start*]. G17:1590
[Ni:S *It*] t143 [Vcb *will* [R:G143 *forever*] *be*] [Ns:e *a baseball mystery*] [Fn?:s *how a team will suddenly start hitting after a distressing slump*] <ebold>. A13:1450
Perhaps [Ni:S *it*] *would be helpful* [Fn:s *if I were to say something . . .*].[11] H21.084

— or as surface object, where Raising to Object has occurred and the remainder of the subordinate clause has been collapsed into the higher clause:

. . . by making [Ni:O *it*] [Ns:j *a responsibility of government*] [Ti:o *to promote individual welfare*] G02:1020
Hamilton, [Fr *who felt* [Ni:O *it*] "[Ns:j *a religious duty*]" [Ti:o *to oppose Aaron Burr's political ambitions*]], . . . G07:1110

§ 5.71 An analysis comparable to that used in cases of Extraposition is not applied in the case of the related construction involving existential *there* (§ 4.444), described by classical transformational theory as produced by *There*-Insertion; in the latter construction the logical subject is regarded as also surface subject, and the word *there*, which because of the nature of its wordtag has no phrase node above it, is not assigned a functiontag:

There_EX is [Ns:s *a devil*] [P:p *among us*].
. . . , it was apparent [Fn:s *that there_EX were* [Np:s *two distinct types*]]. J03:0200

If the subject of a clause with *There*-Insertion falls between *BE* and a participle, the participle is taken as head of a T. . . clause in predicate position, rather than the subject being treated as a guest element interrupting a single V tagma (cf. § 4.444):

[S *There is* [Nns:s *a New South*] [Tg:e *emerging*], . . . S]. G08:0310
[S *There seems* [Ti:s *to be* [R:m *almost*] [Ns:s *a conspiracy of silence*] [Tg:e *veiling it*] Ti:s] S]. G01:1330

---

[11] This construction should not be confused with that of the example quoted in § 5.40, *If they avoid the use of . . . it is because it is taboo*, where the *if* clause expresses a condition and the emphasized *it* is analysed as logical as well as surface subject.

In a case such as:

There_EX [Vwp *were said*] [Ti:S *to be* [Np:s *wolves*] [P:p *in the mountains*] Ti:S].

the verb agreement is paradoxical in terms of SUSANNE function-tagging, which treats the Ti as subject of *were said*. Classical transformational grammar would explain this case by saying that *wolves* had been Raised into the main clause, triggered verb agreement with *were*, and was then shifted back into the Ti when *there* was inserted in the main clause; but the SUSANNE scheme indicates nothing of this.

§ 5.72   In *But there seemed* [Ti:s *to be* [Ns:s *some difference of opinion as to how far the board should go, and whose advice it should follow* Ns:s] Ti:s]. A10:0420 the Ns *some difference . . .* has been displaced from its logical position at the beginning of the Ti, but by the rule about lowest possible attachment of dislocated elements (§ 5.7) it remains a daughter of the Ti. Cf. *There seems* [Ti:s *to be* [Ns:s *an intruder*] [P:p *in the garden*] Ti:s].

§ 5.73   In a cleft construction, where the extraposed element is formtagged Fn (§ 4.308), this is tagged as logical subject, the *it* as surface subject, and the focused element as guest:

[Ni:S *It*] *was* [P:G123 *to him*] [Fn:s *that Barton had sent Dill* q123 . . .]. N07:0470

. . . and [Ni:S *it*]*'s usually* [P:G123 *under just those conditions*] [Fn:s *that help is called for* c123]. F22.035

For clefts where the extraposed element is an Fr, see § 5.85.

RELATIVE CLAUSE FORMATION, *WH*-FRONTING, WHIZ DELETION

§ 5.74   The relationship between a relative pronoun and its antecedent is indicated by the indexing mechanism; if a zero relative pronoun is used then a ghost node is inserted in order to carry the appropriate functiontag and index. The functiontag on the ghost will show the underlying logical role of the antecedent within the relative clause, except that if the relativized item is subject of a passive clause the ghost is functiontagged :S rather than :o or :i. A ghost indexed to the antecedent is also inserted in cases where Whiz Deletion has removed both the relative pronoun and the finite verb of an underlying relative clause, provided that what remains is a non-finite clause (T. . . or Z) which follows rather than precedes the head.

§ 5.75   If a constituent moved leftwards by *Wh*-Fronting remains a daughter of its "logical mother", no special annotation is called for; but *wh-* items moved into a separate tagma have their source indicated via the ghost system.

I like [Ns:o123 *the man* [Fr [Nq:o123 *who*] [Ny:s *you*] *met*]]
I like [Ns:o123 *the man* [Fr [Ny:s *you*] *met* o123]]
... *having* [Ns:o193 *the first carefree, dreamless sleep* [Fr *that* [Nas:s *she*] *had known* o193 [Fa:t *since they dropped down* ...] Fr] Ns:o193] N13:1270
[Ns:s123 *The reason* [Fr *we subtract the correction term* <formul> c123]] *is that* ... J19.203
[Ns@:193 *a picture* [Fr [Nap:s195 *they*] m197 [Vdc *could* [R:G197 *scarcely*] *afford*] [Ti:o s195 *to present* o193 *to the public* Ti:o] Fr] Ns@:193] G22:1290
[Nq:o *Who*] [Vod *did*] [Nns:s *John*] [Vr *meet*]?
[S? [Nqp:o *What additional roles*] *has* [Ns:s *the scientific under-standing of the 19th and 20th centuries*] *played* S?]? G11:1370
[Nq:G123 *What*] [Vo *do*] [Ny:s *you*] [Vr *keep*] [Ds:o *this*] [Ps:p *in* 123]? — *What* is logically a daughter of the P *in what*, so becomes a guest when separated from its preposition by *Wh*-Fronting
I don't know [Fn?:o [Dq:G158 *what*] *you're* [P:e *up_to_II=* 158] Fn?:o], ... N12:0810
[Nq:G123 *Who*] *did* [Ny:s *you*] *say* [Fn:o [Ny:s *you*] *met* o123]?
I like [Ns:o123 *the man* [Fr [Nq:G123 *who*] [Nns:s *John*] *said* [Fn:o s123 *was* [Ncs:e *an Albanian*]]]]
... [Ns@:123 *something* [Fr *that* [Nas:s *he*] *had not realized* [Fn:o s123 *existed*] *before* Fr] Ns@:123] G25.076
We encountered [Ncs:o123 *a man* [Tg s123 *shouting* [Ns:o *abuse*]]]
... *occupying* [Np:o121 *seats and vantage points* [Tg s121 *border-ing* [Nns:o *Lafayette Square,* ...] Tg] Np:o121]. A08:0450
she is [Ncs:e123 *a woman* [Tn S123 *consumed* [P:a *by jealousy*]]]
... *the amount of* [Ns:189 *dispersion mode* [Tn S189 [Vn *mixed*] [R:n *in*] [P:w *with the absorption signal*] Tn] Ns:189]. J04:1590
[Nns:s103 *Pennsylvania Avenue,* [Tn S103 *named for one of the original 13 states* Tn], Nns:s103] *perhaps is not* ... A08:0230
[Ms:184 *the one* [Z [J:e *most likely*] [Ti:s s184 *to go*] Z] Ms:184] A08:0970 — see § 5.64 on the analysis of Raising to Subject constructions

This is [Ns:e123 *a good time* [Po *of year*] [Tq [Pq:t *at* [Dq:123 *which*]] *to lay turf* Tq]]. E08.108

that would be [D:e123 *a_lot* [Tf *for* [D:s *a_lot of people*] [Vi *to swallow*] o123 Tf]] B02.050

[Ns:s123 *the man* [Ti *to talk* [P:u *to* 123] *about this* Ti]] *is John.*

§ 5.76   In the case of Ff clauses, or Fa clauses introduced by *wh-* words lacking antecedents (§ 4.291), the Ff or Fa node carries no index; the *wh-* word is indexed only in cases where it needs to be marked as extracted from a separate tagma, as in:

[Ff:s [Dq:G120 *What*] *they are* [P:e *after* 120] Ff:s] *is . . .* G13:0520

. . . to [Ff [Dq:O123 *what*] *I think* [Fn:o s123 *is the clue . . .*] Ff] A19.107

§ 5.77   No ghost is inserted in the case of a non-finite modifying clause *preceding* its head, although some linguists would regard such a clause as arising from Whiz Deletion of a relative clause followed by preposing:

. . . sounded like [Np [Tg [Vg *signaling*]] *Indian scouts*], *. . .* N04:0750

[Ns:o [Tg [Vg *growing*]] *sociological understanding*] G11:0410 *and cause* [Np:o [Tn [Vn *increased*]] *convulsive discharges*]. J17:0390

[Ns:S *the* [Ns [Tn [Vn *adsorbed*]] *water*] *resonance*] J04:1830

In such cases little information is lost by failing to show explicit ghosts — where the participles retain a genuinely verbal sense the ghosts would always be functiontagged :s in the case of Tg and :S in Tn premodifiers; and in other cases, where the participles approach adjectival or nominal status, it would often be artificial to insert ghosts — in sequences such as *its* [Tg *operating*] *procedures* A01:0470, or [Ns [Tg *NURSING*] *HOME*] *CARE* A03:1030, it would be difficult to identify any relationship more specific than modification between the participles and their head nouns.

§ 5.78   No use is made of the index system to link relativized items to antecedents in the case of relative-like A clauses (§ 4.369), the reason being that in such cases the element relativized is often a sense-bearing rather than reference-bearing item, and the SUSANNE scheme in general avoids reconstructing such (cf. § 5.102) — thus in:

The approach . . . may be [Jh:e *analytic,* [A *as it is for Miss Litz*], [Jh+ *or . . .*]]. G09:0950

[Ns:s *the "threshold"*, [A *as the conventional forces strengthening is called*]], *will prove* . . . A04:0670

the items relativized is the predicate *analytic* in the first case, and the noun *threshold* (not the noun phrase headed by it) in the second; and in many other cases the relationship of A clause to the logic of the relative construction is somewhat vague (in *the corporation* [A *as it exists in America today*] G22:0400, is *as it* effectively equivalent to *which*, i.e. indicating a clause with relativized subject — if so, why include the *it*? — or should the clause rather be interpreted along the lines *taken in the form in which it exists today*, that is, with the relativized item playing a role other than subject?). For these reasons, A relatives do not annotate the relationship between relativized item and antecedent even in cases where these can be clearly identified:

at [Ns *the same time* [A *as he sent Cranbrook his copy of the telegram*]] J59.009

§ 5.79 In a relative clause introduced by *that*, the word *that* is regarded as a conjunction, wordtagged CST, rather than a relative pronoun; accordingly the relativized item is indicated by a ghost *which*, if subject of the relative clause, immediately follows *that*:

. . . *to pass* [Ns:o135 *enabling legislation* [Fr *that_*CST s135 *will permit the establishment* . . .]] A01:0620
at [Ns:179 *the very time* [Fr *that_*CST *nationalist fervors can wreak greatest harm* t179]] G02:1430

§ 5.80 *Wh-* adverbs introducing relative clauses are indexed:

till [M:123 *1768*, [Fr [Rq:t123 *when*] *they were delivered* . . .]] J37.080
After all, there was [Ns:s123 *no reason* [Fr [Rq:c123 *why*] *he should come here*]]. N21.025

and *so* (§ 4.312) is treated similarly:

[Ns:o194 *a way* [Fr [R:h194 *so*] *we can carry on without his suspecting us*]] N18:1120

But *like* introducing a relative is treated as a conjunction akin to *that*:

[Ns:o123 *a queer feeling*, [Fr *like_*ICSk *I always get* o123 *when* . . .]] M03.025

§ 5.81 Since a relative pronoun, or its antecedent, may have been moved by some other transformation, and a single antecedent may have multiple relative clauses, a passage containing one or more relative clauses can often have three or more nodes sharing a common index; cf.:

> *I want* [Ns:O123 *the kite* [Fr *I made* o123 *yesterday*]] [Ti:o s123 *to fly*].
> *This is* [Ns:e123 *the woman* [Fr [Nq:s123 *who*] *will teach us* [Fr+ *and* [Nq:S123 *who*] *will be paid accordingly*]]].
> . . . *using* [Ns:o123 *the original lead-210 solution* [Tn *supplied by the Radiochemical Centre*] [Fr [Dq:G123 *which*] *we concluded* [Fn:o s123 *was radiochemically pure*] Fr] Ns:o123] J04.041
> . . . *of* [Ns:123 *the sound complement,* [Fr [Dq:G123 *which*], [Ni:S *it*] *was suggested above (p. 140),* [Fn:o S123 *could be taken as the actual norm* . . .] Fr] Ns:123]. J32.186

§ 5.82 A zero relative which plays no logical role in its clause is not indicated by a ghost — thus no :G element is inserted in the relative clause in:

> *you're* [Ns:e159 *the kind of governor* [Fr *we're* [Jh:e *glad* [Fn *we elected* o159]]]] A06:1390

— likewise no :S element in the Z clauses in:

> [Ms:184 *the one* [Z [J:e *most likely*] [Ti:s s184 *to go*]]] A08:0970
> . . . *who "publishes* [Ns:o123 *a report* [Z [J:e *likely*] [Ti:s s123 *to cause alarm*] [Jh+ *or prejudicial to public safety*] Z] Ns:o123]." A02.084

and no :O element in the relative clause in:

> [Np:o247 *demands* [Fr [Np:s *the dancers*] *find* [J:j *impossible*] [Ti:o *to execute* o247] Fr] Np:o247] G09:1750

§ 5.83 Where the relative pronoun of an Fr is the complement of a prepositional phrase, or the possessive *whose*, this will typically be in a position which would not be phrasetagged were it not for the need for a phrasetag to carry the index (cf. § 5.9):

> [N@:123 *the people* [Fr [Pq:u *with* [Nqo:123 *whom*] Pq:u] *Clause 2 deals* Fr]] H16.117
> . . . *if you lend to* [Ns:123 *someone* [Fr [Nqs:s [Gq:123 *whose*] *credit*] *is not good* Fr] Ns:123], *then* . . . B13.218
> . . . *for* [Nns:123 *Verly Bewicke,* [Fr [Dqp:s *many* [Poq *of* [Nqp [Gq:123 *whose*] *horses*]] *are* [Tn *related to each other*] Fr] Nns:123]. A23.160

§ 5.84 The antecedent of an Fr cannot always be strictly a referring expression co-referential with the relative pronoun. In the example:

> ... *evenings spent at* [G:123 *the vet's*, [G– *the chemist's*] [G+ *and the clergyman's*], [Fr [Pq:G125 *to* [Nqs [Gq:123 *whose*] *society*]] *Sonia now had good hopes of* [Ns *access* 125 Ns]] G:123] K23.150

— logically speaking the antecedent of the Fr is the conjunction of the noun phrases which are stems of the genitive phrases, *the vet, the chemist and the clergyman*; but such a conjunction does not occur as a tagma, so the compound G must be treated as antecedent. (The fact of antecedent and relative pronoun both being possessive in this example is coincidental — the problem would equally arise if the Fr read, say, *with whom Sonia was now well acquainted*.)

§ 5.85 In a cleft construction where the extraposed element is formtagged Fr (cf. § 4.315), the ghost system is used to analyse it as logically a postmodifier of the *it*, cf.:

> [Ni:s125 *It* 123] *was* [Ncs:e *a good school*] [Fr:G123 *I sent him* [Ps:q *to* 125]].
> ... [Ni:s123 *it* 125] *is* [Ns:e *the influence of the mare*] [Fr:G125 [Dq:s123 *which*] *predominates*]. A23.148
> ... [Ni:s172 *it* 171] *was* [Ns:e *a fairly typical landlord*] [Fr:G171 [Nq:s172 *who*] *in the dead of night lugged me up a mountainside* ...] G05:0720
> [Ni:s123 *it* 125] [Vzeb *is not*] [N:e *the Old Country* 127] [Fr:G125 [Pq *on* [Dq:123 *which*]] *they model themselves* Fr:G125], [Nns+:G127 *but the New Jones*]. R01.070

If, however, the antecedent *it* of such a cleft construction is deleted within a reduced clause, the extraposed element must be functiontagged as the whole logical subject and no ghost is reconstructed within it, as in the S– of:

> [S [Ni:s165 *It* 167] *is sex* [Fr:G167 *that* s165 *obsesses them*], [S– [Ns:e *sex*] [Fr:s *that is at the basis of their aesthetic creed*]]]. G13:1050

For clefts in which the extraposed element is an Fa, see § 5.73.

DISLOCATION

§ 5.86 A sequence such as *He is a brilliant man, my father* is analysed as a case of an appositional element within an earlier constituent being displaced to a later position:

[Nas:s *he* 123] *is* [Ncs:e *a brilliant man*], [Ns@:G123 *my father*]

Cf.:

> ... [S+ *and* [Np *three boxers* 123] *reached the semi-finals,*
> [Nn@:G123 [NP1s& *Kasprzyk, Jozefowicz and Gugniewicz*]
> Nn@:G123] S+]. E17.052

§ 5.87   The corresponding analysis is also used:

- when a reflexive pronoun used with emphatic rather than reflexive force is detached from its antecedent:

> [S [Nea:s *I* 123] *made it* [Nos:G123 *myself*] S] P02.186

— emphatic reflexives are not formtagged as appositional,
whether adjacent to or dislocated away from their antecedents.

- in cases of included adverbials (§ 4.23):

> [Ns:S *notice* 199] *would have* [Ti:z t201 [Vip *to* [R:G201
> *first*] *be given* Vip] Ti:z] [Fn:G199 *that...*] A01:1450
> [Np *The limitations of...*] m123 t125 [Vfp *have* [R:G123
> *also*] *been* [R:G125 *recently*] *discussed* Vfp] *by...* J05.046

- shifting of an LE...word, as in:

> [S [Fa *If her naturally healthy desire to grow up is frustrated*]
> 123 *she* [Vc *will* [LEe:G123 *either*] *lose*] *her urge to be
> independent* [S+ *or she will rebel and go her own way
> anyhow*]]. F17.177
> ... *was unable to demonstrate their existence,* [LEe:G174
> *either*] [Pb:h *by* [Np [J 174 *anatomic* [J+ *or physiolo-
> gic*]] *methods*]], *in dogs.* J12:1430 — the fact that the
> co-ordination of adjectives contains a ghost representing
> a pre-co-ordinator is enough to prevent it being analysed
> as a wordlevel co-ordination (but contrast *in* [Np *both the*
> [JJ& *liquid and gas*] *phases*] J06:0200, which does not
> derive from **in the both liquid and gas phases*)

— such cases involve a special additional analytic convention
discussed at § 5.111 below, and detailed analysis of examples
is deferred to that section.

- in cases of Extraposition from NP:

> [Ns:s123 *a performer* 125] *will appear* [R:t *shortly*] [Fr:G125
> [Nq:s123 *who*] *is dressing now*]
> *For every boy and girl...* [Ns:s123 *the day* 125] *comes*
> [Fr:G125 [Rq:t125 *when*] *they must start...*]. H25.149

- and displacement rightwards out of their mother tagma of
  various other "heavy" constituents, e.g. the subordinate conjuncts discussed in § 4.498:

[S *Mr. L. Smith . . . said that* [Np:s123 *many* [Tn S123
employed in public service] 125] *already had three weeks
holiday* [Np+:G125 *and* [R:m *also*] *many white collar
workers . . . ,* [Fr [Nq:s125 *who*] *were winning the day in
negotiations with individual firms* Fr] Np+:G125] S].
A27.014

§ 5.88   The dislocated item will be shown with the formtagging
appropriate to its logical position (although, if it is a single word
moved out of a phrase, it will have to be given a phrase formtag in
order to carry the functiontag and index linking it to its ghost). Thus,
in the A27 case above, the moved element has a formtag containing
plus sign because it is conjoined, not to the S of which it is a surface
daughter, but to the Np within which it occurs in logical structure.

On the other hand, a tagma out of which a constituent has been
dislocated is given the formtagging appropriate to the wording that
remains. Thus, in the example *It was a terrible thing to do* discussed
in § 5.7, the J node dominating *terrible* together with the ghost
representing the logical position of *to do* is not given the Jh subcategory marking the adjective as postmodified.

§ 5.89   When part of a clause IC is dislocated into a position
immediately below the clause node and functiontagged :G, but has
an adjacent tagma associated with it which can be seen as playing
a logical role within the clause — for instance, when a dislocated
appositional element is introduced by an adverbial as discussed in
§ 4.508 — the associated tagma is not itself treated as having been
moved:

he also stresses [N:o *the works* [Po *of these favorite masters*] 168
N:o] [P:p *on tour*], [R:m *especially*] [Nnp@:G168 *Mahler's
First and Fourth Symphonies . . .*]. G06:1180

In his mood, [Ni:s *it* 153] *was* [Ns:e154 *the best way* [Ti *to handle
him* h154]]; [R:m *that_is*], [Ti@:G153 *to show no curiosity
whatsoever*]. N09:0830

— the emphasized constituents are not shown as underlyingly part
of the noun phrases from which the appositional elements have
been extracted.

§ 5.90   As said in § 4.325, the SUSANNE scheme does not treat
sequences such as *more X than . . . , as X as . . . , such X as . . . , so
X that . . .* as involving dislocation; such tagmas are analysed as containing three sister constituents, e.g.:

[Jh:e *more_DAR belligerent_JJ* [P *than the rest of the country*]]
G01:1510

[Np:o *such charges* [P *as poor manners,* . . .]] G01:1790
[Jh– *less eloquent* [P *than Jefferson*]] G07:0850

and even:

[Ns:o *such an inherent sense* [Po *of humor*] [Fc *that it relieves
the strain* . . .]] A14:1530
. . . *revolved around her* [Ds:h *so much* [P+ *and for so long*] [Fc
that now he felt . . .]]. N01:0060

— nothing in the analysis suggests that e.g. *more than the rest of
the country, such as poor manners, so that now he felt* are single
units at a logical level. (In the case of *as X as* . . . there is no
plausibility in a suggestion that the elements before and after the X
form a single logical unit; since these comparative structures are
similar to one another, all of them are analysed as *as X as* . . . must
be analysed.) On the other hand, in examples such as the following
a three-element construction of this kind is broken into two parts
surrounding a fourth element which it might be regarded as a whole
as modifying (though, in SUSANNE terms, the fourth element would
be analysed as a sister of the tripartite construction) — in such cases
the index system is used to link the dislocated part of the tripartite
construction to the earlier parts:

. . . *to resemble* [R:h *more nearly* 185] [Ns:o *the performance of
a rain dance*] [Fc:G185 *than the carrying out of an experiment
in physics*]. G11:1200
. . . *the second education* [R:h *as quickly* 123] *disappeared*
[Fc:G123 *as the first*], . . . D14.043
. . . *to function* [D:h *more* 123] [P:p *in other departments*]
[Fc:G123 *than I have been able to do in the past*]. E11.154
. . . *he* t123 m125 [Vdc *would* [R:G123 *still*] [R:G125 *rather*
127] *sing*] [Fc:G127 *than do anything else*] E11.161
. . . *had mounted* [P:h *at* [Ns *such a rate* 251]] [R:t *recently*]
[Fc:G251 *that I now found* . . .]. N06:1600
. . . *approaches* [Rr:h *much more closely* 123] [P:q *to* [Np
countercurrent [Fc:G123 *than* [P *to crossflow*]] *conditions*
Np] J07.065
. . . *is* h123 [Jh:e *due* [Ds:G123 *as much* 125] [P *to Wicki the
photographer*] [Fc:G125 *as* [P:e *to Wicki the director*] Fc:G125]
Jh:e]. C02.029
It should be [J:e [D *no more* 203] *difficult* J:e] [Ti:s *to deliver
such devices*] [Fc:G203 *than* [Np:o *other weapons*] Fc:G203].
J08:1740

And a two-part tagma *such that . . .* has been broken up in:

> [D:e *such* 142] *is the mystique of planning* [Fc:G142 *that people expect . . .*] J22:0610

— which is accordingly analysed as shown.

§ 5.91 In:

> *The Preminger name worked no miracles with the little man ([I [S he was [R:m only] [J:e little] [R:r physically] S] I]) and he threw in . . .* A18.088

one might think of *only* as having been shifted leftwards out of a logical tagma *only physically*; but in view of the general SUSANNE tendency to treat *only* as not closely cohesive with what it precedes, no dislocation is marked in this case. Likewise, the phrase *more wonderful still* D11.070 might be regarded as a surface reordering of [J *still more wonderful*], but *still more* would not be treated as a tagma within the latter sequence (cf. § 4.199), hence *still* is not dislocated in *more wonderful still*, which is a Jh with three words as ICs.

§ 5.92 Topicalization, where a non-subject is shifted to clause-initial position without a (reduced or full) copy remaining in the logical position — e.g. *strawberries I like*, as opposed to *strawberries, I like them* (for which see § 4.525) — usually calls for no special notation since it merely places the ICs of a clause in a non-standard order. However, the ghost system is used where the topicalized element is only part of a clause constituent, as in:

> [Po:G123 *of those* <bital> d <eital> *that pass through a* <bital> g <eital> *which is not a ray*] [Ms:s *only one* 123] *belongs to* ℱ, . . . J21.036
>
> [S [Po:G120 *Of several methods employed . . .*], *the exchange of inactive chlorine with tagged aluminum chloride at room temperature was found to be* [Nj:e *the most satisfactory* 120]]. J06:0480

EMBEDDED QUOTING CLAUSE

§ 5.93 When a tagma within a passage of direct speech is interrupted by a quoting clause, the quoting clause is formtagged Ss, and the ghost and index system is used to show that the direct speech is logically the object of the verb of quoting; in its surface position the quotation is a "guest":

[O ... "[Q:G117 [S *All my life*", [Ss *he said* o117], "*I tried* S].
[S *I tried*]. [S *I saw you driftin away* ... S]. ... Q:G117]" ...
O] N02:0280

The internal inverted commas used to exclude the Ss from the
quotation are not treated as bounding the Q tagma.

§ 5.94   This system is used only when the quoting clause occurs
medially within a sentence of the direct quotation; if it occurs at a
point which would be a typographic sentence boundary if the
quotation were analysed without the quoting clause, the need for an
Ss tagma is avoided by treating the quotation as a sequence of Q's:

[O ... [S "[Q:o [S *All my life I tried* S] Q:o]", *he said* S]. "[Q
[S *I tried*]. [S *I saw you* ... S]. ... Q]" ... O]

— contrast this with:

"[Q:G175 *Nae_UH*, [Ns" *man*]", [Ss *said Willie* o175], "[S *ye*
must be countin' the echoes S] Q:G175]". A14:1380

where the Ss occurs at an S boundary, but not at a boundary of a
typographic sentence.

§ 5.95   The material interrupted by an Ss need not be formally
speaking "direct speech", formtagged Q: it may be a sequence printed
as indirect speech, or a sequence acting as logical object of a verb
such as *believe* which can never normally take a Q object. However,
because the Ss is regarded as subordinate in surface grammar to its
logical object, in these latter cases the enclosing clause will be
formtagged S, not Fn. Thus:

[S:G151 *It was not*, [Ss *thought* [Nns:s *Pamela*] o151 Ss], *such*
an evil place after all]. N08:0560

[S:G207 *This*, [Ss *he was* [J:e *sure* 207] Ss], *was the way* ...].
N09:1680 — in a sequence *he was sure (that) this was the*
way ..., the nominal clause would be a postmodifier of *sure*
(§ 4.184)

[S:G132 *He could move very quickly*, [Ss *she knew* o132 Ss] ([Fa:c
although he seldom found occasion to do so]), [S+ *but he was*
more wiry than truly strong] S]. N09:0460

§ 5.96   Moreover the Ss analysis can be used where the verb of
the "quoting clause" is intransitive, so that the material logically
subordinate to it is functiontagged :e as discussed in § 5.51:

[S:G249 *This desire*, [Ss *I went on* e249, [Tg:b *growing voluble*
as my conviction was aroused] Ss], *had mounted* ...].
N06:1590

"[Q:G195 *When I was in college*", [Ss *I grinned* e195], "*I re-member . . .* Q:G195]". N18:1140

§ 5.97   If the portion of the quotation following the quoting clause is the kind of material (such as a single "heavy" tagma) which is commonly dislocated rightwards, the analysis which makes the body of the quotation a sister of the verb of quoting and treats the remainder of the quotation as having been moved is preferred:

[S [Fn:o *Not_only*_LE= *were the council there to acknowledge the new Mayor* 123 Fn:o], *said Clr. Hazelden,* [Fn+:G123 *but for the second time in Huddersfield's long history they were to honour their new Mayor with an aldermanic seat* Fn+:G123] S]. A30.062

However, if the material following the quoting clause is part of a Q and surrounded by inverted commas, these will be sisters of the postposed material; rather than adopting an analysis that suggests that a tagma has been moved into a position between a pre-existing pair of inverted commas, the Ss analysis is used:

'[Q:G123 [S *The ball which had been set rolling* <hellip> *did not stop*', [Ss *he wrote later* o123 Ss], '[Fa *until the Education Acts* <hellip> *had revolutionised* <hellip> *administration* <hellip> *throughout the country* Fa] S] Q:G123]'. J39.088

"[Q:G178 [S *This is* [Ns:e179 *a very modest proposal* [Tn S179 *cut to meet absolutely essential needs*", [Ss [Nas:s *he*] [Vd *said*] o178 Ss], "[P+ *and with sufficient 'deductible' requirements to discourage . . .* P+] Tn] Ns:e179] S] Q:G178]". A03:1200

§ 5.98   The containing clause must be of the right form to occur potentially as an element within the Ss clause. The interpolated clauses must be analysed as I rather than Ss in:

Her arrival in Sydney in [N *the autumn,* [Ns+ *or* [I [S? *shall we say*] I] *Sydney's spring* Ns+] N], *would have put . . .* E18.066

"*The recognition of complicity is the beginning of innocence*", [Fr:x *where innocence,* [I [S *I think*]], *means about the same thing as redemption* Fr:x]. G17:1130

This combined experience, on a foundation of [N *very average,* [I [S *I assure you*]], *intelligence and background* N], *has helped . . .* G22:1770

[S *He was* [J:e [J *tall* [J+ *and dark-skinned*]], [Ns− *a half-breed,* [I [S *Wilson thought*]] Ns−] J:e] S]. N05:0600

In the E18 case, what we are invited to say is not something beginning with *or*. One might alternatively treat the whole of *or shall we say Sydney's spring* as an S+ conjoined to *the autumn*, within which *Sydney's spring* is object of *say*; but this would do violence to the logic of the example, which offers *Sydney's spring* as an alternative to *the autumn*. In the G17 case, what I think is not a clause beginning *where* (and *I think* is being used too literally to be analysed as an S! by § 4.447). In the G22 case, the implied object of *assure* is a nominal clause such as *that my intelligence is very average*, but no such clause is overtly present; likewise in the N05 case an object clause such as *that he was a half-breed* has been reduced to a noun phrase functioning as a subordinate conjunct.

§ **5.99**   An Ss may be embedded more than one level deep:

[S:G123 *The establishment of the Overseas Research Council* ... [Vc *will*, [Ss [Ni:S *it*] [Vzp *is hoped*] o123 Ss], *help*] *to strengthen the links* ...]. H10.071

— here the main clause is the logical object of an Ss clause (involving Extraposition) which is included within the verb group of the main clause.

NEGATIVE TRANSPORTATION

§ **5.100**   The ghost and index mechanism is used to mark cases where a negative particle is attached to the verb of a higher clause than the one logically negated, as in *I don't think I have to tell you* ... L10.172 meaning "I think I don't have to tell you ...". Like the shifting of LE ... words (§ 5.87), Negative Transportation involves the special notational convention discussed at § 5.111, and examples are illustrated in detail there.

VP FRONTING

§ **5.101**   There is a difficulty about using the SUSANNE annotation mechanisms to analyse a sequence like *Pass the test he will!*, because the substring that has been preposed, *pass the test*, is not a SUSANNE tagma. (This problem is not simply a consequence of lack of recognition by the SUSANNE scheme of the traditional "VP" category, since even in classical transformational grammar that does recognize VP's these words would not be a constituent of the clause *he will pass the test*.) The solution adopted is to use the Vo and Vr formtags rather than the indexing mechanism:

[Vr *Pass*] [Ns:o *the test*] [Nas:s *he*] [Voc *will*]!

This is not an elegant treatment, since it obscures the fact that (on any obvious view) the words *pass the test* have been moved as a unit; but, since the construction is rather infrequent, the inelegance seems tolerable.

§ 5.102   The analytic practices listed above include many cases where the SUSANNE scheme reconstructs a reference-bearing item (usually a noun phrase) which has been deleted, reduced, or shifted from its logical position. English grammar also contains processes which delete or reduce sense-bearing items. Such processes include Co-ordination Reduction (*John and Mary went to London* from a logical structure of the form [*John went to London*] *and* [*Mary went to London*]), Gapping (*John ate strawberries and Mary salad* from [*John ate strawberries*] *and* [*Mary ate salad*]), and the *Do-So* rule (*John saw the flash and so did Mary* from [*John saw the flash*] *and* [*Mary saw the flash*]).

A fundamental limitation of the SUSANNE analytic scheme is that it makes no attempt to reconstruct sense-bearing, as opposed to reference-bearing, items. The examples just quoted would be analysed within the SUSANNE system as:

[Nn:s [NP1m& *John* [NP1f+ *and Mary*]]] [Vd *went*] [P:q *to London*]

[S [Nns:s *John*] [Vd *ate*] [Ns:o *strawberries*] [S+ *and* [Nns:s *Mary*] [Ns:o *salad*]]]

[S [Nns:s *John*] [Vd *saw*] [Ncs:o *the flash*] [S+ *and* [Ns:h *so*] [Vd *did*] [Nns:s *Mary*]]]

Apart from co-ordinations, reduction is commonly found also in Fc's, and in other constructions which involve partial parallelism of successive tagmas; but no attempt is made to reconstruct their deleted elements:

... [Nas:s *he*] *was* [Jh:e *more puzzled* [Fc *than* [R:t *ever*]]]. N01:0320 — no reconstruction of *he* or *was puzzled* in the Fc

... *it was* [Jh:e *even less inviting* [Fc *than Judith Pierce had made* [Ni:O161 *it*] [Tb:o s161 *seem*] Fc]. N05:1500 — no indication of the logical role of *inviting* within the Fc

[Nap:S243 *We*] *are tempted* [Ti:o s243 *to blame others for our problems* [R:m *rather* [Fc *than look them straight in the face* ...]]]. G22:1640 — no "s243" in the Fc

[Ns+ *and a shift* [P *in the reaction*] [P *from* [Ns *hypo-* [P *to normal*] *reactivity* [Po *of the sympathetic system* Po] Ns] P] [A *as shown by the Mecholyl test*] Ns+] J17:0920 — no reconstruction of the deleted copy of *reactivity* after *normal*

[Ns:S179 *This new force, love of country,* [Tn S179 *superimposed* [P:p *upon* — [Fa *if not displacing*] — [Np *affectionate ties to one's own state*] P:p] Tn],] *was epitomized by Washington.* G07:1640 — the Fa is logically an IC of the Tn but cannot be shown as such (and hence is not functiontagged) ... *ranged* [P:q *from* [Nu 48 [P *to* 74] *percent*]] *last year.* A09:0650

In all such cases the surface structure is analysed in such a way that the first of the two parallel tagmas contains all the elements it needs to be complete (cf. § 4.497) — thus, in the J17 example, the one instance of *reactivity* is included in the Ns *from hypo-* . . . *reactivity* — and nothing is done to show how the gaps in the reduced tagmas are logically filled.

For the simple artificial examples of Co-ordination Reduction listed at the beginning of the section it might be straightforward to devise a notation to show what has been deleted. A notation which adequately reconstructed sense-bearing material in realistically complex texts (including the Fc examples, or authentic examples involving co-ordination), however, would require a major extension to the SUSANNE scheme; this has not been attempted. An item which is *moved* out of the tagma of which it is logically an IC will have its logical position shown by the ghost and index system irrespective of whether or not it is a referring item:

[Fa [J:G123 *Calm*] *though* [Nas:s125 *she*] *strove* [Ti:o s125 *to be* e123] Fa]

Where material is *deleted*, on the other hand, it is reconstructed only if it is a referring item.

§ 5.103   Because reduction operates in a general way to delete any item which is shared between parallel tagmas, irrespective of whether the shared item is sense-bearing, reference-bearing, or purely grammatical, the SUSANNE scheme adopts a general principle that such deletions are not reconstructed, even if the deleted items are reference-bearing constituents: in *John woke up and lit a cigarette*, the scheme will make no attempt to show that *John* occurs logically as subject of the *lit* clause.

§ 5.104   However, where the general approach to logical-grammar annotation would call for a ghost to be created in a subordinate conjunct of a co-ordinate structure, it is not omitted merely because a ghost with the same index is required also in the main conjunct:

> *Let* [Nop:O184 *us*] [Tb:o s184 *look in on* . . . [Tb+ *and* s184 *see what* . . .]]. G03:1220
>
> *from* [Ns:179 *a type of mentality* [Fr [Nea:s181 *I*] +'d en-countered o179 *often enough* [Fr+ *but certainly had not ex-pected* [Ti:o s181 *to find* o179 *here*]]]] N06:0850
>
> *The land over which he sped was* [Ns:e205 *the land* [Fr *he had created* o205 [Fr+ *and lived* [P:p *in* 205] Fr+] Fr]: [Ns@ *his valley*] Ns:e205]. N02:1580

§ 5.105   Because of the limitations discussed above in the logical-annotation scheme, there are real ambiguities in the SUSANNE analyses of co-ordinate structures such as:

> [Np *the extravagant Elizabethan ruffs* [Np+ *and Carolean collars*]] E01.024
>
> [N *their own wholesale department* [Np+ *and depots*]] F41.137

In the former example, it is not explicit whether the collars as well as the ruffs are extravagant; in the latter it is not explicit whether "their own depots" or any depots are included in the co-ordination. (In the second example, the analysis does make it clear that the reference is not to "their own wholesale depots", since this would be treated as wordlevel rather than phraselevel co-ordination.) It might be said that ambiguities such as these are often problematic for human readers and hearers, and that commonly they are re-solved (if at all) by reference to pragmatic rather than narrowly linguistic factors, so that a case could be made for saying that an analytic scheme which fails to treat the alternative readings as grammatically distinct is not inappropriate; but the SUSANNE team would not wish to rest much on this point.

§ 5.106   Because co-ordination reductions are not reconstructed, the functiontag system sometimes has to be used in such a way that a constituent is given a functiontag which logically applies to a deleted element of which that constituent is a modifier; e.g.:

> *The second* . . . *showed* [Np:o *titers of 1:256*] [P:p *in albumin*] [S+ *and* [Ms:o *1:2048*] [Pb:h *by the indirect Coombs test*]]. J09:0220

— *1:2048* is functiontagged :o as direct object, because it is a re-duction of *titer(s) of 1:2048* which is logically direct object of *showed*.

§ 5.107   Conflicts can arise in functiontagging structures including co-ordinations because the functiontag appropriate for one conjunct is not appropriate for the other(s). In *we entertained and were entertained by our neighbours*, the word *We* would be :s in the active clause but :S in the passive clause. The general rule (cf. § 4.497) is that co-ordinations are analysed so that the main conjunct is complete and normal without the subordinate conjunct(s), so the analysis here is:

> [S [Nap:s *We*] *entertained* [S+ *and* [Vwp *were entertained*] [Pb:a *by*] S+] [Np:o *our neighbours*] S]

Cf.:

> [S [Fn?:s162 *Whether a concept analogous to the principle of internal responsibility operates* ...] *is* [Jh:e *less obvious*] [S+ *and* [Jh:e *more difficult*] [Ti:s *to establish* o162] S+] S].
> G02:1120

— if the sentence had run *Whether a concept ... operates ... is more difficult to establish*, the Fn? would be functiontagged :S rather than :s.

Similarly, a co-ordination itself takes one functiontag but sometimes the separate conjuncts considered separately would call for distinct functiontags: again the choice appropriate to the main conjunct prevails. Thus, in both of the following cases:

> *A lot of people will roam the streets* [P:p *in costumes and masks,* [Tg+ *and having a ball*] P:p]. N18:1200
> ... *to articulate them precisely* [P:p *on the spot* [P+ *and on the basis of quick and accurate diagnostic assessments*] P:p].
> J24:0890

the main conjunct is a clear Place adjunct (for *in costumes and masks* see § 5.128 below), but the subordinate conjunct taken in isolation would be a Manner adjunct, functiontagged :h (for *having a ball* see the *carving in a road* example in § 5.148 below).

LIMITS AND EXCEPTIONS TO THE LOGICAL-ANNOTATION SYSTEM

§ 5.108 For the avoidance of doubt, we now survey some further grammatical phenomena which were classically handled by transformational rules but where the SUSANNE scheme does not need to use its ghost and index mechanism because the facts are adequately represented without it. Thus, nothing corresponding to Dative Movement is needed — as we have seen, *I wrote John a letter* is given an analysis "in its own right" rather than as derivative from *I wrote a letter to John*. Likewise Complementizer Deletion has no reflex: *I want John to go* is not regarded as a mutilated form of an underlying **I want for John to go*. Preposition Deletion is reflected in the scheme only indirectly, through the fact that subordinate clauses are sometimes functiontagged in terms of a missing preposition whose nature is implied by the identity of the higher verb (§§ 5.36, 5.134). In a passive clause lacking an agent, the SUSANNE analysis does not reconstruct a putative deleted logical subject (which would often be a quite artificial procedure). Since the formtagging system provides a symbol identifying imperatives, it would be redundant also to reconstruct the deleted elements *you will*. And the SUSANNE scheme includes no analogue of Particle Movement, relating *John looked the number up* to *John looked up the number*; the surface parsing scheme makes *up* an IC of the clause in both cases (the words *looked up* are not grouped as a single constituent even when adjacent), and the functiontag :n adequately marks the relationship between particle and verb.

§ 5.109 It should be said also that the SUSANNE analytic scheme uses indices only in the specific ways listed above. There are obvious potential extensions to the indexing system, under which it might be used to mark co-reference more generally: for instance between non-emphatic reflexives and their antecedents, and/or between non-reflexive anaphoric pronouns and their antecedents. The SUSANNE scheme does not use indices for these additional purposes.

§ 5.110 This means that on occasion co-referential items both bearing indices may have different indices, as in:

[Nns:s117 *The Mayor*] *declined* . . . [Ti:o s117 *to confirm or deny the reports* [Fn *that* [Nas:s121 *he*] *had decided* [Ti:o s121 *to run*] . . .]. A07:0370
[S* *Let* [Nop:O104 +'s 106] [Tb:o s104 *get one thing straight*], [Ny@:G106 *you and me*] Tb:o] S*]. N07:0090

— in context it is clear that in the A07 example *he*, indexed 121, and *The Mayor*, indexed 117, are the same man, but this case of co-reference is not one of the categories recognized by the SUSANNE annotation system; likewise, in the N07 example, the appositional element *you and me*, indexed 106, is co-referential with the whole Nop from which it has been extracted, and this Nop is indexed 104 to mark the fact that it has been raised out of the Tb, but these are separate grammatical relationships and the SUSANNE scheme gives no reason to link them with a common index. Cf. also the example from N09 quoted in § 5.89 above. There, the Ti@ needs an index as dislocated from appositional position after *it*; *the best way* needs an index as antecedent of the relative Ti. The main verb *was* asserts co-reference between the items so indexed; but the co-reference expressed by equative verbs is not a category marked in the SUSANNE scheme, so the indices are different.

§ 5.111   Any item functioning as one or another complement-type in a clause is invariably annotated with the appropriate functiontag. Since functiontags appear only in the parse field, not the wordtag field, this rule occasionally conflicts with the principle according to which certain categories of wordtag (§ 4.58) are immediately dominated by clause nodes without intervening phrase nodes. Consider for instance the example:

The answer is of course yes. G11:0120

Here, *yes* is clearly the predicate complement of the subject, and must therefore take the :e functiontag; yet *yes* is wordtagged UH and a terminal node labelled UH would normally be directly dominated by the S node.[12] A similar contradiction arises, more frequently, between the requirement that items displaced into other tagmas must take the :G functiontag, and the fact that certain types of word have no corresponding tagmatags: for instance, Negative Transportation (§ 5.100), as in *I don't think I have to tell you . . .* L10.172, moves the word *not* or *+n't* into a clause other than the one to which it logically belongs, but the wordtag XX has no corresponding phrasetag which might be supplemented by a :G functiontag.

The solution in such cases is that, where a wordtag from the list lacking corresponding tagmatags is required to be dominated by a node including a functiontag, the formtag for the latter node will be a copy of the wordtag. Thus, interjections functioning as complements are analysed as in:

[S [Ns:s *The answer*] *is of course* [UH:e *yes*_UH]].
. . . the crowd . . . voted [UH:h *no*_UH] A01:0980
I told him [UH:o *no*_UH +, [Fn– *that I had had a very happy childhood*] UH:o].[13] G12:1390
[S [UH:e *Yes*_UH], [Nns:s *the Maestro*] *assented*]. G06:0470 — for the choice of the :e functiontag, cf. § 5.51

---

[12] In a case where a word taking no tagmatag might be seen as playing an adjunct (rather than complement) role in a clause, normally the nature of the wordtag will adequately indicate its function, so there is no rule that adjunct functiontags must be shown in such cases: in a sentence such as *He was, yes, desperate* one might think of *yes* as fulfilling the role of a Modality adjunct, but it is simply treated as a UH word directly attached to the S node.

[13] Here, a UH is the main conjunct of a co-ordination whose subordinate conjunct is a clause; given the rule that a UH acting as clause complement is tagmatagged UH, this analysis follows.

Similarly, a functiontag can be added to a wordrank formtag derived from a wordtag lacking a corresponding tagmatag, e.g. UH&, UH=, thus:

> [S [UH&:o *Yes*_UH — [UH– *yes*_UH] — [UH+ *and yes*_UH] UH&:o], [Nns:s *Edward*] *admitted*]. L14.178

Negative Transportation examples are:

> *I* [Ve *do* [XX:G123 +*n't*] *think*] [Fn:o *I* [V *have* 123] [Ti:z *to tell you . . .*]] L10.172
> . . . [Ns@:199 *one thing* [Fr *I just* [Ve *do* [XX:G200 +*n't*] *think*] [Fn:o *there* [Vzb *is* 200] s199 Fn:o] Fr] Ns@:199], . . . N11:1190

(The formal V subcategory e marks the V which is negated at the surface, not the V logically negated.)

This rule is also regularly invoked in cases where the first element of a "double conjunction" is shifted into a position preventing it from being analysed as a sister of the conjoined items (§ 5.87), as in:

> . . . *the midwife, knowing that the afterbirth is ready to pop out,* [LEe:G123 *either*] *asks her* [Ti 123 *to relax while her tummy is pressed gently,* [Ti+ *or else to take a deep breath and . . .*]]. F32.144
> *When necessary, we should make it clear* [Fn:o *that* [Np:s123 *countries which . . .*] 124 [Vce *will* [LE=:G124 *not_only*_LE=] *lose*] *our sympathy* [Fn+ *but also risk their own prospects for orderly development* Fn+] Fn:o]. J22:0280

GHOST PLACEMENT

§ 5.112 While the logical interpretation of the SUSANNE annotation scheme depends purely on the labels of nodes and their constituency (mother/daughter) relationships, rather than on the left-to-right ordering of ICs of a tagma (which is normally determined by surface grammar), it is clearly desirable to adopt some conventional system for left-to-right placement of ghosts with respect to the full constituents of a tagma. Surface grammar leaves us free to insert ghosts wherever we prefer below their mother node, but it would be inconvenient if ghost placement varied unsystematically from example to example.

§ 5.113 The general SUSANNE approach is to locate a ghost wherever within a sequence of ICs the corresponding full constituent would most naturally be located. In the case of a relative clause with zero relative pronoun, the ghost representing the relativized item will begin the clause if it is functiontagged :s or :S; though, if the relative is introduced by the conjunction *that*, a subject ghost will immediately follow *that*. If functiontagged :o, the ghost will be placed immediately after the verb (or, if there is a full indirect object, immediately after that). Thus:

[Ns:s149 *The one thing* [Fr [Nap:s *they*] *had* o149 [R:h *in_common*] Fr] Ns:s149] N07:0830

Having [Ns:s151 *nothing else* [Ti [Vi *to do*] o151] *except wait for my forms to be processed*], . . . N06:0540

[Fr [Dq:G173 *which*] *he makes* [Ns:o *little effort* [Ti [Vi *to conceal*] o173 [R:m *even*] [P:p *in the presence of Southern friends*] Ti] Ns:o] Fr] G01:0510

[Ns:s123 *The advice* [Fr *I gave* [Nns:i *Mary*] o123 Fr] Ns:s123] *was* . . .

§ 5.114   Where an Ss has subject following verb, the object ghost is placed after both:

"[Q:G175 *Nae_UH,* [Ns" *man*]", [Ss *said Willie* o175], "[S *ye must be countin' the echoes* S] Q:G175]". A14:1380

§ 5.115   If the ghost has an adjunct functiontag, it will normally be placed at the end of the clause:

It was [Fa:G220 *when he attempted to end the relationship*] [Fn:s *that the murder took place* t220]. A20:1700

. . . *falling into* [Ns:113 *the creek* [Fr [Pb:G116 *by* [Dq:113 *which*]] [Nap:s114 *they*] *persisted* [P:u *in* [Tg s114 *playing* p116] P:u] Fr] Ns:113]. N10:0210

[S [Po:G219 *Of Gustavus Adolphus and Charles XII*] [Ni:S *it*] *is* [J:e *unnecessary*] [Ti:s *to speak* r219] S]. G18:1720

But if the clause also contains full adjunct tagmas, the ordering of the ghost relative to these is decided in terms of which ordering of adjunct-types is most natural; the example:

I've noticed [Ns:o187 *the way* [Fr *you've been looking* [P:u *at me*] h187 [Fa:t *ever since we met*]". N18:1020

is analysed as shown, because *you've been looking at me that way ever since* . . . is a more natural sequence than . . . *looking that way at me ever since* . . . or . . . *looking at me ever since we met that way* (with *that way* an IC of the main clause). An object ghost is placed before rather than after the particle of a phrasal verb:

[Ns:123 *the word* [Fr *I looked* o123 [R:n *up*] Fr] Ns:123]

§ 5.116 If a relative clause contains an overt relative pronoun, this will of course appear at the beginning of the clause irrespective of its functiontag, as a consequence of the English rule of *Wh*-Fronting ([Ns:123 *the house* [Fr [Dq:o123 *which*] *we bought*]]); but in a case of a zero relative pronoun, it would be alien to the SUSANNE philosophy to assume that this resulted from a *wh-* pronoun which was first fronted and then deleted, leaving no concrete clue to its underlying form or position. The SUSANNE analysis is [Ns:123 *the house* [Fr [Nap:s *we*] *bought* o123 Fr]], not [Ns:123 *the house* [Fr o123 [Nap:s *we*] *bought* Fr]]. A subject ghost is placed at the end of its clause in:

> ... [Ns@:199 *one thing* [Fr *I just* [Ve *do* [XX:G200 +*n't*] *think*] [Fn:o *there* [Vzb *is* 200] s199 Fn:o] Fr] Ns@:199], ... N11:1190

because the presence of *there* makes it clear that an overt subject would have to be clause-final.

§ 5.117 In the case of included adverbials, logically these are to be shown by means of ghosts as clause ICs (and consequently given functiontags showing their adjunct roles), but the concept of a natural ghost location does not in general apply, since very often the surface position of an included adverbial medially within a clause IC is in fact more natural in English than any position between clause ICs would be. Ghosts for included adverbials are therefore conventionally placed immediately before the clause IC within which the adverbials occur (this is sometimes a position where they might occur in surface grammar, but is often a quite "unnatural" position). Thus:

> *American and free-world policies* h215 [Vc *can* [R:G215 *marginally*] *affect* Vc] *the pace* ... J22:1840
> *It* c121 [Vcp *may,* [R:G121 *however*], *be noted* Vcp] *that* ... G18:0320
> ... *the nation* h180 m182 [Vzf *has,* [P:G180 *to some degree*] [R:G182 *at_least*], *broadened* Vzf] *the capacity* ... G02:1470

This rule applies even if it results in a ghost being the first constituent of a sentence:

> [O [S c174 [N:s *The natural world* [Rsw:G174 *then*], *plus poetry and some kinds of art,* N:s] *receives* ... S]. ... O] G05:0800

§ 5.118 Unfortunately, there is a problem with the rule of the preceding section, which was not appreciated until a very late stage

in the construction of the SUSANNE Corpus, concerning adverbials
included within co-ordinations. As discussed in § 4.211, an element
functioning adverbially will normally be analysed as a sister rather
than daughter of a clause IC, even if logically it applies specifically
to that IC rather than to the clause as a whole: ... *to occur* [R:m
only] [P:p *within a limited range...*] J25.090, not ... *to occur*
[*only* [*within a limited range...*]]. This means that, if the example
had read ... *to occur within only a limited range...*, the SUSANNE
included-adverbial treatment, which yields an analysis ... *to occur*
m123 [P *within* [R:G123 *only*] [Ns *a limited range...*] P], is a
plausible one — it gives an underlying constituent structure comparable to what can occur as the surface structure. However, where a
clause IC is a co-ordination, an adverbial included within it may
apply only to a subordinate conjunct (whether placed within that
conjunct, or between it and the main conjunct). Thus, in the sequences which are currently analysed as:

> *Is* [Ni:S *it*] *not a fact,* [Fn:s *that... the lapse of time* [Vc *will*
> *weaken* [V+ *and* [P:t *in the end*] *destroy* V+] Vc] *it* Fn:s]?
> D14.081
> ..., [Fa:t *while on the other side the black ones were grouped,*
> [J:b *dark* [J+ *and* [R:m *almost*] *sinister* J+] J:b], *to hang and*
> *creep down as if in despair* Fa:t]. E23.141
> *We walked* [P:q *down the Rue de L'Arcade,* [R:q *thence*] [R:q
> *along*] [P– *beside the Madeleine*] [P+ *and across to a sidewalk*
> *cafe...* P+] P:q]. G12:0400
> ... *you could cut out the apéritif* [S+ *and serve* [N:o123 *a glass*
> *of light non-vintage port* 125] [P:w *with the Boston Cream*
> *Pie*]; [Ns+:G125 *or* [R:m *perhaps*] [R:m *even better*], *an*
> *inexpensive dessert wine...* Ns+:G125] S+]. E19.084

there is no satisfactory point at which to place a ghost representing
the logical position of the phrases *in the end, almost, perhaps, even
better, thence, along.* The normal SUSANNE rules require these
phrases to be given :G functiontags in their surface position, linked
by indices to ghosts carrying appropriate adjunct functiontags which
would be inserted before the main conjuncts (the Vc, J, P, and in
the last case presumably before the N *a glass of port*, even though
the subordinate conjunct has been dislocated away from this). But
if that were done, the logical-annotation scheme would fail to express the fact that the adverbials apply only to one conjunct, not to
the whole co-ordination.

§ 5.119   Since the analysis of co-ordinate structures permits co-ordination to be analysed as occurring between high-level tagmas, with reduction of subordinate conjuncts, one solution would be to adopt a rule saying that, wherever a co-ordination includes an adverbial applying to a subordinate conjunct, the co-ordination must be analysed as a co-ordination of clauses, however heavily this implies that the subordinate conjunct(s) are reduced: the apparent "included adverbials" would then be ICs of appropriate clauses, and the ghost system would not be needed. For some of the examples quoted above, this rule would give reasonable results:

[S *We walked down the Rue de L'Arcade,* [S– [R:q *thence*] [R:p *along*] [P:p *beside the Madeleine* P:p] S–] [P+ *and . . .*] S]
[S+ *and serve* [Ns:o *a glass of . . . port*] [P:w *with the . . . Pie*]; [S+ *or* [R:m *perhaps*] [R:m *even better*], [Ns:o *an inexpensive dessert wine . . .*] S+] S+]

But analyses such as:

[Fn:s . . . [Vc *will weaken*] [Fn+ *and* [P:t *in the end*] [V *destroy*] Fn+] [Ni:o *it*] Fn:s]
[Fa:t *while . . . the black ones were grouped,* [J:b *dark*] [Fa+ *and* [R:m *almost*] [J:b *sinister*] Fa+], *to . . .* Fa:t]

seem fairly clearly contrary to a natural understanding of the structure of the co-ordinations; and in other cases again the rule suggested would yield results that seem more or less absurd. For instance, the *not just* phrase (§ 4.535) and the *even* added as an afterthought in the sequence currently analysed as:

. . . , [Tg:b *the result being somehow* [J:e *as ineffective,* [R:m *not just*] [J– *dusty-grey* [J+ *but muddy,* [J– *slimy*] [R:m *even*] J+] J–] J:e] Tg:b]. R03.099

would force the passage to be treated as a co-ordination of Tg's rather than J's; and, in the sequence currently analysed as:

<bbold> [S *Spahn not only is* [N:e *a superior pitcher* [Ns+ *but a gentlemanly fine fellow,* [Ns@ *a ball player's ball player,* [A:m *as they say in the trade*] Ns@] Ns+] N:e] S] <ebold>. A13:1180

since the closing remark *as they say in the trade* applies only to the immediately preceding phrase *a ball player's ball player,* the analysis would have to be something like:

[S *Spahn not only is a superior pitcher* [S+ *but* [N:e *a gentlemanly fine fellow,* [S– [Ns:e *a ball player's ball player*], [A:m *as they say in the trade*] S–] S+] S]

— despite the fact that one would not think of analysing *but a gentlemanly fine fellow* as a reduced clause, were it not for the words tacked on to the end of a conjunct subordinate to it.

§ 5.120   These analyses seem so unnatural that the SUSANNE scheme as it stands rejects them. SUSANNE Corpus analyses of co-ordinations which contain included adverbials applying only to subordinate conjuncts leave the adverbials in their surface positions, and provide labels showing their adjunct functions at those positions. This treatment is of course entirely at variance with the normal rule that functiontags (other than :G) mark roles within clauses, and should therefore apply to clause ICs only. It must be honestly stated that, with respect to the annotation of adverbials applying to sub-ordinate conjuncts, the present state of the SUSANNE parsing scheme is unsatisfactory.

Adjunct Categories

§ 5.121   The Gothenburg Corpus classified adjuncts into six func-tional categories, including a large miscellaneous group which ac-counted for 37 per cent of all adjuncts. This scheme was not always applied to individual cases in a consistent fashion. In order to im-prove on this classification scheme, the SUSANNE team consulted *CGEL*, pp. 479 ff., as a relatively authoritative survey of adjunct types. (*CGEL* uses the term "adverbial", because it reserves "ad-junct" for use in a narrower sense.) *CGEL* distinguishes seven main categories for adjuncts, most of which have subcategories so that at the finer classification level there are twenty-four categories. (There are many correspondences between Gothenburg categories and *CGEL* main categories and subcategories, as one would expect — if there were not, the task of imposing a classification on Corpus examples would seem very artificial.)

§ 5.122   *CGEL* describes its categories as "semantic roles"; but it also notes (e.g. p. 489) that there are significant correlations between semantic roles and grammatical properties of adjuncts. The fact that such correlations exist is the most important reason for including a classification of adjunct functions in the SUSANNE annotation scheme.[14]

[14] Incidentally, *CGEL* at one point, p. 487, claims that its adjunct function scheme has the property that a clause may never contain two non-co-ordinated adjuncts bearing the same function; that is, it claims that the property regarded by Joan Bresnan (§ 5.16 above) as distinguishing complements from adjuncts is equally true of adjuncts provided these are classified in an adequately refined manner. However, this claim is questionable, and a later passage in *CGEL*, p. 648, appears to retract it. The SUSANNE scheme explicitly makes no such claim.

§ 5.123   The SUSANNE scheme does not simply take over the *CGEL* classification unaltered. That would have been inappropriate for several reasons. Despite its remarks just alluded to about correlations between meaning and grammar, the *CGEL* scheme is arguably at some points unduly influenced by aprioristic conceptual analysis as opposed to the inherent organization of the language; also, there are a few cases where *CGEL* adjunct categories apply to items treated by the SUSANNE scheme as complements or vice versa; and *CGEL* covers prepositional phrases separately from other adjuncts (in its chapter 9), so that adjunct functions realized exclusively by prepositional phrases tend to be omitted from the general *CGEL* scheme. Furthermore there would have been practical difficulties, even if it had been desirable, in moving from the six-way Gothenburg classification all the way to the twenty-four subcategories of the *CGEL* scheme. Therefore the SUSANNE adjunct classification scheme evolved as a compromise between the Gothenburg categories, the *CGEL* categories, and the categories which emerged as coherent groupings during the task of classifying all the adjuncts in the Corpus. The result is a scheme of ten adjunct functions.

§ 5.124   It is worth noting that the SUSANNE scheme makes no use of a "miscellaneous" adjunct category. During the work of creating the SUSANNE Corpus, a "miscellaneous adjunct" symbol was in fact provided by which analysts were allowed to indicate that a particular adjunct fell outside the definitions of the ten specific categories; but it was an understood principle of the project that use of this symbol was discouraged — where possible, analysts were asked to find ways of extending one of the ten specific adjunct categories to cover "awkward cases", logging any such extensions so that precedents would be followed consistently. After all adjuncts had been functiontagged along these lines, the residue of some 6 per cent that had been given the "miscellaneous" tag were examined; rather than forming a patternless rag-bag of diversity they proved to group into a few fairly coherent classes. Consequently, by making a few clear-cut modifications to the ten specific category definitions it was possible to eliminate the "miscellaneous" category altogether.

That is not to say that one can always assign English adjuncts to one of the ten categories defined here without ever encountering difficult borderline cases — natural language is never that neat. Of course there are such cases, and many such are discussed below. However, it is claimed that the difficult cases explicitly discussed here offer a rather complete picture of the extent to which the ten adjunct categories leave grey areas between them; there are not, it is believed, many adjuncts in the SUSANNE Corpus not mentioned here but which raise further difficulties of classification, different from the cases which are discussed. (Undoubtedly there will be some cases that have been missed, but it is claimed that there are not many.)

§ 5.125 Naturally there will always be further classification problems stemming from the fact that English is ambiguous; it is possible for a competent English speaker to take a form of words one way or another way, and the alternatives might lead to different adjunct functiontags. No grammatical annotation scheme can remove that sort of indeterminacy. But, modulo choice of interpretation of a text's wording, it is claimed that the ten adjunct categories offer a classification scheme that is comparable, in completeness and in predictability, to more traditional dimensions of grammatical classification.

§ 5.126 Since the *CGEL* subcategories are defined and illustrated in considerable detail, the following exposition of the SUSANNE adjunct-classifying scheme proceeds largely by specifying which *CGEL* subcategories can be grouped together under particular SUSANNE functiontags.

:p, :q PLACE AND DIRECTION

§ 5.127 *CGEL* has a broad category of Space adjuncts, which it subdivides into adjuncts of "position", "direction", and "distance", illustrated by the following examples:

- *CGEL* "position":

  He lay on his bed.
  They are strolling in the park.

- *CGEL* "direction":

  They drove westwards.
  She walked down the hill.
  Their houses face towards the sea.
  She walked to the bus stop.
  She walked from the school.

- *CGEL* "distance":

  They had travelled a long way.
  She had driven (for) fifty kilometres.
  He hadn't gone far.

(*CGEL* further subclassifies the "direction" group using the concepts "goal" and "source".) SUSANNE uses the name Place, :p, for the *CGEL* "position" class, and adopts the *CGEL* Direction class unchanged, symbolizing it :q. On the other hand the SUSANNE scheme treats the *CGEL* "distance" group as part of the Manner/ Degree category, :h. Place and Direction adjuncts answer *where* questions, while "distance" adjuncts are elicited by questions using the phrase *how far*; and distance adjuncts are often realized as noun phrases, which is not true of the Place or Direction categories.

§ **5.128** *In* preceding clothes, shoes, or hat is functiontagged as a preposition of Place:

> *he looked dapper **in a lightweight summer suit, brown silk tie and**...* N06:1380
> *What would you have done **in Montero's moccasins?*** N04:0180

§ **5.129** Direction (rather than Place) is used in e.g.:

> *Steinberg left Germany for the United States, **by_way_of Switzerland**.* G06:0830 — *for the United States* here is also Direction
> *dances that "moved [P:q **all over the stage**]",*... G09:1040

Place rather than Direction is used for e.g.:

> *how many fans purposely stayed away **from Bears Stadium** last year* A13:1610

In ... *their second skin has a light dusty cast **to it**.* G04:1540, *to it* is regarded as an idiomatic paraphrase of *about it* or *on it* and is functiontagged :p. *To* phrases are treated as metaphorical Place adjuncts also in:

> *there's not much **to it*** A12:0410
> *There was more **to this** than Jones had told him.* N01:1040

§ **5.130** The Place and Direction adjunct categories raise in an acute form a general problem which to some extent affects all the semantic aspects of the SUSANNE annotation scheme, namely how to analyse figurative (metaphorical) usage (cf. § 4.3). The general SUSANNE approach in connection with adjunct classification is that when an originally figurative usage clearly ranks in modern English as a "dead" metaphor, and one whose current usage relates it clearly to a SUSANNE analytic category different from the category relevant to its figurative origin, then the annotation reflects the current usage; but when a metaphor is still to some extent "alive", or when a metaphor is dead but no specific SUSANNE category offers itself as clearly appropriate to the current usage, then the figurative language is annotated as if it were intended literally. In borderline cases the presumption is in favour of analysing figurative uses as if they were meant literally.

§ 5.131   It is particularly common for locative expressions to be used in extended, non-spatial senses. When the extension is from space to time (*in the morning, between 5 and 6 p.m.*, etc.), the adjunct is assigned to the Time category. But when a basically spatial expression refers neither to space nor to time but to some more abstract relationship, the principle just quoted commonly causes it to be assigned to the SUSANNE Place or Direction categories. This would apply for instance to the great majority of figurative or abstract uses of prepositional adjuncts quoted on pp. 685–7 of *CGEL*.[15] Compare also:

- Place:

  In his only attack on the Republicans, Hughes said . . .
  A06:1420

  "*To prevent hoodlums from infiltrating the state as they did
  in the Republican administration in the early 1940s*".
  A06:1570

  Among other acts, Teller and Austin are accused of . . .
  A20:1410

  *the hours spent in purely diagnostic study may equal or
  exceed* . . . J24:1420

  He hadn't shown up too well in their eyes, . . . N05:1070

  *but what a young woman half his age saw in him was a
  mystery* . . . N18:0720

  My future lay solely with the hall, . . . N06:0920

  But I shall campaign on the Meyner record . . . A06:1500

  . . . , *quantum yields* . . . *have been observed at 85°.* J06:0050

  At 100 Amp the 360 cycle ripple was less than 0.5 V . . .
  J02:1120

  as effective as the polyphosphates [P:p *over the relatively wide
  range of conditions* [Tn *met* [P:p *in practice*]]] J05:0680

  . . . *have led the field of somewhat less important writers in
  a sort of post-bellum renaissance.* G08:0170

  She wondered what had taken place . . . *between him and his
  wife.* N10:0270

  *They wouldn't o' stood no chance with you in a plain,
  straight-out shoot-down*". N11:1010

---

[15] An exception would be *travelling at* (*over*) *60 m.p.h.*, where the *at* phrase is a SUSANNE Manner adjunct.

- Direction:

> *he jerked* **to attention** N14:1290
> *she would be baited* **into a tantrum** N09:0850
> *he had come* **into possession of the family estate** *and had . . .*
> G18:0870
> *A concentration distribution has been derived* **from radar**
> **observations** *. . .* J07:1630
> *. . . using our rifles* **on them!** N04:0150
> *leading an Evanston policeman* **on a high speed chase** *. . .*
> A20:1730
> *. . . ran the Grizzlies' winning streak* **to four straight.** A13:0060
> *to have been carved* **from the same material** G04:1370

But in a case analogous with the last, *Shah Abbas II in about 1657 built,* **of sun-baked brick, tile, and stone,** *the present bridge.* G05:0920, the link with a spatial metaphor is too tenuous and the *of*-phrase is analysed as a Manner adjunct, functiontagged :h (since Manner covers "means", § 5.141); likewise :h is used in the cases:

> *Hague had made a virtue* **of ruthlessness** *all of his life.* N07:1550
> *. . . spectacle she was making* **of herself,** *. . .* N03:0430
> *. . . was built up* **from the material fed from between the blocks**
> *. . .* J03:0280
> *concentrated* **from very dilute solutions** J09:1020

In *Haying time was* **close at hand,** *. . .* N11:0760 the physical meaning of the emphasized P is so concrete that :p is used despite the clear reference to time.

§ 5.132 The fact that a metaphorically spatial expression appears in complement position is not used in order to avoid giving it a :p or :q functiontag:

> *. . . the group has* [Np:o *no candidates for the charter*
> *commission*] [P:p **in mind**] [P:t *at present*] A05:1490 —
> P:p not P:j

§ 5.133 A case where the :p functiontag is frankly used for want of a more appropriate alternative is in:

> *. . . and limit sizes* **to larger than a few microns.** J07:1800

— the *to* phrase cannot be regarded as a prepositional object, although the preposition is thoroughly determined by the identity of the verb, since *limit* has the object *sizes*; metaphorically, to *limit* X *to* Y is to force X to remain within Y, hence Place.

§ 5.134 Sometimes the *to* of a Ti can simultaneously be a directional *to* justifying the :q functiontag, since sequences like

... *to to* ... are systematically reduced to single words in English; thus [Dp *Those who are sexual deviants*] *are naturally drawn* [Ti:q *to join the beatniks*]. G13:1570 can be regarded as, logically, ... *drawn to* [*to join* ...].

:t   TIME

§ 5.135   *CGEL* subclassifies time adjuncts into:

- "position", e.g.:

  She drove to Chicago **on Sunday**.
  He was there **last week**.

- "duration", e.g.:

  I shall be staying here **till next week**.
  Washington delayed his counter-attack **until the following spring**.
  I've been staying here **since last week**.
  I stayed (**for**) **three weeks**.

- "frequency", e.g.:

  How often *do you go to the theatre?*
  I like to go **frequently**, *but* ... *I've been only* **three times** *this year*.

- "relationship", e.g.:

  I was already writing my novel in 1980 and I'm afraid it is **still** *in progress.*
  He had visited his mother **already** *when I saw him yesterday.*

These are all indifferently functionagged :t in the SUSANNE scheme. Arguably there would be as strong a case for separating "frequency" from other time adjuncts as there is for separating "distance" from space adjuncts (§ 5.127 above); but the Gothenburg and *CGEL* schemes agree in placing frequency expressions under the Time heading, and the SUSANNE scheme follows suit.

§ 5.136   Note that *still* as "even now" is a Time adjunct, but *still* as "nevertheless" (e.g. **Still** *you should have visited him*) is classified as Contingency (§ 5.158).

§ 5.137   A borderline case analysed as a Time adjunct is the *to* phrase in:

those nights when he slept alone by his campfire and waked suddenly **to the hoot of an owl or the rustle of a blade of grass** ... N02:0790

§ 5.138   An example of the operation of the presumption in favour of literal interpretation would be the analysis of *while* clauses such as:

> *At one side of the stage a dancer jumps excitedly; nearby, another sits motionless, **while still another is twirling an umbrella**.* G09:1470

The concept expressed by *while* here is on the borderline between a concrete relationship of simultaneity and a more abstract relationship, that might be paraphrased *whereas*, which in SUSANNE terms would be classified under Contingency. The general presumption favours the concrete interpretation and this *while* clause is functiontagged :t. However, :c is used for:

> *Mr. Martinelli has, in recent weeks, been of the opinion that a special town meeting would be called for the vote, **while Mr. Bourcier said that a special election might be called instead**.* A05:1400

§ 5.139   The *when* clause is functiontagged :t in terms of its literal interpretation in:

> *How could he comprehend her need **when he himself was innocent**?* N08:0940

§ 5.140   *In* meaning *while* can introduce a :t phrase:

> *Direct proportionality ... has also been assumed* [P:t *in* [Tg *obtaining the value in the last column ...*]]. J06:1800
> [P:t *In* [Tg *taking account of seventeen years of law practice*]], *Adams concluded ...* G07:1230

And cf.:

> *the economic atmosphere favoring growth of the individual, who,* [P:t *in turn*], *would help us ...* G22:1600

In the case of ***In this test**, 130 gallons of a suspension ... was aerosolized.* J08:0820, the preposition is being used to express a vague metaphorical relationship ambiguous between Time and Place; since there is no neutral functiontag, the fact of *in* being primarily a spatial preposition justifies the :p tag.

:h   MANNER/DEGREE

§ 5.141   This functiontag covers the great majority of adjuncts which answer questions asked by the word *how*, together with some related adjunct types for which *how* would not be used. It comprises three of the four subcategories listed under the *CGEL* main category "process" (*CGEL*, pp. 482–3), namely:

- "manner", e.g. *casually, with deference, carefully, slowly, like John, just as John does*
- "means", e.g. *by bus, through insight*[16]
- "instrument", e.g. *with a fork, using a dictionary, by means of interrogation, . . . had erred* [Pb:h *by "encouraging the removal" of Prince Souvanna*]. A04:1700

(The fourth *CGEL* "process" subcategory, namely "agentive", is in SUSANNE terms a complement rather than adjunct function.)

§ 5.142 The SUSANNE :h category also comprises the various subcategories of the *CGEL* "degree" group (*CGEL*, pp. 485–6), namely:

- "amplification":

  *I **badly** want a drink.*
  *She is **increasingly** adding to her work load.*

- "diminution":

  *He doesn't like playing squash (**very**) **much**.*[17]
  *She helped him **a little** with his book.*

- "measure":

  *He likes playing squash **more than his sister does**.*
  *She had worked **sufficiently** that day.*

§ 5.143 The SUSANNE scheme treats "distance" adjuncts, as in *go **much further than this*** G01:1720, which *CGEL* classifies under "space" as we saw earlier, as naturally grouped with the "measure" subcategory under the functiontag :h.

§ 5.144 *CGEL* quotes *He doesn't play squash (**very**) **much*** as a case on the borderline between "degree" and "time" (either frequency or duration). In SUSANNE terms adjuncts such as *much, a lot* express degree and are functiontagged :h. The fact that playing squash is a predicate for which "high degree" entails either "high frequency" or "long duration" is seen as primarily a fact about the game of squash rather than about the logic of English.

---

[16] *CGEL* gives a third illustrative example, *in mathematics*, but out of context this does not appear to represent "means"; it may be an error.

[17] *CGEL* treats *+n't . . . very much* in this example as a single discontinuous degree adjunct. In SUSANNE terms the adjunct consists only of the R phrase *much* or *very much*.

§ 5.145 Postposed *all*, *both*, *each* (cf. § 4.217) are tagged as R:h items.

§ 5.146 A premodifier to a subordinating conjunction introducing an Fa will be functiontagged :h —

[Fa:t [Np:h *two hours*] *after Mr. Kennedy flew in*] A28.036
[Fa:t [R:h *shortly*] *after the Maguires joined it*] N10:0240
[Fa:t [R:h *ever*] *since we met*] N18:1030

§ 5.147 *So* as a pro-form, e.g. in the *do so* construction, is word-tagged as a pronoun (PN1z), and tagmatagged as a noun phrase, Ns, but it is functiontagged :h as an expression of manner.

§ 5.148 Some borderline cases assigned to the :h category are:

- expressions involving *on the basis of . . .* , *on a . . . basis*:

    the thermal radiation which might be predicted [P:h *on the basis of the known temperature of Mars*] J01:0330
    They "operate [P:h *on a volume basis*]", *it was contended,* . . . A05:0900

- prepositional phrases in *as* of the type:

    [P:h *as part of a larger development effort*], *however, it may gain wide acceptance* J22:1040 — this sort of *as* phrase cannot be functiontagged :e as discussed in § 5.43: the verb *gain* does not assert that "it" is "part of a larger . . . effort"

- *with* or similar phrases after *share*:

    a capillary bed [Tn *shared* [P:h *in_common_with the pulmonary artery*] . . .] J12:1740

- Tg clauses amplifying a higher verb, as in:

    They had spent a million dollars, [Tg:h *carving in a road, putting up buildings, drilling their haulage tunnel*]. N07:0900
    . . . to get into their costumes, cover their faces with masks and go [Tg:h *adventuring*]. N18:0260

Logical subjects are not reconstructed in clauses playing this role (reconstruction of deleted logical constituents is done in main and complement clauses, not in adjunct clauses).

- scores or voting tallies or results occurring in adjunct positions, e.g.:

    . . . they dropped their sixth straight spring exhibition decision . . . [P:h *by a score of 5 to 3*]. A11:0030
    . . . one that beat Anson, [M:h *3-0*], *in a 1953 district game.* A12:0270

the privilege resolution which the House voted [R:n *through*]
[M:h *87-31*]. A01:1480
... *the crowd* ... *voted* [UH:h *no*] ... A01:0980

— and, by analogy:

... *was fined* [Nu:h *$100*] *yesterday* ... A20:1720

§ 5.149 *In* phrases are often functiontagged :h as "manner"
adjuncts (e.g. the N03 and A13 cases below) or "instrument" adjuncts (e.g. the J23 and A09 cases below):

... *fell in a heap.* N03:1400
crushing the Reds in a humiliating 13-5 barrage Monday in the
loosely played finale. A13:1670
[P:h *In* [Tg *providing for these inner individual functions*]],
religion undertakes ... J23:0820
... *the city also intervened in the Hughes bankruptcy case in*
U. S. District Court [P:h *in a move preliminary to filing a claim*
there]. A09:0370

§ 5.150 The preposition *to* indicates "instrument", therefore :h, in:

That guiding principle of the Hoover Administration fell to the
siege guns of the New Deal; ... G02:0740

— and the *before* phrase is likewise functiontagged :h in *it crumpled*
before the onslaught of the powerful streams, ... N07:1400. In the
semantically rather similar *and you fall for a pass by his own*
nephew N18:1560, however, the preposition *for* is so closely determined by the verb *fall* (in this sense) that the functiontag is :u
rather than :h.

§ 5.151 In the sequence *The Dreadnought was built* [P *on de-*
signs supplied by the United States in 1959] ... A20:0050, the
preposition *on* (which normally expresses Place or Time) is used for
a relationship more commonly expressed by *by, according_to*, or the
like, and the P is functiontagged :h as would be usual with the latter
prepositions. Likewise *under* introduces an :h phrase in:

The Republicans must hold a primary under the county unit
system ... A01:1050
Under his supervision, the state fire-fighting agency developed
... A06:1240
[Tn+ *and exposed under identical conditions*][18] J06:1210

---

[18] The noun *conditions* in a case like this does not imply that, since Contingency covers
(inter alia) statements of conditions, the phrase must be tagged as a Contingency adjunct. It
is the semantic relationship between prepositional complement and containing clause expressed by the preposition, not the head noun of the prepositional complement, which is
primarily relevant for choice of functiontag.

The functiontag :h is used for the *in* phrase of *to loosen the dirt particles and dried matter in the presence of water . . .* J05:1160.

In *Those writers [Tn known collectively as . . .]* G08:0120, *collectively* is functiontagged :h.

§ 5.152   In *shot himself to death* A01:1820, *squeeze him to death* N11:1180, *to death* is functiontagged :h as representing the "degree of completeness" of the shooting or squeezing.

:m   MODALITY

§ 5.153   This SUSANNE functiontag covers all the *CGEL* subclasses listed under the same heading, namely:

- "emphasis" on the positive or negative truth value of a clause, e.g.:

  *She has **certainly** been enthusiastic about her work.*
  *She hasn't been enthusiastic **at all** about her work.*

- "restriction" of the scope of the assertion, e.g.:

  *She has been enthusiastic **only** about her work.*
  *She **alone** has been enthusiastic about her work.*

- and what *CGEL*, perhaps rather infelicitously, calls "approximation", as in:

  *She has **probably** been enthusiastic about her work.*
  *She has not **really/exactly** been enthusiastic about her work.*
  *She has **hardly** been enthusiastic about her work.*
  *I've **almost** finished painting the bathroom.*

§ 5.154   The *CGEL* subcategory "approximation" is used to include elements whose function is to comment on the authority for a proposition, e.g.:

*She has **allegedly** been enthusiastic about her work.*
*She has been, [A:m **as she puts it**], enthusiastic about her work.*

This latter example is extended by the SUSANNE scheme in order to use the :m functiontag for the emphasized phrase in:

*What if the President himself, **in the language of the military,** "goes ape"?* G03:0960

— which refers not to the manner of going ape but the way the comment is expressed. Cf. also *But [A:m **as I have said before**], if . . .* A07:0470.

(*CGEL* adds here the example *She has been, **if I may say so,** enthusiastic . . .* ; but in keeping with the general SUSANNE principle of analysing in terms of literal meaning rather than pragmatic force this case would be treated under the SUSANNE scheme as a conditional clause and classified under Contingency.) With the exception just stated, all the *CGEL* Modality examples are functiontagged as Modality adjuncts in the SUSANNE scheme also. This is a case where the broad *CGEL* category seems more coherent than the subcategories into which *CGEL* divides it: thus the adverb *even* is closely comparable to *only* (though it does not express "restriction"), and again is given the :m functiontag, as are *also* and *too* (as an adjunct). *In addition, furthermore, after all, moreover, likewise, in conclusion, in other words, of_course, instead, for one thing,* and tagmas introduced by *in addition to*..., *except*..., *apart from*..., *instead_of*..., *rather than*... in functiontagged positions are tagged :m.[19] For logicians "modality" refers primarily to concepts of possibility and necessity, and adjuncts expressing these concepts are given the :m functiontag although the *CGEL* Modality subcategories do not very clearly embrace them; thus:

> *we* m159 [Vef *have not* [R:G159 **necessarily**] *assured*] *ourselves* ... G11:0900

§ 5.155   Adverbs such as *further, somehow, naturally, as_usual* are functiontagged :m when occurring as "sentence adverbs", e.g. with *further* paraphrasing "also" or *somehow* paraphrasing "for some reason", as in:

> ... *it* m185 [Vzp *is* [R:G185 **further**] *suggested*] *that a hypothalamic imbalance may play an important role* ... J17:2110
> *and* **further** *his Lordship desir'd that I would send the Constable* ... G35.174
> ... *they* **somehow** *made me expect to see him launch into a vaudeville tapdance routine* ... N06:1400
> *which,* **oddly enough**, *is not reflected* ... G08:0280
> *the variety of soils and fabrics* [Tn **normally** *encountered in the washing process* Tn], ... J05:1860

but they are functiontagged :h when modifying a verb or predicate adjective, e.g. with *further* paraphrasing "more fully" (or "more far"), *somehow* paraphrasing "in some way", or the like, as in:

> ... *to send in more men, not weaken it* **further** *by desertion.* B01.122

---

[19] But in *"Perhaps" stands in_place_of commitment.* G12:1490 the P represents "where the word stands", and is therefore treated in terms of its literal sense as a Place adjunct functiontagged :p.

*Both, of course, were remarkable feats and **further** embossed the
fact that baseball rightfully is the national pastime.* A13:1060
— **embossed** seems to be a malapropism

*... agents that are associated **naturally** with epidemic disease.*
J08:1590

*... this unwholesome, chilling atmosphere that was **somehow**
grotesquely alive.* N08:1430

*but can even be eliminated from it **altogether**.* G09:1720

§ 5.156   Likewise, prepositional phrases may be functiontagged
:m when acting as "sentence adverbials" although similar phrases
modifying verbs would be given other functiontags; for instance :m
is used for the emphasized phrases in:

***By (1)**, the image of this pencil is a ruled surface ...* J21:0980 —
i.e. it follows from (1)

*... are reputed, **in the accepted wisdom**, to describe ...* G02:1870

In:

*... [A:m **just as all the buildings have not fallen** ...], [Rs:m **so**]
the values which wanted them ... have not all disappeared.*
G05:0300

both the A clause and the adverb *so* refer not to manner in which
falling or *disappearing* were carried out but to the truth values of
the two propositions, so again both are functiontagged :m. (The
word *just* is included within the A clause by analogy with the rule
of § 4.304 for Fa clauses.)

§ 5.157   *As such* as an Fa (§ 4.371) is functiontagged :m.

The CS= *in_so_far_as* (spelled as two words in American English)
introduces an :m clause:

*... to be remarkably like that of man, [Fa:m **insofar_as this can
be ascertained from** ...].* J12:0820

Apposition-introducing elements, e.g. *for_example*, are functiontagged :m when in positions requiring functiontags.

A phrase such as *on the other hand* is on the border between
Modality (cf. *for one thing*) and Contingency (cf. *however*): the
functiontag :m is chosen.

Against all expectation is functiontagged :m at N14:0290.

:c   CONTINGENCY

§ 5.158   This functiontag covers adjuncts which express the various
relationships that mathematical logicians have attempted to formalize

by means of the connectives of the propositional calculus, together with similar adjuncts which have no translations into mathematical logic because they involve subjective concepts such as purpose. The Contingency category includes, among others, the various adjuncts which answer *why* questions.

The SUSANNE Contingency category coincides with the *CGEL* category of the same name, which is subdivided and exemplified as follows:

- "cause", e.g. *She died of cancer; she helped the stranger out of a sense of duty.*
- "reason", e.g. *He bought the book because of his interest in metaphysics.*
- "purpose", e.g. *He bought the book so as to study metaphysics.*
- "result", e.g. *He read the book carefully, so he acquired some knowledge of metaphysics.*
- "condition", e.g. *If he reads the book carefully, he will acquire some knowledge of metaphysics.*
- "concession", e.g. *Though he didn't read the book, he acquired some knowledge of metaphysics.*

Adverbs and adverb phrases standardly functiontagged :c include: *all_the_same, consequently, however, in any case, anyway, in that case,*[20] *in_vain, nevertheless, otherwise, so, then* (in non-temporal uses), *therefore, thus, yet.*

Conjunctions introducing clauses functiontagged :c include: *although, because, despite, even_though, if, in the event that, provided_that, since* (in non-temporal uses), *whereas.* And the inverted type of Fa discussed in § 4.294 will normally be functiontagged :c.

§ 5.159 *As it happens, As luck had it* N14:0370, and related forms are functiontagged :c.

§ 5.160 A phrase beginning *regardless of . . .* will normally be tagged Jh:c (*regardless of* is not treated as a grammatical idiom); and cf.:

> <bbold> Baylor <ebold> *worked out in the rain Monday — [N:c mud or no mud]* <hellip> A12:1140
> *For better or for worse, we all now live in welfare states, . . .* G02:1100

---

[20] However, the *case* phrases in *containing 0.2 of an atmosphere of added oxygen in one case and added moisture in another* J06:1340 are functiontagged :r rather than :c — here *in . . . case* does not mean "if . . . is so".

§ **5.161** The preposition *for* introduces a Contingency phrase when it paraphrases "despite" or "because of", as in:

> *Even Hemingway, **for all his efforts to formulate a naturalistic morality**... never maintained that sex was all.* G13:0010
> *... has been under fire **for its practices in**...* A01:0430

For phrases are also functiontagged :c when identifying a rate of pay for which someone works, as in:

> *He agreed to do the job **for £500***
> *"We'll work **for our keep**",...* N01:1090

— since this relates to purpose; and consequently the functiontag :c is also used as in ... *the city could hire a CD director **for about $3,500 a year**...* A05:0130, although from the employer's viewpoint "purpose" is irrelevant, and as in ... *contracted to do the repairs **at a cost of $500 for each joint**.* A09:0450, although the preposition *at* does not make the element of motive salient, and as in *Jim Gentile bounced a hard shot off Kunkel's glove and beat it out **for a single**,...* A11:0560, where the link with the "pay for work" concept is only metaphorical.

§ **5.162** *Wh-...-ever* words introduce Contingency adjuncts,[21] as in:

> *Finally, **whatever the techniques used**, a twin goal is common to...* J24:1090

A *to* phrase as in **To his faint surprise** *Russ held up his hand.* N14:1020 expresses result and is accordingly given the :c functiontag.

§ **5.163** *On* represents purpose, therefore :c, in *to watch his plane take off **on a combat mission*** N15:0350; and the *in* phrase is regarded as expressing purpose in [P:c *In an apparent effort to head off such a rival primary slate*], *Mr. Wagner talked*... A07:0210.

§ **5.164** *With* is roughly equivalent to "because of", and introduces a Contingency adjunct, in:

> [P:c *With* [N *the rapid rate of closure*, [Ns– *the approach from below*...] N] P:c], *there would be only a moment when damage could be done.* N15:1470

---

[21] Compare the highly reduced construction in:

[N:c *Red man or white man*, [N– *pacifist or killer*]], *the forest would accept* [Nop:o *them*] *all*... N08:0860

— the N:c phrase is logically equivalent to "whether they were red man or...", though the logical-grammar notation cannot indicate this.

And compare:

> [P:c *With all his musical activities*], *did he have the time* ...?
> G06:1350
> ... *no tax increase would be possible* [P:c *without consent of the*
> *General Assembly*] A05:1690

The type of *without* + Tg phrase discussed in § 4.367 is P:c.

§ 5.165   The sequence *so that* (wordtagged RRz CST) introduces a Contingency phrase, the analysis being as follows:

> *It was turned away*, [R:c *so* [Fc *that for a second Martin*
> *thought* ...]] K06.083

§ 5.166   The prepositional idiom *thanks_to* introduces a :c phrase.

§ 5.167   *In this light* is roughly equivalent to *in this case*, therefore P:c, in *"In this light we need 1,000 churches in Illinois,* ...
A10:1580; likewise [P:c *Upon consideration of the variety of* ...],
it is little wonder that ... J05:1850. (On the other hand, a literal
usage such as *... in broad daylight it was even less inviting* ...
N05:1490 is given the Place functiontag :p.)

§ 5.168   In the American English construction which has *go/come*
immediately preceding a Tb, the latter is functiontagged :c as a
purpose clause:

> *Let's go* [Tb:c *get the boy*]". N07:1140

§ 5.169   Prepositional phrases are functiontagged :c as related to
purpose in:

> [S [Nns:s *Mitchell*] *was* [P:c *for using it*], [S– [Nns:s *Jones*] [P:c
> *against*]], [S+ *and* ...] ... S]. A06:0050
> *leagued against a hostile, persecutory world* G13:1390
> *Sheeran* ... *is running against the Republican organization's*
> *candidate,* ... A06:1080
> *"I ain't drawin' against you"* N12:1050
> *The suit was filed later in the day in Common Pleas Court 7*
> *against the Hughes company* ... A09:0340
> *The golfing fathers ruled in his favor.* A14:1670

— note that in the last case the borderline between :c (which was
chosen) and :h is very debatable.

:r   RESPECT

§ 5.170   This term is used in the sense of *with respect to*; prepositional phrases introduced by the latter phrase or by *about* (in

the "concerning" sense) or *in connexion with* are typical examples of Respect adjuncts. The *CGEL* examples are:

> *So far as travelling facilities are concerned, we have obviously made a popular decision; but with respect to the date, many people are expressing dissatisfaction;*
> *She helped him a little with his book.*
> *She talked learnedly about Kant.*
> *They are advising me legally.* — that is, "with respect to the law", not "in a legal manner" which would correspond to the function-tag :h

CGEL also lists an example *He has always been frightened of earwigs*. In SUSANNE terms *frightened* is an adjective by the "dictionary test", and therefore the Po *of earwigs* is an IC of the Jh phrase headed by *frightened* — it is not a clause IC, and consequently no functiontag is assigned to the Po. A SUSANNE example comparable to the *CGEL* example is:

> *he was* [Tn:e *excited* [P:r *about* [Tg *his son's having received the Prix de Rome in archaeology*]]] G06:1500

§ 5.171   *CGEL* further discusses various cases which it regards as being on the border between Respect and other categories. Under the SUSANNE system, the P phrase in *He is working in a factory* is a clear Place adjunct, irrespective of whether it is seen as answering the question "Where is he working?" or the question "What is he doing?" — the SUSANNE approach avoids delving behind the literal meaning of a text to represent its pragmatic force; and the Tg's in *they split their sides laughing, he's busy writing*, as we saw above, are categorized as Manner/Degree (:h) adjuncts.

§ 5.172   The *with* phrase is functiontagged :r in *had nothing to do with him* N09:1200.

§ 5.173   The emphasized phrase in *worth X to me* is tagged P:r, and hence this analysis is used also in:

> *Even* [P:r *for those who have been observing the political scene a long time*], *no script from the past is worth very much . . .* A08:0640
> *The prospect of cutting back spending is an unpleasant one* [P:r *for any governor*]. A08:1710

(Cf. § 5.33 on experiencers as prepositional objects, :u — the cases listed here as :r are felt to be less closely cohesive with the predicates of their clauses, but this distinction is difficult to make precise.)

§ 5.174 A number of extended uses of originally locative expressions fit sufficiently clearly within the Respect category to be functiontagged :r, e.g.:

> ... *for saving large tracts of open land **from the onrush of urban
> development**.* A06:1630
>
> *In some areas, the progress is slower than in others. **In agriculture**, for example, ... elaborate rituals tend to persist ...*
> G11:1540
>
> *the role played by the Supreme Court **in that transformation***
> G02:0460
>
> *micelles **in themselves** do not contribute significantly ...* J05:1440
>
> *Varani has been fired **on charges of accepting gifts from the
> contractor**.* A09:0180
>
> *... the Longhorn team that will be heavily favored Saturday **over
> Oklahoma** in the Cotton Bowl.* A12:0080
>
> ***From the standpoint of the army of duffers**, however, this was
> easily the most heartening exhibition ...* A14:1280

Also cf.:

> *depend on someone **for assistance***
>
> *... amounted to* [Nu:177 *$634,517,000,* [Z s177 [Ns:e *a 4 per
> cent increase*] [Tn:r ***compared to the corresponding period of
> last year***] Z] Nu:177] A19:1610
>
> *... they formed what they **officially** styled "The Confederate States
> of America".* G10:0460 — not *"in an official manner"*, which
> would be :h, but *"with respect to official purposes"*
>
> *the issues of* [Ns [Tn [Vn *centralized*] [P:r *vs.* [Tn *limited*]]]
> *government* Ns] G07:1730
>
> ***Both** turned in top jobs **for the second straight game**.* A12:0770

§ 5.175 The use of *with* in an exclamation, as in *"To hell **with**
him!"*, is functiontagged :r (the *to hell* phrase is functiontagged :q).

§ 5.176 The *of* phrase in the idiomatic construction *what of ...*
(not a grammatical idiom) is functiontagged :r, e.g.:

> [L? [Dq:e *What*] [Rsw:c *then*] [Po:r *of the positive arguments for
> their being composed for gentle ears*] L?]? F27.082

§ 5.177 The *for* phrase as in *If it were not **for an old professor
who made me read the classics** I would have been stymied ...*
N18:0040 is somewhat arbitrarily given the :r functiontag; and so
is the prepositional phrase of (British) *named **after** ...* , (American)
*named **for** ...* : [Ns:o137 *an avenue* [Tn S137 *named* [P:r *for
Bankhead McGruder, ...*] Tn] Ns:o137] G08:0410.

§ 5.178   This functiontag covers phrases introduced by *with* where this means "together with", "accompanying" (as opposed e.g. to "by means of" or "in view of"), and in a few cases phrases introduced by *without* in the converse sense. A clause containing a comitative phrase can commonly be paraphrased by a clause in which the comitative element is co-ordinated with one of the complements; thus

[Nns:s *John*] *arrived* [P:w *with Mary*].

is roughly equivalent to:

[Nn:s *John and Mary*] *arrived.*

Corpus examples include:

*The lawyer **with whom I studied law** . . .* A05:1060
*Fulton legislators "work **with city officials** to pass enabling legislation* . . . A01:0610
*All Dallas members voted **with Roberts,** except Rep. Bill Jones* . . . A02:1130
. . . *he will take up the matter **with Atty._Gen. J. Joseph Nugent** to get "the benefit of his views".* A05:0610
*All his people ask for is no more war. But he plunges into yet another, this time **with Norway,** and* . . . G18:1450
. . . *take* [N:o *counsel*] ***with the men who made the nation.*** G07:0060

and the metaphorical *my dear friend Dimitri Mitropoulos is no longer **with us,*** . . . G06:1260.

As examples involving *without*, CGEL gives:

*She went **without her children.***
*You never see him **without his dog.***

§ 5.179   The adverb *together* will normally be functiontagged :w (but see § 5.42).

§ 5.180   A *with* phrase as in *he took his Winchester **with him*** N01:0220, or *They, too, have fragments of the go code **with them.*** G03:1770 is functiontagged :w. On the other hand, the similar phrase in *It has nothing of the proud stride of the trained runner **about it,*** . . . G04:0180 is regarded as a metaphorical use of a Place adjunct (cf. § 5.129), and functiontagged :p.

§ 5.181   A number of cases listed as "comitative" in CGEL, p. 702, would not be functiontagged :w in the SUSANNE system.

In **Without you, I'm not going**, the *without* phrase paraphrases "if you are not going" and is treated as a Contingency adjunct; likewise the *with* phrase of **With all the noise, she was finding it hard to concentrate** (cf. § 5.164). In **It all started with John('s) being late for dinner**, the *with*-clause is a Manner adjunct. In **Curry with rice is my favourite dish**, the *with* phrase is a postmodifier within the noun phrase headed by *curry*, hence according to SUSANNE annotation rules takes no functiontag. In cases like:

> **With every leaping stride of the horse beneath him** he crossed one
> more patch of earth ... N02:1590
> ... a single powerful jab that sent Gyp reeling wildly [Tg+ and
> crashing down **with a whining groan**]. N14:0670

the *with* phrase is functiontagged :h, not :w.

§ 5.182   *With* phrases as clause ICs in which *with* paraphrases "having" are functiontagged :w, as in:

> He was [Po:e *of short, stocky, powerful build*], [P:w *with fiercely*
> *curling black hair and* ...]. G16.163 — cf. § 4.367
> [Np:s123 *firms* [Z s123 [P:w *with an annual turnover of £½m.*]
> [R:h *each*] Z] Np:s123] G72.181 — cf. § 4.372

§ 5.183   The Comitative adjunct category is very infrequent, applying to fewer than eight per thousand of the adjuncts in the SUSANNE Corpus. With one exception (see :k below), categories of this degree of specialization are not recognized elsewhere in the adjunct system. It may have been an unjustified decision to create a separate Comitative category in the annotation scheme; a better approach might have been to treat "comitative" as a subclass of one of the larger adjunct categories (presumably :h). Since the work of identifying Comitative instances has been done, however, :w tags have been allowed to stand in the SUSANNE Corpus. Users who prefer to treat :w as a homograph of :h are free to do so.

:k   BENEFACTIVE

§ 5.184   The benefactive functiontag is applied to elements fulfilling semantic roles akin to indirect objects, but which are not indirect objects and are not paraphrasable as such (so that neither of the functiontags :i, :u applies). These elements include those *for* phrases in which the *for* is undeletable (as in *I have found a place for the magnolia tree*, as opposed to *I have found a place for Mrs Jones* — cf. § 5.32 — or *she gave me a scarf for her son*, where the indirect object slot is filled and the *for* phrase identifies a more remote participant), together with phrases introduced by semantically similar prepositions which are never deleted, such as *on_behalf_of*. In to *win more and more people* **to the national effort** J22:1680 the emphasized phrase is functiontagged :k — a commoner way of expressing the same sense would use the *for* of the *scarf* example instead of *to*.

§ 5.185   The idiomatic usage in *Hez could see* **for himself** N13:0540 is functiontagged :k.

§ 5.186   This functiontag is even less frequent than the Comitative tag, applying to fewer than three per thousand SUSANNE adjuncts. The only substantial reason for recognizing it as a distinct category is the fact that the indirect-object construction implies that beneficiary roles have special significance within English grammar, so some residual category seems to be needed for those beneficiaries which cannot be expressed as indirect objects. An alternative might be to treat ":k" elements as cases of Contingency, :c, since the benefactive relationship is one of purpose.

:b   ABSOLUTE

§ 5.187   *CGEL*, p. 1120, uses this term for Tg, Tn, and verbless clauses containing an overt subject which function adverbially but are not linked to their higher clause by a subordinating conjunction or a preposition, as in:

> **No further discussion arising**, *the meeting was brought to a close.*
> **Lunch finished**, *the guests retired to the lounge.*
> **Christmas then only days away**, *the family was pent up* [sic] *with excitement.*
> *The boy came on to the porch and sat down,* [L:b **his gaze on Morgan as if half expecting him to shoot and not really caring**]. N01:0440
> *The company grew out of efforts* [Pb *by* [Np *two completely inexperienced men in their late twenties* Np] Pb], [Tg:b [Ds:s **neither**] **having a formal education applicable to**... Tg:b]. G22:1810 — the presence of a separate subject *neither* for the Tg prevents it being treated as a postmodifier of *men*

§ 5.188   The SUSANNE scheme extends this category in various respects. Thus W clauses, which are introduced by a preposition but resemble the cases above in describing circumstances in which the proposition of the higher clause obtains or obtained without explicitly identifying the relationship between that proposition and the circumstances identified, are always functiontagged :b, as in:

But [W:b *with the months moving on — and the immediate confrontations with the Communists showing no gain for the free world —*] *the question arises:* ... A04:0930

— and cf. the following examples, where a W has been reduced to a P:

Congress starts another week tomorrow [P:b *with sharply contrasting forecasts for the two chambers*]. A07:0730
... he ... abandoned his career at the bar, [P:b *with considerable financial sacrifice*]. G07:1260
We are in a wilderness [P:b *without a single footstep to guide us*]. G07:0160
The valley was only a few hundred yards wide [P:b *with just about room enough for a properly performed hundred-and-eighty-degree turn*]. N15:0640

§ 5.189   In:

As first Chief Justice, *his strong nationalist opinions anticipated John Marshall.* G07:0900

the word *as* means something like *when*, but if the phrase were *when first Chief Justice* it would be tagged as an Fa:t within which the effect of the understood *he was* would be represented by the functiontag :e on the N *first Chief Justice*; with the word *as* the whole is a P, therefore there is no possibility of making explicit the role of the N by giving it a functiontag, so the whole is P:b.

§ 5.190   The functiontag :b is also applied to Tg's, and to non-finite clauses and phrases in which the verb *being* is understood, which apply to the subject of the higher clause to describe an action carried out by the subject or a state the subject is in which is simultaneous with the action or state described by the higher clause (while again leaving inexplicit the nature of the relationship between the two propositions):

The gunman nodded, [Tg:b *slipping the picture into his breast pocket,* [Tg– *saying nothing*] Tg:b]. N07:1760
(or: **Slipping the picture into his breast pocket,** *the gunman nodded.*)
"We'll double teams **zigzagging up the mountain,** *Harmony"* N13:1700
Almost equal in size to a honeybee, <bital> A. armata <eital> *is much more beautiful in color...* J10:1170
Incapable of self-delusion, *the Founding Fathers found...* G07:0070

Note that in the Tg cases just cited, the Tg is not "amplifying" the higher verb, as in the examples given in § 5.148 — in *spent a million dollars, carving in a road,* . . . , the Tg *carving in a road* identifies how the money was spent; *zigzagging up the mountain* is not the result of doubling teams but merely the circumstance in which this will be done.

§ 5.191   With these examples of Tg:b contrast *She remained squatting on her heels* G04:1270, where the Tg is complement of *remained* and functiontagged :e.

§ 5.192   In a clause functiontagged :b as above, no ghost constituent is reconstructed to represent the missing subject (cf. § 5.148). (However, if a :b clause contains a subordinate clause of a type which would normally have a missing constituent reconstructed via a ghost node, this may be indexed to an antecedent outside the :b clause — [Nns:s113 *Nate*] *turned his head,* [Tg:b *attempting* [Ti:o s113 *to speak* . . .] Tg:b]. N13:0290.)

§ 5.193   *CGEL* gives the Absolute examples:

> *Persuaded by our optimism, he gladly contributed* . . .
> *Confident of the justice of their cause, they agreed to put their case* . . .

and cf. the authentic example:

> *Gaunt was compelled to give up his search for an elusive foe,* [S+ *and,* [Jh:b *afraid* [Ti *to return home without something to show*] Jh:b], *he foolishly attempted* . . . S+] G01.013

But the further example listed by *CGEL* at the same point, *To climb the rock face, we had to take various precautions,* would be classified under the SUSANNE scheme as a Contingency rather than Absolute adjunct since *to* makes explicit that the subordinate clause expresses the "purpose" of taking precautions: a Ti will not be functiontagged :b. In many Tg cases a relationship will be sufficiently explicit to justify a more specific functiontag; thus in *Assuming the weather is halfway decent that day, hundreds of thousands of persons will mass along this thoroughfare* . . . A08:0180 the Tg expresses a condition and hence is tagged as a Contingency adjunct.

§ 5.194   As *CGEL* points out, a common phenomenon which is regarded as a solecism in English is for the type of non-finite clause or phrase described in § 5.190 to occur with the understood subject not the same as the subject of the higher clause — as in *Driving to Chicago that night, a sudden thought struck me.* Cases of this kind are often described by the term "dangling participle"; *CGEL* uses the term "unattached clause". The functiontag :b applies to constructions of these types irrespective of whether they are correctly attached or unattached. Since the ghost system is not used to reconstruct deleted subjects in adjunct clauses, SUSANNE annotations do not reveal whether or not an Absolute adjunct is correctly attached.

§ **5.195** The asyndetically co-ordinated clause ICs quoted in § 4.518 from LOB texts C01 ([L *Demure one moment* , [L– *decisive the next*]], *she caught* . . .), C07, and M02 all consist of :b adjuncts.

THE PREPOSITION *FROM*

§ **5.196** Adjuncts introduced by the preposition *from* are often particularly problematic with respect to functiontagging. The category most "literally" associated with this preposition is Direction, :q, and this is often applied where the concept of directionality is more abstract:

> . . . *a meeting . . . brought enthusiastic responses* **from the audience.** A01:0880
> *The most positive element to emerge* **from the Oslo meeting** . . . A04:0010
> . . . *the shooting had been done* **from a distance of 300 yards.** N11:0370
> *straightened* **from his lax slouch** N03:0590
> *woke up* **from her winter sleep** J10:0460
> *They expected greater things* **from him,** . . . N05:1080
> . . . *can even be eliminated* **from it** *altogether.* G09:1720
> *It is apparent* **from the above and from experimental evidence** *that* . . . J02:0400

But in other cases *from* introduces a Respect adjunct, :r —

> *the Russian instruments are isolated* **from the skin** J07:1150
> *"These actions should serve to protect . . . the court's wards* **from undue costs** *and its . . . servants* **from unmeritorious criticisms",** . . . A01:0490
> *trying to keep them* **from falling into the creek** . . . N10:0210
> *Pennsylvania Avenue . . . perhaps is not the most impressive street in the District of Columbia* **from a commercial standpoint.** A08:0230

or a Contingency adjunct, :c —

> *an embankment that had become soft and spongy* **from the rains** A14:1590

as would be expected from the explanation of Piddington and Minnett (1949) J01:1820

The men in Pettigrew's were tired from a night's drinking,... N02:1000

the cattlemen who had been facing bankruptcy from rustling losses N11:1600

From the preceding remarks, it is clear that... J21:1180

the pattern known from the sleep-wakefulness cycle J17:1080

or an instrument adjunct, :h —

I write about Northern liberals from considerable personal experience. G01:0140

The DEAE-cellulose, containing 0.78 mEq of N/g, was prepared in our laboratory... *from powdered cellulose, 100-230 mesh.* J09:0750

The radius is calculated from the mass by assuming... J07:1390

or, with certain verbs, as a prepositional object, :u —

an international inspection system which will prevent Laos from being used as a base for Communist attacks on... A04:0780

a line... *marking the upper limits of tidewater would roughly divide the Old South from the new,*... G01:1010

Other Functiontags

:n PARTICLE OF PHRASAL VERB

§ 5.197   For the concept "phrasal verb" see *CGEL*, pp. 1152 ff.; the distinction between phrasal and prepositional verbs (e.g. *call up* = "summon" v. *call on* = "visit") is elaborated on pp. 1166–7.

The particle of a phrasal verb, whether adjacent to the verb or postposed, is tagged R:n —

[S *They* [Vd *called*] [R:n *up*] [Ns:o *the dean*] S].
[S *They* [Vd *called*] [Ns:o *the dean*] [R:n *up*] S].

The preposition of a prepositional verb, by contrast, forms a P:u with its complement:

[S *They* [Vd *called*] [P:u *on* [Ns *the dean*]] S].

With so-called phrasal-prepositional verb constructions (*CGEL*, pp. 1160–1), the particle is R:n and the preposition initiates a P:u —

Why don't you [Vr *look*] [R:n *in*] [P:u *on Mrs Johnson*] [P:p
on your way back]?
We put [Ns:o *our success*] [R:n *down*] [P:u *to hard work*].

:X PROPOSITIONAL RELATIVE CLAUSE

§ 5.198 Some relative clauses, and non-finite clauses of the types
(such as Tg) which regularly share the noun-postmodifying functions of standard relative clauses, have as antecedent not a nominal
expression but the whole clause, or a predicate expression (a sense-
rather than reference-bearing element) within the clause, of which
they form an IC. Such tagmas are functiontagged :x (and contain no
index linking them to their antecedents). Their interpretation is always
appositive rather than restrictive.

> [S [Nas:s *He*] [Vd *left*] [R:t *early*], [Fr:x [Dq:s *which*] *surprised*
> [Neo:o *me*] Fr:x] S].
> [S [Nns:s *John*] [Vzb *is*] [J:e *witty*], [Fr:x [Dq:o *which*] [Ny:s
> *you*] [Vce *cannot say*] [Po:r *of Peter*] Fr:x] S]. — the ante-
> cedent is *is witty*, rather than the entire main clause
> [S . . . [Ns:s *the bill*] [Vd *passed*], [M:h *114 to 4*], [Tg:x *sending
> it to the Senate, where a similar proposal is being sponsored by
> Sen. George Parkhouse of Dallas* Tg:x] S]. A02:1200
> [S [Np:s *They*] [R:h *all*] [Vd *occurred*] [P:t *during my service
> with the Trinity House*], [Fr:x [Dq:s *which*] *is not altogether
> surprising when one remembers . . .*] S]. F22.032
> [S+ *and the consequence is,* [Fn:e *the brain monopolises the nu-
> tritive supply,* [Fn+ *and is developed to the detriment of
> the merely physical powers*], [Fr:x [Nqs *the result* [Poq *of
> which*]] *is,* [Fn:e *that the man is more feeble . . .*] Fr:x]
> Fn:e] S+]. D14.025

Clauses formtagged A frequently act as propositional relatives (the
examples in § 4.370 will all be functiontagged :x). And an *as* phrase
is functiontagged :x in:

> [S+ *but former Gov. Stratton commuted her term to 75 years,
> making her eligible for parole,* [P:x *as one of his last acts in
> office* P:x] S+]. A20:1670

:Z COMPLEMENT OF CATENATIVE

§ 5.199 *CGEL*, pp. 136–7, points out that there is a cline in English between modal verbs such as *can, might*, and main verbs which

take non-finite clause complements, such as *hope* (*to* . . .), *enjoy* (. . .*ing.* . .). All these verbs are followed by further, non-finite verbs; but clear cases of modal verbs group with the following verbs into a single verb group, heading a single clause, whereas the non-finite verbs following verbs such as *hope* or *enjoy* form separate verb groups heading subordinate clauses. *CGEL* lists the following classes of intermediate verbs:

- "marginal modals", e.g. *dare, need, ought to, used to*
- "modal idioms", e.g. *had better, would rather/sooner, BE to, HAVE got to*
- "semi-auxiliaries", e.g. *HAVE to, BE about to, BE bound to, BE going to, BE obliged to*
- "catenatives", e.g. *APPEAR to, HAPPEN to, SEEM to, GET* + past participle, *KEEP* + present participle

CGEL discusses a number of criteria for placing particular verbs in these intermediate classes rather than in the polar classes represented by *can* and *hope* respectively.

The SUSANNE scheme provides a special analytic structure for the intermediate cases (which are referred to generally as "catenative" structures within the SUSANNE scheme — it is unclear why *CGEL* reserves this term for one of its four intermediate categories). The subordinate clause is given the functiontag :z, and, unlike in the case of complement clauses following ordinary main verbs, no subject is reconstructed via the ghost/index system in a :z clause.

> *if their problem-solving behavior is* [Ti:z *to be constructive* . . .] J24:1030
> *It's bigger* [Fc *than it has* [Ti:z *to be*] Fc], . . . N05:0140
> "[Ni:s159 *It* 161]*'s Ben Arbuckle* [Fr:G161 *we* [Vaut +'re *going*] [Ti:z *to talk* [P:r *about* 159] Ti:z] Fr:G161]". N12:0820
> *You* [Vd +'d] [R:m *better*] [Tb:z [V *sleep*]]". N01:1580

§ 5.200　Additionally, five words which commonly introduce catenative constructions have special wordtags in this function: *about* RPK, *bound* VVNK, *going* VVGK, *ought* and *used* VMK. Thus:

> *You* [Vaet +'re *not going*_VVGK] [Ti:z *to marry a miserable invalid*]. P17.170
> *He* [Vsb *was*] [R:m *just*] [R:e *about*_RPK] [Ti:z *to leave the hotel on his quest*] *when* . . . P12.125
> *They* [Vct *ought*_VMK] [Ti:z *to have a pleasant time*]. B04.095
> *There*_EX [Vzpt +'s *bound*_VVNK] [Ti:z *to be* [Ns:s *someone*] [P:e *on guard*] Ti:z], . . . N03:0490

For the analysis of the N03 case, cf. § 5.71.

§ 5.201   If the catenative clause is passive, the subject of the higher clause will be functiontagged :S rather than :s, as in:

if [Nap:S *they*] *are* [Ti:z *to be applied to man*] J12:1570
... *read* [Ns:o123 *the letter* [Fr [Dq:S123 *which*] [Vsb *was*] [R:e *about*_RPK] [Ti:z *to be sent to her husband* . . .] Fr] Ns:o123].
K23.144

§ 5.202   "Catenative constructions" for the purpose of applying the :z functiontag do not cover exactly the same range of constructions listed by *CGEL* under its four categories.

§ 5.203   On one side, the *CGEL* "marginal modals" *dare, need* are analysed as ordinary modals, wordtagged VMo, when functioning like other modals (occurring as leading verb in a sequence, followed by a base-form verb without *to*); the catenative analysis is used for cases like:

*Certainly, she wouldn't dare*_VV0v [Tb:z *ask her father afterward*]. N10:0380 — *dare* not the leading verb
*we need*_VV0t [Ti:z *to hear some voice* . . .] A10:0570 — *need* is followed by *to*

§ 5.204   On the other side, some of the *CGEL* intermediate cases are analysed under the SUSANNE scheme as two-clause constructions of a standard type not requiring the :z functiontag. Among the verbs listed under the *CGEL* "catenative" subcategory, *APPEAR HAPPEN SEEM* are analysed in the SUSANNE scheme as introducing Raising to Subject rather than catenative constructions:

[Nns:S123 *Sam*] [Vde *did* [XX:G125 +*n't*] *appear*] [Ti:s s123 [Vi 125 *to realize*] [Ns:o *the importance of the problem*] Ti:s]

rather than:

[Nns:s *Sam*] [Vde *did* [XX:G125 +*n't*] *appear*] [Ti:z [Vi 125 *to realize*] [Ns:o *the importance of the problem*] Ti:s]

§ 5.205   Furthermore, some of *CGEL*'s "semi-auxiliary" constructions are of the form *BE* + adjective + *to* (e.g. *BE able to, BE willing to*): SUSANNE treats the Ti in such cases as postmodifying the adjective within a Jh:e, and again the functiontag :z is not needed. SUSANNE treats the *BE obliged to* construction as simply the passive version of *X OBLIGE Y to*, since the latter construction is also normal and the meaning of the passive version is predictable from that of the active version, hence *BE obliged to* is not catenative. Contrast *BE bound to, BE supposed to*: the construction *X BIND*

Y to . . . is quite unusual in modern English, and neither this nor the fairly standard active construction *X SUPPOSE Y to* . . . has the semantically modal force of *BE bound to* (= "must"), *BE supposed to* (= "ought"), hence the :z functiontag *is* used for the latter constructions.

§ 5.206   *CGEL* states that the boundary between the intermediate cases and the clear main verb + non-finite clause constructions is difficult to draw unambiguously. In borderline cases, the SUSANNE scheme chooses whether or not to apply the :z functiontag by reference to the "independence of subject" test (*CGEL*, pp. 126–7). Thus Tg:z is used in the analysis of *KEEP Verbing* sequences, but *fail to, manage to, get to* are analysed within the SUSANNE scheme as ordinary Equi or Raising constructions:

[Nns:S123 *Sam*] *failed* [Ti:s s123 *to realize* . . .]
[Nns:s123 *Sam*] *managed* [Ti:o s123 *to solve it*]

not:

[Nns:s *Sam*] *failed* [Ti:z *to realize* . . .]
[Nns:s *Sam*] *managed* [Ti:z *to solve it*]

After the verbs *begin, start, cease,* a Ti is given the :z functiontag but a Tg is not:

[Fa:t *As we began* [Ti:z *to converse*] *in the lounge of his Fifth Avenue hotel*], . . . G06:0150
Some opposition to the home rule movement started [Ti:z *to be heard*] *yesterday,* . . . A05:1610
. . . *that John Jay never ceased* [Ti:z *to be the friend of Peter Van Schaack*]". G07:1570
. . . *against* [Np:191 *the teamsters,* [Fr [Dq:s191 *which*] *began* [Tg:o s191 *organizing city firemen*] *in 1959* Fr] Np:191]. A09:1660
[Nns:s170 *Andy Ross*] *had just started* [Tg:o s170 *swinging an ax at his second willow*] *when* . . . N11:0790

§ 5.207   Two additional construction-types analysed using the SUSANNE functiontag :z are that of *BE well advised to, BE a fool to*; as in:

He'd be [Ns:e *an idiot*] [Ti:z *to let them stay*] N01:1050

— and the *so as to* construction, as in:

. . . *is very often extremely finely divided* [R:c *so* [A *as* [Ti:z *to exhibit colloidal properties*] A] R:c]. J05:0890

□ 6 □
SPEECH

§ 6.1 Spoken English is not a separate language from written English, and many of the annotation conventions devised for the written language carry over unchanged to spoken English. But it is obvious that the spoken language includes distinctive properties of its own, which require additional annotation conventions.

§ 6.2 Techniques for grammatical annotation of written English have existed, if not necessarily formalized as fully as in the present work, for a very long time. By contrast, comparable techniques applicable to the spoken language scarcely exist. Roger Moore, a leading British authority on automatic speech recognition, has written recently of the "overwhelming need for agreed standards of . . . annotation . . . normal, everyday, *non-prepared speech* is replete with repetition, false-starts, repairs, partial utterances, 'uhms' and 'errs' etc. . . . it is essential that there should be orthographic transcription conventions for such events" (Moore 1992). It is not surprising that there should be a large disparity in the degree of maturity of annotation techniques for the two language modes. Speech needs to be transcribed in some permanent form before the work of devising structural annotations can begin, while writing is already in such a form. The electronic research resources needed in order to develop annotation techniques systematically have been available for a longer time in the case of written English: the Brown Corpus became publicly available in 1964, while the first sizeable machine-readable corpus of spoken English, the (British) London-Lund Corpus (on which see Svartvik 1990), became available in electronic form only in 1980. At the time of writing, no machine-readable corpus of spoken American English is yet available, though Wallace Chafe is developing one at the University of California, Santa Barbara (see Chafe *et al.* 1991).

§ 6.3 The present author's research team has put some effort into studying the problems of structural annotation of spoken English, and into extending the SUSANNE scheme to deal with these problems, in connection with a project on automatic parsing of spoken English,[1] and also in the author's own case as a member of the Text Encoding Initiative working group on speech annotation. The speech annotation scheme developed in connection with the research project just referred to (which for convenience will here be called the SUSANNE speech annotation scheme, though historically the acronym SUSANNE was not associated with this project) is far less fully elaborated, and has been applied to a much smaller sample of material, than the scheme for written English defined in earlier chapters. However, the general immaturity of this area of the discipline means that even our limited scheme may be worth presenting. It draws together research from a number of sources not all of which are widely available.

§ 6.4   The SUSANNE speech annotation scheme is based on the experience of annotating a small sample drawn from the London-Lund Corpus. The genres of speech represented in the London-Lund Corpus can be classified rather unambiguously into what might be called "private" and "public" speech — the former comprising relaxed dialogue between pairs or small groups of participants, and full of phenomena typical of speech such as dysfluencies, repetitions, changes of tack in mid-tagma, etc., the latter comprising material such as formal speeches to an audience, radio talks, etc., which attempt to a greater or lesser extent to emulate the edited, finished style usual in written prose (and which in some cases may actually be read from written scripts). Categories 1 to 9 of the London-Lund Corpus are private speech, categories 10 to 12 are public speech. Our work used the private speech, since this contains in concentrated form the various problems needing to be solved; our annotated speech corpus (which is not in the public domain) includes parsetrees for every fiftieth "speaker's turn" — that is, stretch of continuous speech by a single speaker — in London-Lund categories 1 to 9, totalling very roughly 7,000 words. The examples discussed below are all drawn from the texts printed in Svartvik and Quirk (1980), which contains most of the material from categories 1 to 3.

The Base Transcription

§ 6.5   The examples quoted below from London-Lund are shown in a transcription derived from the electronic Corpus, but processed by our research group to suit the purposes of grammatical analysis. Briefly, the reformatting represents the London-Lund dialogues as

[1] The project "A speech-oriented stochastic parser", Ministry of Defence reference no. D/ER1/9/4/2062/151, was sponsored by the Speech Research Unit of the Royal Signals and Radar Establishment (now Defence Research Agency), Malvern. Unfortunately this research was terminated prematurely as a consequence of career developments alluded to in Ch. 1.

a sequence of "turns", in the above sense, by individual speakers (in the original Corpus, a single turn does not always appear as a continuous segment), and it eliminates the rich London-Lund annotation of prosodic features such as intonation, while representing the wording itself in an easily legible manner.

§ 6.6   One reason why our analyses ignore prosodic information is that there is no straightforward way to bring it into a relationship with the grammatical issues with which the SUSANNE scheme is concerned. Undoubtedly the two kinds of phenomena are related, but the relationship is a subtle and indirect one. An independent reason, though, is that our research on grammatical analysis of speech has been oriented to the task of automatic speech recognition, and it seems quite unlikely that prosodic information of the kind represented in the London-Lund Corpus will be reliably identified in the output of automatic speech recognition systems developed in the foreseeable future. Current ASR systems normally limit their target to that of outputting sequences of words. There is plenty of evidence, dating back for instance to Lieberman (1967), to show that prosodic features of speech are only to a limited extent grounded in physical properties of the speech signal, and that much of the detail of what we think we hear as, for instance, differential levels of stress on different syllables is in reality a perceptual construct. On the basis of his understanding of the language structure, the hearer unconsciously supplies a prosodic pattern for a heard utterance which does not physically contain such a pattern. If that is so, then it is arguably more appropriate to develop a grammatical annotation system for speech based on the wording of utterances alone than on a version of the utterances that includes prosodic information: the prosodic properties derive from the grammatically annotated wording, rather than the grammatical analysis deriving from the prosodically annotated wording.

§ 6.7   Thus our transcriptions omit all symbols relating to "tone unit", "nucleus", "booster", and "stress", in terms of the List of Symbols on pp. 21 ff. of Svartvik and Quirk (1980). Pauses, which *may* have more physical reality, are represented in the transcriptions by hyphen and full-stop characters: a full stop represents "Brief pause (of one light syllable)", hyphen represents "Unit pause (of one stress unit or 'foot')", and longer pauses are represented by a sequence of one or more hyphens followed by zero or one full stop, corresponding to the length of the pause.[2] Where the London-Lund

---

[2] Occasionally a pause will be represented by hyphen(s) and full stop(s) in some other combination, as a consequence of the fact, discussed below, that our transcriptions unite segments of a speaker's turn which in the original Corpus are split in order to show simultaneous speech by another speaker.

Corpus uses IPA phonetic transcription to represent non-verbal speech sounds or distorted syllables or words, we replace the IPA symbols with conventional equivalents using the ordinary roman alphabet — for instance short shwa, long shwa, and syllabic [m] are shown as *uh er mm* respectively. An isolated phoneme is often shown as a letter immediately followed by a hyphen, to indicate that the letter is used for its phonetic value rather than as a complete word. (The phonetic equivalences used are not specified in detail in the present work, which is primarily concerned with grammatical annotation rather than base transcription; our phonetic notation is slightly less detailed than that of the electronic London-Lund Corpus, which is in turn slightly less detailed than that of the original, hard-copy Corpus.)

§ 6.8   Wording transcribed as incomprehensible by the London-Lund Corpus compilers is shown within angle brackets, where the compilers have supplied a reconstruction of the words believed to be intended, and otherwise is represented by question marks, one per syllable where the number of syllables is indicated. Asterisk indicates a non-speech noise, e.g. laugh or kiss, with multiple asterisks standing for longer noises. Curly brackets surround "contextual comments", e.g.:

{ . clears throat}

— where the full stop shows the length of the event described, by the same code as used for pauses.

§ 6.9   When a single word is spoken with an internal pause, the part-words are prefixed by hyphens (without intervening space) to indicate that they are parts of a longer word, thus *remember* spoken with a short pause before the final syllable appears as:

–remem . –ber

§ 6.10   Reference numbers in the London-Lund Corpus identify successive "tone units", which are phonetically defined segments of a spoken utterance. A speaker's turn may include more than one tone unit; and the London-Lund numbering of the tone units making up a single turn will not necessarily be sequential. Where speakers talk simultaneously, the tone units are numbered in time order, and the Corpus includes notation showing precisely how the material overlaps. This information has little relevance for grammatical analysis, and our transcriptions unite the tone units of one speaker's turn into a continuous sequence: our convention is to use the London-Lund reference number of the first tone unit of a turn to number the whole turn. Thus, turn 1.1.13 represents a turn by speaker B which comprises tone units 13, 14, 15, 16, 18, and 20 of the text identified on p. 34 of Svartvik and Quirk (1980) as "S.1.1"; it runs in our transcription (compare the original London-Lund transcription shown by Svartvik and Quirk, loc. cit.) as:

> *Well what you do is to – – this is sort of between the two of us what you do is to make sure that your own . candidate is . . that your . there's something that your own candidate can handle – – <I won't be a minute> – – ? ? ? – – – ,*

In Svartvik and Quirk (1980) each text name is prefixed by the characters "S.", which appear to play no role in distinguishing one text from another and do not appear in the electronic Corpus; this document ignores that prefix and identifies London-Lund texts by two-part numbers, "1.1", "2.12", and so on, where the first number is a text category and the second an individual text within the category.

§ 6.11 Where, as in the case of turn 1.1.13 just quoted, the last tone unit of a turn is marked[3] as "incomplete", a comma ends the turn in our transcription.

§ 6.12 Turns are given an initial capital letter like written sentences, and words are shown with any internal hyphenation, apostrophes, or capitalization required by conventional orthography. Apart from that, punctuation appears in the transcriptions only to represent phonetic features as discussed above: thus, turns constituting statements or questions are not ended with full stops or question marks to show their grammatical status.

It should also be mentioned that, to protect speakers' privacy, the London-Lund compilers replaced all proper names occurring in the recorded utterances with different, prosodically similar names in the transcriptions.

Grammatical Annotation of Speech

§ 6.13 Within our parsetrees for spoken utterances, root nodes, labelled O, dominate turns. Where spoken English is fully fluent, the grammar of a turn is normally analysed in the same way as the corresponding wording would be analysed if appearing in writing: a turn may consist of one or more S tagmas and/or lesser grammatical units. Obviously an O in speech will never have a punctuation mark as a daughter, but it may have a pause as daughter (see below).

---

[3] By a "2" in column 24 of the electronic Corpus, cf. Svartvik and Quirk (1980: 32).

§ **6.14** Asyndetic co-ordination is not recognized immediately below an O in the analysis of speech (and will probably be little needed at any level of a speech parsetree). In writing, an O daughter may be a tagma having the structure [S ... [S– ...]], identified as a single tagma by orthographic cues such as semicolon rather than full stop between the clauses, and lack of capitalization on the second clause. These cues are absent in speech, so a sequence of tagmas at the top level is treated as a co-ordination only if the last of them, at least, is preceded by a conjunction. Even when a main clause is preceded by a co-ordinating conjunction, in the analysis of written English it can be treated as an S+ attached directly to the root node, and accordingly in the parsing of speech a main clause will be analysed as a subordinate conjunct only if there is further evidence, apart from a conjunction, that it is acting as such (for instance if it has been reduced by deletion of material logically shared with the preceding tagma).

§ **6.15** We have made no attempt to apply the SUSANNE logical-grammar annotation scheme to speech, and the examples shown below include only word and surface-grammar tagging. In the case of spoken utterances whose logic is unambiguous, we do not know of special problems that would make it difficult to apply the annotation scheme of Chapter 5, but there may be such difficulties. The problem of utterances whose logic is unclear, which can create difficulties for the logical annotation of written language, would certainly be very salient in the case of spoken language.

§ **6.16** As with examples cited elsewhere in the present book, when citing examples of annotated speech below we show only those aspects of the annotation relevant to the point at issue, omitting information which is not germane and might clutter the page confusingly.

§ **6.17** A new wordtag is needed to label "distorted words" — attempts to produce a word which are broken off prematurely or fail in some other way to constitute an adequate articulation of the word. The tag FD is used for this purpose. In the annotation of spoken utterances in general it would be necessary to devise guidelines for deciding when a word is sufficiently distorted to be tagged FD rather than taking the wordtag of the word which the speaker intends; but in our work this decision was left to those who compiled the London-Lund Corpus — if they found a word sufficiently distorted to transcribe it other than in its conventional orthographic form, we tag it FD.

§ **6.18** Where a word occurs in a distorted form but is not involved in a speech repair (see below), the structure and labelling of the parsetree above it is chosen in terms of the analyst's surmise about the speaker's grammatical intentions. In cases where long sequences of words are distorted or inaudible to the point of incomprehensibility, as often happens in the London-Lund Corpus, there will be no basis for choosing a parsetree. We have simply omitted such passages from the material we analysed, because the aim of the present scheme is to propose annotational norms for spoken English utterances assuming that one understands them — incomprehensible speech is a different sort of problem, and not our concern here. When words were physically incomprehensible but the Corpus compilers were sufficiently confident of the words intended to supply them within angle brackets, our parses treat the words as if they were spoken normally.

§ 6.19 Apart from the matters discussed above, there are three main areas in which the SUSANNE scheme of earlier chapters needs to be extended to handle spoken English. These are:

- pauses
- discourse items
- speech repairs

and they will be dealt with in the chapter-divisions following this one.

§ 6.20 Incidentally, some of the phenomena for which this chapter offers annotation norms when they occur in speech do also occur in written English, even if much less saliently, and are sometimes assigned different analyses by earlier chapters when occurring in written English. Thus, §§ 4.522 ff. define a structure for speech repairs as found in written representations of informal speech which is quite different from the structure that this chapter will assign to identical repairs if they occur in speech itself. An obvious question, now that the conventions of the present chapter have been established, would be whether the written-language annotation conventions ought to be revised to bring them into line where they conflict.

The author is inclined to think that this is not desirable. In the first place the speech annotation conventions simply have not yet been tested sufficiently for it to be safe to let them override well-established conventions laid down for written prose. But furthermore, a written representation, say in a novel, of a stretch of a dialogue containing a dysfluency is really a different category of thing from a dysfluency actually occurring in speech. The passage from the novel is a well-formed English sequence which uses the resources of written English competently in order to represent a particular phenomenon (which in this case happens to be the phenomenon of a speaker making an error of performance); the dysfluency in speech is a performance error. Special annotation conventions devised to represent performance errors surely are not appropriate to represent competent, well-formed examples of language. Accordingly, there are no plans to revise the SUSANNE Corpus of written English to modify its annotations in line with the conventions of the present chapter.

Pauses

§ 6.21 Spoken language includes many so-called "filled" and "silent" pauses. Silent pauses are what the name suggests: stretches of time within a speech turn during which the speaker utters no sound — or that at least is the naïve view of the matter: it may in fact be that pauses too are perceptual constructs, and that many of the phenomena heard by the Corpus compilers as silence and represented by them with hyphens and full stops were physically realized as processes such as lengthening of a preceding phoneme, without any silence, but we cannot enter into such questions here. "Filled pause" is the term used for sounds such as *er, mm*, made by a speaker during a turn but not functioning to realize any particular word — filled pauses may serve to notify other dialogue participants that the speaker is retaining the turn while he formulates his next words, but again it is not for us to go into the purpose of such items.

§ 6.22 Since pauses in speech are to some extent akin to punctuation in writing, our scheme assigns them wordtags beginning Y.... . (The similarity between spoken pauses and written punctuation should not be overstated, but we have to devise wordtags somehow.) A silent pause of any length is treated as a single "word" tagged YP; a filled pause of any length, and irrespective of the particular sound involved, is treated as a single "word" tagged YM.

§ 6.23 A filled pause may coincide phonetically with a meaningful word. A short shwa vowel may be a brief filled pause, or may be the indefinite article *a*. A syllabic [m] may be a filled pause or, at least in British English, an informal synonym for *yes* — as in e.g.:

   ...that's perfectly all right is it   2.6.440
   Mm   2.6.451

Our scheme assumes that acting as a filled pause is a distinct identifiable grammatical role for a sound: a syllabic [m] will be a "word" that is sometimes tagged YM as a filled pause and sometimes tagged UY as a Positive discourse item (see below), just as the word *shed* is sometimes tagged NN1c and sometimes VV0t; we assume that context will normally disambiguate in either case.

§ 6.24   The rule for attaching pauses to parsetrees is the same as in the case of written punctuation marks (§ 4.65): a pause is attached as high as is possible without doing violence to the analysis of the surrounding wording.

Discourse Items

§ 6.25   We take the term "discourse item" from the work of the Lund group, for words or short set phrases which are characteristic of speech rather than written language because they serve pragmatic functions which are applicable to speech but scarcely or not at all applicable to writing, rather than serving semantic or grammatical functions. As Anna-Brita Stenström points out (1990: 137–8), the mere fact that a vocabulary item occurs only or mainly in speech does not in itself make it a discourse item. Her example is *really*, as used four times in London-Lund turn 2.2.16:

> But I don't *really* know that I'm going to be a vast amount of help to you . I was interested in your advertisement and and um – – . uh but uh I gather you're after <an> enormous amount of information and I don't *really* know that I've got – you know whether what I've got is uh of any help I mean it's *really* for you to decide *really* – – –

This word is far more characteristic of speech than of writing, but in all the cases quoted, and probably in other cases, it acts rather clearly as an adverb of Modality and thus serves a semantic rather than a pragmatic function. On the other hand *yes, you know* are examples of items which are both much more characteristic of speech than of written language and, when they occur in speech, commonly have only a pragmatic function; thus these are discourse items.

§ 6.26   A spoken item having a characteristic pragmatic function can be recognized as a discourse item although the same spoken word or phrase on other occasions functions semantically. For instance *well* is very common as a discourse item (*well I don't know*), but obviously *well* can also function in speech, with no noticeable difference in pronunciation, as the adverb corresponding to *good*. (Likewise *you know* may have its literal sense in speech — *You know Mrs Hogben, I think?* — though it may possibly be that pragmatic and semantic uses of *you know* tend to be distinguished by degree of stress on the pronoun.) In cases like these, our scheme treats the word or phrase as grammatically ambiguous: *well* receives one wordtag, RR, as an adverb, and a different wordtag, UW, as a discourse item. *You know* is tagged UE= as a discourse item, as PPY VV0v in its literal use.

§ 6.27 Papers by Anna-Brita Stenström (1990) and by Bengt Altenberg (1990) in a recent collection of articles on the London-Lund Corpus (Svartvik 1990) jointly represent the fullest empirically based attempt to classify discourse items known to us. (An earlier classification scheme by the Lund group, which differed in some details and included very little explanation of its categories, was published in *CAE*, pp. 179 ff., and also appears with slight changes in Svartvik 1990: 101 ff.) Stenström's and Altenberg's papers seem to be based on analysis of the same 50,000-word subset of the London-Lund Corpus, and between them include both extensive discussion, with examples, and frequency data. Our scheme is based on these papers together with the 1987 classification, though there are minor (unexplained) differences between each pair of these three schemes; and our scheme makes some additional modifications.

§ 6.28 Our classification of "discourse items" in fact draws the boundary round this concept more tightly than do the Lund researchers. For us, "discourse items" are limited to items which, if analysed according to the written-English annotation scheme, would be tagged UH (or UH=), together with the type of short set phrase which § 4.447 of the written-English scheme treats as S! tagmas: that is, items that are grammatically independent, not integrated structurally into larger utterances, and which are listable rather than constructed by productive rules of grammar. (We do not attempt to provide exhaustive lists, however.) Our scheme handles discourse items by providing a range of wordtags beginning U. . . , which subdivide the single crude category UH that suffices for written English because discourse items are so infrequent there.

§ 6.29 It is true that, for instance, *sort of* in *this is sort of between the two of us* (from turn 1.1.13, quoted above) serves a specific pragmatic function of hedging an assertion that might otherwise sound too bald, and that tag questions such as *isn't it* ("Q-Tags" in Stenström's scheme) serve a pragmatic function of inviting the hearer to associate his authority with that of the speaker behind the latter's assertion. But at the same time these items are usually integrated grammatically with their context; thus, a tag question can be *isn't it, couldn't she,* and many other forms depending on the form of the preceding clause. The phrase *sort of* occurs in typical adverbial environments and logically modifies the following tagma, as adverbs standardly do. The analytic scheme set out in earlier chapters is essentially based on grammatical structure, and it would be a very large undertaking to adapt it so that it *both* continued to reflect grammar *and* simultaneously showed the pragmatic functions of grammatically integrated "discourse items". A phrase like *sort of* will for us merit a U. . . tag, rather than its standard RR= tag, only in the (surely) rare cases where it is disconnected from a grammatical context, e.g. in *It's early, sort of* (in which case it will be tagged as an Engager, UE=).[4]

§ 6.30 Since our concept of "discourse item" is narrower than that of the Lund group, a fortiori it is much narrower than Diane Litman and Julia Hirschberg's concept of "cue phrase" (Litman and Hirschberg 1990, see especially n. 4; see also Hirschberg and Litman 1993), though the central examples *now* and *well* studied by Litman and Hirschberg are discourse items in our terms.

§ 6.31 The full set of SUSANNE discourse-item wordtags, with examples as in Anna-Brita Stenström's paper, is as follows.

UA	Apology	*pardon sorry excuse_me I'm_sorry I_beg_your_pardon*
UY	Positive	*yes yeah yup mhm*
UN	Negative	*no*
UR	Response	*ah fine good uhuh oh OK quite really right sure all_right fair_enough I'm_sure I_see very_good*

Under Response, Stenström also lists *that's good, that's it, that's right, that's true*; from our point of view these are regular clauses, which do not require to be given special wordtags as fixed clichés. The border between UY and UR seems blurred, since UR contains many items almost synonymous with "yes"; Bengt Altenberg merges UR, UY, and also UN into one large class of "Response" items. But there does seem to be some justification for distinguishing *yes* and its reduced forms, together with assenting sounds consisting essentially of a syllabic [m], from other ways of expressing assent, in that the former but not the latter can be produced virtually unconsciously by a hearer responding to a flow of conversation; assenting forms such as *OK, right* seem to reflect more conscious thought. Therefore we have retained Stenström's classification.

UP	*please*	
UT	Thanks	*thanks thank_you*

---

[4] Anna-Brita Stenström quotes an example which purports to include *sort of* in a grammatically disconnected role (1990: 139, example (5)), but her example could equally be seen as a case where *sort of* is functioning as an adverb in a clause which is interrupted immediately after the occurrence of the phrase.

UG	Greeting	*hi hello good_morning/evening/ ... Happy_ New_Year how_are_you how_do_you_do*
UX	Expletive	*damn gosh hell good_heavens the_hell for_goodness_sake good_heavens_above oh_bloody_hell* (but not *fuck off* from Stenström's list, since — like Altenberg's class of Orders, e.g. *give over* — this is parsed as a S* clause rather than a discourse item)
UE	Engager	*I_mean mind_you you_know you_see as_you_know do_you_see* (includes *sort_of kind_of sort_of_thing* when disconnected from a grammatical context, as in *It's cold, sort of*)

The Lund term for this group is Softeners, but the pragmatic function seems rather to be that of drawing the hearer into association with the speaker's viewpoint.

UW		*well*
UI	Initiator	*anyway however now* (as utterance initiators)
UB	Smooth-over	*don't_worry never_mind*

The two following categories are introduced by Altenberg (1990: 183):

UK	Attention Signal	*hey look*
UL	Response Elicitor	*eh what*

Altenberg (loc. cit.) gives *eh* and *right* as examples for Response Elicitor, but it is not clear when *right* has this function; on the other hand, the word *what* seems comparable to *eh*.

§ 6.32 The tags UP and UW are intended to be used for one specific word each. All other discourse-item tags may in principle cover a range of words and phrases, which in some cases, e.g. UX, will include many items not listed above, though in the case of UN, for instance, it is not clear that any word in non-regional British English other than *no* would take this tag. (For American English, two-syllable sounds such as *uh-uh* said on a falling pitch function as synonyms of *no*.)

Speech Repairs

§ 6.33 Probably the most challenging issue in the grammatical annotation of speech is the assignment of structure to "speech repairs", which are a phenomenon having no close analogue in written language.

§ 6.34   The fullest previous treatments of this issue known to us are Levelt (1983), and unpublished work based on Levelt's by Howell and Young (1990 — see also their 1991). (Allwood *et al.* (1990) is also important, but is less concerned with defining annotation techniques.) All of these studies are founded on empirical data. Levelt used a corpus of 959 speech repairs in Dutch elicited in a well-defined experimental task (describing examples of a class of geometrical figures), while Howell and Young used 1,142 speech repairs extracted from the London-Lund Corpus, together with instances from a corpus of dictaphone recordings.

Original Utterance

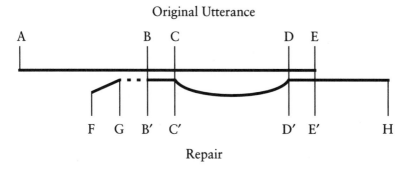

Repair

Figure 6.1

Levelt proposed, and Howell and Young accepted, a rather elaborate scheme for analysing speech repairs which might be represented diagrammatically as in Fig. 6.1 (adapted from Levelt's Fig. 2, p. 45). The speaker utters material from A to E. He breaks off his utterance at E, the "moment of interruption"; "rewinds" to some earlier point B; goes through an "editing phase", which may include production of an "editing term" (e.g. *er, no*), represented by F–G, and/or a pause, G–B′; after which he repeats B–E with changes, as B′–E′, then continues to H. The stretch B′–E′ may begin with a segment B′–C′ (the "retrace") which simply repeats the corresponding segment of B–C unchanged, and likewise B–E may end with a segment D–E (the "delay") which is repeated unchanged in the repair. The segments C–D and C′–D′ which differ as between original utterance and repair are called the "reparandum" and the "alteration" respectively.

Levelt assumes that A–B followed by B′–H, that is the material which remains if B–B′ is removed — perhaps identifiable as what the speaker would have said if he had chosen his words more carefully in the first place — will be parsable as a normal utterance. He calls a repair *well-formed* (1983: 78) if, within this material, point B (= B′) is syntactically a suitable point to begin a co-ordination. He appears to claim at least implicitly that speech repairs commonly are "well-formed" in this sense. (Levelt's position here is perhaps not wholly clear, though cf. Levelt (1989: 486–7). One interpretation of his discussion is that he draws a distinction between ideal "competence" and imperfect "performance" in speech repairs, akin to Noam Chomsky's competence/performance distinction for linguistic behaviour in general: speakers aim to make "well-formed" speech repairs but sometimes fail to do so.)

§ 6.35 In view of its empirical basis, Levelt's scheme has seemed worthy of detailed description. However, our experience with London-Lund data led us to the conclusion that a scheme as elaborate as this cannot be made to fit the range of dysfluencies that occur in practice.[5] Howell and Young (1990) claim that Levelt's scheme shows promise with their dictaphone material, but this is an unusual hybrid genre, in that the speaker's intention is not merely to convey his message but to create good written prose; thus, while the dysfluency of the material may be characteristic of speech, the underlying grammar is that of writing. (Probably the dysfluency too is conditioned by the fact that the speaker does not need to keep speaking in order to hold the turn.)

The speech repairs extracted by Howell and Young from the London-Lund Corpus seem to have been selected as cases where the speaker corrects himself, rather than cases where the speaker amplifies, repeats himself, or changes tack. Corrections are the type of editing most amenable to Levelt's analytic scheme, yet Howell and Young nevertheless often find themselves having to analyse their data in terms of compound and embedded repairs — leading to structures which seem implausible psychologically, and which often require apparently unmotivated selection between alternative analyses. (For instance, when a correction is itself corrected, a decision may be needed as to when the speaker stops correcting the correction and resumes correcting the original.) See also Howell and Young (1991: 741).

We prefer to avoid such artificial issues. Furthermore, for present purposes we need to define analyses not just for corrections but for the whole range of speech management phenomena as we find them

---

[5] Some might argue that a scheme for annotating English cannot be based on data from Dutch, but the present author would not make this objection: it is doubtful whether the general nature of speech repairs differs significantly as between two closely related Germanic languages.

in the data, without selection. There is an important difference between the motivation of Levelt's approach to speech-repair description, and ours: Levelt aimed to produce a tightly constrained predictive theory of how humans do (and how they do not) go about repairing their speech, as a contribution to theoretical psychology (so that for Levelt an observed repair that his notation could not handle would be an interesting scientific counterexample), whereas our aim is to devise a flexible notation that makes as few assumptions as possible about what speakers do and do not do, so that it can successfully reflect whatever happens to occur in the data. For us an example that our notation could not describe would be merely a nuisance.

§ 6.36 For these reasons, the SUSANNE annotation scheme deliberately adopts an approach which is less informative than Levelt's: in his terms, our speech-repair annotations identify the "moment of interruption", E, but do not attempt to identify many of the other lettered points in Fig. 6.1. On the other hand, our scheme does address the issue of how to fit the analysis of a speech repair into a wider parsetree, an issue which Levelt's and Howell and Young's work did not consider.

§ 6.37 In the SUSANNE scheme, the interruption point (Levelt's "moment of interruption" — conceptually the point where the speaker first notices an error) is represented as a terminal node in the parsetree. Like a ghost node, this is an analytic device corresponding to no concrete elements of the utterance; in terms of SUSANNE field structure, it would be represented by a record containing a hyphen in the word field, and some special wordtag (we propose using the tag YR for this purpose) in the wordtag field. Our corpus of annotated speech has not in fact to date been cast in the SUSANNE field format; in the present document we shall indicate interruption points by the simple symbol "#".

§ 6.38 An interruption point is attached as daughter to the lowest parse node such that both the material immediately preceding and the material immediately following the interruption (other than hesitation phenomena) can be seen as attempts to realize that node. Thus, in the example:

> ... *and that any bonus he anything he gets over that is a bonus* ... 2.2.669

the analysis, omitting irrelevant details, will be:

[Fn+ *and that* [Ns *any bonus* [Fr [Nas *he*]] # *anything* [Fr [Nas *he*] [Vz *gets*] [P *over that*] Fr] Ns] *is a bonus* Fn+]

The interruption is a daughter of the Ns following *that*, because *any bonus he* and *anything he gets over that* can both be seen as attempts to produce a subject for the nominal clause.

Another way of looking at this is that the grammatical oddity of a speech repair is confined below the node to which the interruption point is attached; that node itself will be normal with respect to its environment of mother and sister nodes. (An Ns is standard between the *and that* and the verb of an Fn+, but in edited English one will not find a sequence like *any bonus he anything he* . . . realizing an Ns.)

§ 6.39 The material before and after an interruption point will not necessarily represent tagmas with identical formtags. Consider some possible variations in the wording of the above example:

1. . . . *and that any bonuses he anything he gets over that is a bonus* . . .
2. . . . *and that any bonus he whatever he gets over that is a bonus* . . .

In (1), *any bonuses he* is an uncompleted Np, whereas *anything he gets* . . . is an Ns. In (2) we have Ns versus Ff.

These pairs of sequences are still counted as attempts to realize the same node: the criterion for that is function with respect to the wider grammatical environment (in this case, subject of the Fn+) rather than form. Therefore the tree structure and placement of the interruption point is unaffected by these variations. For the label of the node dominating the interruption point, the rule is that where the formtags of the parts on either side of the interruption point would be alternative subcategorizations of a common main category, the label of the entire node will be a neutral tag including just the elements that would be common to the formtags of both (all) parts (provided this is a valid formtag), and where the relationship between the sequences separated by interruption point(s), and the limitations on valid formtags, make a neutral formtag impossible, a compound formtag is created by placing the formtags for the parts on either side of a # symbol. Thus in (1) above, Np and Ns give N for the node dominating the interruption point, since N is a valid formtag neutralizing Np and Ns. In (2), Ns and Ff give Ns#Ff. In a hypothetical example:

he likes to tell people telling people what to do

where the formtags for the sequences either side of the interruption point are Ti and Tg, there is no valid formtag "T" so the analysis would be:

[Ti#Tg *to tell people # telling people what to do*]

In cases where a node dominates three or more subsequences separated by interruption points, even if they cannot all be classified under one neutral formtag, the length of the compound tagmatag for the node will be minimized by representing adjacent subsequences with single neutral tags wherever possible, for instance one would write not, say, Np#Ns#Ff but N#Ff.

§ 6.40 A tagma whose right boundary immediately precedes an interruption point will commonly be incomplete: in the *bonus* example, the interruption point is preceded by an Fr consisting solely of a subject. Because any pre-interruption tagma is likely to be incomplete, and because it is not always easy to determine whether a particular tagma in this situation is complete or not, no special annotation is used to mark tagmas which are in fact incomplete.

§ 6.41 In the example, the material following the interruption marker is a fresh attempt to realize the tagma to which the marker is attached, from the beginning — *anything* is an appropriate first word for an Ns. But this will not always be the case. Suppose the utterance had run:

. . . and that any bonus he money he gets over that is a bonus . . .

— then *money* would restart the Ns beginning at the point between *any* and *bonus*. One might think of representing this fact by inserting a second type of marker, different from #, between *any* and *bonus* (in Levelt's terms, marking point B):

[Ns *any* $ *bonus* [Fr *he*] # *money* [Fr *he gets over that*]]

Our system chooses not to do this, for several reasons. In cases where wording following an interruption resumes in the middle of a tagma, it is not clear that speakers are always careful to ensure that their new wording fits grammatically on to the earlier wording: if they do not, locating point B would be a scarcely meaningful exercise. Furthermore, the interruption point is a psychologically real phenomenon, often associated with audible hesitation, but point B has no special status for the speaker at the time when he reaches it: it acquires a theoretical significance only later, through the speaker's decision about how to proceed after interrupting himself. For an empirically based annotation scheme such as ours, a general commitment to mark point B in a speech repair would involve inappropriately deep and debatable analysis. In many cases it is likely that point B will coincide with the left boundary of the tagma to which the interruption point is attached, as it does in the 2.2.669 case quoted in § 6.38.

§ **6.42** A tagma may be broken off prematurely without any attempt to complete it. In this case an interruption-point marker is placed at the end of the word sequence, attached to the highest node which clearly requires additional daughters in order to be well formed. This will often be the lowest node above the last word. Thus, a (hypothetical) utterance *she was going into the* — would be analysed:

[S [Nas *she*] [Vsg *was going*] [P *into* [N *the* #]]]

— an N needs more wording after *the*, but the P needs no daughter after the N and the S needs no daughter after the P. (It might of course have been the speaker's intention to add extra material within the S following the P, but the grammar of what was actually said gives no reason to predict this.)

Where the London-Lund transcribers have implied that a turn is incomplete by marking its last tone unit as discussed in § 6.11, our analysis attaches a comma as the last daughter of the O node dominating the turn.

§ **6.43** If silent or filled pauses occur adjacent to an interruption point, as is common, these are analysed as following rather than preceding the interruption point, and as sisters to it. (If pauses were analysed as preceding interruption points, they would have to be treated as daughters of the lowest preceding tagma, since otherwise there would be tagmas which were imperfect because of the interruption but were not immediately followed by the # mark. This would run counter to the general SUSANNE principle that punctuation is attached as high in the tree as possible.)

§ **6.44** The "before" and "after" of a speech repair can be individual words, as in:

Yes I think they they they have ... 1.9.375

— in which case the logic of the system discussed above would give a tagma [*they* # *they* # *they*] which as a whole functions as a word tagged PPHS2.[6] We do not want to use wordtags unaltered as tagmatags, so we use the character # as a suffix to form a tagmatag for a speech repair realizing a word (cf. the suffixes & = for other kinds of wordrank tagmatag); thus the analysis is:

---

[6] One might query the term "repair" for a case such as this where, according to the transcriptions provided by the compilers of the London-Lund Corpus, each one of repeated attempts to realize a constituent was successful. It is far outside the purview of the SUSANNE annotation scheme to enquire why multiple successful realizations of words or tagmas occur; they are very common in practice, and in this work the term "speech repair" is intended to include them.

[PPHS2# *they*_PPHS2 #_YR *they*_PPHS2 #_YR *they*_PPHS2]

If the "before" and "after" words are different and have different wordtags, then the label for the node dominating the repair links the distinct wordtags with a # character, as discussed earlier, and also adds a # after the last wordtag to show that the whole is a tagmatag. Identical tags for adjacent words appear once only in the compound tag (but partially similar wordtags are not reduced to "neutral" tags). The wordtag FD is ignored in constructing such compound tags, unless *all* the words separated by interruption points are distorted in which case the tagmatag is FD#. Thus the examples:

... and . we . I uh I uh do have ... 3.4.40
Tuh– Tom Blandermore 1.9.374

receive the analyses:

[S+ *and* ._YP [Na [PPIS2#PPIS1# *we* # . *I* # *uh I*]] *uh* [Vk *do have*] ...]
[Nns [NP1m# *Tuh*–_FD #_YR *Tom*_NP1m] *Blandermore*_NP1s Nns]

§ 6.45   Analytic problems can arise from the fact that the segments of an utterance which are repeated or modified in a speech repair tend to be phonologically defined segments, which do not necessarily coincide with grammatical tagmas as recognized by the SUSANNE scheme. Consider for instance the speech turn:

No I'll I'll I'll have a nasty French one – ,   2.10.543

Phonologically, an enclitic forms a word with the stem to which it is suffixed: the speaker has made three attempts to realize the word *I'll*. Grammatically, however, +*'ll* forms a tagma with *have*. The smallest tagma which the successive instances of *I'll* can each be regarded as attempting to realize is the entire S; the analysis must be:

[O *No*_UN [S [Nea *I*] [Vcx +*'ll*] # [Nea *I*] [Vcx +*'ll*] # [Nea *I*] [Vc +*'ll have*] [Ns *a nasty French one*] S] –_YP , O]

Enclitics such as reduced auxiliary verbs are an extreme case in English of inconsistency between phonologically motivated and grammatically motivated segmentation, but the problem outlined here is a more general one. The SUSANNE rule is that the constituency structure assigned to spoken utterances, including that assigned to utterances involving speech repairs, depends on the grammar of the utterances alone even in cases where the nature of the repair is manifestly determined by phonological considerations which clash with the grammatical structure.

Examples

§ 6.46   The closing section illustrates the above principles by applying them to a few speech turns taken from the London-Lund Corpus. As usual, only those aspects of the annotation which relate to the issues discussed in this chapter are displayed; further labelled bracketing is implied straightforwardly by the conventions defined in earlier chapters.

[O [S* [V *Go*] [P *to*] # [V *find*] [R *out*] [Np *the right seminars* [Ti [Vi *to go*] [P *to*]]] S*] [S [Ds *that*] [Vzb +*'s*] [Ff *what I did when I first came*] S] O] 1.5.9

[O <*Well*>_UW [S [Fa *if you just write to Paxted College*] ._YP *erm*_YM [Ny *you*] [Vc +*'ll get*] [Nos *him*] S] –_YP [S+ *and* [Nas *he*] [Vzb +*'s*] [Ns *a* #] S+] , O] 1.9.389

Contains a turn-final interruption point.

[O *Yes*_UY [S [Nea *I*] [V *think*] [Fn [Nap [PPHS2# *they* # *they* # *they*] Nap] [V *have*] – ._YP [Np *transcripts* # –_YP *er*_YM *transcriptions* [I [S? *shall I say*] I] [Np– *not transcripts* [S@ *transcripts are uh what the Bishop has*] Np–] Np] Fn] S] O] 1.9.375

Since *transcriptions . . . not transcripts* is most naturally analysed as an asyndetic co-ordination, it must be a phraselevel co-ordination (*not transcripts* is a phrase rather than a word), therefore *transcripts . . . transcriptions* is a phraselevel rather than wordlevel repair.

[O [Np *Transcriptions* [Po *of* . [Dp *quite a lot of* [Np [DD2# *these* # . *these*] *county monographs in the Peak District*]]] Np] [S+ *and* – *this is* [Jr *much easier* [Ti *to* #] *uh* [I [S *we can go through theirs* S] I] [Fc *than* [Ti [Vi *to* . *uh work*] [P *through the county monographs*] Ti] Fc] Jr] S+] [S+ *and I* [Vc *must get*] # *uh I* [Vfg +*'ve been meaning*] [Ti [Vi *to get*] [Ns *hold of him*] Ti] [P *for a long time*] S+] O] 1.9.381

This turn is by the same speaker as the one above, and is that speaker's next turn; however, the London-Lund compilers treat it as a separate turn. The Jr headed by *easier* appears to be of the intended general structure *much easier to X than to Y*, but the X item has been omitted and a grammatically independent statement interpolated in its place. Despite the clear semantic parallel between the two occurrences of *get* in the last S+ clause, the SUSANNE analytic scheme does not allow them to be treated as sister words.

[O [S [Nas *He*] [Vz *doesn't live*] [P *in*] S] # . –_YP *yes*_UY [S+ *but*_CCB [Nas *he*] [Vz *doesn't . live*] [P [II# *in* # *in* # *in*] ._YP *er*_YM *Tundraland* P] [R *at_all*] S+] O] 1.9.398

Analysed as a repair at the O rather than S level, because *yes* would not normally be treated as part of the S+ (§ 4.458).

[O <*What*>_UL [S [P *because_of periodicity*] [Ny [PPY# *you* # *you* # *you*]] # S] , O] 1.9.423

From the context it is fairly clear that the repeated *you* is intended to be completed as *you mean*. Since this assumed phrase is being used with its literal meaning, rather than being interpreted as an Engager discourse item it is regarded as comprising the subject and head verb of a clause in which *because of periodicity* is the preposed object; it follows that the clause must be closed with an interruption point.

[O *Oh*_UX [S [Nea *I*] [Ve *don't think*] # [Nea *I*] [Ve *don't think*] [Fn *I ever went to see mine*] S] O] 1.12.1376

[O *Right*_UR *well*_UW [S* *let +'s* # *er* – – . *let +'s* [Tb *look at the applications*] S*] – *erm* – [S* *let me just* [Tb *ask initially* [Ds *this*] – – [I [S *I discussed it with er Reith er* [S+ *but we'll . have to go into it a bit further* S+] S] I] – [S?@ *is it* # *is it* [P *within* [N *our*_APPG] P] # *erm er . are we* [Jh *free er* [Ti [Vi *to er draw*] [R *up*] [Ns *a* [J *rather . exiguous*] *list* – [Po *of* [N *people* [Ti *to interview*] N] Po] – – *er that's_to_say*_REX [M@ *three* [M+ *or four*] *only* M@] Ns] Ti] Jh] S?@] Tb] S*] . [S *that's perfectly all right* [Iq [S? *is it*]] S] O] 2.6.440

The question is attached in sentential apposition to the Tb clause which introduces it. The word *our* is given an N phrasetag although consisting of a single word and daughter of a phrase, because it is an incomplete version of something which, if complete, would contain more than one word and would therefore require a phrasetag.

[O [S [Ns *That*] [Vdcb *would be*] [Ff *what would be expected*]] . [S? [Dq *what*] # *er I_mean*_UE [Voa *are*] [Ny *you*] [Vrg *asking*] [Fn? *whether . it would be normal to have a much bigger list than this* Fn?] S?] , O] 2.6.452

The word *what* appears to be the beginning of a direct question which is aborted after its first word.

[O *Mm*_YM [R *not necessarily*] [S [Ni *it*] [Vzb *+'s*] [R *en–*_FD]
[Ni *it*] [Vzb *+'s*] [R *entirely*] [P *up to us*] S] , O] 2.6.458

The syllable *en–* is tagged FD as a "distorted word", but the
analyst's knowledge that it represents the beginning of *entirely* is used
in order to assign it the phrasetag R.

[O [Fa *Cos* [P *in* [Nns [NP1t# *Boreham–*_FD # *Borehamwood*]
Nns] P] *it was* [Ns *a r–*_FD # *a regular blizzard* Ns] Fa]
*I_mean*_UE [S <*it*> *didn't really settle very much* S] – [S+ *but
er it was quite a blizzard* [Fa *cos Sabre was out in the back
garden* [Fa+ *and* [Ns *this huge Alsatian*] – <*I_mean*>_UE [R
<*rea–*>_FD] [R *sort_of*] [Vn *covered*] [P *in* [N [FD# *s–*_FD
*s–*_FD] N] # . [II# *in* # *in*] [Np *flakes of snow*] P] Fa+] Fa]
S+] . [S *it was really* [P *like* [Ns <*a*> *sort_of beautiful um* . *er
wolf* [P [II# *in* # *in*] *the Arctic* P] Ns] P] [Tg *watching him
sort_of wander about in the garden* Tg] S] O] 2.13.1046

The Fa+ is analysed on the assumption that the speaker intended a
finite clause along the lines *this huge Alsatian was covered . . .* , and
that the finite verb was omitted in error. The closing Tg is regarded
as having undergone Extraposition, that is the assumed logical
structure of the last S is: [*watching him wander about . . .*] *was
like a beautiful wolf in the Arctic*.

Arguably, it misrepresents the reality of the spoken language to
take the occurrence of a CS word *cos* (an informal spoken
equivalent of *because*) at the beginning of a clause as requiring an
analysis in which the clause is subordinated to the preceding clause.
In the example, *cos Sabre was out . . .* is shown as subordinate to
the *was quite a blizzard* clause, and because the *Alsatian* clause is
linked by *and* to a clause which is analysed as subordinate, it is
itself treated as an Fa+, and thus attached three levels below the
root node. Just as in analysing speech we normally treat S+ clauses
as attached directly to root nodes rather than to preceding S clauses
(§ 6.14), so it may be that realistically we ought to treat *cos Sabre
was out . . .* as a sister rather than daughter of the *quite a blizzard*
clause. However, this would lead to large questions about when
clauses beginning with subordinating conjunctions are to be analysed as genuinely subordinate, if it is accepted that subordinate
clauses are to be recognized in some cases even in speech. We have
not to date gained enough experience with the grammar of speech
to suggest answers to questions of this order, and therefore adopt
the most straightforward solution, namely to apply the same rules
as would apply if the words were written.

[O [S [Ni *It*] [Vzb +'s] [J *most unfair*] [Fa *because*] S] # .
*well*_UW . *no*_UN [S [R *perhaps*] [Ni *it*] [Vzeb +'s *not*] [J
unfair] S] – [S *Ella loves the little one*] – [S *that's her favour-*
ite] O] 2.13.1060

In the Corpus, this turn begins with incomprehensible material
identified as "several sylls murmur": our analysis simply omits this.
Again the discourse items *well, no* lead to the repair being analysed
at O rather than S level.

HOW TO GET THE SUSANNE CORPUS

The SUSANNE Corpus is distributed electronically by the Oxford Text Archive over the international network Internet. Anyone with physical access to Internet is welcome to take a copy; he needs no permission from the author or from the Archive, and there are no controls over how copies are used. The only restrictions are matters of honour rather than law: it would not be a friendly act to set up as a rival distributing centre for this resource, and, since the chief reason for creating the SUSANNE Corpus was to promote the SUSANNE annotation scheme, the author would be particularly sorry to see another group transpose the SUSANNE annotations into an alternative system and publish the new version in order to promote the other scheme. (But there is obviously no objection to research groups converting SUSANNE annotations into their preferred equivalents for their own local use; this may often be an appropriate thing to do.)

If users of the Corpus produce publications based on it, the Economic and Social Research Council (UK), and the author's employer, the University of Sussex, would undoubtedly welcome an acknowledgement of their roles as SUSANNE sponsor and grantholder respectively.

Release 1 of the SUSANNE Corpus was finalized in September 1992. Release 2, which eliminates a number of errors found in Release 1 and incorporates some small modifications in annotation conventions, was finalized in June 1993; and Release 3, correcting errors discovered in the process of completing the manuscript of this book, will be circulated before the book is in print. It is anticipated that subsequent releases will be produced as further errors come to light, but after the present work goes to press the annotation conventions to which the Corpus conforms will not normally be modified (unless the definitions of the conventions in the preceding chapters prove to contain inconsistencies). A section in the electronic documentation file accompanying successive releases of the Corpus will identify the nature of any such modifications.

At any time, the instructions which follow will secure a copy of whichever is currently the most up-to-date release of the Corpus.

The sixty-five files of the SUSANNE Corpus (annotated versions of sixty-four Brown texts, and a documentation file) are held by the Oxford Text Archive in compressed form: in order to reduce file transfer time, the whole Corpus is compressed into single files in two alternative formats, one suitable for Unix users and the other for users who have access only to a PC. To retrieve either version, proceed as follows:

1. `ftp black.ox.ac.uk` [or `ftp 129.67.1.165`]
2. *At the login prompt, type:* anonymous
   and at the password prompt, type your e-mail address
3. `cd ota/susanne`
4. *Unix users:* `get susanne.tar.Z`
   PC users: `get susanne.zip`
5. `quit`

To get the compressed file into a usable state on your home system, if you are a Unix user:

```
uncompress susanne.tar.Z
tar -xf susanne.tar
```

— if you are a PC user:

```
pkunzip -x susanne.zip
```

You should now have the sixty-five SUSANNE files in the form described in the present book.

If you already have a copy of the Corpus and wish to discover whether a newer release is available, at step 4 the command:

```
get SUSANNE.doc
```

will retrieve a copy of just the documentation file, in uncompressed form; this begins with version information about the current release. Unix users can do:

```
get SUSANNE.doc "|more"
```

to view this file on screen without copying it into their home filestore.

In case of difficulties which cannot be resolved by an ftp expert on your local system staff, e-mail enquiries may be sent to the Oxford Text Archive at archive@black.ox.ac.uk or archive@vax.oxford.ac.uk. The author will be pleased to receive correspondence on the contents of the Corpus, e.g. identifying errors for correction in future releases, by post at the following address:

School of Cognitive and Computing Sciences
University of Sussex
Falmer, Brighton BN1 9QH, England

Apart from the SUSANNE Corpus, most of the electronic data resources discussed in this book (various corpora, and the CUVOALD computer-usable dictionary), as well as many further resources, are obtainable (against payment, and subject to various restrictions on use) either from the Oxford Text Archive, e-mail address as above, or from ICAME, the International Computer Archive of Modern English, in Bergen, Norway, e-mail icame@hd.uib.no. Details and order forms are distributed with successive numbers of the *ICAME Journal*. Exceptionally, the Tagged Brown Corpus is distributed only by its American creators, who can be contacted at:

Box 1978
Brown University
Providence, RI 02912, USA

The format of the SUSANNE Corpus, as described in Chapter 2, is designed to make it easy to write software to process the entire Corpus and extract statistics of any required kinds. Some researchers use analysed corpora in a different way, searching for and visually inspecting individual examples of particular grammatical configurations. This mode of research can be facilitated by software which allows the user to specify configurations of interest and automates the search process. Readers may therefore like to know that Martin Corley of the University of Exeter (e-mail M.M.B.Corley@uk.ac.exeter) has been developing such software for SUSANNE; those interested should contact him.

□

BIBLIOGRAPHY

Place of publication is included only for publishers who do not list a London office.

AARTS, J., and VAN DEN HEUVEL, T. (1985), "Computational tools for the syntactic analysis of corpora", *Linguistics*, 23: 303–35.

AKMAJIAN, A., and HENY, F. (1975), *An Introduction to the Principles of Transformational Syntax*, MIT Press.

ALLWOOD, J., et al. (1990), "Speech management: on the non-written life of speech", *Nordic Journal of Linguistics*, 13: 3–48.

ALTENBERG, B. (1990), "Spoken English and the dictionary", in Svartvik (1990).

ANDERSON, J. M. (1976), *On Serialization in English Syntax*, R. O. U. Strauch (Ludwigsburg).

BLACK, E., et al. (1993) (eds.), *Statistically-Driven Computer Grammars of English: The IBM/Lancaster Approach*, Rodopi (Amsterdam).

BRESNAN, JOAN (1982), "Polyadicity", in Joan Bresnan (ed.), *The Mental Representation of Grammatical Relations*, MIT Press.

BRISCOE, E. J. (1990), "English noun phrases are regular: a reply to Professor Sampson", in J. Aarts and W. Meijs (eds.), *Theory and Practice in Corpus Linguistics*, Rodopi (Amsterdam).

BURT, MARINA K. (1971), *From Deep to Surface Structure: An Introduction to Transformational Syntax*, Harper & Row.

CHAFE, W. L., et al. (1991), "Towards a new corpus of spoken American English", in Karin Aijmer and B. Altenberg (eds.), *English Corpus Linguistics: Studies in Honour of Jan Svartvik*, Longman.

CHOMSKY, A. N. (1957), *Syntactic Structures*, Janua Linguarum 4, Mouton (The Hague).

—— (1964), *Current Issues in Linguistic Theory*, Janua Linguarum, series minor, 38, Mouton.

—— (1965), *Aspects of the Theory of Syntax*, MIT Press.

—— (1968), *Language and Mind*, Harcourt, Brace & World (New York).

—— (1976), *Reflections on Language*, Temple Smith.

DIK, S. C. (1968), *Coordination: Its Implications for the Theory of General Linguistics*, North-Holland (Amsterdam).

DOWTY, D. (1982), "Grammatical relations and Montague grammar", in Pauline Jacobson and G. K. Pullum (eds.), *The Nature of Syntactic Representation*, Reidel.

ELLEGÅRD, A. (1978), *The Syntactic Structure of English Texts*, Gothenburg Studies in English 43, Acta Universitatis Gothoburgensis (Gothenburg).

ELSNESS, J. (1984), "*That* or zero? A look at the choice of object clause connective in a corpus of American English", *English Studies*, 65: 519–33.

FILLMORE, C. J. (1968), "The case for case", in E. Bach and R.T. Harms (eds.), *Universals in Linguistic Theory*, Holt, Rinehart & Winston.

FLIGELSTONE, S. (1992), "Developing a scheme for annotating text to show anaphoric relations", in G. Leitner (ed.), *New Directions in English Language Corpora*, Mouton de Gruyter (Berlin).

FRANCIS, W. N., and KUČERA, H. (1982), *Frequency Analysis of English Usage: Lexicon and Grammar*, Houghton Mifflin (Boston).

—— (1989), *Manual of Information to Accompany a Standard Corpus of Present-Day Edited American English, for Use with Digital Computers* (corrected and rev. edn.; 1st edn. 1964), Department of Linguistics, Brown University (Providence). [Cited in the text as *BCUM*.]

FRIES, C. C. (1952), *The Structure of English*, Harcourt, Brace & World (New York).

GARSIDE, R. G., and LEECH, FANNY (1987), "The UCREL probabilistic parsing system", in Garside *et al.* (1987: ch. 6).

—— *et al.* (1987) (eds.), *The Computational Analysis of English: A Corpus-Based Approach*, Longman. [Cited in the text as *CAE*.]

GAZDAR, G. M., *et al.* (1985), *Generalized Phrase Structure Grammar*, Blackwell (Oxford).

Hart's Rules for Compositors and Readers at the University Press Oxford (1983) (39th, rev. edn.), Oxford University Press (Oxford). [Cited in the text as "Hart's Rules".]

HIRSCHBERG, JULIA, and LITMAN, DIANE (1993), "Empirical studies on the disambiguation of cue phrases", *Computational Linguistics*, 19: 501–30.

HOCKETT, C. F. (1968), *The State of the Art*, Janua Linguarum, series minor, 73, Mouton (The Hague).

HOFLAND, K., and JOHANSSON, S. (1982), *Word Frequencies in British and American English*, Longman.

HOWELL, P., and YOUNG, K. (1990), "Speech repairs: report of work conducted October 1st 1989–March 31st 1990", unpublished report, Department of Psychology, University College London.

—— —— (1991), "The use of prosody in highlighting alterations in repairs from unrestricted speech", *Quarterly Journal of Experimental Psychology*, 43A: 733–58.

JOHANSSON, S. (1978), *Manual of Information to Accompany the Lancaster-Oslo/Bergen Corpus of British English, for Use with Digital Computers*, Department of English, University of Oslo (Oslo). [Cited in the text as *LCUM*.]

—— (1986), *The Tagged LOB Corpus Users' Manual*, Norwegian Computing Centre for the Humanities (Bergen). [Cited in the text as *TLCUM*.]

KATZ, J. J. (1971), *The Underlying Reality of Language and its Philosophical Import*, Harper & Row.

LANGENDOEN, D. T. (1969), *The Study of Syntax: The Generative-Transformational Approach to the Structure of American English*, Holt, Rinehart & Winston.

LEECH, G. N. (1987), "General Introduction", in Garside *et al.* (1987: ch. 1).

LEVELT, W. J. M. (1983), "Monitoring and self-repair in speech", *Cognition*, 14: 41–104.

—— (1989), *Speaking: From Intention to Articulation*, MIT Press.

LIEBERMAN, P. (1967), *Intonation, Perception, and Language*, Research Monograph 38, MIT Press (Cambridge, Mass.).

LITMAN, DIANE, and HIRSCHBERG, JULIA (1990), "Disambiguating cue phrases in text and speech", in H. Karlgren (ed.), *Papers Presented to the 13th International Conference on Computational Linguistics* (Helsinki), ii.

MARCUS, M. P., *et al.* (1993), "Building a large annotated corpus of English: the Penn Treebank", *Computational Linguistics*, 19: 313–30.

MATTHEWS, P. H. (1981), *Syntax*, Cambridge University Press.

MITTON, R. (1986), "A partial dictionary of English in computer-usable form", *Literary and Linguistic Computing*, 1: 214–15.

MOORE, R. K. (1992), "User needs in speech research", paper circulated at the Workshop on European Textual Corpora, Pisa, Jan. 1992.

OBERMEIER, K. K. (1989), *Natural Language Processing Technologies in Artificial Intelligence: The Science and Industry Perspective*, Ellis Horwood (Chichester).

QUANG PHUC DONG (1969), "Phrases anglaises sans sujet grammatical apparent", *Langages*, 14: 44–51.

QUIRK, R., *et al.* (1972), *A Grammar of Contemporary English*, Longman (Harlow). [Cited in the text as *GCE*.]

—— (1985), *A Comprehensive Grammar of the English Language*, Longman. [Cited in the text as *CGEL*.]

SAG, I. A., and POLLARD, C. (1991), "An integrated theory of complement control", *Language*, 67: 63–113.

SAMPSON, G. R. (1975), *The Form of Language*, Weidenfeld & Nicolson.

—— (1987a), "MT: a nonconformist's view of the state of the art", in Margaret King (ed.), *Machine Translation Today: The State of the Art*, Edinburgh University Press (Edinburgh).

—— (1987b), "Evidence against the 'grammatical'/'ungrammatical' distinction", in W. Meijs (ed.), *Corpus Linguistics and Beyond*, Rodopi (Amsterdam).

—— (1989a), "Language acquisition: growth or learning?", *Philosophical Papers*, 18: 203–40.

—— (1989b), "How fully does a machine-usable dictionary cover English text?", *Literary and Linguistic Computing*, 4: 29–35.

—— (1991), "Analysed corpora of English: a consumer guide", in Martha Pennington and V. Stevens (eds.), *Computers in Applied Linguistics*, Multilingual Matters (Clevedon).

—— (1992a), "SUSANNE: a deeply analysed corpus of American English", in G. Leitner (ed.), *New Directions in English Language Corpora*, Topics in English Linguistics 9, Mouton de Gruyter (Berlin).

Sampson, G. R. (1992*b*), "Probabilistic parsing", in J. Svartvik (ed.), *Directions in Corpus Linguistics: Proceedings of Nobel Symposium 82, Stockholm, 4–8 August 1991*, Mouton de Gruyter (Berlin).

—— and Haigh, R. (1988), "Why are long sentences longer than short ones?", in Merja Kytö *et al.* (eds.), *Corpus Linguistics, Hard and Soft*, Rodopi (Amsterdam).

—— *et al.* (1989), "Natural language analysis by stochastic optimization: a progress report on Project APRIL", *Journal of Experimental and Theoretical Artificial Intelligence*, 1: 271–87.

Somers, H. L. (1987), *Valency and Case in Computational Linguistics*, Edinburgh University Press (Edinburgh).

Sperberg-McQueen, C. M., and Burnard, L. (1990), *Guidelines for the Encoding and Interchange of Machine-Readable Texts* (Draft: Version 1.0), Association for Computers and the Humanities/Association for Computational Linguistics/Association for Literary and Linguistic Computing (Chicago and Oxford).

Starosta, S. (1988), *The Case for Lexicase: An Outline of Lexicase Grammatical Theory*, Pinter.

Stenström, Anna-Brita (1990), "Lexical items peculiar to spoken discourse", in Svartvik (1990).

Stockwell, R. P., *et al.* (1973), *The Major Syntactic Structures of English*, Holt, Rinehart & Winston.

Svartvik, J. (1990) (ed.), *The London-Lund Corpus of Spoken English: Description and Research*, Lund Studies in English 82, Lund University Press (Lund).

—— and Quirk, R. (1980) (eds.), *A Corpus of English Conversation*, C. W. K. Gleerup (Lund). [Cited in the text as *CEC*.]

Taylor, Lolita, *et al.* (1989), "The syntactic regularity of English noun phrases", in *Proceedings of the Fourth Annual Meeting of the European Chapter of the Association for Computational Linguistics*, University of Manchester Institute of Science and Technology.

Tesnière, L. (1965), *Éléments de syntaxe structurale*, 2nd edn., Klincksieck (Paris).

Thomason, R. H. (1974) (ed.), *Formal Philosophy: Selected Papers of Richard Montague*, Yale University Press.

Vennemann, T. (1984), "Typology, universals and change of language", in J. Fisiak (ed.), *Historical Syntax*, Mouton (Berlin).

Weber, Rose-Marie (1983), "Behind the slash", *Visible Language*, 17: 390–5.

Winograd, T. (1983), *Language as a Cognitive Process*, i: *Syntax*, Addison-Wesley.

INDEX OF TOPICS AND
SYMBOLS

The general names for the principal parts of speech, e.g. noun, preposition, are not separately indexed; however each SUSANNE wordtag, and some specialized wordclass descriptions such as 'possessive pronoun', are given index entries. Entries for idiomtags ending in equals sign are included with entries for the corresponding wordtag without equals sign.

The word 'versus' in subentries is abbreviated 'v.' in accordance with British convention (the American equivalent is 'vs').

INDEX OF WORDS, PHRASES, AND AFFIXES